MILLER'S
INTERNATIONAL
ANTIQUES
PRICE GUIDE

1993 AMERICAN EDITION

MILLER'S
INTERNATIONAL
ANTIQUES
PRICE GUIDE

1993 AMERICAN EDITION

COMPILED AND EDITED BY

JUDITH AND MARTIN MILLER

VIKING
STUDIO
BOOKS

HOW TO USE THE BOOK

Miller's uniquely practical *International Antiques Price Guide* has been compiled to make detailed information immediately available to the consumer.

The book is organized by category of antique: e.g. Pottery, Porcelain, Furniture, etc. (see Contents List on page 6); within each major category there are sub-categories of items in alphabetical order: e.g. basket, bowl, candlestick, etc., and these in turn are ordered by date. There are around 10,000 photographs of antiques and collectibles, each with a detailed description and price range. There is also a fully cross-referenced index at the back of the book.

This 1993 Edition contains 144 pages in full color — illustrating over 1,500 exceptional or attractive pieces.

In addition to individual entries there are special features throughout the book, giving pointers for the collector — likely condition, definitions of specialist terms, history, etc. — together with general articles, chapter introductions, glossaries, bibliographies where further reading is important, tables of marks, etc. As all the pictures and captions are new every year the selection of items included quickly builds into an enormously impressive and uniquely useful reference set.

PRICES

All the price ranges are based on actual prices of items bought and sold during the year prior to going to press. Thus the guide is fully up-to-date.

Prices are *not* estimates; because the value of an antique is what a willing buyer will pay to a willing seller, we have given not just one price per item but a range of prices to take into account regional differences and freak results.

This is the best way to give an idea of what an antique will *cost*, but should you wish to *sell* remember that the price you receive could be 25-30% less — antique dealers have to live too!!

Condition

All items were in good merchantable condition when last sold unless damage is noted.

ACKNOWLEDGEMENTS

Judith and Martin Miller wish to thank a large number of International auctioneers, dealers and museums who have helped in the production of this edition. The auctioneers can be found in our specialist directory towards the back of this edition.

Copyright © Millers Publications 1992.

**Viking Penguin, a division of Penguin Books USA Inc.
375 Hudson Street, New York New York 10014, U.S.A.**

**Penguin Books Canada Ltd.
10 Alcorn Avenue, Suite 300
Toronto, Ontario, Canada
M4V 3B2**

Designed and created by
Millers Publications
The Cellars
High Street
Tenterden, Kent
TN17 2JA, England

All rights reserved.
First published in 1992 by Viking Penguin, a division of Penguin Books USA Inc.
ISBN: 0-670-84500-0

Bromide output by Final Word,
Tonbridge Kent, England
Color originated by Scantrans,
Singapore

Printed and bound in England by
William Clowes Ltd., Beccles and London

Editor's Introduction

by

Judith Miller

Martin and I started *Miller's Antiques Price Guide* in 1979. We produced a book which we believed was greatly needed by virtually everyone who had some interest in antiques, whether professional or as a collector.

We firmly believed that what was needed was a guide to the antiques market which was photographically illustrated, with detailed, concise descriptions and price ranges. The last 13 years have convinced me that this is what the buying public want. Initially, of course, we produced the kind of book that Martin and I wanted — and since we now sell well in excess of 100,000 copies of the British edition, it would seem we were not alone. The book in its various editions is now used all over the world as a major reference work to antiques and since we use in the region of 10,000 new photographs every year, the issues of the British Guide provide an unrivalled source to 100,000 different antiques.

Seven years ago we decided, in conjunction with Viking Penguin, to produce a U.S. edition of the Guide. We were convinced that the U.S. market needed the clear, high quality photographs, detailed descriptions, and the price ranges which give a "ball-park" figure for the thousands of items featured in *Miller's International Antiques Price Guide*. These price ranges are researched from sold items and give readers an essential tool for buying and selling antiques and collectibles. We are constantly trying to improve our product and give the U.S. consumer information relevant to the antiques market in the States.

One interesting development I have noticed over the years is that the antiques market is becoming more international. Of course, each country has a special interest in items made by native craftsmen and it is the general trend that such pieces will sell better at a major saleroom in their country of origin. However, to balance this, when general prices achieved at auction in New York, London, Geneva and Hong Kong are compared, they show a striking similarity.

We try to include as many color photographs as is possible, and this year we have well over 1,500 items illustrated in color, all of which have been on the market in the year prior to compilation. All the pieces included, either in color or black and white, are antiques which have been available through dealers or auction houses; they are not museum pieces. The result is a strongly visual and encyclopedic reference guide to recognizing and buying antiques, to detecting trends and to planning one's future collecting. On my monthly trips to the U.S. I am in constant touch with dealers, antiques centers and auction houses to check and verify prices.

Finally our thanks are due to all those experts whose invaluable help and guidance has contributed so much toward this new edition.

CONTENTS

A bronze and ivory figure of a dancer, clad in a tightly fitting body suit, her arms outstretched, on a stepped onyx base, inscribed D. H. Chiparus, base replaced, depatinated, left hand reglued, c1925, 24in (62cm) high.
$23,000-30,000

POTTERY

The pottery market has shown no great improvement this year and contrives to be the most recession-hit of all the ceramic sections. Rumours of a scandal involving fake early English pottery being sold onto the market have not helped the top end of specialist sales, despite assurances that all of these pieces are now accounted for and have been taken off the market. The market trends of the past two or three years remain the same. The rare and unusual pieces continue to attract high prices whilst the more mundane items fail to sell. Good quality late British ceramics, such as Wemyss, Moorcroft, Minton etc. continue to sell well if they are unusual, new to the market and in perfect condition. Majolica pottery continues to attract high prices for the rare and unusual. A George Jones majolica strawberry set from around 1870 realised $3,400 at Sotheby's in Sussex.

Wemyss ware continues to attract extensive interest from collectors with surprisingly high prices being realised for the rare and unusual pieces. One of many salerooms offering Wemyss last year was Andrew Hartley of Ilkley, who sold a 12 inch wide oval basket with apple decoration for $1,125, a 6.25 inch high pottery goose for $950, and a 12.25 inch high black and white cat for $2,200.

Interest in Moorcroft pottery remains high although there has been a noticeable drop in prices for the more common pieces. Wedgwood's highly decorative and skilful 1920s Fairyland Lustre wares continue deservedly

A Toby jug, wearing a black hat, painted in blue, green and brown, restored, 10.5in (26cm).
$720-1,000

to rise in price for the perfect pieces. Sotheby's Sussex saw a pair of 10 inch high vases with the 'Imps on a bridge and Tree House' pattern realise a double mid-estimate $5,600 and a 6 inch diameter 'Woodland Bridge' bowl fetched nearly $3,400 against an expected $850-1,200. Taking into account the artistry and production difficulties of Wedgwood's Fairyland Lustre wares they still appear to be very good value for money compared to the dubious merits of many of the highly priced contemporary Staffordshire factory studio ceramics of the various popular lady designers.

A Prattware barrel, probably Bristol, c1820, 6.5in (16.5cm) high.
$720-900

A not too often mentioned corner of the pottery market is that of the tile collector. Tiles still represent very good value for money; good examples being available for as little as $25-35 for a 19thC Staffordshire example. English 18thC delft tiles range from $85-255 whilst complete tile pictures can fetch many thousands of pounds. Andrew Hartley of Ilkley sold an interesting tile picture last year which was dated 1913 and inscribed 'After Edmund Dulac' by Mowbray Jeffrey. Comprising eighty tiles, the picture in the Art Nouveau style, measured 5ft by 4ft and realised $5,000.

A pottery flask, 16thC, 6in (15cm).
$600-750

English blue and white printed earthenware has always been popular with collectors and the rare and sought after patterns still continue to realise high prices. A 'Durham Ox' pattern meat plate was sold by Spencers, Retford, for $2,900. Blue and white printed earthenware Staffordshire figures and commemorative ware are all sectors of the pottery market that seem to be riding the recession with ease. This is probably because these markets are based around a sizeable and knowledgeable group of collectors.

Bottles

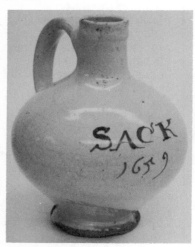

A rare delft bottle, inscribed and dated 'Sack 1659', 6in (15cm) high.
$3,600-5,000

A West Country bottle, late 19thC, 6.5in (16cm) high.
$70-80

Bowls

A London delft, blue and white bowl, c1770, 9in (23cm) diam.
$360-500

A Lambeth delft blue and white bowl, c1760, 12in (31cm) diam.
$6,000-7,000

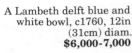

A Wedgwood creamware bowl by Millicent Taplin, early 20thC, 8in (20cm) diam.
$900-1,000

A Bristol delftware polychrome fluted punch bowl, some chips, cracks and restoration, c1735, 12in (31cm).
$4,000-5,000

A pair of English delft flower bowls, probably London, some chips and restoration, c1700, 7.5in (19cm).
$4,000-5,000

A Nevers bowl, restored, c1790, 12.5in (32cm) diam.
$700-750

A delft blue and white barber's bowl, c1720, 10in (25cm) diam.
$7,000-7,200

A Mason's posy bowl, impressed mark, c1815, 7.5in (19cm) long.
$350-450

Boxes

A Victorian majolica sardine box, with integral stand and cover, decorated in typical palette, damaged, unmarked, 9.5in (24cm) wide.
$900-1,200

An early Quimper box and cover, c1800, 5in (13cm) diam.
$400-500

A money box, 18thC, 4in (10cm) high.
$180-360

A slipware money box, probably Buckley, c1890, 10in (25cm) wide.
$350-400

Busts

A Staffordshire bust of Queen Victoria, c1820, 6in (15cm) high.
$1,400-1,700

An Enoch Wood bust of Plato, decorated in coloured enamels, 13in (33cm) high.
$720-1,000

Commemorative

A Staffordshire bust of Milton, 12in (31cm) high.
$900-1,000

A bust of Alexander I of Russia, decorated in enamel and gold leaf, inscribed E. Wood on rear, c1800, 11in (28cm).
$900-1,050

A Staffordshire pearlware plate, commemorating the death of Princess Charlotte, entitled 'Great Britain mourn her, Princes weep', all within a border moulded with fruiting vine and picked out in purple lustre, minor chips, impressed retailer's mark Clark's China Shop, Glasgow, c1817, 7in (17cm).
$600-800

A Doulton Lambeth brown glazed jug, made for Bullards & Sons Ltd to commemorate the 60th year of Queen Victoria's reign, 8.5in (21cm) high.
$360-540

A Shelley loving cup, commemorating the Coronation of George VI, colourfully gilded and enamelled with printed double portrait medallion beneath elaborate blue acanthus swag, the reverse depicting the Royal Princesses, 4in (10cm) high.
$600-700

A Copeland Spode three-handled loving cup, colour enamelled with portrait of Edward VIII flanked by crusaders, Britannia surrounded by ships and elaborate Royal coat-of-arms, the inside rim with roses, restored, 5.5in (14cm) high.
$720-900

A Staffordshire jug to commemorate the Coronation of Queen Victoria, transfer printed in black with 2 bust portraits, relevant dates and a border of roses and diapering, 19thC, 6.5in (17cm) high.
$700-900

British Commemorative Pottery

* the earliest wares available to collectors tend to be the blue-dash chargers of the late 17thC

* there has always been a strong royalist or political theme on chargers

* of the blue-dash chargers, the 'Royals' tend to be more valuable than, say, the Duke of Marlborough - the late delft dishes with Queen Anne or George I are very sought after

* a lot of the delftware is damaged but this does not severely affect value, rarity is more important

* the 19thC saw an absolute glut of 'royal' items particularly Victoria - these should only be bought in good condition

* American collectors always seek out Jubilee items.

A commemorative jug depicting the marriage of Princess Louise and Marquis of Lorne.
$250-360

A Paragon china cup, saucer and plate, brown printed with portrait of Princess Elizabeth, with gilt and red lined rim, by Marcus Adams, produced with special permission of the Duchess of York.
$300-400

An Edward VIII Coronation mug, by Ewenny potteries, c1937, 3.5in (9cm) high.
$35-70

A pipe commemorating Admiral Nelson inscribed on the front of the bowl 'Nelson' and 'Forever' on the rear, c1802, 9in (22.5cm) long.
$1,500-1,800

A Wade Heath Art Deco style jug, enamelled blue and orange, with colour printed portrait medallion of George VI and Elizabeth, the reverse with Princess Elizabeth, 5.5in (14cm) high.
$70-145

Cottages and Pastille Burners

A Staffordshire cottage, possibly by Walton, with a lamb lying amongst foliage, c1825, 4in (10cm) high.
$350-500

Cow Creamers

A North Country pottery cow creamer, c1820, 6in (15cm).
$1,000-1,500

A South Wales pottery cow creamer, c1840, 6in (15cm).
$450-550

A cow creamer with flower knop on the cover, sponged in brown, ochre and yellow on green base, c1800, 7in (17.5cm) wide.
$1,300-1,500

A Fell (Newcastle) cow creamer and cover, sponged in purple/lilac with green base.
$900-1,000

A Prattware creamware cow creamer, sponged with horizontal lines in ochre and black, horns restored, 5in (13cm) high.
$720-1,000

A Prattware cow creamer and cover, sponged in ochre, brown and green, c1800, 5.5in (14cm) high.
$1,100-1,300

A large Staffordshire Prattware cow creamer, sponged in yellow, ochre, blue and black, c1800, 8in (20cm) wide.
$1,300-1,500

A Swansea Pottery cow creamer with red and pink lustre on a green base, c1820, 7in (17.5cm) wide.
$400-500

A Yorkshire type cow creamer, 19thC, 7in (17.5cm) wide.
$300-500

Cups

A Foley faience loving cup by Wileman & Co., depicting a Yorkshireman's coat-of-arms, c1892, 4.5in (11cm) high.
$60-70

Two Quimper egg cups, c1925, 3in (7.5cm) wide.
$90-120

Two ironstone egg cups, unmarked, c1818, 3in (7.5cm) high.
l. damaged, **$110-145**
r. **$220-270**

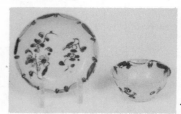

A C. J. Mason cup and saucer, c1830, 5.5in (14cm) diam.
$140-180

A C. J. Mason cup and saucer, with pseudo Chinese seal mark, c1840, 5.5in (14cm) diam.
$200-240

A Quimper egg stand, c1890, 8in(20cm) high.
$400-500

A Staffordshire miniature tea bowl and saucer, hand painted and enamelled, salt glazed, c1765, saucer 2.5in (6cm) diam.
$1,500-1,700

Ewers

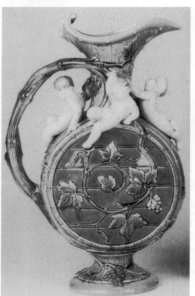

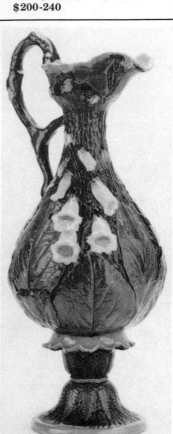

A Prattware stirrup cup, modelled as the Pope and the Devil, with ochre and yellow Papal hat and green hair, c1780, 6in (15cm) high.
$500-780

Two Minton majolica ewers, impressed with the artist's monogram and various marks, model number 900, date code for 1862, 15in (38cm) high.
$2,200-3,000

A pair of English majolica ewers, moulded with foxgloves on a bark and leaf ground, with a turquoise interior, small chip, c1860, 16in (40.5cm) high.
$1,000-1,500

Figures - Animals

A Staffordshire bird, c1770, 3.5in (8.5cm) high.
$1,700-2,500

A matched pair of Staffordshire pottery birds, each with orange beak and gilt markings, perched on blue-washed rocks sprigged with moss, small crack, 11in (28cm) high, and a Staffordshire pottery group of two birds perched above a nest of three eggs.
$750-1,200

A Prattware bird, decorated in yellow, ochre, blue and green, 8in (20cm).
$2,500-3,000

A Staffordshire tree group of canaries, decorated in coloured glazes, c1790, 8in (20cm).
$2,000-3,000

A Staffordshire greyhound with a hare in his mouth, c1850, 11.5in (29cm).
$250-285

A Staffordshire figure of a floppy eared rabbit, with brown patched animal crouching on the oval base, 19thC, 6in (15cm).
$800-1,200

A Yorkshire cow, calf and figure group, decorated in ochre, green, black and blue on a white ground, 6in (16cm) wide.
$1,700-2,000

A Staffordshire cow and milk-maid group, c1860.
$350-450

A Staffordshire figure of a floppy eared rabbit, with brown patched animal crouching on the oval base, 19thC, 6in (15cm).
$800-1,200

A pair of Staffordshire spaniels, decorated in red and white, c1860, 8in (20cm).
$360-540

A Staffordshire Whieldon type hollow sporting dog, in brown and green glazes, c1775, 4in (10cm).
$900-1,000

A pair of Staffordshire pottery zebras, each beast striped black with flaring mane, c1900, 8.5in (21.5cm).
$750-900

A creamware bull baiting group, decorated in enamel colours, the bull in pinkish brown, with black and white terrier, c1800, 7in (18cm).
$1,200-1,700

A Staffordshire model of a ram and lamb, on a mound base with bocage to rear, with green and brown enamel decoration, c1825, 5in (13cm).
$500-550

A pair of Salt pottery bocage figures, one inscribed 'Sportsman' depicting a man with his shotgun, powder flask and hound, his lady companion entitled 'Archer' with a bow, arrow and straw target, slight damage, one inscribed Salt, 7in (17.5cm).
$900-1,500

Figures - People

A figure, probably made at Pill Pottery, Newport, run by H. Davies, c1840, 8in (20cm).
$550-650

A Prattware figure of Bacchus, showing a domestic scene, decorated in ochre, green and brown, on a high square base, c1800, 10in (25cm).
$900-1,500

A Prattware coloured figure of a girl holding oranges in her apron, c1815, 10in (25cm).
$400-500

A Prattware figure of a hurdy gurdy player, with acanthus leaf decoration and underglaze colours of blue, brown, ochre and green, on a square base c1800, 10in (25cm).
$900-1,200

A Leeds figure of Minerva, Goddess of Wisdom, decorated in brown, turquoise, black, blue and red, c1790, 11in (28cm).
$1,700-2,200

A Pill Pottery, Newport, Gwent, figure, damaged, c1840, 7in (18cm).
$1,700-2,200

A hollow Prattware figure of Spring, modelled as a young lady holding a basket of flowers, decorated in yellow, brown, white, ochre, blue and green, c1800, 6in (15cm).
$600-900

A Prattware figure of Summer, with a cornucopia of flowers, c1810, 6.5in (16cm).
$650-750

A Staffordshire Obadiah Sherratt type Dandies group, decorated in enamel colours, c1820, 7in (18cm).
$1,000-1,400

A pair of Staffordshire figures, Protestantism and Popery, c1850, 9in (23cm).
$2,250-2,500

Staffordshire Figures of the Victorian Era

A Staffordshire figure of Topsy and Eva, c1852, 9in (22.5cm), B.26/84.
$600-650

A pair of Staffordshire figures of Havelock and Campbell, in blue coats with turquoise sashes, c1857, 9in (22.5cm), C/35 (176-177).
$1,200-1,500

A Staffordshire figure of Miss Nightingale and The Wounded Soldier, she in green skirt, pink blouse and blue veil, he in brown coat with blue sling, c1855, 10in (25cm). C/55 (143).
$1,500-1,700

A Staffordshire figure of William Wallace, the Scottish Champion, in plumed hat and plaid kilt, holding a round shield and a sword in his right hand, cracked, 17.5in (44cm), I/6.
$250-400

A Staffordshire figure entitled Soldiers Dream, the soldier wearing blue coat and white, green and red kilt, with ochre sash, c1854, 14in (35.5cm), C/73 (210).
$750-850

Staffordshire Figures

The letters and figures in brackets refer to the book *Staffordshire Portrait Figures,* by P.D. Gordon Pugh.

A pair of Staffordshire figures of cricketers, decorated in pale colours with blue coats, c1865, 10in (25cm), F/6 (11,12).
$1,500-1,700

A Staffordshire figure of The King of Sardinia, in blue coat and pink cape, on coloured base, c1854, 13in (33cm), C/102 (300).
$850-950

A Staffordshire figure of the Begging Sailor, wearing blue coat with pink bag, and a child wearing a pink coat, c1854, 16in (40.5cm), C/81 (236).
$1,200-1,500

A Staffordshire figure of Jenny Lind as Alice in Meyerbeer's opera, wearing a blue and yellow dress, c1847, 13.5in (34.5cm), E/80 (158).
$1,200-1,700

A Staffordshire figure of Romeo and Juliet, played by the Cushman sisters, c1852, 10.5in (26.5cm) E/1A (1).
$1,200-1,700

Two Staffordshire figures of The King of Sardinia, and Garibaldi, c1860, 10.5in (26.5cm), C/102 (298-299).
$900-1,200

A Staffordshire figure of The Sailors Return, c1855, 12.5in (32cm), C/71 (197).
$600-900

A pair of Staffordshire figures of Omer Pacha and The Sultan, both in navy coats with yellow saddle blankets, c1854, 10in (25cm), C/64 (166 and 167).
$1,200-1,500

In the Ceramics section if there is only one measurement it usually refers to the height of the piece.

Flatware

A Bristol delft blue oak leaf charger, mainly blue, yellow and green, repaired, c1700, 14in (35.5cm).
$2,000-3,000

A Dutch Delft child's plate, c1760, 6.5in (16cm).
$110-180

When a child left home the mother would make a hole in the plate so that it could never be used again, and it would be hung on the wall by a piece of string.

A Rothwell, Leeds, plate, decorated in sponged glazes of brown and emerald green, stippled brown to reverse, c1775, 9.5in (24cm).
$400-500

A pair of Ashworths teapot stands, with double landscape decoration, c1865, 6in (15cm).
$180-250

A Desvres hors d'oeuvre dish, c1890, 12in (30.5cm).
$250-300

A Dutch Delft plate, c1760, 6.5in (16.5cm). **$100-130**

A C.J. Mason dessert plate, with painted floral bouquet, 8in (20cm). **$350-400**

A Middlesbrough Pottery child's plate, with daisy relief moulded border, the central panel with transfer printed nursery rhyme 'Hey Diddle Diddle' , c1845, 7in (18cm). **$70-145**

A child's plate, with verse by Isaac Watts, possibly Llanelly Pottery South Wales, 6.5in (16cm).
$70-145

A Bristol delft blue charger, depicting Adam and Eve, repaired, c1700, 14in (35.5cm).
$3,000-4,000

A Quimper comport, c1900, 9in (23cm) diam.
$275-350

A Minton majolica 'Lazy Susan', with encaustic decoration in white, purple, ochre, brown, turquoise and green, revolving on a flared foot, cracks to rim, impressed mark and model number 799, c1873, 18in (46cm) diam.
$1,200-1,700

A Nevers plate, decorated with a peacock, 9in (23cm).
$400-650

A Rouen plate, c1770, 9in (23cm).
$450-550

A red painted daisy plate, 'The Sick Donkey', Anthony Scott, Sunderland, c1845, 6in (15cm).
$150-230

A child's plate, with relief moulded border of flowers in dark red, the central panel with transfer print of 'Grandad' with related verse, probably Staffordshire, c1840, 7in (18cm).
$85-135

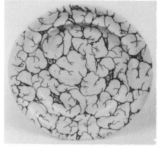

A Swansea Pottery plate, with black and white underglaze sheet pattern transfer, Lazuli pattern, Dillwyn & Co., c1850, 10.5in (26cm).
$150-190

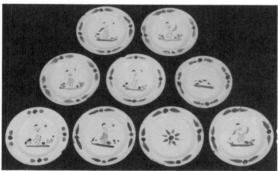

Nine underglaze painted moulded miniature plates, c1810, 3in (8cm).
$450-650

A Fremington, Devon, dish with combed slip, c1890, 12in (30.5cm) wide.
$240-280

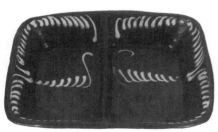

A Sunderland or Newcastle dish, 11in (28cm) wide.
$70-85

A Davenport blue and white platter, impressed mark, c1830, 21in (53cm) wide.
$250-300

A creamware dish, decorated with flowers in underglaze blue and dated 1778, 16in (41cm) diam.
$700-800

A child's plate, Joseph series, c1850, 6.5in (16cm).
$65-80

A slipware plate decorated in brown, cream and ochre, late 18thC, 8.5in (21cm).
$4,200-5,000

A slipware charger, late 18thC, 13in (33cm).
$1,700-2,500

A rare relief moulded alphabet plate, impressed Fordy & Patterson, Sheriff Hill Pottery, Newcastle, Gateshead, c1825, 3.5in (9cm).
$550-750

An Hispano-Moresque copper lustre charger, with central boss, painted concentric bands of stylised leaves and flowers, 16thC, 15.5in (39cm).
$1,700-2,000

Inkstands

A Quimper inkstand, c1890, 10.5in (26cm) wide.
$650-800

A Mason's Ironstone inkwell, Old School House pattern, c1815, 2.5in (6cm) diam.
$550-700

A rare Mason's inkstand, decorated in green enamel with gilt, impressed mark, c1815, 5in (13cm).
$1,150-1,250

A Mason's Ironstone inkstand, with black printed mark, replaced lids, c1835, 12in (31cm) wide.
$1,350-1,500

A Georgian inkstand, decorated in blue and ochre, green shell tops, mid-19thC, 15in (38cm) wide.
$1,000-1,200

Jardinières

A George Jones Majolica jardinière, with dark blue ground, moulded in relief with a frieze of half-length figures of sea gods and goddesses, turquoise glazed interior and yellow line rim, on a spreading foot, incised monogram, painted pattern number 2784, c1880, 23in (59cm) wide.
$6,000-8,000

A Mintons large pottery jardinière.
$1,400-1,950

Jars

An English delft blue and white drug jar, 7in (18cm).
$1,200-1,700

Jugs

A Bristol pearlware puzzle jug, decorated with flower sprays, inscribed initials, dated August 11th - 1819, probably painted by William Fifield, repaired, 5in (13cm).
$900-1,220

A Claypits Pottery jug, green, c1900, 7in (18cm).
$70-145

A London delft, blue and white drug jar, c1730, 4in (10cm).
$900-1,500

A delft puzzle jug, probably Liverpool, c1740, 7in (17cm).
$2,000-2,500

A pair of Davenport jugs, pink and purple lustre decorated with flowers and named, c1830, 8.5in (21cm).
$1,200-1,700

A Davenport ewer, with blue and white underglaze transfer pattern, c1835, 9in (23cm).
$180-260

A Drabware jug, c1810, 3.5in (9cm).
$70-100

An English delftware puzzle jug, inscribed with the usual verse, Liverpool, chipped, c1760, 7in (17cm).
$2,000-2,700

Three Nottingham saltglazed bear baiting jugs, mid-18thC.
$17,000-20,000

A Quimper wall font and basin, 18in (46cm) complete.
$2,000-2,700

A Mason's sparrow beek jug, c1815, 2.5in (6cm).
$300-370

A creamware beer jug, decorated with roses and flower sprigs, in the Leeds manner, inscribed Drink it up under the spout, strap handle, c1780, 7in (18cm).
$500-650

A Staffordshire saltglazed puzzle jug, decorated in scratch blue and white, c1760, 7in (18cm).
$4,250-5,000

A Staffordshire bear jug and cover, decorated in tones of beige and brown, c1780, 8in (20cm).
$5,000-6,000

A Minton 'Majolica' jug, modelled in high relief with peasant figures dancing and a man seated beneath the spout, the foot with a formal border of crosses and studding, all glazed in tones of green, blue, yellow, brown and white, registration and impressed marks, shape number and date code for 1865, 10in (25cm).
$1,300-1,600

A pottery jug, with black and white transfer of a ship under sail, probably Liverpool, c1810, 5in (13cm).
$170-250

A creamware jug depicting Toby Fillpot, dressed in red coat, pink waistcoat and yellow breaches, on one side, the other The Farriers Arms, in the middle the date 1810, 7.5in (19cm).
$500-700

An earthenware jug, with transfer printed scenes from the Prodigal Son in Georgian costume, 6in (15cm).
$200-250

An underglaze decorated jug, c1795, 7in (18cm).
$330-450

A pink lustre jug, 'Female Archers', marked Fen, 5.5in (14cm).
$500-600

A gravel finish jug, with gadrooned band, c1830, 3in (8cm).
$35-70

A gaudy lustre jug, c1840, 6.5in (16cm).
$120-150

Toby Jugs

A Walton squat type overglaze enamel Toby jug, with blue swirled coat, pink trousers and green base, c1800, 7in (18cm).
$360-540

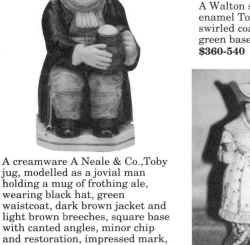

A creamware A Neale & Co.,Toby jug, modelled as a jovial man holding a mug of frothing ale, wearing black hat, green waistcoat, dark brown jacket and light brown breeches, square base with canted angles, minor chip and restoration, impressed mark, incised 15, c1795, 10in (25cm).
$1,500-1,800

A Neale & Co., Toby jug, decorated with overglaze enamels of turquoise coat, buff breeches and blue socks, c1800, 10in (25cm).
$1,200-1,700

An overglaze enamel 'Gin Woman' Toby jug, with yellow hat, black hair, pink face, green and rust dress, c1840, 10in (25cm).
$360-540

A Prattware Toby jug, decorated in yellow and blue patterned jacket and socks, blue waistcoat, yellow breeches, brown hat and shoes, c1790, 10in (25cm).
$1,500-1,700

A cross-legged Toby jug, wearing blue and white transfer printed Willow pattern jacket and hat and brown trousers, c1890, 8in (20cm).
$250-300

An underglaze Toby jug, decorated in Pratt colours of blue coat, yellow waistcoat and ochre breeches, c1840, 10in (25cm).
$250-350

Dr Johnson or 'The Drunken Parson' Toby jug, dressed in black underglaze colours, sitting on a rust Georgian style chair, c1840, 8in (20cm).
$750-1,000

The Nightwatchman or George Whitfield Toby jug, dressed in grey and black coat, the spout forming the chair back, c1890, 7in (18cm).
$360-540

An underglaze snuff taker Toby jug with blue jacket, red breeches, and yellow waistcoat, c1900, 9in (23cm).
$100-160

Mugs

An English delftware blue and white chequer pattern mug, probably Bristol, repaired, 18thC, 5in (12.5cm) high.
$2,500-3,000

An early Victorian pearlware frog mug to commemorate the signing of the Peace Treaty of the Crimean War, printed in underglaze black and naively overpainted in colours with a French and English soldier shaking hands, beneath the scrolled legend 'May They Ever Be United', within Sunderland pink lustre rims and waved line decoration, damaged, 1856, 5in (12cm) high.
$450-550

An English delft named and dated mug, probably Lambeth, with small deep grooved strap handle, painted in blue with a pair of birds perched upon a zig-zag fence flanked by flowering branches, inscribed 'Richard Latham, 1744', below a diapered and stylised flower border, worn, 6.5in (16.5cm) high.
$15,000-17,000

A child's mug, decorated with the alphabet, c1880, 3in (7.5cm) high.
$70-145

A child's mug, c1820, 2in (5cm) high.
$110-180

A child's mug, with alphabet painted in underglaze colour, c1790, 2.5in (6cm) high.
$500-600

A child's mug, Scottish, c1885, 3.5in (8.5cm) high.
$70-145

A child's mug, c1860, 4in (10cm) high.
$90-120

A child's mug, c1870, 3in (7.5cm) high.
$110-180

A marblised tankard, in blue, black and cream on white, c1800, 6in (15cm).
$1,200-1,700

A small banded mug, c1860, 3in (7.5cm) high.
$80-100

A Mocha half-pint mug, c1890, 4in (10cm) high.
$110-180

Plaques

A Staffordshire pearlware plaque, depicting Peace and Plenty before a brazier, with a classical swag surround and decoration, c1790, 5in (12.5cm) high.
$1,200-1,700

A Prattware plaque, depicting the head of a classical female, decorated in typical Prattware palate, c1800, 7.5in (18.5cm) high.
$900-1,500

A Staffordshire plaque, inscribed 'Du of York', decorated in blue, white, ochre and yellow, c1800, 4.5in (11.5cm) high.
$650-750

A creamware plaque of Paris and Oenone in a woodland setting, decorated in enamel with leaf moulded borders, c1800, 9in (22.5cm) high.
$600-700

A Prattware plaque of Bacchus and Venus, decorated in blue, ochre, green, and brown, impressed EC 1801 on reverse, c1801, 8in (20cm) high.
$900-1,500

A pink lustre decorated plaque inscribed 'Duke of Wellington - 131 guns', Anthony Scott, Sunderland, c1840, 9in (22.5cm) wide.
$250-320

Pots

A brownware storage pot, with relief moulding of Victoria and her mother, c1840, 6in (15cm) high. **$150-170**

A rare Prattware plaque of a horse grazing in a rural setting, c1800, repaired, 4.5in (11cm) high.
$750-850

A Desvres (Pas de Calais) Revolutionary faience mustard pot, c1872, 7.5in (18.5cm) high.
$240-280

A Sarreguemines majolica pot, formed as a tree stump with dogs chasing a rabbit into its burrow, complete with handles, 7in (17.5cm).
$170-280

A pearlware baluster shaped mustard pot, decorated in underglaze blue, lid missing, c1790, 4.5in (11.5cm) high.
$200-250

An English delftware bulb pot, London or Bristol, c1760, restored, 5in (12.5cm) high.
$1,200-1,700

An English delftware blue and white posset pot with lid, London or Bristol, c1720, 8.5in (21cm) high.
$3,600-5,000

Posset pots were also made in lead glazed and manganese glazed earthenware and white and brown saltglazed ware. They always had two handles but did not necessarily have a drinking spout. Posset was a wholesome gruel sold in inns and consisted of ale, oats and honey. It was often fortified with brandy.

Services

A Mason's Ironstone dessert service, decorated with a scroll chinoiserie pattern of Orientals seated and standing taking tea in a rocky garden reserved on a tight scroll ground with a lobed panel of trophies, on an elaborately moulded surface, comprising: 13 plates, 2 sauce tureens, covers and stand, 8 various shaped dishes, and a comport, c1820, some damage, plates 9in (22.5cm). **$3,000-5,000**

A Mason's Patent Ironstone part dinner service, comprising: 2 tureens with covers and stands, 16 plates and 11 dishes, early 19thC. **$700-800**

A Wedgwood dessert service comprising: 6 plates, 4 dishes, 1 comport, c1810, comport 5in (12.5cm) high. **$1,700-2,200**

Tea and Coffee Pots

A teapot from the William Greatbatch factory, depicting The Hun August Keppel, hand painted, coloured transfer print, c1780, 6in (15cm). **$4,000-5,000**

A Jackfield teapot, c1755, 3.5in (8.5cm). **$270-350**

A Mason's miniature teapot and cover, 3in (7.5cm). **$650-720**

A Wedgwood creamware teapot and cover, decorated with a Chinaman in a rocky landscape, the reverse with sprays of roses, with Crabstock spout and handle, damaged, c1765, 5.5in (13.5cm). **$1,200-1,700**

A Wedgwood teapot and cover, finely decorated with bouquets of flowers, with Crabstock handle and spout, c1765, 4in (10cm). **$1,250-1,500**

A Mason's teapot and sucrier, decorated with waterlilies, c1815, 7.5in (19cm). **$800-900**

A saltglazed teapot and cover with blue ground, decorated with enamelled red, green and yellow roses, with Crabstock handle and spout, finial repaired, c1760, 4.5in (11.5cm).
$1,800-2,500

A pearlware teapot and cover, decorated with 8 dancing figures, picked out in enamel colours in red, blue and green, c1810, 5.5in (13.5cm).
$750-850

A Redware glazed engine turned teapot, c1770, 4.5in (11cm).
$200-300

A saltglazed teapot and cover, decorated in coloured enamels with roses and blossoms, with Crabstock handle and spout, c1740, 5.5in (13.5cm).
$900-1,500

A Leeds teapot and cover, Dutch decorated with sprays of roses, c1780, 5.5in (13.5cm).
$750-850

Tiles

A London delft blue and white tile, depicting Lazarus in Heaven, and The Rich Man in Hell, c1740.
$70-145

A Liverpool delft blue and white tile, c1760, 5in (12.5cm) square.
$50-80

A Liverpool woodblock transfer print tile, c1757.
$600-700

A Liverpool delft blue and white tile, c1770, 5in (12.5cm) square.
$50-70

A Liverpool delft blue and white tile, c1760, 5in (12.5cm) square.
$50-70

A Liverpool tile, partly restored, 5in (12.5cm) square.
$80-110

A collection of 11 Dutch Delft tiles, each painted in blue with a different animal subject, repaired, 19thC, 6in (15cm) square. **$750-850**

Tureens

An Italian tin glazed maiolica tureen and cover, decorated in blue and white, c1900, 11in (28cm) high. **$180-220**

A Dillwyn & Co. Swansea Pottery lidded tureen, decorated in underglaze blue and white, c1815, 7in (17.5cm) wide. **$180-220**

A swan cheese dish and cover, c1870, 12in (30.5cm). **$360-540**

A Staffordshire pottery bird tureen, decorated in yellow, green, red, grey, brown and blue, 5in (12.5cm) high. **$600-900**

A faience mandolin vase, 11in (28cm). **$360-540**

Vases

A pair of Mason's Ironstone vases and covers of Chinese inspiration, printed and hand coloured with covers similarly decorated beneath an entwined dragon finial, one chipped, impressed and black printed marks, red painted pattern number A/9447/3, c1825, 25in (64cm). **$1,700-2,700**

A London delft blue and white vase, c1750, 5.5in (14cm). **$2,300-3,000**

An English delft blue and white vase, 7in (18cm). **$450-550**

A Staffordshire spill vase, modelled as a rustic man holding a bird's nest, seated by a tree with birds in the branches, with a dog at his side, c1820, 9in (23cm).
$700-900

A Staffordshire bull baiting spill vase, coloured brown, white and green, c1800, 8in (20cm).
$3,600-5,000

A Staffordshire spill vase group entitled 'The Rivals', c1855, 13in (33cm).
$320-500

A pair of Staffordshire creamware triple spill vases of Ralph Wood type, each modelled as entwined green dolphins supporting 3 reed moulded vases enriched in grey and yellow translucent glazes, on foliage moulded brown quatrefoil bases, chipped, c1780, 7.5in (19cm).
$1,200-1,700

A pair of Staffordshire figures of zebras being attacked by snakes with spill holder in the form of a tree trunk, c1860, 6in (15cm).
$350-500

Wemyss

A Wemyss 'combe' flower bowl, painted with large roses and foliage, cracked and chipped, impressed and painted Wemyss, c1900, 8in (20cm).
$680-900

A Wemyss cockerel candlestick, 12in (30cm).
$350-400

A Wemyss three-handled mug, painted with geese, 5.5in (14cm).
$700-1,000

A Wemyss cherry basket, c1920, 4.5in (11cm).
$1,200-1,700

A Wemyss honey pot and cover, painted with bees, 7in (18cm).
$2,700-3,600

A Wemyss biscuit barrel and cover, painted with apples, 5in (12cm).
$400-500

A Wemyss Earshall jug, painted in black with crows nesting in tall spindly trees, divided by a cartouche with 'Earlshall Faire, A.D. 1914' beneath the inscription 'Or whiles a clan o'roosty craws cangle the gether', handle repaired, impressed and painted Wemyss, 8in (20cm).
$450-550

Wemyss Value Points

* quality of painting -especially a large piece painted freely by Karel Nekola

* condition - Wemyss is, by nature, fragile and since many pieces were made for nursery use, many have been damaged, chips can be acceptable but cracks do substantially affect price

* other painters of note include James Sharp, David Grinton, John Brown, Hugh and Christinia McKinnon, also Karel's two sons, Carl and Joseph

* early pieces, particularly with a red border

* unusual subject matters - nasturtiums, gorse, pink flamingos

* beware of unmarked pieces - usually these were rejects or copies from another factory

A Wemyss honey pot and cover modelled as a straw skep, the cover painted with bees on a shaded base, impressed and painted Wemyss, T. Goode & Co., 7in (18cm).
$1,200-1,700

A Wemyss ewer, with high lip, painted with cherries on branches, impressed and painted Wemyss, stamped T. Goode & Co., c1900, 10in (25cm).
$500-700

A Wemyss preserve jar and cover, painted with brambles, 5in (13cm).
$270-350

A Wemyss preserve jar and cover, painted with raspberries, chipped, impressed and painted Wemyss, and stamped T. Goode & Co., c1900, 5in (13cm).
$450-550

A Wemyss honey pot, painted with bees and hive, 5in (13cm).
$450-500

A Wemyss Earlshall jug, painted in black and inscribed 'As the many wintered crow, that leads the clanging rookery home', and Earlshall Faire 1914', impressed and painted mark, 6in (15cm).
$700-900

A Wemyss three-handled mug, painted with plums, 7in (18cm).
$1,000-1,500

Miscellaneous

A Staffordshire cradle with a baby, decorated in yellow ochre and white, early 19thC, 5in (12.5cm) wide.
$720-1,000

A Victorian pottery flour bin, with two lug handles, decorated in underglaze blue with chinoiserie fishermen beneath flower filled baskets and scroll border, damaged, 12.5in (31.5cm) high.
$900-1,500

A Buckley pottery brewing jar, 15in (38cm).
$35-70

A Swansea pottery pierced basket stand, in underglaze blue and white transfer, with 'Ladies of Llangollen' pattern, c1820, 11in (28cm) wide.
$720-1,000

A Staffordshire pottery watch holder, c1830, 7in (18cm).
$360-540

A Ewenny pottery butter churn with lid, c1870, 23in (58cm) high.
$180-360

A pair of delft flower bricks, possibly Liverpool, decorated in blue and white, c1750, 5in (12.5cm) wide.
$1,200-1,700

A Yorkshire puzzle pipe, decorated in Prattware colours, c1800, 11in (28cm) long.
$1,200-1,700

A sauceboat in blue printed Longbridge pattern, 6in (15cm) wide.
$110-180

An English delftware cornucopia wall pocket, probably Liverpool, small crack, inscribed I G I and dated 1748 on reverse, 8in (20cm).
$3,600-5,500

A Minton majolica cheese dish and cover in the form of a bee-skep, with a branch-moulded loop handle, exterior with fruiting blackberry branches, base glazed in mottled pale-blue, on branch-moulded feet, damaged, impressed mark and model number 969, date code for 1865, 14in (35.5cm).
$3,600-5,500

A Bristol delftware bowl, with floral design, c1760, 9in (23cm). **$1,800-2,700**

Three Bristol delftware fluted bowls, probably Brislington, restored, c1830, 7in (18cm) **$1,600-2,700** and a porringer or bleeding bowl, restored, c1725. **$3,600-4,500**

A set of 5 Dutch Delft plates, De Roos factory, each painted with a biblical subject after Lucas van Leyden, rim chips, R mark in underglaze blue, 9in (23cm), c1678. **$7,000-9,000**

An Adam and Eve charger, cracked and chipped, London, c1660, 16.5in (42cm). **$50,000-54,000**

l. An English delftware dated christening bowl, London or Bristol, the exterior with figures and carriages near The Plough Inn, cracked and restored, 1752, 10.5in (26cm). **$40,000-45,000**

A 'Midnight Modern Conversation' punch bowl, the exterior with rural landscape panels, restored, Liverpool, c1750, 10in (25cm). **$18,000-21,000**

An armorial Lambeth delftware caudle cup, inscribed 1674, with paper label, 3.5in (9cm). **$32,000-35,000**

l. A Castelli armorial dish, c1592. **$6,000-7,000**

r. A Castel-durante tondino. **$4,500-5,500**

A dated armorial marriage charger, restored, London, 1673. **$80,000-90,000**

33

COLOUR REVIEW

A pair of Staffordshire rustic musicians, decorated in enamel, possibly by John Dale of Burslem, 4.5in (11cm). **$1,800-2,000**

A pearlware 'Tee Total' figure group, of Obadiah Sherratt type, on a black sponged base, c1830, 7.5in (19cm). **$4,500-6,300**

A pair of figures of Neptune and Venus, by Obadiah Sherratt, on table base, c1825, 9.5in (24cm). **$3,200-4,300**

A Yorkshire pottery horse, c1860, 7in (18cm) wide. **$3,600-4,500**

A selection of Staffordshire models of watch holders and a money box, painted in Pratt enamels, 8 to 11in (20 to 28cm). **$750-2,500 each**

An Obadiah Sherratt group of Dr. Syntax playing cards, c1825. **$5,500-6,300**

A Staffordshire lion, c1820, 7in (18cm) wide. **$2,000-2,700**

A Dixon Austin & Co., watch stand, c1822, restored. **$1,500-1,800**

A Staffordshire pearlware cow group, chipped, c1800, 13in (33cm). **$7,000-8,000**

A creamware Ralph
Wood jug, c1770.
$900-1,200

A Ralph Wood
'Admiral Lord Howe'
Toby jug, c1775, 10in
(25cm).
$8,500-9,000

An Enoch Wood figure
of Fortitude.
$2,500-2,800

A pearlware Toby jug,
c1790, 10in (25cm).
$1,500-1,800

'The Sinner' Toby
jug, c1800.
$3,600-5,500

A Prattware Toby jug,
c1790, 8in (20cm).
$1,500-1,700

A pair of pearlware figures of
Faith and Charity, c1800, 7in
(18cm).
$270-360

A Palissy type
figure of 'La
Nourrice,
probably Avon,
mid-17thC.
$7,000-8,000

A Prattware Rodney's
sailor Toby jug, c1790.
$3,600-5,000

An Obadiah Sherratt group,
c1830. **$720-900**

A 'Lohan' of
Whieldon type,
derived from a
Meissen model,
c1750, 4.5in
(11cm).
$30,500-32,500

A Maiolica group of The
Virgin and Child, probably
Faenza, c1540.
$28,000-30,000

A Staffordshire group of Jenny
Jones and Ned Morgan, c1860, 9in
(23cm).
$720-900

l. A Queen Mary Royal portrait charger, Brislington, c1690, repaired, 13in (33.5cm).
$10,000-11,500

r. An equestrian charger, London, c1670, probably depicting Charles II, repaired crack, 13in (32.5cm).
$32,000-36,000

A delft Queen Anne charger, c1705, probably Bristol, 13.5in (34.5cm).
$18,000-20,000

A delft Queen Anne charger, c1705, probably Bristol, 10in (25cm).
$31,500-33,500

An English delftware charger, probably London, c1690, 12in (30cm).
$4,700-6,500

A Bristol delft tulip charger, c1690, 14in (35.5cm).
$3,250-3,450

A set of 6 octagonal 'Merryman' plates, c1690, 3 repaired, slight glaze flaking, 8in (19.5cm) diam.
$34,000-36,000

l. A Bristol charger, depicting Prince George of Denmark, glaze chip to rim, c1705, 13.5in (34cm).
$19,000-21,000

r. An armorial charger, Southwark, 1651, repaired, 15in (38cm).
$65,000-72,000 .

A delft tulip charger, probably Bristol, glaze damage,13.5in (34cm). **$3,000-4,000**

An Urbino dish, the reverse inscribed Pluto e Proferpina, restored, c1530. **$10,000-11,000**

A Dutch Delft charger, extensively repaired, 13.5in (35cm). **$480-580**

Two Dutch Delft Royalist lobed dishes, with William of Orange and Queen Mary, 9in (22cm). **$1,000-1,500**

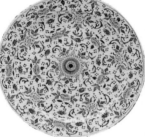

A delft polychrome dish, with allover floral pattern, 13in (33.5cm). **$900-1,000**

A delft polychrome plaque, with 2 Chinese figures in a garden, 14in (35cm). **$1,800-2,000**

A pair of English delft polychrome dishes, with willow and flowering plants, 12in (30.5cm). **$1,200-1,500**

A blue and white delft plate, with a lion, 10.5in (26cm). **$1,000-1,200**

An English delft polychrome plaque, probably Bristol, 14in (35cm). **$550-650**

A blue and white delft dish with figures in a landscape, 14in (35cm). **$700-900**

An English delft polychrome plaque, 14in (36cm). **$2,500-2,800**

An English delft dish, with a Chinaman by a rock, 12.5in (32.5cm). **$1,000-1,200**

A delft polychrome dish, probably London, 14in (35cm). **$1,000-1,500**

37

An Urbino Istoriato dish, painted with the Contest between Pierides and the Muses, repaired, c1540, 15.5in (40cm).
$56,000-60,000

An Istoriato tondino, painted with St Paul healing a woman, perhaps Pesaro, cracked and repaired, c1580, 9in (22.5cm).
$6,500-7,000

A slipware charger, early 18thC.
$18,000-20,000

A Staffordshire dated slipware dish, with stylised bird, minor surface chips, c1790, 14in (35cm).
$9,000-10,000

An Urbino maiolica dish, painted by Francesco Xanto Avelli with a scene from Virgil's Aeneid, restored, dated 1539, 12in (30.5cm).   **$61,000-63,000**

A tondino, Deruta or Siena, some damage, c1510, 9.5in (24cm).   **$4,500-5,500**

A Palissy type dish, probably Le Prè d'Auge, moulded with a coiled snake, rim cracked, early 17thC, 22in (55cm).
$2,500-2,800

A Montelupo dish, depicting figures in a bakery, some damage, late 16thC, 20in (50.5cm).   **$21,000-23,500**

A Staffordshire slipware dish, with a spotted bird surrounded by smaller birds within a pie crust rim, dated 1777, 16.5in (42cm).
$14,500-18,000

A Deruta lustred dish, depicting a mythical beast, minute rim chips, c1525, 17in (43cm).   **$56,000-63,000**

A Cambrian Pottery jug, painted by Thomas Pardoe, depicting a tiger in Indian landscape, chip to spout, c1800, 10.5in (26.5cm).
$8,000-9,500

An inscribed mug, London, some damage, dated 1696, 7in (18cm).
$20,500-22,000

A Don Pottery pearlware jug, early 19thC, 6in (15.5cm).
$3,000-3,200

Two Faenza waisted albarelli, named in Gothic script, some damage and repairs, c1545, 10. 5in (26cm).
$14,500-16,500

A Faenza albarello with Gothic script, c1525, damage and restoration, 12.5in (31.5cm).
$11,000-14,500

A Staffordshire saltglaze bear jug and cover, c1750, 8.5in (21cm).
$3,000-3,600

A Pratt type pearlware jug, painted with flowers, 1817, some damage, 7in (16.5cm).
$800-1,000

A Famiglia Gotica albarello, late 15thC, 11.5in (30cm).
$14,500-18,000

A Staffordshire glazed jug, c1820, restored, 6in (16cm).
$450-650

A Montelupo albarello, cracked, 8in (20.5cm).
$1,600-2,000

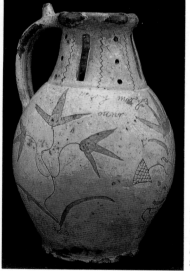

A sgraffito puzzle jug, from Ewenny Pottery, dated June 19th, 1830, slight damage, 13in (33cm).
$2,300-3,200

A creamware baluster jug, possibly Leeds, damaged, dated 1786, 9in (23cm).
$1,500-1,600

A North Italian maiolica albarello, hair crack, with collector's label, 10in (25cm).
$3,000-3,200

A Faenza albarello, mid-16thC, 6.5in (16.5cm).
$5,500-7,000

COLOUR REVIEW

A selection of Wemyss baskets, painted with roses, flowers and fruit, c1900. **$900-2,700 each**

An Urbino cistern, repaired, c1580, 29in (73cm). **$16,500-21,000**

A botanical creamware dessert service, early 19thC, dessert plate 9in (22cm). **$5,000-6,000**

Two Wemyss ewers and basins, c1900. **$1,600-2,500 each**

An Annaberg tankard with pewter lid, c1667. **$26,000-27,500**

A George Jones majolica dessert service, c1870. **$3,500-5,500**

A Nevers faience crucifix base, c1775. **$1,200-1,500**

A French papier mâché model for a tea service, mid-19thC. **$9,500-10,000**

A Wemyss tyg and bucket, c1900, tyg 9in (23cm). **$1,200-2,000 each**

A mug, London or Bristol, c1730. **$5,000-5,500**

A Dutch Delft tureen and cover, c1750. **$4,000-5,000**

A creamware mug, c1782, 6in (16cm). **$1,000-1,200**

A Minton majolica centrepiece, repaired, impressed marks, c1877, 40in (102cm). **$4,500-5,500**

A Wemyss bucket and cover, restored, c1900, 11.5in (29cm). **$3,600-4,5000**

A Newcastle earthenware tea set, c1820, 6in (14.5cm) **$1,800-2,500**

A delft posset pot and cover, mid-18thC, 8.5in, (21.5cm).
$2,500-3,500

A Dutch Delft vase, in Chinese Transitional style, restored, GK monogram in underglaze blue, c1700.
$5,000-5,500

An early delft posset pot, Southwark, Pickleherring, restored, c1630, 5in (13cm) high.
$36,000-40,000

A London delftware plaque, initialled AML and dated 1716.
$8,000-9,500

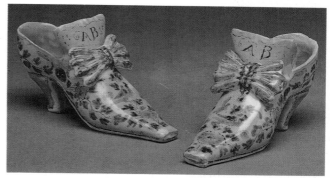

A pair of English delftware shoes, probably London, one tongue restored, dated 1695, 5in (12.5cm).
$32,000-36,000

A hand warmer, in the form of a book, with an aperture at either end, probably London, chipped and restored, late 17thC, 6in (15cm).
$10,500-12,000

Two views of a dated English delftware triangular salt, the sides with a lion, unicorn and dragon in relief, the well inscribed and dated E C 1674, restored.
$59,500-61,000

An English delft drinking vessel, c1650.
$21,000-23,500

l. A pair of English delft child's head flower vases, some damage, c1685, 6.5in (16cm).
$20,000-21,000

r. An English delft candle niche, cracked and chipped, mid-18thC. **$5,500-7,000**

A Meissen gold mounted
snuff box, painted with a
river god, slight rubbing,
c1750, 2.5in (6cm).
$21,000-25,000

Two Meissen quatrefoil centrepieces,
painted with Holzschnitt Blumen,
chipped, c1740, 14.5in (37cm).
$9,500-10,000

A Meissen gold mounted
circular snuff box, c1745, 2in
(5.5cm). **$75,500-81,000**

A St. Cloud silver mounted snuff box,
minor rubbing, c1740, 3in (8cm)
wide. **$7,000-8,000**

A Meissen box and cover, chipped
and restored, restoration and
slight chips, blue crossed swords
mark, c1725, 8in (19.5cm) long.
$38,000-45,000

A Meissen Hausmaler bowl,
crossed swords and J mark,
impressed 6, c1745, 7in (18cm).
$6,000-7,000

A Chelsea fluted teacup and saucer,
tiny chips, painted red anchor mark,
c1754, saucer 5in (13cm).
$2,500-2,700

A Meissen gold mounted yellow
ground oval snuff box, c1740, 3in
(7.5cm) wide.
$75,500-76,500

A pair of Worcester green
camaieu baskets, some chips,
7in (18cm), c1775.
$4,500-5,500

A Meissen gold mounted
snuff box, c1750, 5.5in
(13cm) diam.
$9,500-10,000

A Meissen armorial
chinoiserie teabowl and
saucer, 1731.
$9,000-14,500

A Derby group of Europa
and the Bull, c1765.
$2,500-2,700

A Chelsea figure of a
Judge, c1760.
$4,000-5,000

A group of Juno and a
Peacock, Derby, c1765.
$2,000-4,000

A Chelsea figure group of
Britannia lamenting, c1751,
10in (25.5cm).
$26,000-29,500

A Böttger pagoda figure, c1715, 5in
(13cm).high.
$14,500-18,000

A Meissen armorial teabowl and
saucer, marked, c1730.
$12,000-14,500

A pair of Derby figures, John
Wilkes and General Conway,
c1765. **$2,700-3,000**

A pair of Ludwigsburg figures by
Franz Anton Pustelli, c1760, 5in
(13cm) high.
$5,700-7,000

A Meissen teabowl and saucer, incised and
gilder's mark, c1730. **$5,500-7,000**

A Meissen
yellow ground
coffee cup,
c1730, 3in (7cm)
high.
$24,500-26,000

A Meissen chinoiserie tea
bowl and saucer, c1735.
$54,000-63,000

A Fürstenberg figure of
Frederick the Great, c1800,
19in (48.5cm).
$3,600-4,500

A Sèvres biscuit
figure of Thalie,
impressed, c1808,
12in (30cm) high.
$4,500-5,000

A pair of Chantilly wolves, chipped
and repaired, c1740.
$18,000-27,000

A Meissen figure of Count
Bruhl's tailor, restored, c1880,
marked, 17in (43cm).
$9,500-10,000

A Frankenthal model of
a stork, restored, c1760.
$4,500-5,500

A Meissen
model of a
dove, chipped
and restored,
c1740.
$5,500-6,000

A Meissen model of a
parrot, damaged, c1740,
7in (18cm) high.
$15,000-16,500

A Strasbourg model of a pug
dog, impressed H above F738
above A3, c1770, 4in (10cm).
$7,000-9,000

A pair of Chelsea sporting hounds, with a hare and brace of partridges
under each dog's forepaws, minor chips, c1749, 7.5in (19cm).
$108,000-110,000

A Meissen Paduan
cockerel, incised
L3144, damaged and
restored, crossed
swords mark and
incised, c1880.
$6,000-7,000

A Meissen model
of a guinea fowl,
by J. J. Kändler,
some damage
and restored,
c1745, 6.5in
(16cm).
$4,500-5,500

Two Meissen models of playing bears, by J. J. Kändler, blue
crossed swords at back, minor chips, c1740, 3 and 3.5in (7.5
and 8cm) high. **$10,000-14,500**

A Derby trompe l'oeil plate, minor wear, marked, c1805, 8.5in (22cm). **$3,500-4,500**

A Chelsea two-handled dish, with Arcadian river landscape, stilt marks, c1755, 7in (18.5cm). **$4,500-5,000**

A Swansea dessert plate, painted by Henry Morris, c1820, 8in (21cm). **$1,800-2,800**

A Meissen Schmetterling part dinner service, marked, mid-18thC. **$17,000-18,000**

A pair of Chelsea dishes, restored, marked, c1755, 8in (20cm). **$1,700-1,800**

A Meissen two-handled lobed tray, marked, c1740, 10in (25cm). **$8,000-9,000**

A Meissen dish from the Swan service, marked, c1740, 15in (38cm). **$75,000-80,000**

A Meissen Kakiemon dish, blue crossed swords mark, c1735, 13in (33.5cm). **$10,000-11,000**

A Worcester dish, marked, c1770, 8in (20cm). **$1,000-1,200**

A pair of Chelsea bowls, red anchor marks, c1755, 9in (22.5cm). **$3,500-4,500**

A Nantgarw plate, London decorated, c1820, 10in (25cm). **$5,500-6,000**

A pair of Worcester dishes, one cracked, c1770, 13.5in (34.5cm). **$5,500-6,000**

A Chelsea botanical plate, restored, marked, c1755, 11in (28cm). **$10,500-12,500**

A Meissen cabinet tray, painted with a view of Dresden, c1870, 20.5in (52cm). **$9,500-10,000**

A Sèvres tureen, cover and stand, marked, c1760, 20in (50.5cm). **$40,500-54,000**

A pair of flower tubs and stands, probably Chamberlain's Worcester, c1790, 5in (12.5cm). **$8,000-9,000**

A Longton Hall lobed tureen and cover, restored, c1755, 5in (12.5cm). **$16,500-21,000**

A Vincennes écuelle, cover and stand, damaged, marked, 1753, stand 8in (20.5cm). **$8,000-10,000**

A Coalport botanical dessert service, some damage, impressed and script marks, c1820, 9in (23.5cm). **$6,000-7,000**

A pair of Sèvres bleu lapis ground orange tubs, restored, marked, 1765, 7in (18cm). **$12,000-21,000**

A pair of bough pots, possibly Chamberlains, early 19thC, 8.5in (21.5cm). **$5,500-6,000**

A 'Vienna' tray, painted after F. Laufberger, c1880, 24.5in (62cm). **$4,500-5,500**

Ten Meissen topographical plates, crossed swords in underglaze blue, c1870, 9in (22.5cm). **$16,500-18,000**

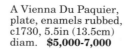

A Vienna Du Paquier, plate, enamels rubbed, c1730, 5.5in (13.5cm) diam. **$5,000-7,000**

A Coalport botanical part dessert service, minor wear and restoration, c1810. **$9,500-10,000**

A Spode botanical part dessert service, minor wear, puce painted mark and pattern number 1100, c1800. **$2,500-3,500**

A Derby dessert service, crowned D and crossed batons mark in iron red, small chips and cracks, c1820. **$3,500-4,500**

A Vienna coffee pot and domed cover, marked, 1796, 8in (20cm). **$1,000-1,100**

A Derby dessert service, painted crown, D and crossed batons, some damage, c1790. **$3,500-4,500**

A pair of Meissen flattened scent bottles, c1745. **$18,000-21,000**

A Höchst part tea and coffee service, puce and gilt wheel marks, gilder's crescent marks, various incised marks, some damage, c1765. **$28,000-29,000**

A Coalport feldspar porcelain botanical dessert service, c1820. **$5,500-7,000**

A Meissen dessert service, painted with reserves of rural landscapes, crossed swords in underglaze blue, incised numerals, one dish with hair crack, c1870. **$10,000-20,000**

A Meissen cabaret set, incised numerals and crossed swords in underglaze blue, c1870. **$14,500-16,500**

A Meissen cabaret set incised numerals and crossed swords, late 19thC. **$2,500-2,700**

A Barr, Flight & Barr dessert service, incised factory marks, c1802, the large oval dish 14in (36cm). **$13,000-16,500**

A pair of Sèvres gilt metal mounted vases, late 19thC, 25.5in (65cm).
$10,000-14,500

A Copenhagen cornucopia vase and cover, c1923, 24in (61.5cm).
$6,000-9,000

A pair of Sèvres pattern gilt metal mounted vases, late 19thC, 43in (110cm).
$22,000-28,000

A pair of Sèvres pattern gilt metal mounted vases, late 19thC, 50.5in (128cm).   **$47,500-51,500**

A French vase, late 19thC, 30.5in (77.5cm).
$3,500-5, 500

A garniture of Sèvres-pattern vases, late 19thC, largest 62in (157.5cm).
$63,000-67,500

A pair of Grainger Lee & Co. Worcester pot pourri vases, c1825, restored, 14in (35cm).
$2,700-3,500

A pair of Sèvres two-handled vases, damage and repair, late 19thC, 17in (43cm).
$4,500-5,500

A garniture of Sèvres vases on gilt stands, marked, c1780. **$3,250-3,500**

A Vienna faux bois ground part coffee service, blue beehive marks, various impressed marks, c1790.
$9,000-10,000

A Flight, Barr & Barr urn, c1825, marked, 12in (31cm).
$2,000-2,700

A garniture of Bow 'frill vases', c1770, marked, 12in (31cm).
$3,500-4,500

A famille rose punch bowl, 2 restored cracks, Qing Dynasty, 14.5in (37cm), late 18thC, 14.5in(37cm). **$29,500-31,500**

A Chinese Lotus pattern tea bowl and saucer, late 18thC. **$200-250**

A famille rose hunting punch bowl, rim restored, Qianlong, 15.5in (40cm) diam. **$9,000-10,000**

A blanc de chine figure of a seated luohan, 17thC. **$9,000-10,000**

A tileworks figure of a lion, chips restored, Ming Dynasty. **$4,500-5,500**

A Compagnie-des-Indes hound, Qianlong. **$7,500-9,500**

A painted pottery horse, restored, Tang Dynasty, 17in (42.5cm) high. **$3,500-5,000**

A Compagnie-des-Indes dog, Qing Dynasty. **$9,500-10,000**

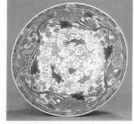

A polychrome bowl, restored, Kangxi, 14.5in (37cm). **$8,500-10,250**

A Kakiemon style shishi, restored, late 17thC. **$19,000-20,500**

A famille rose figure of Budai, 18thC. **$5,500-7,000**

A famille rose punch bowl, Yongzheng, on wood stand, 15in (38cm). **$9,000-10,000**

A set of famille rose figures of Immortals, chipped and restored, Qianlong, 9in (23cm). **$6,000-8,000**

A Sancai pottery ox and cart, minor restorations, Tang Dynasty. **$9,000-10,000**

A set of three doucai dishes, chipped and cracked, 18thC, 15in (38cm) diam. **$10,500-14,500**

A foliate charger, painted in Yuan style, Kangxi, 26.5in (67.5cm). **$3,500-4,500**

A Ming style dish, chipped and restored, Qianlong seal mark and of the period. **$7,000-9,000**

A Ming style dish, with Qianlong seal mark and of the period. **$54,000-56,000**

An Imari shaped dish, 17/18thC, 18in (46cm) diam. **$8,000-9,500**

A Northern celadon saucer dish, Song Dynasty, 7in (18cm) diam. **$11,000-12,000**

A kraak porselein dish in delft style, frits, late Ming Dynasty, c1600, 14in (36cm). **$3,500-4,500**

A kraak porselein dish, late Ming Dynasty, c1643. **$4,500-5,000**

A Ming dish, hairline crack, with encircled Hongzhi six-character mark and of the period, 10.5in (26cm). **$160,000-170,000**

A pair of dragon dishes, with Qianlong seal marks and of the period, 7in (17.5cm). **$16,500-18,000**

A Junyao barbed rim dish, Song Dynasty, 7in (18cm). **$39,500-41,500**

A Kakiemon jar, painted with birds among rocks and peonies, restored, late 17thC, 8.5in (21.5cm). **$18,000-21,000**

A jardinière, with scrolling lotus and key pattern, 19thC, 28in (71cm) diam. **$13,000-15,000**

A ormolu mounted famille rose baluster vase, Yongzheng, 19thC, 18.5in (47cm). **$14,500-18,000**

A pair of famille rose jardinières, with metal liners, on scroll feet, restored, Yongzheng, 13.5in (34.5cm). **$13,000-18,000**

A rouleau vase, painted with phoenix, Kangxi, 18.5in (46.5cm). **$3,500-4,000**

An enamelled moulded baluster vase, Qianlong, 14in (36cm). **$7,000-9,000**

A hu-shaped vase, with 2 taotie fixed-ring handles, Han Dynasty, 17in (43cm). **$5,500-7,000**

An Arita vase, with flowers and Buddhist objects in Wanli style, late 17thC, 21in (51cm). **$10,000-12,000**

A boar's head soup tureen and cover, restored, Qing Dynasty, 18thC, 16in (40cm). **$27,000-29,000**

A Chinese Imari baluster jar, Qianlong, 23.5in (60cm). **$9,000-10,000**

A Henan vase, Song Dynasty, 10.5in (27cm). **$20,000-21,000**

A famille rose ormolu mounted five-piece garniture, restored, Qianlong.
$18,000-21,000

A pair of Canton enamel vases, mid-19thC, 24in (61cm) high.
$3,500-4,000

A beaker vase, restored rim, Kangxi, 17.5in (44cm) high.
$1,500-1,600

A bottle vase, damaged, Tao Kuang mark, Ching Dynasty.
$900-1,000

A pair of Japanese Imari flasks, marked Shin, c1710.
$18,000-20,000

A Transitional wucai baluster vase, c1640, 11.5in (30cm) high.
$8,000-9,000

A famille verte rouleau vase, Kangxi, 18.5in (47cm) high.
$29,500-32,000

A pair of gilt decorated mirror black vases, Kangxi.
$30,000-31,500

A famille rose garniture of vases, well painted, some damage and repair, 1 cover matched, Qianlong, 10.5in (27cm). **$8,000-10,000**

A famille rose mandarin pattern garniture, some restoration, baluster vases, Qianlong, 13.5in (35cm) high.
$16,500-18,000

A pair of Japanese porcelain vases, one with interior firing crack.
$2,000-3,250

COLOUR REVIEW

Four wine glasses on facet cut knopped stems, with cut conical bowls, c1840, 5.5in (14cm). **$650-800**

A pair of ogee rib moulded finger bowls, c1830, 3.5in (8.5cm). **$350-550**

A pair of amethyst carafes, c1850, 7.5in (19cm). **$850-950**

Three finger bowls, 3 to 4in (8 to 9.5cm). **$160-240 each**

A spirit flagon, with loop handle and metal mount, c1830, 7.5in (19cm). **$320-360**

A cranberry enamelled decanter, English, c1890. **$160-210**

An onion shaped carafe, engraved with fruiting vine, 8.5in (21cm). **$450-650**

A pair of spirit bottles with flute cut bodies, c1840. **$1,000-1,200**

A Nailsea bottle with a small loop handle, 8.5in (21.5cm). **$900-1,100**

A cylindrical jar and cover, gilt decorated, c1810, 3in (8cm). **$450-500**

Three spirit bottles, c1835, 11 to 12.5in (28 to 32cm). **$450-750 each**

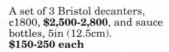

A rare wine glass with mutliple spiral air twist stem, c1750, 6.5in (16.5cm). **$7,500-9,000**

A set of 3 Bristol decanters, c1800, **$2,500-2,800**, and sauce bottles, 5in (12.5cm). **$150-250 each**

Two cream jugs with applied loop handles, *l.* c1800, *r.* North Country soda glass, c1790. **$350-550**

A Baccarat concentric mushroom paperweight, c1850. **$4,500-5,500**

Two wine glasses: *l.* with ogee fluted bowl. **$140-180** and *r.* with cup bowl, c1840. **$300-360**

A Baccarat thousand petalled rose weight, mid-19thC. **$6,000-7,000**

A glass cream jug, 3.5in (9cm) high, c1860. **$250-450**

A selection of Victorian hyacinth vases, c1860-1920. **$35-100 each**

A Stourbridge Webb claret jug, c1897. **$1,500-2,000**

Two Nailsea type water jugs: *l.* c1800, 4.5in (11cm) high and *r.* Wrockwardine, 4in (10cm) high. **$450-800 each**

A Baccarat dated close millefiori weight, marked B/1847, 3in (8cm). **$1,900-2,700**

A cranberry goblet. **$90-125**

A St. Louis fruit weight, mid-19thC. **$1,000-1,800**

A set of 5 wine glasses, with ovoid bowls and flute cut stems, c1840, 5in (12.5cm) high. **$450-650**

Two cream jugs, c1830, 2.5 and 4in (7 and 9.5cm) high and circular salt, c1840, 2.5in (7cm) high. **$180-450 each**

A wine jug, c1800, 8in (20cm) high. **$1,400-1,500**

COLOUR REVIEW

A pair of scent bottles, decorated with enamel and gilt, gold caps and fitted shagreen case, c1760, 1.5in (4cm) high.
$5,500-6,000

A Victorian cranberry glass épergne, with baskets, 21in (53cm) high. **$650-800**

An overlay lustre, c1880, 12in (31cm) high. **$1,200-1,400**

A Bohemian cameo glass vase, c1896.
$450-550

An English cased glass vase, c1880.
$650-800

Three glass scent bottles with brass and silver gilt mounts, *l*. and *c*. c1880, and *r*. c1870, 4 to 5.5in (10 to 14cm) long.
$280-420 each

A Peking glass vase, c1860, 10in (25cm) high.
$900-1,200

A Webb three-coloured cameo vase, attributed to William Fritsche, c1880, 18.5in (47cm).
$9,000-10,000

A set of 4 cut salts, with moulded lemon squeezer diamond feet, c1810, 3in (8cm) high.
$1,500-1,800

Two pairs of English citrine cornucopia, mounted on white marble bases, c1820.
$1,500-1,600 each

Three glass bells, the green one c1890, the 2 cranberry c1880, 13 to 13.5in (33 to 35cm) high.
$180-360 each

PORCELAIN

There has been little change in the porcelain market over the last twelve months. If anything, the pattern of the past two or three years has intensified, with buyers willing to pay record prices for the best items and leaving the regular pieces unsold. There has been a slight increase in interest in 18thC porcelain figures, particularly from the Bow factory, but there has been no real increase in values for some two or three years. The demand for the later British ceramics such as Minton, Crown Derby and Royal Worcester has remained firm but values have not increased. Tablewares have retained their popularity if sold in complete tea or dinner sets but individual pieces are slow selling unless decorated with a rare pattern. After the poor showing of 18thC figures in the auction rooms over the past two or three years the auctioneers have had to readjust their estimates to reflect recent price levels.

A Crown Derby tea service, of Empire inspiration, each piece painted with laurel swags between blue ground borders, gilt with scrolls and foliage above or enclosing a band of flutes picked out in royal blue and gilding, comprising: cream jug, bowl, 2 circular dishes, 12 tea cups, 6 coffee cups, 18 saucers and 12 plates, small hairline cracks, orange printed mark and year code, painted Pattern No. 1654, c1885.
$1,800-2,700

These lower estimates have perhaps encouraged more private buyers into the market with the result that figures are beginning to sell again. Phillips, London, sold a Bow figure of Columbine for $2,635 more than treble the estimate. Similarly, at the same sale, a rare Chelsea red anchor figure, modelled by Joseph Willem as an old beggar wrapped in a cloak, sold for $4,250.

Tablewares are traditionally sub-divided into flatware (plates, saucers etc.) and hollow ware (tureens, teapots etc.). Flatware has always been difficult to sell as individual pieces unless they are examples of a particularly rare pattern or an individual item from a unique service. Hollow wares, with the added interest of shape, are much more decorative and are therefore of more interest to the collector. During the 19thC many factories, such as Minton and Derby, produced specialist cabinet plates, hand painted and gilded to the highest quality, for the sole purpose of display. These plates are miniature works of art and as such are still under valued at $360-900. Complete tea or dinner services are always sought after either by the wealthy collector or the decorator with wealthy clients. Even late services can fetch large sums of money, $7,000 was paid for a 1930s Coalport part tea and dinner service, of 135 pieces, at Sotheby's, Sussex. At some $55 a piece it was probably good value. Had the service been split by the auctioneer the individual prices would probably have averaged much more than $55 and the general collector may have been fortunate enough to own a piece of that particular service. An example of this dilemma for the auctioneer or dealer was the sale of the Barr, Flight and Barr 'Gordon Service' in 1980. Made originally for Sir Willoughby Gordon and kept in the family until the sale, it caused something of a minor furore when Phillips, Edinburgh, divided it into 19 lots. This splitting of the service enabled collectors to have a unique piece of Worcester that would have been denied them had the service been sold complete. It also ensured that these pieces would circulate amongst collectors and reappear on the market from time to time. A pair of plates from the 'Gordon Service' were recently sold by Phillips,

London, for $7,200 the pair, having been sold the first time round in 1980 for $1,500 the pair! Other examples of

A Royal Worcester pierced oviform ewer, the silver form possibly painted by Henry Chair, washed in turquoise and picked out with gilt dots, with foliate scrollwork between bands of white jewelling and joined by the single scroll handle with mask terminal and beadwork border, puce printed mark with year code, registration numbers and shape number 1944, brown printed TIFFANY NEW YORK retailers mark, 1897, 7in (18cm).
$3,600-5,500

the highly decorative Regency painted porcelains continue to sell well. A Flight and Barr 10 inch high yellow ground pot pourri vase and cover with decoration of full blown roses realised $2,900 at the same Phillips sale. Welsh ceramics from the same period, always sought after by a dedicated breed of collectors, have had a boost this year with the sale of the Sir Leslie Joseph Collection. The demand for the later British ceramics, such as Minton, Crown Derby and Royal Worcester, continues on an even keel.

Baskets

A pair of Caughley pierced baskets, decorated in underglaze blue, 8.5in (21.5cm) wide.
$1,000-1,500

A Worcester quatrefoil pierced chestnut basket and cover, moulded with yellow centred puce flowerheads, damaged and repaired, c1765, stand 10.5in (26cm) wide.
$2,700-3,600

Bowls

A pair of Fürstenberg baskets, painted with green and blue flowerheads, the handles and rims enriched with gilding, gilding rubbed, blue F marks inside baskets and impressed NO3 to underside of bases, incised S to one, c1770, 7.5in (19cm) wide.
$2,700-3,600

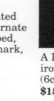

A Worcester footed bowl, colour enamelled with chinoiserie figures, the inner rim decorated in underglaze blue with an ornate border pattern, interior rubbed, blue painted open crescent mark, c1768, 6in (15cm) diam.
$360-540

A Worcester footed bowl, painted in blue with the Precipice pattern, painted open crescent mark, c1765, 8in (20cm) diam.
$360-540

A Bow white squat baluster bowl and cover with loop handles, applied with prunus sprigs, the cover with branch finial, c1752, 5in (13cm) diam.
$3,600-5,500

A Meissen écuelle, cover and stand, painted with scenes of country figures before buildings, bordered by applied trailing vine and foliage, branch handles, gilded details, chipped, crossed swords in underglaze blue and impressed 13, c1880, stand 8.5in (21.5cm).
$3,600-5,500

A Pinxton bowl, enamelled with iron red sprigs, c1799, 2.5in (6cm).
$180-360

A Worcester footed bowl, transfer printed in blue with the Laterre and Mother and Child patterns, hatched crescent mark, c1775, 5.5in (13.5cm) diam.
$360-540

A Worcester bowl, transfer printed in underglaze blue with uncommon European landscapes, c1780, 4.5in (11.5cm) diam.
$180-360

A Worcester blue and white bowl and cover, with shell-moulded handles and pine cone knop, damaged, 18thC, 13in (32.5cm) wide.
$720-1,000

Boxes

A Berlin gilt metal mounted snuff box, the green scale ground reserved with pink ground panels painted in imitation of cameos with The Three Graces and trophies, the base with Cupid blowing bubbles and the interior of the cover finely stippled in colours with a lady at her dressing table trimming her pigtail accompanied by a gallant, base repaired, c1780, 3.5in (8.5cm) wide. **$7,000-9,000**

A German casket with gilt metal mounts, painted with battle scenes alternating with panels of flowers inside an oval gilt frame against a puce scale ground, the inside cover painted with a Royal portrait, impressed eagle mark, late 19thC, 9.5in (24cm) wide. **$3,600-5,500**

A French silver gilt mounted bonbonnière, painted with flowers, the mount with carved borders, 19thC, 3in (7cm). **$1,000-1,500**

A French snuff box and cover, with silver mounts, probably St. Cloud, 18thC, 3in (8cm) wide. **$900-1,500**

A St. Cloud silver mounted snuff box, modelled as a kneeling Chinaman, in an Oriental flowered robe with 3 scattered flying insects, the cover with Oriental flowersprays, reeded silver mounts, damaged and repaired, c1740, 2in (5cm) wide. **$1,200-1,700**

Busts

A Copeland parian bust, modelled as a young maiden with a wreath of ivy tied into her long hair with a ribbon, her head turned slightly to the right, raised on a socle base, restored, impressed COPELAND L 84 and Copyright, c1865, 25in (64cm). **$3,600-5,500**

A Copeland parian bust of Juno, modelled by W. Theed, after the Antique, raised on a low socle base, impressed COPELAND T 28 and copyright, c1851, 23in (59cm). **$7,000-9,000**

A pair of Meissen portrait busts of Prince Louis Charles and Princesse Marie Zéphirine de Bourbon, after the original models by J. J. Kändler, she wearing turquoise, blue, pink, black and gilt, he in gilt, yellow, blue, white and lilac, the bases enriched in gilding, restored, blue crossed swords marks, Pressnummer 77, incised 2764, painted numbers 15, c1880, 6in (15cm). **$1,500-1,800**

Cups

A Miles Mason cup, saucer and bowl, pattern No. 128, The Seasons, bat printed and gilded, c1805, bowl 6.5in (16.5cm) diam.
$180-360
cup and saucer, cup with hairline crack. **$110-180**

A Worcester fluted cup and saucer of Lord Henry Thynne type, each piece painted with a central turquoise and gilt framed circular landscape panel surrounded by arrangements of fruit and scattered insects, within an underglaze blue and gilt rim, saucer cracked, underglaze blue crescent mark, c1772.
$720-1,000

A Böttger Augsburg decorated Goldchinesen two- handled beaker and saucer, gilt in the workshop of Bartholomäus Seuter, the interior and borders richly gilt and edged with C-scrolls, slight damage, stencilled lustre MF monogram marks and incised line to footrim of saucer, c1725.
$14,500-16,500

An English two-handled cup, cover and stand, probably Coalport, painted with flowers in yellow and gilt edged cartouches in a deep blue ground between a pair of angel handles, butterfly finial, late 19thC, 5in (12.5cm).
$900-1,500

A Worcester coffee cup, with grooved loop handle, painted in an unusual and bright palette, c1765.
$1,800-2,700

A Worcester transfer printed coffee cup, with grooved loop handle, printed in sepia with a scene from the Italian Comedy showing Harlequin and Columbine seated beside a table being surprised by Pierrot, c1756.
$720-1,000

A Miles Mason cup and saucer, c1810, saucer 5.5in (14cm) diam.
$110-180

A Miles Mason cup and saucer, with relief moulded decoration, landscape painted panels and gilding, c1805, saucer 5.5in (14cm) diam.
$180-360

A Miles Mason cup, decorated with Boy at the Door pattern, 1796, 2.5in (6.5cm).
$110-180

A Miles Mason cup and saucer, with red bat prints heightened with gilding, c1808, saucer 5.5in (14cm) diam, cup and saucer.
$180-360
bowl 6in (15cm) diam.
$180-360

A Miles Mason Shepherd's bat print and enamelled cup, saucer, and saucer dish, c1805, saucer 5.5in (14cm) diam. cup and saucer **$110-180**
saucer dish 8in (20cm)
$180-360

Ewers

A Derby blue ground ewer, with gilt painted scroll handle, damaged, printed red mark, 14in (35.5cm).
$360-540

A Sèvres ormolu mounted ewer, the ormolu handle moulded with leaves and bulrushes, damaged, blue interlaced L marks, flanked by Z for 1777 and y for Bouillat, the ormolu handle slightly later, 10in (25cm). **$1,800-2,700**

A Royal Worcester blush ivory handled ewer, with floral body decoration with gilding, shape number 1162, puce mark, c1880, 10in (25cm). **$720-1,000**

A pair of Coalport 'jewelled' ewers, decorated beneath a salmon pink ground, green printed marks, gilt pattern numbers V1285, c1885, 8in (20cm).
$900-1,500

Figures - Animals

A Meissen pug dog, after a model by J.J. Kändler, with grey markings and a black muzzle, wearing a green and gilt collar with a purple bow, restored, c1740, 4.5in (11.5cm).
$3,600-5,500

An English porcelain ewer, probably Coalport, the ovoid body applied with a handle, neck and spout in the form of a swan, painted on either side with landscapes and applied with flowers, slight damage, mid-19thC, 11in (28cm).
$720-1,000

A Royal Crown Derby ewer, decorated in cisele gilt with musical trophies, hung from a ribbon tied swag on a salmon pink ground, printed mark in burnt orange, incised 877, 10in (25cm).
$360-540

A pair of Bow models of finches, on pierced scroll moulded bases enriched in turquoise and gilding, damaged, c1765, 6in (15cm).
$2,700-3,600

A pair of Meissen porcelain models of hunting birds, each supported on a tree stump tearing the prey, damaged, l8thC, 11in (28cm).
$7,000-9,000

A pair of Meissen models of thrushes, their plumage naturalistically coloured in shaded brown and grey and with brown markings, on white and blue bases, slight damage, blue crossed swords marks, Pressnummern 123 and 16, incised 113X, painted number 40, c1880, 8in (20cm).
$1,000-1,500

Two English models of spaniels, on yellow tasselled puce cushions, mid-l9thC, 3in (8cm).
$720-1,000

A Meissen white model of a royal eagle, wearing a 'jewelled' gilt crown with white bosses, its beak open aggressively and with boldly painted features, its yellow claws with black talons clasping a 'jewelled' gilt sceptre and a silvered and gilt sword, restored, blue crossed swords mark, Pressnummer 343, incised S63, c1880, 20in (50cm).
$3,600-5,500

A Royal Copenhagen model of an owl, after an original by P. Herder, the bird perched on a cluster of pine and naturalistically coloured, signed, 1911, 13in (33cm).
$1,000-1,500

A group of 3 Meissen monkey band figures, comprising: a conductor, a female harpist and a female hurdy-gurdy player, the conductor's arm damaged and wrist repaired, crossed swords in underglaze blue, incised and impressed numerals, 6.5in (16cm), and a group of 4 Volkstedt monkey band figures, comprising a violinist, a bagpipe player and 2 figures with wind instruments, chips, 19thC.
$2,700-3,600

An English model of a greyhound, on a yellow tasselled puce cushion, restored, mid-l9thC, 4in (10cm).   **$180-360**

A group of Continental monkey band figures, various factories, comprising a conductor and various instrument players, each standing on a circular base moulded with scrolls picked out in gilding, some damage and repair, printed marks, late l9thC, 6in (15cm).
$1,200-1,700

A matched pair of Bow white glazed porcelain figures of recumbent lions, each with a paw resting upon a sphere, damaged, the smaller lion marked B, 3.5 and 4.5in (9.5 and 10.5cm) long.
$2,700-3,600

A set of 13 French dog band figures, adapted from the Meissen monkey band figures, including the conductor, his stand, wind players, brass players and a percussionist, crossed arrow marks in blue enamel possibly for Bourdois & Bloch, 4.5in (11cm).
$1,800-2,700

Figures - People

A pair of Derby figures of a shepherd, in black hat, yellow ground floral trousers, playing a flute, and a shepherdess holding a bouquet of flowers, on rococo pierced scroll moulded bases enriched in turquoise and gilding, c1770, 9in (23cm).
$1,800-2,700

A Derby porcelain group of Procris and Cephalus, in a yellow robe bending over his dying wife touching the arrow in her breast, modelled on a grassy base beneath a stunted tree, chips and restoration to extremities, c1770, 8in (20cm).
$720-1,000

A pair of Chelsea figures of a shepherd and shepherdess, wearing puce and gilt flowered clothes, he in a green hat and his companion in a blue hat, standing before blue and pink flowering bocage, on bases enriched with gilding, damage and restoration, gold anchor marks, c1768, 11in (28cm).
$7,000-9,000

A Copeland parian figure of Sunshine, after William Brodie, minor chips to flowers, impressed factory mark, sculptor's name and title, c1860, 19in (48cm).
$900-1,500

A Minton parian figure of Clorinda after an original by John Bell, chips to inner rim of base, impressed marks and incised February 1848, impressed date code for 1862, 13in (33cm).
$720-1,000

A pair of Chelsea Derby figures he in a red cloak and floral jacket and knee breeches, she in blue bodice and flowered dress, with a sheep at her feet, on a matching base, some damage, 13in (33cm).
$7,000-9,000

A Robinson and Leadbeater tinted parian figure group, entitled 'How Like Grandma', the girl wearing a pink lace trimmed dress with blue sash, dressing a Jack Russell in a white lace cap and coat, seated on a bamboo framed pink plush easy chair, on a shaped base, impressed R & L, 13in (33cm).
$720-1,000

A Royal Worcester figure of The Dodo, modelled by F. G. Doughty, printed mark in black, 3in (8.5cm).
$360-540

A pair of Royal Worcester figures of a huntsman and a fishergirl, coloured in brown and pink with gilt details, one with ends of stick restored, printed and impressed crowned circle mark, c1870, 18in (45cm).
$3,600-5,500

A pair of Royal Worcester figures of Grecian water carriers, each modelled as a Classical maiden wearing bronzed orange, yellow and green robes, carrying an amphora in one hand and with a vase balanced on the head, puce printed shape numbers 2/125 and 'shot enamel' mark, impressed numerals, c1907, 20in (51cm).
$2,700-3,600

An Ansbach group of musicians modelled as a gallant, playing a flute, in a white gilt-trimmed jacket, flowered waistcoat and puce breeches, his companion in a flowered skirt, puce bodice and blue trimmed apron, arbour lacking, restoration, c1770, 4.5in (12cm).
$2,700-3,600

A Dresden figure of a classical lady, blue crossed swords mark, mid-19thC, 10.5in (26cm).
$720-1,000

A pair of Royal Dux figures of maidens, in green and gold flowing robes, one playing a mandolin, the other a tambourine, standing on rocky bases strewn with leaves, some damage, pink patch marks, mid-19thC, 29in (74cm).
$2,700-3,600

A Berlin erotic group, 'The Model', slight restoration, KPM mark, c1870, 13in (33cm).
$900-1,500

A pair of Royal Dux figures of Eastern carpet sellers, coloured in tones of green, red, cream and green, detailed in gilding, her arm repaired, applied pink triangle mark, impressed 465 and 466, early 20thC, 16in (41cm).
$1,800-2,700

A pair of Meissen figures of a fisherman and companion, after models by J.J. Kändler, both restored, c1748, 7in (18cm).
$3,600-5,500

A Höchst figure of a boy as a cooper, after the model by J.P. Melchior, in a puce hat, puce waistcoat, yellow breeches and a brown apron, slight blemish to back, blue wheel mark and incised N97:M48, c1770, 4in (10.5cm).
$1,800-2,700

A pair of Royal Dux figures of water and fruit vendors, each decorated in 'shot enamels', raised on circular bases, minor chip, applied pink triangle mark, impressed 441 and 442, early 20thC, 15in (38cm).
$1,000-1,500

Johann Joachim Kändler (1706-1775)

The first of the 910 monumental animal figures, as commissioned in 1730 by the Elector Augustus for his new palace, were very lifeless and quite unrealistic. Their quality only improved in 1731 when the young J.J.. Kändler began modelling at Meissen. Although Kändler was unable to overcome the firing problems, he studied the animals in the Elector's menagerie and produced lifelike, animated figures.

The project ended in 1733, shortly after the Elector's death and Kändler applied his talents to designing on a smaller scale. From around 1740 until Kändler's death in 1755 Meissen figures replaced table wares as the most sought after of the factory's produce.

The most popular series of figures was the Kändler Harlequins, modelled between 1738-1744.

A pair of Royal Dux figures of a man and woman in rustic dress, each carrying baskets on their shoulders, minor chips to base, applied marks, cl900, 15.5in (40cm).   **$900-1,500**

A French group, modelled as a classical bearded man wearing a crown and loose drapes supporting a young woman, pseudo Derby mark in red, late l9thC, l7in (44cm).
$720-1,000

A Meissen figure of a wheelwright, from the series of Craftsmen modelled by J.J. Kändler and P. Reinicke, in a turquoise tunic, pink breeches, black buckled shoes and a brown apron, arm restored, hammer lacking, chips, blue crossed swords mark to back of base, c1748, 8in (20cm).
$2,700-3,600

A Meissen figure of a boy with a hen, the boy wearing a flowered pink edged robe, on a moulded base with scrolls picked out in gilding, restored chip to base, restoration to fingers and toes, crossed swords in underglaze blue, 19thC, 5.5in (14cm).
$720-1,000

A Meissen group of rustic lovers, modelled as a shepherd and shepherdess, crossed swords in underglaze blue, incised A.41, late l9thC, 7.5in (19cm).
$1,200-1,700

A Fürstenberg figure of a miner, after the model by Anton Carl Luplau, in a black pill box hat, black jacket, apron, breeches and shoes, and red tunic, damaged, blue F mark, late l8thC, 5in (13cm).
$7,000-9,000

A Meissen figure of a chinaman, after a model by P. Reinicke, in a long jacket with indianische Blumen, iron red breeches with yellow edging, black stockings and red shoes, restored and one finger missing, faint blue crossed swords mark, c1740, 6in (15cm).
$1,800-2,700

A Meissen 'Poussah' figure, wearing an orange ground robe scattered with indianische Blumen over his flesh toned body, with green hat, one hand repaired, chip to wing of bird, indistinct crossed swords mark on base, c1745, 7.5in (18cm).
$10,000-12,000

A Lladro group, with figures in a rowing boat on a lake with willow trees, on contemporary base, l8in (46cm).
$900-1,500

A Meissen figure of a youth, clutching a cockerel under one arm, in turquoise hat with puce rosette, white jacket over pale blue trousers and yellow shoes with red bows, repaired, parts lacking and chips, blue crossed swords mark to back of base, c1750, 6in (15cm).
$1,200-1,700

Two Meissen Marcolini figures of a gardener and companion, he in a pink hat, green jacket and patterned breeches, she in a brown bodice and striped skirt, on scroll mound bases enriched with gilding, some damage, blue crossed swords and star marks, impressed H to back of his base and 2 to back of her base, c1790, 5.5in (14cm).
$1,800-2,700

A Meissen Marcolini group of a music lesson, modelled as a young girl in blue and yellow striped dress, her male companion wearing a pale turquoise jacket and purple tunic, attempting to teach her to play a wind instrument, small chips and areas of restoration, crossed swords and dot in underglaze blue, c1800, 5.5in (14cm).
$1,800-2,700

A Royal Worcester figure, 'Kruger', Hadley shot silk shape 223/10, Hadley mark to base, signed Hadley to reverse, c1900, 8in (20cm).
$360-540

A pair of Meissen figures of a shepherd and shepherdess, small chips and areas of restoration, crossed swords in underglaze blue, 19thC, 6in (15cm).
$3,600-5,500

A Vienna group of a peasant and companion, he with a moustache and black hat, buff jacket, patterned shirt, purple breeches with green braces and black boots, she in a yellow bodice, white apron, pink skirt and yellow shoes, on a green mound base edged with gilt scrolls, slight hairline crack to back of her skirt, blue beehive mark, c1770.
$3,600-5,500

Flasks

A Meissen chinoiserie pilgrim flask, painted within gilt quatrefoil cartouches, with Böttger lustre panels, iron red and puce foliage scrolls and gilt shelves supporting purple vases between female mask heads and above moulded gilt gadroons, the neck moulded and gilt with ribs, damaged and repaired, c1730, later gold cover, 3in (7cm).
$7,000-9,000

A Meissen figure of a gallant, wearing a long red coat, gilt edged waistcoat and puce breeches, a green sash over one shoulder, restoration to wrist and hand, crossed swords in underglaze blue, incised 550, 19thC, 9in (23cm).   **$360-540**

Flatware

A Caughley melon shaped dessert dish, blue transfer printed with the full Nanking pattern, c1790, 10.5in (26.5cm).
$180-360

A Sèvres saucer, painted by Falot and gilded by Prevost, reserved on a gold and pink dotted ground within a gold foliate rim, date mark for 1781.
$360-540

A Meissen pilgrim flask, painted within gilt quatrefoil panels with purple scrolls and between female mask heads with iron red plumes, the neck with gilt ribs, damaged, blue crossed swords mark, c1730, later gold cover, 3in (7cm).
$7,000-9,000

A pair of Chamberlain's Worcester Royal Gadroon armorial plates, red script mark, c1820, 10in (25cm).
$1,000-1,500

A Caughley dessert plate, blue printed with the full Nanking pattern, c1790, 8in (20cm).
$180-360

A Caughley blue and white fluted bread and butter plate, transfer printed with Temple pattern, c1780, 7.5in (19cm).
$180-360

A Chelsea strawberry-leaf dish, with incised vein markings enriched in puce, painted beneath a chocolate brown rim, the underside with puce veining, iron red flowers and moulded in relief with a curled strawberry plant terminating in a loop handle, slight damage, red anchor mark, c1756, 9in (22.5cm) long.
$1,800-2,700

A Bow plate, enamelled with the Quail pattern, c1758, 9in (22.5cm)
$720-1,000

A Chelsea shallow dish, painted beneath a brown line rim, slight damage, c1753, 10.5in (26.5cm).
$1,800-2,700

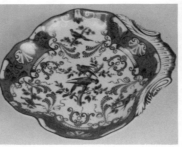

A pair of Coalport shell shaped dessert dishes, painted by John Randell, c1840, 10in (25cm) wide.
$1,000-1,500

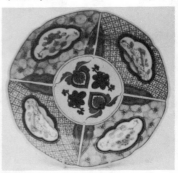

A Derby plate, painted in the Japanese taste, decorated in tones of green, iron red, lilac and blue with gilt detail, slight wear, pseudo seal mark in blue, c1765, 9.5in (24cm).
$180-360

A pair of Coalport plates, each painted with a landscape, pattern No. 4/414, c1840, 8.5in (21.5cm).
$360-540

A Miles Mason porcelain teapot stand, decorated in Boy at the Door pattern, c1805, 7.5in (18.5cm) wide.
$180-360

A Worcester sweetmeat dish of scallop shell form, painted in blue with the Two Peony Rock Bird pattern, blue painted workman's marks, c1755, 4.5in (11.5cm)   **$1,800-2,700**

A Spode blue and white Indian Sporting pattern meat plate, impressed Spode One, 17in (42.5cm) wide.
$900-1,500

A set of 6 Hammersley & Co. dessert plates, each painted with a named bird in its natural setting, within gold decorated pink foliate moulded rims, one damaged, signed E. J. Garnett, 8.5in (21.5cm).   **$360-540**

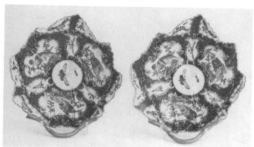

A pair of Worcester blue scale ground dishes, painted with exotic birds and butterflies, with brown tendril handles, blue seal marks, c1770, 8in (20cm) wide.
$2,700-3,600

A Chamberlain's Worcester meat dish with gravy well, and 3 matching deep plates, each painted with the crest of Nevile of Thornley, reserved on a wide orange band painted with scrolling foliage, the centre painted with a flowerhead and gold foliage, meat dish repaired, early 19thC.
$720-1,000

A Worcester plate, transfer printed in blue with the Pine Cones and Butterflies pattern, hatched crescent mark, c1770, 12in (30.5cm).
$360-540

A pair of Worcester blue scale plates of Lady Mary Wortley Montagu type, decorated in the atelier of James Giles, within gilt line circular cartouches, the borders with exotic birds within gilt scroll and flowering foliage cartouches, reserved on blue scale grounds beneath scalloped gilt rims, slight damage, blue square seal marks, c1770, 9in (22.5cm).
$2,700-3,600

A Worcester junket or salad dish, transfer printed in blue with the Pinecone Group pattern, the interior moulded in low relief, the exterior transfer printed in blue, hatched crescent mark, c1770, 10in (25cm).
$720-1,000

A Worcester saucer dish, reed moulded with shaped rim, painted in blue with the Hollow Rock Lily pattern, blue painted open crescent mark, c1760, 7in (17.5cm).   **$720-1,000**

A Worcester Flight Barr & Barr dessert plate with gilded rim, central ivory reserve with painted decoration attributed to Henry Stinton, with gilt scroll and white jewelled border, on deep blue ground, red printed mark, c1825, 10in (25cm).
$7,000-9,000

This pattern was later employed for the 1830 William IV Coronation service, with the Royal Insignia replacing the floral group.

A set of 6 Mintons Cabinet plates, each enamelled with a double rose spray against gilt and silvered stem and leaves, printed and impressed marks and date code for 1885, painted pattern no. G4419/5, 9.5in (23.5cm).
$1,200-1,700

A Worcester blue and white deep dish, printed with the Pine Cone pattern within a diaper and foliate border, slight damage, late 18thC, 15in (39cm).
$1,200-1,700

69

A Worcester footed water basin, painted in blue with the Willow Bridge Fisherman pattern, slight crack, blue painted 'w' workman's mark, c1758, 10.5in (26.5cm).
$1,800-2,700

A Meissen saucer, the centre painted with a bird in flight over a flowering shrub raised on a pierced rock, the underside with birds in flight amongst twigs slight chips, engraved in Dresden, on a café-au-lait ground, underglaze blue caduceus mark and a script letter A, c1725, 4.5in (12cm).
$3,600-5,500

A Meissen blue and white plate, painted within a shaped chocolate line rim, the reverse with a flowering tree and the border with trailing flowering branches, slight chip, blue crossed swords and dot mark, Pressnummer 20, c1740, 10.5in (26cm).
$7,000-9,000

A Meissen armorial plate, painted in purpurmalerei and enriched with gilding, with scattered indianische Blumen, the border with the Arms of the Münchhausen, slight chip, blue crossed swords mark and Pressnummer 16, c1740, 9in (23.5cm).
$7,000-9,000

A Royal Worcester white ground plate, with cobalt blue border, pink panels and gilding, the central panel decorated with still life fruit, pears and damsons, signed R. Sebright, 1913, 9in (22.5cm).
$720-1,000

A Meissen cabinet plate, entitled 'Meleagar u Atalante', after P. Rubens, with the 2 scantily clad figures being united by Cupid, within an elaborate gilt frame and a pierced blue ground border gilt with ovolos and overlapping cash, crossed swords in underglaze blue, impressed numerals and title in black script Meleagar Atalante, nach P. Rubens, c1880, 10in (24.5cm).
$3,600-5,500

A pair of Berlin plates, each painted with figures before Roman ruins, sceptre mark in blue, printed KPM and orb, 19thC, 12.5in (31.5cm).
$1,800-2,700

A Vienna portrait plate, the young girl wearing a white headdress, blue dress with a white lace frilled collar, signed Volk, the dark blue border richly gilt, blue beehive mark, 9.5in (23.5cm). **$2,700-3,600**

A Meissen lobed quatrefoil spoon tray, painted within 2 iron red lines, the border with a band of gilt interlocking scrolls and lines, blue crossed swords mark, Pressnummer 30, gilder's marks 52.L, c1740, 5.5in (14cm) wide.
$1,800-2,700

A Bow Middle Period powder blue plate, c1760, 8in (20cm).
$360-540

A set of 4 Minton dessert plates, each hand painted with a different marine scene, probably by J. B. Evans, pattern no. B1486, c1860, 9in (22.5cm).
$900-1,500

Jars

A pair of Vienna Augustus Rex jars and lids, against a cerise background, gilt detail, mid-19thC, 15in (38cm).
$900-1,500

A Meissen pedestal jar and cover, with handles in the form of writhing snakes, painted in green enamel and gold with figures in gardens, insects and flowers, 18thC, 12.5in (31.5cm).
$1,000-1,500

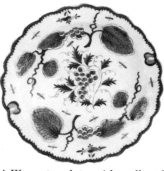

A Worcester plate, with scalloped rim, painted in blue with the Rubber Tree Plant pattern, slight chip, individual pseudo-Chinese four-character mark, c1775, 7.5in (19cm).
$720-1,000

Jugs

A Worcester mask jug, moulded with stiff leaves enriched in yellow, puce and purple, the neck with flowersprays, the rim with a band of moulded leaves and dot pattern and with moulded bearded mask spout, chips to spout and restored footrim, c1770,7.5in (19cm).
$1,800-2,700

A Worcester baluster sparrow beak cream jug and cover, with loop handle, painted with gilt borders on a dark blue ground, the domed cover with flower finial, hairline crack and minute rim chip, blue crescent mark, c1770, 5.5in (14cm).
$720-1,000

A pair of Vienna yellow ground topographical plates, with panels painted with named views of Ankunft des Holländischen/ Schiffes-Amsterdam im Donaukand beim Schanzel./1846 and Der Josefplatz, within broad gilt bands, slight rubbing, blue beehive marks, 1846, 8.5in (21cm).
$180-360

A Royal Worcester blush ivory jug, with coral handle, floral decoration and gilding, puce mark, 1892, 6in (15cm).
$180-360

A Worcester baluster mask head jug, with scroll handle, transfer printed in blue with the Plantation pattern, body crack near spout, unmarked, c1760, 6.5in (16cm).
$110-180

A Lowestoft baluster form sparrow beak jug , painted with Long Elizas in pink, purple, yellow, green and iron red, late 18thC, 4in (9cm) high.
$1,000-1,500

Mugs

A Derby mug, decorated in polychrome with glaze enamels, late 18thC, 4.5in (11cm).
$3,600-5,500

A Longton Hall mug, painted in colours, the rim enriched with a brown line, the handle and surrounding area restored, chip to rim, c1755, 4in (10cm).
$720-1,000

A Plymouth mug, with reeded handle, distinctly painted in coloured enamels below a gilt strapwork border, mid-18thC, 6in (15cm). **$3,600-5,500**

An English mug, with foliate handle, with gold initials, minor damage, 4in (9cm).
$360-540

A buff glazed pearlware mug, bat printed and inscribed in gilt 'Success To The Roe Buck Oyster Club', within a gilt banded border, slight damage, 19thC, 5.5in (14cm).
$180-360

Plaques

A Worcester plaque, painted by R. F. Perling, with a stag, hind and doe in a highland setting, signed Worcester and R. F. Perling, 8 by 9.5in (20.5 by 24cm).
$1,800-2,700

A pair of Royal Worcester miniature plaques, each signed by Raymond Rushton, in original pierced silver mounts, Birmingham 1912, 4in (10cm).
$1,200-1,700

A Staffordshire plaque, painted by Woodhouse, with a pensive family group seated beside trees at the head of a river valley, signed Woodhouse 1838, 6 by 4.5in (15 by 12cm).
$1,200-1,700

A Doccia plaque, after the model by Anton Filippo Weber, with 10 profile bust portraits of various Roman emperors, c1750, 6in (15cm).
$2,700-3,600

A Berlin plaque, painted with the Madonna wearing a diaphanous veil, pink dress and blue robe, seated on a marble bench, unsigned, impressed KPM, impressed Berlin mark, 9 by 7in (22 by 17cm), in a gilt frame.
$1,200-1,700

A 'Vienna' plaque, painted by J. Schiller, within a dark brown border painted and gilt with scrolling foliage and flowers, titled on the reverse H. Makart, Gruppe aus dem Einzug Carl van Antwerpen, underglaze blue beehive mark, painted title, 19thC, 20.5in (52cm), gilt frame
$2,700-3,600

A Berlin plaque, painted in pastel colours with a mother and child, impressed KPM and sceptre, c1890, 9.5 by 7in (24.5 by 18.5cm) framed. **$1,800-2,700**

A Berlin plaque, painted with a portrait of Princess Louise in full court dress of ermine trimmed cloak, gold coronet and gold embroidered white court gown, signed 'C.L.', impressed KPM and sceptre mark, retailer's label and Florentine carved giltwood frame, 9 by 6in (23 by 15cm).
$3,600-5,500

A Berlin plaque, painted in the English style with a bouquet of crimson, pink and white blown roses on a powder green ground, unsigned, impressed KPM and sceptre, 13.5in (35cm). **$900-1,500**

A Vienna plaque, the centre with hand painted panel depicting Samson and Delilah, within a puce and pale blue border overlaid with gilt rococo motif, marked on the reverse Simsons Gefangennahme, 19.5in (49cm) diam, gilt frame.
$3,600-5,500

A Meissen plaque, in the Sèvres manner, painted with a view of Pillnitz on the river Elbe, within a gold foliate reserve and blue rim, set in a gilt plaster frame, inscribed Pillnitz, crossed swords mark, 6in (15cm) wide.
$2,700-3,600

A pair of Sèvres plaques, depicting Buffoon and Marionette, in velvet frames, 6in (15cm) high.
$900-1,500

A Vienna plaque, painted with a panel of Roman Charity, inscribed Cigniani, L. Zeiser, 8.56, impressed beehive mark, numerals 954, late 19thC, 13 by 16in (33 by 41cm), framed and glazed.
$1,800-2,700

A pair of Sèvres type plaques, painted with portraits of Madame de Maintenon and Marie Antoinette, with gilt and blue borders, gilt brass frames, 19thC, 5in (12.5cm). **$720-1,000**

A group of 4 Continental plaques, printed marks, late 19th/early 20thC, 3.5in (9cm) high. **$1,200-1,700**

A German plaque, depicting Amor and Psyche, each scantily clad, flying above the clouds, 10 by 8in (25 by 17cm), in a gilt Florentine frame. **$1,800-2,700**

Pots

A Caughley spittoon, transfer printed with Temple pattern, c1785, 4in (10cm).
$1,800-2,700

A Minton Dresden match holder, design 28, c1835, 5in (12.5cm).
$360-540

Sauceboats

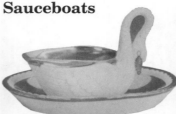

A Sèvres Empire sauceboat and stand, modelled as a white swan, its head and neck forming the handles, the interior solid gilt, the oval stand gilt inside a white feather moulded border, some wear to stand, factory mark in red M. Imp le de Sèvres, c1810, 5.5in (14cm) long.
$900-1,500

Services

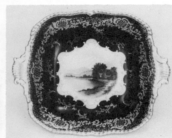

A Coalport part dessert service comprising 7 plates, 9in (22.5cm), and 2 oblong comports, each piece painted and named with an English or Scottish view, signed J. Oldfield, A. Perry, and P. Simpson, with gilt rococo decoration to the blue borders, the views include Loch Awe, Kilchurn Castle, Ullswater, on the Thames, Bassenthwaite Lake, Loch Long, Langdail Pikes, St Michael's Mount and Rydel Water, printed marks, some hairline cracks.
$1,000-1,500

A sauceboat, probably Bow, decorated in relief with a raised border, hand painted and underglazed with blue flower and foliate designs, damaged and cracked, late 18thC.
$110-180

A Worcester sauceboat, moulded with fluted sides, scalloped rim and scroll handle, painted in blue with the Doughnut Tree pattern, unmarked, c1775, 7in (17.5cm)
$360-540

A Copeland dessert service, decorated with salmon pink border and gilt, comprising: 2 oval scallop rimmed bowls with leaf grips, 10in (25cm), 4 square dishes, 8.5in (21.5cm), 3 lobed dishes, 9in (22.5cm), and 20 plates, 9.5in (24cm), with differing pattern numbers.
$3,600-5,500

A Copeland & Garrett Feldspar dessert service, comprising: a comport, 3 shaped dishes and 6 plates, each brightly painted with sprays of flowers within gold foliate reserves on a decorative green band, printed mark, mid-19thC.   **$1,000-1,500**

A residue of a Meissen early morning tea service, painted by C. F. Herold, in red and dark blue, comprising: a teapot and cover, jug and cover, basin, 6 teabowls, and one saucer, crossed swords marks in blue, some chipping.
$40,000-45,000

A Spode part tea service, comprising: a teapot, cover and stand, sugar basin and cover, milk jug, slop bowl, 22 cups and 9 saucers, some damage, Pattern No. 2/578, early 19thC.
$2,700-3,600

A Grainger's Worcester Japan pattern tea and coffee service, decorated with formal floral designs in typical Japan colours, comprising: teapot and cover, sucrier and cover, milk jug, slop bowl, bread and butter plate, 20 cups and 12 saucers, Pattern No. 2013, and a similar bread and butter plate.
$1,800-2,700

A Coalport blue ground part tea and dessert service, brightly painted in iron red, green, blue, yellow and gilding, comprising: a sugar bowl and cover, base inscribed Lord Milford, finial repaired, a milk jug, 2 slop bowls, one inscribed Lord Milford by T. Pardoe, Bristol, 4 muffin dishes and 3 covers, 2 bread plates, one inscribed Pardoe, 28 Bath Street, Bristol, 8 coffee cans, 5 teacups, 10 saucers, one inscribed Lord Milford and another with For Lord Milford by T. Pardoe, Bristol (/) 1812, and 12 side plates, some damage, c1812.
$7,000-9,000

A Meissen tea and coffee service, each painted with small colourful flowersprays, within richly gilt leaf moulded rims, comprising: teapot and cover, a coffee pot and cover, a sugar bowl and cover, a cream jug, 12 cups, saucers and plates, and a cake plate, cancelled crossed swords in underglaze blue, black printed Made in Germany, impressed and painted numerals, 20thC.
$3,600-5,500

A Royal Crown Derby dessert service, with painted central floral bouquets and gilt edges, comprising: 18 plates, 4 dishes, and 2 comports, red printed and impressed marks and pattern number 7698H in red.
$1,200-1,700

A Paris Empire style teapot, sucrier and bowl.
$360-540

> **Miller's is a price GUIDE not a price LIST**

A Chamberlain's Worcester part breakfast and tea service, comprising: 5 plates, 8.5in (21.5cm), 8 plates, 7.5in (18.5cm), 2 slop bowls, 25 cups, and 13 saucers, each piece brightly painted within a white and buff flower embossed border, together with 7 matching cups and 9 saucers, some damage, printed marks, early 19thC.
$1,800-2,700

A New Hall tea service, painted in famille rose style, with a pink diaper border, comprising: a silver shaped teapot, cover and stand, slop bowl, milk jug, and 6 tea bowls and saucers, slight damage and repair, pattern number 173, c1790.
$900-1,500

An English part tea service, comprising: a teapot and cover, sugar basin and cover, milk jug, slop bowl, 2 plates and 12 cups and saucers, each decorated in the Chinese manner with vases, scrolls, boxed and flowers in famille verte enamels, some discolouration, early 19thC.
$720-1,000

A Meissen composite purple ground part tea and coffee service, painted with sprays of Holzschnitt and Deutsche Blumen within brown line quatrefoil shaped reserves, enriched with gilding, comprising: a teapot and cover, hot-milk jug and cover, sugar bowl and cover, 2 coffee cups, 6 teacups and saucers, some repairs and chips, blue crossed swords marks and Pressnummern to some pieces, c1740.   **$10,000-12,000**

A Bloor Derby tea and coffee service, decorated with a turquoise band and gilt flowering branch outline, comprising: pot, stand, slop basin, sucrier and cover, milk jug, 2 dishes, 22 cups, and 12 saucers, red crown and baton mark, c1825.
$3,600-5,500

A Miles Mason blue and white sucrier with cover, cream jug, and tea bowl and saucer, with gilding, c1805.   **$360-540**

A Derby part tea and coffee service, decorated in blue, pink and gilt with a chantilly sprig type decoration, comprising: a teapot and cover, sucrier and cover, milk jug, quatrefoil spoon tray, 2 saucer dishes, 3 coffee cups and 6 tea bowls and saucers, sucrier cover handle restored, and other damage, crown over crossed swords over D over III.
$1,200-1,700

A Meissen outside decorated tête à tête, each piece enamelled with shipping in an estuary scene within gilt borders on a solid turquoise ground, comprising: a tray, 2 cups and saucers, coffee pot and cover, sucrier and cover, and milk jug, slight damage, repaired, deleted swords marks in underglaze blue, late 19thC.
$1,200-1,700

An extensive New Hall tea and coffee service, comprising: 10 saucers, 10 coffee cans, 11 tea bowls, bread and butter plate, sucrier and cover, slop basin, milk jug, teapot, cover and stand, and coffee pot, some damage, pattern No. 480. late 18thC.
$1,200-1,700

Tea & Coffee Pots

A Coalport boat-shaped teapot and cover by Anstic, Horton & Rose, painted with an Imari pattern, c1805, 6.5in (16.5cm).
$360-540

A Meissen teapot and cover, with gilt highlighted animal spout and wishbone handle, painted in colours, with gilt decorated pineapple finial, damaged, crossed swords mark in underglaze blue, and inscribed L in puce, mid-18thC, 4in (10cm) high.
$1,800-2,700

A Miles Mason teapot and cover, with relief decoration and gilding, restored, c1805, 11in (28cm) wide.
$360-540

A Lowestoft teapot and cover, painted in the famille rose palette, within cartouches reserved on an iron red foliate whorl pattern ground with lesser panels of purple foliage, the domed cover with knop finial, c1775, 6in (14.5cm).
$1,200-1,700

A Böttger Hausmalerei teapot and cover, painted in the workshop of Johann Friedrich Metzsch in purpurmalerei, with a purple monogram beneath the spout, chipped and restored, the porcelain c1720, the decoration later, 4.5in (12cm) high.
$7,000-9,000

A First Period Worcester teapot and cover, in underglaze blue, with the Three Ladies pattern, hatched crescent mark, slight chip to cover, c1770, 6in (16.5cm) high.
$1,200-1,700

Vases

Tureens & Butter Tubs

A Chelsea melon tureen and cover, naturally modelled and enriched in yellow and green, repaired, red anchor marks to base and cover, c1756, 6.5in (17cm) wide.
$7,000-9,000

A Meissen tureen and cover, with Dulong moulding and painted with birds within gilt scroll cartouches and scattered Deutsche Blumen, the scroll handles enclosing cauliflower and asparagus, the cover applied with mushrooms, a cauliflower sprig, 2 almonds, a stem of asparagus and a lemon finial, damaged, c1750, 11.5in (30cm) wide.
$3,600-5,500

A Worcester butter tub and cover, transfer printed in blue with the Fence pattern, the cover with applied open flower finial, hatched crescent mark, c1770, 4in (10cm) wide.
$900-1,500

A pair of Worcester, Flight, Barr & Barr green ground two-handled vases, with apple green grounds, the richly gilt foliage moulded scroll handles with anthemion terminals, the rims and feet moulded with a band of white and gilt flowerhead and leaf ornament, on square bases enriched with gilding, damaged and repaired, impressed and script marks, c1820, 8.5in (22cm) high.
$3,600-5,500

A Caughley garniture of 3 vases, painted in the Chamberlain studio at Worcester, probably by George Davis, the necks with blue S-scrolls enriched with gilt flowerhead, foliate and dot ornament, the rims gilt, gilding rubbed, large vase cracked, c1788, 6in (15cm) and 5in (13cm) high.
$1,200-1,700

A Worcester, Kerr & Binns vase, painted by James Bradley Snr., named 'On The Scheld, Holland', c1853, 6in (15cm) high.
$360-540

A Grainger Lee & Co. two-handled pedestal vase, painted below a gold foliate band, the pedestal base enhanced in gold, early 19thC.　**$360-540**

A pair of Chelsea blue ground slender lobed bottle vases, painted within gilt scroll and diaper pattern cartouches reserved on dark blue grounds gilt with flowering foliage, gilt foliate rims, chipped and repaired, c1765, 11.5in (29cm).
$3,600-5,500

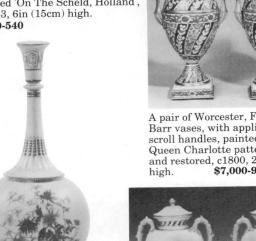

A Royal Worcester biscuit ground vase, with gilded and floral body decoration, shape No. 1149, puce mark, 1894, 17in (43cm) high.
$1,000-1,500

A pair of Worcester, Flight & Barr vases, with applied gilt scroll handles, painted with The Queen Charlotte pattern, chipped and restored, c1800, 20in (51cm) high.　**$7,000-9,000**

A pair of Royal Worcester vases, with covers and inner liners, painted by Stinton on a white ground, signed, one repaired, printed mark in puce, shape number 1927, date cipher for 1905/6, 6.5in (16.5cm) high.
$1,000-1,500

A Royal Worcester biscuit ground vase, with raised floral gilded body decoration, shape No.1764, puce mark, 1896, 14in (35.5cm) high.　**$720-1,000**

A pair of Meissen Schneeballen vases and covers, applied with flowers and floral clusters on the end of green stems and foliage, amongst which small yellow birds perch, the covers similarly decorated and applied with a floral cluster and green stem surmounted by a yellow bird finial, gilt rims, minor restoration, crossed swords in underglaze blue, c1880, 13in (33cm) high.　**$3,600-5,500**

A KPM Berlin two-handled vase and cover, printed and overpainted in colours, between gilt, pink and green borders, Berlin mark in underglaze blue, KPM printed in brown, 17in (43cm) high.
$1,200-1,700

A Vienna vase, painted with a scene after Wouvermanns, on blue and gilt background, gilt handles, 5in (12.5cm) high.
$180-360

A Meissen pot pourri vase and cover, painted with exotic birds between gilt edged puce scale borders, the domed cover with pomegranate finial, repaired, crossed swords mark in underglaze blue, c1770, 8in (21cm) high, with gilt metal base.
$3,600-5,500

A Meissen vase, painted with a view of Wesenstein, other panels painted with coloured sprays of flowers within gold scrolling foliate reserves on a deep blue ground, inscribed Wesenstein, crossed sword mark, 12.5in (32cm) high.
$3,600-5,500

A pair of Helena Wolfsohn vases, painted in the Meissen manner, within ornate gold reserves on a turquoise ground, 19thC, 14.5in (37cm) high.
$1,800-2,700

A Royal Worcester shot silk bamboo double vase, with central handle, shape No. 858, puce mark, 1906, 10in (25cm) long.
$360-540

A pair of large Paris vases, with vine handles, painted on one side with groups of Eastern figures in a garden, on the other a fountain or vases in a similar garden setting, embellished in gold, chipped, 22in (55.5cm) high.
$1,800-2,700

A Meissen (Augustus Rex) vase and cover, with a flower finial, damaged, blue AR mark, incised /// to rim, c1730, the decoration later, 12.5in (32cm) high.
$7,000-9,000

Belleek

Belleek is currently enjoying a steady and deserved growth in popularity and collectability. Founded in 1857, the pottery is still in production on its original site in the little village from which it takes its name in County Fermanagh, Northern Ireland.

It owes its existence to the drive and ambition of three men - John Caldwell Bloomfield, a local entrepreneur and benefactor who donated the site in order to bring work and fame to the area; William Armstrong, a Dublin architect and potter from Worcester who designed, built, and managed the pottery; and William McBirney, a Dublin businessman who financed the venture. Apart from the ready availability of labour and water power, one of the main reasons for the choice of site was an abundance of local deposits of good quality feldspar and other raw materials, but these have since been worked out and now have to be imported.

Initially the pottery only made earthenware, turning out a large range of products including sanitary ware. However, this was not the market in which the founders wished to succeed and Armstrong ploughed back any profit from the earthenware into experiments on parian. Even so it was not until 1863, after at least ten men, together with their knowledge, had been enticed from England (notably the Goss potteries), that Belleek achieved a parian that was marketable.

Belleek won its first Gold Medal at the Dublin Exhibition in 1865. Thereafter it won orders from Queen Victoria and the Prince of Wales and soon this small pottery had become fashionable amongst the nobility. Since then its fortunes have waxed and waned a number of times but

always the high reputation of its work has been maintained.

All Belleek is marked and is relatively easy to date.

A Belleek comport, of a boy and a swan, 1st Period.
$3,600-5,500

* **1st Period 1863-1890**. This mark shows a seated Irish Wolfhound with its head turned to face a Round Tower, on the right of which is an Irish Harp. Below this two sprigs of shamrock border each end of a banner carrying the word Belleek. This mark is usually coloured black, and although other colours are sometimes found this has no special significance.

* **2nd Period 1891-1926**. A furled banner with the words Co. Fermanagh Ireland was added under the first mark.

* **3rd Period 1926-1946**. A circular stamp bearing the Gaelic words 'Deanta in Eirinn' (made in Ireland) and a registration trade mark number 0857 was added below the banner.

All the above marks are known as the black period.

A Belleek four strand woven tray, 24in (61cm) long.
$7,000-9,000

* **1st Green 1946-1955**. The mark remained the same but there was a colour change to green.

* **2nd Green 1955-1965**. To show that the Belleek mark was registered in the USA the letter R within a circle was added above the banner carrying the words Co. Fermanagh Ireland.

* **3rd Green 1965-1981**. The mark was reduced in size and the words Fermanagh were deleted leaving the word Ireland.

* **1st Gold 1981** (still in production). The mark design remained the same but the colour changed to gold.

l. A Belleek spill vase depicting a boy holding a fish, 1st Period, 9in (22.5cm). **$1,200-1,700**
r. A spill vase of a fish, brown and green with gilded fins, 1st Period, 7in (17.5cm). **$360-540**

Baskets are more difficult to date. As a rough guide, early baskets are seldom coloured, are usually three strand and carry the word Belleek or Belleek Co. Fermanagh impressed on pads stuck on the base of the basket. Around 1900 four strand baskets were introduced.

A letter R after the word Belleek is found in Baskets after 1955.

Unlike the parian, Belleek earthenware is not very popular or collectable. Nonetheless, some very handsome and well decorated examples exist and perhaps deserve more credit than they are given.

A Belleek vase, painted on one side with a titled view of The River Erne, Ballyshannon, the handles picked out in gilding, black printed mark, title in black script, post 1891, 10in (25cm).
$1,800-2,700

A Belleek Celtic part tea set, the handles, finials and outlines painted in green, Second Period.
$720-1,000

A Belleek 'Greek' dessert plate, highlighted with turquoise and gilded, First Period.
$360-540

A Belleek tazza on flowered pedestal, First Period.
$1,800-2,700

A Belleek tea set with shamrock pattern, comprising: teapot, sugar bowl, creamer, and 4 cups and saucers, black mark.
$360-540

Two Belleek Nile vases, First Period.
Large **$360-540**
Small **$720-1,000**

A pair of Belleek baskets, with applied flowers and entwined briar handles.
$360-540

A Belleek three-strand covered basket, c1890.
$3,600-5,500

A Belleek thistle vase, and a previously unrecorded shortened example, Second Period.
$360-540

A Belleek shamrock cabaret set, Second period.
$1,200-1,700

One of 35 different sets produced by Belleek.

A Belleek Blarney monogrammed cup and saucer, Second Period.
$720-1,000

A Belleek shell cup and saucer, slight hairline crack, black mark, c1895, saucer 4in (10cm).
$35-70

FURTHER READING

BELLEEK

By Marion Langham
Published by Quiller

ORIENTAL CERAMICS

High quality, combined with an element of the rare and unusual, has been the prerequisite for high prices and demand during the present economic climate. The top end of the Oriental porcelain market, more than perhaps any other, is prone to the fluctuations of international money markets, collecting fashions and effects of the worldwide recession. Early Chinese ceramics of the Song and Tang dynasties are still depressed, although high prices have been attained for good quality Tang tomb figures. The recent fashion for Qing mark and period pieces has continued but only will the rarer, previously unseen pieces fetch record prices. Rare and unusual Chinese export wares of the 18thC continue to be popular but routine famille rose export pieces are having a difficult time. Highly decorative Canton enamel pieces of the 19thC continue to sell for high prices, the demand coming from the decorator market, rather than from collectors.

Good pieces of export ware will fetch high prices no matter where they are sold as international trade buyers search them out. A village hall sale in Yorkshire, saw $6,500 being paid for a good and rare l8thC Chinese porcelain punch bowl painted with a European fox hunting scene encircling the bowl.

Japanese buyers are still in the market for the best of their own ceramics, but at much more subdued price levels than were being fetched two or three years ago. After seeing incredibly high prices recently, Japanese Imari from the last l7thC has now settled down to a steady price level. A pair of 24 inch high Imari vases and covers from the late 17thC sold at Sotheby's Maxwell House sale for the top estimate of $12,000.

Japanese Satsuma pottery is still much sought after, particularly if from one of the well known studios. A signed Kinkozan cabaret set of 9

pieces reached $2,550 in a Heathcote Ball, Leicester, sale. An interesting Satsuma vase, decorated with figures and warriors on a blue ground realised $2,000 at Drewett Neate, Newbury, against a pre-sale estimate of $255-340.

Condition is one of the most important factors in determining the price of Oriental ceramics. A Qianlong mark and period two-handled moon flask was sold by Phillips, Edinburgh, for $25,500. The flask, decorated in underglaze blue and red with the dragon and flaming pearl pattern, had a small, 2 inch, crack to the rim. A perfect example of this type of flask has previously sold for $90,000. To the collector who doesn't worry too much about a small amount of damage there are often bargains to be acquired, normally at about one tenth of the perfect price.

A doucai bowl, painted with ducks among lotus beneath bands of dragons chasing pearls and lanca characters, cracked, underglaze blue Daoguang seal mark and of the period, 6.5in (16cm) diam.
$1,800-2,700

Chinese

Bowls

A Canton famille rose punch bowl, with a gilt ground at the rim, restored, 19thC, 18.5in (47cm) diam.
$3,600-5,500

A Cantonese bowl, painted and gilt with alternating panels of figures on terraces, birds and butterflies among flowers, on a green scroll ground, damaged, 14.5in (37cm) diam.
$900-1,500

A Cantonese bowl, the interior and exterior decorated in famille rose enamels, within gilt and burnt orange key borders, restored, mid-19thC, with later cast gilt brass beaded mounts with Empire style handles and fruit swags, on a quatrefoil foot, 19in (48cm) wide.
$360-540

A Chinese famille rose blue ground medallion bowl, small chips, Qianlong seal mark and of the period, 6in (15cm) diam.
$1,800-2,700

Bearing label for John Sparks Ltd., 128 Mount Street, West London.

A Chinese bowl, on short foot, painted in aubergine with 2 dragons chasing flaming pearls among clouds, above a band of stylised rocks and breaking waves, on a green ground, plain interior, underglaze black Daoguang seal mark and of the period, 6in (15cm) diam.
$3,600-5,500

Chinese dynasties and marks

Earlier Dynasties

Shang Yin, c.1532-1027 B.C.
Western Zhou (Chou) 1027-770 B.C.
Spring and Autumn Annals 770-480 B.C.
Warring States 484-221 B.C.
Qin (Ch'in) 221-206 B.C.
Western Han 206 BC-24 AD
Eastern Han 25-220
Three Kingdoms 221-265
Six Dynasties 265-589
Wei 386-557

Sui 589-617
Tang (T'ang) 618-906
Five Dynasties 907-960
Liao 907-1125
Sung 960-1280
Chin 1115-1260
Yüan 1280-1368

Ming Dynasty

Hongwu (Hung Wu)
1368-1398

Yongle (Yung Lo)
1403-1424

Xuande (Hsüan Té)
1426-1435

Chenghua (Ch'éng Hua)
1465-1487

Hongzhi
(Hung Chih)
1488-1505)

Zhengde
(Chéng Té)
1506-1521

Jiajing
(Chia Ching)
1522-1566

Longqing
(Lung Ching)
1567-1572

Wanli (Wan Li)
1573-1620

Tianqi
(Tien Chi)
1621-1627

Chongzhen
(Ch'ung Chêng)
1628-1644

Qing (Ch'ing) Dynasty

Shunzhi
(Shun Chih)
1644-1661

Kangxi (K'ang Hsi)
1662-1722

Yongzheng (Yung Chêng)
1723-1735

Qianlong (Ch'ien Lung)
1736-1795'

Jiaqing (Chia Ch'ing)
1796-1820

Daoguang (Tao Kuang)
1821-1850

Xianfeng (Hsien Féng)
1851-1861

Tongzhi (T'ung Chih)
1862-1874

Guangxu (Kuang Hsu)
1875-1908

Xuantong
(Hsuan T'ung)
1909-1911

Hongxian
(Hung Hsien)
1916

A Wucai bowl, painted with ruyi cartouches of peony and chrysanthemum on a cell pattern ground, underglaze blue six-character mark, 17thC.
$900-1,500

A pair of Doucai bowls, the exteriors painted with foliate roundels, sprigs of flowers between, the foot painted with a scroll pattern, Jiaqing mark, with ebonised stands, 6in (16cm) diam.
$720-1,000

A Canton famille rose crested punchbowl, painted around the exterior, with a crest beneath the inscription Alexander Crawford Rhodes, 19thC, 16in (41cm) diam.
$7,000-9,000

A famille rose basin, the interior enamelled with 2 pheasants and peonies amidst rocks, the well with 4 floral panels reserved on a diaper and trellis pattern ground, the border with ribboned composite flowersprays below a band of trellis pattern, Qianlong, 15.5in (39cm) diam.
$7,000-9,000

A pair of blue and white soft paste bowls, glaze lines, 18thC, 6.5in (16cm) diam.
$1,200-1,700

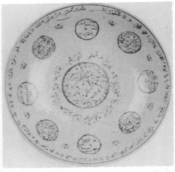

A late Ming Swatow enamelled bowl, the interior containing Arabic script in turquoise and black enamels, an iron red line around the rim, cracked and restored, early 17thC, 15.5in (40cm) diam.
$1,200-1,700

An export bowl for the Dutch East India Company, decorated in tones of underglaze blue, the interior with monogram V.O.C., 9in (23cm) diam.
$3,600-5,500

A famille rose bowl, the interior with gourds on a leafy stem, Jiaqing seal mark, 7in (18cm) diam.
$900-1,500

Cups

A Chinese beaker and saucer, Guangxu 4 character seal mark and period, c1895.
$360-540

A Transitional blue and white tripod surprise cup, modelled in the shape of a lotus leaf, the interior paint with leaf veining, the exterior with a poem, mid-17thC, 2.5in (7cm) diam.
$1,800-2,700

Five famille rose semi eggshell tea bowls, 4 enamelled with a butterfly and flowersprays, a single bloom to the interior, 3.5in (9cm) diam, and one larger, similarly enamelled, 4in (10cm) diam Qianlong.
$2,700-3,600

Figures

A pair of white glazed cockerels, modelled in mirror image, decorated in black, their combs and wattles red, lightly moulded and incised plumage, restored, 18thC, 14.5in (37cm).
$3,600-5,500

A pair of polychrome pheasants, each standing on an outcrop of aubergine with green splashes, their yellow claws naturalistically incised, their feathers brightly enamelled in flame, violet, green, blue and yellow with black details, 19thC, 13.5in (34.5cm).
$3,600-5,500

A stoneware eagle, modelled on a rockwork base, slight touches of ash glaze, chipped, engraved mark kitsu, Bizen Provence, 19thC, 15.5in (39cm).
$1,200-1,700

A pair of white glazed phoenix, modelled in mirror image, with short gold beaks, red crests and beards, cracked and restored, 19thC, 16.5in (42cm).
$1,800-2,700

A pair of blanc de chine cockerels, 19thC, 16in (40cm).
$1,800-2,700

A Sancai glazed pottery horse, all under brown, amber and straw glazes, chipped and restored, Tang Dynasty, 13.5in (34cm).
$10,000-12,000

A buff pottery ox and cart, with 2 large detachable wheels with spokes and large hubs, Tang Dynasty, 9.5in (23cm) long, on fitted wood stand.
$3,600-5,500

A pair of famille rose export figures of elegant lady candle holders, each modelled in mirror image holding a gu-shaped beaker vase wearing long robes with full sleeves, hair tied in a topknot, restored, Jiaqing, 16in (40cm).
$7,000-9,000

A pair of ormolu mounted famille noire figures of boys, wearing tunics, baggy trousers and boots, one with a sword the other mounted as a lamp, damaged, the porcelain 19thC, 13in (33cm).
$7,000-9,000

A set of 9 famille rose figures of Immortals on floral bases, wearing brightly coloured robes and holding their various attributes, some restoration, late Qianlong, 10in (25cm).
$7,000-9,000

A set of 8 famille rose figures of Immortals, on wave pattern bases, wearing brightly coloured robes and holding their various attributes, some restoration, late Qianlong, 9in (23cm).
$2,700-3,600

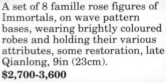

A Tang painted pink pottery figure of a polo player, extensive areas of pigment remaining, restored, 16in (40.5cm) long.
$14,500-16,500

A blanc de chine group modelled as Guanyin and a child, seated on a rocky base, chipped, 18thC, 11in (28cm).
$2,700-3,600

A pair of blanc-de-chine figures of Guanyin and a child, she wearing loose robes and a shawl, the child holding an ingot, restored, 18thC, 16in (40.5cm).   **$2,700-3,600**

A Chinese famille verte figure of Li Tie guai, and a famille rose Immortal, holding a fan and standing on a mound base, both damaged, early 19thC, 8 and 8.5in (20 and 21cm).
$720-1,000

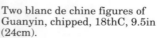

Two famille rose Daoist Immortal groups, each modelled with the 8 Immortals and Shoulao standing on a rockwork and holding their attributes, chipped and repaired, 19thC, 6.5in (16cm).
$360-540

Two blanc de chine figures of Guanyin, chipped, 18thC, 9.5in (24cm).
$1,800-2,700

A blanc de chine figure of Guanyin, the even glaze with a green tinge, chipped, the back with an impressed mark He Chao Cong, 17thC, 15in (37.5cm) on wood stand.
$14,500-16,500

Flatware

A pair of dragon dishes, painted in underglaze blue and washed in yellow with a dragon in pursuit of the flaming pearl amidst clouds, the border with 2 further dragons, all against a blue ground, some damage, seal mark of Daoguang in blue, and period, 10in (25cm).
$1,800-2,700

A famille verte charger, 19thC, 21in (53cm).
$360-540

A Chinese dish, minor rubbing to glaze, Qianlong, 17in (43cm).
$1,000-1,500

A Junyao saucer dish, with shallow sides, under a pale blue glaze, thinning at the rim, the centre with a crescent shaped purple splash and 2 small circles, Song Dynasty, 7in (17cm).
$3,600-5,500

A pair of famille verte deep dishes, painted with scrolling peony flowerheads and foliage, minute rim frits, Kangxi, 11in (28cm).   **$720-1,000**

A set of 7 famille rose plates, 4 octagonal and 3 circular, decorated within an underglaze blue border, some cracked, Qianlong, 9in (23cm).
$1,000-1,500

A pair of famille rose dishes, decorated in bright enamels, the ground enriched with multi-coloured blooms, small chips, Qianlong, 15in (38cm).
$3,600-5,500

A Chinese saucer dish, Daoguang mark and period, c1845, 10in (25cm).   **$900-1,500**

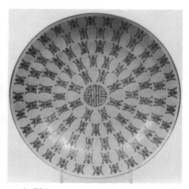

A Chinese saucer dish, cracked and restored, Tongzhi mark and period, c1868, 9in (23cm).
$1,000-1,500

A late Ming Japanese market blue and white moulded saucer dish, rim frits, encircled Chenghua six-character mark, Tianqi, 8.5in (21.5cm).
$1,800-2,700

A late Ming blue and white saucer dish, Jiajing six-character mark and late in the period, 14in (36cm).   **$2,700-3,600**

A famille rose saucer dish, the interior enamelled, exterior plain, rim chip, encircled Yongzheng six-character mark and of the period, 8in (19.5cm).
$1,800-2,700

A famille rose dish, painted at the centre beneath a band of pink trellis pattern, the well reserved with 4 cartouches of precious emblems, the border with 8 Daoist Immortals, slight rubbing and chip, early Qianlong, 13.5in (35cm).
$3,600-5,500

A Longquan celadon dish, the interior carved with a peony spray below petals, beneath everted rim, the countersunk base with an unglazed ring burnt orange in the firing, rim crack, 14th/15thC, 17in (43cm).
$2,700-3,600

A Chinese blue and white deep dish, decorated with trailing floral border, the centre with figures in a landscape and pagodas, c1750, 15in (38cm).
$360-540

A famille rose dish, Qianlong, 14in (35cm).
$2,700-3,600

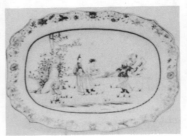

A famille rose meat dish, painted and gilt within a gilt chain border, minute rim frits, Qianlong, 12.5in (31cm) wide.
$1,200-1,700

A Canton famille rose commemorative plate, painted in the centre with 3 Portuguese ships within a band inscribed QUARTO CENTENARIO DO DESCOBRIMENTO DA INDIA, surmounted by the Royal arms of Don Carlos I, within 2 rows of butterflies, ducks, fish and floral sprays, minute rim chip, 19thC, 10in (25cm).
$1,000-1,500

Four Cantonese warming dishes, 19thC.
$1,800-2,700

An enamelled plate, the interior painted en grisaille and gilt, the border with a blue enamelled Y-pattern ground below a band of scrolling foliage, rim chips, Yongzheng, 8.5in (21cm).
$3,600-5,500

Nanking

In the 18thC the bulk of Chinese export porcelain for the West was the now well known blue and white, commonly called 'Nanking' after the port from where it was shipped. Nanking is on the lower Yangtze river, to which the porcelain was sent by boat from Ching tê Chên via the Po-yang lake in Kiangsi province.

Three Chinese Imari dishes, each with a vase of flowers within a central medallion below a qilin, birds and prunus, lotus sprays at the well, early 18thC, two 11.5in (29cm), one 13in (33cm).
$3,600-5,500

A blue and white deep dish, painted with 4 exotic fantailed fish swimming amongst lotus heads and water plants within a band of peony, lotus, hibiscus and dense foliage at the well, the border with 4 broad clusters of peony and stylized flowers, small rim chips and frittings, c1750, 17.5in (45cm).
$10,000-12,000

A pair of Chinese Imari 'Dame-au-Parasol' plates, painted after a design by Cornelis Pronk, on an iron red diaper ground, restored, c1735, 9in (23cm).
$1,500-2,000

An iron red European subject baptism plate, painted with the Baptism of Christ in a wooded riverscape below the Holy Spirit in Dove form, surrounded by 4 winged cherubs and a bird holding ribboned flowersprays above a cartouche inscribed Mat.3.16, small rim chip, Qianlong, 10.5in (27cm).
$2,700-3,600

Jars

Garden Seats

A pair of Canton famille rose garden seats, painted with figure and bird panels around pierced cash between gilt stud borders, late 19thC, 19in (48cm).
$3,600-5,500

A blue and white baluster jar and cover, cracked and restored, Kangxi, 20.5in (52cm).
$2,700-3,600

A Chinese Imari silver mounted milk jug, the domed silver cover with coat-of-arms below a crest and the motto Recte Faciendo Neminem Timeas, handle chipped and cracked, the porcelain 18thC, the mounts 19thC, 10.5in (26cm).
$7,000-9,000

A pair of Canton famille rose baluster jars and covers, with Buddhistic lion finials, on wood stands, late 19thC, 17.5in 45cm).
$3,600-5,500

A Cantonese garden seat, in famille rose et verte enamels and gilt, 19in (48cm),
$1,200-1,700

A pair of blue and white soft paste miniature jugs and covers, the covers and handles pierced, minute chips, jade character mark, Kangxi, 4in (10cm).
$2,700-3,600

A Transitional oviform jar, c1640, 11.5in (29cm).
$2,700-3,600

Hollow Ware & Services

A Chinese famille rose teapot, c1770, 4in (10cm). **$360-540**

Two Chinese blue and white vegetable tureens and domed covers, with strawberry finials, painted with fishermen in mountainous river landscapes, early 19thC, 9in (23cm) diam. **$360-540**

A Canton 'Cadogan' wine pot, the peach shaped body painted on one side with figures and on the other with birds, insects and flowers on a foliate decorated gold ground, minor damage, 6in (16cm). **$180-360**

A Canton 'Cadogan' famille verte wine pot, painted with 6 panels of figures and birds on branches, 6.5in (16cm). **$180-360**

A famille rose tureen, cover and stand, with iron red hare head handles and knop finial, enamelled with mixed floral sprays within flame shaped aubergine hatched borders and spear head around the foot, Qianlong, 14.5in (37cm) long. **$7,000-9,000**

A famille rose monogrammed teapot and cover, each side of the body enamelled with a cypher containing the letters spelling Sir Joshua Reynolds for whom the service was made, below an underglaze blue Fitzhugh pattern border repeated around the flat cover, with a straight spout and entwined double strap handle, c1785, 9.5in (23cm) wide. **$7,000-9,000**

A white glazed rococo style tureen and cover, modelled from a European faience original, supported on 4 paw feet, moulded with irregular flutes and ridges, the sides set with scrolling handles, the cover modelled as a curled leaf with spiralling stem finial, small chips, Qianlong, c1760, 12in (31cm) wide. **$10,000-12,000**

A famille rose tureen and cover, modelled after a European silver original, supported on 4 claw feet, decorated with flowersprays, applied at either side with elaborate frond handles, the cover similarly decorated and surmounted by a rococo scroll finial, chipped, Qianlong, 12.5in (32cm) wide. **$3,600-5,500**

A famille rose armorial tureen, cover and stand, decorated predominantly in blue enamel, iron red and gilt with a crest above the motto Sub Umbra Alarum Tuarum, crack to rim of stand, c1800, stand 14in (36cm) wide. **$3,600-5,500**

A famille rose Mandarin pattern part tea service, enamelled with a dignitary seated in a chair being attended by his wife, a child and a female servant in the garden of a dwelling, with floral panels reserved on gilt and grisaille borders, comprising: a silver mounted teapot and domed cover, a milk jug and domed cover, baluster tea caddy and domed cover, an octagonal lobed spoon tray, a hexagonal lobed spoon tray, a large tea bowl and saucer, 6 tea bowls and saucers, Qianlong. **$3,600-5,500**

A Chinese exportware toy tea service, each piece painted with flowersprays and a puce scale border, comprising: teapot, cover and stand, hot milk jug and cover, tea caddy, spoon tray and 6 cups and 4 saucers, some damage, Qianlong.
$900-1,500

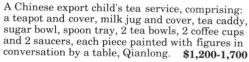

A Chinese export child's tea service, comprising: a teapot and cover, milk jug and cover, tea caddy, sugar bowl, spoon tray, 2 tea bowls, 2 coffee cups and 2 saucers, each piece painted with figures in conversation by a table, Qianlong.   **$1,200-1,700**

The residue of a Canton famille rose dinner service, each piece with a panel of figures meeting by a veranda framed by a border of butterflies amongst scattered flowers, comprising: an oval dish, oval vegetable dish and cover, 4 rectangular vegetable dishes and 2 covers, a pair of oval dishes, 4 liners and 2 covers, some damage, early 19thC.
$2,700-3,600

Vases

A blue and white dinner service, painted with figures amidst pavilions in a river landscape, comprising: 4 tureens, 3 wine coolers with mask handles, a sauceboat, 5 oval dishes, 95 plates, 13 soup plates, 2 strainers, 1 hot water plate, 16 saucer dishes, 37 foliate rim plates, 4 foliate rim saucer dishes, a sauceboat stand and a blue and white part dinner service painted with a boy riding a buffalo beside 2 figures and a pavilion in a wooded river landscape, comprising: a floral rim dish, 12 floral rim plates, 8 floral rim soup plates, and 11 plates painted with ladies on a terrace, 9in (22.5cm), 2 shaped octagonal dishes, painted with rocks, trees and peonies on a terrace, 10in (25cm) and 2 sauceboats, 10.5in (26cm), and 8in (20cm), cracks and chips, all Qianlong.
$27,000-36,000

A Chinese blue and white bottle, Wanli period, 11.5in (29cm) high.
$2,700-3,600

A pair of Transitional Wucai baluster vases and covers, each enamelled on an iron-red trellis pattern ground, beneath an underglaze blue bud finial, slight damage, c1640, 15in (38.5cm) high.
$3,600-5,500

A pair of Chinese famille verte vases of square tapering form, with waisted cylindrical necks, decorated with exotic birds, flowers and foliage, one rim damaged, retrospective Kangxi marks, 19thC, 16in (41cm) high.
$1,200-1,700

A pair of Canton famille rose baluster vases, each with swan handles, 3 handles restored, 19thC, 25in (64cm) high.
$3,600-5,500

A pair of Chinese blue and white vases, the low baluster body filled with leaf shaped landscape panels in insect medallions in a lotus scroll ground, under a broad neck with bell shaped mouth, one rim chipped, 19thC, 17in (43.5cm) high.
$1,800-2,700

A Chinese famille rose vase, 18thC, 6in (15cm) high.
$360-540

A bottle vase, painted in underglaze blue and copper-red with kylins, with gilt metal mounts, cracked, 18in (46cm) high.
$7,000-9,000

A pair of Canton famille rose square baluster vases and domed covers with Guanyin finials, reserved on a ground of scrolling flowers and fruit embellished with exotic birds and butterflies, the covers similarly decorated, slight damage, 19thC, 21.5in (55cm) high.   **$7,000-9,000**

A famille rose vase, with tall flaring neck painted and gilt with shou medallions, surrounded by flowerheads and scrolling leaves, underglaze blue Guangxu six-character mark and of the period, 15.5in (39.5cm) high.
$1,200-1,700

Did you know

MILLER'S Antiques Price Guide builds up year by year to form the most comprehensive photo reference library available.

A Chinese vase, delicately decorated in pastel shades and iron red, 19thC, 10.5in (26.5cm) high.
$720-1,000

A Chinese finely enamelled vase, Daoguang, 5.5in (13.5cm) high.
$720-1,000

A pair of famille noir vases, decorated and heavily gilt with scrolling lotus and shou symbols between bands of lappets, underglaze blue Kangxi six-character marks, l8in (45.5cm).
$1,200-1,700

A pair of Samson famille rose rouleau vases painted with birds and butterflies among peonies issuing from pierced rockwork on blue grounds, 18.5in (47cm) high.
$1,000-1,500

A pair of Chinese famille verte vases, the necks applied with iron red Buddhistic lions, hairline cracks, 19thC, 24in (61cm) high, on wood stands.
$1,800-2,700

A lustrous black glazed garniture comprising: a pair of squat baluster vases and domed covers with knop finials, and a pear shaped vase decorated in gilt, 19thC, vases 17.5in (44.5cm).
$3,600-5,500

A Chinese famille rose vase, 24in (61.5cm) high.
$360-540

A pair of Chinese clobbered flattened vases, with angular handles, painted and gilt with bands of scrolling lotus and peonies on green, red and black grounds, 11in (28cm) high.
$720-1,000

Clobbered: In the late 18thC it was the practice in Europe to enhance the value of simple blue and white porcelain from China with overglaze enamelling - now called clobbering. Most clobbering was done in Holland but a small amount was done in the London decorators' workshops.

A pair of Canton vases, each brightly painted with panels of strolling figures in conversation, reserved on a green hatched ground, damaged, 24in (61cm) high.   **$1,200-1,700**

A pair of Cantonese vases, decorated in famille rose colours, with reserved panels of warriors and other figures in interiors and alternate panels with vases of flowers and insects, restored, 19thC, 10in (25cm) high.
$360-540

A famille rose oviform enamelled vase, the interior and base with a turquoise glaze, Qianlong seal mark, 9in (22.5cm) high.
$2,700-3,600

A pair of Canton famille rose flaring vases, with pierced covers, each painted with figure panels divided by relief gilt squirrels and vines, with gilt handles, the lightly domed pierced covers with matching decoration, 19thC, 9in (23cm) high. **$3,600-5,500**

A pair of famille rose lobed baluster enamelled vases and covers, the shoulders with 2 lion mask fixed ring handles, the domed covers with flowersprays below a Buddhistic lion finial, one cracked, one restored, Qianlong/Jiaqing, 24in (61cm) high. **$7,000-9,000**

A carved celadon meiping, decorated under a thick creamy celadon glaze stopping around the foot to expose the body burnt orange in the firing, 14thC, 10in (25.5cm) high. **$3,600-5,500**

An Imari triple gourd vase, brightly painted in iron red, green and yellow enamels, with gilt on underglaze blue, rim chipped, Kangxi, 12.5in (32cm) high. **$3,600-5,500**

Miscellaneous

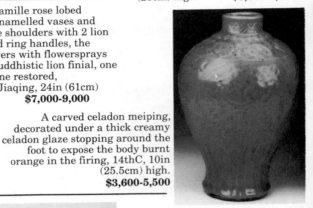

A painted Cizhou pillow, modelled as a recumbent tiger with a broad mouth, pierced nostrils and bold eyes, freely painted with black stripes on a flame coloured ground, its back with a cream ground panel containing a bird within a lozenge, Jin Dynasty, 14.5in (37cm) wide. **$3,600-5,500**

A Chinese blue and white bidet, of waisted form, Qianlong/Jiaqing, 24in (61cm) long, on a four-footed mahogany stand. **$1,800-2,700**

A Transitional blue and white double gourd ewer, painted with lotus and peony sprays and cloud scrolls, strut crack, c1640, 9in (23cm). **$2,700-3,600**

A blue and white jardinière, painted in smokey blue tones, 19thC, 21.5in (54in). **$3,600-5,500**

A pair of Rhodes Kuthaya style baluster jars and domed covers, with twin lion head loop handles, painted with flowering stems on a whorl pattern ground, 15in (38cm) high. **$2,700-3,600**

A Chinese blue and white pilgrim flask, replacement silver neck and cover, 19thC, 9in (23cm). **$360-540**

Japanese
Bowls

An Imari bowl, painted against a predominantly iron red ground between further brocade borders, ho-o mon within, Meiji period, 15in (38cm).
$1,000-1,500

A Satsuma bowl, the exterior enamelled with a dragon, the inside filled with the 18 Rakkan, signed, Meiji period, 5in (13cm).
$720-1,000

A Kenji Imari style bowl, kiku signature, mid-18thC, 12.5in (31.5cm). **$3,600-5,500**

A porcelain bowl by Zengoro Hozen, his son Wazen, or grandson Tokizen, finely painted in underglaze blue in late Ming style with 2 immortals on a raft, the exterior with dragons and Buddhist objects, the rim with brown edge, signed Dai Nihon Eiraku tsukuru, 19thC, 7.5in (19cm) wide. **$1,800-2,700**

An Imari bowl, painted and gilt to the interior, the exterior with panels of chrysanthemum sprays and stylised heads on geometric grounds, damaged, c1700, 10in (25cm). **$1,800-2,700**

An earthenware bowl by Kizan, painted in enamels and gilt with 2 panels showing a formal and an informal picnic, the interior with mille fleur, the base with ho-o, Meiji period, marked Dai Nihon Kizan tsukuru, 5in (12.5cm).
$3,600-5,500

An Imari bowl, painted and gilt with a design of bijin holding parasols, 10in (25cm), and a set of 6 quatrefoil bowls painted and gilt with flowersprays and geometric patterns, 7in (17.5cm). **$360-540**

A Kakiemon bowl, decorated in enamels and slight gilt with pine and prunus, the everted rim with scrolling peonies within a brown edged rim, footrim drilled with one hole, late 17thC, 5.5in (13.5cm).
$1,800-2,700

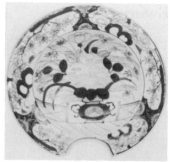

An Imari barber's bowl, painted and gilt within a border of panels of trees, rockwork and buildings, chipped, c1700, 11in (28cm).
$1,000-1,500

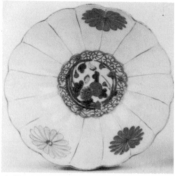

A fluted Imari bowl, decorated in typical coloured enamels and gilt on underglaze blue, early 18thC, 8.5in (21.5cm). **$3,600-5,500**

An Imari barber's bowl, early 18thC, 11in (28cm).
$1,800-2,700

Imari

Most Japanese porcelain was manufactured in and around the town of Arita, in the province of Hizen. The factories of Arita were within eight miles of the port of Imari, the market town of the district, and the place to which all porcelain was carried before being shipped to Nagasati for export to Europe.

The term 'Imari' survives to describe a certain type of decoration on Arita wares, namely underglaze blue, with on-glaze iron red and gold decoration.

Ewers

A large Arita ewer, decorated in underglaze blue with peonies between floral and geometric bands, drilled towards the foot, c1670, 11in (28cm).
$1,800-2,700

An Arita blue and white moulded kendi, late 17thC, 8in (20cm).
$1,800-2,700

An Arita ewer.
$1,000-1,500

A pair of Arita ewers, decorated in underglaze blue with figures in a garden, damaged, c1670, 10in (25cm).   **$1,800-2,700**

Figures

A Kutani group of 5 cats, comprising: a mother and 4 kittens, each asleep with their paws tucked beneath them, with gilt fur markings and orange bows, Taisho period, 11in (28cm) and 2.5in (6.5cm) wide.
$1,000-1,500

A Satsuma earthenware figure of Fugen Bosatsu, by Kizan, the female deity seated on an elephant, decorated in enamels and gilt, foot of goddess restored, marked Dai Nihon Satsuma yaki Kizan, Meiji period, 13in (33cm) high.
$3,600-5,500

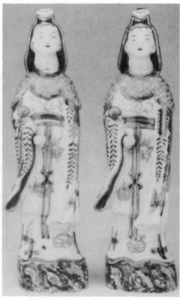

A pair of Imari figures of ladies, wearing high cowls and flowing robes, each holding a flowerspray, slight damage and repair, 16in (41cm) high.
$720-1,000

A porcelain duck, the plumage ornithologically correct, the eyes touched in black, slight damage, possibly Mahuzu Kozan, Meiji period, 8in (20cm) wide.
$1,000-1,500

An Hirado white glazed model of a tiger, 6in (15cm) high.
$720-1,000

Flatware

An Arita dish, decorated in underglaze blue with floral designs, late 17thC, 12.5in (31.5cm).
$1,800-2,700

Two Imari dishes, decorated in underglaze blue, iron red, black enamel and gilding with a bijin and attendants, both with a rivetted crack, 19in (49cm) and 18in (45.5cm).
$3,600-5,500

An Imari charger, decorated in underglaze blue, iron red, enamels and gilding, 19thC, 17.5in (45cm).
$3,600-5,500

An Imari plaque painted with panels, 18in (46.5cm).
$360-540

A large Imari dish, the iron red ground filled with a profusion of peony painted in underglaze blue, detailed in black lacquer, slight damage, 25in (63cm).
$1,200-1,700

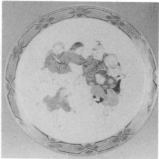

An Arita dish, framed by a border of panels filled with dots between intersecting blue lines, Meiji period, 21.5in (54.5cm).
$720-1,000

An Imari charger, painted and gilt with a central ho-o medallion within a border of three panels of cranes, sages and birds among the Three Friends, on a floral and geometric design ground, 24.5in (63cm). **$2,700-3,600**

An Imari saucer dish, decorated in iron red and gilt on underglaze blue, c1700, 21in (54.5cm).
$7,000-9,000

An Imari foliate rimmed charger, decorated in iron red and gilt on underglaze blue, late 19thC, 25in (64cm).
$3,600-5,500

An Arita blue and white charger, containing the letters V.O.C., surrounded by a ho-o bird perched among flowers and foliage, the rim with 6 shaped rectangular panels alternately containing the shochikubai.
$21,000-27,000

Two Imari chargers, painted and gilt with shaped and scroll panels of maple, wisteria, bijin and landscapes, 18in (46cm).
$720-1,000

A Imari charger, painted with panels of mountain landscape and kara shi shi on gilt and blue ground with cranes amidst clouds, and gilt and red phoenix in shaped panels, 21.5in (54.5cm).
$360-540

A Nabeshima style dish, decorated overall in underglaze blue with finely scrolling foliage, the exterior with larger scrolls, the tall tapering foot with 'comb' design, 19thC, 19in (48cm).
$2,700-3,600

An Arita blue and white charger, painted with a roundel enclosing the letters V.O.C., surrounded by 3 ho-o birds, one perched on a rock, the other in flight amongst pomegranate and peony sprays, within a border of 6 alternate panels of peony and shochikubai sprays divided by vertical bands of stylised flowerheads and foliage, late 17thC, 14.5in (37.5cm).
$21,000-27,000

An Arita blue and white charger, late 17thC, 23in (58cm).
$7,000-9,000

An Imari charger, decorated with 2 galloping fabulous animals with a phoenix overhead, the floral lattice border with groups of pendant hexagons painted with flowering branches and formal designs, 24in (61cm).
$1,200-1,700

Hollow Ware

A large blue and white jardinière, raised upon 3 dwarf cabriole legs, 19thC, 25in (64cm) diam.
$1,800-2,700

A Kakiemon cup and an Arita saucer, the cup decorated in iron-red, green, blue and black enamels and gilding with floral sprays, the saucer of multi-lobed form with floralsprays, damaged, late 17thC, cup 2.5in (6.5cm), saucer 5in (13cm).
$1,200-1,700

An Arita blue and white silver mounted coffee pot and cover, on 3 shaped feet, the loop handle decorated with scrolling foliage, the porcelain late 17thC, the mounts 19thC, 13in (33cm) high.
$7,000-9,000

> **Miller's is a price GUIDE not a price LIST**

An Hirado jar and cover, modelled as a conch shell in blue, brown, cream and green glazes, the shell encrusted conch moulded with crabs and limpets, slight damage, 18thC, 11in (28cm).
$3,600-5,500

Vases

Three Arita blue and white jars and covers, damaged and covers repaired, late 17thC, 18.5in (47cm).   **$10,000-12,000**

A Imari fluted jar, painted and gilt in coloured enamels and underglaze blue, c1700, 16in (41cm).
$7,000-9,000

A pair of Imari vases, painted against an iron red ground, damaged and repaired, Meiji period, 36in (92cm), on wood stands. **$900-1,500**

A pair of Satsuma vases, damaged, signed in gold within the pattern, 6in (15cm).
$900-1,500

A pair of Satsuma vases, painted and gilt with continuous scenes, signed Renji, 7in (17.5cm).
$1,200-1,700

A pair of Satsuma vases, painted and gilt with continuous scenes, damaged, 11in (28cm) high.
$1,200-1,700

A pair of Satsuma vases, reserved on a brocade ground, fitted with pierced gilt brass stands, 12in (30.5cm). **$2,700-3,600**

An Imari vase, traditionally decorated with blue, rust and gilt floral designs, early 19thC, 18in (46cm).
$720-1,000

A Samson Imari jar and domed cover, with knop finial, painted and gilt, 33in (83.5cm).
$10,000-12,000

A pair of Kutani vases, applied with butterfly handles, one repaired.
$1,800-2,700

An Imari bottle vase, moulded in relief and painted in underglaze blue, iron red and gilding with sprays of kiku and peonies, c1800, 7in (17.5cm) high.
$1,800-2,700

A pair of Kutani vases, enamelled, with mask and tongue handles, 11in (28cm).
$1,200-1,700

A pair of Imari vases, each in the form of Benkei clinging to a giant leaping carp, decorated in underglaze blue, iron red, enamels and gilding, damaged, c1800, 9in (23cm).
$7,000-9,000

Benkei, a hero of the 12thC, as a boy was nicknamed Oniwaka (young demon) and is often depicted exhibiting great feats of strength.

A Satsuma vase, of butterfly outline, one side filled with a panel of bijin, the other with samurai on a shore, signed, Meiji period, 4in (10cm)
$720-1,000

A large Satsuma quatrefoil vase, painted and heavily gilt with panels of officials, ladies and children before buildings in mountainous landscapes, 19.5in (49.5cm).   **$2,700-3,600**

An Imari garniture, comprising: jar and cover, and a pair of beaker vases, all decorated in underglaze blue, iron red, slight black enamel and gilding, beaker vases restored, c1800, jar and cover 19in (48cm).   **$3,600-5,500**

A pair of Satsuma double gourd vases, painted with Rakkan, signed, Meiji period, 8.5in (22cm) high.
$900-1,500

An Imari vase and cover, decorated in underglaze blue, iron red, enamels and gilding, with panels of bijin and attendants, with a wood stand, Meiji period , 25in (64cm) high.
$2,700-3,600

An Imari vase, decorated in underglaze blue, iron red and gilding with ho-o among flowering trees, c1800, 13in (33cm) high.
$2,700-3,600

An Imari vase, painted beneath the shoulder with a repeated panel showing a bird descending to a blossoming branch, 3 ho-o panels on the shoulder reserved in a flower strewn blue ground, c1800, 10.5in (26.5cm).
$720-1,000

A Kutani millefiori vase, signed, Meiji period, 12in (30.5cm).
$1,800-2,700

A blossom vase for the tea ceremony room, (Hanaike), Ko-Kiyomizu-Edo, 14in (36cm).
$3,600-5,500

A pair of Kutani vases, each painted in brilliant enamels and gilding with figures in a landscape, marked fuku (happiness), Meiji period, 11.5in (29.5cm) high.
$2,700-3,600

A Kutani vase, decorated in white and coloured enamels and gilding with chrysanthemum, marked Kutani Taniguchi, Meiji period, 14in (36cm).
$2,700-3,600

A pair of Satsuma earthenware vases, decorated in typical palette, 17.5in (44cm).
$7,000-9,000

A pair of Satsuma earthenware vases, by Fuzan, each with 4 panels of bijin, birds and flowers, reserved on a blue ground, marked Fuzan, Meiji period, 6.5in (16.5cm).
$3,600-5,500

A pair of Imari moulded trumpet necked vases, decorated in iron red and gilt on underglaze blue with 2 panels of vases of flowers divided by massed flowers and foliage, late 19thC, 22.5in (58cm).
$7,000-9,000

A pair of Imari vases, each painted with cockerels, bats, chrysanthemum, peony and blossoming branches, within moulded hexagonal panels, late 19thC, 18in (46cm).
$7,000-9,000

A pair of Satsuma earthenware vases by Gyokushu, each decorated in enamels and gilt with landscapes and still life, signed Gyokushu, one rim chip repaired, 4in (11cm) high.
$2,700-3,600

An Imari bottle vase, decorated in underglaze blue, iron red and gilding, with shaped panels of kiku and peonies reserved on birds and trees, c1800, 10.5in (26.5cm) high.
$2,700-3,600

An Hirado reticulated and double skinned vase, c1860, 6in (15cm).
$1,800-2,700

GLASS

Bowls

A green glass finger bowl, c1800, 4.5in (11cm) diam.
$110-180

Two Stourbridge bowls, c1880, 5.5in (14cm) and 6.5in (16.5cm) diam.
$110-180

A butter dish, with prism cutting above and below a band of relief diamonds, star cut base, notched rim with 2 fan cut handles, c1810, 7.5in (18.5cm) wide.
$720-1,000

An English sugar bowl, engraved with a fruiting vine, with pedestal stem and star engraved foot, c1880, 5in (12.5cm) diam.
$110-180

A butter dish, cover and stand with diamond, prism and blaze cutting, the domed cover with a mushroom finial, c1825, 5in (12.5cm).
$360-540

A fruit bowl, with kettle drum body, turn-over rim and cut with diamonds and splits, on a bobbin knopped stem and square lemon squeezer foot, c1800, 9.5in (24cm) diam.
$1,200-1,700

A pair of Georgian style cut glass bowls, with crenellated rims over steep diamond faceted sides, late 19thC, 9in (22.5cm) diam.
$1,200-1,700

A Victorian glass bowl and stand with silver cover, etched with trailing water lilies and lotus blossoms, the flat silver cover crested and with further water lily finial, by C. T. & G. Fox, London, 1859, fully marked, 6.5in (16.5cm) diam., 9oz of silver.
$1,000-1,500

An opalescent vaseline bowl, 5.5in (14cm) diam.
$70-145

Decanters

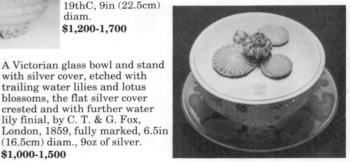

A dish, cut with small diamonds and fluting, serrated on a short cut stem and notch cut rim, conical star cut foot, c1810, 6in (14.5cm).
$360-540

A pair of plain decanters, with three neck rings and cut mushroom stoppers, c1800, 8in (19.5cm).
$1,200-1,700

A pair of cut glass decanters, with an engraved crest, c1780, 12.5in (32cm) high.
$2,700-3,600

GLASS - PRICE TRENDS

In my previous three reviews I made the point that glass had bucked the trend compared with other areas of collecting by moving up sharply in price. Over the past year, however, as the recession has deepened, prices have stabilised and are generally not very different from twelve months ago.

The demand for early English glass is still strong, with good quality pieces being very much in demand. Victorian glass on the other hand has fared poorly, this is due in part to the lack of interest being shown by overseas buyers, particularly the Americans who are normally avid collectors.

Continental glass is selling but when one looks at the sale results ordinary façon de Venise, Venetian and South German glass make up most of the unsold lots.

Returning briefly to English glass, there seem to be quite a lot of 'Beilby' enamelled glasses appearing on the market. The quality of these does vary a lot and while a glass with poor decoration or restoration can be had for as little as £500 a good glass with ordinary fruiting vine decoration and a gilt rim cannot be had for much less than £1,200. Jelly glasses are becoming quite hard to find and it is not unusual to find an early or mid-18th century example with, perhaps, a ribbed bowl, air beaded knop and domed foot making in excess of £80.

In conclusion, I sense that more glass is now coming on to the market and, if the economy does pick up as predicted, prices should not advance too rapidly. Now, therefore, is a good time to buy good quality examples when they become available.

R. G. Thomas
April 1992

A set of 3 cruciform decanters, with bladed string rings, c1730, 11.5in (29cm).
$2,700-3,600

An octagonal moulded decanter, with annulated string ring, c1730, 8in (19.5cm).
$720-1,000

A pair of near Rodney type plain decanters, with monogram 'BB', 3 plain neck rings and target stoppers, c1800, 8in (20cm).
$1,800-2,700

A pair of decanters, engraved 'WMW' below a hatched rose and laurel leaf garland, with target stoppers, c1770, 10in (25cm).
$1,800-2,700

A pair of heavy cut decanters, with cut mushroom stoppers, c1810, 8.5in (21cm).
$1,800-2,700

A Bristol blue decanter, engraved with gilding and 'Noyeou', French, c1760, 9in (22cm).
$720-1,000

A pair of decanters with ovoid bodies, broad flute cut, 3 neck rings and target stoppers, c1820, 8.5in (21cm).
$900-1,500

A pair of tapered decanters, with a band of looped egg and tulip engraving, with lunar cut bevelled lozenge stoppers, c1780, 9in (23cm).   **$1,800-2,700**

Three spirit decanters, with ovoid bodies, c1810:
l. flute cut base and angular neck rings, with mushroom stopper, 7in (18cm)
c. plain body and neck rings, with target stopper, 7in (18cm)
r. flute cut base and neck, cut neck rings, with mushroom stopper, 7.5in (19.5cm).
$180-360 each

A magnum decanter, cut with flutes, prisms, diamonds, cut neck rings, star cut base and cut mushroom stopper, c1810, 10.5in (27cm).
$1,200-1,700

A green glass Whiskey decanter, c1850, 10in (25cm).
$180-360

Three decanters with ovoid bodies, c1810:
l. fluted base and neck, with mushroom stopper, 8.5in (21.5cm)
c. plain body, target stopper, 9in (22.5cm)
r. fluted base and neck, with mushroom stopper, 8.5in (21cm).
$360-540

A pair of Continental enamelled glass decanters, with titled oval portrait medallions of Field Marshal, Duke of Wellington and Admiral Nelson, 19thC, 9.5in (23.5cm).
$1,000-1,500

A blue glass Claret decanter, c1850, 10in (25cm).
$180-360

Three cut decanters:
l. body cut with strawberry diamonds and flutes, with cut mushroom stopper, c1820, 8.5in (21cm)
$360-540
c. body cut with diamond and flute cutting, with cut mushroom stopper, c1810, 8in (20.5cm).
$360-540
r. body cut with strawberry diamonds, flutes and prisms, with mushroom stopper, c1825, 8in (20.5cm).
$360-540

A liqueur decanter and 2 glasses, 9.5in (24cm) and 3.5in (9cm).
$110-180

A green glass Rum decanter, c1850, 10in (25cm).   **$180-360**

Three decanters:
l. with ovoid plain body, 3 plain neck rings, with plain mushroom stopper, c1800, 9in (23cm)
$360-540
c. with straight sided body flute, diamond and prism cut, 2 cut and one annulated neck rings, with cut mushroom stopper, c1820, 9in (23cm)
$360-540
r. with tapered body, 3 bladed neck rings, with cut lozenge stopper, c1800, 9in (23cm).
$360-540

A Georgian cut glass tumbler, 3.5in (9cm).
$35-70

A commemorative rummer, the ovoid bowl engraved with Admiral Lord Nelson's catafalque, the reverse side engraved 'Lord Nelson, Jan'y 9, 1806', 5.5in (14.5cm).
$1,800-2,700

An ale glass, engraved with hops and barley, on lemon squeezer foot, c1790, 4.5in (11.5cm).
$180-360

A rummer, the ovoid bowl on a collared stem with domed, moulded, lemon squeezer base, c1800, 5.5in (14cm).
$110-180

A rummer, the ovoid body engraved with Nelson's funeral car, the reverse side 'Jan'y 9, 1806', 5.5in (14.5cm).
$1,800-2,700

A set of 4 pale green wing flutes, with drawn slice cut stems, engraved with fruiting vines, c1830, 4.5in (11cm).
$360-540

Three flutes, the conical bowls on cut baluster stems, c1850, 7in (17.5cm).
$180-360

A bucket rummer, with hollow knop containing a silver coin for 1817, 6in (15cm).
$360-540

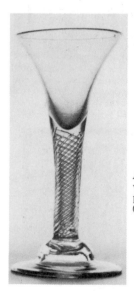

A drawn trumpet bowl wine glass, with air-twist stem and domed partially folded foot, c1740, 6.5in (16.5cm).   **$360-540**

A pair of bucket shaped bowl rummers, engraved with monogram WB, within a leaf cartouche, with knopped stems, and plain conical feet, c1825, 6.5in (16cm).
$180-360

Three panel moulded rummers, the ovoid bodies with a band of floral and leaf decoration, c1810, 4.5 to 5in (11 to 12.5cm).
$110-180

An Anglo-Venetian ale glass, the deep round funnel bowl with wrythen and pincered decoration, a short knopped stem and folded conical foot, c1700, 5in (13cm).
$1,200-1,700

A rummer, the cup shaped bowl engraved with the rare motif of St George slaying the dragon, the reverse side with monogram T.E.B. and date 1818, plain stem, square, domed, lemon squeezer foot, 6.5in (16cm).
$1,800-2,700

An English wine glass, with opaque spiral twist stem, 18thC.
$1,800-2,700

A set of 14 wine glasses, with deep round funnel bowls on stems with single series spiral cable air-twists, on plain conical feet, c1745, 7in (18cm).
$10,000-12,000

A Lynn wine glass, the horizontally ribbed round funnel bowl on a stem with a double series opaque twist and plain conical foot, c1760, 5.5in (13.5cm).
$1,200-1,700

Three wine glasses, with double series opaque twist stems, and plain conical feet, c1760, 5 to 6in (13 to 15cm).
$360-540

A trumpet bowl wine glass, drawn stem with multiple spiral air twist, plain conical foot, c1750, 6.5in (16.5cm).
$360-540

l. A firing glass, with trumpet bowl, on a drawn stem with multiple spiral air-twists, on a thick flat foot, c1745, 4.5in (11cm)
$360-540
r. A wine glass with similar bowl and stem, on a plain conical foot, c1745, 6.5in (16cm).
$360-540

A glass, with multiple series opaque twist stem on a thick foot, c1760, 4.5in (11.5cm). **$180-360**

A large drawn trumpet bowl wine glass, with air-twist stem and folded conical foot, c1745, 8in (20cm). **$360-540**

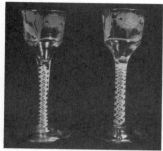

Two wine glasses, the ogee bowls engraved with a Jacobite rose and bud, and thistle, double series opaque twist stems, plain conical feet, c1760, 6in (15.5cm).
$720-1,000

Three wine glasses, bowls, with double opaque twist stems and plain conical feet, c1760, 5.5 to 6in (13.5 to 15cm).
$360-540

A pair of wine glasses, with round funnel bowls, engraved and polished with a floral band, on stems with double series opaque twists and plain conical feet, c1760, 6in (15cm).
$1,000-1,500

A gilded green wine glass, 18thC, 5in (13cm).
$180-360

Two opaque twist wine glasses with round funnel bowls, engraved with fruiting vines, double series opaque twist stems and plain conical feet, 6in (15.5cm).
$360-540 each

Three glasses with double series opaque twist stems, and plain conical feet, c1760:
l. with a bell bowl, 6.5in (16.5cm)
c. with an ale bowl, engraved with hops and barley motif, 7.5in (19cm)
r. with ogee bowl, 6in (15cm).
$360-540 each

A wine glass, the ogee bowl engraved with a sunflower and sprig, on a stem with a double series opaque twist, and plain conical foot, c1760, 5in (13cm).
$360-540

A trumpet drawn wine glass, with spiral air-twist stem and basal knopped stem with domed foot, 7in (18cm).
$720-1,000

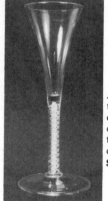

A mixed twist flute, with slender trumpet bowl on a stem with central opaque white gauze, and outer pair of spiralling air-twist threads, on a plain conical foot, c1760, 7.5in (19cm).
$720-1,000

A Beilby funnel bowled wine glass, enamelled in white with trailing grapes and vine leaves on a double series opaque twist stem, on spreading foot, foot chipped, c1760, 6in (15cm).
$900-1,500

A wine glass, with round funnel bowl engraved with fruiting vine motif, on a double series opaque twist stem and plain conical foot, c1760, 6in (15cm).
$720-1,000

A Beilby wine glass, the ogee bowl decorated with white enamel fruiting vine, on a stem with a double series opaque twist, with plain conical foot, c1775, 5.5in (14.5cm).
$3,600-5,500

A wine glass with round bowl, finely engraved with Jacobite rose and moth, polished in parts, with double series opaque twist stem and plain conical foot, c1765, 6.5in (16cm).
$1,200-1,700

A mixed twist flute, the trumpet bowl on a stem with annulated collar and slender stem, with a central opaque white gauze and a pair of outer air threads spiralling, on a plain conical foot, c1770, 7.5in (19cm).
$1,200-1,700

A firing glass, with ogee bowl on a short stem with double series opaque twist stem, thick terraced firing foot, c1760, 3.5in (9.5cm).
$720-1,000

An ale glass with deep round funnel bowl, engraved with hops and barley motif, with double series opaque twist stem and plain conical foot, 7.5in (19cm).
$360-540

An unusual ale glass, with deep ogee bowl engraved with hops and barley, on a stem with multiple spiral air-twist and plain conical foot, c1750, 7.5in (18.5cm).
$1,000-1,500

Firing Glasses

Firing glasses are always short stemmed. They are dram glasses or small wines made with a specially strong, thick foot for use at meetings. When a toast was drunk the members would strike the table simultaneously with their glasses, the noise was said to resemble the firing of a musket.

A large drawn wine glass with tear drop stem, domed and folded foot, c1720, 9in (22.5cm).
$360-540

A short cordial glass, the trumpet bowl on a drawn stem with multiple spiral air-twist, and plain conical foot, c1745, 4.5in (11cm).
$720-1,000

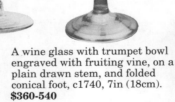

A wine glass with trumpet bowl engraved with fruiting vine, on a plain drawn stem, and folded conical foot, c1740, 7in (18cm).
$360-540

One goblet and two wine glasses, with trumpet bowls and plain drawn stems with air tears, c1745, 6 to 7.5in (15.5 to 18.5cm).
$180-360

l. An ale glass, with deep round funnel bowl engraved with a barley motif, on a plain drawn stem, and plain conical foot, c1750.
$360-540
r. A wine glass, the ogee bowl on a plain stem, and folded conical foot, c1750.
$180-360

Did you know

MILLER'S Antiques Price Guide builds up year by year to form the most comprehensive photo reference library available.

Two wine glasses, with plain stems and folded conical feet, c1748, 7 to 7.5in (18 to 19cm).
$360-540

A Jacobite wine glass, the trumpet bowl engraved with Jacobite rose, two buds and a star, on a plain drawn stem with air tear, and plain conical foot, c1750, 6.5in (16cm).
$1,800-2,700

A green wine glass, late 18thC, 5in (13cm).
$110-180

An ale glass, with deep round funnel bowl engraved with hops and barley motif, on a plain stem and folded conical foot, c1750.
$360-540

A glass with bell bowl, engraved with a vine and grapes, on a drawn stem with tear and folded foot, c1770, 6in (15cm).
$180-360

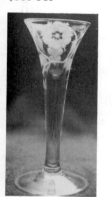

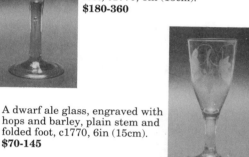

A dwarf ale glass, engraved with hops and barley, plain stem and folded foot, c1770, 6in (15cm).
$70-145

An English glass with bucket bowl, engraved with grapes and vines, on a plain stem and folded conical foot, c1770, 6in (15cm).
$180-360

A green wine glass, c1780, 6in (15cm).
$180-360

A Jacobite wine glass with trumpet bowl, engraved with a Jacobite rose, two buds and an oak leaf, on a plain drawn stem and plain conical foot, c1750, 6in (15.5cm).
$2,700-3,600

A green wine glass, with baluster stem, c1880, 4in (10cm).   **$35-70**

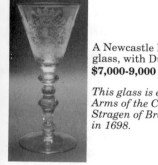

A Newcastle light baluster wine glass, with Dutch engraving.
$7,000-9,000

This glass is engraved with the Arms of the Count van der Stragen of Brabant, created Count in 1698.

A green wine glass, on a faceted stem, with gilding, c1820, 6in (15cm).
$180-360

A toastmaster's glass, the deceptive conical bowl straight on to an inverted baluster knop with air tear, on a folded conical foot, c1720, 4in (10.5cm).
$1,200-1,700

A heavy baluster wine glass with conical bowl, mushroom and base knop stem, on domed folded foot, c1720, 6in (15cm).
$1,200-1,700

Two heavy baluster wine glasses, with solid sections to bowls containing an air tear, knopped stems, folded conical feet, c1720, 5.5 to 6in (14to 15cm).
$1,800-2,700

Three balustroid wine glasses:
l. with waisted bucket bowl,
inverted baluster knopped stem,
and folded conical foot, c1720,
5.5in (14cm).
$1,000-1,500
c. with trumpet bowl, multi-
knopped stem, and plain conical
foot, c1740, 7in (18cm)
$1,200-1,700
r. with bell bowl, hollow inverted
baluster knop stem, and folded
conical foot, c1720, 6.5in (16cm).
$1,200-1,700

A balustroid cordial glass, the bell
bowl on a stem with cushion drop
and true baluster knops, on a
domed folded foot, c1720, 5.5in
(14cm).
$900-1,500

Three balustroid wine glasses:
l. with trumpet bowl, drawn with
swelling knop and air tear stem,
on plain conical foot, c1720, 6.5in
(16.5cm)
$1,200-1,700
c. with bell bowl, stem with
annulated and base knops, folded
conical foot, c1720, 6in (15cm)
$1,000-1,500
r. with bell bowl, stem with
central ball knop, plain conical
foot, c1725, 6.5in (17cm).
$720-1,000

A gin glass, the trumpet
bowl on a balustroid stem
with shoulder, inverted
baluster and base knops,
on a folded conical foot,
c1720, 5in (12.5cm).
$360-540

A baluster wine glass, with
a bell bowl, on inverted
baluster and base, knopped
stem, on plain domed foot,
c1720, 6in (15cm).
$1,200-1,700

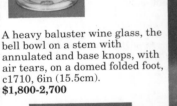

Three balustroid wine glasses,
two with bell bowls and domed,
folded feet, one with trumpet
bowl, 'kit-kat' stem, and plain
conical foot, c1720, 5.5 to 6.5in (14
to 16cm).
$900-1,500 each

A heavy baluster wine glass, the
conical body with solid section, on
a stem with inverted baluster and
base knops and air tear, on a
domed folded foot, c1710, 7.5in
(19cm). **$2,700-3,600**

A balustroid wine glass, the bell
bowl on a stem with base ball
knop, on a plain folded foot,
c1740, 6.5in (16.5cm).
$720-1,000

A heavy baluster wine glass, the
bell bowl on a stem with
annulated and base knops, with
air tears, on a domed folded foot,
c1710, 6in (15.5cm).
$1,800-2,700

A balustroid wine glass, the
conical bowl on a stem with an
unusual cylinder knop with air
tear, on folded conical foot, c1720,
5.5in (14cm).
$1,200-1,700

A heavy baluster wine glass, with
trumpet drawn bowl, tear to stem
and knop, domed foot, small chip
to foot, c1720, 6.5in (16.5cm).
$720-1,000

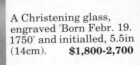

A Christening glass,
engraved 'Born Febr. 19.
1750' and initialled, 5.5in
(14cm). **$1,800-2,700**

A Newcastle type goblet, the round funnel bowl engraved with fine band of scrolling and floral decoration, with Newcastle type knopped and air beaded stem, on a plain conical foot, c1750, 7in (18cm).
$1,800-2,700

A 'Newcastle' light baluster goblet, the round funnel bowl engraved with a border of floral swags pendant from tied tassels, on a multi-knopped inverted baluster air beaded knopped stem, on a plain conical foot, c1750, 7in (18cm).
$2,700-3,600

A balustroid wine glass, the round funnel bowl engraved with a band of fruiting vine, on a stem with shoulder, angular inverted baluster and base knops, domed folded foot, c1730, 7in (17.5cm).
$1,000-1,500

A balustroid wine glass, on a folded conical foot, c1750, 6in (15cm).
$360-540

A 'Newcastle' light baluster goblet, on a multi-knopped stem, with a plain conical foot, c1750, 7in (18cm).
$1,800-2,700

A Newcastle type goblet, engraved with the Royal coat-of-arms, Newcastle knopped air beaded stem, c1750, 7.5in (18.5cm).
$2,700-3,600

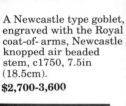

A Newcastle type wine glass, engraved with a band of floral meander with perched parrots, on a light baluster stem, with shoulder ball and inverted baluster knops, on a plain domed foot, c1750, 7in (18cm).
$1,800-2,700

A balustroid goblet, engraved with a band of scrolling, foliage and exotic birds, with a multi-knopped stem, on a plain domed foot, c1750, 7.5in (19cm).
$1,800-2,700

A green mead glass with incised knop stem, c1760, 5.5in (14cm).
$1,200-1,700

Two facet stem wine glasses with round funnel bowls, diamond cut stems, and plain conical feet, c1770, 4.5 to 5.5in (11.5 to13.5cm).
$180-360

l. A wine glass with diamond cut knopped stem, c1770, 6in (15cm).
$180-360
c. An ale glass, engraved with a band of stars and printies, on a diamond cut stem, c1770, 7in (18cm).
$360-540
r. A wine glass with pan top bowl, on a drawn hexagon cut stem, c1770, 5.5in (14cm).
$1,000-1,500

A Bristol blue moulded goblet, c1810, 6in (15cm).
$180-360

A Newcastle engraved goblet, the stem with angular and inverted baluster air-beaded knops, on a plain conical foot, c1750, 7.5in (18.5cm).
$1,800-2,700

A green glass facet funnel bowl on balded knop stem, c1840, 4.5in (11.5cm).
$35-70

A set of 10 green cut glass wine glasses, c1830, 5.5in (14cm).
$360-540

A green cut glass wine glass, 4.5in (11cm).
$35-70

An amethyst cut glass wine glass, c1840, 5.5in (14cm). **$110-180**

A Newcastle light baluster goblet, on a plain domed foot, c1750, 7in (18cm).
$1,800-2,700

Three wine glasses, with multiple spiral air-twist stems, on plain conical feet, c1750, 6 to 7.5in (15.5 to 18.5cm).
$720-1,000

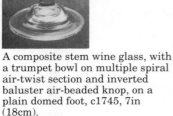

l. A wine glass, with bell bowl on a stem with multiple spiral air-twist and shoulder knop, on a plain conical foot, c1745, 6.5in (16.5cm).
$720-1,000
r. A wine glass, with trumpet bowl on a drawn stem with multiple spiral air-twist, on a folded conical foot, c1745, 7in (18cm).
$360-540

A composite stem wine glass, with a trumpet bowl on multiple spiral air-twist section and inverted baluster air-beaded knop, on a plain domed foot, c1745, 7in (18cm).
$1,200-1,700

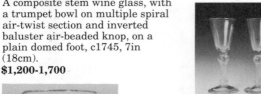

A set of 6 wine glasses, the round funnel bowls on stems with multiple spiral air-twists and shoulder and centre knops, on a plain conical feet, c1750, 6in (15cm).
$3,600-5,500

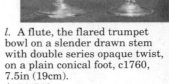

l. A flute, the flared trumpet bowl on a slender drawn stem with double series opaque twist, on a plain conical foot, c1760, 7.5in (19cm).
$360-540
r. A dwarf wrythen ale glass, with conical bowl, on a short stem with cushion knop, on a plain conical foot, c1800, 5in (13cm).
$35-70

A wine glass, engraved with a fruiting vine, on a stem with multiple spiral air-twist and shoulder knop, on a plain conical foot, c1750, 6.5in (16cm).
$1,000-1,500

Dessert and Jelly Glasses

A sweetmeat glass, the double ogee bowl with a dentillated rim, on a stem with centre ball knop, on a plain domed foot, c1750, 3.5in (9cm).
$720-1,000

An unusual sweetmeat glass, on a moulded pedestal stem, on a plain domed foot, c1750, 5.5in (14cm).
$360-540

A sweetmeat glass, with double ogee bowl and dentillated rim, on a Silesian moulded stem with star studded shoulders with coiled collars at each end, on a domed folded foot, c1730, 5.5in (14cm).
$1,000-1,500

Jugs

A Bristol blue cream jug, c1800.
$180-360

A water jug, the pillar with moulded decoration, with prism cut neck and serrated rim, on star cut base, with applied strap handle, c1830, 7in (18cm).
$180-360

A Georgian cut glass footed jug, with applied handle, c1800, 10in (25cm).
$180-360

A North Country clear soda glass jug, with wrythen body and translucent blue rim, with applied handle, c1800, 5in (13cm).
$360-540

A jug, the bowl engraved with a barrel and coopers tools, with inscription' Mr N. Player, P.O.K.H.S., and date July lst 1828', with heavy strap handle, 8.5in (22cm).
$1,200-1,700

A cut cream jug, on scalloped cut foot, with cut strap handle, on star cut base, c1810, 4.5in (11.5cm).
$360-540

A water jug, cut with small diamonds below a deep band of flute cutting, notched rim, and cut strap handle, c1810, 6.5in (16cm).
$720-1,000

A pair of enamelled Continental glass claret jugs and stoppers, each painted with clusters of vine and holly between pincered ribs, late 19thC, 9in (23cm).
$360-540

A cranberry and opaque cider set, moulded with irises, comprising a jug with applied loop handle, and six cylindrical tumblers.
$360-540

A Bristol blue cream jug, c1800, 4.5in (11.5cm).
$70-145

A wrythen Bristol blue cream jug, with folded rim, c1840, 3in (8cm).
$70-145

A late Victorian silver mounted glass claret jug, decorated with a satyr mask, vines and bunches of grapes, with wrythen decorated handle, the hinged cover with heraldic lion and shield finial, having a star cut flared base, London, 1876, maker's mark C.B., 11in (28cm).
$900-1,500

A cut glass magnum claret jug, c1790, 10.5in (26.5cm).
$1,800-2,700

A pair of Victorian frosted glass and silver mounted claret jugs, raised on a circular foot, inscribed on foot Green & Co. Fecit London, 1867, 13.5in (34.5cm).
$10,000-12,000

A late Victorian cut glass claret jug, engraved with flowers and scrolls in a rock crystal effect, the silver top embossed with foliage and a humming bird, the hinged gadrooned edge cover with a chased finial, the handle decorated with a cartouche and garrya flowers, makers William Hutton & Sons, London 1894, 11in (28cm).
$1,800-2,700

A late Victorian diamond, hob nail and panel cut glass claret jug, with silver mounts to the rim, the hinged cover with baluster finial and acanthus capped inverted S scroll handle, Birmingham 1889, maker's mark H & T, 10.5in (26cm).
$720-1,000

Paperweights

A millefiori glass paperweight, the four central white and green cut canes surrounded by 2 concentric circles of coloured canes, possibly Clichy, 2.5in (6cm) diam. **$720-1,000**

An Italian micro-mosaic paperweight, the oval panel depicting St Peter with lapis lazuli border and mounted on a black slate base, c1860.
$900-1,500

A pair of Edward VII silver mounted engraved glass scent bottles, decorated with anthemion shells and daisies, with similarly decorated hinged covers with glass stoppers, William Comyns, London 1907, 7in (18cm).
$720-1,000

Scent Bottles

A pair of blue moulded scent bottles, English, c1890, 8in (20cm).
$180-360

A scent bottle in the form of a two handled amphora, applied with vari-coloured agates, with slide-action dispensing mechanism and chain and loop attached, late 19thC, 2.5in (6.5cm). **$360-540**

A gold mounted gem set bloodstone scent bottle, the neck and hinged cover chased and engraved with acanthus leaves and scrolling foliage and set with red stones and a pearl, 19thC, 2in (5cm).
$1,800-2,700

Two cut glass scent bottles with silver gilt mounts:
l. c1880, 3.5in (9cm) long
$110-180
r. c1860, 3.5in (9cm) long
$180-360

A silver topped quilted satin scent bottle, with Jules Barb decoration, 2.5in (6.5cm).
$180-360

A purple glass double scent bottle, with scroll engraved silver gilt stoppers.
$360-540

A Webbs cameo glass scent bottle, the blue body etched with flowers, leaves and a bee, the cover engraved with flowers, 5in (13cm).
$360-540

Vases

A pair of opaque green glass vases, on veined marble bases, late 19thC, 7.5in (18.5cm) high.
$720-1,000

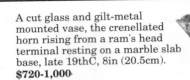

A cut glass and gilt-metal mounted vase, the crenellated horn rising from a ram's head terminal resting on a marble slab base, late 19thC, 8in (20.5cm).
$720-1,000

An opalescent vaseline glass fan-shaped vase, 6in (15cm).
$70-145

Two English celery vases:
l. with moulded pedestal, 1880, 10in (25cm)
$35-70
r. gadrooned and scalloped, c1770, 10in (25cm).
$35-70

A turquoise trailed posy vase, with clear collar, English, c1890, 4in (10cm).
$35-70

A Victorian engraved hyacinth vase, 8.5in (21cm).
$35-70

A Continental hyacinth vase, with enamel decoration, c1870, 5.5in (14cm).
$70-145

A selection of hyacinth vases.
$35-70

A cut glass celery vase, c1880, 10.5in (26.5cm).
$35-70

A pair of gilt-bronze, white marble and glass cornucopia vases, each in the form of a fluted vase supported by ram's mask, 1830, 11in (28cm).
$2,700-3,600

Miscellaneous

Two unusual toddy lifters, c1810, 5.5 and 6.5in (14 and 16cm). **$180-360 each**

A tankard with baluster body, folded rim, and gadrooned base, on a plain conical foot ring, with reeded handle, c1790, 6in (15cm). **$720-1,000**

Two toddy lifters, c1810, 5.5 and 6in (13.5 and 14.5cm). **$180-360**

A storm shade candlestick, on an ormolu mounted blue drum base, c1790, 18.5in (47cm). **$1,000-1,500**

A cut glass pickle jar and cover, c1825, 5.5in (14cm). **$180-360**

A pair of cut pickle jars, on lemon squeezer feet, c1810, 6in (15cm). **$720-1,000**

A pair of ormolu and cut glass candle lustres, c1830, 16.5in (42cm). **$21,000-27,000**

A storm shade candlestick, ormolu mounted, with a Wedgwood base, c1800, 16.5in (42cm). **$1,200-1,700**

An unusual wine glass cooler, with two pouring lips, c1820, 4in (10cm). **$180-360**

A Stourbridge green opalescent over white night light, c1880, 4.5in (11cm). **$180-360**

A pair of confitures, with slice cut rims, raised on stepped circular bases with slice and star cut feet, mid-19thC, 8.5in (21cm).
$180-360

A storm shade candlestick, with blue and gilt drum base, c1800, 13.5in (34.5cm).
$720-1,000

Two Stourbridge pink opalescent night lights, c1880, 4 to 5in (10 to 13cm). **$180-360 each**

A pair of 18thC style candlesticks, the cylindrical stems terminating in bell shaped feet, all facet cut, chipped, 10in (25.5cm).
$360-540

An unusual wine urn, c1790, 13in (33cm). **$14,500-16,500**

A pair of cranberry glass salts, 2.5in (6.5cm) diam.
$110-180

A Victorian glass centrepiece, engraved with holly leaves and berries, 16.5in (42cm).
$180-360

Irish Glass

An Irish cut glass footed bowl, c1825, 10in (25cm) diam.
$1,800-2,700

A Victorian blue glass bird feeder, with blue stopper, 5.5in (14cm).
$70-145

An Irish boat-shaped fruit bowl, with knop stem, on a moulded oval foot, c1700, 12in (31cm).
$2,700-3,600

An Irish cut glass bowl and cover, c1790, 11in (28cm).
$1,000-1,500

An Irish spirit bottle, c1800, 9in (23cm). **$110-180**

An Irish bowl, with typical herringbone design, c1800, 10in (25cm) diam.
$360-540

Two Irish cruet bottles, for oil and vinegar, c1800, 6.5in (16.5cm).
$35-70

An Irish glass library candlestick, c1790, 5in (13cm).
$180-360

An Irish cut glass preserve dish and cover, c1800, 7in (18cm) diam.
$360-540

An Irish jug, c1790, 6in (15cm).
$720-1,000

An Irish cut glass decanter, c1810, 8.5in (21.cm).
$180-360

An Irish cut glass decanter, c1785, 11in (28cm).
$180-360

An Irish butter dish, the body and domed lid cut with small diamonds and prisms, c1810, 6.5in (16cm) diam.
$720-1,000

An Irish rummer, c1790, 6in (15cm).
$180-360

l. An Irish decanter, with 3 annulated neck rings, and moulded mushroom stopper, probably Cork Glass Co.,c1810, 8in (20cm).
$360-540

r. An Irish decanter, with base moulded fluting extending underneath, a plain lozenge (disc) stopper, indistinctly marked Waterford Co. Cork, 9in (23cm).
$720-1,000

An Irish decanter, with engraved anchor design, on a rib moulded base, c1790, 12in (31cm).
$720-1,000

An Irish moulded glass tantalus, with japanned wood base and metal trim, c1800, 9.5in (24cm).
$360-540

A pair of Irish glass salts, c1790, 3in (8cm).
$360-540

A set of 4 Irish glass salts, c1790, 3in (8cm).
$1,000-1,500

A rummer, possibly Irish, c1800, 4.5in (11.5cm).   **$70-145**

An Irish cut glass decanter, c1820, 9.5in (24cm).
$180-360

An Irish ribbed glass rinser, c1790, 4.5in (11cm) diam.
$110-180

An Irish spirit decanter, with moulded fluting at the base, and 2 bladed neck rings, the body engraved with 3 thistle sprays, with flat circular grid moulded stopper, marked underneath Edwards Belfast, c1810, 7in (18cm).
$1,000-1,500

OAK AND COUNTRY FURNITURE

Beds

A 17thC style oak cradle, with arched canopy, panelled sides and ball finials, 44in (111.5cm) long.
$900-1,500

An oak tester bedstead, the headboard with 2 nulled panels above rectangular panels and channel-moulded stiles and muntins, the tester with lozenge carved panels and on 2 turned posts with square feet, 17thC and later, 54.5in (138cm) wide.
$14,500-16,500

A Federal stained birchwood and pine four-post bedstead, Massachusetts, with central shaped pine headboard between turned head posts, reeded and turned foot posts, on vase shaped feet, with tester, c1805, 78in (199cm) long.   **$7,000-7,500**

An oak cot, 18thC.
$720-1,000

An oak tester bed, dated 1517, 51in (130cm) wide.
$7,000-9,000

An oak bed, the headboard basically 17thC with later top, the footboard incorporating some 17thC pieces, with 2 associated side-rails, 84in (213cm) long.
$3,600-5,500

An oak headboard, some pieces deficient, incised E D K D, mostly 17thC with later braces, 65.5in (166cm).
$1,000-1,500

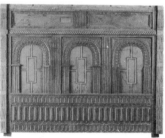

Bureaux

An early Georgian oak bureau, with fitted interior, on bracket feet, 29.5in (75cm).
$3,600-5,500

An oak bureau, with fall front and 2 long drawers having moulded decoration, on 2 baluster front legs, c1940, 30in (76cm).
$180-360

An oak bureau cabinet, with double domed cornice and 2 conforming fielded panel doors, fitted interior, on bun feet, early 18thC and later, 38in (96.5cm).
$2,700-3,600

An oak bureau bookcase, 18thC.
$1,800-2,700

A Chippendale carved walnut bureau, Pennsylvania, with fitted pigeonholes, small drawers and central fan-carved prospect door, with concealed 2 drawer pull-out cupboard section, upright document drawers, 4 thumb-moulded and graduated long drawers, on ogee bracket feet, restored, c1780, 38in (96.5cm) wide.
$3,250-3,750

An oak bureau, with brass handles and escutcheons, on bracket feet, 18thC, 37.5in (95cm).
$3,600-5,500

An 18thC style oak bureau, with later all-over carved decoration of religious panels, the fall flap enclosing a fitted interior, over one dummy, 2 short and 2 long drawers, on bracket feet, 36in (91.5cm).
$1,000-1,500

A Queen Anne applewood bureau, with hinged lid enclosing pigeonholes and 4 small drawers, 4 graduated long drawers below, on bracket feet, some repairs, 34.5in (87.6cm) wide.
$4,800-5,200

A Chippendale carved mahogany ox-bow front bureau, Massachusetts, with thumb-moulded hinged lid, 4 shaped and graduated long drawers, on cabriole legs on claw-and-ball feet, some repairs, 42.5in (108cm) wide.   **$3,000-4,000**

An oak bureau, with brass drop replacement handles, supported on carved bracket base, mid-18thC, 34in (86cm).
$1,200-1,700

Cabinets

A George III oak bureau, the fall revealing mahogany veneered stationery compartments, c1760, 39.5in (100cm).
$1,800-2,700

An oak cabinet-on-stand, veneered in walnut and ebony, 17thC, the stand of later date with plain turned supports, 40in (101.5cm).
$3,600-5,500

A Charles II oak and parquetry cabinet-on-stand, the stand with spirally-twisted legs and double gateleg action to the front, on bun feet, restorations to interior, 45in (114cm).
$3,600-5,500

A walnut and oak bureau, with crossbanded fall, on bracket feet, mid-18thC with later veneered on oak carcass, 37in (94cm).
$1,800-2,700

An oak cabinet, carved with initials 'M.E.', early 18thC, adapted, 62.5in (159cm).
$3,600-5,500

Chairs

A Charles I oak open armchair, incised 'RM 1640' with 3 smaller 'RM', the scroll arms and splayed seat on turned supports joined by a box stretcher, with carved apron, additional support to base of back.
$1,800-2,700

A Charles II oak panel back armchair, with a fluted and scroll cresting rail, the back with mitred mouldings flanked by stop fluting, the solid seat above square and turned legs joined by peripheral stretchers, reconstructed.
$720-1,000

A Charles II oak armchair, with old repairs, c1670.
$1,200-1,700

A Shaker birchwood stencilled child's armchair, black painted, No.1, late 19thC.
$1,400-1,600

A James II oak open armchair, the toprail carved '1686', flanked by animal scrolls, with later solid seat, on baluster legs joined by square stretchers, one front foot with later section, the feet shortened, Westmoreland.
$3,600-5,500

A set of 4 Charles II oak side chairs, on bobbin-turned legs joined by a turned front stretcher, the back seat-rail incised 'WS'.
$7,000-9,000

An oak child's wainscot chair, 17thC, 33in (83.5cm) high.
$1,800-2,700

The serpent strapwork and snail-like creatures flanking the cresting are two of the most distinctive features of Lake District furniture. Distinctive forms appear on dated furniture continuously from as early as the 1620s until as late as the 1740s.

A Shaker birchwood child's rocking chair, No.1, late 19thC.
$3,800-4,200

A North Country shepherd's wing chair, with original painted decoration, c1780.
$3,600-5,500

A black painted turned maple rush seat ladderback open arm chair, Delaware River Valley, c1750.   **$6,000-6,500**

A set of 4 ash spindle back chairs, on pad and ball feet joined by stretchers, late 18th/early 19thC.
$1,200-1,700

An oak wainscot chair, 17thC.
$2,700-3,600

A set of 6 elm Lancashire spindle back dining chairs with rush seats and club front legs, 19thC.
$2,700-3,600

A pair of panel back chairs, with foliate carved shaped cresting rails, the panels carved with scrolling foliage and flowers and the solid seats on baluster turned legs with similar front stretchers, late 17thC.
$720-1,000

A Yorkshire ash panel back open armchair, with planked seat and on bobbin turned legs joined by box stretchers, with additional later back stretchers and front seat moulding, mid-17thC.
$3,600-5,500

A pair of William and Mary beechwood chairs, with cane splats, the cane seats above square and turned legs joined by stretchers, restored, c1690.
$720-1,000

A red painted plank seat Windsor rocking chair, c1820.
$1,100-1,500

A Welsh primitive oak and ash comb back armchair, with semi-circular seat and triple splayed legs.
$1,000-1,500

A yew wood and elm Windsor armchair, with a pierced splat back and turned splayed legs joined by crinoline stretchers, on later turned ash feet, early 19thC.
$1,000-1,500

A set of 4 yew, ash and elm low back Windsor chairs, on turned legs with crinoline stretchers.
$3,600-5,500

A pair of James II oak side chairs, on C-scroll legs joined by turned stretchers and by a high pierced scrolled front stretcher.
$3,600-5,500

Two elm and fruitwood Mendlesham open armchairs, each with spindle back inlaid with boxwood, one with vase-shaped splat, with solid seat on turned tapering legs joined by turned H-shaped stretchers, early 19thC.   **$1,800-2,700**

A matched set of 8 North Country spindle back dining chairs, in fruitwood and ash, including one elbow chair, with rush seats, turned legs and stretchers, early 19thC.   **$3,600-5,500**

A yew and elm Windsor chair, 19thC.
$360-540

A matched set of 8 ash and beechwood spindle back chairs, including 2 armchairs, with rush seats, on turned tapering legs ending in pad and ball feet, late 18th/early 19thC.
$3,600-5,500

A yew and elm Windsor armchair, with spindle filled hoop back and horseshoe arms, solid seat and on baluster turned legs joined by stretchers, stamped Hubbard, early 19thC.
$900-1,500

A pair of William and Mary walnut side chairs, each with vertical railed back surmounted by a scroll cresting and flanked by turned supports, the planked seat on turned legs joined by a turned front stretcher, on bun feet, one with repair to one front and one back leg.
$3,600-5,500

An elm and yew wood child's Windsor armchair, the back legs fruitwood, 19thC.
$1,000-1,500

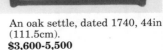

An oak settle, dated 1740, 44in (111.5cm).
$3,600-5,500

A set of 8 Windsor elbow chairs, 19thC .
$3,600-5,500

A turned maple and hickory red painted high chair, with upholstered seat, early 19thC.
$1,000-1,500

An oak chair, with folding steps, turned spindle back and legs and solid seat, 19thC.
$360-540

A set of 6 spindle back chairs and 2 armchairs, in ash, with rush seats, c1840.
$3,600-5,500

A Gothic carved oak pew, the uprights carved with foliage and heraldic beasts, the associated solid seat with crewel-work loose cushion, on solid supports, lacks back, restored, late 15th/early 16thC, 44in (112cm).
$2,700-3,600

An elm and fruitwood Windsor chair, with comb back, solid splat and cabriole front legs.
$1,800-2,700

Chests

An oak chest of drawers with hinged lid, c1690.
$1,800-2,700

An oak chest of drawers, with oak drawer linings on side runners, with applied mouldings to drawer fronts, lozenges with painted black centres, c1665, 36in (91.5cm).
$1,800-2,700

A George III oak chest-on-chest, 39in (99cm).
$1,800-2,700

An oak chest of drawers, with original yew wood handles, c1680, 36in (91.5cm).
$2,700-3,600

A William and Mary oak chest, with later top, above 4 moulded doors with panelled sides, on later bracket feet, 40in (102cm).
$1,000-1,500

An oak chest of drawers, with bracket feet, c1770, 36in (91.5cm) wide.
$1,000-1,500

A bone-inlaid oak and fruitwood chest, in 2 sections, with star-shaped inlay flanked and divided by simulated fluting above 2 drawers with conforming decoration, on bun feet, restored, 17thC, the applied decoration probably later, 44in (112cm).
$3,600-5,500

An oak coffer, with plain top over 4 carved panels to the front, 18thC, 48in (122cm).
$1,000-1,500

An oak chest of drawers, with applied geometric mouldings and bun feet, c1690, 36in (91.5cm).
$2,700-3,600

An oak laburnum and fruitwood chest, in 2 parts, with cleated top, dentil frieze, conforming uprights and on later bracket feet, late 17thC, 45in (114cm).
$3,600-5,500

A James I style carved oak coffer, the hinged top above a gadrooned frieze flanked by grotesque masks, the triple arched front with foliate carving and central heraldic shield surmounted by the date '1625' and flanked by figural pilasters, on stile feet, early 20thC, 68in (173cm).
$1,800-2,700

A Queen Anne oak and mahogany chest, with crossbanded drawers, on later bun feet, c1705, 34in (86cm).   **$1,200-1,700**

A panelled oak coffer, outlined with chip carved mouldings, the top inlaid with various devices and the date '1588', the front with crosses within lozenges, the sides applied with later lozenges, on stile feet, 16thC, 37.5in (95cm).
$1,800-2,700

An oak six-plank chest, with scratch carved decoration, c1700, 24in (61.5cm).
$1,000-1,500

A Charles II carved oak coffer, the moulded hinged top above a strapwork scroll frieze and twin lunette panel front, on tall stile feet headed by shaped angle brackets, 47in (120cm).
$1,800-2,700

An oak coffer, with plain triple panelled hinged lid over 2 plain panels to the front, on block supports, 18thC, 43in (109cm).
$360-540

An oak chest, with 3 panelled carved front and plank top, c1670, 51.5in (130cm).
$1,000-1,500

Miller's is a price GUIDE not a price LIST

An elm chest, with plank top and carved panelled front, c1670, 42in (106.5cm).
$900-1,500

An oak commode, on bronze lion paw feet, late 19thC.
$2,700-3,600

Reputedly once the property of Sir William Russell Flint.

A Charles II oak coffer, with hinged top enclosing an interior with till, the panelled front carved with '1671 IT', on stile feet, with later cleats, one back foot spliced, 50in (127cm).
$1,800-2,700

A carved oak chest, with 3 panels and quatrefoil motif, c1670, 48in (122cm).   **$1,800-2,700**

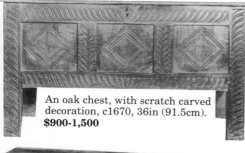

An oak chest, with scratch carved decoration, c1670, 36in (91.5cm).
$900-1,500

An oak coffer, with plain hinged top and front, 18thC, 35in (89cm).
$360-540

A Charles II oak coffer, with hinged moulded top, inscribed on the reverse 'P.R. 1680' within a circle, the front carved with scrolling foliage and sea monsters around 3 geometric carved and inlaid panels, above 2 drawers inlaid with scrolling foliage, restored, South Yorkshire, 58in (147cm).   **$7,000-9,000**

An oak and fruitwood chest, lead scratch carved with compass decoration, c1690, 42in (106.5cm).
$1,200-1,700

A carved oak coffer, c1800, 44in (111.5cm).
$1,000-1,500

Cupboards

An oak cupboard, the top and sides carved with Romayne panels flanked and divided by foliate capitals, on moulded canted rectangular base and gothic bracket feet, Flemish or French, extensive restoration, later top, drawer, supports, back and base, 34in (86.5cm).
$2,700-3,600

An oak court cupboard, early 18thC.
$3,600-5,500

A mid-Georgian oak cupboard, back feet replaced, restorations to cornice, West Wales, 59.5in (151cm).
$3,600-5,500

A Yorkshire oak press cupboard, with turned bulbous supports, the frieze drawer with gadrooned decoration over 2 panelled doors, carved strap work surround and stile supports, 17thC, 50.5in (128cm).
$3,600-5,500

An oak tall standing corner cupboard, in 2 sections, the panel doors enclosing shaped shelves, 18thC, 85in (216cm) high.
$900-1,500

A Queen Anne oak press cupboard, the moulded cornice above a pair of arched fielded panelled doors, the base with a triple fielded panel front and a pair of drawers below, on stile feet, c1700, 60in (152cm).
$1,800-2,700

An oak spice cupboard with rosewood inlay, c1690, 12in (31cm) square.
$720-1,000

A George III oak press, with moulded cornice above 2 arched fielded doors divided by reeded pilasters, the base with 3 short and 2 long drawers, on block feet, 55in (140cm).
$2,700-3,600

A Continental oak and ebony inlaid cupboard, 17thC, 38in (96.5cm).
$2,700-3,600

A Welsh oak press deuddarn, the moulded cornice with turned pendant finials above triple recessed ogee panel doors, the base with 3 frieze drawers and a pair of panelled cupboard doors, on stile feet, 18thC, 58in (147cm).
$3,600-5,500

A George III oak aumbry, the sides in pine, the base now with 2 dummy frieze drawers and a pair of panel doors, on stem feet, the interior now with hanging space and a shoe rest, altered, c1790, 39in (99cm).
$1,800-2,700

A French Provincial oak armoire, with conforming front apron, on cabriole front supports, 18thC, 60in (152cm).
$7,000-9,000

An oak clothes press, with later moulded cornice, 2 doors with ogee moulded fielded panels, 3 false and 3 real drawers below, on stile feet, mid-18thC, 53in (134.5cm).
$1,800-2,700

An oak press cupboard, outlined with punched decoration, with projecting frieze, on turned supports, on reeded stile feet, 51in (129.5cm).
$3,600-5,500

An enclosed oak cupboard, with yew wood inlay and applied geometric mouldings, c1645.
$3,600-5,500

A two-stage oak cupboard, with wave pattern cornice, centre ogee panel flanked by similar doors, over 3 fielded panels with 2 drawers below, panelled sides and ogee feet, mid-18thC, 63.5in (161cm).
$3,600-5,500

A carved oak livery cupboard, in 2 sections, the upper portion with 2 ornately carved doors, the lower portion with 2 doors, with a fitted shelf, 46in (116.5cm).
$720-1,000

A French provincial elm and fruitwood armoire, with arched moulded cornice, above a pair of arched fielded panelled doors enclosing an interior with a drawer, on angled cabriole legs, late 18th/early 19thC, 48in (122cm).
$2,700-3,600

Dressers

A Charles II oak dresser base, with associated moulded top, the back re-supported, 79in (201cm).
$3,600-5,500

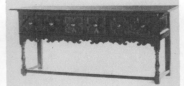

A William and Mary oak dresser base, the baluster turned legs joined by stretchers, drawers relined, c1690, 74in (188cm).
$3,600-5,500

A William and Mary oak dresser base, with an open plate shelf, the 3 frieze drawers with mitred mouldings and walnut veneers, with 3 panelled doors and bun feet, partially reconstructed, 72in (183cm).
$3,600-5,500

A William and Mary oak dresser base, the drawers with mitred mouldings and fruitwood veneers, on square and baluster turned legs, restored, 72in (183cm).
$3,600-5,500

An oak dresser, on bracket feet, restored and with alterations, 18thC, 58in (148cm).
$3,600-5,500

An oak dresser base, on stile feet, part early 18thC, 58in (147cm).
$3,600-5,500

An oak dresser, the inverted breakfront base with 4 central drawers flanked by a pair of fielded panel cupboard doors, on bracket feet, part 18thC, 76in (193cm).
$1,800-2,700

An oak dresser, 18thC, 70.5in (178cm).
$3,600-5,500

A George II oak dresser base, with shaped apron and cabriole legs ending in pad feet, formerly with an open shelf back, 71in (180cm).
$3,600-5,500

An oak dresser base, with unusual legs, c1740, 80in (203cm).
$7,000-9,000

A George II oak dresser, the raised open shelf back with a moulded cornice and valanced frieze, the base with 3 drawers, on turned tapering legs ending in pad feet, c1750, 68in (172cm).
$3,600-5,500

An oak dresser base, with 3 fascia drawers with brass drop handles, contemporary delft rack with stepped and moulded cornice, shaped frieze, 3 moulded shelves, on shaped supports, early 18thC, 76in (193cm).
$3,600-5,500

A mahogany banded and inlaid oak low dresser, with some original pierced handle plates, mid-18thC, 72in (182.5cm).
$3,600-5,500

An oak Welsh dresser, the later delft rack with stepped and dentil pediment over 2 shelves with panel backs, over a base with mahogany crossbanding to the top, fluted pillar sides, enclosing 9 drawers with mahogany crossbanded fronts and brass swan neck handles, the whole supported on short bracket feet, 93in (236cm).
$1,800-2,700

A George III oak and pine dresser, with chamfered square legs joined by a platform stretcher, restored, late 18thC, 55in (139cm).
$7,000-9,000

A late George III oak and pine Welsh dresser, with arched panelled doors below, flanking 3 simulated drawers, on block feet, 53in (134cm).
$3,600-5,500

An oak dresser and rack, with dentil moulded cornice and open shelves above 3 drawers, on square legs, part 18thC, 75in (190cm).
$1,800-2,700

A George III oak dresser, the moulded cornice above an open shelf back, the pair of frieze drawers above baluster turned and square legs joined by a platform stretcher, on bracket feet, possibly reduced in width, c1790, 46in (117cm).
$3,600-5,500

A pair of oak dresser bases, probably adaped from a single dresser base, each with rectangular top above 2 frieze drawers and waved apron, on baluster turned uprights and block feet, part 18thC, 46in (117cm).
$3,600-5,500

An oak dresser, with baluster turned uprights and bun feet, joined by an undertier, 94in (239cm).
$2,700-3,600

An oak dresser and rack, with moulded dentil cornice and waved frieze, 18thC and later, 70in (178cm).
$3,600-5,500

An oak Welsh dresser, with chamfered legs joined by an undershelf, on block feet, 18thC, 61in (154.5cm).
$3,600-5,500

An oak dresser base on straight feet, having 3 fielded panelled doors and 3 drawers over, 18thC, 71in (180cm).
$3,600-5,500

Stools

A child's joint stool, with baluster turned legs, c1640, 14in (35.5cm) square.
$900-1,500

A country stool, 19thC, 25in (64cm) high.
$35-70

A Charles II oak bench, lacking 2 spandrels, 81in (205cm) long.
$7,000-9,000

An oak joint stool, c1650, 18in (45cm).
$1,200-1,700

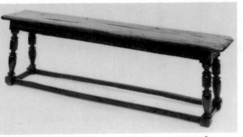

A pair of oak benches, with plain tops and reeded friezes, on turned legs with plain stretchers, 17thC, 63in (160cm).   **$720-1,000**

An oak joint stool, 17thC, 23in (59cm) high.   **$2,700-3,600**

Tables

An oak oval gateleg dining table, with plain top, frieze drawer, turned supports and plain stretchers, 60in (152cm) extended.
$1,800-2,700

A small oak side table, with turned legs and box stretchers, c1700.
$720-1,000

A Charles II oak gateleg table, with bobbin turned supports and gates, feet reduced, 56in (142cm).
$7,000-9,000

An oak gateleg table, with twin-flap top and one panelled drawer, on later bun feet, restorations to top, some replacements to legs, top extended, part late 17thC, 60in (153cm).
$2,700-3,600

A Charles II oak and later painted double action gateleg table, made up, 49in (125cm).
$1,800-2,700

A George I oak gateleg table, the top with a frieze drawer, c1720, 60in (151cm) extended.
$3,600-5,500

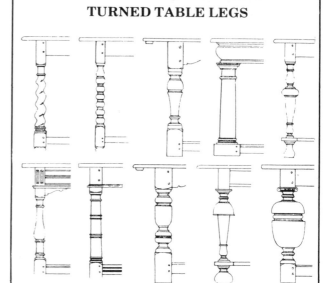

Oak & Country Furniture
TURNED TABLE LEGS

A Tuscan 17thC style walnut refectory table, made up, on shaped trestle supports, 57.5in (146cm).
$3,600-5,500

A cherrywood refectory table, with plank top and plain frieze, formerly with slide, now fixed, on square legs joined by plain stretchers, early 19thC, probably French, repaired, 90.5in (230cm).
$2,700-3,600

An oak refectory table with detachable elm top, 18thC, 75in (190.5cm).
$1,800-2,700

An Elizabeth I style carved oak refectory table, made up, including 17thC components, 69in (176cm) long.
$1,800-2,700

A oak gateleg table, with later top, associated frieze drawer, on twist-turned legs joined by similar stretchers, mid-17thC, 62in (157cm).
$7,000-9,000

A William and Mary oak side table, the overhanging moulded top above a frieze drawer, on baluster turned and square legs joined by stretchers, c1690, 27.5in (70cm).
$1,800-2,700

A William III oak gateleg table, the associated top with a frieze drawer, the turned and square legs joined by stretchers, c1700, 56in (143cm).
$3,600-5,500

An oak cricket table from West Wales, c1780.
$360-540

A Charles II oak side table, on bobbin turned legs joined by a conforming front stretcher, 34in (87cm).
$3,600-5,500

A William and Mary small oak side table, c1690, with later bun feet, 24in (61cm).
$1,000-1,500

An oak gateleg table, 31.5in (80cm).
$1,800-2,700

A William and Mary oak gateleg table, the top with a frieze drawer, the baluster turned and square legs joined by stretchers, top restored, c1690, 59in (150cm).
$1,800-2,700

A lowboy, with 3 drawers, shaped frieze and pad feet, c1750, 26.5in (67.5cm).
$1,800-2,700

An oak side table, with moulded edge to the elm top, frieze drawer, on baluster turned legs with square stretchers, 17thC, 34in (86.5cm).
$900-1,500

An oak side table, on turned baluster legs joined by box stretchers, late 17th/early 18thC, 36in (91cm).
$1,000-1,500

A George II oak side table, on cabriole legs with pad feet, damaged, 31in (79cm).
$1,800-2,700

An oak side table, with swan neck brass handles and escutcheons, shaped central and side aprons, supported upon shaped legs with pad feet, 19thC, 28in (71cm).
$720-1,000

An oak lowboy, the 3 drawers with herringbone inlay, on rounded cabriole legs terminating in pad feet, c1725.
$2,700-3,600

An oak side table, with 2 early additional frieze drawers, late 17th/early 18thC, 36in (91cm).
$1,200-1,700

An oak lowboy, early 18thC, 36in (91cm).
$1,200-1,700

An oak lowboy, with square cabriole legs, and shaped frieze, c1740.
$1,800-2,700

An oak lowboy, c1780, 30in (76cm).
$2,700-3,600

A George I oak side table, the top with cusped corners, c1720, 32in (81cm).
$1,800-2,700

An oak side table, with 2 plank top, single drawer to frieze, supported on 4 chamfered square legs, 18thC, 29in (74cm).
$720-1,000

An oak lowboy, with 3 plank top and moulded edge, with a single oak lined drawer, brass swan neck handles and escutcheons, late 18thC, 31.5in (80cm).
$1,200-1,700

A Flemish oak centre table, the bulbous turned legs joined by peripheral stretchers, on bun feet, top split, part 17thC, 50in (127cm).
$1,800-2,700

An oak hall table, with full width fitted drawer with brass peardrop handles, supported upon turned legs with stretchers, early 18thC, 32in (81cm).
$2,700-3,600

A William and Mary oak tea table, the double fold-over top revealing a well, the turned and square legs joined by stretchers, minor restoration, c1690, 30in (76cm).
$3,600-5,500

An oak 17thC style draw-leaf table, 75.5in (192cm).
$3,600-5,500

An oak livery table, with cupboard, c1625.
$2,700-3,600

A pine tavern table, with scrubbed top and cream painted base, c1820, 30in (76cm).
$900-1,500

A George IV oak dining table, by Alexander Norton, with central section and 2 rectangular end sections, the moulded top inset with simulated green leather, the gothic panelled frieze on turned tapering arcaded legs carved with acanthus and headed by paterae, each end painted in Gothic script 'KESTEVEN', with trade label of JAMES LATHAM LTD. HIGH CLASS VENEERS BANDINGS MOULDINGS INLAYS TIMBER 124 CURTAIN RD LONDON EC, inscribed in ink *'Curtis Mawer Silver St. Lincoln'*, some replacements to frame, 216in (549cm).
$7,000-9,000

This table was part of the furnishing of Kesteven Sessions, at Sleaford, Lincolnshire by the firm of Alexander Norton of 14 Bulstrode Street, Manchester Square, London. The building itself was designed by Henry Edward Kendall (1776-1875) and completed in 1830. The account of the furnishings, totalling £537. 19s. 0d. was 'allowed and confirmed' by the Sessions on 23rd October 1830 and still exists in the Lincolnshire Archives Office.

A South German walnut and oak side table, with moulded top above one fielded panelled drawer, with later flat stretcher and block feet, restored, part late 17thC, 42in (107cm).
$3,600-5,500

An oak serving table, the top with foliate carved edge above a scroll carved frieze, on 6 foliate carved baluster uprights on block feet joined by stretchers, part 17thC, reconstructed, 84in (214cm).
$2,700-3,600

A James I style oak refectory table, early 20thC, 120in (305cm).
$2,700-3,600

Miscellaneous

An oak apprentice piece kitchen cabinet, inlaid with mahogany, Welsh, early 19thC, 21in (53cm).
$1,200-1,700

A set of Victorian oak 3 tread library steps in Gothic Revival style, with a turned post and chamfered legs, c1870.
$2,700-3,600

An oak door surround, the top rail carved with a crest of a mask flanked by scrolls and shields and the date 1614, early 17thC, 51in (129.5cm).
$2,700-3,600

An elm dough bin, c1820, 48in (122cm).
$360-540

Did you know

MILLER'S Antiques Price Guide builds up year by year to form the most comprehensive photo reference library available.

FURNITURE

FURNITURE

Another year has passed and the antique furniture business appears as difficult to summarise as ever. The major auction houses have all seen a reduction in turnover during the past year, but this is due just as much to the lack of quality items offered for sale as to the prices attained.

Early English furniture has, for many years, been considered of significantly less value than comparable items of a later period; this has been particularly true of chests of drawers. However, there are signs of movement in this area. Bonhams recently sold a Charles II oyster veneered and marquetry chest for $21,000 which represents an unusually high price when compared with its Regency equivalent. At a Midland saleroom a few months ago three court cupboards sold for well over their pre-sale estimates, making between $10,000 and $13,500 each. Of early furniture, small oak and country pieces remain most popular. At Lawrence's of Crewkerne a rare Charles II food hutch recently made over $9,000, and a Queen Anne oak chest nearly $10,000.

A Chippendale period mahogany serpentine fronted commode, c1760, 45in (114cm) - sold for **$36,000** at Phillips Oxford.

Georgian furniture, probably the backbone of the British antiques trade, has followed the same trend as in previous years. Genuine pieces with a fine colour, impeccable provenance and in good condition have been selling as they always will. Christie's sold the Messer Collection, some of the finest furniture to come on the market in recent times, and attained excellent prices, including the St Giles

armchairs (a pair) at $470,000, and a superb pair of dolphin armchairs at $485,000. A stunning mahogany commode, attributed to the workshop of Thomas Chippendale and one of the best examples available of the English Director period, was sold for $1,500,000.

A George II walnut elbow chair - sold for **$63,000** at Phillips Cornwall.

Phillips have also reported excellent prices and interest in English furniture from their provincial rooms. Among their most notable sales are a Chippendale period serpentine front commode, sold for $40,000 at Oxford and a glorious George II walnut elbow chair sold for $90,000 in Cornwall.

Regency furniture continues to be sought, often, at present, by interior designers and decorators rather than dealers and collectors. Sotheby's Sussex recently sold a Regency sofa table at twice the pre-sale estimate.

Victorian furniture, again, must be of the highest standard of both crafts-manship and materials to tempt a buyer and, as before, furniture of high quality has been selling very well. Bonhams report a very healthy demand for good Victorian furniture, especially small walnut pieces.

The market for Continental furniture is enjoying a buoyancy unusual in the United Kingdom. Most French and Italian furniture,

especially fine quality examples that demonstrate the style of the country of origin, has been selling extremely well. Biedermeier furniture, long a favourite of the cognoscenti, is now enjoying a more popular appeal and consequently enjoys a very steady demand with both dealers and in the salerooms.

It is fair to say that good lots, realistically reserved, do continue to sell, while less worthwhile items remain a block on the market. Significant exceptions to this rule are the well-publicised house sales that appear very successful. Sotheby's raised $3,400,000 at Castle Howard in Yorkshire late last year, with just about every lot doubling or trebling their estimate.

There is a popular belief that there has never been a better time to buy, this depends entirely on what you are looking for. It is certainly a good time to buy ordinary pieces whose values are depressed, but it is as difficult today to find a wonderful piece at a bargain price as it has ever been.

A Charles II oyster veneered and marquetry chest - sold by Bonhams for **$21,000**

Hopefully the next year will see more and more furniture of better and better quality offered for sale. The prices will certainly be keen. However, the old warnings and advice are as relevant as ever. Buy what you like and what you can live with rather than for investment. Buy the very best you can afford and buy from reputable auction houses and dealers, who will always be willing to offer help and advice.

Beds

A mahogany framed child's cot, with caned sides and hood, on turned supports, 19thC.
$720-1,000

A Napoleon III ormolu mounted mahogany day bed, covered with white and beige striped silk, the mattress covered in conforming material, with 2 bolsters and 2 shaped cushions, 83in (210cm) long.　　　**$3,600-5,500**

A mahogany and boxwood strung four poster bed, with moulded arched canopy and polygonal uprights with stiff-leaf headings, 52in (132cm) wide.
$1,800-2,700

A Dutch marquetry double bed, with mattress, mid-19thC, 52in (132cm).
$3,600-5,500

A French walnut bedroom suite in the Louis XV style, comprising: a double bed with rococo scroll carved surmounts, floral carved foot on dwarf cabriole supports, 66in (167.5cm) wide, an armoire, 54in (137cm) wide, and a bedside cupboard with inset marble.
$3,600-5,500

An Empire ormolu mounted mahogany lit-en-bateau, with velvet head and footboard, the plinth base with a Bacchic mask within a wreath of roses flanked by rose trails, lacking mattress, 49in (124.5cm) wide.
$7,000-9,000

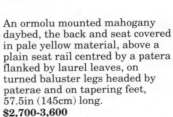

An ormolu mounted mahogany daybed, the back and seat covered in pale yellow material, above a plain seat rail centred by a patera flanked by laurel leaves, on turned baluster legs headed by paterae and on tapering feet, 57.5in (145cm) long.
$2,700-3,600

An Empire ormolu mounted mahogany
lit-en-bateau, the panelled head and footboard
with turned toprail and a column headed by a
swan below a star, with dished panelled
frontrail, on bun feet, lacking mattress and
box spring, with inscription *meuble 3 a Cigne*
(sic), 78in (198cm) long.   **$7,000-9,000**

An Empire style cream painted and parcel gilt
lit-en-bateau, the conforming footboard with fruiting
finials, on turned feet carved with acanthus, 42in
(106.5cm).   **$7,000-9,000**

A French double bedstead in the Japanese style,
the beechwood framed panelled head and foot inset
with 2 panels boldly carved with floral sprays and
with gold lacquer shibayama panel of flowers and
leaves and 2 small panels inlaid with mother-
of-pearl, stamped G Siardot (?), 19thC, 62in
(157cm) wide   **$2,700-3,600**

A French ormolu mounted
mahogany lit-en-bateau, with
later panelled headboard and side
boards mounted with ducks'
heads, the scrolled end board
centred by billing doves and a
laurel wreath, on giltwood paw
feet, with modern mattress, some
mounts probably re-casts and
some later, lacking finials, 19thC,
80.5in (205cm) long.
$7,000-9,000

Bonheur du Jour

A Louis XVI green painted lit
d'alcove, with arched padded
sides within conforming moulded
frame, carved with entrelac and
headed by pinecone finials, on
short tapering fluting legs headed
by paterae, upholstered in
celadon floral silk, 71in (180.5cm)
long.
$3,600-5,500

Miller's is a price
GUIDE not a price
LIST

An Edwardian inlaid rosewood
bonheur du jour, with inlaid urn
decoration, satinwood stringing
and shell motifs, with brass
gallery, inset leather surface, and
2 frieze drawers, supported on
square tapering legs, 36in
(91.5cm).
$1,200-1,700

An Italianate bonheur du jour, the doors inset with pietra dura vase and floral design, brass stringing, drawer and slide below, 19thC.
$2,700-3,600

An inlaid rosewood bonheur du jour, with brass fretwork decoration, on cabriole supports, with bronze mounts, 19thC, 34.5in (88cm).
$3,600-5,500

A German rosewood bonheur du jour, with leather lined writing surface, above 3 frieze drawers, on foliate carved baluster turned legs, mid-19thC, 44in (112cm). **$1,200-1,700**

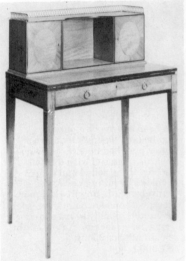

A George III satinwood and tulipwood veneered bonheur du jour, the superstructure with a pierced brass gallery, concave central shelf to an open compartment, flanked by a pair of oval panel doors, enclosing a drawer, banded in ebony above a leather inset writing flap and a fitted drawer, later gilt brass handles to the segmented front, on square tapering legs, c1790, 29.5in (75cm).
$21,000-27,000

A Louis XV style ormolu-mounted kingwood bonheur du jour, with hand painted and gilded porcelain plaques, supported upon shaped cabriole legs, 19thC, 28in (71cm).
$7,000-9,000

Breakfront Bookcases

A late George III mahogany architectural breakfront library bookcase, the upper section with broken apex pediment over dentil carved cornice, with 4 sets of adjustable shelves, brass shaped lock escutcheons, 94in (238cm).
$14,500-16,500

A mahogany breakfront library bookcase with moulded cornice, 63in (160cm) wide.
$7,000-9,000

A Victorian mahogany breakfront bookcase, the glazed upper section fitted with 4 doors enclosing adjustable shelves, the lower portion fitted with 4 drawers to frieze and 4 panel doors below, on plinth base, 111in (282cm). **$10,000-12,000**

A carved mahogany library breakfront bookcase, the arched cavetto and dentil cornice above 4 astragal glazed doors enclosing fixed shelves, the lower fitted with cupboards and standing on a plinth form base, 133in (287cm).
$7,000-9,000

A mahogany breakfront bookcase, the lower section with 4 arched panel doors on plinth base, parts 19thC (adapted), 122.5in (311cm).
$3,600-5,500

A Victorian mahogany breakfront library bookcase, with arched and moulded cornice, glazed and leaf carved doors enclosing adjustable shelving, over 3 arched cupboard doors, on plinth base, 64in (162.5cm).
$7,000-9,000

An Edwardian mahogany crossbanded Georgian style breakfront library bookcase, crossbanded and inlaid with satinwood, with angled broken trellis fretwork pediment with urn finial, triple opening astragal glazed doors with 3 internal shelves, base with 3 upper drawers, brass swan neck handles with pierced backplates, cupboards beneath having single panelled doors with fitted shelves, 72in (182.5cm).
$7,000-9,000

A George IV mahogany breakfront bookcase, with moulded cornice, 4 glazed doors with arched astragals and on a plinth base, 117in (297cm).
$3,600-5,500

Bureau Bookcases

An Edwardian mahogany boxwood and ebony strung bureau bookcase, with overall rosewood bands, on bracket feet, 39in (99cm).
$1,800-2,700

An Edwardian mahogany and boxwood strung bureau bookcase, with moulded cornice above a pair of astragal glazed doors and hinged slope enclosing a fitted interior, above 4 drawers, on bracket feet, 42in (106.5cm).
$2,700-3,600

A Regency mahogany breakfront bookcase.
$10,000-12,000

Use the Index

Because certain items might fit easily into any number of categories, the quickest and surest method of locating any entry is by reference to the index at the back of the book.
This has been fully cross-referenced for absolute simplicity.

A Georgian mahogany bureau with additional bookcase, the top with stepped pediment over 2 glazed astragal doors enclosing adjustable shelves, over an inlaid fall flap enclosing a fitted interior, over 3 small and 3 long drawers, on bracket feet, 45in (114cm). **$1,800-2,700**

A lady's Sheraton Revival satinwood bureau bookcase, painted with baskets, floral garlands and ribbands, the upper section with swan neck pediment above a bookcase enclosed by glazed doors, the base with fitted bureau, on bracket feet, 32in (81cm). **$14,500-16,500**

A walnut bureau bookcase, the upper part with a cavetto moulded cornice above 2 glazed doors enclosing adjustable shelves and 4 small drawers, 2 candle slides, the fall front enclosing a fitted interior, the drawer fronts and interior feather and cross-banded, on bracket feet, 37in (94cm). **$10,000-12,000**

Dwarf Bookcases

A Regency brass inlaid rosewood and simulated dwarf bookcase, the frieze with panels of stylised foliage above open shelves flanked and divided by foliage, on later turned feet, adapted, 72in (182.5cm). **$7,000-9,000**

A mid-Victorian walnut breakfront dwarf bookcase, with moulded cornice, above open shelves between acanthus carved mouldings on plinth base, 94in (239cm). **$2,700-3,600**

Library Bookcases

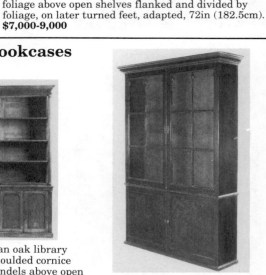

A Regency rosewood dwarf bookcase, with scrolling foliate brass inlay, the crested ledge back above 3 open tiers between walnut banded side panels, on bracket feet, 46.5in (118cm). **$2,700-3,600**

An early Victorian oak library bookcase with moulded cornice applied with roundels above open shelves flanked by similar roundel uprights with 2 slides below, on a plinth base, 76in (193cm). **$2,700-3,600**

A George III mahogany bookcase, with dentil cornice, 2 astragal glazed doors, 2 panelled doors on a plinth, astragals altered, 66.5in (168cm). **$3,600-5,500**

An Edwardian mahogany bookcase, inlaid overall with boxwood lines and chequer stringing, with moulded cornice above a pair of astragal glazed doors enclosing shelves above 2 drawers and 2 panelled doors, on a plinth base, 49in (125cm).
$2,700-3,600

A Regency mahogany secrétaire bookcase, with moulded cornice above 2 glazed cupboard doors enclosing shelves, the base with deep secrétaire drawer with cockbeaded panel, above panelled doors enclosing 3 sliding shelves, flanked by fluted pilasters, on fluted melon feet, 43in (109cm).
$3,600-5,500

A Federal maple secrétaire bookcase, with raised cornice, 3 urn finials, arched glazed doors, hinged baize lined writing slope, and 3 graduated drawers on bracket feet, late 19thC, 31in (79cm) wide.
$2,000-2,500

Secrétaire Bookcases

A late Victorian walnut secrétaire bookcase.
$1,200-1,700

A George III mahogany secrétaire bookcase.
$3,600-5,500

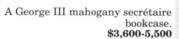

A mahogany secrétaire bookcase, with broken arch pediment above 2 glazed doors enclosing 2 fixed shelves, the base with a moulded edge above 5 long drawers, enclosing a fitted interior, on shaped ogee bracket feet, early 19thC, 48in (121cm).
$2,700-3,600

A George III mahogany secrétaire bookcase.
$3,600-5,500

A George III secrétaire bookcase.
$3,600-5,500

Bookcases

A William IV bookrack, with central division and scroll ends, with bobbin turned uprights, on bun feet, 16in (41cm).
$1,200-1,700

A satinwood revolving bookcase, the brass bound top decorated with trellis pattern inlay, the open tiers below fitted with brass wirework panels, on dwarf cabriole legs with pad feet, 18.5in (47cm).
$3,600-5,500

A late Victorian stained oak revolving bookcase, with gabled top and simulated tiling, carved with the inscription 'The Tabard Inn' and on the frieze 'The True University of These Days' above asymmetrically arranged shelves carved with various other inscriptions, on 4 splayed legs, attributed to Richard Norman Shaw, 76in (193cm) high.
$1,000-1,500

A walnut and feather banded bureau, with ledged fall enclosing fitted interior, on bun feet, top and base associated, restored, 18thC, 32.5in (82cm).
$2,700-3,600

A walnut and feather banded bureau, on bracket feet, later veneer, fall front damaged, mid-18thC, 30in (76cm).
$3,600-5,500

Bureaux

An early Georgian walnut bureau, inlaid overall with feather and crossbanding, the hinged fall enclosing fitted interior, on bracket feet, restored, 36in (92cm).
$3,600-5,500

A walnut bureau, with satinwood line inlay, the fall enclosing fitted stepped interior with numerous shaped drawers, 2 short and 3 long drawers beneath, on bracket feet, 18thC, 36in (92cm).
$3,600-5,500

A walnut and feather banded bureau, with hinged fall enclosing a fitted interior, on bracket feet, restored, possibly previously with bookcase top, 18thC, 33in (84cm).
$3,600-5,500

A Georgian mahogany bureau, the fall front fitted with pigeon holes and a well, 2 drawers below flanked by fluted side columns, opening to reveal 4 small drawers, 24in (61cm).
$1,800-2,700

An early Georgian fruitwood bureau, with hinged fall enclosing a fitted interior, on later bracket feet, the fall warped, restored, 34in (86cm).
$2,700-3,600

A walnut bureau, early Georgian design, with crossbanded top and sloping fall front enclosing a fitted interior, on bracket feet, 37.5in (95cm).
$3,600-5,500

A walnut and feather banded bureau, the sloping fall front enclosing a fitted interior and well, on bracket feet, 18thC and later, 37in (94cm).
$2,700-3,600

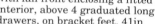
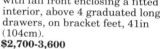

A George III mahogany bureau, with fall front enclosing a fitted interior, above 4 graduated long drawers, on bracket feet, 41in (104cm).
$2,700-3,600

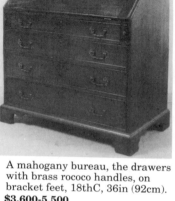

A mahogany bureau, the drawers with brass rococo handles, on bracket feet, 18thC, 36in (92cm).
$3,600-5,500

A Georgian mahogany bureau, 34in (86cm).
$2,700-3,600

A George III mahogany bureau, the fall front opening to reveal fitted interior including semi-secret document drawers, with later brass loop handles, pierced back plates and lock escutcheons, on bracket feet, 36in (92cm).
$1,800-2,700

A mid-George III mahogany bureau, with hinged fall front enclosing a fitted interior, above 4 graduated drawers, on later bracket feet, 38in (97cm).
$3,600-5,500

A George III mahogany bureau, the hinged fall front above 4 long graduated drawers, on bracket feet, 36in (92cm).
$1,200-1,700

A Georgian mahogany bureau, the plain fall front enclosing an interior of drawers, pigeon holes, small cupboard and secret compartments, over 4 long drawers with brass swan neck handles, on turned supports, 42in (106cm). **$2,700-3,600**

A mid-George III mahogany bureau, with replaced top above hinged fall front enclosing fitted interior, with 4 graduated drawers below, on bracket feet, one foot loose, one missing, 42in (106cm). **$1,800-2,700**

An early Victorian mahogany cylinder bureau, with three-quarter galleried top above hinged fall enclosing fitted interior with leather lined slide and central ratcheted writing slope, above 3 drawers to either side, on plinth base, 48in (122cm). **$2,700-3,600**

A mid-George III mahogany bureau, with hinged fall enclosing fitted interior with central mirrored compartment, on shaped bracket feet, the fall front warped, 39.5in (101cm). **$2,700-3,600**

A George III mahogany bureau, with inlaid interior, on ogee bracket feet. **$7,000-9,000**

A George III mahogany bureau, with 4 long graduated drawers, on bracket feet, 33in (84cm). **$2,700-3,600**

A mahogany bureau, with hinged fall enclosing fitted interior, on outswept bracket feet, possibly Danish, late 18th/early 19thC. **$2,700-3,600**

A George III mahogany bureau. **$1,800-2,700**

A Georgian mahogany bureau, the plain fall front enclosing an inlaid and fitted interior, on splayed feet, 39in (99cm). **$2,700-3,600**

A George III mahogany bureau, with sloping fall front enclosing small drawers and a cupboard, on later bracket feet, some restoration, 34in (86cm). **$2,700-3,600**

A mid-George III mahogany bureau, the hinged fall front enclosing fitted interior, on bracket feet, 42in (106cm).
$1,200-1,700

A late George III mahogany and later inlaid bureau, with hinged fall enclosing fitted interior, above 4 graduated drawers, on bracket feet, 42.5in (108cm).
$3,600-5,500

A French kingwood and parquetry bureau de dame, the sloping fall front opening to reveal a fitted interior, green baize writing surface, shaped apron, on square section cabriole supports, with gilt metal foliate cast mounts to the top, lock escutcheon and knees, mid-19thC, 24in (61cm).   **$3,600-5,500**

A marquetry bureau de dame, of bombe form, on cabriole legs, 19thC.
$3,600-5,500

A French mahogany and floral marquetry bureau à pente, the hinged front enclosing fitted interior above 2 frieze drawers, on cabriole legs with gilt clasps and sabots, 26in (66cm).
$2,700-3,600

A late Louis XVI ormolu mounted mahogany bureau à cylindre, with three-quarter pierced galleried inset white and grey marble top, above 2 panelled drawers and a cylinder enclosing a gilt tooled inset leather writing slide and a pair of open compartments above a pair of open drawers, the frieze fitted with a pair of panelled drawers, on circular tapering fluted legs, 32.5in (82cm).
$7,000-9,000

A French bureau de dame, decorated with kingwood crossbanding and inlaid flowers, surmounted by a pierced scrolling balustrade, the serpentine shaped fall front with ormolu border opening to reveal 3 small drawers and a well, on scrolling tapering legs terminating in sabots, 19thC, 28in (71cm).
$2,700-3,600

A French Vernis Martin mahogany and ormolu mounted bureau de dame, the top with 3 frieze drawers above a panelled cylinder and hinged fall decorated with pastural scenes, opened by a frieze drawer below, on square tapering legs, 35in (89cm).
$3,600-5,500

A French tulipwood and kingwood banded bureau à pente, with hinged fall front enclosing fitted interior above 2 frieze drawers and waved apron, on cabriole legs with gilt sabots, 33.5in (85cm).
$2,700-3,600

Bureau Cabinets

A Milanese walnut and ebony bureau cabinet, 31in (79cm) .
$3,600-5,500

A Dutch walnut and marquetry bureau cabinet, 18thC, 40in (101.5cm).
$27,000-36,000

A mahogany bureau and associated cabinet, with cavetto cornice, mid-18thC, on later bracket feet, 39.5in (100cm).
$3,600-5,500

A George III mahogany bureau and associated cabinet, the sloping flap enclosing a cupboard, drawers and pigeon holes, a brushing slide and 4 graduated long drawers below, on moulded bracket feet, some alteration, 45.5in (115cm).
$3,600-5,500

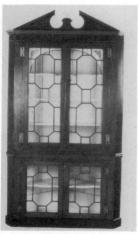

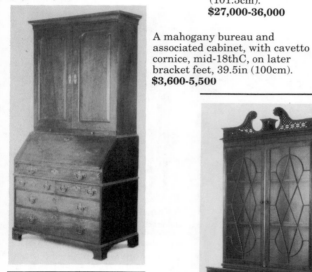

A George III style mahogany display cabinet, with pierced swan neck pediment and double astragal doors, the stand with 3 drawers, on reeded and tapered legs, 43in (109cm).
$1,800-2,700

An Edwardian mahogany Art Nouveau style display cabinet, with central leaded glass door flanked by similar bowed side panels above stylised foliate marquetry panels, inlaid with pewter and copper, on tapered square legs, c1910, 35in (90cm).
$2,700-3,600

Display Cabinets

A George III mahogany corner display cabinet, with broken pediment, upper doors enclosing a white and painted arcaded interior with gilt cherub motifs, 48in (122cm).   **$2,700-3,600**

A Victorian walnut breakfront display cabinet, applied with gilt brass foliate mouldings, the cavetto frieze inlaid with scrolling foliage, 60in (152cm).
$3,600-5,500

An Edwardian inlaid mahogany china cabinet, with fixed bowed centre panel, 44in (112cm).
$1,000-1,500

An Edwardian inlaid walnut display cabinet, 23in (59cm).
$180-360

An Edwardian satinwood and marquetry vitrine, crossbanded overall and inlaid with geometric lines, with mirror backed interior, 3 velvet lined shelves, with convex fronted glazed sides, on square tapering legs and block feet, 50in (128cm).
$2,700-3,600

A Sheraton Revival period mahogany display cabinet, with moulded cornice and top frieze, on splayed rectangular legs, 42in (107cm). **$720-1,000**

A mahogany corner display cabinet, with moulded cornice, canted corners, an astragal glazed door and 2 panelled doors above a shaped apron, 39.5in (100cm).
$3,600-5,000

A French gilt metal mounted, tulipwood, parquetry and marquetry display cabinet, inlaid overall with trellis and rosette on an amaranth ground, with green velvet lined interior, on cabriole legs headed by floral clasps, marble top repaired, reverse stamped 1883G, inscribed in chalk GORDON LAWERENCE 27382, 20thC, 49.5in (126cm).
$3,600-5,500

A Dutch 18thC style walnut bombé display cabinet, with brass loop handles, pierced shaped back plates and lock escutcheons, on heavy claw-and-ball front feet, 50in (127cm).
$7,000-9,000

A French rosewood and gilt metal mounted bombé vitrine, with C-scroll arched cresting and a pair of glazed panel doors with painted panels below of 18thC figures in pastoral settings flanked by similar panels, on angled splayed legs with gilt sabot, one pane damaged, late 19thC, 32in (81cm).
$3,600-5,500

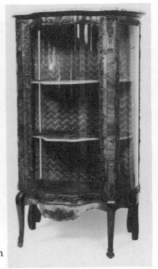

A mahogany display cabinet, with plain gallery back, inlaid stringing decoration and painted ribbon and garland designs, 2 glazed astragal doors, enclosing shelves, over 2 drawers, on square tapering legs, 42in (107cm).
$900-1,500

A Louis XV style kingwood vitrine, with bronzed metal mounts, serpentine fronted internal green velvet lined shelves with matching back, on shaped legs and rouge marble detachable top, 19thC, 33in (84cm).
$2,700-3,600

A Hepplewhite style mahogany breakfront display cabinet, the pediment with carved gadrooning, leaf and wheat ear designs, each door with a central oval floral medallion, Prince of Wales feathers and carved acanthus leaves, 76in (193cm).
$3,600-5,500

A George III style satinwood cabinet-on-stand, with kingwood crossbanding, boxwood and ebony stringing and inlaid with urns, swags and scrolling foliage, on tapering square legs with spade feet, 22in (56cm).
$1,800-2,700

A Continental red tortoiseshell display cabinet, with mirrored back, plinth base, on bracket feet, one section of back foot lacking, one detached, hinges stamped JC PATENT, 19thC, 48in (122cm).
$14,500-16,500

Side Cabinets

Cabinets-on-Stands

A Louis XV style kingwood and marquetry secrétaire cabinet-on-stand, of serpentine outline, applied with gilt brass foliate mounts, the scagliola top with pierced brass gallery, the conforming stand with a fitted drawer, on cabriole legs joined by an undertier, 33in (84cm).
$3,600-5,500

A Spanish tortoiseshell and ivory inlaid cabinet-on-stand, late l8thC, 33in (84cm).
$3,600-5,500

A George IV rosewood breakfront dwarf side cabinet, 52.5in (133cm).
$3,600-5,500

A Georgian satinwood demi-lune side cabinet, with shaped apron, the 3 crossbanded doors with string inlay and original brass escutcheons, 4 hexagonal tapering legs surmounted ormolu mounts, 29in (74cm).
$1,000-1,500

A Regency rosewood side cabinet, with later hardwood top, the doors flanked by gilt brass mounted freestanding columns, on reeded bun feet, 38in (97cm).
$1,200-1,700

A William IV rosewood side cabinet, with an associated coromandel tapering three-tier galleried superstructure, with a pair of glazed doors and a plinth base, c1830, 28.5in (72cm).
$2,700-3,600

A Chinese cabinet, with ivory panelled doors, l9thC, 45.5in (115cm).
$1,200-1,700

A William IV rosewood side cabinet, with arched ledged scroll carved mirrored back, on plinth base, 76in (193cm).
$2,700-3,600

A William IV rosewood inverted breakfront side cabinet, with brass grilles and green cloth backing, on plinth base.
$2,700-3,600

A Regency rosewood dwarf side cabinet, with three-quarter pierced brass gallery, 52in (132cm).
$2,700-3,600

A Regency rosewood side cabinet, with brass inset frieze, tapering side pillars with ormolu capitals, the cupboard with 2 adjustable shelves, double opening doors with floral needlepoint glazed panels with black background, on crescent shaped base,45in (114cm).
$3,600-5,500

A Victorian walnut side cabinet, crossbanded with rosewood and with satinwood stringing, 2 fitted red velvet lined shelves, double opening ormolu mounted panelled doors with hand painted and gilded portrait plaques and ormolu ribbon finial, 45in (114cm).
$2,700-3,600

A Victorian burr walnut veneered breakfront credenza, with moulded edge top, inlaid frieze with stringing and gilt brass mounts, the central cupboard plush lined with a shelf, enclosed by a panelled door with floral porcelain plaque, the serpentine sides with shelves enclosed by glazed doors, on a shaped plinth, 53in (135cm).
$3,600-5,500

A Victorian figured walnut and ormolu side cabinet.
$1,800-2,700

A mid-Victorian inlaid walnut breakfront side cabinet, the top with brass beaded edge above a central glazed door flanked by turned uprights with gilt cappings and open compartment with doors below centred by jasperware plaques, on turned feet, 68.5in (173cm).
$3,600-5,500

A Victorian burr walnut credenza.
$3,600-5,500

A Victorian ebonised and burr walnut credenza, with curved ends, painted porcelain door panel, foliate brass mounts and beaded outlines, 60in (152cm).
$2,700-3,600

A brass mounted mahogany side cabinet, with hinged lid enclosing a fitted interior above a panelled frieze and 2 panelled doors, on toupie feet, probably Dutch, late 18thC, 52in (132cm).
$3,600-5,500

A Victorian burr walnut inlaid breakfront credenza, with gilt brass appliques, 61in (155cm).
$3,600-5,500

An Edwardian inlaid rosewood side cabinet, with satinwood stringing and marquetry inlaid decoration of urns and scrolling leaves, the back with nine bevelled glass panels, numerous display shelves with turned galleries, 48in (122cm).
$1,200-1,700

A walnut and amboyna pot cupboard, 31in (79cm).
$360-540

A Napoleon III ebonised, ormolu mounted, tortoiseshell and brass inlaid credenza, of broken D-shaped outline, the top with egg-and-dart border above a frieze with female mask mounts, on plinth base, slight damage, 84in (213cm).
$3,600-5,000

A mid-Victorian walnut floral marquetry and ormolu mounted side cabinet, with foliate scroll inlaid frieze and similarly inlaid glazed panelled doors flanked by female mask mounts, on plinth base with waved apron, 31in (79cm).
$2,700-3,600

A Victorian walnut breakfront credenza, with inlay and gilt metal mounts.
$2,700-3,600

A Dutch kingwood side cabinet, the panelled door set with a ribbon tied Japanese lacquer dish, on square tapering legs, c1790, 28in (71cm).
$3,600-5,500

Chiffoniers

A Regency rosewood and banded chiffonier, with brass three-quarter galleried mirrored ledged back top with turned supports, above a frieze drawer flanked by ormolu maidens with 2 panelled doors below, on turned feet, 36.5in (93cm).
$2,700-3,600

A William IV chiffonier, veneered in rosewood.
$1,800-2,700

A Regency mahogany and ebony string inlaid two-stage chiffonier, the lower stage with reel and leaf decoration enclosing shelving and 2 drawers, on reeded base with turned supports, 44in (111.5cm).
$1,200-1,700

A William IV rosewood chiffonier, the mirrored back carved with lotus, acanthus and scrolls, the top with gadrooned edge, the reeded supports also carved with lotus and acanthus and on a concave plinth base, 54in (137cm).
$1,800-2,700

A William IV mahogany chiffonier, the raised back with moulded edged shelf with turned and gadrooned column supports and shaped smaller shelf below on similar supports, 2 glazed and brass grille cupboard doors enclosing adjustable shelving, on bun feet, 42in (106.5cm).
$2,700-3,600

A William IV mahogany chiffonier, with half-reel turned beading, the shelved upstand above base with 2 frieze drawers and 2 cut velvet inset doors, on lobed bun feet, 56in (142.5cm).
$2,700-3,600

A late Regency rosewood chiffonier, the triple tiered ledge back with pleated silk panels and scroll bracket supports, above a rectangular top and 2 frieze drawers with 2 silk panel doors below, on plinth base, possibly adapted, 28in (72cm).
$1,800-2,700

Chiffoniers

The chiffonier became popular during the late 18thC and is basically a small shallow cabinet with a shelf and perhaps a drawer below the top of the cabinet section. Many cheap chiffoniers were produced in the Victorian era, lacking the refinement of those made in the Regency period.

Canterburies

A George III mahogany music canterbury, the hooped divisions above a drawer with turned legs on brass casters, c1805.
$3,600-5,500

A late George III mahogany canterbury, with wavy rail uprights, swept rectangular top and a drawer to the base with turned knob handles, on ring turned tapering supports with brass caps and casters, 16in (41cm).
$3,600-5,500

A Regency mahogany folio canterbury, with 4 divisions, on turned feet with casters, c1810.
$3,600-5,500

A late George III mahogany canterbury, with 4 divisioned top above a drawer, on square tapered legs, 18in (46cm).
$3,600-5,500

A Victorian rosewood canterbury, 20in (51cm).
$2,700-3,600

A late Georgian mahogany canterbury.
$2,700-3,600

A Victorian walnut canterbury, with 4 arched divisions, on turned tapering spindle supports, shaped and pierced sides with carved scroll decoration, single drawer with turned knob handles, turned baluster supports with brass toes and casters.
$1,800-2,700

A mid-Victorian figured walnut canterbury, the oval top with 2 handles, 3 division undershelf and drawer, on casters, 24in (61cm).
$1,200-1,700

A late George III mahogany canterbury, the top with spindle turned sides and apron drawer below, on baluster turned legs and casters, some slat divisions missing, 55.5in (140cm).
$2,700-3,600

A William IV rosewood 3 division canterbury, with pierced lyre ends carved with flowerheads flanked with spindle turned uprights, with single frieze drawer, on gadrooned and turned tapering legs.
$2,700-3,600

A William IV mahogany double canterbury, the crested toprail with egg-and-dart moulding above 6 slatted divisions and baluster turned lotus leaf lappeted lower rail between reeded and finial supports, the base with 2 apron drawers, on reeded turned tapering legs and brass casters, 55in (140cm). **$10,000-12,000**

A Regency mahogany 4 division canterbury, c1810, 20in (51cm). **$1,800-2,700**

A Victorian walnut canterbury, 19in (48cm). **$1,000-1,500**

Open Armchairs

A George III mahogany Gainsborough type open armchair, upholstered in olive green floral damask, on square chamfered legs. **$3,600-5,500**

A pair of George II mahogany armchairs, the upholstered seats now covered with floral tapestry, the chamfered square legs joined by H-shaped stretchers, damaged and old repairs, c1750. **$3,600-5,500**

A George III black japanned and gilt armchair, with cane seat and turned splayed legs, c1800. **$1,200-1,700**

A George I walnut armchair, with a solid vase shaped splat and an upholstered seat, on cabriole legs joined by waved H-shaped stretchers, minor restorations, c1720. **$2,700-3,600**

A Regency reclining library chair. **$1,200-1,700**

A Chippendale mahogany open armchair, Philadelphia, on cabriole legs ending in claw-and-ball feet, 19thC. **$32,000-35,000**

A pair of William IV mahogany library armchairs, upholstered in red ochre leather, on reeded legs. **$3,600-5,500**

A Restauration mahogany fauteuil, the padded back and seat covered in floral patterned cotton, the scrolled arms with reeded terminals on sabre legs headed by lotus leaves, repair to end of one arm.
$1,800-2,700

A pair of Louis XVI beechwood fauteuils by Pierre-François-Joseph Corbisier, each covered in patterned cotton, with moulded frame, on turned tapering fluted legs headed by paterae and pointed feet, stamped P F J CORBISIER, previously gilt.
$3,600-5,500

A Chippendale carved mahogany armchair, Philadelphia, with cabriole legs and claw-and-ball feet, possible restoration, c1770.
$220,000-250,000

A pair of French giltwood open armchairs, each with laurel band padded seat, arms and seat covered in grey striped floral silk, the seat rails carved with entrelac, on fluted beaded twilled tapering legs headed by lotus leaf, late 19th/early 20thC.
$7,000-9,000

A pair of carved walnut Louis XIV style high back elbow chairs, with floral tapestry backs and stuffover seats, on turned legs united by a floral and scroll arched stretcher to the front.
$1,800-2,700

A pair of Louis XVI grey painted fauteuils, each covered in floral needlework in imitation of tapestry, the moulded frame on turned tapering stop fluted legs headed by paterae, on turned feet.
$3,600-5,500

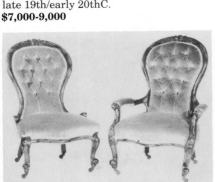

A Victorian walnut and button upholstered armchair, together with a companion occasional chair, the frames with simulated figuring and stylised leaf crestings, the serpentine seats on cabriole legs with casters, slight worm damage, c1860.
$1,800-2,700

A Victorian walnut open armchair, upholstered in floral woolwork and crimson velour, on fluted cabriole front supports carved at the knees with flowerheads, terminating in knurl and peg feet and ceramic casters.
$1,200-1,700

A Victorian mahogany salon armchair, on leaf carved cabriole legs, c1860.
$2,700-3,600

A mid-Victorian oak master's chair, the arched back with dentil moulded cornice above a pair of carved figures on lion's mask brackets flanking geometric panels with cherub masks with carved inscription above, the drop-in loose cushion seat with acanthus carved baluster turned legs headed by lion's masks, the Greek inscription translated reads: God is not mocked; for what a man soweth that shall he also reep, the seat carved Made 1841, carved on seat rail J Sutt, 1841. **$900-1,500**

A pair of French beech fauteuils of Louis XV design, with floral needlework upholstery back and seat, foliate carved outswept arms and cabriole legs with scroll feet. **$2,700-3,600**

A Chippendale walnut open armchair, Southern, on square moulded legs, reduced in height, c1770. **$1,500-2,500**

A pair of Edwardian Sheraton revival painted satinwood open armchairs, each with crested shield shaped cane panel back decorated with an oval portrait of a lady above a serpentine fronted cane seat, flanked by swept arms, on square tapering legs and splayed feet, including squab cushion. **$1,200-1,700**

A pair of carved giltwood Adam period armchairs, the seats covered in blue dralon, moulded paterae fronts to turned fluted leaf carved legs and fluted feet, one repaired, c1770. **$3,600-5,500**

A pair of Regency carvers. **$2,700-3,600**

A Louis XV giltwood fauteuil, with padded back and seat upholstered in pale floral brocade, with foliate cresting and scroll arms, on cabriole legs, re-gilded, and a matched giltwood fauteuil. **$1,800-2,700**

A George III mahogany library armchair, with upholstered back and overstuffed seat with later covering, acanthus leaf and flower carved arm supports and similarly decorated cabriole front legs with claw-and-ball feet. **$3,600-5,500**

A Flemish walnut open armchair, covered in blue velvet with dished acanthus carved and beaded arms, on baluster turned legs joined by turned stretchers, restored, late 17thC. **$3,600-5,500**

Miller's is a price **GUIDE** not a price **LIST**

Upholstered Armchairs

A pair of mahogany wing armchairs of mid-Georgian design, upholstered in green floral damask, on mask headed cabriole legs with paw feet.
$3,600-5,500

A Chippendale mahogany wing armchair, New England, c1785.
$2,000-4,000

A George IV mahogany and button upholstered armchair, covered in nailed green hide, ring turned legs on brass casters, c1825.
$2,700-3,600

A late George III mahogany bergère armchair, with panelled cresting rails and stiles, red leather upholstered arm pads, baluster turned arm fascias applied with split balusters, cane panelled back, arms and seat, panelled seat rail and short sabre front supports with casters, damaged.
$2,700-3,600

A Georgian style mahogany porter's chair, the canopy supported by 4 detachable carved pillars, with upholstered seat and back, on reeded baluster legs with casters, 76in (193cm) high.
$1,200-1,700

A Queen Anne walnut wing armchair, Boston Area, Massachusetts, with cabriole legs ending in pad feet, repairs, c1750.
$13,500-15,000

A small upholstered low seat drawing room chair.
$360-540

A Victorian rosewood drawing room chair.
$720-1,000

A rosewood and simulated rosewood nursing chair, on foliate headed cabriole legs, possibly Continental, mid-19thC.
$720-1,000

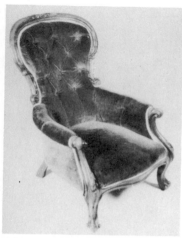

A Victorian open armchair, with mahogany show frame carved with foliate scrolls, buttoned rounded back and seat in green velvet, scroll arms, and leaf carved cabriole legs.
$900-1,500

A William IV mahogany bergère, with deeply curved caned back, sides and seat, the padded arms and squab cushion covered in buttoned green leather, on lotus carved turned legs and brass caps, restored.
$3,600-5,500

A Directoire grey painted and parcel gilt bergère, upholstered in yellow patterned cotton, on turned tapering feet headed by paterae, later blocks, the seat rail with later fillets to front and back.
$1,800-2,700

A set of 4 French walnut framed fauteuils, the shaped show wood frames with carved leaf cresting, C and S-scroll mouldings, scroll arm terminals, on cabriole supports with carved cartouche ornament to knees, upholstered in cream floral brocade, 19thC.
$3,600-5,500

An Anglo-Indian hardwood bergère armchair, the scroll back with reeded uprights and arms, on turned and reeded front supports, 19thC.
$1,200-1,700

A Victorian mahogany framed shaped back gentleman's chair, with shaped arm terminals, leaf carved to serpentine frieze and squat circular front legs.
$1,200-1,700

A black lacquered and gilt chinoiserie decorated four-piece bergère suite, comprising a sofa, a pair of armchairs and a stool, each with caned back and solid vase splat and double caned arms, on cabriole legs with pad feet, the sofa 66in (168cm).
$3,600-5,500

Miller's is a price
GUIDE not a price
LIST

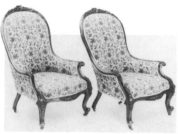

A pair of Victorian walnut show frame armchairs, with tulip carved moulded crests and terminals to the arms, serpentine front seats to front cabriole legs, on china casters.
$3,600-5,500

Corner Chairs

A Victorian satinwood frame corner seat, upholstered in buttoned green damask, on moulded cabriole legs with scroll toes and casters, restored.
$900-1,500

A Queen Anne cherrywood corner chair, Connecticut, with cabriole legs and pad feet, one front leg return replaced, c1765.
$10,000-12,000

A pair of Italian carved walnut armchairs, the solid tub shaped backs with foliate scroll crestings above griffin cartouches and griffin arms, the serpentine seats on splayed legs with scrolled knees and hairy paw feet, including loose squab cushions, c1870.
$2,700-3,600

Dining Chairs

A set of 6 George III mahogany shield back dining chairs, including 2 similar style carvers, each with carved wheat ear back supported upon square tapering legs with spade feet, the seats upholstered in red leather.
$3,600-5,500

A set of 11 Queen Anne style walnut dining chairs, including 2 open armchairs, each with floral needlework drop-in seat, on C-scroll and shell headed cabriole legs with trefid pad feet, damaged.
$3,600-5,500

A set of 4 mid-George III mahogany ladder back dining chairs, each with waved toprail and horizontal bars above drop-in seats, on square chamfered legs joined by stretchers.
$1,200-1,700

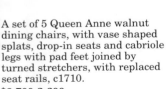

A set of 5 Queen Anne walnut dining chairs, with vase shaped splats, drop-in seats and cabriole legs with pad feet joined by turned stretchers, with replaced seat rails, c1710.
$2,700-3,600

A George I walnut dining chair.
$720-1,000

A set of 8 George III style mahogany dining chairs, including 2 armchairs, with pierced vase shaped splats and drop-in seats, on chamfered square legs, c1900.
$2,700-3,600

A set of 6 George III design mahogany dining chairs, each with pierced interlaced splat above a padded drop-in seat, on cabriole legs with claw-and-ball feet and foliate headings.
$1,200-1,700

A set of 6 late George III design mahogany dining chairs, including 2 open armchairs, each with shield shaped back, pierced vase splat with inlaid paterae and carved husks above bowed padded seat, on square channelled tapering legs with spade feet.
$2,700-3,600

A set of 4 George III mahogany chairs, the serpentine crestings above pierced splats and drop-in seats, the chamfered square legs joined by stretchers, c1770.
$2,700-3,600

A set of 6 George III mahogany ladder back dining chairs, with pierced interlaced splats and dished tapestry upholstered seats, on moulded square legs joined by stretchers, c1770.
$3,600-5,500

A set of 8 George III mahogany dining chairs, including 2 later armchairs, the slat backs carved with flower heads, with floral needlepoint covered padded seats, on tapered square legs and spade feet, damaged, c1790.
$2,700-3,600

A set of 6 late George III mahogany dining chairs, each with channelled uprights and 2 pierced bars above drop-in seat, on square tapering legs joined by stretchers.
$2,700-3,600

A set of 6 late George III mahogany dining chairs, each with arched back with pierced vase splat above drop-in seat, on square chamfered legs joined by stretchers, re-blocked.
$1,800-2,700

A set of 6 George III mahogany dining chairs, with arched crest, wave patterned splat backs, dished upholstered seats and chamfered square supports and stretchers.
$1,200-1,700

A set of 6 William IV dining chairs, each with scroll carved bar toprail and horizontal splat above drop-in seat, on sabre legs joined by stretchers, restored.
$2,700-3,600

A set of 6 George III mahogany dining chairs, with green damask covers, the backrails inset with spheres, on ring turned supports.
$3,600-5,500

A set of 18 George III style mahogany dining chairs, including 2 armchairs, with pierced strapwork splats and drop-in seats, on chamfered square legs, 20thC.
$7,000-9,000

A set of 7 Regency mahogany dining chairs, including one carver and a matched carver, each with a bowed toprail and crossbar, above a padded drop-in seat, on sabre legs.
$3,600-5,500

A set of 14 George III style mahogany dining chairs, including a pair of armchairs, with pierced vase shaped splats above nailed hide uphostered seats, on fluted tapered square legs with spade feet, c1905.
$10,000-12,000

A set of 6 mid-Victorian rosewood balloon back dining chairs, on cabriole legs with scroll feet, and 2 similar mid-Victorian rosewood dining chairs, one damaged.
$1,800-2,700

A set of 6 early Victorian mahogany dining chairs, each with deep bar toprail and channelled uprights above padded seats, on turned tapering legs.
$2,700-3,600

A set of 6 late Regency mahogany dining chairs, each with a scroll bowed bar toprail and crossbar above a padded drop-in seat, on sabre legs.
$2,700-3,600

A matched pair of Regency beech dining chairs, in simulated rosewood finish, with canework seats, one stamped I.C., brass inlaid roundels to backs.
$360-540

THERE ARE MANY ANTIQUE
SHIPPERS IN BRITAIN BUT...

... few, if any, who are as quality conscious as Norman Lefton, Chairman and Managing Director of British Antique Exporters Ltd. of Burgess Hill, Nr. Brighton, Sussex.

Thirty years' experience of shipping goods to all parts of the globe have confirmed his original belief that the way to build clients' confidence in his services is to supply them only with goods which are in first class saleable condition. To this end, he employs a cottage industry staff of over 50, from highly skilled antique restorers, polishers and packers to representative buyers and executives.

Through their knowledgeable hands passes each piece of furniture before it leaves the B.A.E. warehouses, ensuring that the overseas buyer will only receive the best and most saleable merchandise for their particular market. This attention to detail is obvious on a visit to the Burgess Hill showrooms where potential customers can view what must be the most varied assortment of Georgian, Victorian, Edwardian and 1930s furniture in the UK. One cannot fail to be impressed by, not only the varied range of merchandise, but also the fact that each piece is in showroom condition awaiting shipment.

As one would expect, packing is considered somewhat of an art at B.A.E. and the manager in charge of the works ensures that each piece will reach its final destination in the condition a customer would wish. B.A.E. set a very high standard and, as a further means of improving each container load, their customer/container liaison dept, invites each customer to return detailed information on the saleability of each piece in the container, thereby ensuring successful future shipments.

This feedback of information is the all important factor which guarantees the profitability of future containers. "By this method" Mr. Lefton explains, "we have established that an average £10,000 container will immediately it is unpacked at its final destination realise in the region of £17,500 to £25,000 for our clients selling the goods on a quick wholesale turnover basis."

In an average 20-foot container B.A.E. put approximately 75 to 100 pieces carefully selected to suit the particular destination. There are always at least 10 outstanding or unusual items in each shipment, but every piece included looks as though it has something special about it.

Burgess Hill is 15 minutes away from Gatwick Airport, 7 miles from Brighton and 39 miles from London on a direct rail link, (only 40 minutes journey), the Company is ideally situated to ship containers to all parts of the world. The showrooms, restoration and packing departments are open to overseas buyers and no visit to purchase antiques for re-sale in other countries is complete without a visit to their Burgess Hill premises where a welcome is always found.

BRITISH ANTIQUE EXPORTERS LTD,
SCHOOL CLOSE, QUEEN ELIZABETH AVENUE,
BURGESS HILL, WEST SUSSEX RH15 9RX, ENGLAND.
Telephone BURGESS HILL (04 44) 245577.
Fax from USA 011 44 444 232014
Tel from USA 011 44 444 245577

MEMBER
LAPADA
MEMBER

A set of 8 Hepplewhite style
mahogany dining chairs, with
woolwork drop-in seats, on square
tapering supports tied by plain
stretchers, two with outward
scroll arms, late 19thC.
$3,600-5,500

A set of 8 Victorian carved walnut
balloon back chairs.
$7,000-9,000

An Edwardian seven-piece inlaid
mahogany drawing room suite,
with square tapering legs, and
varying upholstered seats,
including 4 dining chairs, an
open armchair, a two-seater
settee, and a tub chair.
$1,200-1,700

A set of 6 Victorian mahogany
dining chairs.   **$1,200-1,700**

A set of 4 Victorian rosewood
dining chairs.
$1,000-1,500

A set of 6 Victorian mahogany
single dining chairs, with
upholstered backs and seats, each
with a paper label for Urquhart &
Adamson, 13 & 15 Bold Street,
Liverpool.   **$1,200-1,700**

A set of 6 dining chairs, carved in
Carolean taste, with needlework
seats, late 19thC.
$3,600-5,500

James Buckingham
COLLECTION OF ENGLISH PERIOD COPIES
At factory prices

TWIN PEDESTAL DESKS

Also available, L-shape Computer Desks with side returns.

REVOLVING BOOKCASE

BRASS MARQUETRY TOP CHAIRS

BREAKFAST TABLE

ALL ITEMS AVAILABLE IN MAHOGANY WALNUT AND YEW

LOWBOY

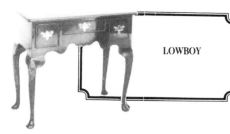

DINING TABLE

FILING CABINET

CHIPPENDALE RIBBON BACK CHAIRS

BACHELOR CHEST

NEST OF 4 TABLES

167

Side Chairs

A Chippendale carved mahogany side chair, Philadelphia, with flaring moulded seat, on acanthus and bellflower carved cabriole legs to front, with claw-and-ball feet, c1770.
$5,500-7,000

A Chippendale carved mahogany side chair, Philadelphia, with cabriole legs on claw-and-ball feet, shell on skirt replaced, c1770. **$5,500-7,000**

A pair of ebony side chairs, carved overall with foliate scrolls and flowerheads, each with pierced rectangular back filled with spirally twisted spindles beneath pierced scrolls, with padded seats covered in later blue and red silk brocade, on spirally twisted turned legs joined by conforming stretchers and later bun feet, Coromandel Coast, India, minor restorations, mid-17thC.
$2,700-3,600

Ebony chairs of this type were imported into England during the second half of the 17th century, and a pair at the Ashmolean Museum are claimed by tradition to have been brought from Portugal in 1661 as part of Catherine of Braganza's dowry.

A Queen Anne figured maple Wethersfield Area, Connecticut, balloon seat side chair, on cabriole legs with pad feet, leg brackets replaced, c1760.
$4,500-6,500

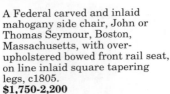

A Federal carved and inlaid mahogany side chair, John or Thomas Seymour, Boston, Massachusetts, with over-upholstered bowed front rail seat, on line inlaid square tapering legs, c1805.
$1,750-2,200

Chests of Drawers

A George III mahogany chest, with green baize lined brushing slide, on ogee bracket feet, restored, 34in (86cm).
$3,600-5,500

A mahogany dressing chest, with brushing slide above 4 drawers, on bracket feet, mid-18thC and later, 34.5in (87cm).
$2,700-3,600

An Edwardian walnut carved window seat, 25in (64cm) wide.
$720-1,000

A mahogany bowfronted chest, with wood knob drawer handles, on splayed bracket feet, 19thC, 40in (102cm) high.
$360-540

A fruitwood and burr walnut veneered chest, inlaid with ebony lines, on bracket feet, early 18thC, 36in (92cm).
$1,800-2,700

A George III mahogany dwarf chest, with brushing slide, on bracket feet, 31.5in (80cm).
$1,800-2,700

A Queen Anne mahogany chest of drawers, Philadelphia, with thumb moulded edge to top, upper drawer fitted with lidded and divided compartments, adjustable mirror, fluted quarter colums, on ogee bracket feet, restored, c1760, 34in (86cm).   **$1,200-1,700**

A mid-George III mahogany chest, with moulded top above 4 graduated drawers, on bracket feet, 36in (92cm).
$2,700-3,600

A George I walnut bachelor's chest, made up, inlaid with feather banding, with fold-over top, on shaped bracket feet, top warped, 39in (99cm).
$7,000-9,000

A Queen Anne walnut chest, inlaid with featherbanding, on bracket feet, 38.5in (98cm).
$2,700-3,600

A George I walnut veneered chest, the crossbanded top geometrically inlaid with boxwood lines, the drawers similarly banded and inlaid, on later bracket feet, 38in (97cm).
$3,600-5,500

An early George III walnut chest, with cockbeaded drawers, pierced brass handles and lock plates, the top three-quarter moulded, on bracket feet, 37in (94cm).
$2,700-3,600

A Victorian mahogany bowfronted chest of drawers, with inlaid banding, the drawers with cock beading.
$720-1,000

A William and Mary walnut and seaweed marquetry chest, with banded and boxwood line borders, on later bun feet, 39.5in (100cm).
$10,000-12,000

A Chippendale carved curly maple chest of drawers, Pennsylvania, with moulded rectangular top, thumb moulded and graduated drawers and scroll cut bracket feet, restored, possibly Lancaster County, c1780, 40in (102cm). **$5,500-6,500**

A William and Mary walnut veneered chest, with later rectangular top, the drawers with crossbanding and ebony stringing, ovolo carcase mouldings, on later bun feet, 39in (99cm). **$1,000-1,500**

A mid-George III mahogany serpentine chest, with 4 graduated drawers, on ogee bracket feet, 41in (104cm). **$2,700-3,600**

A Queen Anne walnut chest of drawers, Philadelphia, with moulded top and drawers, fluted canted corners and on bracket feet, damaged, c1750, 43.5in (110cm). **$9,500-11,000**

A mahogany chest of drawers, with oak lined drawers, brass plate handles and escutcheons, on bracket feet, 18thC, 38in (97cm). **$3,600-5,500**

A Chippendale carved mahogany serpentine front chest of drawers, on cabriole legs with claw-and-ball feet, restored, probably Massachusetts, late 18thC, 39in (99cm). **$6,500-8,000**

A George III mahogany serpentine chest of drawers, 47in (119cm). **$1,200-1,700**

A George III mahogany plan chest, with brass swan neck handles, on block feet, 43in (109cm). **$1,800-2,700**

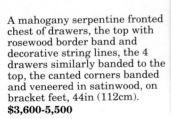

A mahogany serpentine fronted chest of drawers, the top with rosewood border band and decorative string lines, the 4 drawers similarly banded to the top, the canted corners banded and veneered in satinwood, on bracket feet, 44in (112cm). **$3,600-5,500**

A George III mahogany chest, on ogee bracket feet, 41.5in (105cm). **$1,800-2,700**

A mid-Georgian mahogany chest, with original pierced brass drawer handles and key plates, on bracket feet, 31in (79cm).
$1,800-2,700

A pair of walnut chests, with geometric mouldings, on moulded spreading bases and bun feet.
$2,700-3,600

A Chippendale carved walnut chest of drawers, Pennsylvania, with moulded top above 4 thumb moulded graduated drawers, fluted quarter columns, on ogee bracket feet, late 18thC, 39in (99cm).   **$2,000-2,500**

A Federal inlaid cherrywood chest of drawers, probably Rhode Island, c1810, 41.5in (105cm).
$2,000-4,000

A Regency apprentice chest of drawers, 11.5in (29cm).
$360-540

A George II mahogany chest of drawers, the moulded top above a brushing slide and 4 long graduated drawers, on shaped bracket feet, c1770, 33in (84cm).
$2,700-3,600

A late Federal mahogany veneered figured maple and cherrywood tall chest of drawers, probably Pennsylvania, with moulded cornice above 3 short and 5 long graduated cockbeaded drawers, reeded pilasters, on vase feet, c1820, 45.5in (115cm).
$4,000-6,000

A Chippendale carved walnut tall chest of drawers, Pennsylvania, with moulded cornice above 3 small drawers, 5 thumb moulded and graduated drawers flanked by fluted quarter columns, on ogee bracket feet, restored, late 18thC, 46in (117cm).
$3,500-4,500

A walnut and crossbanded bachelor's chest, the folding top with re-entrant corners, above 2 short and 3 long drawers, on bracket feet, 28in (71cm).
$3,600-5,500

A Regency mahogany chest of drawers, with stringing, bowed centre section, 4 long drawers and reeded sides, on sabre legs, 47in (119cm).
$1,200-1,700

A Dutch walnut and marquetry bombé chest of drawers, inlaid overall with vases, birds and flowers, on splayed front legs, late 18th/early 19thC, 33in (84cm).
$2,700-3,600

A Dutch mahogany and marquetry bombé chest, the top centred by a bird perched on an urn of flowers within acanthus scrolls, above 3 long drawers with foliate inlay, on later bun feet, 37.5in (95cm). **$3,600-5,500**

A Dutch mahogany and marquetry bombé chest of drawers, with ornate brass handles, the shaped top inlaid with urn and flowers, the scroll sides on front paw feet, late 18thC.
$7,000-9,000

Chests-on-Chests

A walnut and featherbanded chest-on-chest, with moulded cornice, on bracket feet, the sides split, early 18thC and later, 40in (102cm).
$3,600-5,500

An early George III mahogany tallboy, with cavetto cornice, on bracket feet, 41.5in (105cm).
$2,700-3,600

A George III style crossbanded mahogany tallboy, 44in (112cm).
$1,800-2,700

A George I walnut chest-on-chest, featherbanded throughout, with brass swan neck handles, on later bracket feet, 40in (102cm).
$7,000-9,000

A Channel Islands walnut tallboy, with inlaid string lines, fluted and canted corners, ogee bracket feet, 18thC, 42.5in (107cm).
$7,000-9,000

A George III mahogany tallboy, with cavetto cornice, on bracket feet, 43.5in (110cm).
$1,800-2,700

A George III mahogany tallboy, in 2 parts, the upper with dentil and blind fret cornice, the lower with 3 long drawers below a slide, on bracket feet, 43in (109cm).
$2,700-3,600

A George II mahogany tallboy chest-on-chest, the base drawers with original brass open plate handles and escutcheons, on bracket feet, 39in (99cm).
$3,600-5,500

A Queen Anne style walnut and oyster laburnum veneered small chest-on-chest, on bun feet, c1930, 23in (59cm).
$2,700-3,600

A mid-George III mahogany chest-on-chest, with dentil moulded cornice and blind fret frieze above 2 short and 3 long drawers, flanked by fluted quarter angles, with brushing slide and 3 further drawers below, on bracket feet, damaged, 44in (112cm).
$1,800-2,700

A Regency bowfronted mahogany tallboy, with a shaped pediment, reeded mouldings at the corners, shaped aprons, splay bracket feet, lion mask and ring handles, inlaid ebony string lines, 45in (114cm).
$3,600-5,500

A George III mahogany chest-on-chest, with dentilled cavetto cornice, and chamfered corners, on bracket feet, cornice lacking a corner moulding, c1760, 43.5in (110cm).
$3,600-5,500

A George III mahogany tallboy, with stepped pediment, on splayed bracket feet, 44in (112cm).
$1,800-2,700

A George III mahogany tallboy, with dentil cornice, all with original gilt brass handles and escutcheons, on shaped bracket feet, 43in (109cm).
$2,700-3,600

A walnut chest-on-later stand, the cavetto moulded cornice projecting at the corners, featherbanded, fluted and canted corners, the conforming stand with 3 drawers, on cabriole legs, early 18thC, 42.5in (107cm).
$1,200-1,700

A walnut and feather banded chest-on-stand, the stand with arched apron, on bun feet, re-veneered, early 18thC, 41.5in (105cm).
$3,600-5,500

A William and Mary oyster veneered chest, with fruitwood crossbanding throughout, the top geometrically inlaid with boxwood lines, on a later stand with twist turned supports, bun feet and flat stretchers, restored, 33.5in (85cm).
$3,600-5,500

Chests-on-Stands

A walnut and featherbanded chest-on-stand, the stand with 3 drawers, arched apron and bun feet, early 18thC, top and base later, partly re-veneered, 38.5in (97cm).
$2,700-3,600

A black and gold lacquer decorated chest-on-stand, with moulded cornice, the base with a shaped frieze and 3 oak lined drawers, cabriole legs with pad feet, 18thC with later restoration, 42in (107cm).
$3,600-5,500

A Dutch walnut and marquetry chest-on-stand, decorated overall with scrolling foliate and bird motifs, the banded top with oval panel, on later stand with cabriole legs and pad feet, 18thC and later, 37.5in (95cm).
$3,600-5,500

A Dutch Colonial chest-on-stand, applied throughout with pierced and engraved brass mounts, brass studs and loop handles, the stand with a drawer, on cabriole legs with claw-and-ball feet, 32.5in (82cm).
$1,200-1,700

> **Miller's is a price GUIDE not a price LIST**

Coffers

A Scandinavian painted marriage coffer, the domed lid with initials HRH and MWM above a panelled front painted with legendary scenes, flanked by carrying handles, on block feet, late 19thC, 47.5in (121cm). **$1,200-1,700**

A North Italian walnut cassone, carved with winged dragons and scrolling acanthus, the top inlaid with ebony lozenges and centred by an armorial motif, on bun feet, with carrying handles to the sides, early 18thC, later carving, 55in (140cm). **$1,800-2,700**

A Tuscan walnut cassone, with panelled front and sides, paw feet, 17thC, 55in (139cm). **$1,000-1,500**

Commodes

A George III mahogany bedside commode, the tray top pierced with carrying handles and quatrefoils, above 2 cupboard doors and a sliding commode drawer, on square legs, 22in (56cm). **$1,800-2,700**

A George III mahogany bedside commode, the tray top with waved gallery above 2 cupboard doors and a single drawer as 2 false drawers, on square legs, adapted, 19in (48cm). **$1,800-2,700**

A George III mahogany bedside commode, the tray top with a gallery pierced with carrying handles, above a cupboard door and a sliding commode drawer, on square moulded legs, 21in (53cm). **$1,000-1,500**

A George III mahogany concave front tray top commode, the waved gallery above a tambour front cupboard and deep drawer, on divided square legs, back panel missing, c1780, 23in (58cm). **$2,700-3,600**

Commode Chests

A South German marquetry serpentine commode with bombé sides, inlaid with satinwood and ivory, the legs and sides with scrolling foliage, 19thC, 30in (77cm). **$2,700-3,600**

A Louis XV style kingwood and marquetry bombé commode, applied with foliate cast brass mounts, escutcheons and handles, the pink veined marble serpentine top, drawers inlaid sans travers with scrolling foliage and flowers, on slender splayed legs.
$1,800-2,700

An Edwardian satinwood and tulipwood banded serpentine commode, with chequer inlay, the eared top above a central door with circular panels painted in the manner of Angelica Kauffmann, on spade feet, labelled on reverse The Property of Savoy H, No 101 and maker's label Gill and Reigate, London, W, 48in (122cm).
$7,000-9,000

A French rosewood and kingwood veneered small commode, with brown marble top, drawers with canted sides and gilt bronze mounts throughout, the whole chevron veneered in rosewood with shaped tulipwood crossbanding, c1880, 25.5in (65cm).   **$1,800-2,700**

A George III harewood and tulipwood crossbanded demi-lune commode, the top inlaid with a half fan patera, on square tapered feet, 50in (127cm).
$14,500-16,500

A satinwood demi-lune commode, with rosewood crossbanding, painted with oval plaque after Kauffman and other classical attributes, c1900.
$3,600-5,500

A gilt metal mounted tulipwood and marquetry bombé commode, with moulded serpentine liver marble top, above 2 long drawers inlaid sans travers with flowerheads and foliage, the keeled angles mounted with acanthus and flowerheads, with waved apron, on cabriole legs and scroll sabots, late 19th/early 20thC, 48in (122cm).
$2,700-3,600

A George III mahogany serpentine fronted commode, in the manner of Thomas Chippendale, the top with a floret edge, the cockbeaded drawers with later rococo brass drop handles, the top one fitted with divisions and a frieze covered internal slide, the chamfered angles carved with scrolling acanthus and flowering foliage, the shaped apron carved with C-scrolls, on foliate carved shaped bracket feet, 45in (114cm).
$27,000-36,000

The carved angles also bear a resemblance to the famous 'Moccas Court' commode, from Childwick Bury, Hertfordshire.

An Italian walnut commodino, banded overall in fruitwood, on angled cabriole legs and pad feet, adapted, part 18thC, label with ink inventory number 555, 20in (50cm).
$1,800-2,700

A Regency brass mounted kingwood and walnut commode, with moulded serpentine orange breccia marble top, on bracket feet, remounted, broken marble, with later ink inscription HEDOUIN PERE.
$7,000-9,000

A French commode, with serpentine front and ends, drawer front with matched veneers, ebonised edges and white stringing, decorated with applied gilt metal mounts in the form of female figures, leaves and stalks, fitted with black veined marble top, 19thC, 45in (114cm).
$1,800-2,700

A Louis XV style ormolu mounted kingwood and marquetry serpentine fronted bombé commode, with grey ground multi-coloured marble top, walnut internal veneered doors, tapering legs with pad feet and ormolu mounts, 19thC, 63in (160cm).
$18,000-21,000

A French mahogany commode, with shaped frieze drawer above 3 long drawers, early 19thC.
$1,200-1,700

A Scandinavian brass inlaid mahogany commode, the associated canted black and white variegated marble top above 3 drawers, on tapering feet, restored, formerly with wooden top, 39in (99cm).
$2,700-3,600

A Dutch marquetry bombé commode, inlaid overall, on angled scroll feet, modern, 35in (89cm).
$2,700-3,600

A Dutch rosewood and floral marquetry bombé commode, the undulating top centred by a floral arrangement within a strapwork border, the S-shaped front with 4 long drawers, on bracket feet, late 18th/early 19thC.
$7,000-9,000

A parquetry and marquetry prie dieu commode, on lion front supports, reconstructed incorporating early 18thC German/Italian veneers and inlays, 35in (89cm).
$3,600-5,500

A painted Italianate commode chest, with 3 drawers and brown and red mottled marble top.
$360-540

A French traditional style inlaid walnut commode, with marble top, 3 drawers with ormolu mounts.   **$360-540**

Miller's is a price GUIDE not a price LIST

Cupboards-Armoires

A French walnut armoire, in 2 sections, the red painted interior with 6 shelves and rounded angles, on bun feet, the back feet replaced, mid-18thC, 72in (183cm).
$7,000-9,000

A Franco-Flemish walnut armoire, with rectangular moulded cornice and a lunette carved frieze above 2 panelled doors with large raised cartouche mouldings between pilasters, on inverted plinth base, 64in (163cm).
$1,800-2,700

A French marquetry armoire, inspired by commode made for Louis XV by Jean-Henri Riesener, in Transitional manner, the door inlaid with a marquetry trophy, the lower panel applied with a similar trophy in gilt bronze, with convex corner cupboards, the whole inlaid in pearwood and tulipwood on a kingwood ground, with key, c1885, 73in (185cm).
$27,000-36,000

Corner Cupboards

A pair of mid-Victorian rosewood bowfront corner cupboards, each with scroll crested glazed panelled door enclosing velvet lined interior flanked by pilasters with foliate headings, on plinth bases, 33in (84cm).
$2,700-3,600

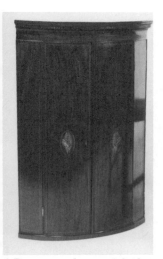

A Regency mahogany inlaid bowfronted corner cupboard, with dentil cornice, blind fretwork beneath, double opening doors with central oval inlaid satinwood and sycamore shell motifs, 3 internal shelves, 30in (76cm).
$720-1,000

A Dutch painted bowfront hanging corner cupboard, the doors depicting St. Catherine of Siena meeting Pope Gregory XI, the interior with shelves, 18thC, 23in (59cm).
$1,200-1,700

A George III mahogany corner cupboard, the dentilled cornice above a lancet astragal door enclosing shaped shelves, the lower part with a pair of panelled cupboard doors, on later bracket feet, alterations, c1790, 42in (107cm).
$2,700-3,600

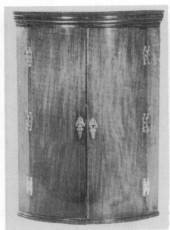

A George III mahogany bowfront
hanging corner cupboard, inlaid
with chequer stringing, the
interior with shelves and 3 small
drawers, c1760, 31in (79cm).
$1,200-1,700

A late George II mahogany corner
cupboard, on plinth base, 86.5in
(220cm) overall.
$2,700-3,600

A George III mahogany
bowfronted hanging corner
cupboard.
$720-1,000

A Chippendale carved walnut
corner cupboard, Pennsylvania, in
2 parts, with an arched, glazed
door and 3 shaped shelves, a pair
of panelled cupboard doors with
painted shelved interior, on ogee
bracket feet, 92.5in (235cm) high.
$5,750-8,000

A Georgian bowfronted corner
cupboard, c1780.
$1,800-2,700

A walnut corner cupboard, the
projecting cornice above a
panelled door flanked by fluted
and stop fluted pilasters with
Ionic capitals, on moulded bracket
feet, Italian or German, c1740,
44in (111cm).
$3,600-5,500

A George III mahogany standing
corner cupboard, the cavetto
cornice with a blind fret carved
frieze, 2 astragal doors enclosing
shaped shelves, on later ogee
bracket feet, restored, c1770, 42in
(107cm).
$2,700-3,600

A Dutch marquetry
double corner
cupboard, 18thC.
$14,500-16,500

A late George III mahogany linen press, with dentil moulded cornice above a pair of panelled doors, on bracket feet, 49in (125cm).
$1,800-2,700

A George III mahogany linen press, with broken arch top and cavetto cornice, the doors with mahogany crossbanded, boxwood and ebony stringing, on bracket feet, 50in (127cm).
$2,700-3,600

A Regency mahogany linen press, with brass lion's head mounts, the broken swan necked pediment above 2 panel doors flanked by reeded columns, on reeded scroll bracket feet, 49.5in (126cm).
$2,700-3,600

A late George III mahogany linen press, on bracket feet, 51in (130cm).   **$1,800-2,700**

A George III mahogany linen press.   **$1,000-1,500**

A George III mahogany linen press, inlaid throughout with stringing, the fluted cornice carved with a swag and paterae above a pair of doors with oval bandings enclosing sliding trays, on later bracket feet, c1780, 51in (130cm).   **$2,700-3,600**

A mahogany linen press.
$1,200-1,700

> **Miller's is a price GUIDE not a price LIST**

A mahogany linen press, with moulded cornice, 2 panelled doors applied with beaded brass mouldings, enclosing sliding trays, the drawers with moulded brass knob handles, on splayed bracket feet, early 19thC, 53in (135cm).
$2,700-3,600

Cupboards-Wardrobes

A mahogany breakfront wardrobe, the broken pediment pierced with trelliswork and centred by an urn above a dentil frieze decorated with ribbons and flowerheads, above 2 blind fret carved panelled doors applied with paterae, the side cupboard doors each with 3 false drawers, the fluted plinth on bracket feet, 19thC, 98in (249cm).
$10,000-12,000

An Edwardian mahogany breakfront wardrobe, with satinwood crossbanding and inlaid with trelliswork, husk swags and lines, on bracket feet, lacking trays to central section, 40in (101.5cm). **$1,200-1,700**

A Regency mahogany wardrobe, the drawers with ebony handles, flanked by 2 long doors each simulated as 2, flanked and divided by reeded and spirally twisted columns, with waved apron, on turned feet, the cornice with 2 later hinged secret compartments, 98in (249cm).
$3,600-5,500

Davenports

A William IV mahogany miniature inverted breakfront wardrobe, of architectural form, with cedar lined drawers flanked by a tall cupboard with panelled door to each side, 21in (53cm).
$3,600-5,500

A Victorian rosewood davenport, the sliding top with fretwork gallery and inset writing surface, the side with pull-out and hinged pen drawer, over brushing slide and 4 real and 4 dummy drawers, the sides on bun feet, one drawer stamped Johnstone Jupe & Co. New Bond, 21in (53cm).
$3,600-5,500

A Victorian curled ash breakfront triple wardrobe, with central mirror door enclosing slides and drawers, flanked by hanging cupboards, on plinth base, 83.5in (212cm). **$900-1,500**

A Victorian mahogany davenport, with a leather inset top above twist columns, with 4 graduated drawers at the side, c1850, 21in (53cm). **$1,200-1,700**

A William IV figured satinwood veneered davenport, with leather inset flap enclosing fitted interior, oak lined drawers, turned feet, 19in (48cm). **$3,600-5,500**

A Victorian figured walnut and marquetry davenport, with inlaid scrolling leaf and flowerhead decoration, tooled leather writing surface enclosing a typical plain interior, over 4 real and 4 dummy drawers, on platform base with carved, curving front supports, 22in (56cm). **$2,700-3,600**

A George IV davenport, with three quarter spindle turned gallery, leather lined fall and fitted interior, flanked by a hinged pencil drawer, on reeded bun feet, stamped M Wilson, 68 Great Queen Street, 24in (61cm).
$3,600-5,500

A mid-Victorian inlaid walnut davenport, the hinged superstructure with pierced three-quarter brass gallery above leather lined fall enclosing a fitted interior, one drawer stamped 20172, 21in (54cm).
$2,700-3,600

A Burmese carved rosewood davenport, late 19thC, 24in (61cm). **$720-1,000**

A Victorian walnut veneered davenport, with small drawers and pigeonholes to the rising stationery compartment, the piano front enclosing a fitted interior, the cabriole front supports carved with flowers and foliage, on turned feet with brass casters, lacking brass gallery, 23in (59cm).
$720-1,000

A William IV rosewood davenport, the sliding top section with a three-quarter gallery, pen drawer and leather lined slope enclosing short drawers, 23in (59cm).
$2,700-3,600

A Victorian walnut veneered davenport, with raised stationery compartment, sloping flap, foliate carved C-scroll front supports, on bun feet with casters, 21in (53cm). **$1,800-2,700**

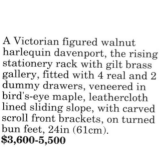

A Victorian figured walnut harlequin davenport, the rising stationery rack with gilt brass gallery, fitted with 4 real and 2 dummy drawers, veneered in bird's-eye maple, leathercloth lined sliding slope, with carved scroll front brackets, on turned bun feet, 24in (61cm).
$3,600-5,500

A Victorian walnut davenport, with crossbanded slope, leather inset reveals a 4 drawer interior, on carved and decorative front supports, 19in (48cm).
$3,600-5,500

An inlaid walnut kneehole desk, with brass ring handles and escutcheons, recessed centre cupboard, distressed, early 18thC. **$1,800-2,700**

A mid-Victorian burr walnut pedestal desk, with leather lined top of broken outline above 3 frieze drawers, 3 drawers to each pedestal, on plinth bases, damaged, 57in (145cm). **$2,700-3,600**

A mahogany kneehole desk, with moulded top above a frieze drawer and an open drawer, above a cupboard flanked by 3 drawers either side, on shaped bracket feet, adapted, late 18thC, 42.5in (108cm).
$1,200-1,700

A Victorian mahogany partners' desk, with rounded leather cloth inset top, above an arrangement of 9 drawers with gadrooned knop handles, opposed by 3 further drawers and a pair of panelled doors, on plinth bases, stamped T. Wilson, 68 Great Queen Street, London, c1850, 72in (183cm). **$7,000-9,000**

A George III mahogany kneehole desk, on bracket feet, 31in (79cm). **$3,600-5,500**

A Victorian mahogany veneered partners' desk, with cloth inset top, wood knob handles, on plinths, 66in (168cm). **$3,600-5,500**

A burr walnut and featherbanded partners' desk, with leather lined top, above 6 frieze drawers, 6 drawers to each pedestal, on plinth bases, 60in (152cm). **$3,600-5,500**

A late Victorian mahogany and ebony strung partners' desk, with leather lined top with reeded edge, on shallow plinth bases, restored, 71in (180cm). **$3,600-5,500**

A George III mahogany tambour top pedestal desk, the interior with small drawers, pigeonholes and adjustable writing inset, the frieze with a real and dummy drawer, fitted as a dressing compartment, c1780, 48in (122cm).
$7,000-9,000

A mahogany Carlton House desk, inlaid with satinwood bands and ebony and satinwood lines, with three-quarter brass gallery, adjustable leather lined writing surface, on square tapering legs, 55in (140cm).
$10,000-12,000

A French style Edwardian lady's kneehole writing desk, with cylinder action, inlaid to drawer fronts and cylinder with coloured woods, 37in (94cm).
$7,000-9,000

A walnut Wooton desk, with amboyna panels, the moulded top and hinged frieze compartment above 2 semi-dome fronted hinged panelled doors enclosing a fall front fitted satinwood and leather lined secrétaire, flanked by numerous stationery compartments, with letter box to the front, on reeded bracket feet, with dummy letter box marked Wooton Desk Co. Indianapolis, IND, Patent October 1874, 39in (99cm). **$3,600-5,500**

A French mahogany piano top desk, the elevated canted top enclosing 3 fall front drawers above a fall front lid, enclosing a pull slide leather lined fitted interior with 3 frieze drawers below, on baluster turned fluted legs, mid-19thC.
$1,800-2,700

A Victorian mahogany pedestal desk, one drawer with paper label inscribed 'Solomon's Office & Household Furniture, Queen Victoria Street, 49in (124cm).
$1,800-2,700

An inlaid writing desk.
$1,800-2,700

An Edwardian inlaid satinwood bowfront desk, with ledged back and finials, above a frieze drawer between 2 quarter veneered panelled doors, on reeded turned tapering legs with gadroon headings, 48in (122cm).
$1,800-2,700

A walnut, ebonised and marquetry kneehole desk, with spindle turned shelved gallery, gadrooned edge and scroll and parquetry inlay, each pedestal similarly inlaid, with cupboard door flanked by fluted uprights, on bun feet, mid-19thC, 55in (140cm).
$3,600-5,500

A Carlton House style mahogany and satinwood banded desk, the raised bowed back with an arrangement of small drawers, compartments and an architectural cupboard, the breakfront frieze with a slide and 3 drawers, on slender tapering square legs and spade feet, c1930, 29.5in (75cm).
$1,800-2,700

Mirrors and Frames

A William and Mary oyster veneered walnut mirror, with bevelled plate in a moulded convex frame, formerly with candle branches, the plate re-silvered, 26in (66cm).
$3,600-5,500

A William and Mary walnut dressing glass, 22in (56cm) high.
$1,000-1,500

A George III carved and gilded frame, the top with eared corners, centred with flowersprays and pendant festoons of husks at the sides, raised egg-and-dart outer edge, alternating rope twist and flower head sight edge.
$720-1,000

A George III design giltwood mirror, the plate between 2 pilasters, on a pierced foliate surround with flowerhead cresting, 49 by 23in (125 by 59cm).
$1,200-1,700

A George III style giltwood architectural wall mirror, with broken pediment, scroll finial and floral decorated shaped frieze, 19thC, 45 by 24in (114 by 61cm).
$1,200-1,700

A George I chinoiserie scarlet and gilt dressing table mirror, made up, with gilt decoration on a scarlet japanned ground, the base with a fall front revealing small drawers and pigeonholes, a serpentined drawer below, on block feet, 37 by 18in (93 by 46cm).
$1,800-2,700

A George IV gold painted overmantel mirror, the plate with an ebonised reeded band, with a foliate cornice and tied reeded pilasters, c1825, 36 by 56in (92 by 122cm).
$1,000-1,500

A mid-George III giltwood and gilt gesso mirror, within C-scroll and trailing foliate surround, 45 by 24in (114 by 61cm).
$1,200-1,700

A George III style satinwood cheval mirror, outlined throughout with ebonised stringing, on down turned splayed legs with brass casters, 68.5in (174cm) high.
$1,200-1,700

A George III giltwood overmantel, 62.5 by 55in (159 by 140cm). **$3,600-5,500**

A George I walnut veneered and giltwood frame mirror, with applied carving to the top and base, sides with trailing fruit, later bevelled glass, missing the surmount, 43 by 25in (109 by 64cm). **$1,800-2,700**

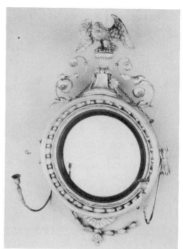

A Regency convex girandole, the ball studded and moulded giltwood frame with a U-shaped candle arm to each side, surmounted by an eagle with scrolling foliage, 40 by 23.5in (101 by 60cm). **$2,700-3,600**

A mahogany framed upright wall mirror, with a boxwood strung frieze, tulipwood crossbanded and boxwood and ebony strung borders, flanked by turned and reeded columns, headed by ebony strung panels, 19thC, 37.5 by 27in (95 by 69cm). **$1,000-1,500**

A William IV mahogany framed cheval glass, with reeded uprights, on scroll carved bases. **$1,200-1,700**

A Regency giltwood convex mirror, the plate in a reeded border edged with foliage and a moulded surround, below a foliate plinth, with an eagle flanked by dolphins, with foliate boss, re-gilt, traces of old gilding, 41.5 by 22in (105 by 56cm). **$1,800-2,700**

A George III style gilt framed pier mirror, the plate with a wave and flame pierced surround, with foliate festoons, with a cabochon surmount and conforming apron, c1900, 60 by 25in (152 by 63cm). **$2,700-3,600**

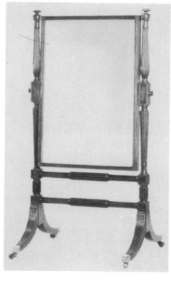

A George IV mahogany cheval mirror, in the manner of Gillow, the plate with a reeded frame, the reeded turned and square supports with mushroom finials, the conforming splayed legs ending in brass capped casters, c1820, 58 by 31in (147 by 79cm). **$3,600-5,500**

A Regency giltwood triple-plate overmantel mirror, the frieze applied with ebonised flowerheads and stars above cluster column uprights, c1810, 61 by 29in (155 by 74cm).
$1,800-2,700

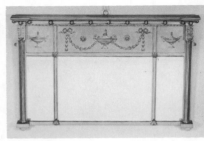

A Regency style giltwood overmantel, the moulded cornice with ball decoration, acanthus leaf finial fluted side columns, 3 bevelled mirror glass panels surmounted by classical urn, ribbon and swag decoration, 19thC, 42 by 28in (107 by 71cm).
$720-1,000

A George III giltwood and gesso pier glass, the 2 plates surmounted by a husk carved pediment, frieze set with 3 classical roundels and flanked by reeded columns with leaf carved capitals, 78 by 36.5in (198 by 93cm).
$1,800-2,700

A Victorian giltwood and gesso overmantel mirror, the surmount decorated in relief with mermaids above a 3 section glass interspersed with turned columns, 64.5 by 31in (163 by 79cm).   **$720-1,000**

A Victorian mahogany and satinwood cheval mirror, the plate on pierced shaped serpentine supports, on splayed feet with casters.
$1,000-1,500

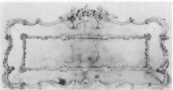

A pair of German gilt mirrors, the plates within 6 subsidiary plates divided by a border of foliate C-scrolls with scallop shells at each corner, surmounted by a rockwork motif flanked by 2 putti, the surround incorporating foliate scrolls, one labelled Carl Brassart, Hgl. Hof-Vergolder, Stuttgart, Specialitat In Zimmer decorationen Von Cartonpierre, re-gilt and slight differences in carving, mid-19thC, 68.5 by 38in (173 by 97cm).
$3,600-5,500

A pair of oval carved giltwood wall mirrors, 18thC.
$14,500-16,500

An Italian giltwood mirror, with divided plate centred by a patera, the frame carved with radiating rays, some losses to extremities, 69 by 62in (175 by 157cm).
$3,600-5,500

A Transitional grey painted and parcel gilt overmantel mirror, with later plate in a moulded foliate surround below a fluted urn with floral cresting and flanked by acanthus scrolls, the sides with leafy trails, the rectangular backboard with later egg-and-dart cornice, part of framing moulding later, 59 by 48in (150 by 122cm).
$3,600-5,500

A Viennese ormolu mounted mahogany and parcel gilt mirror, the cresting with pediment centred by a Bacchic mask above a tablet mounted with Cupid and Psyche, c1830, 62 by 22.5in (157 by 57cm).   **$1,200-1,700**

A Louis XVI grey painted and parcel gilt pier glass, the later divided plate in a lotus leaf and beaded moulded surround with flowerhead top angles, the reverse inscribed in pencil n°1480, reduced in height, 74.5 by 31in (189 by 79cm).
$3,600-5,500

A Victorian giltwood pier glass, c1840, 73in (185cm) high.
$1,000-1,500

A Provincial French carved and gilded frame, 18thC, 50 by 42in (127 by 106.5cm).
$1,800-2,700

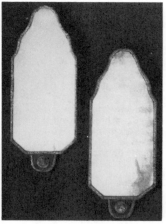

An Italian carved giltwood mirror, the plate engraved with a figure carrying a torch and a coat-of-arms, within a rococo frame with trophies, damaged, 18thC, 49 by 31in (125 by 79cm).
$2,700-3,600

An Italian giltwood mirror, with later plate, reduced in height, re-gessoed and re-gilded, late 17thC, 59 by 46.5in (150 by 118cm).
$10,000-12,000

A pair of Swedish gilt lead mirrors, with shaped plate in a foliate border above an apron centred by a double flowerhead, with filled candle branch sockets, late 18thC, 20 by 8in (51 by 20cm).   **$1,800-2,700**

A Louis XIV carved and gilded frame, with scrolling foliage and flowers flanked by opposed C-scrolls on cross hatched ground, foliate sight edge, 20 by 19in (51.5 by 48cm).   **$720-1,000**

A Victorian giltwood serpentine console and mirror, the arched glass plate surmounted by intersecting scrolling acanthus, the veined white marble top above a similarly carved frieze, on conforming cabriole supports, 126 by 58.5in (319 by 148cm).
$1,800-2,700

A Regency inlaid mahogany toilet mirror, the plate with beaded surround and a patera to each corner, flanked by turned uprights, the D-shaped platform crossbanded in satinwood above 3 frieze drawers, flanked by turned uprights and bun feet, one drawer stamped T Wilson, 38 Great Queen Street, London, 44 by 27in (112 by 69cm).
$1,800-2,700

Screens

A mid-Victorian rosewood pole screen, with polychrome woolwork panel in scrolled surround, baluster column support and tripod base with scroll feet, 54in (137cm).
$720-1,000

A Victorian mahogany pole screen, with a floral tapestry panel, on a tripod dolphin support. **$360-540**

A pair of Regency pole screens, decorated in penwork, on gilt brass mounted ebonised stands with tripod bases, 63.5in (161cm) high.
$1,200-1,700

An early Victorian maple pole screen, the banner with a needlework panel of a dove and prayer book amongst flowers, the triform base with scroll feet.
$720-1,000

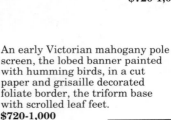

An early Victorian mahogany pole screen, the lobed banner painted with humming birds, in a cut paper and grisaille decorated foliate border, the triform base with scrolled leaf feet.
$720-1,000

An early Victorian stained rosewood cheval firescreen, with profusely carved foliate scroll surround and cartouche shaped woolwork panel in many colours, 45in (114cm).
$1,200-1,700

> **Miller's is a price GUIDE not a price LIST**

A Victorian rosewood pole screen, with woolwork panel of a young lady, on a tripod platform base.
$180-360

A Victorian oak three-fold screen, with carved paterae scrolls and a balustrade above the specimen wood panels of rosewood, bird's eye maple, satinwood, mahogany, kingwood, tulipwood, amboyna, walnut, burr walnut, pollard oak, ash, boxwood, birch and others, 76in (193cm) high.
$1,200-1,700

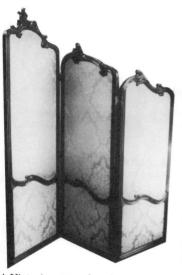

A pole firescreen, the woolwork panel on a dark green background and standing on a mound, 20 by 16.5in (51 by 42cm), on a mahogany baluster tripod stand with hoof feet, 18thC. **$720-1,000**

A Victorian carved mahogany three-fold graduated draught screen, with brocade fabric panels. **$360-540**

A mahogany triple chair back sofa, on shell headed cabriole legs with pad feet, restored, mid- 18thC, 66in (168cm). **$3,600-5,500**

Settees

A George I style giltwood sofa, upholstered in tapestry, the out scrolled arms carved with bell flowers, terminating in eagle masks, on hipped cabriole legs and claw and ball feet, 65in (165cm). **$3,600-5,500**

A George III mahogany triple shield back open arm settee, with pierced wheatsheaf style back, supported on square tapering legs with stretchers, upholstered in rose coloured velvet, 57in (145cm) long. **$900-1,500**

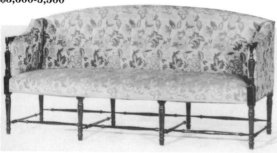

A Regency chaise longue, with scroll end, on curved supports, decorated in white and gilt, green damask cover. **$1,800-2,700**

A George III mahogany sofa, with urn shaped arm supports, on turned tapering legs joined by turned stretchers, c1795, 73in (185cm). **$3,600-5,500**

A carved mahogany sofa, Baltimore, with inlaid seat rail on acanthus and stylised fruit carved animal paw feet, c1830, 90in (230cm) long. **$2,000-2,500**

A mid-Georgian design mahogany and yellow upholstered sofa, on foliate headed cabriole legs with claw-and-ball feet, one arm damaged, 82in (208cm).
$1,200-1,700

A George III brown painted sofa, covered in floral cotton, on turned tapering fluted legs with brass caps, repaired, 71.5in (181cm).   **$1,800-2,700**

A George III mahogany settee, the padded seat covered in pale striped cut velvet, on square tapering legs joined by a later central pine stretcher, repaired, 59.5in (151cm).
$1,800-2,700

Provenance:
Princess Helen Frederica Augusta of Waldeck and Pyrmont was the wife of Prince Leopold, Duke of Albany (d.1884), youngest son of Queen Victoria. She lived at Claremont from 1882-1922. She was the mother of Princess Alice, Countess of Athlone (d.1981).

A mid-Georgian style mahogany sofa, with machine made floral upholstery, the arms with flowerhead terminals, on foliate headed cabriole legs with claw-and-ball feet, 82.5in (209cm).
$1,200-1,700

A Regency style ebonised and gilt sofa, with crimson and blue striped upholstery, scroll ends, scroll arm, reeded seat rail and outswept legs headed by rosettes, 77in (196cm).
$1,800-2,700

A Regency carved rosewood chaise longue, the back and seat with green and cream striped upholstery, the seat rail and turned tapering legs with lotus carved decoration, 79in (201cm).
$3,600-5,500

A Regency mahogany scroll end sofa, of slightly assymetric form, the waved gadrooned top rail, lotus leaf and acanthus carved arms enclosing a floral upholstered back and seat with bolster cushions, on scroll bracket feet, 95in (241cm).
$2,700-3,600

A rosewood framed couch, with single end, carved frame, outswept carved legs, porcelain casters, loose squab and bolster, covered in red brocade, c1830.
$1,200-1,700

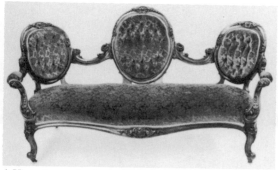

A Victorian walnut settee, with 3 button back panels, each with carved scroll and garland decoration, linked by curving open arms, on an upholstered serpentine seat, on cabriole front legs.
$3,600-5,500

A mid-Victorian satinwood sofa, the back and seat with channelled surround and striped upholstery, vase turned arm supports, square tapering legs headed by paterae, 66in (168cm).
$2,700-3,600

A Victorian love seat, the walnut frame supported by 4 scrolled decorative legs with casters, upholstered in red moquette.
$1,000-1,500

A George III style satinwood and painted settee, the caned back with an ebonised oval caned seat, swag decorated seat rail, on fluted gilt turned legs with brass casters, c1900, 46in (117cm).
$3,600-5,500

An Edwardian mahogany morning room suite comprising: a two-seat settee, inlaid with floral sprays in bone and stained wood, upholstered in gold floral coloured tapestry, on scrolling supports, 2 tub shaped easy chairs and 4 single chairs.
$2,700-3,600

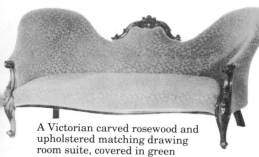

A Victorian carved rosewood and upholstered matching drawing room suite, covered in green moquette, comprising: a sofa and a pair of tub shaped armchairs, with similarly carved supports, c1845.   **$3,600-5,500**

A mid-Victorian carved walnut couch, with serpentine leaf decorated and button upholstered back, upholstered seat with shaped apron, leaf carved cabriole legs with white china casters, 75in (191cm).
$1,800-2,700

A Victorian walnut serpentine chaise longue, the button upholstered back with pierced end rail above seat, on short cabriole legs, with scroll feet.
$1,200-1,700

An Edwardian two-seater open arm settee, in mahogany show wood, re-upholstered in flame pattern material.
$3,600-5,500

A Victorian mahogany frame settee, with carved leaf and scroll decoration, buttoned and upholstered back and seat, carved, curving front supports, on cabriole legs, 82in (208cm). **$2,700-3,600**

An Anglo Indian hardwood sofa, the pierced back with reeded uprights and scrolling reeded horizontals carved with paterae and shells, the ends similarly carved, on reeded baluster turned legs headed by shells, mid-19thC, 104in (264cm).
$1,800-2,700

A French mahogany and gilt metal mounted sofa, of Empire design, applied with gilt paterae and foliate decoration, downswept arms with sphynx uprights, on angled griffin legs, upholstered in green patterned fabric, 65in (165cm).
$3,600-5,500

An Edwardian painted satinwood sofa, the bowed caned back with central panel of figures in a pastoral setting, the bowed caned seat with loose cushion, on turned tapering legs, 47in (119cm).
$3,600-5,500

A walnut framed three-piece bergère suite, comprising: 2 arm-chairs and a three-seater settee, with caned back and sides, carved arms with scroll ends, on cabriole legs with carved shoulders, upholstered loose cushions.
$2,700-3,600

A Regency chaise longue, in simulated rosewood frame, with scroll end and back, on turned supports with brass casters.
$1,800-2,700

A late Victorian painted satinwood double chairback settee, the back with cane panels centred by cherubs, the downswept arms with double cane panels, the upholstered seat with loose squab, on tapering turned legs with brass casters.
$3,600-5,500

Shelves

A pair of mahogany display shelves, with pierced fret sides and fret mouldings, late 19thC, 30in (76cm).
$3,600-5,500

A George III mahogany three-tier open wall shelf, with fretwork tracery sides and galleries, above 2 apron drawers, c1770, 24in (61cm).
$3,600-5,500

A Georgian inlaid and crossbanded mahogany shaped front sideboard, the top with 3 brass finials over a central drawer, flanked by a drawer and cupboard door to one side and a dummy double drawer cellaret to the other, on square tapering legs, 54in (137cm).
$3,600-5,500

A late George III mahogany bowfront pedestal sideboard, outlined with boxwood and fruitwood stringing, the back with double brass rail, crossbanded top, with tambour shutter, on slender bracket feet, 72.5in (183cm).   **$3,600-5,500**

A George III Sheraton style mahogany inlaid serpentine fronted sideboard, with brass side carrying handles, having satinwood stringing, original brass octagonal shaped ringed handles, on 6 square tapering legs with spade feet, 54in (137cm).
$3,600-5,500

A late George III mahogany inlaid and satinwood crossbanded sideboard, of broken D-shaped outline, the top inlaid with a shell motif, on turned legs, 43in (109cm).
$3,600-5,500

Sideboards

A late George III mahogany bowfront sideboard, with central frieze drawer and arched apron drawer, flanked by a deep drawer and cupboard, on turned reeded tapering legs, the top possibly associated, 63.5in (161cm).
$2,700-3,600

A George III inlaid mahogany bowed breakfront sideboard, 52in (132cm).
$2,700-3,600

A Regency mahogany D-shaped sideboard, inlaid with ebony lines, on ring turned tapering legs, 48in (122cm).
$3,600-5,500

A Regency brass inlaid mahogany sideboard.
$7,000-9,000

A Federal mahogany sideboard, New York, on square tapering legs, restored, c1800, 69in (175cm) long.
$3,000-5,000

A mahogany and inlaid sideboard, three quarter scroll fretted brass gallery, ribbed panels and inlaid oval fan medallions, the whole inlaid with floral festoons, ribbons, fan medallions, and decorative bands, square section tapering legs, spade feet, late 19thC, 90in (229cm).
$10,000-12,000

A Federal inlaid mahogany serpentine front sideboard, Middle Atlantic States, restored, c1800, 70in (178cm) long.
$3,500-4,500

A mahogany and chequer strung bowfront sideboard, with satinwood banded top, on square tapering legs with spade feet, restored, late 18thC, 73in (185cm). **$3,600-5,500**

A Regency mahogany sideboard, of broken D-shaped outline with foliate scroll carved galleried back above central frieze drawer and arched apron drawer flanked by a deep drawer and a cupboard, on ring turned tapering legs, 61in (155cm). **$2,700-3,600**

A carved walnut sideboard, the mirror panelled back of architectural form, the drawer stamped Johnstone, Jeanes and Co, 67 New Bond St., London, 5078, 101in (257cm).
$3,600-5,500

A Regency mahogany and ebony strung sideboard, with ledge back above central bowed frieze drawer and apron drawer flanked by a deep lead lined cellaret drawer and a cupboard, on reeded tapering legs, 48in (122cm).
$3,600-5,500

A George IV mahogany sideboard, on ring turned and reeded supports with ball feet, 83in (211cm).
$3,600-5,500

An Edwardian mahogany sideboard, on turned legs, 48in (122cm).
$1,200-1,700

An early Victorian mahogany sideboard, the raised mirror back with scallop carved surmount and panelled pilasters with rosette capitals, the base fitted with 2 frieze drawers on scroll carved front supports and platform base, 69in (175cm).
$900-1,500

Stands

A late Victorian mahogany folio stand, with slatted adjustable sides of slight serpentine outline with incised scroll decoration, on dual reeded scroll uprights joined by a flattened stretcher, 29in (74cm). **$2,700-3,600**

A George III mahogany stand. **$900-1,500**

A wrought iron lectern, with oak plank top and fleur-de-lys detail. **$180-360**

An ebonised and parcel gilt umbrella stand, on a moulded stepped plinth base, 32in (81cm) high. **$2,700-3,600**

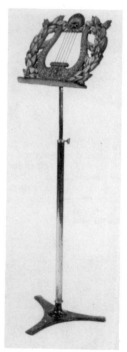

A William IV music stand, the painted and gilt adjustable rest, in the form of a laurel wreath and shell centred by a lyre, the telescopic brass column on a painted cast iron triform base, 55in (140cm) high. **$1,200-1,700**

Did you know

MILLER'S Antiques Price Guide builds up year by year to form the most comprehensive photo reference library available.

A hall/umbrella stand, made from WWI mahogany propeller, 32in (81cm) high. **$70-145**

A late Victorian rosewood and marquetry duet music stand, the twin ratchet adjustable panels inlaid with musical trophies, the adjustable fluted and spiral turned stem on bell flower inlaid splayed tripod supports, c1890, 16in (41cm). **$2,700-3,600**

A Victorian mahogany folio stand with drop side panels, 4 splayed feet and a stretcher. **$2,700-3,600**

197

Steps

A set of mahogany library steps, with gilt tooled leather to the treads, on an open frame, folding over to form a low table, the turned feet on brass casters, early 19thC. **$3,600-5,500**

A set of Regency mahogany and ebony strung library steps, with 3 leather lined rectangular treads, fitted with a commode, and cupboard door with brass handle, 16.5in (42cm).
$7,000-9,000

A Shaker butternut step ladder, Alfred or Sabbath Day Lake, Maine, c1840, 14in (36cm) wide.
$3,500-4,500

Stools

A George II giltwood stool, the stuffed seat covered in grey velvet, the scroll apron with diaper and scallop shells, on moulded cabriole legs, re-gilt and restored, c1755, 26in (66cm).
$3,600-5,500

A George III mahogany stool, with padded top covered in pale floral damask, on chamfered square legs carved with blind strapwork below a scallop shell, on block feet, repair to one leg, 31.5in (80cm).
$3,600-5,500

A mid-Georgian mahogany metamorphic library stool, with padded drop-in seat, on turned legs joined by turned stretchers and short vertical planks forming step treads, 39in (99cm).
$3,600-5,500

An early Victorian rosewood stool, in the Gothic style, with upholstered drop-in seat, on triple cluster legs with carved oak leaf cluster knops and moulded and fretted arched sides, 21 by 17in (53 by 43cm).
$1,200-1,700

A mahogany piano stool, 19in (49cm) high.
$360-540

A Victorian giltwood simulated bamboo stool, with canted padded seat covered in chinoiserie pattern material, with pierced apron, on splayed turned legs joined by X-shaped stretcher with turned boss, redecorated, 24in (61cm).
$1,200-1,700

A pair of Victorian oval rosewood footstools, with padded seats above flower carved aprons, on cabriole legs with scroll feet, c1860, 15in (38cm).
$1,000-1,500

A pair of late Victorian stools of Regency design, with green and gilt decoration, rectangular seats upholstered in buttoned yellow velvet, on ribbon tied X-frame supports with paterae headings, 21.5in (54cm).
$1,800-2,700

A George III mahogany stool, with padded top covered in close nailed yellow leatherette, on 6 canted square supports joined by box stretchers, on block feet, adapted, stretcher restored.
$3,600-5,500

A Victorian grey painted X-framed stool, with a leopard skin seat, c1850, 24in (61cm).
$2,700-3,600

A piano stool with glass marble feet, 20in (51cm) high.
$180-360

A pair of Venetian giltwood stools, with stuffed drop-in seats, pierced aprons, on 4 cabriole legs, mid-18thC, 41in (104cm).
$14,500-16,500

A mahogany duet stool, with well and 4 cabriole legs with shell carved shoulders and claw and ball feet, 20thC, 39in (100cm).
$720-1,000

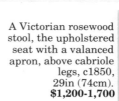

A walnut stool, with serpentine drop-in padded seat covered in green damask, damaged, 26in (66cm).   **$1,800-2,700**

A Victorian rosewood stool, the upholstered seat with a valanced apron, above cabriole legs, c1850, 29in (74cm).
$1,200-1,700

A rococo style carved and giltwood hearth stool, 19thC.
$900-1,500

A Victorian mahogany duet stool, with carved decoration and rising seat, on cabriole legs.
$180-360

An Italian walnut stool, with serpentine padded seat with tassels, a foliate scroll bar to each end, on bearded satyr supports, with later turned feet, late 19thC, 40in (102cm).
$2,700-3,600

A pair of Victorian mahogany stools, with overstuffed close studded seats on turned fluted legs, 30in (76cm).
$1,800-2,700

An early Victorian giltwood stool, the upholstered seat covered in salmon pink fabric, the scroll carved X-frame supports joined by twin turned stretchers, with trade label of Robert Strahan, 24 Henry Street, Dublin, c1850, 22in (55cm).
$1,800-2,700

A pair of George IV white painted and parcel gilt stools, with padded seats covered with floral needlework, on X-shaped end supports carved with acanthus scrolls and centred by a patera, joined by a turned stretcher, on scrolled feet, one with repairs to 3 legs. **$1,800-2,700**

An early Georgian walnut stool, on cabriole legs with square tops and shaped angles, on pad feet, the underside indistinctly inscribed in ink Mont Row, 21in (53cm).
$3,600-5,500

TABLES

Architects Tables

An early George III mahogany architects' table, with fitted frieze drawer with beize lined slide, brass side handles, on square supports concealing columns with brass casters, some alteration, 26in (66cm).
$2,700-3,600

A George II mahogany architect's table, the double rising top self-activating a rising fiddle, with candleslides to the side and split front legs supporting a pull-out drawer, with baize topped surface and compartments beneath, 33in (84cm).
$3,600-5,500

A walnut architect's table, the hinged ratcheted top with adjustable ledge, re-entrant corners and feather-banding flanked by brass candle holders, the front legs sliding open to reveal fitted interior, 36in (92cm).
$3,600-5,500

Breakfast Tables

A George III mahogany snap-top pedestal breakfast table.
$1,800-2,700

A late George III mahogany breakfast table, with reeded edged patent supported top, ebony stringing and wide crossbanding, on tapering ring turned column with 4 splayed legs, brass caps and casters.
$3,600-5,500

A Regency mahogany breakfast table, with rounded corners and reeded edge, on a turned column and reeded downswept legs, with lion's paw feet, c1810, 51in (130cm).
$2,700-3,600

A mahogany breakfast table, with radially veneered top and gadrooned shaft, on scroll carved splayed legs with paw feet, probably German, mid-19thC, 48in (122cm).
$1,800-2,700

A Regency style mahogany crossbanded with satinwood tip-up top breakfast table, with turned central pillar with 4 shaped scroll fluted legs, brass lion's paw feet and casters, 19thC, 48in (122cm) square.
$1,800-2,700

A Regency rosewood breakfast table, the parquetry tip-up top with satinwood banding, on faceted tapering shaft, spreading to tripartite scroll feet, damaged, 42in (106cm).
$1,800-2,700

A Regency mahogany breakfast table, with single plank top, on turned central column and reeded quadruple splay supports with brass caps and casters.
$1,800-2,700

A late Regency mahogany breakfast table, with tip-up top, baluster turned shaft, on 4 splayed legs with paw feet, restored, 46in (117cm).
$1,800-2,700

A Regency mahogany breakfast table, the top inlaid with mahogany segments, tilting on a pedestal base with 3-way plateau and carved paw feet, 54in (137cm).
$3,600-5,500

A Regency design mahogany breakfast table, with crossbanded top in rosewood, on turned shaft and splayed legs, modern, 84in (213cm).
$2,700-3,600

A William IV rosewood breakfast table, with tip-up top, on polygonal baluster turned shaft and circular platform with paw feet, 49in (125cm) diam.
$1,800-2,700

A William IV rosewood breakfast table, with tip-up top and faceted shaft on trefoil platform with paw feet, 47in (119cm).
$2,700-3,600

An early Victorian rosewood breakfast table, with moulded tip-up top, a baluster turned foliate carved shaft, on tripartite hipped splayed legs with cartouche headings and scroll feet, 49.5in (125cm).
$2,700-3,600

A mid-Victorian walnut breakfast table, with quarter veneered shaped oval tip-up top, on baluster turned shaft and splayed scroll legs, 57in (145cm).
$3,600-5,500

A mid-Victorian walnut breakfast table, with quarter veneered tip-up top, foliate carved baluster shaft, on 4 acanthus and scroll carved splayed legs, 46.5in (118cm).
$1,800-2,700

A mid-Victorian burr walnut breakfast table, with tip-up top, baluster turned shaft and quadripartite hipped splayed legs with foliate carved headings, 54in (137cm).
$1,800-2,700

A mid-Victorian burr walnut breakfast table, with oval quarter veneered top, gadrooned shaft, on splayed scroll carved legs, 47in (119cm).
$2,700-3,600

A Victorian walnut and marquetry oval breakfast table, the top inlaid with foliage and flowers, on a carved column and 4 downswept legs with scroll feet, stamped J.L. VIII, c1860, 53.5in (136cm).
$3,600-5,500

A Victorian burr walnut breakfast table, the quarter veneered top with satinwood crossbanding, on a fluted column and 4 leaf carved downswept legs, c1870, 51in (129cm).
$3,600-5,500

A mid-Victorian rosewood breakfast table, of serpentine outline with tip-up top, on faceted bulbous shaft and 4 splayed scroll carved legs, 55in (140cm).
$1,800-2,700

A Victorian coromandel breakfast table.
$2,700-3,600

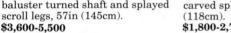

Card Tables

A George III inlaid mahogany folding card table.
$900-1,500

A Queen Anne style walnut and featherbanded card table, the eared hinged top with baize lined surface and playing counters, above a frieze drawer, on shell headed cabriole legs with pad feet, 33in (84cm).
$1,200-1,700

A George III mahogany concertina action card table, with hinged green baize lined top and square legs with scroll angles, on block feet, 36in (92cm).
$3,600-5,500

A George III mahogany D-end folding card table, the frieze drawer with boxwood stringing, on square tapered legs.
$2,700-3,600

A George III mahogany D-shaped fold-over card table, crossbanded and inlaid with satinwood, 36in (92cm).
$1,800-2,700

A late George III satinwood demi-lune card table, inlaid overall with boxwood and ebony lines and rosewood bands, with hinged top, on tapering legs, 38in (97cm).
$3,600-5,500

A George III mahogany and satinwood crossbanded card table, the hinged fold-over top on square tapering legs with spade feet, 37in (94cm). **$3,600-5,500**

A Federal satinwood inlaid mahogany demi-lune card table, New England, probably Rhode Island, with crossbanded frieze, c1800, 36in (92cm) long.
$5,500-6,500

A Federal carved mahogany card table, Haines-Connelly School, Philadelphia, with flowerhead carving on the frieze, on reeded legs and ball feet, c1815, 36.5in (92cm) long. **$1,500-2,500**

A pair of George III satinwood demi-lune card tables, the tops with satinwood and tulipwood crossbanding, on square tapered legs inlaid with boxwood and ebony stringing, 36in (92cm). **$14,500-16,500**

A Regency rosewood and brass inlaid table, the D-shaped fold-over swivel top with baize lining, turned and reeded column support with gadrooned collar, on circular base, 4 splayed feet with star decorated knees and brass lion paw toes and casters, 36in (92cm).
$7,000-9,000

A Regency period rosewood fold-over card table, the revolving top crossbanded with rosewood and shark skin and brass line inlay, on legs with brass inlays and toes, on casters, 36in (92cm).
$7,000-9,000

A Federal inlaid mahogany demi-lune card table, Rhode Island, probably Providence, on line inlaid square tapering legs, repaired, c1805, 35in (89cm) long.
$2,000-3,000

203

A Regency rosewood D-shaped card table, with hinged swivel top and beaded frieze, on square shaft with gadrooned base, on quadripartite platform with scroll feet, 36in (92cm). **$1,800-2,700**

A made-up Regency mahogany card table, on lyre shaped supports, 36in (92cm). **$1,800-2,700**

A Federal inlaid mahogany demi-lune card table, with a line inlaid frieze on line and bellflower inlaid square tapering legs ending in crossbanded cuffs, repaired, c1805, 36in (92cm) long. **$3,500-4,500**

A Federal carved mahogany card table, Haines-Connelly School, Philadelphia, on acanthus carved reeded tapering legs with vase form feet, 36in (92cm) long. **$2,000-3,000**

A William IV rosewood fold-over top card/games table, one side of the interior leaf fitted with a draught board and pegging area, swivel top reveals card storage box, on octagonal tapering column, shaped base, on squat circular feet, 23in (59cm) long when folded. **$1,800-2,700**

A late Regency mahogany card table, with rounded swivel top, scroll carved spandrels, on foliate scroll carved shaft and quadripartite platform with paw feet, 36.5in (93cm). **$1,800-2,700**

A mid-Victorian walnut card table, with serpentine quarter veneered top, on 4 scroll uprights with central finial and 4 splayed legs with scroll feet, 37in (94cm). **$2,700-3,600**

A Victorian walnut card table, with satinwood crossbanded top, on cabriole legs with gilt metal mounts at the knees and sabots, c1860, 39in (99cm). **$3,600-5,500**

A Regency rosewood card table, with rounded fold-over top enclosing a baize lined interior, 36in (92cm). **$2,700-3,600**

A Regency fold-over card table, on plain column with platform base and 4 carved claw supports. **$1,800-2,700**

A Victorian walnut card table, with hinged quatrefoil top, on leaf carved cabriole legs, c1860, 40in (102cm). **$3,600-5,500**

An Edwardian mahogany crossbanded and string inlaid envelope card table, the revolving top with baize lined interior, single frieze drawer with brass knob handles, circular undershelf, on 4 scrolled supports and 4 squared tapering legs with brass toes and casters, 19.5in (49cm). **$720-1,000**

A mahogany demi-lune folding card table, with green baize lined top, on 4 square tapering legs and brown porcelain casters, 24in (61cm) diam.
$180-360

A satinwood demi-lune card table, in the Sheraton manner, the top with crossbanded edge, segmented panels and inlaid Prince of Wales feathers motif, the frieze with crossbanding, stringing, ribbon, swag and shell decoration, the interior with 8 green baize segments, bordered by boxwood stringing, enclosing a central inlaid chequerboard, 36in (92cm).   **$1,800-2,700**

A Chippendale carved mahogany card table, Philadelphia, with bracketed square moulded legs on Marlborough feet, 36in (92cm) long.
$7,000-9,000

A rosewood folding card table, with baize lined swivel top, brass inlay to frieze, on twin supports and spider leg base, decorative brass toes and casters.
$2,700-3,600

A Victorian ebonised and bird's-eye maple card table.
$180-360

Centre Tables

A William IV rosewood centre table, on polygonal ends and dual supports with turned feet, 57.5in (146cm).   **$1,800-2,700**

A Regency rosewood centre table, with leather-lined top and beaded frieze on turned tapering legs, 54in (137cm) wide.
$1,800-2,700

A Victorian walnut centre table, English, inlaid with foliage, on carved cabriole legs, c1855, 59in (150cm) wide.
$2,700-3,600

A burr-elm and parcel-gilt centre table, the top with central ebony and stained yew parquetry feather pattern medallion with yew border, on tapering shaft and inverted tripartite platform base with gilt lions' paw feet, early 19thC, re-veneered, 46in (117cm) diam.   **$3,600-5,500**

A late Victorian walnut and marquetry centre table, the tilt top with central scroll decoration, bordered by scrolling flower and leaf designs, over an inlaid freize supported on a pedestal with 4 turned supports and splayed legs, 34.5in (87cm) wide.
$720-1,000

A Victorian satinwood centre table with serpentine sided top, foliate cartouche and scroll carved frieze, acanthus and cabochon carved baluster end supports, on splayed legs with scroll toes and casters, 54.5in (138cm).
$1,800-2,700

A Regency rosewood centre table in the manner of George Bullock, the tip-up top inlaid in cut brass with a wide band of stylised ivy leaves, the altered baluster stem on a concave sided platform with splayed legs inlaid with brass stars and stringing, ending in brass casters, 50in (127cm) diam.
$3,600-5,500

A mahogany centre table, c1830, **$720-1,000**

An Aesthetic Movement gilt incised rosewood centre table, attributed to Gustave Herter, New York, with black circular marble top above a frieze decorated with gilt trailing ivy, on circular leaf carved standard, with circular feet, c1860, 19.5in (50cm) diam.
$6,500-8,000

A mahogany centre table, with gadrooned edge and faceted baluster shaft, on platform with paw feet, mid-19thC, 45in (114cm) diam.
$1,800-2,700

A mahogany centre table, top inset with various specimen marbles, on baluster turned shaft and 4 splayed legs with scroll feet, mid-19thC, adapted, 26in (66cm) diam.
$1,800-2,700

A Burmese hardwood centre table, the tip-up top with egg-and-dart moulded edge and pierced foliate frieze, on lotus carved baluster turned shaft, on quadripartite platform with scroll feet, mid-19thC, 60in (152cm) diam.
$2,700-3,600

A mid-Victorian walnut, marquetry and ormolu mounted centre table, with cross-banding and floral border, on cabriole legs with gilt clasps trailing to sabots, 42in (107cm) wide.
$2,700-3,600

A late Victorian satinwood and marquetry centre table, inlaid overall with beaded banding, the top centred by a sun-burst with radiating fan pattern and green stained demi-lunes, the frieze with 2 drawers and 4 simulated drawers, reconstructed and adapted from an earlier table, 2 legs re-supported, 54in (137cm) diam.
$10,000-12,000

An Italian rosewood and marquetry table, the top centred by a floral spray within a leafy border, the paterae inlaid frieze including a drawer at one end, on ebonised fluted turned legs, restored, 23.5in (60cm) wide.
$2,700-3,600

A Milanese ebonised centre table, decorated overall with ivory and bone intarsia panels, on square tapering supports with moulded plinth bases, joined by a platform stretcher, damaged, mid-19thC, 55in (140cm) wide.
$2,700-3,600

An Italian walnut centre table, with inlaid marble top and carved border, the tripartite base carved with masks and foliate scrolls, on paw feet, 19thC, 36in (91.5cm) diam. **$1,200-1,700**

A Victorian burr walnut centre table, the quarter veneered tip-up top inlaid with floral swags and motifs, the baluster stem and 4 splayed legs carved with foliage, the toes inlaid with flowers and on casters, 63.5in (161cm) diam. **$2,700-3,600**

A Napoleon III rosewood, ebonised and marquetry centre table, banded with amboyna inner border above waved floral inlaid apron, on cabriole legs with gilt sabots, one sabot missing, 41.5in (105cm) wide. **$2,700-3,600**

A centre table, the top raised on fluted central pillar and 4 subsidiary pillars, the scroll feet with knop surmounts and recessed brass casters, 62in (157cm) diam. **$21,000-27,000**

A Continental centre table, ebonised, with inlaid designs in bone, 19thC. **$720-1,000**

Console Tables

A pair of Italian giltwood demi-lune console tables, with marble veneered tops, early 19thC, 29.5in (75cm). **$2,700-3,600**

A Regency walnut console table with brocatelle marble top, on pieds-de-biches, repaired, 38.5in (98cm). **$3,600-5,500**

A stained wood and gesso console table in the Neo-Classical style with black marble top, oak leaf and acorn frieze, lion monopodia supports and mirrored back, 57in (144.5cm). **$3,600-5,500**

A Louis XVI white painted and parcel-gilt console table, with red and grey veined fossil marble top above a pierced frieze with scrolling foliage centred by a flowerhead, possibly Italian, re-gilt, 32in (81cm). **$2,700-3,600**

A Sheraton style painted semi-eliptical console table, the top centred by a scene of cherubs riding on fishes, contained in a reserve hung by swags and ribbon from a pole, the frieze fluted and decorated with rosettes, on turned fluted legs, united by a concave sided undertier, 19thC, 39.5in (100cm) wide. **$2,700-3,600**

Dining Tables

A Federal mahogany two-part extension dining table, Boston, on baluster and ring turned tapering reeded legs with brass cup feet and casters, and 2 leaves, c1800, 99in (251cm) long when extended.
$6,000-8,000

A Federal mahogany two-part dining table, Philadelphia, with crossbanded apron, on ring turned and tapering reeded legs and ball turned and tapering feet, repaired, c1800, 93in (236cm) long.
$10,000-12,000

A Federal grain painted birchwood drop leaf dining table, New England, painted and grained all over in brown and black on a varnished ground, early 19thC, 36in (915cm) long.
$2,000-3,000

A carved mahogany two-part dining table, Philadelphia, with acanthus carved animal paw feet on brass casters, minor repairs, c1830, 90in (229cm) long when extended.
$5,000-6,000

Display Tables

An Edwardian mahogany inlaid and crossbanded vitreen table, glass cracked, 24in (61cm).
$720-1,000

A pair of gilt-metal mounted mahogany display tables of Louis XVI style, enclosing a velvet lined interior, with panelled sides on fluted turned tapering legs and toupie feet, both locked, one with one foot replaced in wood, c1900, 31.5in (80cm). **$3,600-5,500**

An Edwardian mahogany vitreen table, inlaid with brass, 26in (66cm) wide. **$720-1,000**

Dressing Tables

A dressing table which is part of a mid-Victorian coromandel and amboyna banded ebonised bedroom suite.
$3,600-5,500

An English mahogany veneered bowfront dressing table, the top inlaid with stringing, ivory escutcheons and chased brass bail handles, on swept bracket feet, late 18thC, 43in (109cm).
$7,000-9,000

Dropleaf Tables

A Victorian inlaid rosewood occasional table, the pair of drop-leaves opening to form an oval top above a deep frieze and standing on square tapering supports joined by an under platform, 26.5in (67cm). **$1,200-1,700**

A small Georgian mahogany dropleaf Pembroke table, fitted with 2 small drawers and 2 dummy drawers with brass knob handles, on bobbin turned legs with brass casters, one missing, damaged, 30in (76cm) extended. **$720-1,000**

A Victorian burr walnut and scrolling marquetry inlaid combined games and work table, the top enclosing an inlaid backgammon and chess board above a fitted frieze drawer, 27in (69cm) wide. **$2,700-3,600**

Games Tables

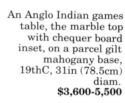

A Victorian figured and carved walnut work and games table, the hinged top inlaid for chess, backgammon and cribbage, with fitted drawer and well below, 23in (59cm). **$1,200-1,700**

An Anglo Indian games table, the marble top with chequer board inset, on a parcel gilt mahogany base, 19thC, 31in (78.5cm) diam. **$3,600-5,500**

An early Victorian inlaid marble chess top table, bordered with bands of coloured geometric and leaf motifs, on burr walnut triform stem with carved base and scroll feet, with plate glass protector, 36in (91.5cm) diam. **$7,000-9,000**

> **Miller's is a price GUIDE not a price LIST**

A Victorian walnut combined games and work table, inlaid throughout with arabesques and stringing, the fold-over top revealing backgammon and chessboards, the frieze drawer above a solid well, on turned end supports with splayed bases joined by a turned stretcher, c1865, 24in (61cm). **$2,700-3,600**

A Syrian parquetry and mother-of-pearl inlaid games table, the swivelling hinged lid with baize lined interior flanked by counter compartments, hinged to reveal backgammon and chess boards on 4 angled faceted uprights joined by a spindle turned upright on 4 splayed legs, late 19thC, 36in (92cm). **$2,700-3,600**

A games table, the mahogany veneered reversible top with counter wells and baize one side, the veneered frieze with slides and small drawers, centred with a scallop shell, on shell carved cabriole legs to claw and ball feet, 31.5in (80cm). **$3,600-5,500**

Library Tables

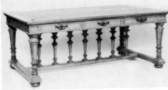

A Victorian light oak library table, each side with 3 drawers, each end with a tooled leather lined writing slide, on spiral turned and carved legs with low 'H' stretchers, 72in (182.5cm).
$3,600-5,500

A Regency rosewood library table inlaid with brass stylised foliate motifs and paterae mouldings, on converging C-shaped end-standards and scroll legs joined by a turned stretcher, with paper trade label, Edwards and Roberts, Upholstery Warehouses, Wardour St, London, 48in (122cm).
$7,000-9,000

A William IV mahogany partners library table, with rounded leather lined top above 2 frieze drawers to either side and beaded frieze on reeded tapering legs, stamped W. Priest, 17 & 24 Water St., Blackfriars labelled Priest's Temple Furniture Mart. 17 & 24 Water Street, Bridge Street, Blackfriars, City, Established for the sale of Superior New and Secondhand Furniture and Office Fittings. Improved Fire-Proof Safes, Doors, Chests....SH and Deed Boxes, 60in (152cm).
$3,600-5,500

William Priest, an Auctioneer and Appraiser, is recorded at this address between 1837-1839; it is probable that he marked secondhand items which were then sold from his warehouse premises.

A William IV rosewood library table, the moulded top lined in gilt tooled black leather with key pattern border with 4 frieze drawers, on solid end standards applied with scrolling volutes and joined by a turned stretcher, on bar and bun feet, 54in (137cm).
$3,600-5,500

A late Victorian walnut library table, with moulded leather lined top, on carved arched supports and twin column end standards with scrolling bar bases joined by a stretcher, 88.5in (224cm) extended.
$2,700-3,600

A William IV rosewood library table, with 2 flush frieze drawers, the leaf scroll volute feet with inset casters, 57in (144.5cm).
$1,800-2,700

A mid Victorian mahogany partners' library table, with leather lined top above 8 frieze drawers, on reeded tapering legs, 96in (244cm).
$7,000-9,000

Nests of Tables

An early Victorian mahogany library table, with rectangular top above 2 frieze drawers and 2 false drawers with a pendant finial at each corner, on pierced spindle turned and scroll carved standard ends joined by a lotus carved inverted U-shaped stretcher, on dual scroll feet, 66in (168cm).
$3,600-5,500

A set of George IV rosewood quartetto tables, the largest table with D-shaped lidded side compartments for chess pieces, the second table top inlaid with a chess board, raised on turned legs united by a turned stretcher, 27in (68cm).
$7,000-9,000

A nest of 4 George III style thuyawood occasional tables, the ebonised beading within tulipwood crossbanding, on simulated bamboo legs and ebony strung splayed feet, largest table 19.5in (49cm).
$1,800-2,700

A nest of 4 George III style mahogany occasional tables, the crossbanded fiddle-back tops centred by an oval flame veneered panel within a band of beading, on simulated bamboo end supports and splayed feet, damaged, c1910, largest table 20in (50cm).
$2,700-3,600

A nest of black lacquered and burr walnut tables, with inlaid satinwood and triangular patterned side stringing, 19thC, largest table 23in (58.5cm).
$1,800-2,700

Occasional Tables

An Easter hardwood occasional table, with front and rear single drawer, on 8 legs richly inlaid with floral patterned bone decoration, 19thC, 24in (61cm).
$720-1,000

A Federal turned curly maple tilt-top candlestand, probably New York State, with tripod base on spade feet, c1820, 22in (56cm) wide.
$2,000-3,000

An Edwardian occasional table, on 4 legs with crossed supports, 24in (61cm) diam.
$360-540

A hand carved Indian table, the top one piece of solid teak, 19thC, 28in (71cm) square.
$360-540

A walnut octagonal inlaid table, 31in (79cm) diam.
$720-1,000

A mahogany snap top occasional table, on vase pedestal and tripod, with felted cover for the top, 28in (71cm) diam.
$360-540

A Queen Anne mahogany and birchwood candlestand, New England, on cabriole legs with snake feet, damaged, c1770, 18in (46cm) diam.
$1,000-1,500

A Dutch satinwood occasional table, with parquetry tilt-top pierced brass gallery, on tripod base, top and base possibly associated, c1800, 25.5in (65cm) diam.
$1,800-2,700

A mahogany snap top occasional table, with pie-crust top, on vase pedestal and tripod, 21in (53cm) diam.
$360-540

A French occasional table, 2nd Empire period, 32in (81cm).
$360-540

Pembroke Tables

A mahogany pedestal Pembroke table with plain top, real and dummy frieze drawers on a turned bulbous stem with quatrefoil base, on 4 fluted curving legs, ending in lion paw casters, 19thC, 40in (101.5cm).
$720-1,000

A carved curly maple tilt-top candlestand, New York State, possibly Albany, the oblong top with scalloped edge, the legs carved with acorns and leaves on scrolled feet, c1815, 20.5in (52cm) long.
$3,500-4,500

A late George III mahogany Pembroke table, with tulipwood banded top above a frieze drawer, on square tapering legs, 39in (99cm). **$3,600-5,500**

A Federal inlaid mahogany Pembroke table, New York, with shaped hinged leaves above a single cockbeaded drawer, on reeded tapering legs, vase form feet brass casters, c1805, 46in (117cm) long when extended.
$2,000-3,000

A late George III mahogany Pembroke table, with rosewood banded hinged top and frieze drawer, on square tapering legs, 39in (99cm).
$3,600-5,500

A George III mahogany and rosewood banded Pembroke table by George Simson, with rounded leaves, on square tapering legs headed by satinwood tablets, outlined overall in boxwood stringing, the drawer with George Simson's trade label, 31in (78cm).
$3,600-5,500

George Simson established his own business by 1787 at 19 St Paul's churchyard where he continued trading until 1839. He subscribed to Sheraton's drawing book in 1793 and was included in the list of master cabinet makers in the 'Cabinet Dictionary' in 1803.

A Sheraton style mahogany inlaid Pembroke table, with oval twin flap top, fitted drawer, on square tapering legs and casters, 19thC, 36in (91.5cm) extended.
$360-540

A George III kingwood Pembroke table, with a broad border crossbanded within a narrow satinwood band, crossbanded end drawer, square section tapering legs with collared feet, edge string lines, brass terminals, casters, 32in (81cm). **$7,000-9,000**

Side Tables

A Queen Anne walnut veneered and elm side table, the quarter veneered top with crossbanding and diagonal banding, on square cabriole legs with pointed pad feet, 31in (79cm).
$3,600-5,500

A Queen Anne oyster veneered walnut and elm side table, the top geometrically inlaid in boxwood, on square cabriole legs, restored, 31.5in (79cm).
$2,700-3,600

A mid-Georgian walnut side table, one drawer with compartments and a simulated short drawer to the front, one short drawer with compartments and candle stand to the side, on lappeted club legs and pad feet, 27in (69cm).
$2,700-3,600

A George III mahogany bowfront side table, c1790, 36in (91cm).
$720-1,000

A Cuban George II side table, with a brass plate handle above a bracketed frieze, on plain turned tapering legs and pad feet, 27.5in (70cm).
$1,800-2,700

A walnut side table, with moulded edge, long frieze drawer, on baluster turned legs joined by square stretchers, early 18thC, 33in (84cm).
$1,800-2,700

A burr elm side table, inlaid overall with kingwood featherbanding, on turned feet, late 17thC, 29.5in (75cm).
$3,600-5,500

A Regency D-shaped side table, the top and frieze with rosewood panels, crossbanded with satinwood and inlaid with string borders, 43in (109cm).
$7,000-9,000

A Victorian mahogany side table, fitted with 2 frieze drawers, turned wood handles, on turned legs.
$360-540

An Italian neo-classical giltwood side table, with liver and green marble top, on turned tapering fluted legs filled with chandelles and headed by paterae, on toupie feet, probably Piedmontese, restored, late 18thC, 53.5in (136cm).
$7,000-9,000

A Dutch mahogany and floral marquetry side table, with dished top above 2 end frieze drawers, on cabriole legs and pad feet, the drawers reconstructed, 31in (79cm).
$2,700-3,600

A grey painted and parcel gilt side table, of Empire design, the concave fronted top with foliate scroll ledge back, on winged female monopodia uprights, 50in (127cm).
$1,800-2,700

A Regency mahogany and ebony strung breakfront serving side table, on reeded tapering legs with paw feet, 80in (203cm).
$3,600-5,500

A Dutch mahogany and marquetry half-round side table, inlaid overall, on square tapering legs, late 18th/early 19thC, 32in (81cm).
$1,200-1,700

A walnut veneered side table, with panels of oyster veneers, oak lining on side liners, spiral twist legs with a shaped stretcher rail, inlaid parquetry 3 pointed stars in ivory, on bun feet, possibly North Italian, 70in (178cm).
$7,000-9,000

Sofa Tables

A mahogany and ebony strung sofa table, on ring turned uprights and dual splayed legs joined by a stretcher, reduced in size, early 19thC, 39.5in (100cm).
$1,800-2,700

A Sheraton period faded rosewood veneered sofa table, banded in satinwood with stringing, the frieze with 2 mahogany lined drawers with brass knob handles, the reverse with dummy drawers, on stretchered trestle ends and splay legs, the brass sabots on casters, c1800, 39in (99cm).
$10,000-12,000

A Regency mahogany sofa table, with rosewood crossbanded top, 2 drawers and 2 false drawers outlined with ebony, on splayed and reeded legs with paterae and brass casters, 61in (155cm).
$3,600-5,500

A rosewood sofa table, on square end standards and spade feet joined by a turned stretcher, adapted, 19thC and later, 57in (145cm).
$1,800-2,700

A Regency brass inlaid rosewood sofa table, the top with 2 frieze drawers, on shaped centre pillar support and umbrella base, with casters, 56.5in (143cm) when extended.
$3,600-5,500

A George IV mahogany sofa table, with crossbanded top, on moulded and hipped sabre legs, c1825, 58in (147cm) when open.
$2,700-3,600

A Regency mahogany pedestal sofa table, with rectangular twin flap top and frieze drawer, on baluster turned shaft and 4 channelled splayed legs, 40in (102cm).
$1,800-2,700

A Regency mahogany and ebony strung pedestal sofa table, with hinged top, on baluster turned shaft and 4 splayed legs, the drawer with label Lord Addington, '7 Gabels', Addington, Nr Winslow, Bucks, 41in (104cm).
$1,800-2,700

A Regency mahogany and calamander crossbanded sofa table, fitted with 2 drawers to one side opposing side with dummies, applied with anthemion decorated brass mounts, 63in (160cm). **$7,000-9,000**

A late Regency rosewood and brass inlaid sofa table, with 2 frieze drawers opposing dummies, on drum feet and casters, allover profusely inlaid with cut brass in a formal floral and foliate design, original turned handles available, 59.5in (151cm) when extended. **$3,600-5,500**

A Regency rosewood sofa table, with satinwood and foliate scroll marquetry inlay, on an inverted tapering octagonal column with concave holly wood banding, brass claw terminals and casters, 61in (155cm) when extended. **$3,600-5,500**

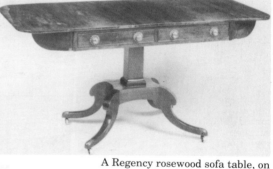

A Regency rosewood sofa table, on a rectangular shaft and inverted quadripartite platform base with hipped splayed legs, extensive restorations, 60in (152cm). **$1,200-1,700**

A George III mahogany sofa table, crossbanded in satinwood, above a pair of real drawers opposing a pair of dummies, with brass box casters, restored, 24in (61cm). **$1,200-1,700**

Use the Index

Because certain items might fit easily into any number of categories, the quickest and surest method of locating any entry is by reference to the index at the back of the book.

This has been fully cross-referenced for absolute simplicity.

A Regency mahogany sofa table, with twin flap top crossbanded in kingwood and edged with gadrooning, the panelled frieze with 2 mahogany lined drawers, 56in (142cm). **$3,600-5,500**

A George IV figured rosewood veneered sofa table, inlaid satinwood and burr wood stringing and banding, gilt brass stamped handles and inlaid brass stringing, the turned stem with a cast gilt brass egg-and-dart moulding, the 4 shaped top splay legs with brass paw sabots, on casters, the twin flaps with restoration, 35in (89cm). **$7,000-9,000**

Sutherland Tables

A mahogany Sutherland table on turned legs and stretchers, mid-19thC, 33in (84cm).
$720-1,000

A Victorian rosewood and simulated rosewood Sutherland table, on tapering turned end supports with down-turned feet joined by pole stretchers, 42in (106.5cm).
$1,000-1,500

A Victorian mahogany double tier Sutherland table, lower tier 30in (76cm) extended.
$360-540

A Victorian burr walnut miniature Sutherland table with carved dual stretchers and turned supports, 21in (53cm).
$720-1,000

A Victorian walnut Sutherland table with quarter veneered burr walnut oval top, spiral turned baluster end supports, on splayed legs with scroll toes and casters, 42in (106.5cm).
$1,000-1,500

Tea Tables

A red walnut semi-circular folding tea table, early 18thC, 30in (76cm).
$1,200-1,700

An inlaid mahogany semi-circular folding tea table, on double fly-leg action, late 18thC, 35in (89cm).
$1,200-1,700

A George II mahogany fold-over top table, with well interior, fitted single swinging leg, supported on 5 cabriole legs, the front with carved shell and swag motifs and shaped brackets, all supported on pad feet, top restored, 35in (89cm).   **$3,600-5,500**

A George III mahogany tea table, on chamfered beaded square legs, restored, 35in (89cm).
$2,700-3,600

A Chippendale mahogany tea table, New York or Philadelphia, on cabriole legs and claw-and-ball feet, underside now painted brown, restored, c1750, 30in (76cm) long.
$26,500-28,000

In the Furniture section if there is only one measurement it usually refers to the width of the piece.

A pair of Regency oak window seats, restored, c1815. **$13,000-15,500**

A Charles II oak box seat joint stool, c1680. **$3,600-4,500**

An oak boarded chest, late 16thC, 39in (99cm). **$2,000-2,500**

A Jacobean fruitwood inlaid and carved oak tester bedstead, 17thC and later, 103in (261cm) long. **$28,000-32,000**

A mid-Georgian oak bookcase. **$6,500-8,000**

A Charles I carved oak armchair, mid-17thC. **$4,000-4,500**

A James I oak open armchair, some replacements. **$10,000-11,000**

A George III oak bureau, the fall revealing stationery compartments, c1760. **$2,200-3,600**

A Charles I oak coffer, c1620, 48in (122cm). **$3,600-4,600**

A George II oak chair, c1670. **$1,500-2,000**

A George I oak bureau bookcase, c1720, 37.5in (95cm). **$10,000-11,000**

A late Elizabethan oak X-frame chair. **$8,000-9,000**

A mahogany crossbanded and inlaid oak low dresser, mid-18thC. **$3,000-5000**

An English oak low cupboard, restorations, late 17thC, 23in (59cm). **$3,200-4,000**

A Dutch oak cupboard, with ebony enrichments, mid-17thC, 72in (182cm). **$16,500-20,000**

A German carved oak chest, c1600, 74in (188cm). **$6,000-6,500**

A Queen Anne oak chest of drawers, c1710. **$3,500-5,500**

A William III carved oak press cupboard, altered, c1700, 69in (175cm). **$3,500-4,500**

A Continental carved oak cupboard, early 19thC. **$320-360**

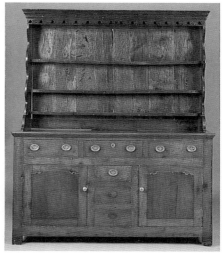

An early Georgian oak low dresser. **$12,000-14,500**

A North Wales oak dresser, in 2 sections, mid-18thC, 64in (162.5cm). **$14,500-18,000**

A Charles II oak refectory table, with four-plank top, c1660, 100in (254cm). **$15,500-17,500**

A George IV oak double-sided library table, with a slide at either end, c1820. **$6,500-8,000**

A George III oak dresser, with matching plate rack, 65.5in (166cm). **$6,500-7,000**

A George III oak dresser, restored, c1780. **$3,600-4,500**

A George III oak dresser, c1780, 73in (185cm). **$7,000-9,000**

A George III inlaid oak Welsh dresser, the back of the upper section of later date. **$10,000-14,500**

A Charles II walnut, elm and ash hanging cupboard, restored, 33in (84cm). **$7,000-9,000**

A Charles I oak armchair, restored. **$2,200-3,200**

An Anglo-Flemish oak cupboard, in 2 parts, c1680. **$4,500-5,500**

A pair of William IV oak card tables. **$6,500-7,500**

A Charles I carved oak credence table, the fold-over top with rear gateleg, c1640, 35in (89cm). **$5,500-6,500**

Paul Hopwell Antiques

Early English Oak

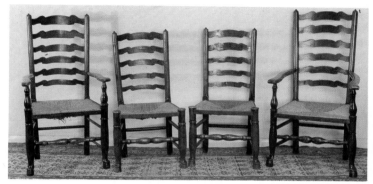

Top: A set of eight (four showing) Georgian ash wavyline ladderback dining chairs. Excellent colour, condition and patination. English c1800.

Centre: A rare George II oak dresser base with a superb arched moulded apron. Standing on cabriole legs with spade feet. Good colour and patination. English c1745.

Bottom: A superb 18th century dresser in oak. Excellent condition, colour and patination. N. Wales c1770.

Furniture restoration service available

30 High Street, West Haddon, Northamptonshire NN6 7AP
Tel: (0788) 510636

A George III mahogany breakfront library bookcase, the lower part cut in 2 parts, c1770, 111in (282cm). **$23,000-27,000**

A George III four-poster bed, with painted cornice, 77.5in (197cm). **$16,500-18,0000**

A George III mahogany tester bedstead, adapted, c1760, 76in (193cm) long. **$33,000-36,000**

A George III mahogany breakfront library secrétaire bookcase, 91in (231cm). **$16,500-20,000**

A Queen Anne bureau bookcase, 19thC decoration. **$29,000-32,000**

A George III mahogany breakfront library bookcase, the cornice with serpentine pediment, c1770, 97in (246cm). **$40,000-45,000**

A Queen Anne bureau bookcase. **$32,000-36,000**

A Second Empire mahogany and ormolu mounted lit en bateau, feet adapted, 91.5in (232cm) long. **$9,000-10,000**

A George III satinwood secrétaire bookcase, the lower part with a fitted secrétaire drawer, c1790, 33.5in (85cm). **$54,000-57,500**

A mahogany and cream painted four-poster bed, part 18thC, 78in (198cm). **$6,500-7,000**

A mid-Victorian mahogany bookcase. **$8,000-10,000**

A George I elm bureau,
c1730.
$15,500-18,000

A George I walnut bureau,
c1725, 41in (104cm).
$8,000-9,000

A Louis XVI ormolu mounted bois satine
bonheur du jour. **$9,000-10,000**

A William and Mary
marquetry bureau, restored.
$12,000-14,500

An early Georgian walnut and burr
walnut bureau, inlaid with
featherbanding, extensively restored and
re-veneered. **$4,500-5,500**

A William and Mary stained
burr elm bureau, banded in
walnut.
$5,500-7,000

A French tulipwood,
parquetry and ormolu
mounted bonheur du
jour.
$12,000-16,500

A George III
bonheur du jour.
$6,500-7,000

A Louis XVI bonheur du
jour.
$60,000-63,000

A Dutch marquetry bureau,
c1770 and later.
$12,000-14,500

A Dutch mahogany and
marquetry bureau, c1780,
marquetry possibly later.
$10,000-14,500

A George II burr elm
bureau, with chequer
stringing, c1750.
$6,500-9,000

A Dutch marquetry bureau,
mid-18thC and later.
$11,000-14,500

An Italian lacca povera bureau, the sloping front enclosing a fitted interior, mid-18thC, 41in (103cm). **$13,000-15,500**

A Portuguese rococo jacaranda bureau, the panelled and carved lid enclosing a fitted interior, 45in (114cm). **$11,000-14,500**

An Edwardian inlaid satinwood and crossbanded cylinder bureau, 42in (107cm). **$9,500-10,000**

A French gilt bronze mounted kingwood free-standing bureau, by Millet of Paris, with 11 drawers and 2 cupboards, 61in (155cm). **$41,500-45,000**

A walnut veneered table bureau, the flap with a book rest and fitted interior, Queen Anne, c1710, 16in (41cm). **$10,000-11,000**

An Italian late Baroque inlaid walnut slant front bureau, with fitted interior, mid-18thC, 50in (127cm). **$18,000-21,000**

An Italian walnut and marquetry bureau, with fitted interior, c1730, 45.5in (115cm). **$75,500-77,500**

A German black and gilt lacquer bureau, with fitted interior, 2 oak lined drawers, on cabriole legs, late 18thC. **$15,500-18,000**

A Louis XIV oyster veneered kingwood and walnut bureau mazarin, the moulded top inlaid with circles and geometric patterns, restored, 30.5in (77cm). **$22,000-24,000**

l. A Louis XVI ormolu mounted mahogany bureau, with fitted interior, c1789, 39.5in (100cm). **$12,500-14,500**

r. A Louis XIV ormolu mounted ebony and amaranth bureau, inlaid in brass and pewter, mid-19thC, 46.5in (118cm). **$72,000-90,000**

A Regency pedestal cupboard, with tambour cupboard, c1805, 15.5in (39cm).
$5,800-6,500

A Regency mahogany pedestal cabinet, each with a pair of panelled and grille filled doors, c1800, 22in (55cm).
$4,500-5,500

A George III serpentine front mahogany side cabinet, in the manner of Thomas Chippendale, the serpentine shaped fielded doors opening to marblized lined sliding shelves, c1775, 47in (119cm) long.
$14,500-16,500

A Regency chinoiserie vitrine, with 2 paper labels PIETRO E GAET.
$58,500-72,000

A pair of Neapolitan painted and parcel gilt display cabinets, mid-18thC.
$6,500-7,000

A Sheraton revival inlaid mahogany and crossbanded display cabinet.
$3,000-3,500

A Venetian red and gilt japanned bureau cabinet, with 2 mirrored doors enclosing fitted interior, mid-18thC.
$60,000-63,000

A Queen Anne walnut bureau cabinet, with fully fitted interior, restored, c1700, 93in (236cm) high.
$40,500-42,500

A George III semi-circular mahogany side cabinet, with crossbanded top and 11 drawers, 35in (89cm) high.
$5,500-6,500

A Victorian inlaid walnut display cabinet, 32in (81cm).
$700-900

A Dutch amboyna display cabinet, the astragal doors enclosing shelves, above 3 long drawers.
$8,000-10,000

An Italian late Baroque scarlet and silver japanned bureau cabinet, with fully fitted interior, mid-18thC, 88in (224cm) high.
$111,500-125,000

A George III mahogany breakfront side cabinet, with 4 central drawers and 1 drawer and a door each side, c1770, 60in (152cm). **$6,500-7,000**

A Goanese rosewood, teak, ebony
and bone inlaid cabinet-on-stand,
late 17thC, 35.5in (90cm).
$32,000-36,000

A William and Mary
walnut and
marquetry cabinet-
on-stand,
reconstructed.
$8,000-10,000

An Augsburg marquetry cabinet,
possibly originally with a fall
front, c1600, 35in (89cm).
$13,000-16,500

A bone, tortoiseshell and ebony
cabinet, Neapolitan or
Spanish, mid-17thC.
$6,000-8,000

A marquetry cabinet, Augsburg or
Ulm, the later conforming stand with
spirally turned legs and waved
stretchers, c1610, 39in (99cm).
$9,000-10,000

A mahogany and
satinwood banded side
cabinet, in the Dutch
manner, c1900, 35in
(89cm).
$4,600-5,500

A Queen Anne walnut cabinet-
on-chest, the doors enclosing a
fitted interior, c1710, 43in
(109cm). **$6,500-8,000**

A pair of George III style bronze mounted
fruitwood inlaid satinwood cabinets, after
a commode attributed to John Cobb.
$20,000-22,500

A Dutch walnut and
marquetry cabinet-on-
stand, adapted.
$12,000-16,500

A boulle and ebonised side
cabinet, c1860, 81in (205.5cm).
$4,500-6,500

An Antwerp painted cabinet,
mounted with repoussé metal
figures, on later ebonised stand
with cabriole legs, 42in (105cm).
$25,000-28,000

A late George III mahogany canterbury, c1810, 18in (46cm). **$3,500-4,500**

A George III mahogany armchair, in French Hepplewhite style, c1770. **$3,000-4,000**

A pair of George II style mahogany library armchairs, with 18thC needlepoint upholstery, on acanthus carved cabriole legs with claw-and-ball feet. **$33,000-36,000**

A George II mahogany library armchair, with cabochon cabriole front legs, c1750. **$6,500-7,000**

A late George III mahogany plate canterbury, 25.5in (64cm) long. **$8,000-9,000**

A Queen Anne walnut shepherd's crook armchair, with needlepoint upholstery, restored, and a similar chair of a later date. **$13,000-17,500**

An early George III mahogany library armchair, covered in tan leather, with moulded arm supports and moulded chamfered legs. **$6,500-7,000**

r. A George IV mahogany canterbury, with a drawer at one end, c1820, 18in (46cm). **$2,800-3,600**

A pair of George III mahogany armchairs, with stuffed backs, arms and seat, c1770. **$7,000-9,000**

A pair of George III mahogany library armchairs, with later needlework covers, c1765. **$19,000-10,000**

A pair of George III mahogany open armchairs, in the French manner, covered in associated 18thC Aubusson tapestry, restored. **$29,000-32,000**

A Regency mahogany plate canterbury, c1820, 25in (63cm). **$4,500-5,500**

A pair of George III mahogany armchairs, c1780.
$18,000-20,000

A set of 9 George III mahogany chairs, c1770.
$7,000-8,000

An early George III carved mahogany armchair, with flower carved arms and supports, c1760.
$5,500-7,000

A pair of giltwood fauteuils, with carved moulded channelled frames, with clasp cresting and centres to the seat rails, on cabriole legs stamped, BAUVE.
$22,000-27,000

A George II carved mahogany armchair, with later wool floral needlework, c1750.
$11,000-12,000

A pair of George III mahogany armchairs, c1770.
$8,200-10,000

A matched pair of Anglo-Dutch mahogany metamorphic wing-backed open armchairs, each with hinged back and seat, in later leather covers, opening to a daybed, restored, mid-18thC, 84in (213cm) long extended.
$38,000-42,000

A George II carved mahogany armchair, in the style of Thomas Chippendale, with drop-in seat, on carved cabriole front legs with claw-and-ball feet, c1755.
$17,500-19,000

A Louis XIV Franco-Flemish armchair, covered in painted leather, c1680.
$6,500-8,000

A Regency mahogany metamorphic library armchair/steps, in the manner of Morgan and Sanders, c1810.
$8,000-9,000

A set of 6 satinwood and painted open armchairs, each splat painted with a mythological figure, restored.
$18,000-21,000

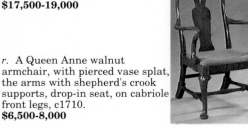

r. A Queen Anne walnut armchair, with pierced vase splat, the arms with shepherd's crook supports, drop-in seat, on cabriole front legs, c1710.
$6,500-8,000

A Regency mahogany
library bergère, repaired.
$28,000-30,500

A George I walnut needle-
point wing armchair, repaired
c1720. **$57,500-63,000**

A pair of early George III mahogany
armchairs, with carved and pierced
splats. **$18,000-21,000**

A walnut wing armchair,
one foot spliced, labelled.
$13,000-16,500

A George I wing
armchair, some
restoration.
$5,500-6,500

A George III
mahogany framed
and buttoned
leather porter's
armchair, c1780.
$4,500-5,500

A George III mahogany
wing armchair, c1770.
$5,500-7,000

A Queen Anne walnut
wing armchair, restored.
$16,500-20,000

A pair of mid-Victorian
ebonised spoonback
chairs. **$6,500-7,000**

A set of 9 George III mahogany
dining chairs, c1790.
$17,500-19,000

A set of 6 Regency chinoiserie
japanned armchairs, with caned seats,
c1805. **$25,000-27,000**

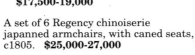

A George II walnut
armchair, c1750.
$2,600-3,600

COLOUR REVIEW

A George II mahogany wing armchair, with carved front cabriole legs, c1730.
$16,500-18,000

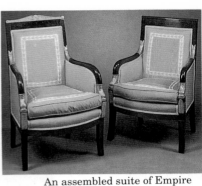

A pair of walnut bergères, with channelled cabriole legs, restored.
$7,000-9,000

An assembled suite of Empire mahogany and parcel gilt seat furniture, early 19thC, 3 pieces.
$8,000-10,000

A Louis XV white painted and gilded bergère, stamped I.B. Boulard.
$14,500-16,500

A Regency caned mahogany bergère, with anthemion carved toprail, scrolled arms and leaf carved front legs, c1815.
$12,000-14,500

A pair of ormolu mounted mahogany bergères, the moulded frames mounted with entrelac, very distressed cover, late 19thC. **$22,000-27,000**

A William IV mahogany bergère, in leather cover, c1830.
$6,500-7,000

A Queen Anne walnut easy chair, probably Rhode Island, c1770, 48in (122cm) high.
$42,000-45,000

A set of 8 walnut dining chairs, with velvet seat covers, extensively restored, part 18thC.
$22,000-27,000

l. A George IV caned mahogany library bergère, with panelled frame and circular reeded front legs, c1825.
$4,600-6,500

230

A set of 8 rosewood and gilt chairs, with curule legs set with bosses, c1810. **$24,000-28,000**

A set of 14 Regency mahogany dining chairs, with curved toprail and crossbar, c1825. **$16,500-17,500**

A set of 12 George III style mahogany 'Gothick' dining chairs, by Edwards & Roberts. **$28,000-30,000**

A set of 14 mahogany dining chairs, with cabriole legs. **$25,000-27,000**

A pair of Piedmontese giltwood chairs, with curved backs. **$16,500-17,500**

A pair of George III mahogany hall chairs, c1805. **$2,700-3,600**

A pair of George II mahogany hall armchairs, with solid shell shaped seats, on cabriole front and raked back legs, 40in (101cm) high. **$65,000-70,000**

A set of 4 George II walnut side chairs, on cabriole legs with later eagle-head brackets, restored, c1745. **$36,000-45,000**

A pair of George II mahogany hall chairs, c1766. **$7,000-9,000**

A George III mahogany library bergère chair, c1780. **$6,000-7,000**

A set of 6 mahogany dining chairs, c1815. **$4,500-5,000**

A set of 8 grained rosewood and gilt dining chairs, c1810. **$21,000-23,000**

A pair of George I style walnut dining chairs. **$800-900**

231

A George I burr walnut tallboy, with chevron and crossbanding, c1720, 70.5in (179cm) high. **$18,500-21,000**

An early Georgian walnut chest-on-chest, 69.5in (176cm) high. **$10,000-12,000**

A walnut and marquetry chest-on-stand, late 17thC and later, 48.5in (123cm) high. **$7,500-9,500**

A William & Mary japanned chest-on-stand. **$7,000-10,000**

A William & Mary oyster veneered walnut and marquetry chest, on later bun feet, 37.5in (95cm). **$9,500-10,500**

A Queen Anne walnut veneered chest, with pine sides, c1710. **$3,600-4,500**

A George II walnut veneered tallboy, c1730, 69in (175cm) high. **$11,000-13,000**

A George III mahogany chest, on scroll bracket feet, c1760, 36in (92cm). **$7,000-9,000**

A George III mahogany chest-on-chest. **$17,000-18,500**

A George I inlaid burr walnut bachelor's chest, restored. **$9,500-10,500**

l. A William & Mary walnut and marquetry chest-on-stand, with elaborate floral inlay, 2 short and 3 long drawers, the stand with an inlaid drawer, restored, c1690, 51in (129cm) high. **$28,000-32,000**

A George I walnut bachelor's chest, in feather banded wood, c1720, 36in (92cm). **$30,000-36,000**

A German walnut chest of drawers, with 4 long drawers and cabriole feet, c1740, 36in (92cm). **$20,000-22,000**

A parcel gilt walnut chest, North German or Danish, mid-18thC, later marble top, 34.5in (87cm). **$36,000-40,000**

An Irish Georgian mahogany blanket chest-on-stand, the stand with 2 drawers and a carved apron, cabriole front legs with claw feet, mid-18thC. **$4,500-6,000**

A pair of George III serpentine mahogany chests, c1770, 44in (111cm). **$9,500-11,000**

A mahogany veneered chest, on turned feet, mid-19thC, 13.5in (34cm). **$270-360**

A Victorian mahogany military chest, with recessed handles, on turned legs. **$1,800-2,200**

A Hepplewhite period yew wood secrétaire chest. **$14,500-16,500**

A Genoese walnut chest, the 4 panelled drawers with cherub head handles, with carved decoration, late 17thC, 60.5in (153cm). **$16,500-18,000**

A walnut and crossbanded chest, on later cabriole feet, possibly Swedish, c1720, 28in (72cm). **$14,500-16,000**

A Regency mahogany bowfront chest, c1800, 28.5in (72cm). **$3,600-4,500**

A Wellington chest, early 20thC, 42in (107cm) high. **$650-720**

A German parquetry chest, with serpentine front, 3 long drawers, carved projecting corners and paw feet, mid-18thC, 43in (109cm). **$12,000-14,500**

An Italian walnut chest of drawers, of inverted breakfront form, with panelled top and 4 long drawers, 35in (90cm). **$9,000-10,000**

A satinwood serpentine commode, crossbanded overall in amaranth, with one mahogany lined and 3 cedar lined drawers, on splayed bracket feet, restored, 41in (104cm).
$7,500-9,000

A George III pair of semi-circular harewood commodes, crossbanded in satinwood, c1780, 33in (84cm) high.
$9,000-10,000

A Louis XV ormolu mounted kingwood and tulipwood marquetry commode, mid-18thC, 31in (78.5cm).
$16,500-18,000

A Louis XV ormolu mounted tulipwood parquetry commode, with marble top, signed M. Criard, 34in (86cm).
$9,000-10,000

A George II mahogany chest of drawers, c1755, 38.5in (98cm).
$5,500-7,000

A pair of George III sycamore, rosewood and tulipwood inlaid satinwood commodes, on moulded plinths, composed in part of 18thC elements, 50in (127cm) long.
$33,000-36,000

A French Louis XV kingwood serpentine commode, with moulded breccia marble top, 2 drawers veneered with end-cut marquetry and overlaid with acanthus, alterations, c1750, 55in (139cm). **$22,000-24,000**

A Louis XV ormolu mounted tulipwood commode, signed P. Roussel, JME, mid-18thC.
$9,500-11,000

A Louis XV ormolu mounted amaranth and marquetry bombé commode, restored, stamped J.C. ELLEAUME JME.
$11,000-13,000

A George III marble top inlaid satinwood and harewood demi-lune commode, with marble top. **$10,000-12,000**

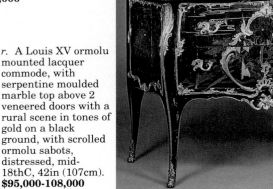

r. A Louis XV ormolu mounted lacquer commode, with serpentine moulded marble top above 2 veneered doors with a rural scene in tones of gold on a black ground, with scrolled ormolu sabots, distressed, mid-18thC, 42in (107cm).
$95,000-108,000

A painted and lacca povera commode, with a marble top, Southern French or North Italian, mid-18thC.
$40,000-45,000

A North Italian walnut inlaid commode, c1790, 49in (124cm). **$27,000-29,000**

A Louis XVI tulipwood commode, with grey marble top, c1780, 44in (111cm). **$10,000-12,000**

An early George III serpentine fronted mahogany chest, the top with gadrooned edge, c1760, 44in (111cm). **$14,500-18,000**

A George III satinwood and marquetry demi-lune commode, c1775. **$235,000-245,000**

A Louis XV ormolu mounted tulipwood, kingwood and fruitwood marquetry commode. **$50,000-54,000**

A pair of German rococo walnut and tulipwood commodes. **$140,000-150,000**

A German rococo brass mounted kingwood commode, with marble top, restored. **$14,500-16,500**

An Italian marquetry commode, c1830, 52in (132cm). **$7,000-10,000**

A Louis XV/XVI ormolu mounted tulipwood and fruitwood marquetry commode, with marble top, signed M.B.Evald, late 18thC, 37in (94cm). **$15,000-18,000**

A French mahogany commode, after the model by Beneman and Stockel, locked shut, c1910. **$11,000-14,500**

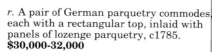

r. A pair of German parquetry commodes, each with a rectangular top, inlaid with panels of lozenge parquetry, c1785. **$30,000-32,000**

A satinwood davenport, English, c1830, 22in (26cm). **$4,500-5,500**

A George IV mahogany writing desk, c1820, 36in (91cm). **$5,500-6,500**

A Victorian walnut kidney shaped desk, with moulded top and 8 drawers, c1840, 51.5in (131cm). **$18,000-27,000**

A George IV mahogany Carlton House desk, with hinged bookrest above 3 drawers and turned legs, c1820, 55in (140cm). **$15,000-16,500**

A George III satinwood and later gilt tambour top writing desk, crossbanded in mahogany, restored, 42.5in (108cm). **$7,000-9,000**

A George IV rosewood davenport, inlaid overall with boxwood lines, 18in (46cm). **$3,600-4,500**

A Franco-Flemish marquetry and ebony kneehole desk, with 5 small drawers within hinged cover and fall front, 40in (102cm). **$12,000-14,500**

A German rococo walnut and parquetry cylinder desk, on cabriole legs and scroll feet, late 18thC, 47in (119cm). **$15,000-17,000**

A Victorian mahogany partners' desk, with leather lined moulded top above 3 drawers, and 3 drawers in each pedestal, 67.5in (172cm). **$7,000-9,000**

A burr walnut veneered kidney shaped walnut desk, with leather lined top, 7 drawers and ebonised mouldings, 60in (153cm). **$18,000-20,000**

A George II walnut wall mirror, c1730, 30in (75cm) high. **$5,500-7,000**

A George II parcel gilt walnut wall mirror, 31in (79cm) high. **$5,500-6,500**

A William and Mary seaweed marquetry mirror, with bands of scrolling foliage, with a barber's pole moulding, 31.5in (80cm) high. **$7,000-8,000**

A walnut mirror, c1730, 41in (104cm) high. **$3,600-4,500**

A pair of George II giltwood pier mirrors, each with coat-of-arms and eagle's heads, 64in (163cm) high. **$42,000-45,000**

A giltwood and gesso mirror, c1730, 43in (110cm) high. **$10,000-12,000**

A giltwood wall mirror, c1725, 60in (151cm) high. **$7,000-8,000**

A George I giltwood pier mirror, c1715, 49in (124cm) high. **$8,000-9,000**

A George I giltwood wall mirror, with leaf decorated moulded frame, 33in (84cm) high. **$15,000-16,500**

A pair of George II giltwood mirrors in the Kent style, repaired, 76.5in (194cm) high. **$180,000-215,000**

A George I, James Moore style, giltwood wall mirror, 55.5in (141cm) high. **$30,000-35,000**

A Queen Anne giltwood wall mirror, c1710, 36in (90cm) high. **$7,000-8,000**

A George II giltwood
and plaster
overmantel mirror,
c1755.
$9,000-10,000

A George III
giltwood mirror,
restored.
$9,000-10,000

A George II carved giltwood
mirror, c1755, 62in (157cm)
high.
$12,000-14,500

A Scottish giltwood
pier mirror, late
18thC, 67in (170cm)
high.
$21,000-24,000

A pair of George III
giltwood oval mirrors,
each with later plate.
$17,000-20,000

A George II giltwood
wall mirror, c1730,
34in (86cm) high.
$5,500-7,000

A George III giltwood
pier mirror, c1755.
$24,000-28,000

A George III
giltwood mirror.
$18,000-20,000

A pair of Queen Anne
giltwood wall mirrors,
with replaced plates,
c1710, 51in (130cm) high.
$20,000-21,000

A George III giltwood wall
mirror, the frame carved with
rococo scrolls and flowers, c1765,
55.5in (141cm) high.
$10,000-12,000

A pair of George III
giltwood mirrors.
$22,000-24,000

A George II
giltwood wall
mirror, c1730.
$5,500-7,000

A giltwood wall
mirror, c1755.
$12,000-14,500

A Queen Anne
black japanned
toilet mirror,
c1705.
$4,500-5,500

An Italian gilt
framed mirror.
$3,000-4,500

A mahogany shield shaped
box base toilet mirror, with 3
drawers, early 19thC.
$350-450

A Swedish Baroque polychrome
painted dressing mirror, early
18thC, 30.5in (77cm) high.
$40,000-45,000

A Scandinavian ebonised
and tortoiseshell mirror.
$6,000-7,500

A Spanish mirror, c1680, 67.5in
(171cm) high.
$44,000-46,000

A pair of Venetian mirrors, in a
framework of engraved glass panels,
c1700. **$110,000-120,000**

An Irish oval wall
mirror, early 19thC.
$7,000-9,000

A German black and gilt
japanned mirror, early
18thC, 57.5in (146cm) high.
$7,000-10,000

A George III giltwood overmantel
mirror, 48in (122cm) high.
$9,500-10,500

A George II carved grey
painted wall mirror, c1750,
68.5in (173cm) high.
$43,000-45,000

COLOUR REVIEW

A mahogany sideboard, c1780, 66.5in (169cm). **$7,000-8,000**

A satinwood inlaid mahogany sideboard, c1780, 60in (163cm). **$18,000-19,000**

A George III mahogany bowfront sideboard, c1780. **$10,000-12,000**

A George III inlaid sideboard, 18thC, 62in (157cm). **$16,500-18,000**

A George III mahogany sideboard, c1780, 84in (214cm). **$18,000-20,000**

A mahogany serpentine sideboard, remodelled, 18thC, 71in (181cm). **$6,000-9,000**

A George III mahogany bowfront sideboard, c1785, 72in (183cm). **$16,500-18,000**

A George III mahogany sideboard, c1800, 66in (168cm). **$5,500-7,000**

A George III bowfront mahogany sideboard, c1780, 66.5in (169cm). **$9,000-10,000**

A George IV bowed breakfront mahogany sideboard, c1820, 84in (214cm). **$4,500-5,500**

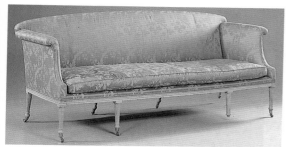

A George III painted sofa, with stuffed back, arms and seat, the beaded frieze on reeded circular legs, 88in (224cm) long. **$3,600-4,500**

A George III mahogany camel back sofa, with stuffed back, arms and seat, Chinese fret legs and stretchers, c1760. **$10,500-12,500**

A George III mahogany sofa, with stuffed back, arms and seat, on 3 square front legs with stretchers, c1770. **$9,500-12,000**

A George II carved mahogany settee, with upholstered back, arms and drop-in seat, mid-18thC, 62in (157cm) long. **$14,500-16,500**

A George III mahogany settee, with needlework upholstery, on stop fluted square chamfered legs, restored, c1770, 96in (246cm) long. **$10,000-12,500**

A George II walnut settee, with out-turned arms terminating in lion's heads, carved cabriole legs, c1740. **$7,000-9,000**

A Queen Anne giltwood sofa, the wing back and out-scrolled arms detachable from the padded seat, restored, c1700, 99in (252cm) long. **$5,500-8,000**

A George II mahogany double chair back settee, restored, c1755, 55in (140cm) long. **$17,000-19,000**

A George III fine carved mahogany sofa, with serpentine back and seat, moulded padded arms and 4 fluted circular front legs, c1780, 81in (205cm) long. **$17,000-20,000**

A Swedish painted and parcel-gilt sofa, perhaps by Ephraim Ståhl, c1810, 92in (233cm) long. **$7,650-10,000**

An Italian neo-classic beechwood settee, with loose cushion seat, on circular tapering stop-fluted legs headed by paterae, 79in (200cm) long. **$7,650-8,500**

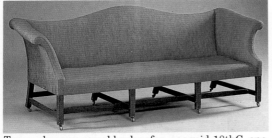

Two mahogany camel back sofas, one mid-18thC, one modern, 86in (218cm) long. **$15,300-17,000**

A carved mahogany couch or window seat, probably Scandinavian, c1830, 94in (238cm) long. **$20,400-22,000**

A suite of giltwood furniture, comprising a sofa and 8 armchairs, with piastre moulded frames, Rome or Turin, c1780, 98in (249cm) long. **$85,000-119,000**

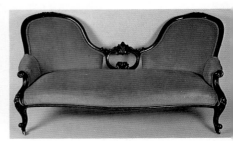

A Victorian walnut double backed settee, with serpentine seat, cabriole legs, scroll feet with ceramic casters. **$1,700-2,500**

An Italian grey painted settle, with putti and a winged angel, late 17thC, 84in (213cm) long. **$24,650-26,350**

A Venetian cream painted and parcel gilt sofa, painted overall with flowers, on cabriole legs, damaged and restored, mid-18thC, 87.5in (222cm) long. **$5,250-6,800**

A Louis XV beechwood marquise, with flower carved moulded frame, cabriole legs, possibly reduced from a sofa, mid-18thC, 34in (86cm). **$6,000-7,650**

A mahogany sofa, covered in yellow silk, with scrolled terminal arms and acanthus headed cabriole legs, 62.5in (159cm). **$7,650-9,350**

A George III mahogany low whatnot, with 3 shelves and slatted ends, the tapering legs with brass caps and casters, c1800, 29.5in (75cm) wide.
$3,400-5,000

A George IV mahogany stick stand, c1820, 28in (71cm).
$8,500-9,350

A George II mahogany two-tier dumb waiter, with revolving tiers, c1760, 35in (89cm) high.
$7,650-9,350

A Regency mahogany two-tier dumb waiter, c1810, 27.5in (70cm) diam.
$5,000-6,000

A George IV mahogany whatnot, with bead and reel turned frame, c1820, 40in (101cm) high.
$4,250-5,000

A George III mahogany whatnot, c1800, 52in (130cm).
$6,000-7,650

A George III mahogany what-not, 60in (152cm).
$3,400-4,250

A George III mahogany dumb waiter, c1780, 46in (117cm) high.
$3,750-5,000

A George IV mahogany four-tier whatnot, with drawer, c1820, 60.5in (154cm) high.
$2,550-3,400

A mahogany four-tier whatnot, with drawer, 19thC.
$950-1,100

A Swiss or Austrian carved wood hall stand, late 19thC, 85in (216cm) high.
$2,000-3,000

COLOUR REVIEW

An Empire giltwood tabouret pliant, on channelled carved X-shaped supports, restored, later seat base, 25.5in (65cm).
$14,450-16,000

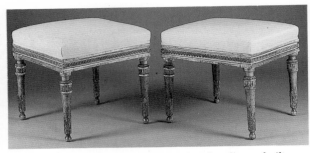

A pair of Italian neo-classic green painted and parcel gilt tabourets, with panelled carved seat rails, on circular tapering legs, both seat rails branded MR, late 18thC.
$17,850-19,550

A painted stool, with Louis-Philippe's inventory mark, LP beneath a crown, c1800.
$4,600-6,300

A pair of Dutch walnut stools, c1720, 17in (43cm).
$19,550-21,250

A Louis XVI painted stool, with loose cushioned seat, c1780, 30.5in (77cm).
$5,000-6,000

A pair of Regency marble mounted parcel gilt rosewood pedestals, c1820, 37in (94cm) high.
$13,600-15,300

A George II style carved and silver painted stool, c1920, 36in (92cm).
$3,750-5,000

A monumental Regency giltwood stool, with needlework covered drop-in seat, leaf carved legs on block bases, damaged, 29in (74cm).
$22,000-23,800

A pair of Empire mahogany tabourets, carved with laurel leaves, joined by baluster shaped stretchers with claw feet, early 19thC, 20in (51cm).
$11,000-12,750

A pair of George II red walnut stools, restored, c1740, 32in (55cm).
$18,700-20,400

A pair of North European white painted and parcel gilt window seats, with cane filled arms and seats, late 18thC.
$4,700-6,400

r. A George II walnut stool, with contemporary embroidery drop-in seat cover, 18in (46cm).
$13,600-14,450

r. A pair of William IV mahogany stools, with rococo carving, c1835, 24in (61cm).
$6,800-8,500

244

A George III serpentine mahogany card table, c1770, 37in (94cm). **$5,000-6,000**

An Irish Georgian walnut card table, with candlestand corners and counter wells, c1740. **$5,000-6,800**

A George II concertina action card table, the cabriole legs with foliate cabochons, c1755. **$4,250-5,000**

A Dutch marquetry and mahogany card table, the fold-over top revealing a baize inset and playing card motifs, the frieze and sides with drawers, on cabriole legs with claw-and-ball feet, c1750, 30in (76cm). **$6,000-6,800**

A pair of George III inlaid satinwood crossbanded and painted demi-lune card tables, each hinged flap opening to reveal a baize lined surface, minor restorations to veneers, decoration of a later date, late 18thC, 38.5in (97cm) wide. **$42,500-51,000**

A pair of George III rosewood card tables, each with a fold-over top above a boxwood strung frieze, c1790, 38in (96.5cm). **$10,200-12,000**

An Irish Georgian card table, with baize lined interior, candlestands and counter wells mid-18thC, and a modern copy. **$5,000-6,000**

A George III satinwood and marquetry card table, the top crossbanded in mahogany, c1775, 36in (92cm). **$3,400-4,250**

A George II concertina action card table, with interior candle-stands and wells, c1740, 33in (84cm). **$3,400-4,250**

A late Louis XVI mahogany card table, with hinged semi-circular top and square tapering legs, 44in (112cm). **$5,000-6,800**

A William and Mary walnut card table, with crossbanded top, restored, c1690, 30.5in (78cm). **$12,000-13,600**

245

A George IV brass inlaid rosewood card table, with swivel top, c1820, 36in (92cm). **$6,000-7,650**

A pair of satinwood card tables, the fold-over tops crossbanded in rosewood, c1825, 35.5in (90cm). **$6,000-8,500**

An ebonised and inlaid fold-over top card table, the top with brass reeded border, on 4 turned supports, early 19thC, 35.5in (90cm). **$1,000-1,200**

A Regency amboyna, maple, bird's-eye maple, specimen-wood and parcel gilt centre table, with tilt-top, 52.5in (133cm) diam. **$42,500-46,000**

A late George II mahogany centre table, with associated crossbanded top, c1755, 25.5in (64cm). **$26,350-28,000**

A George IV pollard elm and marquetry card table, with swivel top, c1820, 36in (92cm). **$4,250-6,000**

A pair of William IV mahogany card tables, with swivel crossbanded tops, c1835, 36in (92cm). **$6,000-6,800**

A Russian brass mounted mahogany, walnut and marquetry card table, late 18thC. **$8,500-10,200**

A pair of late George III mahogany card tables, c1805, 36in (92cm). **$6,000-7,650**

A Regency mahogany centre table, with 2 frieze drawers each side, 45in (114cm). **$8,500-10,200**

A Regency calamander and coromandel banded centre table, 54in (137cm). **$6,000-7,650**

A pair of George III giltwood consoles, with white marble tops, restored, c1770, 44.5in (114cm). **$61,200-68,000**

A Restauration mahogany centre table, with granite top, c1825, 43.5in (110cm) diam. **$12,000-15,300**

A William IV brass mounted parcel gilt rosewood and burr elm centre table, c1835, 51.5in (131cm). **$15,300-18,700**

An Empire centre table, attributed to Jacob-Desmalter, after a design by Percier and Fontaine, c1805, 36in (91cm) diam. **$62,000-68,000**

A Restauration mahogany centre table, with marble top, stamped Jacob, c1830, 37.5in (96cm). **$58,650-60,350**

A William IV rosewood centre table, the top inlaid with squares of specimen marble and hardstone, c1835, 31in (79cm). **$32,300-34,000**

A George IV brass inlaid rosewood centre table, with tilt-top banded with foliage, 60in (152cm) diam. **$11,000-12,750**

A mahogany and gilt brass mounted centre table, 24in (61cm) diam. **$3,400-5,000**

A brass inlaid mahogany centre table, c1820, 31.5in (80cm). **$4,250-5,000**

A George IV mahogany centre or breakfast table, with rosewood crossbanding to top, c1820, 56in (142cm) diam. **$11,000-12,750**

A Regency giltwood centre table, with moulded marble top and heavily carved supports, some damage, 36in (92cm). **$34,000-42,500**

COLOUR REVIEW

A George II mahogany concertina action card table, banded in pearwood, c1740. **$7,650-9,350**

A Regency mahogany breakfast table, the tilt-top with reeded edge, repaired, 59in (150cm) diam. **$12,000-13,600**

A George III crossbanded satinwood card table, c1785. **$6,800-8,500**

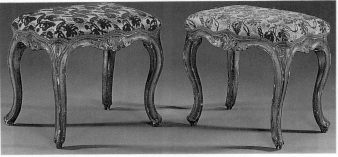

A pair of Italian giltwood stools, with serpentine stuffed seats, the moulded front seat rails centred by rococo cartouches, on cabriole legs, mid-18thC, 21.5in (55cm). **$9,000-10,500**

A George III mahogany architect's table, c1765, 36in (92cm). **$8,500-10,200**

A George III mahogany card table, crossbanded in satinwood and veneered in segments, c1780. **$4,250-6,000**

A George III mahogany breakfast table, the finely figured top with a broad mahogany crossbanding, restored, 60in (152cm) long. **$5,000-6,800**

A pair of Swedish painted stools, c1800, 15in (39cm) wide. **$5,000-6,000**

A George IV brass inlaid rosewood veneered card table, the top crossbanded in calamander, c1820. **$5,000-6,000**

An Italian giltwood stool, the sides and legs ornately carved, possibly Sicilian, mid-18thC, 24in (61cm) wide. **$12,000-13,600**

An Italian neo-classic walnut and parquetry card table, with inlaid playing surface, late 18thC, 35in (89cm). **$12,000-13,600**

A Regency style mahogany dining table, the top inlaid with ebony lines, with downward reeded base, 54in (137cm). **$9,350-11,000**

A George III mahogany three-pedestal dining table, c1810 and later, 126in (320cm) extended. **$14,450-20,400**

An early George III mahogany twin pedestal dining table, with one leaf, on turned spreading shafts, 77.5in (197cm). **$17,000-25,500**

An Anglo-Irish mahogany two-pedestal dining table, with reeded edge, c1825, 80.4in (204cm) extended. **$8,500-12,000**

A Venetian walnut marquetry dressing table, c1770, 38.5in (98cm). **$20,400-26,350**

A George II mahogany triple-top games table, with baize lined interior, c1740, 34.5in (88cm). **$4,700-6,400**

A Dutch fruitwood and marquetry centre table. **$5,000-8,500**

A George III mahogany games table, c1805. **$6,800-7,650**

A Venetian black japanned dressing table, mid-18thC. **$11,000-12,750**

A George IV mahogany twin-pedestal dining table, with later extra leaf, restored, top and bottom possibly associated. **$9,350-12,000**

A French kingwood extending table, c1920. **$7,650-9,350**

A George III mahogany Wilkinson's patent dining table, with 3 leaves, c1810, 88.5in (224cm) extended. **$13,600-17,000**

An Irish Regency mahogany draw-leaf pedestal dining table, leaf scratched, c1820, 72in (183cm) extended. **$6,800-8,500**

A pair of marble inset rosewood tables, c1840, 36in (91cm). **$15,300-17,000**

A rosewood and calamander library table, c1805. **$14,450-17,000**

An red tortoiseshell boulle occasional table, c1850. **$7,650-8,500**

A Regency inlaid mahogany library table, restored, c1820, 66in (168cm) long. **$12,000-17,000**

A Federal mahogany library table, with inset green leather lining, Boston, early 19thC, 85in (216cm) long. **$15,500-20,500**

A Charles X ormolu mounted rosewood guéridon, mid-19thC, 33in (84cm) diam. **$15,300-18,500**

A George IV mahogany library table, with curved ends, 2 drawers, and spindle filled end supports, c1820, 40in (102cm). **$5,000-6,000**

A marble topped rosewood occasional table, 25in (63cm) diam. **$3,600-5,000**

A George IV occasional table, c1820. **$2,500-3,500**

l. A parquetry games table, German or Austrian, mid-18thC. **$13,500-17,000**

r. A mahogany 3-pillar dining table, c1820, 123.5in (314cm). **$31,000-34,000**

l. A mahogany library table, with moulded leather lined top, 3 drawers and pierced fret brackets, c1770, 59.5in (151cm) long. **$12,000-13,600**

r. A pair of mahogany toilet tables, each with divided top enclosing apertures and rising mirror, c1770. **$29,750-32,300**

A pair of George III inlaid mahogany tulipwood and rosewood crossbanded Pembroke tables, c1770, one pair of stretchers later. **$32,300-39,000**

A George IV marble topped pedestal table, c1825. **$4,250-5,000**

A pair of George IV mahogany pier tables, c1820, 42in (106cm). **$7,250-8,500**

A pair of George III harewood and satinwood oval occasional tables, c1780, 16.5in (42cm). **$5,000-6,800**

A pair of Italian neo-classic walnut night tables, each with a frieze drawer and hinged fall front, on square tapering legs, 16in (41cm). **$21,250-23,800**

A George III inlaid satinwood Pembroke table, late 18thC. **$6,500-8,500**

A Regency brass mounted ebony Pembroke table, early 19thC. **$31,000-34,000**

A pair of Federal mahogany Pembroke tables, each with 2 drop leaves, a single long drawer with incised moulded edge, on square tapering legs, New York, c1800, 30in (76cm) long. **$8,500-10,000**

A Russian ormolu mounted Empire centre table. **$20,400-24,000**

A satinwood veneered Pembroke table, c1780. **$5,000-6,800**

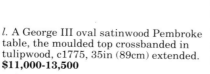

An English serpentine mahogany centre table, in Chippendale style, 42in (106cm) long. **$5,000-8,500**

l. A George III oval satinwood Pembroke table, the moulded top crossbanded in tulipwood, c1775, 35in (89cm) extended. **$11,000-13,500**

A George III yew wood Pembroke table, the twin flap top crossbanded with mahogany, 38in (97cm) open **$12,750-14,450**

A pair of George IV pier tables, c1820, 26.5in (68cm).
$3,700-4,250

A George IV mahogany side or serving table, the moulded frieze with a drawer, on carved scrolling front legs, 88in (224cm) wide.
$6,000-6,800

A George III mahogany serving table, with rosewood crossbanded top, 36in (92cm) wide.
$3,500-4,250

A pair of giltwood pier tables, in the manner of Thomas Johnson, each with removable marble tops supported on a tree with rocky base, 19thC, 33in (84cm) wide.
$51,000-54,000

A Dutch satinwood centre table, inlaid with sycamore, c1790, 40in (102cm) wide.
$3,700-4,250

A George III harewood Pembroke table, c1780, 35in (89cm) wide open.
$3,500-4,250

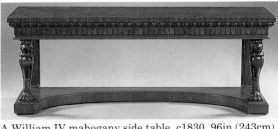

A William IV mahogany side table, c1830, 96in (243cm).
$12,000-15,300

An Anglo-Indian rosewood veneered library table, c1830, 60in (152cm).
$5,500-6,500

A satinwood Pembroke table, c1785. **$5,000-6,000**

A George III painted mahogany Pembroke table, c1780, 40in (102cm).
$8,500-10,000

A pair of Italian carved giltwood pier tables, depicting Summer and Autumn, c1800, 34in (87cm) wide.
$46,000-51,000

A pair of George IV mahogany side tables, with brown English marble top, 72.5in (184cm) wide.
$6,800-8,500

A Regency ebonised and parcel gilt console table, c1810, 50in (127cm).
$5,500-6,500

A George I walnut lowboy, restored, c1715, 30in (76cm).
$11,000-12,750

An early Georgian walnut lowboy, restored, 32in (81cm).
$11,000-12,000

A pair of Portuguese rosewood side tables, each with 2 drawers in the panelled frieze, part 18thC, 47.5in (121cm). **$12,000-13,500**

An Irish George II style mahogany side table, c1900, the top possibly associated, 55in (140cm).
$7,650-10,000

A George III satinwood and marquetry side table, the top crossbanded in kingwood, c1775, 68in (173cm). **$10,000-12,000**

A George II mahogany side table, c1730, 27.5in (70cm). **$7,500-8,500**

A Regency plum pudding mahogany side table, the top banded in amboyna, 42in (106.5cm).
$7,500-9,500

A pair of Louis XV rococo painted console tables, each with serpentine fronted moulded white marble top, possibly reduced in size, 28.5in (72cm).
$12,000-13,600

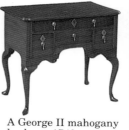

A George III mahogany Pembroke table, by George Simson, with flame figured top, the drawer with maker's label, 40in (101.5cm).
$14,500-17,000

A George II mahogany lowboy, c1740.
$6,000-6,800

A Queen Anne gilt gesso side table, restored and re-gilt, c1710.
$3,500-4,500

A George III rosewood sofa table, the top with partridgewood banding between double lines of boxwood, 63in (160cm) long. **$22,000-25,500**

A carved giltwood side table, with painted top, and carved legs, Italian or Austrian, mid-18thC, 66in (168cm). **$4,250-5,000**

A Restauration mahogany centre table, c1820. **$6,000-7,650**

A Regency ebonised and bird's-eye maple sofa table, restored, 58.5in (148cm). **$6,800-10,000**

A Régence ormolu mounted boulle marquetry side table, with marble top, the front and sides veneered with panels of boulle marquetry and brass, c1725, 39in (99cm). **$340,000-382,500**

A George III mahogany 3-pedestal dining table, with 3 additional leaves, late 18thC. **$37,000-43,000**

A Restauration parcel gilt mahogany centre table, c1825, 38in (97cm) diam. **$24,000-27,000**

A pair of Biedermeier Hungarian ashwood side tables. **$6,800-10,000**

Two Roman carved giltwood side tables, with marble tops, c1730, 48.5in (123cm). **$36,000-39,000**

A late George III rosewood sofa table, with amboyna and kingwood crossbandings, 56in (143cm). **$11,000-13,600**

A George II mahogany card table, with a drawer, 32.5in (82cm). **$4,250-5,000**

An Austrian walnut centre table, with parquetry top, mid-18thC. **$9,500-12,000**

A Regency satinwood veneered sofa table, cross-banded with calamander, c1810, 63.5in (161cm) open. **$6,800-7,800**

A mahogany sofa table, on leaf carved reeded hipped sabre legs, part c1820, 58.5in (149cm) open. **$3,500-5,000**

A George II mahogany tripod table, c1730. **$3,500-4,250**

A George III japanned side table, chinoiserie decorated within floral borders, c1770. **$12,000-13,600**

An inlaid mahogany tripod table. **$4,250-5,000**

A George II carved mahogany tripod table, c1755, 33in (84cm) diam. **$27,000-34,000**

An early George III mahogany tripod table, with birdcage support. **$18,500-20,500**

A George II mahogany tripod table, top split. **$6,500-8,500**

A Piedmontese giltwood console table, in the manner of Bonzanigo, late l8thC. **$12,000-14,000**

An early George III mahogany tripod table, 24.5in (62cm) diam. **$37,000-41,000**

A George II mahogany tripod table, c1755, 30in (76cm) diam. **$9,500-12,000**

A George III brass bound mahogany wine cooler, with metal liner, 20in (51cm) wide. **$16,500-18,000**

A Regency mahogany wine cooler, with metal liner, on paw feet, 39in (100cm) wide. **$36,000-40,000**

A set of Edwardian library steps, converting to a chair. **$1,000-2000**

A Victorian ormolu mounted hexagonal mahogany wine cooler, with pomegranate finial, 20in (51cm) wide. **$3,600-4,500**

A mahogany cellaret, c1780, 21in (54cm) wide. **$4,500-5,500**

A mahogany and iron library ladder, 19thC, 59in (150cm) high. **$4,500-5,500**

A mahogany cellaret, c1770, 19in (48cm) wide. **$6,000-7,000**

A George III mahogany cellaret, c1780, 19.5in (50cm) wide. **$5,500-6,000**

A pair of George III mahogany buckets, with pierced sides, brass band and liner, late 18thC, 13in (32cm) high. **$10,000-11,000**

A Regency mahogany wine cooler, restored, 29in (74cm) wide. **$7,000-8,000**

An Irish mahogany brass bound turf bucket, mid-18thC. **$5,500-6,000**

A five drawer chest, c1880, 42in (107cm). **$720-800**

A Co.Clare bed, c1820, 66 by 70in (168 by 178cm). **$2,000-3,000**

A harness cupboard, c1820, 60in (152cm). **$2,200-2,500**

A housemaid's cupboard, c1890, 96in (244cm) high. **$1,800-2,800**

A bureau, c1780, 42in (107cm). **$2,700-3,000**

A linen press, with brushing slide, c1790, 48 by 80in (122 by 203cm). **$2,200-2,400**

A French glazed cupboard, c1870. **$1,700-2,000**

A French cupboard, c1870, 76in (193cm) high. **$2,200-2,400**

An English corner cupboard, c1770. **$1,000-1,200**

A Scandinavian chest of drawers, c1860, 48 by 50in (122 by 127cm). **$720-800**

A breakfront bookcase, c1820, 168in (427cm) wide. **$4,000-4,500**

An Irish food cupboard, c1850, 58in (147cm) wide. **$2,200-2,400**

An Irish glazed cupboard, c1850, 82in (208cm) high. **$2,200-2,500**

COLOUR REVIEW

A Welsh dresser, c1820, 58in (147cm) wide. **$1,700-2,500**

An Irish fiddle front dresser, c1820, 50in (127cm) wide. **$2,000-2,500**

A Scottish dresser, c1860, 52in (132cm) wide. **$900-1,000**

An Irish dresser, c1840, 78in (198cm) high. **$1,200-1,500**

An Irish dresser, c1850, 49in (124.5cm) wide. **$1,200-1,500**

An Irish dresser, c1880, 80in (203cm) high. **$1,000-1,200**

A Scottish dresser, c1860, 55in (139.5cm) wide. **$1,400-1,600**

An Irish dresser, c1860, 80in (203cm) high. **$1,400-1,600**

An Irish dresser, c1860, 60in (152cm) wide. **$2,800-3,200**

An Irish dresser, c1880, 52in (132cm) wide. **$1,500-1,700**

An Irish settle, c1880, 75in (190.5cm). **$720-800**

A French buffet, c1850, 52in (132cm) wide. **$1,200-1,500**

An Irish cupboard, c1820, 54in (137cm) wide. **$1,500-1,700**

An English press cupboard, c1840, 88in (223.5cm) high. **$1,200-1,500**

A single wardrobe, c1850, 40in (101.5cm) wide. **$1,000-1,200**

A Danish single door wardrobe, c1870, 40in (101.5cm). **$650-725**

A French buffet base, c1880, 44in (111.5cm) wide. **$650-725**

An Irish four-door cupboard, c1850, 65in (165cm). **$1,500-1,700**

A double wardrobe, c1890, 48in (122cm). **$800-900**

A Southern Irish corner cupboard, c1850, 45in (114cm). **$1,800-2,000**

A set of 4 Coade stone figures representing The Seasons, designed by John Bacon, c1779, 73in (185cm) high. **$125,000-145,000**

A pair of carved stone urns, early 18thC, on associated plinth. **$12,000-14,500**

A Flemish marble figure of Minerva, early 18thC, 72in (183cm) high. **$72,000-80,000**

An Italian white marble fountain bowl-on-stand. **$4,000-5,500**

A bronze figure, early 20thC. **$9,000-10,000**

A pair of French cast iron figures of putti, late 19thC, 51in (130cm) high. **$9,000-10,000**

A carved sandstone model of a lion passant gardant, c1880, 85in (216cm) **$20,000-22,000**

l. A pair of Japanese bronze cranes, late 19thC, 81in (206cm) high. **$5,500-7,000**

Two matching serpentine brass fenders, pierced and engraved with unicorns and cherubs, mid-19thC, 53in (135cm) wide. **$9,000-10,000**

An English marble chimney surround, early 19thC, 75in (190cm) wide. **$6,000-9,000**

A Victorian steel fire curb and 3 steel and brass fire irons, c1860, 54.5in (138cm). **$2,000-2,500**

A Regency Coalbrookdale floral pattern seat, seat rails damaged, 46in (116.5cm) wide. **$3,000-4,000**

A George III steel basket grate, with Royal arms, 32.5in (82cm). **$2,500-3,500**

A brass and steel basket grate and surround, c1800, 38in (96cm) wide. **$2,500-3,500**

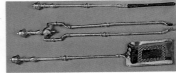

A set of 3 Regency brass fire irons, shovel 27.5in (70cm). **$2,000-2,200**

A William IV brass fender, c1835, 35.5in (90cm). **$4,500-5,500**

A set of 3 Regency steel fire irons, shovel 30in (75.5cm). **$1,200-1,500**

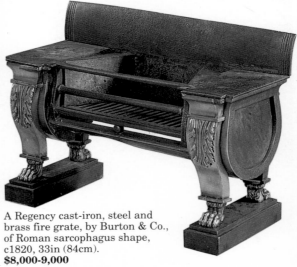

A Regency cast-iron, steel and brass fire grate, by Burton & Co., of Roman sarcophagus shape, c1820, 33in (84cm). **$8,000-9,000**

A Regency rosewood tea table with plain frieze and U-shaped support on a concave sided platform with 4 sabre feet, brass foliate caps and casters, 36in (92cm).
$1,800-2,700

A William IV rosewood D-shaped tea table, with beaded edge on turned lotus-carved shaft with gadrooned base and 4 acanthus carved splayed legs with scroll feet, 36in (92cm).
$2,700-3,600

A William IV rosewood tea table with D-shaped top and baluster-turned faceted shaft with lappeted base, on quadripartite platform with scroll feet, 42in (107cm).
$1,200-1,700

An early Victorian rosewood D-shaped tea table, the hinged top inlaid with butterflies and sprays of flowers, on cabochon carved baluster turned shaft and 4 floral headed cabriole legs with scroll feet, 39in (99cm).
$1,800-2,700

A Dutch mahogany tea table, the double fold-over breakfront top revealing a well with compartments, the frieze containing a small drawer, on fluted and stop-fluted tapered square legs ending in block feet, 31in (79cm).
$2,700-3,600

A late George III mahogany fold-over tea table, on 4 turned columns and raised on quadruple platform base, with 4 reeded swept sabre supports, all having brass cappings and casters, 40in (101.5cm).
$1,800-2,700

This table is probably Scottish, and is similar to the work of William Trotter, the Edinburgh cabinet maker.

A Scottish Regency mahogany, rosewood crossbanded, boxwood and ebony lined tea table, on bobbin turned tapering supports, 38in (97cm).
$1,200-1,700

Tripod Tables

A mid-George III mahogany tripod table, with bird cage action lobed top, on vase turned shaft and 3 splayed legs, restored, 20.5in (51cm).
$1,800-2,700

A George III mahogany tripod table with bird cage action, the tip-up top above a baluster turned shaft, on hipped splayed legs with pad feet, 36in (92cm).
$1,200-1,700

A Dutch mahogany and marquetry inlaid tripod table, the tip-up top decorated with flowers, parrots and butterflies with a chequered border, on hipped splayed legs and pad feet, damaged, c1800, 29.5in (75cm).
$1,800-2,700

A Georgian red walnut bird cage top tripod table, c1780.
$1,200-1,700

A George III style mahogany tripod table, the shaped tilt-top on cabriole legs ending in egg and claw feet, 37.5in (95cm).
$1,200-1,700

A George III mahogany tripod occasional table, with dished top above a bird cage and gun barrel turned column, on ogee supports and pad feet, 20in (50.5cm).
$1,800-2,700

Work Tables

A late Regency crossbanded work table in rosewood, with original silk bag, double fronted frieze and dummy drawers, 18in (46cm).
$2,700-3,600

A Regency rosewood work table with sliding well on column uprights with brass cappings, on dual splayed legs joined by a turned stretcher, 21in (53cm).
$1,800-2,700

A Regency rosewood crossbanded mahogany drop-leaf work table, with 2 frieze and 2 dummy drawers, the wooden sewing box re-covered, the table in need of further restoration, 32in (81cm) extended.
$1,800-2,700

A Victorian walnut games and work table, the burr walnut fold-over top set with a Tunbridge ware panel depicting Eridge Castle within geometric bands and opening to reveal chess and backgammon boards, the frieze with a drawer above sliding work compartment, on turned end supports with foliate carved splayed feet joined by a pole stretcher, 23in (59cm).
$1,800-2,700

A George III mahogany work table of Louis XV style, the eared serpentine fronted top with a silk lined rising firescreen behind, above a velvet lined slide and false drawer, with one side drawer and waved apron, on cabriole legs joined by an undertier, screen replaced, restorations, 20in (50.5cm).
$2,700-3,600

A Victorian burr walnut veneered top work table, inlaid stringing, the fitted interior with fretwork above a fabric covered work box, the turned spiral twist supports, on leaf carved open scroll capped legs with casters, turned connecting stretcher, 25in (64cm).
$720-1,000

A mid-Victorian mahogany writing table, the leather lined top with hinged fitted compartment above 2 frieze drawers on fluted tapering legs, stamped Gillow, L1126, restored, 36in (92cm).
$2,700-3,600

An Edwardian mahogany and marquetry writing table, the writing surface lacks lining, on tapering legs inlaid with trailing foliage, stamped Joseph Hide, Market Place, Kingston, 42in (107cm).
$3,600-5,500

A George III zebrawood veneered writing table, outlined throughout with boxwood stringing, the crossbanded top enclosing a fitted interior with adjustable tooled leather writing slope, 19in (48cm).
$1,800-2,700

Teapoys

A Victorian walnut teapoy, the crossbanded top enclosing a fitted interior containing 2 oval caddies above a band of lobing, raised on a fluted column and 3 leaf carved scrolling legs, c1850, 18.5in (47cm).
$1,800-2,700

A George IV golden wood veneered sarcophagus shaped teapoy, inlaid with chequer banding, the sides with brass decorative ring handles, the interior with a mahogany lift-out mixing box and 2 caddies with fielded sliding covers, the leaf carved stem on shaped top splay legs, the brass sabots on casters, 18in (46cm).
$720-1,000

A mahogany teapoy, c1830.
$1,800-2,700

Whatnots

A George IV mahogany two-tier whatnot, the top hinged to form an adjustable reading slope, the lower tier with a drawer, on turned supports and turned lopped feet, fitted casters, c1825, 20.5in (52cm).
$1,800-2,700

Washstands

A Sheraton period washstand.
$720-1,000

A mahogany washstand in the Gillows manner, the interior with lidded compartment and provision for bowl and accessories, the frieze with one false and 2 real drawers, on tapering reeded legs with brass casters, early 19thC, 33in (84cm).
$720-1,000

A Victorian walnut three-tier serpentine fronted whatnot, with pierced gallery, turned finials, wrythen fluted supports, plain shelves, single drawer to the base, on turned legs, 22in (55.5cm).
$1,800-2,700

A mid-Victorian mahogany whatnot, on ring turned tapering supports, 18in (46cm).
$1,800-2,700

A Regency mahogany three-tier lectern whatnot, the top above a finialled base with drawer, joined by turned supports and vertical cross stretchers, on baluster turned legs and brass casters, 19.5in (50cm).
$3,600-5,500

l. A Victorian three-tier walnut graduating whatnot, with shaped outline.
$1,200-1,700
r. A Victorian walnut Canterbury with fretted sides and drawer under.
$1,800-2,700

A mahogany butler's tray, with folding sides and collapsable stand, mid-19thC.
$1,200-1,700

Miscellaneous

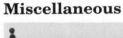

A Regency painted towel rail, 25in (64cm).
$180-360

A Black Forest carved and stained hat and umbrella stand, in the form of a large bear and 2 cubs, around a tree, 82in (208cm) high.
$3,600-5,500

An Edwardian mahogany three-tier cakestand, 36in (92cm) high.
$360-540

A Victorian mahogany boot rack, supported between 2 turned uprights and trestle base, terminating in bun feet, c1880, 38in (97cm).
$360-540

A walnut butter cooler, the oval brass banded sides with heart pierced lifts and 2 hinged covers, 18thC, 13.5in (34cm).
$3,600-5,500

PINE FURNITURE
Chairs

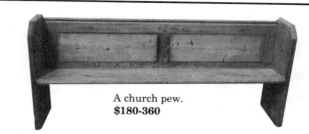

A church pew.
$180-360

A high/low chair, c1880.
$180-360

A child's rocker.
$35-70

A high/low rocking chair, c1890.
$180-360

A school chair.
$35-70

A side chair, with a new seat, 31in (79cm) high.
$110-180

Chests

An English plan chest, c1880, 48in (122cm).
$720-1,000

An English chest of drawers, c1890, 36in (92cm).
$360-540

A chest of drawers, c1840.
$720-1,000

A chest of drawers, c1820.
$720-1,000

A miniature waxed chest of drawers, 11in (28cm).
$70-145

A chest of drawers, 19thC, 36in (92cm).
$180-360

An Austrian mule chest, totally
original, including lock and key,
48in (122cm).
$720-1,000

A miniature chest of spice
drawers, c1890, 18in (46cm) high.
$360-540

A chest of drawers, 40in (102cm).
$360-540

A chest of drawers, c1870, 32in
(81cm) high.
$360-540

A Scandinavian or South German
chest of drawers, 44in (112cm).
$360-540

A green painted pine child's
blanket chest, probably New
England, on ball feet, early
19thC, 25in (64cm) long.
$1,500-2,000

Commodes

An English bank
of drawers,
c1890, 89in
(226cm).
$1,000-1,500

A child's painted commode, 24in
(61cm) high.
$110-180

Cupboards

A wall cupboard.
$70-145

A step commode, c1860, 18in
(46cm). **$180-360**

A two-door glazed cupboard,
originally with metal mesh,
c1825, 72.5in (183cm) high.
$1,200-1,700

A glazed cupboard with enclosed
drawers, c1870, 15in (38cm) high.
$360-540

A German bedside cupboard.
$180-360

A glazed two-piece bookcase, c1880.
$1,200-1,700

An English corner cupboard, c1870, 27in (69cm). **$360-540**

A late George III standing corner cupboard, the moulded cornice with foliate carved frieze above a central lion's head and spandrels with paterae and trailing husks, single arched astragal glazed door between reeded uprights, with a panelled door below between similar uprights, 32.5in (82cm).
$1,800-2,700

A Chippendale carved and red painted pine and poplar corner cupboard, Delaware River Valley, restored, c1800, 88.5in (225cm) high.
$3,500-5,500

A mid-Georgian corner cupboard, with breakfront moulded cornice above a recess with open shelves and semi-domed top, flanked by moulded uprights, 48in (122cm).
$1,200-1,700

Desks

A Scandinavian pine desk, with oak top, c1910, 51in (130cm).
$720-1,000

A three-piece partners' desk, 51in (130cm) long. **$1,200-1,700**

A Regency simulated bamboo desk, with new leather top, c1820, 45in (114cm).
$1,800-2,700

A fitted desk, with new sledge feet, c1870, 48in (122cm) high.
$1,200-1,700

A desk, with black china knob handles, new leather top, c1860, 47in (119cm) long. **$1,200-1,700**

Dressers

A painted pine low dresser, c1700, 60in (152cm).
$2,700-3,600

A Danish dresser base, c1895, 40in (102cm).
$720-1,000

A Welsh glazed dresser, c1880, 39in (99cm).
$1,200-1,700

A Scottish dresser, c1880, 49in (125cm).
$720-1,000

A two drawer sycamore dresser base, 63in (160cm) long. **$720-1,000**

Stools

A pine stool.
$35-70

A beech piano stool, c1890, 22.5in (57cm) high. **$110-180**

Tables

A Federal cherrywood and pine scalloped top tea table, New England, early 19thC, 35in (89cm) long.
$2,500-3,500

A Welsh drop-leaf table, c1865, 34in (86cm).
$180-360

A cheese table, with turned legs 18 by 18in (46 by 46cm).
$70-145

A three drawer writing table, c1820, 31.5in (79cm) high.
$1,200-1,700

272

273

Washstands

A washstand, with one door and one drawer, c1880, 40in (102cm) high.
$720-1,000

A dressing table/washstand, c1870, 55in (140cm) high.
$720-1,000

An original painted washstand, 36.5in (93cm) high. **$360-540**

A pine washstand.
$110-180

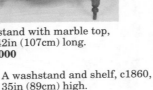

A washstand with marble top, c1880, 42in (107cm) long.
$720-1,000

A washstand and shelf, c1860, 35in (89cm) high.
$180-360

Miscellaneous

A pine tub, 27in (69cm) diam.
$180-360

Pine shelves, 21in (53cm).
$110-180

A pine box c1880, on a new stand, 22in (56cm) high. **$110-180**

A German painted and decorated pine marriage bedstead, the shaped headboard painted with a lady and a gentleman standing in a landscape, with floral and leaf motifs in polychrome, and an inscription 'Johann and Maria Katharina' and the date '1824', with turned footposts, the tester panel overhead painted with bucolic landscapes within medallions in polychrome, 50.5in (128cm) wide.
$3,600-5,500

A Scandinavian painted beech spinning wheel, c1860, 37in (94cm) high.
$180-360

A pine tray, on a new stand, 22in (56cm) high. **$110-180**

A plant stand, 28in (71cm) high. **$110-180**

A pine easel, 43in (109cm) high. **$70-145**

IRISH FURNITURE

A glazed pine bookcase, c1870, 49in (124cm). **$720-1,000**

A pine chiffonier, c1870. **$360-540**

A bed-settee, unrestored, c1800. **$720-1,000**

A Co. Galway pine cottage dresser, c1840. **$1,000-1,500**

A pine dresser, c1870. **$1,200-1,700**

A chest of drawers, unrestored, c1835. **$1,000-1,500**

A glazed cupboard, unrestored, c1840. **$720-1,000**

A dresser, c1890. **$1,000-1,500**

A Co. Galway pine cupboard, c1840. **$1,000-1,500**

WHAT IS AN ARCHITECTURAL ANTIQUE?

Broadly speaking, antique architectural elements fall into two categories; architectural salvage which covers reclaimed building materials, such as bricks, paving stones, roof tiles and balustrading, and architectural antiques which covers statuary, garden ornaments and chimneypieces.

BUYING AND SELLING ARCHITECTURAL ANTIQUES

Despite the enormous increase of interest in architectural antiques in recent years it is not an easy area for collectors. Unlike other specialist fields, such as porcelain or clocks where a massive amount of information on individual items and their values is readily available, there are only a small number of books currently in print on the subject, and few of these give even rudimentary advice on prices.

The first and most important rule for collecting architectural antiques is 'buy what you like'. There are two main reasons for this: First because you can live happily with your purchases even if they do not prove to be a good investment in financial terms. Secondly, you are unlikely to be misled by fashion. In recent years certain materials and manufacturers have drastically increased in price, only to fall rapidly back to more sensible levels. An example of this are the products of the Coalbrookdale foundry in Shropshire - notably cast iron garden seats and fountains - which, after a boom in prices in the mid 1980s, are now so debased by later copies that only the very rarest pieces achieve even moderate results at auction.

The second rule is to pay as much as you can reasonably afford. As in other fields of collecting you will, on the whole, get what you pay for and you are unlikely to buy good pieces at very low prices.

With reasonable luck and good judgement, however, it is perfectly possible to buy pieces which will not only enhance the appearance of your house and garden but may, in a few years time, provide a good return on your investment.

There are four main choices when buying and selling; auctions, specialist dealers, general dealers and demolition yards. The classic argument in favour of buying at auction goes as follows:- dealers buy at auction. When a dealer sells he must be charging the auction price plus his profit margin, therefore it must be cheaper to buy at auction.

The specialist dealer does at least deal in the goods 365 days a year, as opposed to 2 or 3 days for the auctioneer. Although the price he offers the vendor may be below an auctioneer's estimate, the seller has the certainty of a sale at a fixed price with no hidden charges. For the buyer, provided he takes the precaution of obtaining an invoice with a full description of the piece, including date of manufacture, material and any known provenance, he secures himself against most eventualities.

Many general dealers also carry architectural antiques in their stock. The advantage and disadvantage of buying from general dealers is the same. They may not know exactly what they have. Thus, whilst it is possible that a bargain may be secured, the reverse may also be true. Again it is important that the item is described fully on the invoice.

Demolition yards are theoretically most likely to yield bargains for the purchaser. Their stock-in-trade is usually architectural salvage, but they do occasionally deal in antique garden ornaments and fireplaces. A vendor may recognise the value of a piece even though it is tucked away in a dusty corner, and many an unsuspecting buyer has been fooled by dirt and disorder.

MATERIALS

Broadly speaking, the materials most commonly encountered fall into two categories; the carved and the moulded, or cast. The carved category includes marble and stone (but beware of the term bonded marble, which is cement made from marble dust and then cast). The cast and moulded materials include cast and wrought iron, bronze, brass, lead, spelter (a cheaper and lighter alloy), terracotta and cement, or reconstituted stone.

A decorative cast iron fountain, 42in (107cm) high.
$1,800-2,700

Because it is relatively cheap to cast items, they are far more likely to be modern reproductions than carved pieces. Indeed, the only substantial source of carved reproduction pieces is Northern Italy, where vast quantities of relatively high quality limestone pieces are still produced. Cast materials, on the other hand, have all been reproduced with varying degrees of success in recent years. Lead pieces are mostly produced in England, bronzes in Italy and the Far East, terracotta in Italy and Spain, and cast stone almost everywhere.

There is, of course, nothing wrong with modern reproductions, provided they are correctly described, but they may not appreciate in value and cannot reasonably be described as architectural antiques.

ARCHITECTURAL ANTIQUES
Bathroom Ware

A baby's W.C., 10.5in (46cm) high.
$180-360

A Rufford & Co, stoneware bath, complete with mahogany surround and mahogany encased thunderbox, restored, c1890, 90in (229cm) long.
$7,000-9,000

Provenance: Knowsley Hall, Knowsley, Lancashire, the residence of the Earl of Derby.

A copper bath, 65in (165cm) long.
$2,700-3,600

A copper bath, 54in (137cm) long.
$900-1,500

A French 3 bowl hairdressers' shop fitting, 168in (427cm) long.
$1,200-1,700

A blue and white Trent Sanitary Closet, 18.5in (47cm) high.
$180-360

An Edwardian porcelain wash basin, T.C. Brown, Westhead, Moore & Co., of Stoke-on-Trent, with Queen Alexandra's Royal Warrant, 19in (48cm).
$720-1,000

A bathroom chrome radiator towel rail, 37.5in (95cm) high.
$180-360

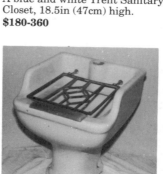

A Victorian mop sink.
$110-180

A Victorian scalloped basin, with brass taps, plug and chain.
$720-1,000

Bird Baths

A carved sandstone bird bath, 30in (76cm) high.
$1,000-1,500

A Yorkshire carved stone bird bath, 37.5in (95cm) high.
$720-1,000

A granite bird bath, 19thC, 39in (99cm) high.
$1,000-1,500

Chimney Pots

A chimney pot, 39in (99cm) high.
$70-145

Chimney pot, 42in (107cm) high.
$70-145

A chimney pot, with crown top and square base, 24in (61cm) high.
$35-70

A chimney pot, 29in (74cm) high.
$70-145

A square chimney pot, 37in (94cm) high.
$35-70

Doors & Gates

A pair of church doors.
$360-540

ARCHITECTURAL ANTIQUES

WHAT TO LOOK FOR

* LEAD

Lead is one the most difficult materials to identify. After a few years exposure to the elements and a little judicious waxing, new lead and old are visually indistinguishable. However, early leadwork was primarily of very high quality and the finish and detail on 18thC figures is very good, whereas modern pieces suffer by comparison. Fingers are often clumsy, hair badly detailed and faces expressionless. Also, figures in reduced scale (i.e. less than lifesize) are almost certainly late, although often misleadingly described as 18thC. Genuine 18thC lead cistern tanks which make delightful planters, should have some evidence of having been used as cisterns, usually signs of an inlet pipe around the top rim and a tap hole at the lower edge.

An original mahogany lead-lined cistern.
$360-540

* BRONZE

Contrary to popular opinion, it is possible to produce virtually perfect copies of antique originals and green patination, which many take to be a sign of age, is easily applied. The underside of the piece should be examined and not look too clean and if there is wear in the patination it should be in places where it would occur naturally as the piece was handled over the years. Remember that signatures and foundry marks are as easy to fake as the piece itself.

* CAST IRON

Probably the most widely reproduced of all materials. If you are buying garden ornaments or furniture purported to be antique, first lift them. If they are light they are probably aluminium. If they are heavy, look at the finish. Casting marks, the little protruding spots of metal, were carefully removed in Victorian

castings and any that were not would long since have been worn away. As with bronze, foundry marks are commonly faked.

* STONE

The two stones most commonly encountered are limestone and sandstone. Common types of limestone include Portland stone (grey/white) and Bathstone (yellow). Common sandstones include York stone (dark yellow weathering to black/green) and red sandstone. Broadly speaking, limestone is preferred for statuary and sandstone for architectural elements. Beware of pieces where the surface has broken down, as they may be beyond restoration. Limestone is generally more popular than sandstone because many people do not like the black and green colour of weathered sandstone. Sandstone is also more brittle and although it will take fine detail, it is susceptible to damage.

* MARBLE

There are many native British marbles, but the white marbles used in sculpture are mostly Italian. True statuary marble, the most highly prized and now virtually unobtainable, is a creamy white colour and has little or no veining. Carrara, or second statuary, is a bluer white with some degree of veining and is harder and thus more resistant to the British weather. Once the surface of the marble has broken down and become sugary, it is often beyond restoration.

Modern marbles, often dazzlingly white and imported from India, can be readily identified by their crystalline nature.

A weathered marble statue of a seated wounded cupid working on his net, late 19thC, 26in (66cm) wide. **$1,000-1,500**

When buying marble statuary look for signs of quality carving in high relief, arms and hair carved away from the body and true proportions.

* TERRACOTTA

Terracotta (red earth in Latin) has been used since pre-classical times. It is resistant to weathering and thus ideal for exterior statuary and planters. The most desirable colour is yellow and the least, brick red. Oil jars have become a highly popular decorative feature in gardens in recent years, but because terracotta is a fragile material, genuine ones are rare and they are still produced in considerable quantities in Southern Europe. Genuine oil jars will probably have some signs of glazing on the interior.

A terracotta urn, 28in (71cm) high. **$360-540**

* RECONSTITUTED STONE

Although debased by inferior modern castings, reconstituted stone has a long and honourable history. One of the earliest types used in England was Coadestone (named after Eleanor Coade, its inventor). Starting in 1769, the Coade factory produced an enormous number of pieces of the highest quality, and signed pieces fetch high prices.

Look for the same signs of quality as in marble carvings. The lines of cast pieces should be crisp and the material free from aggregate and air holes. As with carving, the casting should be free and confident.

A pair of wrought iron gates, early 20thC, each gate 90.5 by 59in (229 by 150cm). **$1,200-1,700**

A French cast iron fountain figure of a putto seated on an upturned ewer, late 19thC, 28in (71cm) high. **$1,200-1,700**

From an original model by Mathurian Moreau, 1821-1912.

A pair of wrought iron gates, each of arched rectangular form, early 20thC, each gate 86 by 54in (173 by 137cm). **$1,200-1,700**

Fountains

An original Victorian cast iron fountain, in tazza form with egg-and-dart mouldings, 38in (97cm) high. **$1,200-1,700**

A cast iron figural fountain, the standard cast with egrets, supporting a foliate cast bowl, probably Fiske, N.Y., late 19thC, 48in (122cm) high. **$2,500-4,000**

> **Miller's is a price GUIDE not a price LIST**

A cast iron 3-tiered fountain, the welled base with a lily pad and frog cast rim, central standard formed as 3 egrets, stamped J.W. Fiske, N.Y., late 19thC, 110in (279cm) high. **$10,500-15,000**

A Vicenza stone lion fountain mask, mid-20thC, 28in (71cm). **$1,000-1,500**

Fireplaces

A Louis XVI style white marble chimneypiece, mid-19thC, 51 by 71in (130 by 180cm).
$7,000-9,000

A cast iron fireplace, with tile decoration, 38in (97cm) square.
$720-1,000

A cast iron fireplace, 38 by 30in (97 by 76cm).
$720-1,000

A painted wood fire surround, 54 by 70in (137 by 178cm).
$720-1,000

A Victorian carved oak chimneypiece with overmantel, c1880, 97 by 102.5in (246 by 260cm).
$1,200-1,700

A cast iron fireplace, with inlaid tiles and brass hood, 38in (97cm) square.
$720-1,000

A duck's nest hob grate, 23 by 31in (59 by 79cm).
$720-1,000

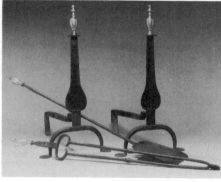

A pair of brass and wrought iron knife blade andirons, attributed to Isaac Conklin, New York, c1810, together with brass and wrought iron tongs and shovel.
$2,500-3,500

A Federal pine fireplace mantle, the projecting cornice above an urn carved tympanum, surround flanked by leaf carved and fluted pilasters, painted light green, 55.5in (141cm) high.
$1,000-1,500

A pair of cast iron andirons and fire grate, Shields Foundry, early 19thC, andirons 21in (53cm), grate 14in (36cm) high.
$4,500-5,500

A pair of Louis XV style bronze and gilt bronze chenets, in the form of scantily draped children warming themselves at flaming braziers, c1900, 14in (35cm) high.   **$1,800-2,700**

A set of 6 fireplace tiles.
$70-145

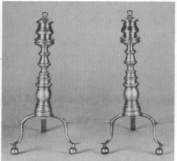

A set of polished steel fire irons, with faceted pommels, comprising: a pierced shovel, a pair of tongs, a poker and a pair of fire iron supports, with scrolling arms, fluted and spirally turned knopped shafts and scrolling pierced trefoil bases, 26in (66cm) high.
$1,800-2,700

A pair of seamed brass andirons, each with ring turned shaft and hipped downswept legs with ball feet, restored, possibly American, early 19thC, 16in (40cm) high.
$1,800-2,700

Garden Furniture

A Coalbrookdale Rustic pattern cast iron seat, with diamond stamp for 7th April, 1851, and numbered 78766, c1860, 50in (127cm).
$1,800-2,700

A carved stone garden seat, with high back and lion's feet, 65in (165cm).
$3,600-5,500

A pair of painted cast iron armchairs in 'Curtain' pattern, by S. S. Bent & Sons, New York, late
$750-1,000

A pair of carved stone benches, early 18thC, 73in (185cm).
$3,600-5,500

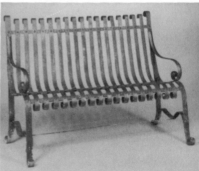

A painted strap iron bench, late 19thC, 45in (114cm) long.
$1,500-2,000

A pair of painted cast iron lyre back armchairs, signed Robert W. Wood, Philadelphia, 19thC.
$3,000-5,000

A wrought iron garden seat, the curved low back with 3 lyre shaped splats, with slat seat, on spade feet, 19thC, 84in (213cm).
$2,700-3,600

Pumps

A cast iron pump, 61in (155cm). **$110-180**

A cast iron water pump, early 19thC, 57in (144.5cm). **$720-1,000**

An Irish cast iron pump, A. Clyde, Ballymena, 51in (129.5cm). **$110-180**

A small cast iron water pump, 27in (68cm). **$110-180**

An iron water pump. **$110-180**

Roof Tiles

Hand made plain clay tiles. **$70-145 per hundred**

Hand made clay roof tiles. **$110-180 per hundred**

Hand cut stone tiles. **$900-1,500 per tonne**

A pair of early stone griffin ridge tiles, 25in (63.5cm) high. **$1,800-2,700**

Staddle Stones

A staddle stone. **$110-180**

A matched set of six staddle stones, 18th/19thC, 31.5in (80cm) high. **$1,800-2,700**

A staddle stone, 28in (71cm) high. **$110-180**

Stands

A cast iron hall stand, with registration stamp for 20th July 1846, 114in (290cm) high.
$1,800-2,700

A Coalbrookdale cast iron hall table, inlaid with marble top and with indistinct registration stamp, the backplate stamped No. 49 and centred with a mirror, 86in (218cm) high.
$2,700-3,600

This design is registered in the 1875 Coalbrookdale Catalogue.

A lead head of a classical woman, mid-18thC, 14in (36cm) high.
$1,800-2,700

Statues

A wirework Statue of Liberty topiary figure, painted green, c1960, 96in (244cm) high.
$2,500-3,500

A lead statue of Father Time with flowing beard and moustache, lacking scythe, 56in (142cm).
$7,000-9,000

Four female standing figures, spring, summer, fall and winter, inscribed Wheeler Williams, 1934, Albastone, 41in (104cm) high.
$35,500-40,000

A pair of Italian composition stone figures of putti musicians, modern, 59in (150cm).
$1,800-2,700

A sandstone group of putti at play, with a dog, 19thC, 32in (81cm) high.
$7,000-9,000

A pair of Italian terracotta busts of Dante and Petrarch, the poets both crowned with laurel, 19thC, 29in (74cm) high. **$3,600-5,500**

A pair of recumbent stone lions, mid-18thC, 38in (96.5cm) long.
$3,600-5,500

Sundials

A sandstone sundial, with square column, the vertical dial with bronze gnomon beneath a pyramid top, on a stepped square base, early 20thC, 91in (230cm).high.
$1,800-2,700

A Georgian sundial, 39in (99cm) high.
$3,600-5,500

A stone water trough, marked Horses 1813.
$720-1,000

An Italian grey and white marble jardinière, late 18thC, 34in (86cm) wide.
$10,000-12,000

Troughs & Planters

A pair of lead planters, the sides cast with a band of cherubs below ropework edges and rams' mask terminals, 32in (81cm) wide.
$1,800-2,700

A pair of lead garden flower tubs, the bodies with rams' heads and decorated with a frieze of cherubs beneath rope edges, on bun feet, 18in (46cm) diam.
$1,200-1,700

An Italian rosso Verona marble jardinière, late 17thC, 126in (320cm) long.
$10,000-12,000

A pair of marble mortars, 22in (55.5cm) wide.
$360-540

A marble sarcophagus trough, 3rd/4thC, 74in (188cm) wide.
$18,000-21,000

Urns

A pair of painted cast iron egret base urns, with leaf cast bowl, attributed to J.W. Fiske & Co., New York City, c1893, 36in (92cm) high.
$4,500-6,000

A painted cast iron egret and griffin urn, on shaped pedestal with 3 standing cranes and moulded base, by J.W. Fiske & Co., New York City, c1893, 58in (147cm) high.
$3,000-3,500

A Coadestone memorial urn, with plaque inscribed Ann Finch, O.B., 21 Sept. 1792, on a square foot stamped Coade London 1793, 30in (77cm) high, on a panelled pedestal inscribed with a funerary verse, 24in (61cm).
$3,600-5,500

A white painted cast iron garden urn, on a separate square stepped plinth, 52in (132cm) high.
$720-1,000

A pair of carved stone urns, each on associated square plinth, late 17th/early 18thC, 27in (69cm) high.
$3,600-5,500
Formerly at Newby Hall, Yorkshire.

A Medici reconstituted stone vase, early 19thC, 45in (114cm) high.
$7,000-9,000

A pair of composition fruit filled campana urns, on square bases, 28in (68.5cm) high.
$1,200-1,700

A pair of white marble urns, mid-19thC, 29.5in (75cm) wide.
$2,700-3,600

A pair of composition urns, with everted lips, the baluster bodies decorated with drapery swags upon spreading socles and square plinths, 24in (61cm) high.
$1,800-2,700

A pair of Victorian cast iron urns, 27in (69cm) high.
$900-1,500

An Italian white marble model of the Warwick urn, on associated plinth, early 19thC, 27in (68cm) high.
$1,800-2,700

Windows

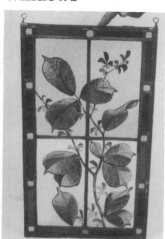

A stained glass panel, 18 by 10.5in (46 by 25cm). **$360-540**

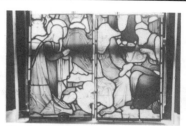

Two stained glass religious scenes, 28 by 16.5in (71 by 42cm). **$720-1,000**

A stained glass window, with City of London crest, 21 by 25in (53 by 64cm). **$360-540**

A stained glass window, 23in (59cm) square. **$720-1,000**

A stained glass panel, 18 by 10.5in (46 by 25cm). **$360-540**

A stained glass panel, with grapes, 12in (30.5cm). **$70-145**

A stained glass window, with Newcastle crest, 21 by 25in (53 by 64cm). **$360-540**

A stained glass framed panel. **$360-540**

Miscellaneous

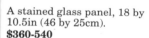

A decorative radiator, c1890. **$360-540**

A Stuart lead cistern, dated 1666 and initials I.F., 47in (119cm) wide. **$3,600-5,500**

A decorative radiator, 38in (96.5cm). **$360-540**

An owl nest opening, for building into a barn or house gable end, 6in (15cm). **$360-540**

CLOCKS

Prices and the recession

Oddly enough, the prices for good 'honest' clocks have not been too badly affected by the recession. On the contrary, prices for clocks in the lower and middle price bands have continued to rise. More expensive clocks have not always reached their estimated value but this could, in part, be due to the fact that higher priced 'top of the range' clocks are a highly specialised area.

A late Victorian ebonised chiming bracket clock, with arched brass dial signed on shield John Jackson, Portsea, triple-train fusee movement, striking on 8 bells and a gong, with matching bracket.
$1,800-2,700

Makers

The great majority of British clocks made before about 1820 were actually made by the man whose name appears on the dial (except of course that the 'white' dial on those types of clocks was bought from a specialist dial maker). After 1820 an increasing number of clocks were bought pre-made by specialists with just the finishing touches being carried out by the local retailers. Bracket and other spring driven clocks pre-1850 are also slightly different. Certain makers specialised in this area and supplied both the engraved and white dial form of bracket clocks to retailers. Even famous

London clockmakers bought in spring clocks in this way, making them little more than retailers as far as spring clocks were concerned.

For famous makers and retailers the name will have a considerable bearing on price, especially with London makers. With provincial clocks the name is not nearly as important in affecting price, with the exception that in each county there was a handful or so of makers who were particularly skilled, famous or highly reputed within their own areas. Clocks by such makers, and especially early ones before about 1750, will carry a premium because of the name. Makers are still coming to light today, whose work is little known but may be of exceptionally high quality, and buyers who can learn to recognise features indicative of high quality may be fortunate in locating a clock where the maker's name has not yet attracted this quality premium in price. Many makers, including a few of exceptional ability, have escaped being recorded in the standard reference texts, so a clock might still be a very fine one even if by a maker as yet unrecorded.

A French ivory mantel clock, with a 2.5in (6.5cm) enamel dial, movement No. 4153, with platform cylinder escapement, outside countwheel striking on a bell, fluted half column case surmounted by a tazza, raised on scroll feet, 11in (28cm).
$3,600-5,500

A mahogany longcase clock, the 12in (31cm) arched and silvered the dial signed Graham, Grafton Street, Soho, 94in (238cm).
$3,600-5,500

Special and Complicated Clocks

The field of musical and quarter-chiming clocks can be a difficult one for the unwary. Such a clock in fine mechanical condition and expertly restored will cost considerably more than a simple hourly-striking version. But beware of such clocks in <u>un</u>restored condition, as the restoration of these can be very difficult and costly - this applies especially in the case of musical clocks, some of which once may have played tunes which are now unrecognisable and therefore may be impossible to restore. Any clocks with missing trains (sets of gears) may well appear to be bargains, but even when restored such clocks will not rival in price a complete original one of the same type. Again, a highly-complex or unusual clock with vital parts missing may prove impossible to restore. Remember with any British clock before about 1850 parts are not interchangeable and anything missing has to be purpose-made. With imported clocks after about 1850 there is a greater chance that a restorer may have spare parts which can be used, <u>if</u> you can locate a restorer with enough spares.

Bracket Clocks

An English bracket clock, the enamel dial with Roman numerals and inscribed Thos. W. Field, Aylesbury, the 8-day 'A' plate timepiece movement with fusee drive, the inlaid mahogany case with domed pediment, open brass fishscale sideplate and fan form inlaid reserves, on brass ball feet, 18in (46cm).
$1,200-1,700

A walnut cased bracket clock, by Garrard, Westminster chimes movement, the dial with silvered chapter ring and gilt metal mask spandrels, 15.5in (39cm).
$720-1,000

An ebonised bracket clock, signed James Chater, London, with rococo spandrels and date aperture, the movement formerly with a third musical train and a foliate engraved and signed backplate, in an associated black painted oak case carved with a dragon surmount and caryatid columns, with nest of bells, 27in (68cm).
$1,800-2,700

A carved oak bracket clock, with German movement and Westminster chimes, early 20thC, 18in (46cm).
$360-540

A George II ebonised bracket clock, the 7in (18cm) dial signed in the stopped pendulum aperture Geo Hide, with calendar aperture, the 5-pillar movement with rack and bell striking and now with anchor escapement, in an inverted bell top case with carrying handle, shell and leaf cast brass door frets and ball-and-claw feet, one pillar missing, c1740, 19in (48cm).
$1,800-2,700

A mahogany bracket clock, in mid-18thC style, with a broken arch brass dial and gong striking movement, c1920, 9.5in (24cm).
$720-1,000

A William & Mary ebonised striking bracket clock, with foliate handle to basket top, later finials, cast gilt mask and foliate sound frets to the sides, on later turned brass feet, the 8in (20cm) square dial signed Al: Irving London, 16.5in (42cm).
$3,600-5,500

A Regency mahogany bracket clock, the painted convex dial signed Jas McCabe, Royal Exchange, London, No. 881, strike/silent lever above, reverse of dial scratched James McCabe, Royal Exchange, 881, 6084, similarly signed fusee and chain movement No. 6084, anchor escapement, bell-striking, pull repeat, c1820, 16in (41cm).
$2,700-3,600

A Neuchatel bracket clock, with 9in (23cm) enamelled dial painted with putti at a fountain, the movement rack striking now on 2 gongs, the waisted case with verre eglomisé panels and painted with garlands, 28in (71cm).
$1,800-2,700

A late Victorian chiming bracket clock, the arched brass and silvered dial with subsidiary dials for chime/silent and chime on 8-bells/Cambridge chimes, the repeating movement chiming on the quarter hours, in gilt brass mounted ebonised case, 24in (61cm).
$1,800-2,700

A late Victorian chiming bracket clock, with 7.5in (19cm) dial and subsidiary dials for chime/silent and chime selection for Westminster 8-bells/10-bells, the movement with a further 4 gongs and one other for the hour, the ebonised and imitation tortoiseshell case set with ornate gilt brass mounts, 28in (71cm).
$3,600-5,500

Carriage Clocks

A brass grande sonnerie carriage clock, the white enamelled dial and backplate signed C.J. Klaftenberger, with subsidiary alarm dial, the gorge case with bevelled glasses, the rear glass engraved Presented to Surgeon Major Logie, M.D., Royal Horse Guards by L. Wickham Esq., Feb. 1874, 5.5in (14cm), in leather travelling case.
$3,600-5,500

A silver cased carriage clock, with a plain white enamel dial, platform lever escapement, the case of large size die-struck with masks and leafy scrolls, with carrying handle and resting on knurled bun feet, London 1891, 4.5in (11cm).
$1,000-1,500

An 8-day repeating carriage clock, with alarm, No. 187, the white enamel dial signed Chas. Frodsham, Clockmaker to the Queen, 84 Strand London, the chapter ring with Roman numerals and alarm dial below, the lever movement striking the hour and half-hour on a bell, in gilt brass gorge case, 6in (15cm), and outer travelling case.
$1,200-1,700

A French brass carriage clock, inscribed Dent 61 Strand London, enclosing an 8-day movement, striking with 2 hammers on a single gong, 7in (18cm), and contemporary leather travelling case with brass key.
$720-1,000

A French gilt brass carriage clock, with a white enamelled dial and bell striking movement, in a one-piece case with bevelled glasses and moulded pillars, 5in (13cm).
$720-1,000

A French carriage clock, with hour repeater and alarm, on bell, white enamel dial, retailed by Hall & Co., Manchester, movement stamped 'B' within a circle, c1900, 6in (15cm), and case with key. **$1,800-2,700**

A French gilt brass repeating carriage clock, with cream enamel chapter ring, leaf scroll engraved mask, gong striking movement, the case with upper and lower pierced friezes and with fluted columns and bail handle, 6in (15cm), and leather travelling case.
$720-1,000

A brass carriage clock, with a white enamel dial and engine turned frost gilt mask, the movement numbered 4451, the case plain, on bracket feet, with bail handle, 3in (8cm).
$720-1,000

Garnitures

A gilt metal mounted veined cream and brown marble clock garniture, the movement numbered 8608 and striking on a bell, some damage to eagle, clock 20in (50cm) high overall, urns 17in (42.5cm). **$720-1,000**

A French clock garniture, the clock with an enamelled dial, signed T. Simpson et Cie, Paris, with blue Roman numerals and regulator square above XII, the centre painted with military trophies, the 8-day movement by Japy Frères, striking on a bell, the gilt metal case cast overall with diaper and scrollwork, incorporating 3 small enamel panels, the finial in the form of an armoured bust, 12in (31cm), with accompanying candelabra, all on giltwood stands and under glass domes.
$1,800-2,700

A French white marble and gilt brass clock garniture, the four-glass clock gong striking, the bevelled glasses mounted with garlands and with a vase surmount, c1800, clock 18.5in (47cm) high. **$3,600-5,500**

A French boulle clock garniture, with a 5.5in (14cm) cartouche dial, bell striking movement, in a waisted case with gilt brass scroll mounts and putto finial, 17in (43cm), and a pair of 4-light candelabra.
$1,800-2,700

Miller's is a price
GUIDE not a price
LIST

A clock garniture, the 8-day movement by Marti & Cie, in parcel gilt bronze mounted black marble case, surmounted by a bronze model of the Warwick vase, 19thC, 19in (48cm), the side pieces in the form of Medici vases, 18in (46cm).
$1,800-2,700

Lantern

A George I miniature brass lantern timepiece with alarm, the arched dial signed Massey London, with brass chapter ring, central alarm disc, pierced single steel hand, the movement with verge escapement and bob pendulum, alarm on bell above, lacking gallery frets and one side door, 8in (25cm) high.
$2,700-3,600

A brass striking lantern clock, with pierced blued hand, the movement with anchor escapement and countwheel strike on bell above, enclosed within pierced brass frets, 15in (38cm) high.
$1,200-1,700

A George III lantern clock for the Turkish market, with a 9in (22.5cm) dial with scroll and flower spandrels and signed Isaac Rogers London in the arch above, the posted movement with verge and short pendulum escapement and countwheel bell striking, c1770, 14in (35.5cm) high.
$2,700-3,600

A brass winged lantern clock, with a 6.5in (16.5cm) chapter ring, engraved dial, and central alarm disc, the central fret signed Peter Closon at London fecit, the movement now with verge escapement, outside countwheel and with central anchor pendulum, with an oak bracket and weight, with alterations and replacements.
$2,700-3,600

A George II lantern timepiece with alarm, the dial signed John Belling Bodmyn 1753 beneath the chapter ring with central alarm disc, pierced blued single hand, the movement with verge escapement and alarm striking on bell above within engraved pierced gallery frets, spurs to back feet, 9in (23cm) high.
$7,000-9,000

A brass lantern clock, in 17thC style, with central alarm disc, verge escapement and bob pendulum, 8in (20cm), on a stained oak bracket.
$1,800-2,700

Longcase

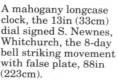

A William III walnut and floral marquetry longcase clock, the 10in (25cm) brass dial signed Humphry Adamson, London, the 8-day bell striking movement with outside countwheel, with restoration and replacements, the formerly rising hood with plain pilasters, convex shoulder moulding, skirt replaced, 78.5in (199cm).
$18,000-21,000

An oak longcase clock, with 8-day rack striking 4-pillar movement, with 12in (31cm) brass dial, the chapter with inner calendar ring, the circular boss in the arch signed R. Holborn, Tadcaster, 89in (226cm).
$1,200-1,700

A carved oak 8-day striking longcase clock, by Ben Kimberly, Catshill, 18thC, 90in (228.5cm).
$1,200-1,700

A William IV automaton mahogany longcase clock, the 12in (31cm) dial signed And'w Rich, Bridgwater, with seconds dial, calendar sector, and an automaton scene in the arch of Adam and Eve, with rack and bell striking movement, the trunk door crossbanded with rosewood and flanked by similar pillars, 91.5in (232.5cm).
$2,700-3,600

A mahogany longcase clock, the 13in (33cm) dial signed S. Newnes, Whitchurch, the 8-day bell striking movement with false plate, 88in (223cm).
$7,000-9,000

A Chippendale carved walnut longcase clock, by Adam Brant, New Hanover, Pennsylvania, engraved brass dial with phases of the moon, seconds and calendar date register, cast spandrels on dial missing, c1785, 102in (259cm) high.
$12,000-18,000

A George II burr walnut longcase clock, the 12in (31cm) dial signed Jn°. Berry, London, with seconds dial, calendar aperture, mask and leaf spandrels and a strike/silent dial in the arch, the movement with rack and bell striking in a flat top case with brass capped hood pilasters, some pieces replaced, 84.5in (215cm).
$3,600-5,500

An 8-day longcase clock, the white dial with a blue ground colour, by Samuel Deacon of Barton, in original oak case, 1806, 87in (221cm).
$3,600-5,500

A Federal inlaid mahogany longcase clock, by Simon Willard, Roxbury, Massachusetts, the white painted dial with phases of the moon and seconds register, restored, c1805, 96in (244cm) high.
$30,000-35,000

A George III mahogany longcase clock, the 14in (36cm) painted dial indistinctly signed Jn° Houghton, Chorley, the false plate signed Walker & Finnemore, the movement with rack and bell striking, in a well figured case with swan neck cresting and inlaid throughout with shells, fans and flowerheads, 87.5in (222cm).
$1,800-2,700

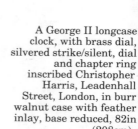

A Federal inlaid cherrywood longcase clock, New England, probably Vermont, face and works probably of different origin from case and pierced crest and feet replaced, c1800, 90in (229cm) high
$6,000-8,000

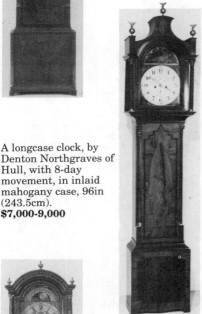

A longcase clock, by Denton Northgraves of Hull, with 8-day movement, in inlaid mahogany case, 96in (243.5cm).
$7,000-9,000

A mahogany longcase clock, the 12in (31cm) arched brass dial signed on a plate Warburton, W. Hampton, with 8-day bell striking movement, 92.5in (234cm).
$2,700-3,600

A George II longcase clock, with brass dial, silvered strike/silent, dial and chapter ring inscribed Christopher Harris, Leadenhall Street, London, in burr walnut case with feather inlay, base reduced, 82in (208cm).
$2,700-3,600

A George II black japanned longcase clock, the dial signed Thomas Johnson, Richmond, with subsidiary seconds ring and calendar aperture, pierced blued hands, mask and foliate spandrels, the 5-pillar rack striking movement with anchor escapement, 88in (224cm).
$2,700-3,600

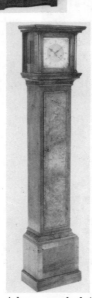

A longcase clock in early 18thC style, the brass dial with silvered chapter ring inscribed Tho. Lee, London, calendar aperture, the 4-pillar 8-day movement striking on a bell, in walnut veneered case, 69.5in (176cm).
$1,200-1,700

An exceptionally small 8-day white dial longcase clock, by McGregor of Ayton, Scotland, in original oak case, c1810, 79in (200.5cm).
$3,600-5,500

A Scottish mahogany longcase clock, the 13in (33cm) silvered dial signed Chas. Merrilies, Edinburgh, subsidiary seconds and date dials, 8-day bell striking movement, the drum hood with concave brass bezel, 80.5in (204cm).
$1,800-2,700

A George III longcase
clock, the painted dial
decorated with flowers
and Britannia in an oval,
the 8-day movement with
calendar and seconds
dials and striking on a
bell, the inlaid mahogany
case with carved swan
neck pediment and
corner columns, 82in
(208cm).
$2,700-3,600

A Victorian mahogany
longcase clock, with
painted figurative
spandrels representing
the seasons, the centre
with Christ in the
Wilderness, white
chapter ring inscribed
Blackhurst Over,
subsidiary seconds dial,
the well-figured trunk
and inspection door with
inlaid string lines, 8-day
bell striking movment,
90in (228.5cm).
$1,800-2,700

A Yorkshire longcase
clock by James
Whitworth, Lussley, the
12in (31cm) arched brass
dial with rolling moon in
the arch, subsidiary
seconds and date pointer,
8-day 4-pillar rack
striking movement with
anchor escapement,
82.5in (209cm).
$1,800-2,700

A mahogany longcase
clock, the painted dial
indistinctly inscribed,
enclosing an 8-day
movement with seconds
and date dials, 19thC,
88in (223.5cm).
$1,200-1,700

Mantel Clocks

A Federal mahogany, curly maple
and eglomise pillar-and-scroll
mantel clock, labelled Eli Terry,
Plymouth, Connecticut, some
small areas of sky repainted on
lower panel, 31in (79cm) high.
$3,000-5,000

A mahogany and brass inlaid
mantel clock, the 6in (15cm)
cream dial signed Catchpool,
Bishopsgate St., London, twin
fusee movement, with pull repeat,
the backplate with engraved
border, c1820, 16.5in (42cm).
$1,800-2,700

A French champlevé enamel and
gilt metal mantel clock of lyre
form with Japy Frères movement
striking on a bell, the base set
with two putti, late 19thC, 13in
(33cm).   **$1,800-2,700**

An Empire bronze and ormolu
mantel clock, the twin train
movement with bell strike, the
white enamel dial with Roman
and Arabic chapter ring, inscribed
Le Sieur à Paris, with engine
turned bezel, 14in (5.5cm).
$3,600-5,500

A late Victorian chiming mantel clock, the dial with 3 subsidiaries, the substantial triple-train fusee movement chiming on 8 bells and striking on gongs, the architectural case inlaid with swags and scrolls, gilt brass mounts, 23.5in (60cm).
$2,700-3,600

A gilt brass perpetual calendar mantel clock, the 3in (7.5cm) white enamelled dial signed Cotonie, Paris, and with subsidiary dials for day, date and month, with silk suspension and Japy Frères movement, the associated case with leaf engraved and pierced mask, 8.5in (21cm).
$1,200-1,700

A Regency brass inlaid mahogany mantel clock, the painted dial with regulation and strike/silent dials, the movement with engraved backplate signed John Moore, Clerkenwell, pull repeat, the arched case with fishscale frets and moulded lower frieze, 20in (51cm).
$1,800-2,700

A Louis Philippe ormolu automaton mantel clock, with an enamel dial and a silk suspension movement signed Guyerdet & Bouilly à Paris, striking on a gong in the base, the case in the form of a fortified chateau with a ship and a rowing boat rolling realistically on the choppy 'water' below, the automaton movement with 3 cams and mounted in an inlaid rosewood plinth, dome cracked, c1840, 25in (64cm).
$7,000-9,000

A French gilt mantel clock, the 3in (7.5cm) dial painted and signed Achille Brocot, bell striking, the case with pink porcelain panels and lion's masks, 14.5in (37cm), with dome and plinths.
$1,800-2,700

A Napoleon III oval 4-glass perpetual calendar mantel clock, the bell striking Marti movement No. 6635 with Brocot escapement and mercury pendulum, the 2-piece enamel dial centred by a colourful calendar indicating date, day of the week and month, an aperture above showing moon phases, in a gilt brass oval four-glass moulded case, c1870, 15in (39cm).
$3,600-5,500

A small French gilded case mantel clock, with small drum case striking movement, with a silvered Roman numeral dial, 19thC, 5in (13cm).
$720-1,000

Regulators

A mahogany Vienna regulator, with 7in (18cm) milk glass dial, cast and chased bezel, movement with square plates, deadbeat escapement, micrometer adjustment to the crutch, ebonised wood rod pendulum with brass bob, case lacking cresting, 37.5in (95cm).
$1,800-2,700

A mahogany Vienna regulator, with 7in (18cm) enamel dial, engine turned bezel, movement with square plates, c1830, 43in (110cm).
$3,600-5,000

A mahogany Vienna regulator, with 7in (18cm) 2-piece enamel dial indistinctly signed, florally cast bezel, movement with arch top square plates, deadbeat escapement, ebonised wood rod pendulum with brass bob, dial cracked, c1845, 37in (94cm).
$1,800-2,700

A Victorian Vienna regulator with walnut and beech case, decorated with typical split turnings, unusual keyhole shaped glass covering white enamel dial, 8-day movement striking on single gong, 57in (145cm).　**$2,700-3,600**

Skeleton Clocks

A brass York Minster skeleton clock, by Alfred Smith of Huddersfield, with an 8in (20cm) skeletonised silvered chapter ring, 6-spoke wheels, twin fusee movement, rack and snail strike on a gong and bell pull repeat, stamped on base and on an ebonised plinth, c1860, 21in (53cm).
$3,600-5,000

A Victorian balance wheel skeleton clock, with 4.5in (11.5cm) chapter ring, fusee movement with 6-spoke wheels, pierced barrel covers, maintaining power and deadbeat escapement with vertical balance and lever, in a scroll frame on a stepped rosewood plinth, c1850, with later glazed cover, 12.5in (32cm).
$2,700-3,600

A brass skeleton clock, the frame of scroll form, the 2-train fusee movement with bell striking and pull repeat, 5-spoke wheels, the 5.5in (14cm) silvered chapter ring inscribed J. D. Taylor, Liverpool, wood base, 19thC, 13in (33cm), on an ebonised stand with glass dome.　**$1,000-1,500**

An early Victorian month going skeleton clock, attributed to Parker and Pace, Bury St Edmunds, with 8.5in (21.5cm) silvered chapter ring, twin fusee movement driving the intermediate pinion and a 4-wheel train with deadbeat escapement and cylindrical bob pendulum, the backplate of solid arched form, the frontplate consisting of interlocking scrolls, marble base with glass dome, c1850, 11.5in (29cm).
$2,700-3,600

Table Clocks

A George III mahogany table clock, the 8in (20cm) silvered dial signed William Lindsey, London, central calendar, strike/silent in the arch, engraved flower spandrels, 5-pillar bell striking fusee movement, verge escapement and well engraved backplate, c1790, 17in (44cm).
$2,700-3,600

William Lindsey was apprenticed in 1759.

A Charles II ebony veneered table clock, with 6.5in (16.5cm) dial, calendar aperture, cherub spandrels, 5-pillar bell striking movement signed Henry Younge in ye Strand, verge escapement, formerly quarter repeating with unusual circular rack mounted on the front plate, well moulded case with small domed top, brass carrying handle and claw feet, verge rebuilt, c1680, 12in (30cm).
$14,500-16,500

Henry Younge was apprenticed in 1659 to Thomas Taylor and Free of the Clockmakers' Company from 1672; he worked in London until c1685. This clock was made soon after the introduction of rack striking and has a most unusual and efficient form of circular rack. Although the quarter repeating work has been entirely removed the 3-stepped quarters snail can still be seen on the minute wheel.

A Germanic striking table clock with alarm, the gilt movement signed Kriedel London on the top plate, with foliate pierced and chased footed lock, chain fusee for the gong, resting barrel for the bell in hinged base, pull wind alarm from the central disc in the silver champlevé arcaded dial, with blued steel hour hand and later minute hand, and similarly signed on the outer concentric alarm ring, c1700, 4in (10cm) dial diam.
$7,000-9,000

A Swiss cylinder paperweight table clock, the three-quarter plate keywind movement with going barrel, plain cock with steel regulator, plain 3-arm gilt balance with blue steel spiral hairspring, white enamel dial with subsidiary seconds, Roman numerals, blue steel hands, domed gunmetal case with silver bezel and a folding strut for use as a desk clock, c1870.
$70-145

Wall Clocks

A George IV mahogany wall clock, the 15in (36cm) painted dial signed J. R. Parker, Walsingham, weight driven movement with tapered plates, 5 wheels in the train and anchor escapement, the case with moulded wood bezel, c1830, 53.5in (136cm).
$2,700-3,600

A mahogany and boxwood gaming wall clock, with framed and glazed baize lined dial, the frame surmounted by turned boxwood chess pieces, the twin going barrel movement with anchor escapement and strike on gong, frame 20in (51cm) square. **$1,200-1,700**

A Dutch Zaandam striking and alarm wall clock.
$3,600-5,000

A German Black Forest wall clock, with strike and alarm, the 3.5in (9cm) enamel dial with central alarm disc and set on a colourfully decorated porcelain surround, the wood plated weight driven movement with outside countwheel, gong striking and top mounted alarm bell, the frame with the original side doors, gong missing, c1860, 8in (21cm).
$1,000-1,500

A George III mahogany wall clock, the 13in (33cm) painted dial signed T. Banks, Preston, the false plate signed Finnemore, 2-train rack and bell striking weight driven movement, teardrop case outlined with ebony and box stringing, veneered in well figured wood, c1800, 62in (157.5cm).
$2,700-3,600

> **Miller's is a price GUIDE not a price LIST**

A mahogany drop dial wall clock, the 12in (31cm) brass dial signed Thos. Pierce, Jnr., Bristol, twin fusee movement, bell striking, trunk with glazed lenticle, 27.5in (70cm).
$1,000-1,500

A Victorian Gothic quarter chiming wall clock, signed W. Potts & Sons, Leeds, with blued spade hands, the massive 5-pillar triple chain fusee movement with anchor escapement chiming on 8 bells via 8 hammers and striking on gong on backboard, 35in (89cm) high.
$3,600-5,000

A French picture wall clock, with silvered dial enclosing an engine turned panel, the movement striking the quarters on 2 graduated bells, and with sunburst pendulum, 19thC, 21in (53cm).
$1,000-1,500

Miscellaneous

A Continental walnut and boxwood strung cuckoo clock, the alabaster dial with cartouche chapter ring and enamel Roman numerals, the twin train movement striking on a gong, with bellow mechanism, 19thC, 19in (48cm).
$1,000-1,500

WATCHES

A Thomas Earnshaw 18ct. gold hunter cased half quarter repeating watch, hallmarked 1847, case maker's mark AC, 2 small chips around the edge, 4.9cm.
$1,800-2,700

A gold open faced keyless lever watch, by Patek Philippe, Geneve, with short length of 18ct. gold chain, 5.3cm.
$1,200-1,700

A Swiss yellow metal hunter cased quarter repeating key wind pocket watch, the movement with compensated lever movement, repeating on 2 gongs with 2 hammers, white enamel dial with gold hands and subsidiary seconds dial, in an engine turned case with repeating slide in the band, with gold 'tipsy' key, 5cm.
$1,200-1,700

A pink gold hunter cased keyless lever watch, No. 57032, matt gilded movement signed Deutsche Uhrenfabrikation Glashütte, gold escape wheel and pallets, compensation balance, blued steel spiral spring and regulator with micrometer adjustment, white enamel dial, signed Deutsche Uhrenfabrikation Glashütte I/S, Lange & Söhne, plain Louis XVI-type case, the three covers with the Lange stamp, c1910, 5.5cm.
$2,700-3,600

An 18ct. gold open faced key wind watch, the full plate fusee movement with lever escapement, plain gold 3 arm balance and signed French, Royal Exchange, London, hallmarked 1826, hinge to back cover defective, 4.2cm.
$360-540

An 18ct gold open faced key wind watch, the full plate fusee movement with lever escapement, compensated balance, engraved cock and signed Wm. Simcock, Warrington, with small inspection on cover and hallmarked 1872, 4.6cm.
$360-540

A spherical glass magnifying paperweight deck watch, by the New Haven Clock Co., 19thC, 7.5cm.
$360-540

A lady's silver and enamel cased fob watch, enamel chipped to rear.
$110-180

An 18ct. gold cased quarter repeating keyless lever pocket watch, with unsigned movement, white enamel dial with Arabic numerals and subsidiary seconds, the minutes divided into fifths, the back inner case engraved 'A Happy New Era, 1901', the outer case with monogram inlaid with blue enamel, some damage.
$1,200-1,700

A gentleman's pocket watch by Record, with nickel case and Swiss lever movement, with GWR insignia on the reverse.
$180-360

A rare George III watch alarm, by
W. Gossage.
$720-1,000

An 18ct. gold minute repeating
pocket watch.   **$3,600-5,000**

An 18ct gold open faced key wind
watch, signed Jas. Whitlaw,
Edinburgh, hallmarked 1826,
5.3cm.
$360-540

A silver hunter cased verge
watch, for the Turkish market,
the full plate fusee movement
with pierced and engraved cock,
Turkish signature, and silvered
regulator dial, the white enamel
dial with Turkish numerals,
unmatched hands and signed
Ralph Gout, London, case hinge
defective, hallmarked 1834,
4.9cm.
$360-540

A Massey lever in a silver open
face case, full plate gilt keywind
fusee movement with signed and
numbered dust cover, Harrison's
maintaining power, engraved cock
with diamond endstone, polished
steel Bosley regulator, signed
Hunt & Son Yarmouth 39248,
hallmarked London 1825, maker's
mark IHM, 5.3cm.
$360-540

Wristwatches

A gentleman's silver cased
wristwatch, with jewelled Swiss
lever movement, finished and
retailed by Benson, c1930.
$180-360

A gentleman's wristwatch, by
Longines, in a gold case, c1930.
$180-360

A lady's stainless steel cased
Rolex Oyster Perpetual
wristwatch, the silvered dial with
applied gilt metal line batons
with aperture for date, in a case
of plain form on articulated
stainless steel Rolex bracelet
strap.
$360-540

A paste set metal wristwatch, by
the Aircraft Watch Co., with
Swiss cylinder movement, c1930.
$70-145

A gentleman's yellow gold oyster perpetual wristwatch, the movement stamped Rolex Perpetual, Trigger Screw, Vis. Tirette 000, the silvered dial inscribed Rolex Perpetual, Chronometer, import mark for Glasgow 1937, on 9ct. expanding bracelet.
$2,700-3,600

A gentleman's silver wristwatch in a cushion shaped case, c1925.
$70-145

A Tourneau gold calendar and moonphase chronograph wristwatch, the matt silvered dial with outer date ring and central date hand, dagger 5-minute marks, subsidiary dials for running seconds, elapsed minutes and hours combined with phases of the moon, apertures for day and month, sweep centre seconds operated by two buttons in the band, the case with screwed back and maker's mark, numbered 1024324, the signed movement jewelled to the centre, 3.5cm.
$1,800-2,700

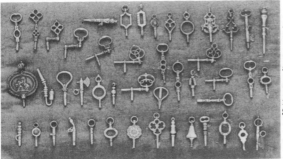

A collection of 46 steel watch keys, one in the form of a pipe, another a pistol, on a green cloth mount.
$2,700-3,600

BAROMETERS
Chronometers

A 2-day marine chronometer, by Victor Kullberg, No. 6357, the 4in (10cm) silvered dial signed and numbered, the movement with Earnshaw spring detent, escapement, palladium spring, compensated balance, spotted movement, gold hands and fully numbered, with brass gimbal and box, in a 3-tier mahogany case.
$2,700-3,600

An 8-day marine chronometer, originally made for use with vacuum, glass and pump now missing, unsigned movement with reversed fusee, Earnshaw spring detent escapement, Z-balance, free sprung, 4in (10cm) silvered dial, the whole gimballed in mahogany carrying case with door at the front for access, c1800.
$10,000-12,000

A 2-day marine chronometer with integral balance, with later unsigned spotted movement with Earnshaw spring detent escapement, Guillaume integral compensated balance, blued steel helical spring, free sprung, restored silvered dial signed A. Lange & Söhne, Glashütte B/Dresden No. 79, Roman numerals, subsidiary dials for seconds and up-and-down, in brass box also numbered, stamped 671E and with crowned M, in brass bound rosewood box with flush handles, later key, diameter of bezel 5in (12cm).
$3,600-5,000

Stick Barometers

A Regency mahogany bowfront stick barometer, with ogee top, glazed vernier scale signed G. C. Dixey, London, moulded ebonised cistern cover to shaped base, restored, 38.5in (97cm).
$2,700-3,600

A mahogany stick barometer, the bone plates signed H. Hughes, 59 Fenchurch Street, London, with mercury thermometer, the case with arched top and turned cistern cover, 36.5in (93cm).
$1,200-1,700

A mahogany bowfronted stick barometer, with step pediment and bowfronted thermometer to main trunk, with original ebony urn cistern cover to the base, c1835.
$3,600-5,000

A George I walnut barometer, by J Halifax of Barnsley, 6in (15cm) dial with mask spandrels, finely engraved centre scrolling leaves, the richly coloured chevron veneered trunk outlined in stringing and set with engraved recording dial, c1720.
$54,000-63,000

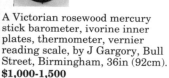

A Victorian rosewood mercury stick barometer, ivorine inner plates, thermometer, vernier reading scale, by J Gargory, Bull Street, Birmingham, 36in (92cm).
$1,000-1,500

A mahogany stick barometer, the paper plates signed Manticha Fecit, the case with exposed tube, fluted corners and rectangular cistern cover, 38.5in (97cm).
$1,000-1,500

A mahogany stick barometer, with round top, glazed door to main dial, exposed tube on front of case and hemispherical cistern cover, c1800.
$2,700-3,600

A mahogany stick barometer, with silvered brass dials and long thermometer to the front of case, c1790.
$2,700-3,600

A George II mahogany stick barometer, with later wood finial to cavetto arched top, the dial with foliate border engraving, moulded cistern cover, 38in (97cm).
$1,000-1,500

Wheel Barometers

A flight of 3 walnut barometers, by C. H. Chadburn & Son, with 8, 10 and 12in (20, 25 and 31cm) dials, with patented rack and pinion movement, dated 1861.
$7,000-9,000 the set

An oak cased aneroid barometer, in Art Nouveau design, by Negretti & Zambra, London, 11.5in (29cm).
$180-360

An Edwardian Regency style mahogany aneroid wall barometer, crossbanded with satinwood, with thermometer box, 8in (20cm) silvered dial, J. Lucking & Co., Birmingham, 34in (86cm).
$720-1,000

A Sheraton design mahogany banjo shaped barometer, by Catelly & Co, Hereford, the case inlaid with shells and chequered stringing.
$1,200-1,700

A carved oak aneroid barometer, with printed 8in (20cm) dial, by Coombes of Davenport, unrestored, c1910, 33in (84cm).
$180-360

An oak cased combination clock and barometer, in anchor design with rope carved pattern around bezels, 8-day clock movement, 21in (53cm).
$720-1,000

A mahogany and inlaid wheel barometer, with 8in (20cm) silvered dial, signed Josh. Frigerio, 281 High Holborn, and alcohol thermometer, the case with architectural pediment inlaid with shells and stringing, 38.5in (98cm).   **$720-1,000**

SCIENTIFIC INSTRUMENTS

Dials

A brass miner's dial, the silvered dial engraved Francis Thomas, Engineer, Marazion, Cornwall, in brass box with spirit level and hinged sight enclosed by a hinged lid with integral sight, with engraved scale plates to the sides, on a tripod fitment with pinion 2-way revolutionary movement and clamping screw, small crack to glass, 18thC.
$180-360

An ivory and enamel compass dial barometer, signed Abraham Optician Cheltenham, with graduated mercury thermometer, compass needle, carved border decoration, in plush lined leather case, enamel cracked, 4.5in (11cm) diam.
$360-540

An English brass universal equinoctial dial, signed Thos Rubergall, Optician to the King, 27 Coventry Str.t, London, with silvered brass hour ring, hinged latitude arc and gnomon, compass rose inset with spirit levels, on 3 levelling screws, in original sharkskin covered and velvet lined case, c1830, 5in (13cm) wide.
$2,700-3,600

An Andreas Vogler brass universal equinoctial dial, engraved with foliage, inset compass with hinged latitude arc, hour ring and gnomon, 2in (5cm) with original printed list of cities and latitudes, in leather and card case, distressed, 18thC.
$720-1,000

A German silvered brass horizontal sundial, unsigned, the plate engraved with hour scales and minute divisions, decorated with scrolls, incorporating a compass with iron needle and brass cap, a folding string gnomon and 3 adjustable levelling screws, in original chamois leather lined shaped case, the cover with traces of embossed decoration, 18thC, 7.5in (19cm) long. $2,700-3,600

A Continental universal equinoctial ring, c1740, 4.5in (11.5cm) high.
$1,000-1,500

A brass universal equinoctial ring dial, unsigned but engraved on the equinoctial ring James Heron's Present to W. Campbell at Rosemount April 3 1769, and an hour scale III-XII-IX, the meridian ring calibrated on one side with 0°-90° scale, the other side with a quadrant scale, the pivoted bridge with sliding pin-hole sight calendar and declination scales, 18thC, 3in (8cm) diam.
$1,200-1,700

A horizontal sundial, probably English, the brass plate engraved with hour scale, scrolling decoration and monogram, mounted with sliding gnomon and rotating above shaped brass plate engraved with 4 quadrants, late 18thC, 7in (18cm).
$2,700-3,600

Globes

A lacquered and silvered brass universal equinoctial compass dial, signed on the hour ring Je Ramsden London, the hour scale divided IIII-IIX-VIII with minute sub-divisions and scrollwork decoration, with spring loaded gnomon, the silvered latitude arc engraved 0°-60°, the silvered compass dial with level and cross bubble, engraved in 4 quadrants, with needle on jewelled pivot with clamp, on 3 adjustable screw feet, damaged, in shaped fishskin covered case, late 18thC, 7in (18cm) wide.
$2,700-3,600

An 18in (46cm) terrestrial globe, by Blades, East and Blades, 22 Abchurch Lane, London, mounted in brass meridian within horizontal ring of calendar and zodiac scales, on mahogany stand with stretcher, inset with a silvered dial compass, 41.5in (114cm) high.
$3,600-5,000

A terrestrial globe, by W. & A. K. Johnston Ltd, early 20thC.
$7,000-9,000

A Charler Bloud ivory diptych dial, the upper outer face with equinoctial pin-gnomon dial with decorative geometric engraved decoration, upper inner face with silver volvelle, mis-shapen, lower inner face with analemmatic magnetic dial, lacking magnetic needle, glass cover and hinged latitude arm, the base with rotating silver disc engraved with calendar and operating the analemma, signed Fait et Jnue par Charles Bloud Dieppe, late 17thC.
$1,800-2,700

A 2in (5cm) terrestrial globe, the maker's label inscribed MALBY & Co Houghton Str. Newcastle St. Strand, dated 1842, the paper gores delicately coloured, the globe with steel axis pin, in a mahogany case with domed cover, mid-19thC, 3in (8cm) high.
$2,700-3,600

A Malby 18in (46cm) terrestrial globe, published by Edward Stanford , 55 Charing Cross, London, Jan. 1st 1883, the gores with analemma and lines of variation, the engraved brass meridian circle divided in 4 quadrants, with hour ring, the printed horizon circle with zodiac and calendar scales supported on an oak tripod stand with compass, needle and glass missing, late 19thC, 45in (114cm).
$3,600-5,000

A G. M. Lowitz 5in (13cm) celestial globe on stand, the sphere applied with well engraved and hand coloured gores, mounted in brass meridian and horizontal ring applied with coloured print of calendar and zodiac scales, on 4 turned and ebonised wood legs, on oak base, 1747.
$3,600-5,000

Surveying

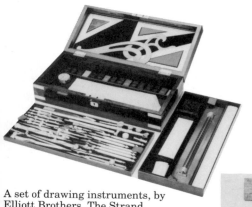

A lacquered brass surveying level, signed on the finely engraved compass dial Cole Fecit, the compass star engraved with scrolls, the dial with 2 scales, one in 4 quadrants, the other 0°-360°, with maker's trade label, in fitted oak carrying case, late 18thC, 25.5in (65cm).
$2,700-3,600

A set of drawing instruments, by Elliott Brothers, The Strand, London, in a purple velvet lined 3-tiered rosewood box with plaque inscribed Elliott Smith, 13.5in (35cm).
$3,600-5,000

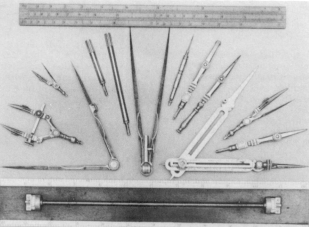

An octant, by H. Hughes, Fenchurch Street, London, in original fitted case, early 19thC.
$360-540

A lacquered brass level, by Thos. Cooke, York, with inserted bubble level, draw tube focusing, 1.25in (3cm) lens, limb attached to body tube by fixed column and levelling screw on bayonet tripod mount with screw adjustment, in fitted mahogany case with trade label.
$720-1,000

Thomas Cooke 1807-68.

A part set of W. & S. Jones drawing instruments, with nickel silver instruments, including triangular compasses, proportional compasses, wheel pen, beam compasses, miniature compasses, ivory and ebony parallel rule, in mahogany case, early 19thC, 13in (33cm).
$1,800-2,700

A lacquered brass part surveying level, telescope missing, signed on the silvered compass rose, Martin London, with fine blued steel needle on agate pivot, with rack adjustment, silvered vernier with folding magnifier, telescope mounting and staff socket, in fishskin covered fitted case, 18thC, 5in (13cm).
$360-540

A gunner's quadrant, the brass base frame stamped C.T.D.E.M and dated 1612, engraved with flower and foliate decoration, the quadrant with stamped numerals with scale 45°-0°-45° each end of the quadrant terminating with the head of a mythical beast, with plummet indicator, and fitted to base frame by twin screws and lugs, the base drilled and tapped at each end, early 17thC, 5in (13cm) wide.
$2,700-3,600

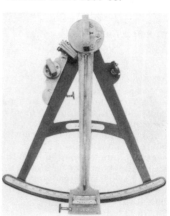

A E. & G .W. Blunt ebony octant, with ivory scale, vernier and maker's plaque, brass index arm, peep-hole sight and set of coloured filters, American, c1835, 10.5in (26cm) radius.
$720-1,000

Telescopes

A 4in (10cm) brass reflecting telescope on stand, signed G. Adams at No 60, Fleet Street, London, Instrut. Maker to his MAJESTY K. G. III, late 18thC, 27in (69cm), together with a spare reflector and fragment of Dixey trade label.
$1,800-2,700

A 4in (10cm) Broadhurst Clarkson & Co. brass refracting telescope on stand, 55in (140cm) tube, in pine case, with 5 eyepieces including a prismatic lens, late 19thC.
$2,700-3,600

A 2in (5cm) brass refracting telescope on stand, the tube with rack and pinion focusing, mounted on bracket above tapering column and folding tripod base, signed R. & J. Beck, 31 Cornhill, London, c1880, 33in (84cm).
$1,200-1,700

A 3in (8cm) brass refracting telescope on stand, signed on tube Newton & Co, Opticians to the Queen, 3 Fleet Street, London, mid-19thC, 41in (104cm) tube, in mahogany case, with 3 oculars.
$1,800-2,700

A brass refracting telescope on stand, by G. Carter, Exeter, the 3in (8cm) tube with rack and pinion focusing, on turned brass column and folding tripod base, early 19thC, 41in (104cm), in fitted wood case with additional eyepieces.
$720-1,000

A brass 2in (5cm) 5-draw refracting telescope, signed James Jeffreys, St. Johns Street, London, with lens cap and eyepiece, dust slide and mahogany outer body tube, with associated folding tripod and accessories, in fitted mahogany case, 19thC, 13in (33cm).
$1,800-2,700

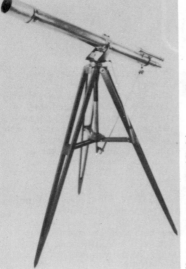

A 4.5in (11cm) refracting telescope, signed T. Cooke & Sons, York, the 64in (163cm) long body tube with rack and pinion focusing, lens hood and star finder, mounted on a trunion with geared azimuth motion, the centre column supported from the mahogany tripod by folding locking arms, the steadying bar with later body tube attachment, late 19thC.
$2,700-3,600

A 4in (10cm) reflecting telescope, signed on the backplate, JAMES SHORT LONDON, the 24in (61cm) long tube with screw-rod focusing, lens cap and star finder telescope, with fine gear alt-azimuth mounting with tangent screw fine adjustment, on pillar support and folding tripod stand, the cabriole legs terminating in pad feet, 18thC.   **$2,700-3,600**

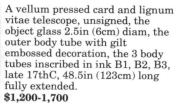

A vellum pressed card and lignum vitae telescope, unsigned, the object glass 2.5in (6cm) diam, the outer body tube with gilt embossed decoration, the 3 body tubes inscribed in ink B1, B2, B3, late 17thC, 48.5in (123cm) long fully extended.
$1,200-1,700

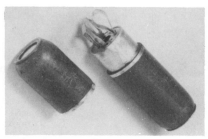

A refracting telescope nécessaire, probably French, the green painted wood tube with gold and silver mounts, fitted with tweezers, spatula, needle and pricker, late 18thC, 3.5in (9cm) long.
$1,800-2,700

A 3-draw vellum and paper card telescope, unsigned, with 1in (3cm) object glass, 'Augsburg' type paper covered draw tubes, leather outer cover, horn and mahogany fittings, 18thC, 56in (142cm) fully extended.
$1,800-2,700

A brass 3.5in (9cm) refracting telescope, signed on the backplate NEGRETTI & ZAMBRA LONDON, the 49in (125cm) long body tube with rack and pinion focusing, star finder and lens cap raised on a tapering pillar support, with solar filters, in fitted mahogany carrying case, with brass drop handles, late 19thC, 52in (132cm) long.
$2,700-3,600

A Steward 3in (8cm) brass refracting telescope, the tube with rack and pinion focusing, mounted on bracket above tapering column and supporting strut, folding tripod base, 37.5in (95cm) long tube, late 19thC.
$720-1,000

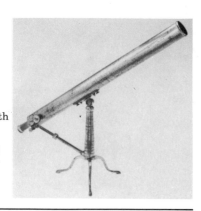

Microscopes

A refracting and reflecting brass telescope, the tube inscribed Newton and Co., Opticians, 3 Fleet St., Temple Bar, London, together with original mahogany box with Newton and Co. paper label, 7 alternative eyepieces, 62in (157cm) long.
$3,600-5,000

A lacquered brass 'Culpeper' type miscroscope, unsigned, simple draw tube focusing, the stage signed Adams London and united with the mahogany plinth base by scroll supports, with diamond shaped feet, the plinth base with accessory drawer, pyramid shaped mahogany case, with further accessory drawer, early 19thC, 18in (46cm).
$1,800-2,700

A compound monocular miscroscope, signed on the trade card E. Culpeper Sculp. London, with brass eyepiece and turned lignum vitae mount, single draw applied with green vellum, the wooden tube with grey rayskin cover, circular stage raised on 3 brass columns above reflector and lignum vitae base, in original oak pillar case with drawer of accessories including 5 objectives, stage condensor, fishplate, live box and large glass stage plate, 1730, 14in (36cm) high.
$7,000-9,000

A binocular microscope, by C. Collins, 157 Great Portland Street, London, with accessories, in mahogany case, 18.5in (47cm). **$720-1,000**

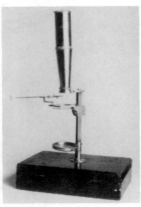

An English brass Cary type botanical microscope, the mahogany case containing compound tube, racked supporting column, side reflector, c1830.
$360-540

A brass binocular microscope, by Baker, 244 High Holborn, London, in fitted mahogany case with many accessories including objectives, oculars and condenser
$1,000-1,500

A compound monocular microscope, with turned lignum vitae eye piece, pasteboard tube with grey rayskin covered binding, shaped brass stage on wooden base of later date, together with 2 objectives, fishplate, reflector and wheel of specimen mounts, mid-18thC, 13.6in (34cm) high.
$3,600-5,000

A brass compound monocular microscope, with sliders and some accessories, 18thC, 11in (28cm) high, and a small pocket telescope by Ramsden.
$2,700-3,600

A brass monocular compound microscope, signed Baker, 244 High Holborn, London, the bar limb construction with rack and pinion focusing, mechanical stage and sub-stage, large plano/concave mirror, the tube engraved 'Presented to Thomas Hodge by the Honourable the Commissioners of Inland Revenue for proficiency in Chemistry shown at the Examinations held by Professor Frankland at the close of the session 1871-72', 19in (48cm) high, together with 3 objectives, 2 oculars and live box.
$1,000-1,500

A lacquered brass compound monocular microscope, unsigned, probably Dutch, late 18thC, 9in (22cm) long. **$1,800-2,700**

A binocular compound microscope, signed Ross London 5303, with A-shaped base mounted with 2 columns supporting sub-stage, circular stage and binocular tubes, in mahogany case with bench condenser, c1885, 16in (41cm) high.
$1,000-1,500

A brass compound monocular microscope, signed Thos. D. King, Optician Bristol, No 203, Paris 1855, on tripod base, in mahogany case with 6 oculars, camera lucida, bench condenser and separate 2 cases of specimen slides, 18in (46cm) high.
$1,800-2,700

A brass compound binocular microscope, signed Negretti & Zambra, of Ross-type design with fine focusing by calibrated milled screw, mechanical stage and sub-stage and large plano-concave reflector, in mahogany case with monocular tube, 6 oculars, 4 objectives, analyser, polariser and live box, late 19thC, 19.5in (49cm) high.
$1,800-2,700

A compound binocular microscope, signed Ross London 5394, focusing by micrometer screw and rack and pinion, rotating circular stage with sub-stage assembly and plano-concave mirror, on A-shaped base, 20in (51cm) high, together with 5 oculars, 4 objectives, Lieberkuhn, live box, dark ground condenser, other accessories and 3 boxes of specimen slides, c1885.
$1,800-2,700

A brass monocular microscope, on a shaped base inscribed Nachet et Fils, 17 Rue St. Severin, Paris, in a fitted mahogany carrying case with 2 spare oculars, 2 objectives by R. and J. Beck, an R. and J. Beck objective case and 2 boxes of tiny glass specimen slides.
$360-540

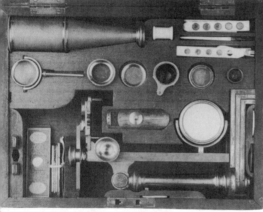

A brass compound monocular microscope, signed on the folding tripod stand Dollond London, with accessories, incomplete, in fitted mahogany case, mid-19thC, 11in (28cm) wide.   **$1,800-2,700**

A screw barrel microscope, signed E. Culpeper Fecit on the screw barrel, turned ivory handle, 7 numbered objectives, ivory talc box, black/white disc and stage forceps, set of ivory and brass specimen slides and a small booklet of instructions, in green velvet lined fishskin covered case, early 18thC, 5in (13cm) wide.
$3,600-5,000

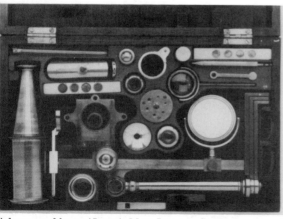

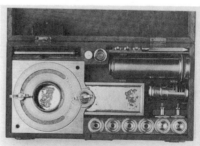

A lacquered brass 'Jones's Most Improved' type compound monocular microscope, signed on the folding tripod stand Cary London, in baize lined and fitted mahogany case, 19thC, 11in (28cm) wide.
$2,700-3,600

A polished and lacquered brass solar microscope, signed on the base plate DOLLOND. LONDON, with Wilson screw-barrel extension, brass slide and other accessories, in fitted mahogany case, 12in (31cm) wide.
$1,800-2,700

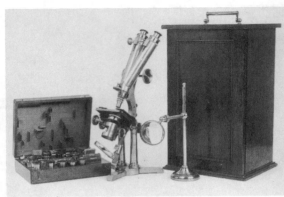

An oxidised and lacquered brass binocular microscope signed Henry Crouch, London, No. 722, with draw tube eye piece adjustment, rack and pinion focusing, nose piece fine focusing screw, prism, double nosepiece, limb with central axis, circular stage, detachable sub-stage condenser, plano-concave mirror, on jointed arm on 'Y' shaped foot, in fitted mahogany case, with accessories, late 19thC, 15.5in (39cm) high.   **$720-1,000**

A lacquered brass compound binocular microscope, signed on the stand Smith & Beck, 6 Coleman St, LONDON, No. 1885, with rack and pinion coarse and micrometer fine focusing, prism, mechanical stage, sub-stage wheel condenser, plano-concave mirror and an extensive range of accessories in supplementary case including double nosepiece, 3 objectives, Abbe condenser and other items, with a bull's-eye condenser, in mahogany carrying case with brass handle, 19thC, 20in (51cm) high. **$3,600-5,000**

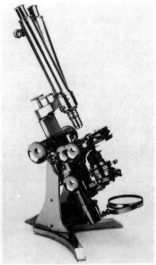

A brass binocular compound aquarium microscope, signed on the base Ross, London 3227, c1875, 16in (40cm) high, in original mahogany case with Ross Ltd documentation and original catalogue, pricing the microscope at £21 and the case with accessories at £2.10s., accessories include 4 oculars and 3 objectives. **$3,600-5,000**

A lacquered brass compound binocular microscope, signed on the Y-shaped stand ROSS London No. 3701, with rack and pinion coarse and fine focusing, micrometer differential screw extra fine adjustment, the base of the body tubes engraved Wenham's Binocular by Ross, London, 19thC, 25.5in (65cm) high. **$2,700-3,600**

A Cuff type compound monocular microscope, unsigned, the body tube located on a limb from the rectangular section vertical pillar, with internal rack and pinion adjustment to the stage, bull's-eye condenser and plano-concave mirror, with scroll support on mahogany veneered oak plinth base, with accessory drawer containing a numbered set of 6 objectives, ivory sliders, sprung stage and other items, in pyramid shaped mahogany case, with supplementary drawer, early 19thC, 19.5in (49cm) high. **$3,600-5,000**

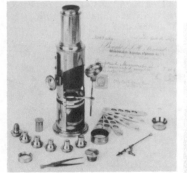

A lacquered brass Martin's type drum microscope, with draw tube and rack and pinion focusing, rack work mounted to outer body tube, circular 2-tier stage with internal spring to stage, concave mirror on circular foot, in fitted case with accessories, 11in (28cm) wide.   **$1,200-1,700**

A lacquered and oxidised brass compound binocular microscope, signed on the horseshoe stand Swift & Son, 81 Tottenham Court Rd., London W., 19thC. **$1,800-2,700**

MEDICAL INSTRUMENTS

An English mahogany medicine chest, with brass carrying handles, early 19thC, 9in (23cm) wide.
$2,700-3,600

A set of 25 eyes varying in sizes, iris and scleral colouring, in a fitted case with 25 sub-divisions, box clasp signed L.Z. PARIS, 6.5in (16cm).
$180-360

A pair of Benjamin Martin type iron Martins Margins, with large ring ends, counter sunk non-slotted screws, inserted horn visuals, repaired, c1750, lenses 1in (3cm) diam.
$180-360

An apothecary's mahogany travelling medicine chest, with brass carrying handles, the lid opening to reveal a fitted compartmented interior, early 19thC, 10in (25cm) wide.
$720-1,000

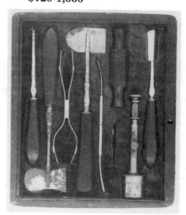

An English trephine set, the brass mounted and fishskin covered case fitted with 2 Hay's saws, elevator, crown saw, tweezers, case restored, late 18thC, 9in (23cm) wide. **$1,800-2,700**

A pair of spring framed spectacles, inset into the inner cover of the book Breviarium Theologicum, published 1702, pigskin binding with tooled decoration, probably German.
$7,000-9,000

It is extremely rare to find a book used as a housing or case for a pair of spectacles.

A pair of 'Nuremberg' single wire rim nose spectacles, in flat edged grooved copper wire, German c1670, 1.5in (4cm) diam. lenses.
$1,800-2,700

An English leather reading glass, with thumb extension, lens with grey colouration, 3in (8cm) diam., chipped, c1650, 5in (13cm) long.
$2,700-3,600

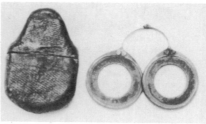

A pair of Martin's Margins rivet nose spectacles, from the circle of James Ayscough, horn frame, horn insert, with a steel folding bridge, reduced aperture lenses, 1in (2cm) diam, power of +2 on each, invented by Benjamin Martin, in original fitted papier mâché case, c1760, 3in (8cm) high.
$3,600-5,000

A pair of steel surgical forceps, with join and parallel action jaws, a knuckle triangular blade with serrated face, signed blade 'Plum' with flat smooth horn face, central parallel plate lock, 18thC, 6.5in (16cm) wide.
$180-360

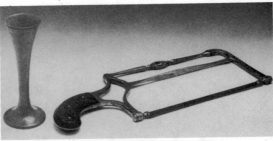

A home medicine chest by Springweiler and Co., London, the mahogany case with sunken brass handle and hinged front, the interior fitted with glass bottles, balance scales and a glass pestle and mortar, early 19thC, 8.5in (21cm) high.
$1,200-1,700

A Dr Butcher's bone saw, with ebony handle and steel frame with screw tension, English mid- 19thC, 13in (33cm) long, and a monaural stethoscope, in turned beech, 5.5in (14cm) high.   **$900-1,500**

An amputation bone saw, signed W. & H. HUTCHINSON, SHEFFIELD, Instrument Makers to the Royal Navy, with carved lion, crown and unicorn on shaped ebony handle, 15in (38cm) long.
$180-360

A pair of folding eyeglasses, with riveted steel bridge engraved 6, leather rims, English, c1750, 1.5in (4cm) diam.
$3,600-5,000

The style is depicted on the trade card attributed to James Ayscough of London.

A Weiss set of surgeon's amputation instruments, the brass bound mahogany case with badge engraved Dr. Settle, fitted interior with bone saw, 2 Hay's saws, set of liston knives, 2 tourniquets, tweezers, ligatures and needles, signed along the lock mounting Weiss's Improved Air Tight Case, 62 Strand, London, c1840, 15in (39cm) wide.
$2,700-3,600

An English cased trephine set, in fishskin covered case with red velvet lining, fitted with hand drill with 2 crown heads and an arrowhead, ivory handled brush, bone remover and 2 lenticulars with rosewood handles, late 18thC, 9 by 7in (23 by 18cm).
$2,700-3,600

An English carved ivory phrenology head cane handle, the head engraved with numbered sections of the skull, with corresponding characteristics including 'Indivuality, Wonder, Ideality and Imitation', the base with screw thread, mid-19thC, 3in (7cm) high.
$1,800-2,700

A silver nipple shield, hallmarked London 1801, together with a silver pap boat hallmarked 1769, with beaded rim, 4.5in (11cm) long.
$720-1,000

A John Weiss & Sons cased surgical instrument set, the brass bound oak case fitted with 2 lift-out trays, containing dental instruments, trepanning set, Liston knives, scalpels, bone saws, bullet extractors, clamps and others, c1900, 18in (46cm) wide.
$1,800-2,700

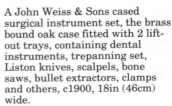

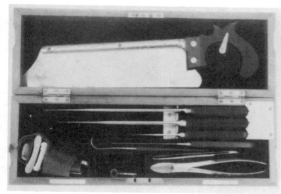

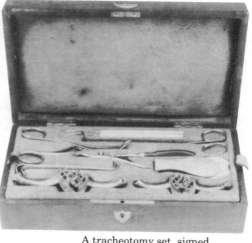

An amputation set, by S. MAW Son & THOMPSON LONDON, ALDERSGATE St. LONDON, and MAW LONDON, with bone saw, finger saw, tourniquet, 3 liston knives and other items, with chequered grip ebony handles, in a velvet lined brass bound mahogany case, c1870, 14.5in (37cm).
$1,200-1,700

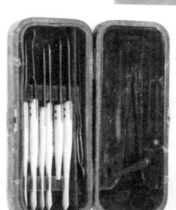

A tracheotomy set, signed Mathieu, with lift-out tray containing 4 silver graduated tracheotomy cannulae, folding tongue depressor, 2 retractors, a hooked spreader with ebony chequer grip handle, 2 forceps and 2 ivory handled lancets, in mahogany case with brass fittings, brass plate inscribed Dr. Mauricel, with suede interior and accessories, 10in (25cm) wide.
$1,800-2,700

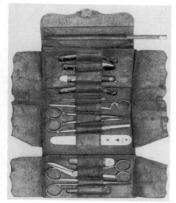

A surgeon's pocket set, signed Manufactured by H. Schively at his Surgical Instrument Manufactury No 75 Chestnut St Philadelphia, with 6 smooth ivory handled lancets, in velvet lined paper covered wooden case, 19thC, 7in (17cm) wide.
$180-360

A similar set is displayed at the Virginia Apothecary Shop, Williamsburg U.S.A.

An English surgeon's pocket instrument set, in red leather case fitted with a variety of instruments including a silver tongue depressor, hallmarked London 1802, a number of scalpels with tortoiseshell guards, scissors, probes, early 19thC, 6in (15cm) wide.   **$900-1,500**

A Fowler's ceramic phrenology head, lettered with transfers and with underglaze blue lining, late 19thC, 12in (31cm) high.
$1,800-2,700

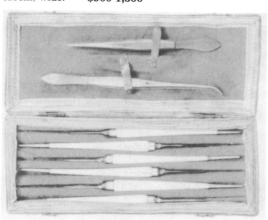

A set of French scalpels, in steel with ivory handles, in original leather case with cloth and metal braid, c1800, 9in (23cm) wide.
$720-1,000

A pair of French obstetric forceps, indistinctly signed LS EI and stamped with maker's symbol, with central locking pin, straight limbs and flat cross shaped ends, late 18thC, 18in (46cm) long.
$720-1,000

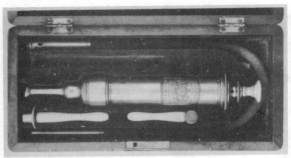

A brass enema, by Salt & Son, cutlers to the Queen and surgical instrument manufacturers, Birmingham, with cord attachment, ivory handled plunger and nozzles, in velvet lined fitted mahogany case, 11in (28cm).
$360-540

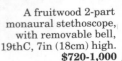

A fruitwood 2-part monaural stethoscope, with removable bell, 19thC, 7in (18cm) high.
$720-1,000

External aspect nerves, arteries, veins and muscles of the head, with maker's label Lehrmittelwerke Berlinische Verlagsanstalt GmbH. Berlin N.W.87, with descriptions of the various numbered areas in both Latin and English, study in wax, in black painted glazed case, 9.5in (24cm) high, and another study of the diseases of the teeth, 12.5in (31cm) wide.
$720-1,000

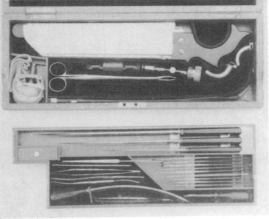

A field surgeon's amputation set, signed Young Edin. and Evans and Co. London, the instruments with smooth ebony handles, including a large bone saw, small bone saw with hinged back, trephine with chequer grip handle, silver tracheotomy tube, cross legged forceps, trocar and cannulae, Liston knives, in velvet lined fitted brass bound mahogany case, 17.5in (45cm) wide.
$1,800-2,700

An ebony monaural stethoscope, with student's listening outlet, c1870, 8in (20cm) high.
$1,000-1,500

A French plaster ecorché, after Bouchardon, the figure with various muscles and tendons named in ink, on oval base, 19thC, 23in (59cm) high.
$1,800-2,700

A black painted tin ear trumpet, 4in (10cm) diam.
$180-360

A Rein & Son silver plated ear trumpet, with scrolling decoration and simulated ivory earpiece, mid-19thC, 6in (15cm) high, together with a silver shaving cream warmer, hallmarked London 1900, with cylindrical container mounted above burner, 6in (15cm) extended.
$1,200-1,700

A set of male urethral sounds, with 4 graduated sounds and an adjustable urethral dilator with ivory handles and chrome rod, in satin lined case, 15in (38cm) wide.
$360-540

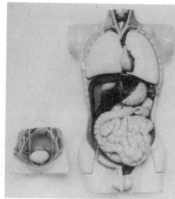

A plaster anatomical male demonstration model, each piece numbered in order of assembly, with an additional section for female uterus.
$360-540

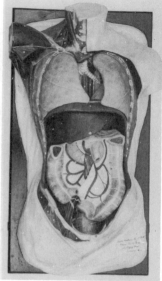

An English Adam, Rouilly & Co painted plaster anatomical model of the human torso, with removable organs, on baseboard, early 20thC, 30in (76cm) high.
$900-1,500

A Dr. D'Odredanne's patent ether apparatus, the brass and copper instrument with paper exhalation bag, marked Collin, French, c1906, 9in (23cm) long.
$720-1,000

A double leg amputee's hardwood crutch with arm rest, spirally reeded stem with brass stringing and bone ferrule, early 19thC, 24in (61cm) high.
$360-540

A Rein brass 'London Dome' ear trumpet, with floral engraving to the surface and pierced cover to the trumpet opening, c1865, 6in (15cm) long.
$720-1,000

A black painted tin ear trumpet, with wooden earpiece, 6.5in (16cm).
$180-360

A leather and iron surgical corset and neck brace, with metal strapwork to spine, hips and neck, cloth shoulder straps and front tying bodice, WWI.
$180-360

An English carved ivory phrenology head handle, of dark yellow patina with head inscribed with numbered segments and corresponding characteristics listed around the base, mid-19thC, 4in (10cm) high, on mounting pin.
$2,700-3,600

Dental Instruments

A silver toothbrush, hallmarked 1801, in leather case with powder holder, 5in (13cm) long, together with a silver tongue scraper hallmarked London 1813, 4in (10cm) long, and a tongue depressor 5in (13cm) long.
$1,000-1,500

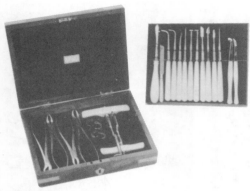

A set of dental instruments, signed Read with maker's label for Thomas Read & Co., manufacturers of Chirugical Instruments, Parliament St. Dublin, with octagonal ivory handles, steel instruments including 2 steel tooth keys with fluted cranked shafts, smooth ivory handles with removable claws, 4 steel forceps, pull-out tray with part set of steel shaft and smooth ivory handled scalers with 2 replacement instruments, including small finger saw, in mahogany brass bound case, early 19thC, 9in (23cm) wide.
$1,800-2,700

A set of 5 educational dental views, Made for the Dental Board of the United Kingdom by Educational & Scientific Plastics Ltd., Croydon, Surrey, in clear plastic and wood display cases, 13 by 18in (33 by 46cm).   **$360-540**

A dentist's surgery suite, comprising DMC Ltd leather upholstered adjustable chair with footrest, spittoon on stand, mouthwash stand, cases of dentures, c1900, approx. height of chair 47in (120cm).
$1,000-1,500

CAMERAS

An Eastman Ordinary Kodak camera, No. 1218, the film back stamped 1800, with lens and string set shutter, rollfilm polished wood body.
$1,800-2,700

A metal body hanging advertising sign in the shape of a film box, with hanging panel and mounting bracket, with cream, orange and blue painted text 'Made in Great Britain Ensign Film. Films Developed and Printed', Houghton-Butcher Mfg. Co. Ltd., London.
$180-360

This sign dates from the 1920s and features the Ensign house colours and design of the period.

An Eastman Kodak 35mm Ektra camera, No. 3363, with a magazine back No. C-4758 and a Kodak Ektra 50mm f/1.9 lens, Kodak rangefinder, Kodak right angle viewfinder, a Kodak waistlevel finder and a copy instruction booklet, in maker's fitted leather case.
$1,000-1,500

A 5 by 4in (13 by 10cm) wet-plate sliding box portrait camera, No. 676, with a brass bound J.H. Dallmeyer lens No. 5729, inset label J.H Dallmeyer, Optician, London, a brass bound lens with flange.
$1,800-2,700

A 3.5 by 4.5in (9 by 12cm) Ernoflex folding reflex model II camera, No. 1094064, with a Carl Zeiss Jena Tessar f/4.5 18cm lens no. 563546, film pack adapter and 3 double darkslides, in a fitted metal case, Ernemann-Werke, Dresden.
$360-540

A brass mounted mahogany plate view camera, by J.H. Dallmeyer of London, with rack and pinion focusing, fine focusing adjustment by rack and pinion on the lens, and individual slide aperture control, applied with a mahogany plaque inscribed J.H. Dallmeyer, Optician, London, together with 3 double and 2 single dark slides and a viewing screen, slight damage, c1861.
$2,700-3,600

A Jahagee Kine Exakta camera, No.484441, with round magnifier in hood and Jahagee Anastigmat Exakta f/3.5-5.4cm lens, No. 751738, in a brown leather carrying case, together with 3 instruction booklets, an extension tube, an Adon patent telephoto lens by J.H. Dallmeyer, London, No. 67349, an Ilford photo electric light meter and lens hood.
$360-540

A Jos-Pe 3 colour camera, No. 585, with top mounted sportsfinder, 3 backs, a Steinheil Quinar anastigmat f/2.5 10.5cm lens No. 165091 in a dial set compound shutter and 6 single metal slides, in maker's fitted leather case.
$2,700-3,600

A quarter plate mahogany body pinhole camera, with removable back panel and a brass bound lens section with screw lens cap with pinhole, pivoting shutter and engraved James Dixon & Sons, Sheffield.
$360-540

A Leitz screw-fit Elmar f/4.5 135mm lens, with barrel engraved 573, a FODIS rangefinder, early black WINKO right angle viewfinder and 3 Leitz filters, in a Leitz leather outfit case.
$360-540

A Kern-Paillard Bolex stereo outfit, comprising a Kern stereo f/1.6 20mm lens No. 212972 lens hood, viewfinder stereo masks, viewfinder mounting bar, a Kern Yvar stereo 12.5mm f/2.8 lens No. 210441, instruction booklet Bolex Stereo Movies and polarising glasses, in maker's fitted box.
$180-360

A W. Kunik Petie Vanity outfit, comprising a 16mm Petie camera in a red leather covered vanity case, with powder compact, lipstick holder, spare film holder and instruction sheet, in maker's box, W. Kunik, West Germany.
$360-540

A single speed Leica Motor, No. 911, with fixed 2-speed button.
$1,200-1,700

A Leitz 35mm restored grey Leica IIIc camera, No. 390330K, with a Leitz Elmar f/3.5 50mm lens, No. 93147, in maker's leather ever ready case.
$1,000-1,500

A Ross 3 by 3in (8 by 8cm) twin lens reflex camera, with a brass bound Ross, London, Rapid Symmetrical 5in (13cm) viewing lens, a brass bound taking lens in a Koilo shutter and 2 double darkslides.
$1,000-1,500

A Leitz screw-fit non standardised Elmar f/4.5 135mm lens, with barrel numbered 359.
$180-360

A 35mm Red Flag 20 camera, No. 770184, with a Red Flag 20 f/1.4 50mm lens, No. 770015, in ever ready case, a Red Flag 20 f/1.4 35mm lens, No. 77140, in maker's plastic keeper and a Red Flag 20 f/2 90mm lens, No. 760037, in maker's plastic keeper.
$2,700-3,600

A Nikon outfit, comprising a 45mm Nikon S3 camera, No. 6304070, with a Nippon-Kogaku Nikkor-S.C f/1.4 5cm lens, No. 387998, in maker's ever ready case, Nikon S3 instruction booklet, a Nikon leather outfit case containing a Nippon Kogaku Nikkor-P f/2.5 10.5cm lens, No. 925644, aperture defective, in leather case, a W-Nikkor.C f/3.5 2.8cm lens, No. 716580, in leather case, a Nikon 2.8 optical finder in leather case, a Nippon Kogaku, Tokyo, Universal finder, No. 545235, engraved Nikon in leather case and lens hoods.
$2,700-3,600

A tropical folding plate camera, with retailer's plaque A Stegemann, Berlin, the brass reinforced teak body with double extension, rack and pinion focusing, red morocco bellows, Tessar 18cm f/6.3 lens, shutter 1/150 to 1 sec. 3 by 4in (8 by 10cm) in ground glass screen, together with 3 double plate holders.
$360-540

A Leitz 35mm Leica MDa camera, No. 1254651, in maker's leather ever ready case, a Leitz Super-Angulon 21mm f/4 lens No. 1646648 and lens hood, in maker's plastic keeper, 21mm SBKOO finder in leather case.
$1,800-2,700

A Newman & Sinclair 35mm NS cinematographic camera, No. 761, with polished duraluminium body, built in recording watch mounted on front panel and marked 761 PATT 5875, a Ross, London Xpres 2in (5cm) f/3.5 lens No. 195469 a Ross, London Xpres 4in (10cm) f/3.5 lens, No. 177106, a Ross, London Xpres 6in (15cm) f/3.5 lens, No. 177153, each panel engraved 761, and a film magazine marked 761, in maker's fitted leather case.
$1,200-1,700

A Voigtländer Bijou camera, with a Voigtländer Heliar 10cm f/4.5 lens, No. 98607, focal plane shutter, focusing screen missing, and retailer's plate The Westminster Photographic Company Ltd., 119 Victoria St., S.W.
$900-1,500

A Newman & Guardia quarter plate Reflex camera, No. SR.1838, with rising focusing hood, a Carl Zeiss Jena Tessar f/4.5 150mm lens, No. 91868, a Carl Zeiss Distar lens 3/IV, No. 4209, instruction booklet The Newman & Guardia Reflex Self focusing cameras, 3 N & G double darkslides and a film pack adapter, in a fitted pigskin case.
$360-540

A Marion & Co., quarter plate tropical reflex camera, No. M.1596, with polished teak and lacquered brass fitted body, a Carl Zeiss Jena Tessar f/4.5 15cm lens, No. 204595, a Carl Zeiss Jena Magnar f/10 45cm lens, No. 218422a (sic) and 6 tropical double darkslides, in a fitted leather case.
$7,000-9,000

A complete run of 6 volumes of British Journal Photographic Almanac 1917-1963, Henry Greenwood and Co in yellow paper wrappers, the remainder in green cloth.
$720-1,000

A 7 by 3.5in (18 by 9cm) boxform detective stereoscopic camera, with rack and pinion focusing, a pair of lacquered brass barrel Wray, London, 5in (13cm) stereo lenses Nos. 6542 and 6543, set in a roller blind shutter.
$360-540

A camera obscura, probably French, the walnut case with iron hinged lid opening to shaped folding panel inset with projection lens and folding mirror, the base with 3 folding sides opening to receive drawing paper, c1800, 23in (59cm) sq. **$1,800-2,700**

A 7 by 3.5in (18 by 9cm) brass and mahogany stereoscopic tailboard camera, with a pair of Wray, London, 5in (13cm) Stereo lenses, Nos. 9284 and 9285, in a roller blind shutter and 3 double darkslides, in maker's fitted canvas case.
$1,000-1,500

A Leitz Fiman Leica developing drum outfit, comprising a metal stand with handle and attached 6in (15cm) diam. glass drum and a 6 by 8in (15 by 20cm) glass chemical dish. **$180-360**

A 7 by 3.5in (18 by 9cm) brass and mahogany hand and stand camera, with red leather bellows and a pair of Wray, London, 5.5in (14cm) Rapid Rectalinear lenses, Nos. 7043 and 7044, set in an integral sliding shutter and internal self-collapsing septum.
$720-1,000

An ebonised wood pedestal stereoscope, with decorated gilded designs, a pair of focusing eye pieces, hinged lid and internally contained stereocards.
$720-1,000

A Newman & Guardia quarter plate Nydia collapsable camera, No. 1064, with a Ross, London Homocentric 5.5in (14cm) f/6.3 lens, No. 66322 and Newman & Guardia changing back, in maker's leather case.
$720-1,000

SILVER
Baskets

A George II bread basket, engraved with a coat-of-arms within a rococo cartouche, by Edward Aldridge, 1759, with blue glass liner, 17in (43cm) wide, 52oz.
$10,000-12,000

A set of 4 William Pitts II dessert baskets, on cast leaf scroll feet, the centres engraved with contemporary coats-of-arms, one piece of foliage missing, London 1821, 12.5in (32cm) wide, 143oz.
$14,500-16,500

A William IV sweetmeat basket, chased and embossed with scrolling foliage, the centre with a relief view of Abbotsford, chased swing handle, maker's Taylor & Perry, Birmingham 1836, 5in (13cm), 3oz.
$360-540

A Georgian silver boat shaped fruit basket, with engraved handle, pierced rim and matching foot, maker JS, London 1909, 5in (13cm) high, 22oz.
$1,800-2,700

A George V basket, the pierced scalloped bowl with gadroon edging, scrolling mermaid handle, and 3 dolphin supports, maker's mark indistinct, London 1912, 10in (25cm) wide, 38oz.
$3,600-5,000

A George V bread basket, engraved with a presentation inscription, raised on 4 acanthus leaf, cabochon and C-scroll supports, terminating in stylised hoof feet, maker's mark rubbed, London 1924, 13in (34cm) wide, 1278gr.
$1,800-2,700

A Victorian cake basket, by Robinson, Edkins & Aston, Birmingham 1843, 12in (30cm) diam., 795gr.
$900-1,500

A George III sugar basket, faceted boat shaped with formal bright cut band, crested and initialled below a scalloped rim, spreading foot and swing handle, London 1787, 7in (18cm), 6oz.
$720-1,000

A George IV cake basket, by Robert Garrard, in mid-18thC style, the centre engraved with the Haddington family armorials, London 1823, 14in (36cm) diam., 62oz.
$7,000-9,000

A cake basket, the body embossed with wrythen scrolls and chased flowerheads and foliage, engraved crest to centre, folding handle, entwined with foliage, London 1832, 14in (36cm) diam., 41oz.
$1,800-2,700

A mid-Victorian cake basket, maker's mark A.C. over T.P., London 1867, 11.5in (30cm), 1,115gr.
$1,000-1,500

A Victorian dessert basket, oval shaped on a spreading foot, scroll and flower embossed and lattice pierced, London 1890, 12in (31cm), 23oz.
$1,000-1,500

A mid-Victorian sugar basket, by Joseph Angell, allover pierced and engraved with strapwork, with frosted glass liner, slight splitting, Birmingham 1875, 6in (16.5cm) high including handle, 145gr.
$360-540

A Victorian boat shaped cake basket, with gadroon edging above pierced and bright cut sides, on spreading pedestal base, by Thomas Bradbury and Sons, Sheffield 1900, 12 .2oz.
$360-540

A Victorian shell shaped basket, the pierced scalloped bowl with gadroon edging, scrolling mermaid handle and on 3 dolphin supports, by Goldsmiths and Silversmiths Co. Ltd., London 1900, 35.4oz.
$3,600-5,000

A late Victorian quatrefoil pierced cake basket, on applied shell and scrolling foliate feet joined by scrolling mounts with ball finial, the basket die-stamped with rococo flowers, shells, scrolling foliage and beading, by James Dixon & Son, Sheffield 1900, 12in (31cm), 20.25oz.
$1,200-1,700

A Victorian silver gilt dessert basket by George Fox, in the manner of Paul de Lamerie, crest engraved on the underside, London 1874, 14in (36cm) wide, 62oz.
$10,000-12,000

A Victorian silver sugar basket, in neo-classical style, boat shaped with rope twist edges and swing handle, bright cut and pierced body and oval foot, Birmingham 1861, 8.5oz.
$360-540

A Victorian bread basket, with pierced and embossed floral and trellis decoration to border, London 1898, 11in (29cm) diam, 9oz.   **$360-540**

A late Victorian silver cake basket, with heavy embossed and chased decoration, pierced detail, double rope twist swing handle, Birmingham 1899, 16oz.
$360-540

A cake basket, part scroll pierced shaped oval, with ribbon tied reeded rim, spreading foot, swing handle, Sheffield 1912, 12in (31cm), 24oz.
$720-1,000

An oval cake basket, by S. J. Phillips, the pierced sides applied with ribbon tied husk swags centred by a pair of oval cartouches cast with profile portraits, beaded borders, pierced loop handles and 4 panel feet, London 1907, 11.5in (29.5cm), 23oz. 9dwt.   **$1,800-2,700**

A pair of Victorian baskets, each on 3 dolphin feet, by William Gibson and John Langman, 1895, 11in (28.5cm) wide, 83oz. **$10,000-12,000**

A pair of pierced circular silver comports, with flower decorated rims, leaf surmounted and flower decorated bases, London 1909, 6in (15cm) wide, 19oz. 15dwts. **$900-1,500**

A pair of Edwardian oval dessert baskets, embossed and pierced fret decorated with beaded foliage borders and cartouche shape panels, with spray lifts, on chased cast rococo legs with shell feet, and scroll stretchers, maker's James Dixon & Sons, Sheffield 1908, 9.5in (24cm), 23.5oz. **$900-1,500**

l. and r. A pair of late Victorian baskets, the central oval panels engraved with an initial, London 1900, 9in (23cm) wide, 820gr. **$1,200-1,700**
c. A late Victorian bowl, of lobed quatrefoil form, stamped and pierced with scrolls, foliage and flowerheads, on a similar openwork foot, Sheffield 1898, 10in (25cm) wide, 309gr. **$360-540**

Beakers

A French bell shaped beaker, engraved with foliage and shells and with 3 oval panels depicting a water well, a fountain and a windmill, by Louis-Jacques Berger, Paris 1798/1809, 5in (13cm), 5.75oz.   **$360-540**

A pair of silver beakers, by Jacob Hurd, Boston, c1737, each marked near rim Hurd script in oval punch, 5.5in (14cm) high, 16oz. **$83,000-90,000**

Bowls

A George II Irish bowl, on spreading foot and with moulded rim, by Peter Racine, Dublin 1734, 7.5in (19cm) diam., 19oz. **$3,600-5,000**

A George III two-handled bowl with monteith rim, engraved with armorials within a frame of scrollwork, with devil's mask drop ring handles and notched, pierced rim on spreading base, maker's mark W. B., London 1817, 11in (28cm), 100.8oz. **$7,000-9,000**

A silver covered punch bowl, Tiffany & Co., New York, made for the World's Columbian Exposition, Chicago, 1893, with gilt interior, marked on base and numbered 11232/3218, 29.5in (75cm), 490oz.   **$45,000-60,000**

A Victorian silver rose bowl, London 1891, 8.5in (21.5cm) wide. **$1,200-1,700**

A silver punch bowl, Gorham Mfg.
Co., Providence, RI, on 4
conjoined grapevine feet with
matching cast grapevine rim,
1897, 16.5in (42cm) diam.
$5,000-7,000

A pair of silver punch bowls, with
half-fluted design, London 1896,
10in (25cm) diam.
$2,700-3,600

A pair of French silver gilt finger
bowls, each chased with a single
foliate band incorporating a
monogrammed cartouche below
an applied gadroon rim, c1880,
5.5in (14cm), 16oz.
$720-1,000

A heavy silver bowl, decorated
with embossed sea creatures on
dolphin supports, London 1899,
36oz.   **$2,700-3,600**

A late Victorian punch bowl, by
Martin Hall & Co., London 1889,
13.5in (34.5cm) diam., 2,530gr.,
and an Edwardian Old English
pattern ladle engraved with
crests, London 1909, 311gr.
$7,000-9,000

A circular footed punch bowl, with shaped floral
rim, 13in (33.5cm) diam., and 12 matching cups,
3in (7.5cm), silver embossed with floral decoration,
maker WAH, Birmingham 1952, bowl 76oz,
cups 54oz.   **$2,700-3,600**

A late Victorian floral and foliate-
chased two-handled christening
bowl, with a pierced rising shaped
circular foot and applied with a
pierced rim, engraved with a
crest, Wakely and Wheeler,
London 1897, 8in (20cm), 10.25oz.
$720-1,000

Boxes

An Edwardian silver foliate
engraved card case, Birmingham
1902, 3in (8cm) wide.
$110-180

A Victorian jewel casket, by
George Edwards & Son,
Edinburgh, bombé oblong,
embossed with putti and
arabesque panels above baluster
supports, ovolo, stiff leaf and
mask borders, the hinged domed
cover with recumbent classical
maiden within a lattice and shell
border, velvet lined, lock and key,
1887, 7in (18cm) wide.
$1,800-2,700

A silver trinket box, with finely
inlaid tortoiseshell lid,
Birmingham 1919, 5in (13cm)
diam.
$720-1,000

An American fruit bowl, chased in
high relief with a frieze of
acanthus leaves with various
flowers and foliage above, applied
with a floral and foliate scroll rim
and on a shallow rising circular,
Jacobi & Jenkins, Baltimore,
Maryland, c1898, 8in (20cm),
23oz.
$1,000-1,500

A biscuit barrel, with hinged cover and integral stand, on 4 paw and rosette feet, Sheffield 1898, 8in (21cm), 968gr.
$1,800-2,700

A George II toilet box and cover, the detachable slightly domed cover engraved with a coat-of-arms, the base later engraved with a crest, by Charles Kandler, 1727, 3in (8cm) diam., 6oz.
$3,600-5,000

A Charles II plain tobacco box, the detachable cover engraved with a coat-of-arms, the base engraved with a monogram, maker's mark indistinct, 1671, 4in (10cm) high.
$2,700-3,600

A casket, Dutch or German, the body embossed with tavern and coaching scenes between mask headed corner volute supports, the cover with scene of Napoleon greeting Josephine with attendant officers and ladies in waiting, gilt interior with inscription, fitted lock, import mark Chester 1905, 9.5in (24cm) wide, 43oz.   **$2,700-3,600**

A card case, die struck with a bagpiper playing for his ladies, London 1897, 4in (10cm), and 2 other boxes.
$720-1,000

An Edwardian silver embossed pill box, Birmingham 1901, 1in (3cm) diam.
$70-145

A Victorian silver box, embossed with hunting scenes, Schoonhoven, Netherlands, 1887, 1.5in (4cm) high.
$110-180

A Norwich silver 2 sectioned box, with cut corners, central hinge, the lid engraved with shells and acanthus scrolls, each base of the interior marked with the maker's mark of Elizabeth Haselwood, c1700, 3 by 2in (8 by 5cm).
$7,000-9,000

A Continental silver tobacco box, the cover chased with putti at play, the sides flat chased with shells and scrolls, 4.5in (12cm).
$360-540

A Scottish silver gilt double snuff box, with cut corners, bright cut with foliage borders and engraved with military trophies, thistles, roses and Royal Crown, the cover and base with presentation inscription, maker's mark RH, probably for R. Hexton, Edinburgh, c1800, 3.5in (9cm) long, 6oz.
$3,600-5,000

The inscription on the lid reads 'A Testimony of Gratitude, Esteem & Attachment from the OFFICERS of the MID LOTHIAN REGIMENT to their Much Respected Friend and Lieut. Coll. SIR JAMES FOULIS BARt, Drogheda Septr 22nd 1800'. The base is engraved with the name of the Colonel, The Earl of Ancram, together with further names of Captains, Lieutenants and Cornets.

A Continental fan sh **$1,000-1,500** decorated all over with cherubs, flowers and scrolling foliage, import mark for London 1913, 7in (18cm) wide, 7.9oz.
$720-1,000

Candelabra

A pair of Japanese style silver and other metals two-light candelabra, Tiffany & Co., New York, with detachable nozzles, marked on bases and numbered 5162/9806/282, c1878, 10in (25cm) high, 29oz gross.
$42,000-60,000

A pair of silver seven-light candelabra, Gorham Mfg. Co., Providence, RI, in Louis XVI style, marked on bases and stamped with code MMX, 1907, 27.5in (70cm) high, 426oz 10dwts.
$27,000-35,000

A pair of George II table candlesticks, one engraved with an earl's arms, crest and initial below similar knopped stems and lapped shell moulded sconces, detachable stiff leaf nozzles, William Gould, London 1751, 10in (25cm) high, 48oz.
$3,600-5,000

A pair of George III square based candlesticks, having leaf decorated corners, with baluster stems with spool shape candle holders, detachable nozzles, by William Cafe, London 1770, 9in (23cm), 27oz.   **$3,600-5,000**

A George II candlestick, matching snuffers and tray, each engraved with a coat-of-arms, by James Gould, 1729, candlestick 6in (15cm) high, tray 6.5in (17cm) long, 22oz.
$21,000-27,000

The arms are those of Newman.

A pair of George III candlesticks, engraved with a coat-of-arms and crest, by John Lloyd, Dublin, c1770, 12in (31cm), 52oz.
$7,000-9,000

Candlesticks

A pair of Queen Anne candlesticks, engraved with a coat-of-arms within a scalework cartouche, by William Denny, 1702, 8in (20cm) high, 18oz.
$3,600-5,000

A pair of George III candlesticks, with corded border and flower and foliage decoration engraved with a coronet and initial B, by Joseph Craddock and William Reid, 1819, 12in (31cm), 107oz.
$7,000-9,000

A pair of George IV table candlesticks, engraved with a crest, marked on bases and extension nozzles, by Samuel Whitford, London 1852, 8in (20cm), 32oz.
$3,600-5,000

A set of 4 George II cast silver
candlesticks, by John Cafe,
marked on bases, 1745, 7in
(18cm), 61oz.
$10,000-12,000

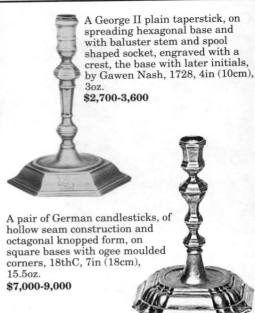

A George II plain taperstick, on
spreading hexagonal base and
with baluster stem and spool
shaped socket, engraved with a
crest, the base with later initials,
by Gawen Nash, 1728, 4in (10cm),
3oz.
$2,700-3,600

A pair of German candlesticks, of
hollow seam construction and
octagonal knopped form, on
square bases with ogee moulded
corners, 18thC, 7in (18cm),
15.5oz.
$7,000-9,000

A set of 4 table candlesticks, 8in
(20cm). **$1,200-1,700**
and a pair of candlesticks, 4in
(10cm).
$360-540

A pair of William IV chamber
candlesticks, by Paul Storr,
London 1832, the bases inscribed
Storr & Mortimore 88, 6.5in
(16cm) diam. 28.9oz.
$7,000-9,000

*The crest is that of the Earls of
Cork, probably for Edmund, 8th
Earl of Cork 1767-1856.*

A set of 4 George IV silver gilt
candlesticks, engraved twice with
crest and Earl's coronet, by
Robert Garrard, 1823, one nozzle
1825, 13in (33cm), 180oz.
$18,000-21,000

Four George II candlesticks, with
detachable nozzle and ovolo
borders, engraved with a crest, by
John Cafe, one 1752, one 1754
and two 1755, 9.5in (24cm) high,
81oz.
$14,500-16,500

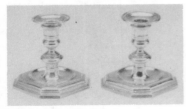

A pair of cast desk-top
candlesticks, with shaped square
bases and knopped stems, by
Asprey, London 1962, and a pair
of detachable Britannia Standard
circular nozzles, 27.81oz.
$720-1,000

A William IV chamber
candlestick, with reeded edging,
detachable nozzle and conical
extinguisher, by Henry Wilkinson
and Co., Sheffield, 1835, 6in
(15cm) diam. 11.2oz.
$720-1,000

A Regence ormolu mounted boulle bracket clock and bracket, signed Mynuel à Paris.
$4,500-6,000

A Louis XIV ormolu mounted brass inlaid tortoiseshell boulle marquetry bracket clock, 39in (99cm).
$6,000-6,800

An English repeating carriage clock, by James McCabe, London, c1860, 8.5in (21cm).
$8,500-10,000

A gilt brass mounted ebonised musical and chiming bracket clock, by Higgs & Evans, London, c1780, 26in (66cm) high.
$18,000-21,000

A Regency mahogany bracket clock, with brass stringing. **$4,250-6,000**

A 6 bell quarter pull repeat bracket clock, with original verge escapement, London, c1760.
$9,350-11,000

A bronze and cut glass mounted musical japanned bracket clock, by George Prior, London, c1770, 32in (81cm).
$20,500-25,500

A Regency bracket clock, London.
$5,000-6,000

A Louis XV ormolu mounted brass inlaid rosewood and tortoiseshell boulle marquetry bracket clock, by François Clement, 18thC.
$4,250-5,000

A French Napoleon III boulle bracket clock and bracket, Paris, 1850.
$6,800-7,800

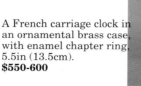

A French carriage clock in an ornamental brass case, with enamel chapter ring, 5.5in (13.5cm).
$550-600

An 8-day striking ebony veneered bracket clock, with 6.25in silvered chapter ring, by John Bushman, London, works restored, c1695.
$17,000-20,500

COLOUR REVIEW

A Scottish, mahogany longcase clock, 13.5in dial signed John Johnson, Galway.
$8,000-9,000

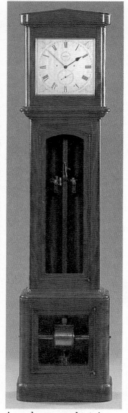

A mahogany electric longcase clock, by Alexander Bain, London,, c1845, 82.5in (209cm).
$65,000-72,000

A walnut musical longcase clock, by Nicholas Lambert, c1730.
$18,000-20,000

A quarter striking calendar and tidal longcase clock, Isaac Nickals Wells, c1750.
$32,000-40,000

A lacquered longcase clock, 18thC.
$18,000-20,000

l. A walnut marquetry longcase clock, c1695.
$15,000-16,500

A three-train longcase clock, 18thC.
$6,000-7,000

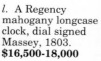

A chiming and musical longcase clock, by Claudius de Chesne, c1720.
$11,000-12,000

l. A Regency mahogany longcase clock, dial signed Massey, 1803.
$16,500-18,000

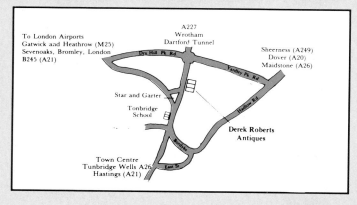

A German neo-classical ormolu-mounted longcase clock, late 18thC.
$28,000-30,000

l. An oak longcase clock, the brass dial with moonphase, c1770.
$7,200-8,200

l. A mahogany longcase clock, with moon-phase and calendar, c1770.
$13,000-15,000

l. A burr yew longcase clock, London, c1695.
$27,000-30,000

A small Scottish longcase clock, c1810.
$4,500-5,500

A gilt bronze mounted and brass inlaid rose-wood longcase clock, signed John Jones, London, 18thC.
$20,000-21,000

An oak painted dial longcase clock, c1810.
$4,500-5,500

A burr walnut month going longcase clock, Daniel Quare, London, c1705.
$45,000-54,000

An olivewood marquetry longcase clock, by Thomas Tompion, London, c1680.
$125,000-160,000

l. A mahogany longcase clock, London, c1790.
$14,500-16,500

An olivewood month going striking longcase clock, by Joseph Knibb, London, c1680.
$108,000-145,000

An ebonised longcase clock, Thomas Tompio London, No. 53 c1710.
$108,000-145,0

l. A olivewood and walnut longcase clock, Fromanteel & Clarke, c1700. **$24,500-26,500**

l. A Dutch mahogany musical automaton longcase clock, dial signed Cs. Both, late 19thC. **$8,500-10,000**

l. A Dutch

l. A mahogany longcase clock, with Battledore & Shuttlecock automata, c1810. **$7,750-8,500**

A small oak and mahogany longcase clock, c1840. **$5,000-6,000**

l. A mahogany, boxwood strung and inlaid 8-day longcase clock, by Garland, Plymouth, c1830. **$7,750-8,500**

A walnut longcase clock, 11in latched dial signed Fromanteel and Clarke, c1700. **$16,000-17,850**

A Charles X ormolu and bronzed mantel clock, Thomire & Ce, 19thC. **$13,500-15,500**

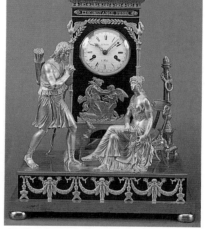

An Empire ormolu and bronze mantel clock, the dial signed Le Paute à Paris, 21.5in (54.5cm). **$10,500-12,000**

A Louis XV ormolu mounted corne verte mantel clock, signed Martin à Paris, 43in (109.5cm). **$15,500-16,000**

A Louis Philippe ormolu and Baccarat mantel clock, 16in (41cm). **$2,500-3,500**

A bronze mantel clock, with twin fusee movement signed by Webster, London, c1850. **$6,800-7,800**

A Charles X ormolu and bronze mantel clock, 21.5in (55cm). **$3,500-4,500**

COLOUR REVIEW

An Empire ormolu mantel clock, the 4.75in enamel dial signed Jean Perin à Paris, c1810, 19.5in (49.5cm).
$6,000-7,000

A Louis XVI ormolu mantel clock, the dial inscribed Petitdant à Paris, late 18thC, 14.5in (36.5cm).
$19,000-21,000

An ormolu and white marble Directoire mantel clock, the 4.75in enamel dial signed Coteau, c1795, 15in (38cm).
$6,000-7,000

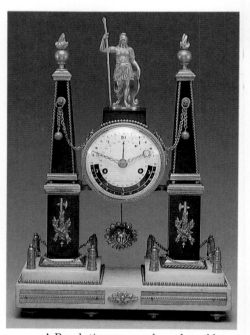

A Regency ormolu mounted griotte marble striking mantel clock, by Benjamin Vulliamy, 12in (30.5cm).
$13,000-14,500

A Second Republic silvered and gilt brass mantel clock, Japy Frères bell striking movement and Brocot escapement, c1850, 29in (73cm).
$6,000-7,000

A Revolutionary ormolu and marble mantel clock, 4in enamel dial signed Duval à Paris, c1795, 17in (43cm).
$12,000-14,500

A Louis XVI ormolu and marble mantel clock, the enamel dial inscribed Lepaute H. Du Roi, late 18thC, 23in (58.5cm).
$17,000-18,000

A French bow-sided porcelain mounted ormolu mantel clock the movement with maker's stamp of J.B. Delettrez, c1870.
$4,500-5,500

l. A Louis XVI ormolu mounted marble mantel clock, the dial signed Le Pareur, c1790, 22in (55cm).
$5,500-6,500

334

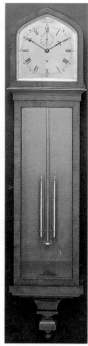

An Austrian rosewood regulator, c1850. **$10,000-12,000**

A Louis XIV ormolu mounted brass inlaid tortoiseshell and ebony mantel clock, 20in (50cm). **$8,500-9,500**

An electrically wound wall regulator with Riefler deadbeat escapement, c1905. **$44,000-47,500**

A gilt bronze 4-glass mantel clock, 11in (28cm). **$650-800**

A Louis XV ormolu and Meissen mantel clock, c1750. **$7,000-8,000**

A mahogany month going wall regulator, by Charles Frodsham, late 19thC. **$22,000-24,000**

An Austrian mahogany regulator clock, by Gustaf Becher. **$550-650**

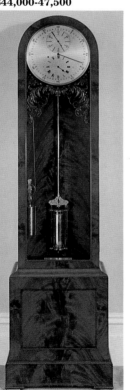

An English mahogany regulator, with jewelled dead beat escapement, 71in (180cm), c1860. **$12,000-12,750**

r. A mahogany weight driven table regulator, by Benjamin Martin, c1775, 25in (64cm). **$31,500-33,500**

A French bow-sided porcelain mounted mantel clock, c1870, 20in (51cm). **$3,500-4,500**

A mahogany quarter striking table clock, by Francis Perigal, London, c1800, 18in (46cm). **$7,500-8,500**

An ebony veneered table clock, by Joseph Knibb, c1680, 13in (33cm). **$36,000-45,000**

An ebony veneered quarter repeating table clock, by Jonathan Lowndes, c1690 **$9,000-12,000**

An ebony veneered basket top table clock, by Johannes Fromanteel, c1690, 13in (33cm). **$11,000-12,500**

A mahogany musical table clock, by Eardley Norton, c1780, 29in (74cm). **$18,000-25,000**

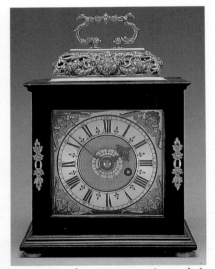

An ebony veneered quarter repeating and alarm basket top table clock, by Henry Jones, c1690, 12in (31cm). **$18,000-27,000**

An ebonised quarter repeating table clock, dial signed Ja. Boyce London, c1700. **$9,500-10,500**

A walnut grande sonnerie table clock, by Edward Bird, c1685, 21.5in (55cm). **$36,000-45,000**

A silver mounted quarter repeating walnut table clock, c1690. **$17,000-18,000**

An Arabesque marquetry table clock, by George Etherington, c1695. **$25,000-32,000**

A brass bound ebonised chiming table clock, c1785. **$10,000-11,000**

An ormolu mounted ebonised musical clock, 7in enamel dial signed George Prior, c1780.
$30,500-37,500

A night clock, early 20thC, 10in (25cm). **$250-350**

A French inlaid striking balloon clock, c1900.
$1,500-2,500

An ebonised brass bound chiming table clock, by William Webster, c1765.
$11,000-12,000

A Gothic oak quarter chiming clock, by William Roskell, c1880.
$1,200-1,600

An American ship's striking clock, The Goldsmiths & Silversmiths Co., in heavy brass case, 9in (23cm) wide.
$270-350

A Louis XVI ormolu mounted Paris porcelain musical automaton clock, the dial signed Ardiot.
$20,500-21,250

A Victorian brass skeleton clock, with a single fusee movement, inscribed Widenham, London.
$1,000-1,200

An American inlaid rosewood 8-day wall clock, late 19thC.
$650-700

A japanned clock with wood dial, by John Longhurst, Kingston.
$4,500-5,000

A black and gilt japanned tavern clock, by John Wright of Dorking, c1790.
$7,500-8,500

An iron chamber clock, South German/Swiss, dated 1693.
$14,500-15,500

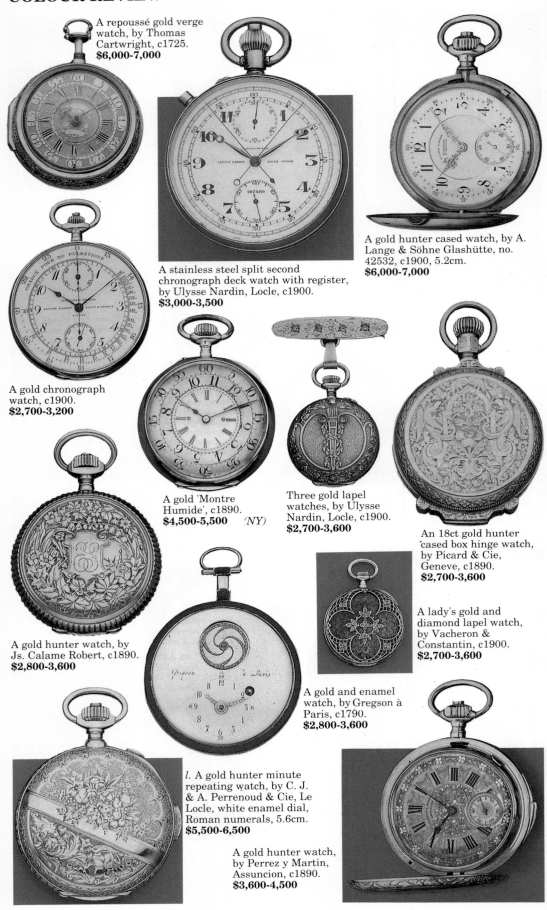

A repoussé gold verge watch, by Thomas Cartwright, c1725. **$6,000-7,000**

A stainless steel split second chronograph deck watch with register, by Ulysse Nardin, Locle, c1900. **$3,000-3,500**

A gold hunter cased watch, by A. Lange & Söhne Glashütte, no. 42532, c1900, 5.2cm. **$6,000-7,000**

A gold chronograph watch, c1900. **$2,700-3,200**

A gold 'Montre Humide', c1890. **$4,500-5,500** (NY)

Three gold lapel watches, by Ulysse Nardin, Locle, c1900. **$2,700-3,600**

An 18ct gold hunter cased box hinge watch, by Picard & Cie, Geneve, c1890. **$2,700-3,600**

A gold hunter watch, by Js. Calame Robert, c1890. **$2,800-3,600**

A lady's gold and diamond lapel watch, by Vacheron & Constantin, c1900. **$2,700-3,600**

A gold and enamel watch, by Gregson à Paris, c1790. **$2,800-3,600**

l. A gold hunter minute repeating watch, by C. J. & A. Perrenoud & Cie, Le Locle, white enamel dial, Roman numerals, 5.6cm. **$5,500-6,500**

A gold hunter watch, by Perrez y Martin, Assuncion, c1890. **$3,600-4,500**

A gold hermetic Movado watch, 18k, silvered matte dial, luminescent Arabic numerals and hands, c1940.
$4,000-5,000

A gold and enamel hunter cased minute repeating watch, c1890.
$10,000-12,000

A Viennese gilt metal and enamel watch, with scent compartment, late 19thC.
$2,000-2,500

A gold and enamel hunter cased watch, Le Roy à Paris, c1830.
$1,700-2,700

A gold open faced dress watch, signed Breguet, c1930. **$3,000-3,700**

Two gold open faced watches, Universal Geneve, c1930 and Piguet & Co., c1920.
$2,500-3,500

A lady's gold, enamel and diamond open faced lapel watch, c1900.
$2,700-3,500

A gold, enamel and pearl lapel watch, Patek Philippe & Co., c1900, 2.7cm.
$2,700-3,500

A gold hunter cased pocket chronometer, Dent no. 26605, London c1860.
$5,000-5,500

A gold and enamel hermetic Movado watch, c1945, 2in (4.7cm) long.
$4,250-5,000

A gold open faced watch, Patek Philippe & Co., no. 121841, c1905, 5.6cm.
$3,000-4,000

A gold open faced watch with Guillaume balance, Patek Philippe & Co., no. 162718, extra, 23 jewels, dial and movement signed, c1915.
$5,000-6,000

A gold hunter cased watch, J. Assmann, Dresden, no. 3223, c1880, 5.1cm.
$5,500-6,500

COLOUR REVIEW

A gold Rolex Oyster Perpetual calendar watch, c1949. **$27,000-29,000**

A gold Rolex Oyster Perpetual calendar watch, c1950. **$3,500-4,000**

A gold watch, by Patek Philippe & Co., c1925. **$7,650-8,500**

A gold jump hour watch, with moon phases, dial signed DF. **$32,300-35,700**

A gold watch, by E. Gübelin, c1950. **$2,500-3,500**

A gold 'Helm' watch, by Cartier, c1935. **$54,500-59,500**

A cushion calendar watch, by Patek Philippe & Co., c1928. **$308,000 -340,000**

A white gold self winding watch by Patek Philippe & Co., 1965. **$2,000-2,500**

A stainless steel watch, by Universal Geneve, Aero-Compax, c1940. **$4,250-5,000**

A stainless steel watch, by Ulysse Nardin, Locle, c1945. **$2,000-2,500**

A stainless steel chronograph watch, by Gallet. **$2,000-2,500**

A Rolex Oyster cosmograph, Daytona, c1970. **$5,000-6,000**

A stainless steel and gold watch, by Movado, c1945. **$2,000-2,500**

A gold and enamel automatic 'bridge' watch, by Cartier. **$20,500-22,000**

A stainless steel and gold watch, by Vacheron & Constantin, c1950. **$2,500-2,700**

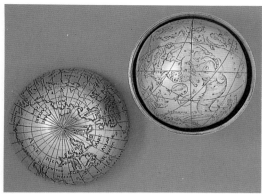

A silver 'Mother and Child' terrestrial/celestial globe couplet, early 19thC, unsigned, 2in (5cm) diam. **$5,500-7,000**

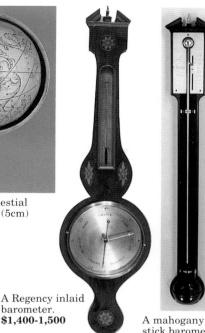

A Regency inlaid barometer. **$1,400-1,500**

A mahogany stick barometer, by Tangate, 18thC. **$1,800-2,000**

A mahogany wheel barometer, by Levy & Co., Bristol, c1845. **$1,000-1,200**

A pair of miniature table globes, by J. Wyld, c1840, 10in (25cm) high. **$8,000-9,000**

A silver miniature armillary sphere, signed J. Chapotot, 18thC. **$4,500-5,500**

A metal celestial globe, possibly Persian, 13in (33cm) high. **$8,000-9,000**

A Regency bowfront mahogany stick barometer, by Bate. **$5,600-6,000**

A 12in time globe, by Juvet & Co., late 19thC. **$1,500-2,000**

l. A mahogany stick barometer, by J. M. Ronkett, 19thC. **$2,200-2,700**

A pair of Cary's celestial and terrestrial library globes, each in a William IV mahogany stand, 1820 and 1836. **$36,000-45,000**

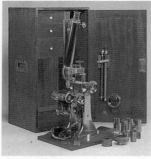

A Ross Wenham's binocular compound microscope, c1865. **$4,500-5,500**

A brass 4in refracting telescope, by Ross London, 19thC, 67in (107cm) long. **$6,000-7,500**

A brass horological compendium, dated 1605. **$20,000-22,000**

A Stegmann solar microscope, by Cassel, dated 1759, 9.5in (24cm) long. **$4,500-5,500**

A brass Ottoman equatorial dial, signed Abu l-Fath Ali, dated 1161H (AD 1748). **$12,500-14,500**

A sundial and nocturnal, dated 1650, 4in (10cm) long. **$6,000-7,000**

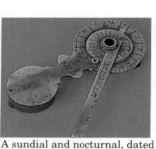

A boxed Wilson Screw microscope set, c1920. **$650-800**

A brass 5in reflecting telescope, signed Thomas Morton, 19thC. **$9,000-10,000**

The 'Berselius' astrolabe, with dedication dated 1522. **$90,000-105,000**

A lacquered brass compound binocular microscope, signed Powell & Lealand, dated 1895. **$7,000-9,000**

A combination microscope and 3-draw telescope. **$3,200-4,200**

A brass refracting telescope, by J. H. Steward, body 41in (104cm). **$900-1,000**

The Globe typewriter, by The American Typewriter Co., with original tin cover, c1893. **$180-280**

An exhibition multi-blade knife with 32 blades, stamped Wlaszlovits Stos, inlaid with mother-of-pearl, 8in (20cm) long. **$2,000-2,500**

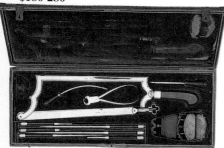

A set of Boullay amputation instruments, French, late 18thC, case 22.5in (57cm) long. **$6,800-7,800**

An Animatographe No. 4 cinematic projector, by R. W. Paul, c1900. **$750-1,000**

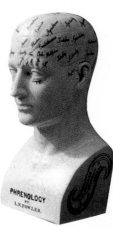

A Phrenology head by L. N. Fowler, early 20thC, 18in (46cm) high. **$1,000-1,500**

An x-ray tube, early 20thC. **$110-145**

A marine chronometer, by Thomas Earnshaw, London, No.724, c1800, in gimballed mahogany carrying case, with brass plaque inscribed John S. Buckwell, Brighton. **$26,350-30,500**

A large slide rule calculator, c1920. **$210-280**

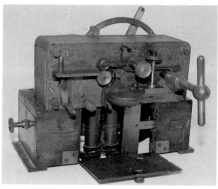

A clockwork telegraph receiver, by Elliott Bros, c1870. **$350-450**

A Dutch pierced silver bread basket, by Dirk Blom, Amsterdam 1767, 10in (25cm) long, 1,581.5gr. **$49,000-68,000**

A Scottish George II silver bread basket, the base engraved with a coat-of-arms, by James Ker, Edinburgh 1745, 13in (33cm) long, 61oz. **$35,700-42,500**

A silver centrepiece, by Robert Garrard, 1861, 18in (46cm). **$6,800-8,500**

A George III seven-light silver candelabrum centrepiece, by Paul Storr, 1817, 18in (46cm) high, 447oz. **$34,000-39,000**

A silver gilt centrepiece, by Brahmfeld & Gutruf, Hamburg, c1860, 39in (99cm) high. **$29,000-34,000**

Six Victorian silver candlesticks, 4 by John Hunt and Robert Roskell, 1886, 2 by Robert Garrard, 1874, one nozzle by Craddock and Reid, 1820, 12in (30cm) high, 208oz. **$18,700-25,500**

A James II silver gilt two-handled porringer and cover, by Robert Cooper, 1688, 7.5in (19cm) high. **$8,500-13,500**

A silver oil and vinegar frame, by Paul de Lamerie, 1723, 8in (20cm) high, 18oz. **$19,500-24,000**

A silver gilt two-handled cup, engraved with inscription and date 1844, by Paul Storr, 1821, 15.5in (39cm) high, 114oz. **$12,000-17,000**

A silver sugar box and 2 tea caddies, by Edward Cornelius Farrell, London 1817, 6 and 6.5in (15 and 17cm) high, 87oz. **$12,000-15,500**

An inverted helmet-shaped ewer, by John Bodington, 1712, 10in (26cm). **$19,500-23,000**

Twenty George III silver soup plates, by John Houle, engraved with armorials and crests, 1818, 10.5in (26.5cm) diam, 491oz. **$19,500-23,000**

A George III silver-gilt tray, by Benjamin & James Smith, London, 1810, 30in (77cm) long, 237oz. **$103,700-110,500**

A George IV silver presentation tea tray, by Benjamin Smith, London, 1827, 31in (79cm) long, 203oz 12dwt. **$10,200-11,000**

A set of 12 George III dinner plates, 1768, 9.5in (24cm) diam, 153oz. **$15,300-18,700**

A set of 4 George III silver gilt wine coasters, Robert Garrard, 1818. **$35,700-42,500**

A 4-piece silver tea set, Birmingham 1920, 47oz. **$750-900**

A pear-shaped teapot, stand and lamp, 1713. **$29,000-30,500**

A George II silver cream boat, Paul de Lamerie, London, 1744, 4.5in (12cm) long, 5oz 6dwt. **$10,000-13,500**

A silver jardinière, by Robert Garrard, London, 1863. **$27,000-29,000**

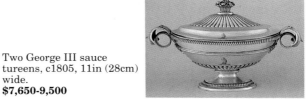

Two George III sauce tureens, c1805, 11in (28cm) wide. **$7,650-9,500**

A set of 4 silver salt cellars, by John Hunt and Robert Roskell, 1852, each base stamped Hunt & Roskell late Storr & Mortimer, 7in (18cm) high, 108oz. **$26,500-34,000**

A silver wine cooler or tureen and cover, The Goldsmiths & Silversmiths Co. Ltd., London 1912, 20in (50cm) long. **$21,250-25,500**

A set of 4 silver salt cellars, with hooved stems and gilt interiors, by Robert Hennell, London 1776, 4.5in (11cm), 22oz 3dwt. **$7,650-9,500**

A silver mounted mirror plateau, by Paul Storr for Storr & Mortimer, London 1826, 14 by 18in (36 by 46cm). **$64,500-71,500**

A George III tureen, cover and liner, engraved twice with a coat-of-arms, by Paul Storr, 1805, the liner 1834, 16in (40cm) long, 158oz. **$17,000-20,500**

A silver ginger jar and 2 similar vases, the jar and one vase by W.W. Williams, 1869, the other by William Mann, 1856, 224oz. **$18,000-20,500**

A silver soup tureen, stand, cover and liner, by Paul Storr, 1819, 352oz. **$59,500-85,000**

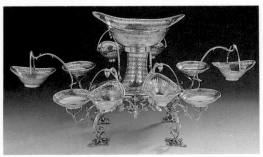

A silver and cut glass épergne, 1807, 58oz. **$8,500-12,000**

l. An Irish ten-branch épergne, by Thomas Jones, 1789. **$23,000-30,500**

A silver vase, by Paul Storr, 1838, 235oz 2dwt. **$18,700-22,000**

A bronze figure of Lord
Kitchener, signed Sydney
March, 1911.
$12,000-16,500

A pair of bronze and gilt bronze chenets, mid-
19thC, 23in (58cm) wide.
$20,000-21,000

A bronze of 'Teucer',
signed Hamo
Thornycroft, c1900.
$23,000-27,000

A bronze of Penelope,
stamped J. Cavelier, 19thC.
$4,500-6,000

A Florentine bronze of a pacing horse,
from the workshop of Pietro Tacca,
17thC, 9in (23cm) high.
$28,000-30,000

A bronze of a girl,
'La Toilette', signed
Pradier, c1860.
$9,000-12,000

A bronze of a mower, signed Hamo
Thornycroft R.A., early 20thC, 25in
(64cm) high. **$20,000-25,000**

A bronze of Pandora,
signed Pradier Scpt.,
mid-19thC.
$6,000-7,000

A bronze of
Nature, signed E.
Barrias, late
19thC.
$12,000-14,500

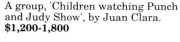

A group, 'Children watching Punch
and Judy Show', by Juan Clara.
$1,200-1,800

A bronze of Diana
Victorious, signed Carrier
Belleuse, late 19thC.
$23,000-27,000

A cock and hen pheasant, Viennese,
with Bergman monogram, late 19thC.
$2,700-3,600

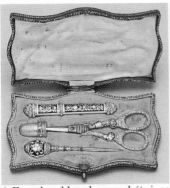

An Empire gilt bronze table centrepiece, signed Thomire à Paris, c1815, 27.5in (70cm) high. **$43,000-51,000**

A French gold and enamel étui, each piece enamelled with flowers, in original fitted leather case, c1830. **$900-1,000**

An Italo-Flemish bronze wine cooler, with scroll handles and paw feet, 17thC, 37in (94cm) diam. **$12,000-15,500**

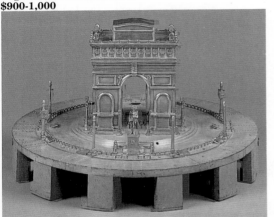

A pair of French bronze models of the Medici vase, on square stepped Siena marble plinths, mid-19thC, 17.5in (44cm) high. **$7,650-9,500**

A steel and brass model of the Arc de Triomphe in Paris, on a grey painted wooden base and block feet, c1920, 19in (48cm) high. **$6,000-10,000**

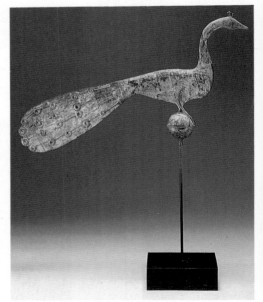

An 18ct gold and enamel City of London freedom casket, maker's mark A.P., Chester 1888, 8in (20cm) wide, in original silk-lined case. **$26,500-34,000**

l. A French model of a bull, the head to sinister, on oval base signed I. BONHEUR, 19thC, 8in (20cm) wide. **$3,500-4,500**

r. A Dutch or Flemish oval brass wine cooler, with lion's mask handles and paw feet, 33in (84cm) wide. **$12,500-14,500**

A gilded and moulded copper peacock weathervane, possibly A.L. Jewell, Massachusetts, c1860. **$17,000-20,500**

A pair of Siena marble and bronze jardinières, trough shaped, with tapering sides centred by Bacchic masks, on scroll legs, 18in (46.5cm).
$10,500-12,000

An Italian marble figure of a fisherboy, by Bazzanti, late 19thC,
$17,000-24,000

A marble head of an emperor, Italian, 17thC, 32in (81cm) high.
$44,000-47,500

An Italian white marble bust, mid-19thC, 27in (69cm) high. **$7,650-9,500**

A white marble vase, c1760, 38in (96cm) high.
$6,500-8,500

A marble bust of Lady Ribblesdale, 1804, 29.5in (75cm) high. **$10,000-12,000**

A Napoleon III ormolu-mounted griotte marble urn, 21in (53cm) high.
$3,500-5,000

A pair of Italian marble busts after Bernini.
$8,000-9,500

A pair of Italian marble plinths, mid-19thC, 43.5in (110cm).
$24,500-26,500

A pair of ormolu-mounted Porphyry urns, late 19thC, 12in (30.5cm) high. **$30,500-32,500**

A pair of marble busts of Roman emperors.
$8,000-9,500

A Neapolitan carved giltwood and polychrome group of the Virgin and Child, 18thC, 17.5in (44cm) high. **$2,700-3,600** Two others. **$750-1,500 each**

A pair of ivory reliefs of the Flagellation and the Mocking of Christ, within gilt and eboniséd wood frameworks, Austrian or North Italian, late 17thC. **$20,000-30,000**

A French terracotta bust of a lady, signed A. CARRIER, 19thC, 26in (66cm). **$8,000-10,000**

A gilt and painted wood group of St. George and the Dragon, restored, c1480. **$40,000-45,000**

An Upper Rhenish painted lindenwood figure of St. Cecilia, c1480, 28in (71cm) high. **$72,000-90,000**

An Upper Rhine polychrome and giltwood figure of St. John, some damage and restoration, c1485, 61.5in (156cm). **$36,000-54,000**

A late Elizabeth I pearwood cup and cover, 11in (28cm) high. **$18,000-21,000**

An Upper Rhine painted wood group of Adam and Eve, comprising 3 separate carvings, early 17thC, figures 28 and 29in (71 and 74cm), tree 47in (119cm) high. **$45,000-54,000**

A Dieppe ivory architectural cabinet-on-stand, carved and engraved, with 7 concealed drawers, mid-19thC, 66in (168cm) high overall. **$34,000-40,000**

A Dieppe ivory carved centre table, mid-19thC, 36.5in (93cm) wide. **$9,000-12,000**

A Swiss singing bird box, in white metal serpentine shaped case, 4in (10cm) wide. **$1,500-2,000**

A gold and agate vinaigrette, early 19thC. **$4,250-5,000**

A new French Plan to invade England

A Staffordshire enamel patch box, late 18thC, 1.5in (4.5cm). **$5,250-6,500**

A Staffordshire enamel patch box, late 18thC, 1.5in (4.5cm). **$3,500-5,000**

A gold snuff box, interior inscribed 'Mrs Ann Lind to John Gray 1793', 3in (8cm). **$4,250-5,000**

A Staffordshire enamel patch box, late 18thC, 2in (4.5cm). **$1,200-1,500**

A 2-colour gold snuff box, by C. M. Weishaupt, Hanau, the lid with an oval chased floral flourish, c1825, 3in (8cm). **$3,500-4,250**

A 2-colour gold snuff box, engine turned, with engraved roundels, French, c1870, 3in (7cm). **$3,500-5,000**

A silver-gilt and enamel snuff box, Birmingham, 1825. **$2,000-2,500**

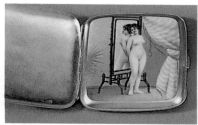

An enamelled cigarette case, with secret compartment, c1910, 3.5in (9cm) long. **$1,600-2,000**

A Staffordshire enamel patch box, titled R. McGuire, late 18thC, 1.5in (4cm). **$3,000-3,500**

A silver box with enamel-inset screw-on cover, probably South German, mid-18thC, 2in (5cm). **$1,000-1,200**

A gold and enamel Swiss snuff box, by Rémond, Lamy & Co., Geneva, with painted lid by Jean-Louis Richter, c1802, 3in (8.5cm). **$9,000-10,000**

COLOUR REVIEW

A 2-colour gold, tortoiseshell and enamel powder box, Paris, 1789. **$4,500-5,500**

A painted and carved cedar box, probably American Indian, 19thC, 23.5in (60cm) long. **$5,500-7,000**

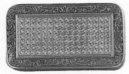

A Swiss snuff box, by Jean-George Rémond & Co., c1810, 3in (8cm). **$1,500-1,600**

l. A French lacquer travelling
l. A French lacquer travelling necessaire and bodkin case, with silver mounts, c1790, 6.5in (16.5cm). **$6,000-7,000**

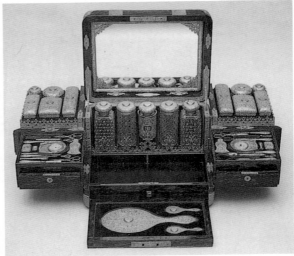

A Victorian calamander toilet box, makers G.B., G.W.B. and J.B. & S. Mordan & Co. **$21,000-25,000**

A tortoiseshell piqué toilet box, Naples, c1740, 6in (15.5cm). **$3,600-5,500**

A gilt-bronze surtout, c1820, 9.5in (23cm). **$3,000-3,500**

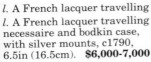

A tortoiseshell and jewelled gold piqué snuff box, c1750, 2in (5cm). **$2,700-3,600**

A Restauration gilt-bronze lion, the plinth concealing a well, c1825, 10in (25cm). **$4,500-6,000**

A French bodkin case, late 18thC, 6in (15cm) long. **$9,000-9,500**

A lapis lazuli snuff box, with silver gilt mounts, by Luigi Mascelli, Rome, c1815. **$4,500-6,000**

A French gilt and embossed leather playing card case, c1780, 3in (7.5cm) square. **$900-1,000**

Casters

A pair of sugar casters, by Walker & Hall, Sheffield 1931.
$360-540

A Victorian sugar caster, of urn form, with 2 curved side handles, gadrooned rim, ornate chased and pierced concave sided top with boss finial, London 1891, 8.5in (21cm), 13oz. **$720-1,000**

A George I silver sugar caster, with inset restricting sleeve to the pierced top, maker's mark WE, London 1718, 6in (15cm), 7oz. **$720-1,000**

Centrepieces

A Victorian dessert stand, the circular base applied with beading, and cast in high relief with entwined scaly dolphins and putti holding reins, the dolphins tails supporting a large gilt lined shell shaped bowl, by Frederick Elkington, 1875, 12.5in (32cm), 84oz.
$10,000-12,000

A George V dessert stand centrepiece, the central bowl with pierced decoration, supported on a panelled tapering stem with 3 scroll branches, with similarly decorated swing handled baskets, on a monogrammed shaped circular base, by Walker & Hall, Sheffield 1920, 13in (33cm), 43.7oz.
$1,800-2,700

A table centrepiece, the central boat shaped bowl issuing from a foliate sheathed baluster stem flanked by 2 similar smaller bowls, issuing from foliate sheathed scrolling branches, on a lobed quatrefoil base raised upon 4 acanthus leaf, scroll and shell feet, with cast scroll and foliate angles, 15in (38cm).
$720-1,000

An early George V three-piece table suite, comprising an èpergne, the central trumpet vase with pie crust rim enclosing foliate piercing, flanked by 3 smaller trumpet vases, the 3 scroll branches hung with shallow baskets, one handle missing, each raised on 3 lion paw feet, from a high domed base, engraved with a monogram, and a pair of trumpet shaped posy vases, by Walker & Hall, Sheffield 1910, 2931gr.
$3,600-5,000

An early George V small èpergne, the central trumpet shaped posy vase surmounted by a basket, stamped and pierced with flowerheads and pendant husks, flanked by 2 similar smaller bowls on scroll branches, on a swept circular foot, London 1910, 10.5in (26cm), loaded.
$720-1,000

Cups

A silver cann, by Samuel Tingley, New York, repaired, marked on base ST script in conforming punch and N.York script, also in conforming punch, c1770, 5in (13cm) high, 12oz 10dwts.
$2,000-2,500

A George II silver gilt inverted bell shaped cup and cover, later applied with a drapery cartouche enclosing a crest, the cover later engraved with an inscription, by John Tuite, 1730, the cover with maker's mark struck twice only, 12in (31cm), 83oz.
$3,600-5,000

The inscription reads 'Presented to John Nash Esqr. by LADY GREY EGERTON, in testimony of the sincere esteem and regard of his departed friend SIR JOHN GREY EGERTON BART. 1825.'

A Victorian cup and cover, with two handles in griffin and scroll form, embossed and chased with decorative cartouches, female masks, bands of ribbon tied oak foliage and other formal designs, inscribed 'Debrooghur Races 1872, Presented by Wm. Minto', lacking finial, maker's mark JD and S, Sheffield 1870, 13.5in (34cm), 35.25oz.
$1,200-1,700

A Scottish Victorian cup and cover, engraved with a coat-of-arms within a strapwork and ribbon cartouche, the detachable cover chased and engraved with strapwork, foliage and grotesque masks and with pointed finial, the base engraved with a presentation inscription, by Rait, Glasgow, 1888, 29in (74cm), 177oz.
$3,600-5,000

A Victorian loving cup, of tapering cylindrical form with C scroll handles, inscribed 'Jhansie Sky Races, 1879, Jhansie Cup', possibly by Robert Pringle, Sheffield 1878, 6.5in (16cm), 29.75oz.
$720-1,000

A 1912 Olympic Trophy, Art Nouveau loving cup, in sterling silver inscribed on all 3 sides, presented to Fred W. Kelly winner of the 110 metre hurdles, Olympic Games, Stockholm, Sweden 1912, by the Los Angeles Evening Herald, his vaulting figure is etched on one of the sides, 11in (28cm) high.
$3,000-4,000

'The Calcutta Cup', a Victorian cup and cover of campana shape, the two handles in the form of elaborate swans' heads with outstretched wings, the ovoid knop to the stem embossed and chased with masks, the domed cover surmounted by a figure of a horse and rider, inscribed 'The Calcutta Cup, Jorrhant Races, 1878 won by', maker's mark C and W, Birmingham 1869, 25in (64cm), 132.5oz.
$3,600-5,000

Coffee and Chocolate Pots

A George II pear shaped coffee pot, cast with rocaille ornament, the body chased with flowers, foliage and scrolls, the curved leaf-capped spout with vacant rococo cartouche, the domed cover with flower finial, the body engraved with 2 vacant foliate cartouches, by Thomas Whipham, 1757, 10in (25cm), 32oz.
$3,600-5,000

A George III baluster coffee pot, husk swag and paterae chased incorporating engraved armorials, similarly chased spreading foot and domed cover, stylised bud finial, leaf capped curved spout, wood scroll handle, by Charles Wright, London 1776, 12in (31cm), 30oz.
$3,600-5,000

A George III coffee pot, with later composition double scroll handle, marked on base and cover, Courtauld & Cowles, London 1769, 12.5in (32cm), 33oz.
$3,600-5,000

A George III plain vase shaped coffee jug, stand and lamp, engraved with a crest, by Paul Storr, 1801, 13in (33cm), 48oz.
$3,600-5,000

A George IV coffee pot, with inverted pear shaped baluster body, flower cluster chased and ribbed at intervals incorporating armorials, above a spreading foot, loop handle, domed cover with flower finial, London 1824, 10in (25cm), 33oz.
$1,000-1,500

A Maltese coffee pot, with wood scroll handle, Rosso, c1840, 9.5in (24cm), 29oz. **$2,700-3,600**

A matched pair of café au lait pots.
$360-540

A Continental plain bellied coffee pot, with scroll handle and leaf and bud finial, early 19thC, 6in (15cm).
$720-1,000

A George III coffee pot, monogrammed, crested and decorated with scrolls, flowers and foliage, with wood handle, on spreading base, maker's mark W.C., London 1762, 10in (25cm), 22.9oz. **$1,800-2,700**

A George III coffee pot, with baluster body, later armorial engraved, above a spreading foot, with leaf wrapped curved spout, ivory scroll handle and stepped domed cover, with stylised bud finial, gadroon borders, marked on body and cover, W. & R. Peaston, London 1771, 11.5in (29cm), 28oz. **$3,600-5,000**

A George II chocolate pot, engraved with a crest, swan neck spout, flat domed hinged cover with detachable turned finial and ivory scroll handle, on spreading base, Isaac Cookson, Newcastle 1732, 10in (25cm), 29.2oz. **$7,000-9,000**

A George III beaded vase shaped coffee pot, later chased with drapery swags and arabesques, with a later added scroll handle and domed hinged cover with stylised artichoke finial, engraved with a crest, the pot London 1778, the handle with Victorian hallmarks, 12.5in (32cm), 31.75oz. **$1,800-2,700**

Cutlery

A George III silver shovel caddy spoon, by Joseph Taylor, Birmingham 1810, 2in (5cm). **$180-360**

A silver pierced ladle, Tiffany & Co., New York, the stem cast in high relief as a pair of embracing putti, monogrammed HHF, marked on bowl, c1910, 13.5in (34cm) long, 15oz 10dwts. **$2,000-2,500**

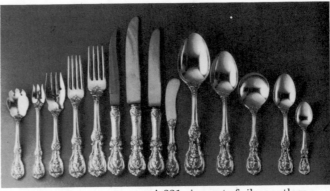

A 321 piece set of silver cutlery, Reed & Barton, Francis I pattern, a few pieces engraved M above 38, 20thC, 399oz 10dwts. **$12,000-13,000**

A pair of cased silver fruit spoons, the bowls and stems finely chased with flowers and foliage, scrolled terminals to handles, London 1885/6. **$360-540**

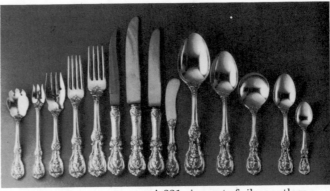

A George III Old English pattern table service, comprising: 24 spoons and forks, 12 teaspoons, by Richard Crossley, 1798, 1801/2/3, with 12 table and cheese knives, and 2 carving knives and forks, with steel blades and prongs, 1964 and 12 fish knives and forks with silver blades and prongs, Sheffield 1965, in fitted wood case, 113oz. **$7,000-9,000**

A 185 piece Kings pattern silver dinner service. **$3,600-5,000**

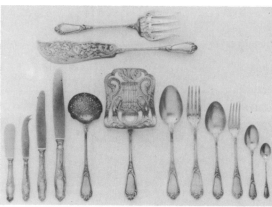

A mid-Victorian travelling apple corer, the tapering cylindrical hollow handle enclosing the screw action blade, engraved E.B.N., by George Unite, Birmingham 1875, 5.5in (14cm), 30gr.
$360-540

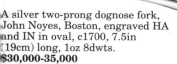

A silver two-prong dognose fork, John Noyes, Boston, engraved HA and IN in oval, c1700, 7.5in (19cm) long, 1oz 8dwts.
$30,000-35,000

A French silver gilt table service, comprising: 60 spoons, 84 forks, 12 fish knives and forks, 12 dessert knives and forks, a soup ladle, 20 various serving spoons and forks, a ham bone holder, 12 table knives with steel blades, 12 each pineapple, cheese and caviar knives, the majority with maker's mark HS, late 19thC, 8,150gr.
$14,500-16,500

Dishes

A William IV soup plate, the edges decorated with moulded flowers and scrolls, by W. K. Reid, London 1835, 30.5oz.
$720-1,000

Two George I meat dishes, each with ovolo border, engraved with a coat-of-arms, by David Willaume I, 1725, Britannia Standard, 13 and 14in (33 and 36cm) long, 75oz.
$3,600-5,000

A silver porringer, by Edward Webb, Boston, marked in bowl EW in rectangle, c1700, 5in (13cm) diam, 5oz 10dwts.
$12,000-14,000

A pair of entrée dishes and covers, with gadrooned borders, detachable handles, Sheffield 1933, 101oz.   **$1,800-2,700**

A silver chafing dish, cover and lampstand, Tiffany & Co., New York, in Chrysanthemum pattern, ivory handles, the dish with removable liner, the stand with detachable top rim, covered lamp with remote wick adjustment, the reservoir of ring form with flower form cap, c1905, 9in (23cm) diam, 106oz gross.
$15,000-18,000

A Continental dish, chased with a seraphim surrounded by symbols of the Evangelists, the underside nielloed with birds, letters and a date 1777, 4in (10cm), and a Continental circular dish chased with flowers and foliage, 5in (13cm).   **$2,700-3,600**

An early George III silver meat dish, of shaped oval design, with gadrooned edge, by Sebastian and James Crespell, London 1764, 21oz.
$720-1,000

A pair of George III entrée dishes and covers, with loop handles, the domed covers with turned finials, by M. Fenton and Co., Sheffield 1791, 15in (38cm), 52.75oz.
$2,700-3,600

Inkstands

A Scottish silver and hardstone inkwell, by Aitchisons, Edinburgh 1855, 5.5in (14cm).
$2,700-3,600

A Victorian inkstand, with applied shell punctuated gadroon border and pierced corner panel supports, complete with two silver capped glass wells, extinguisher and nozzle, fully marked, Charles Stuart Harris, London 1898, 10.5in (26cm), 32oz.
$3,600-5,000

A silver novelty inkwell-cum-vesta case, in the form of a starboard ship's lantern, London 1894, 2in (6cm).
$720-1,000

A Victorian cast inkwell, the canted sides decorated with leafy panels below a Celtic frieze, the platform with cast gallery of entwined sea nymphs and shells, the plain faceted glass bottle with silver mounts and mermaid cover, on 6 foliate paw feet, by Robert Garrard, London 1870, 5in (13cm) wide, 19oz 13dwt.
$1,800-2,700

A silver lantern inkwell, with red lens, the hinged cover with stamp recess, by S.J., London 1894, 2in (6cm).
$720-1,000

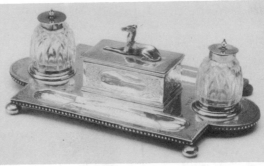

A Victorian inkstand, with presentation inscription, beaded edging, central rectangular reservoir with dog finial, 2 cut glass wells, Birmingham 1890, 10in (25cm) long, 11.3oz.
$1,200-1,700

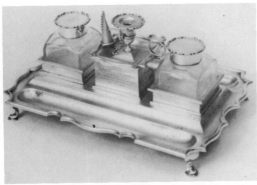

A partners' inkstand, the 2 glass wells with silver mounts, a taperstick with nozzle and extinguisher, with shaped moulded borders, on 4 hoof feet, by Goldsmiths and Silversmiths Co., London 1904, 62.5oz.
$2,700-3,600

The taper holder frame inscribed to The Rev. Charles L. Lovett-Cameron, M.A. Vicar of Mortimer.

An Edwardian inkwell, the single girdled cylindrical pot centred by a hinged domed cover, enclosing pottery liner, flanked by 5 pen apertures, on a circular reeded flange foot, by R. & S. Garrard and Co., London 1904, 5in (13cm) diam., 285gr.
$720-1,000

An Italian inkstand, chased with
rococo scroll and rocaille borders,
enclosing a central pomegranate
finial and 2 detachable cylindrical
wells, similarly chased and
pierced and with hinged covers,
pad supports, Turin c1770, liners,
the wells unmarked and possibly
later, 10.5in (26cm) wide.
$7,000-9,000

Jugs

A George II plain beer jug, on
spreading moulded foot, with leaf-
capped double scroll handle and
moulded rim and spout, by Fuller
White, 1748, 7in (18cm), 29oz.
$7,000-9,000

An early Victorian covered jug,
the pear shaped body embossed
with panels of foliage, engraved
with a crest, the moulded border
with floral sprays, rococo moulded
hinged cover with cast flower
finial, leaf-capped engraved scroll
handle, on floral leaf spray scroll
feet, by Mortimer & Hunt,
London 1843, 7in (18cm), 17oz.
$1,200-1,700

A Victorian ewer, the plain bellied
body with narrow cylindrical neck
and beaded border, the cover with
coronet finial above a
Staffordshire knot, simple handle,
on spreading foot, by Stephen
Smith, London 1864, 9.5in
(24cm), 19oz 16dwt.
$1,200-1,700

A Japanese style silver water
pitcher, by Tiffany & Co., New
York, with monogram BVRE,
marked and numbered
5051/3885/933, c1880, 9in (23cm)
high, 36oz.
$23,000-25,000

A Charles II plain inkstand,
maker's mark on base, IM
between pellets, c1680, 5.5in
(13cm) wide, 18oz.
$7,000-9,000

A silver and tortoiseshell
mounted leather blotter, with
reed and tie border, by John
Collard Vickery, London 1912,
11.5 by 8.5in (29 by 21cm).
$720-1,000

A George III hot water jug, with
coronet and crest engraved
baluster body, gadroon ring foot
and rim, domed cover with turned
finial, raffia covered loop handle,
by John Barbe, London 1763, 10in
(25cm), 17oz.
$1,200-1,700

Did you know

*MILLER'S Antiques
Price Guide builds up
year by year to form the
most comprehensive
photo reference library
available.*

Mugs & Tankards

Two Georgian pint mugs, both later foliate scroll chased baluster above spreading bases, leaf-capped double scroll handles, London 1798 and Newcastle 1744, 5in (13cm), 20oz.
$720-1,000

A George II tankard, by Robert Williams, 1728, 7in (18cm), 24oz.
$3,600-5,000

A George II baluster tankard, engraved with a presentation inscription within a rocaille cartouche hung with swags of fruit and flowers, by William Shaw & William Priest, London 1752, 8in (20cm), 24oz. 10dwts.
$2,700-3,600

The inscription reads 'The gift of Susannah Hacking 50 years a faithful servant to the Rossell family.'

A silver tankard, by Andrew Tyler, Boston, marked AT, c1721, 7.5in (19cm) high, 26oz 10dwts.
$20,000-30,000

A silver tankard, by Jacob Hurd, Boston, marked I. Hurd, c1728, 8in (19cm) high, 24oz 12dwts.
$35,000-45,000

A pair of George III mugs, engraved with armorial crests, 3.5in (9cm).
$3,600-5,000

A silver tankard, by Jacob Hurd, Boston, marked with Hurd script in oval, c1737, 7.5in (19cm) high, 25oz.　　**$50,000-60,000**

A pair of George III mugs, engraved with coat-of-arms, crest and initial between reeded bands and with leaf-capped handles, maker's mark worn, possibly C.F. for Charles Fox, London 1815, 5in (13cm), 23.8oz.
$1,200-1,700

A George III pint mug, with double scroll handle, inscribed beneath 'Trav'ling o'er we now thank Heaven, Are arrived at Thirty Seven, and may no bitter cup reach thee, unless that cup resembles me', by Samuel Welles, London 1760, 5in (13cm), 11oz.
$1,200-1,700

A George III tankard, engraved with an armorial crest, the hinged flat cover engraved with monogram, bracket handle with bar pierced thumbpiece, by Henry Chawner, London 1787, 7in (18cm), 47.5oz.
$3,600-5,000

A silver tankard, by Andrew Tyler, Boston, marked AT, c1721, 7.5in (19cm) high, 26oz 4dwts.
$30,000-40,000

A Victorian trophy in the form of a covered tankard, with mask spout, the body embossed and chased, inscribed 'Jorehant Races 1877-78' and 'Mouse Cup won by', by Frederick Elkington, London 1874, 12in (31cm), 45oz.
$3,600-5,000

A pair of George III salt cellars, by Robert and David Hennell, London 1798, 5in (13cm), and a pair of closely matching Victorian salt cellars, by Edward and John Barnard, London 1861, 14oz. **$720-1,000**

Salts

A set of 10 silver gilt salts, 10 matching casters and 10 salt spoons, by Tiffany & Co., New York, in Georgian style, after originals by Dorothy Mills, London, c1940, casters 5.5in (13cm) high, 63oz.
$3,000-3,500

A set of 4 Irish William IV heavy cast salt cellars, on lion mask and paw feet, maker's mark WN, marks rubbed, blue glass liners, one replaced, 4in (10cm) diam. 33oz.
$1,200-1,700
and a Victorian mustard pot en suite, London 1840, 10.5oz.
$720-1,000

A pair of Victorian salts, with shell, flower and mask chased borders, on mask and scroll feet, by Joseph Angell, London 1829, 4in (10cm), and a pair of King's pattern crested salt spoons, London 1829, 12oz.
$720-1,000

Salvers

A George II salver by John Tuite, on 4 scroll feet, with moulded border, engraved with a coat-of-arms and motto, by John Tuite, 1733, 13in (32.5cm), 30oz.
$3,600-5,000

The arms are those of Cowper, presumably for William, 2nd Earl Cowper, died 1764.

A George I Britannia Standard small pedestal salver, with raised reeded edge, raised upon a waisted socle and stepped circular foot, the underside engraved E * P, by David Hennell, London 1718, 6.5in (17cm) diam., 269gr.
$2,700-3,600

A George III salver, the borders moulded with a band of roses and other flowers, maker's mark W S, 1817, 11in (28cm), 40oz.
$1,800-2,700

A George II waiter on hoof feet, with applied shell and scroll rim and plain ground, maker's initials I.M., in script, London 1751, 6in (15cm), 7oz.
$720-1,000

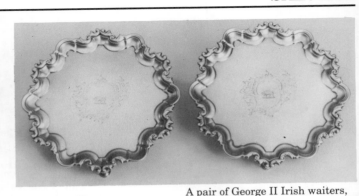

An early George II pie crust salver, the central panel probably later, flat chased with rococo scrolls, foliage and scallop shell enclosing an engraved crest, raised on 4 acanthus leaf sheathed knurl feet, by John Tuite.
$1,000-1,500

A Queen Anne Britannia standard pedestal salver, on a waisted socle and stepped foot, the underside engraved ICF, by Jno Read, London 1707, 7.5in (19.5cm) diam., 289gr.
$1,800-2,700

A pair of George II Irish waiters, the serpentine moulded borders with leaf scrolls, centred by cartouches with a boar crest, on cast scroll pad feet, by William Williamson, Dublin, c1750, 6.25in (16cm), 16.5oz.
$2,700-3,600

A silver waiter, by Joseph Richardson Sr., Philadelphia, inscribed, marked IR, c1770, 6.5in (16.5cm) diam., 8oz 10dwts.
$30,000-40,000

A silver stand, marked A. Rasch & Co., Philadelphia, c1820, 8in (20cm) diam., 16oz 10dwts.
$2,000-2,500

A silver alms dish, by Jacob Hurd, Boston, marked Hurd, c1737, 12in (31cm) diam., 18oz 8dwts.
$60,000-80,000

A late George III salver, the gadrooned border with acanthus leaf angles, raised on 4 stiff leaf and rosette feet, by Paul Storr, London 1814, 12in (30.5cm) diam., 949gr.
$2,700-3,600

A George IV salver by William Eley, in the mid-18thC taste, on hoof feet and with an applied shell and scroll rim, the ground engraved with a crest, London 1824, 8in (20cm), 10.5oz.
$1,000-1,500

A Victorian waiter by George Richard Elkington, London 1867, 8in (20cm), 10.5oz.
$360-540

A George III oval waiter, 9in (22.5cm) wide.
$1,000-1,500

An early George V presentation salver, with pie crust border, raised on 4 stepped hoof feet, centrally bright cut engraved with the coat-of-arms of George Nathaniel Curzon, First Marquess Curzon Kedleston and the facsimile signatures of the Cabinet of 1916/17, including Lloyd George, Austen Chamberlain, Bonar Law, Lord Derby, Balfour and other members, maker's mark C.S. & H.S., London 1916, 20in (51.5cm) diam., 3,500gr.
$2,700-3,600

A Victorian salver by John Harris, on 4 openwork scroll feet and with cast Bacchanalian mask and trailing vine border, engraved with a band of demi-putti, vines and scrolling foliage, the centre engraved with a coat-of-arms, 1840, 25in (63.5cm) diam., 187oz.
$10,000-12,000

A George IV salver by John Mewburn, armorial engraved within a broad band of flat chased scrolls, vine and lattice, raised and applied scroll and shell border, on volute supports, 23in (59cm) diam., 138oz.
$3,600-5,000

A Victorian salver by Robert Harper, the centre engraved with floral festoons, scrolling foliage and monogram above the date 1878, bead edge, claw and ball feet, London 1876, 8.5oz.
$360-540

A William IV Scottish salver by J. McKay, on foliate and shell feet, with an applied foliate, shell and floral rim, the ground chased with a frieze of arabesques and with contemporary presentation inscription, 1830, 12in (31cm), 29.75oz. **$720-1,000**

Sauceboats

A pair of George II sauceboats by J. S. Harman, each on spreading moulded foot and with shaped rim and double scroll handle, 8.5in (21.5cm), 30oz.
$1,800-2,700

A late George III pap boat by Crespin Fuller, the plain oval bowl with applied double reeded border, London 1808, 4.5in (11cm), 55gr.
$180-360

A French two-handled double lipped oval sauceboat with shaped reeded border and fitted oval stand, late 19thC, 10in (25cm).
$720-1,000

A late Victorian sauceboat and cover by Walker & Hall, the boat with beaded border, acanthus leaf sheathed double C scroll handle, raised upon 3 stepped hoof feet with scallop shell terminals, the lift-off cover with ivory finials, Sheffield 1899, 560gr.
$720-1,000

A pair of George III sauceboats with punched bead rims and leaf capped flying scroll handles, each on 3 pad feet, maker's mark W.S. possibly that of William Skeen, London 1768, 20.1oz.
$1,800-2,700

A pair of silver sauceboats in
George III style, by the
Goldsmiths and Silversmiths
Company, on oval stepped bases,
London 1931, 18oz.
$720-1,000

A pair of George III sauceboats,
by Daniel Piers with shaped rim,
leaf capped scroll handles, 3 short
shell and scroll feet, initialled and
crested, London 1749, 25.5oz.
$1,200-1,700

Services

A George IV three-piece tea set by
Joseph Angell, the basin and jug
with gilt interiors, fully marked,
London 1823, 50oz.
$2,700-3,600

A William IV four-piece tea and
coffee set by Edward Barnard &
Sons, the basin and jug with gilt
interiors, fully marked, London
1836, 79oz.   **$3,600-5,000**

A Victorian silver gilt tea service,
in the German taste, by William
Cooper, comprising: a teapot with
curved spout and hinged domed
cover, a two-handled sugar basin
and a cream jug, 1842, teapot 5in
(12.5cm) high, 25oz.
$3,600-5,000

Miller's is a price
GUIDE not a price
LIST

A silver five-piece tea and coffee
set, with matching two-handled
oval tea tray, by Reed & Barton,
Taunton, Ma., Francis I pattern,
engraved with foliate monogram,
comprising: teapot, coffee pot,
covered sugar bowl, creamer,
waste bowl and tray, c1950, tray
31in (79cm) long, 285oz.
$10,000-12,000

A Victorian four-piece tea and
coffee set, by Edward Barnard &
Sons, London, the basin and jug
with gilt interiors, fully marked,
1850, 68oz.
$3,600-5,000

A Victorian four-piece tea and
coffee set by Frederick Francis,
London, fully marked, 1852, 78oz.
$1,200-1,700

A Victorian three-piece silver tea service, the sugar basin and cream jug with gilt interiors, London marks for 1857, 47oz.
$1,800-2,700

A silver six-piece tea and coffee set with similar two-handled tray, by Gorham Mfg. Co., Providence, comprising: teapot, coffee pot, covered sugar bowl, creamer, waste bowl, and kettle on lampstand, engraved with monogram, c1907, kettle 14.5in (36.5cm) high, 337oz 10dwts.
$11,000-13,000

A Victorian three-piece tea set by John Samuel Hunt, the pot with facetted curved spout, flat cover and ivory button the basin and jug with gilt interiors, fully marked, 1860, 49oz.
$2,700-3,600

A Victorian three-piece tea set by John Sherwood & Sons, Birmingham, the basin and jug with gilt interiors, fully marked, 1862, 45oz.
$1,800-2,700

A William IV four-piece tea and coffee service by Jonathan Haynes, 1831 and 1833, coffee pot 9.5in (24cm) high., 82oz.
$3,600-5,000

A Victorian four-piece tea and coffee set by H. W. Curry, the pots with rocaille scroll moulded curved spouts, domed covers and convolvulus finials, the basin and jug with gilt interiors, fully marked, London 1868, 82oz.
$3,600-5,000

A Victorian four-piece tea and coffee service by George Richard Elkington, 1856, coffee pot 10in (25cm) high, 84oz.
$3,600-5,000

A Victorian silver gilt punch set by Martin Hall and Co. Ltd., the jug and beakers on 3 ball feet and engraved with a band of trailing vines, 1872, jug 10in (26cm), 177oz.   **$7,000-9,000**

A Victorian four-piece tea and coffee set, the pots with wood handles and buttons, Birmingham, 1897, 76oz.
$1,800-2,700

A Victorian silver presentation tea set by G. Martin Hall & Co. Sheffield, comprising: an ovoid teapot with flattened loop handle, domed hinged lid with urn finial, pedestal base and allover chased leaf, flower and geometric decoration, 8.5in (21cm), matching cream jug and sugar bowl, London 1874, and a matching coffee pot, London 1872, 11in (28cm) high, 71oz. 5dwts.
$3,600-5,000

A Victorian four-piece tea and coffee set by Edward Charles Brown, each piece engraved with ornate cartouches, the scrolled handles moulded foliage, inscribed Debrooghur Races 1877-78, Presented by J. Berry White Esqr and Cunningham Hudson Esqr, and Jokai Plate won by, London 1876, 81oz.
$3,600-5,000

A silver six-piece tea and coffee set with matching two-handled tray, by Tiffany & Co., New York, Chrysanthemum pattern, monogrammed RAV, comprising: teapot, coffee pot, covered sugar bowl, creamer, waste bowl, and kettle on lampstand, kettle 14in (35cm) high, 489oz. **$32,000-42,000**

A silver tea service by James Dixon & Sons, executed in the Waterloo pattern after a Paul Storr original of 1815, comprising: a spirit kettle, teapot, hot water jug, sugar bowl, milk jug, slop basin, 2 stands and an oval serving tray, Sheffield 1925, 350oz., in original oak chest. **$10,000-12,000**

An Edward VII three-piece tea service, with reeded girdles above lower bodies, applied decoration and scroll handles on spreading bases, London 1904, 41.6oz. **$900-1,500**

A Japanese style silver six-piece tea and coffee set, Gorham Mfg. Co., Providence, RI, comprising: teapot, coffee pot, covered sugar bowl, creamer, waste bowl, and kettle on lampstand, monogrammed W, each signed in Japanese, numbered 8745, c1897, coffee pot 9in (23cm) high, 130oz.
$6,500-8,500

A four-piece tea and coffee set, the pots with composition handles and buttons, Sheffield, 1932/33, 52oz. **$1,200-1,700**

A Victorian five-piece tea and coffee set.
$3,600-5,000

A Victorian silver gilt three-piece Bachelor's tea set by Finnegan's Ltd., initial engraved, with loop handles, the pot with straight spout and domed cover with flower finial, fully marked, Dublin 1898, 30oz. **$2,700-3,600**

A silver tea service by Walker & Hall, Sheffield 1959, 53oz.
$720-1,000

A Victorian four-piece tea and coffee set.
$1,800-2,700

Tea Kettles

A Victorian embossed plated tea urn with chrome lid, scrolled handles and tap to front, on dome stem to a square base with ogee feet, embossed detail over, 17in (43cm) high.
$360-540

A silver tea urn, by R. & W. Wilson, Philadelphia, engraved Eliza Bruce, c1840, 16in (40.5cm) high, 100oz. **$7,000-8,000**

An early George V small tea kettle on a stand, London 1913, and a burner, London 1896, 1,302gr.
$720-1,000

A George IV tea kettle and stand, by John Edward Terrey, with plain detachable lamp, the kettle with curved spout and partly wicker-covered swing handle, the cover with shell and foliage finial, chased overall with shells, scrolls, foliage and scrollwork on a matted ground the kettle and burner engraved with a crest, 1829, 14in (36.5cm) high, 81oz.
$3,600-5,000

Make the most of Miller's

Unless otherwise stated, any description which refers to 'a set' or 'a pair' includes a valuation for the entire set or the pair, even though the illustration may show only a single item.

A mid-Victorian tea kettle-on-stand with burner, probably by Stephen Smith, engraved with a continuous band of ivy and a crest, with fixed overhead handle and hinged domed cover, the fluted domed stand with cast acanthus leaf apron raised upon 3 double C scroll supports on leaf feet, London 1867, 2,239gr.
$1,800-2,700

A late Victorian tea kettle on a stand with burner, with fixed overhead acanthus leaf sheathed handle, raised on an arcaded and rosette pierced cylindrical stand on 3 lion paw feet with mask terminals, hinge damaged, 17.5in (45cm) high. **$720-1,000**

A mid-Georgian silver tea kettle on a stand by Thomas Whipham, with part wicker covered swing loop handle, cone finial on hinged lid and allover embossed rococo decoration, the stand with similar pierced decoration, on 3 scrolled supports, London 1739, 15.5in (39cm), 78.25oz.
$3,600-5,000

Tea Caddies

A pair of George II vase shaped tea caddies and sugar box, by Samuel Taylor, engraved with a coat-of-arms, 1753, in fitted silver mounted wood case, sugar box 6in (14.5cm) high, 31oz.
$7,000-9,000

A George III tea caddy, by Thomas Chawner, the domed cover with ivory finial, engraved with a coat-of-arms and monogram within bright cut escutcheons, the base with the inscription 'The Gift of Maria Blizard to her Niece and God-daughter Hester Carter Smith', 1786, 6in (14.5cm) high, 12oz.
$3,600-5,000

A pair of George II tea caddies, by William Soloman, each chased with bands of scrolls, foliage and rocaille ornament and engraved with initials, 1758, each with original lead lining, 4.5in (11.5cm) high, 46oz.
$7,000-9,000

A pair of early George III vase shaped tea caddies, by Samuel Taylor, London 1764, and Benjamin Brewood, London 1763, the slightly domed covers with cast flowerhead finials, one engraved G, one cover with lion passant only, 5.5in (14cm) high.
$1,800-2,700

A George III tea caddy by Hester Bateman, the domed cover with urn finial, London 1789, 5in (13cm) wide, 10.25oz.
$2,700-3,600

A tea caddy with repoussé decoration of rococo design, London 1893, 6in (15cm) high, 8oz. **$720-1,000**

A pair of George III tea caddies and matching sugar box, by William Vincent, with detachable domed covers and rose finials, each later engraved with a crest and initials within a ribbon tied foliage cartouche,1769, and a pair of sugar tongs, c1770, contained in a silver mounted japanned oblong case with lock plate and key, sugar box 5in (13.5cm) high, 28oz.
$7,000-9,000

Teapots

A George I teapot by John Gorsuch, with curved decagonal spout, hinged domed cover and baluster finial, engraved with a crest, 1726, 6in (15.5cm), 19oz.
$18,000-21,000

A late George III teapot by Joseph Craddock and William Reid, with melon fluted ivory finial and with polished fruitwood scroll handle, London 1813, 565gr.
$720-1,000

A George IV Bachelor's teapot by Rebecca Emes and Edward Barnard, the hinged domed cover with mushroom finial and with acanthus leaf sheathed loop handle, London 1823, 411gr.
$720-1,000

A George IV melon shaped silver teapot by the Barnards, with bud and leaf finial to lid, scrolled handle, cast 4-footed base, London 1842, 26oz.
$720-1,000

A George III teapot and stand by Robert Hennell, the teapot engraved with a coat-of-arms, 7in (17.5cm) high, the stand conforming in outline and similarly engraved with armorials within a foliate band, and on 4 ball feet, 7in (17.5cm) long, 19oz. 17dwt.   **$2,700-3,600**

A George III teapot by Robert and David Hennell, with straight spout, domed cover, wooden handle and finial, bright cut with 2 vacant cartouches and formal bands, London 1796, 13.25oz.
$1,200-1,700

A George III teapot by Robert and David Hennell, engraved crest and initials within shield shaped cartouches, engraved wrigglework and reeded borders, tapering spout, scroll wood handle, London 1796, 11.5oz.
$1,200-1,700

A George III teapot by Thomas Robins, with bright cut band above crests and initials within wreaths, with ivory finial and angular handle on 4 ball feet, London 1805, 7in (18cm) high, 19.2oz.
$720-1,000

A George III teapot and stand by Crispin Fuller, the pot with straight spout, domed cover with green stained ivory finial and later wood loop handle, the stand with reeded border and panel supports, London 1794, fully marked, 6.5in (16.5cm) high, 21oz.
$3,600-5,000

A William IV compressed melon fluted teapot by Edward, Edward Jnr., John and William Barnard, London 1834, 9.5in (24cm), 17oz.
$1,200-1,700

A George III teapot, festoon bright cut and crest engraved compressed vase shaped, ring foot, everted collar, wood loop handle and button, London 1805, 5in (12.5cm), 21oz.
$720-1,000

A Victorian silver teapot with fluted base rising curved spout, hallmark 1899.
$180-360

A late George III teapot probably by Thomas Wallis, with ivory finial, ebonised reeded angular handle and raised upon 4 spherical feet, the shield shaped panel later engraved with a presentation inscription, London 1806, 796gr.
$900-1,500

Trays

A George III tray by John Crouch, on 4 foliate feet, and with shell, oak leaf, acorn and gadrooned border, with similar scroll handles, engraved with a coat-of-arms, 1808, 29.5in (75cm) wide, 195oz.   **$14,500-16,500**

A tea tray by James Dixon & Sons, centred by a presentation inscription, gadrooned borders interrupted by foliate shells, on 4 openwork supports, Sheffield 1909, 29.5in (75cm), 6,760gr.
$3,600-5,000

A George III tea tray, engraved with scrolling flowers and foliage with a gadrooned border and reeded handles, maker's mark I.M. possibly for John Mewburn, London 1818, 26in (66cm) wide, 118.6oz.
$2,700-3,600

> **Miller's is a price GUIDE not a price LIST**

A silver two-handled tea tray, by Tiffany & Co., New York, in Regency style, inscribed, c1977, 26.5in (67.5cm) long, 122oz 10dwts.
$8,000-9,000

A Victorian silver engraved two-handled footed gallery tray, with pierced rim, London 1898, 22in (55.5cm) long, 70oz.
$2,700-3,600

Tureens

A late Victorian tureen, cover and liner, of inverted baluster oval form richly repoussé with flowerheads and scrolls, maker's mark W.W. over BT, London 1900, 2,910gr.   **$7,000-9,000**

A soup tureen and cover by James Dixon & Sons, engraved with a crest and presentation inscription below the gadroon border, reeded loop handles and pedestal base, Sheffield 1909, 15.5in (39.5cm) wide, 2,103gr.   **$3,600-5,000**

Two two-handled soup tureens and covers, one tureen Dublin, perhaps John Gumley, c1760, the other tureen and the 2 covers E. J. & W. Barnard, 1840, 15in (38cm) wide, 163oz.
$14,500-16,500

Four George III sauce tureens and covers by Henry Chawner, engraved either side with a coat-of-arms and motto below reeded borders, similar loop handles and pedestal bases, the crested covers with urn finials, 9in (22.5cm) 2,122gr.
$14,500-16,500

A pair of William IV entree dishes by William Bateman, with covers and handles, each with gadrooned borders and detachable foliate scroll handle, the covers engraved with a coat-of-arms and plumed helmet, 1830, 11.5in (29cm) wide, 114oz.
$3,600-5,000

Miscellaneous

A silver vase designed by William Codman and chased by Frederick A. Jordan, The Gorham Co. Martelé, 950 Standard, retailed by Bailey, Banks & Biddle, Philadelphia, marked on base, numbered 657, signed, 1898, 18in (46cm) high, 77oz 10dwts.
$28,000-32,000

A pepperette, cast in the form of a spaniel's head, Birmingham 1905, 2in (4.5cm) high.
$110-180

A George III barrel shaped silver nutmet grater crested at each end, maker's mark S.M.
$360-540

A silver novelty propelling pencil, by Sampson Mordan, in the form of a rowing boat with well modelled planking, oars and rigging, c1890, 2.5in (6cm).
$720-1,000

A late Victorian wafer holder of escallop shell form, opening to reveal pierced hinged grilles, and with rustic cast stand and overhead handle, 10in (25cm) high.
$360-540

A pin cushion in the form of a jockey's cap, with 3 ribbed segments and brim, Birmingham 1891.
$110-180

A George III large plain circular saucepan, the body of shaped outline and with turned wood handle, engraved with a crest, maker's mark worn, presumably Benjamin Gignac, 1769, 6in (15cm) high, 32oz.
$7,000-9,000

An Edwardian silver child's rattle, Birmingham, 1902, 5in (12.5cm) long.
$110-180

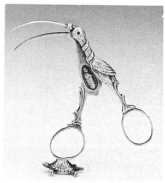

A pair of late Victorian ribbon threaders or sugar nips, in the form of a running stork, with one blue stone eye, the body enclosing a baby wrapped in swaddling bands and the stork raised on the back of a tortoise, London import marks 1890, 40gr.
$720-1,000

Although these items are often called ribbon threaders, this pair has no eyelet in the beak.

A late Victorian silver novelty pepperette in the form of a fish, maker's mark indistinct, London 1884, 4.5in (11cm) long, 82gr.
$360-540

A pair of Victorian harlequin sugar nips, maker's mark indistinct, Birmingham 1872, 63gr.
$360-540

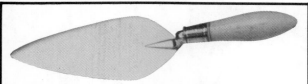

A George IV presentation trowel with inscription, used by Frederick, Duke of York, with a turned ivory handle, maker's mark W.K., London 1823, 15in (38cm) long. **$1,000-1,500**

A model of a milkmaid, with detailed costume, holding 2 jugs and a basket of fruit above a stepped oval base of 17thC style, detachable head, German, 19thC, 11.5in (29.5cm) high, 18oz. **$1,200-1,700**

A silver model of a bulldog, by Gorham Mfg. Co., Providence, RI, modelled by E. E. Codman, retailed by Shreve, Crump & Low, signed, c1930, 6in (15cm) long, 29oz. **$4,500-5,500**

SILVER PLATE
Candlesticks

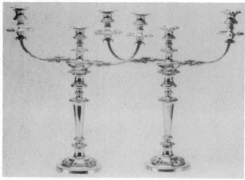

A pair of Sheffield plate candelabra, the shaped circular bases, knopped tapering stems, drip pans and detachable nozzles with scroll reeded edging, 20in (51cm) high. **$1,000-1,500**

A pair of electroplated Corinthian column five-light candelabra, the stepped square bases, drip pans and detachable nozzles with beaded edging, 20.5in (52cm) high. **$2,700-3,600**

A set of 4 Sheffield plate table candlesticks, the circular bases, fluted tapering stems and detachable nozzles with beaded edging, 11.5in (29cm) high. **$1,000-1,500**

A pair of electroplated three-light candelabra, with detachable nozzles and stepped square bases with gadrooned edging, 18.5in (47cm) high. **$1,000-1,500**

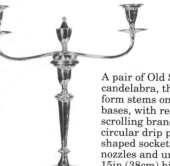

A pair of Old Sheffield plate candelabra, the tapering vase form stems on spreading circular bases, with reeded borders, the 2 scrolling branches supporting circular drip pans, campana shaped sockets with detachable nozzles and urn finials, c1790, 15in (38cm) high. **$720-1,000**

Services

An electroplated four-piece tea and coffee service, engraved with scrolling acanthus and with scroll handles on spreading bases, the teapot and coffee pot with strawberry finials.
$720-1,000

A plated oval shaped four-piece tea service, by Mappin & Webb, comprising: a teapot, hot water jug, milk jug and sugar basin, on 4 claw feet, together with a plated tray by Mappin & Webb, 25in (63.5cm), and a pair of sugar tongs.
$360-540

Tureens

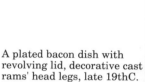

A pair of electroplated rounded entrée dishes with detachable acanthus handles and gadroon edging, on 2 warming bases with 4 acanthus supports, 14in (36cm).
$720-1,000

A Sheffield plate oval soup tureen, by Matthew Boulton & Co., c1825, 15.5in (40cm) wide.
$1,800-2,700

A plated bacon dish with revolving lid, decorative cast rams' head legs, late 19thC.
$720-1,000

Miscellaneous

A plated two-handled floral patterned tray with vine decorated rim, 25in (64cm) long.
$180-360

An electroplated two-division oil lamp with revolving boat-shaped reservoir, supporting 2 burners, decorated with masks and scrolling acanthus and with central carrying handle, on spreading pedestal base with reeded edging, together with 2 glass funnels, shades missing, stamped Patent Wild & Wessel Berlin, 25.5in (65cm) high.
$1,800-2,700

An Old Sheffield plate kettle-on-stand, the kettle with repoussé foliate scroll decoration and engraved with a coat-of-arms and crest, the stand with burner and raised on scroll feet, 15in (38cm) high overall.
$720-1,000

A Victorian parcel gilt and silver electro-type tankard.
$1,800-2,700

A graduated matched set of 5 electroplated salvers, each engraved with a vacant circular panel within a frame of Greek key pattern and within a pierced border with beaded edging, small salver 12in (31cm) diam. **$1,800-2,700**

A plated near complete canteen, by Walker & Hall, comprising: a 12 place setting including ivory hafted fish and dessert services, together with a pair of entrée dishes, a four-piece tea and coffee set, toast rack, butter dish, a pair of cruet stands, and accessories, in a carved oak cabinet-on-stand with cabriole legs and casters, 31.5in (80cm) wide.
$3,600-5,500

An electroplated two-division biscuitière, with hinged scalloped bowls each with a pierced retaining grille on a stand with chased decoration and central carrying handle, 11in (28cm) high.
$720-1,000

A Sheffield plate argyle, of cylindrical form, engraved with crest within a wreath and with engraved ribbon-tied festoons and fronds, with beaded edging, detachable cover and wood scroll handle, 5in (13cm) high.
$720-1,000

WINE ANTIQUES

A wagon-form double wine coaster, the circular coasters with pierced sides, with shaped square join between, on 4 wagon wheels, with swivelling reeded pull and baluster handle, c1810, 16in (40.5cm) long.
$720-1,000

A pair of George III silver wine coasters, probably by Robert Hennell, pierced with bright cut decoration enclosing crested cartouche, with turned mahogany bases, marks rubbed, London 1792.
$1,800-2,700

Two silver crested, pierced and bright cut wine coasters, London 1777, 4.5in (11.5cm) diam.
$1,800-2,700

A pair of George III wine coasters, by J. W. Story & William Elliott, with wooden bases centred by a circular boss engraved with a crest, London 1809, 7in (17.5cm) diam. **$1,800-2,700**

A pair of Regency red lacquer ribbed wine coasters, with Sheffield plated rim and ring handles, 5.5in (14cm) diam.
$1,000-1,500

Miller's is a price GUIDE not a price LIST

374

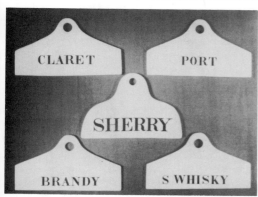

A selection of Victorian pottery cellar bin labels, with black enamel lettering, impressed with Farrow & Jackson, Wedgwood, Minton, Copeland and Spode. **$35-70 each**

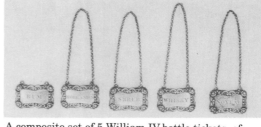

A composite set of 5 William IV bottle tickets, of shaped rounded rectangular form, the borders stamped with rosettes and acanthus leaves, engraved 'Noyeau' and 'Shrub,' Sheffield 1836, maker's mark S.W. and Co, and 'Rum', 'Hollands' and 'Whisky', Sheffield 1830, by S. C. Younge and Co., on belcher link chains, some damage. **$360-540**

A selection of silver or enamel decanter labels, 18th and 19thC. **$110-180 each**

A walnut tantalus, supporting 4 square decanters with faceted stoppers, in a case with hinged lid, 20thC. **$720-1,000**

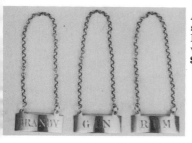

A set of 3 George III Scottish silver labels, by Matthew Crow, Edinburgh, c1805, 1.5in (4cm) wide. **$360-540**

A silver decanter label of goblet and festoon shape, engraved with rare name 'CARLOWITZ', London 1880, maker's initials JA over JS. **$110-180**

A Victorian engraved and shaped silver wine label, Birmingham 1847, 2in (5cm). **$110-180**

A Derby porcelain wine taster's tastevin, the bowl decorated with sprigs of blue flowers, c1770. **$720-1,000**

A multi-tool with spoon and fork, including a small corkscrew, with a plastic handle simulating a stag's antler, c1920. **$35-70**

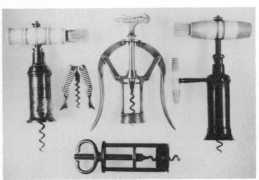

Five antique corkscrews, including a Thomason type, **$360-540,** lady's legs, **$110-180,** Heeley A1 Double Lever, **$70-145,** an all steel bone handled King's Screw, **$360-540,** and an iron open frame corkscrew, **$360-540**

A George III all steel pocket picnic corkscrew, the sheath inserts through the ring to form a handle, c1790.
$110-180

A French pinion assisted side wind corkscrew, open framed nickel plated, c1880.
$110-180

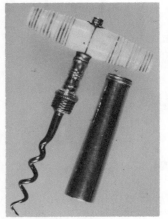

A German 'Naughty Nineties' corkscrew, in celluloid and nickel silver, the lady's legs flesh with pink and white striped stockings.
$110-180

A George III silver and ivory handled pocket corkscrew with silver sheath, stamped with maker's initials.
$360-540

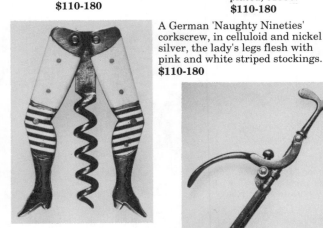

A cast steel side lever corkscrew, known as the 'Royal Club', with brass oval plaque, Charles Hull's Patent of 1864.
$720-1,000

A cast iron bar corkscrew, named the 'Original Safety', 19thC.
$110-180

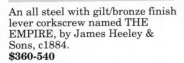

An all steel with gilt/bronze finish lever corkscrew named THE EMPIRE, by James Heeley & Sons, c1884.
$360-540

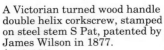

A Victorian turned wood handle double helix corkscrew, stamped on steel stem S Pat, patented by James Wilson in 1877.
$110-180

An all steel concertina corkscrew with copper finish, stamped The Pullezi, Heeley's Original Patent.
$70-145

A brass bar cork drawer, named 'The Slam', with cast iron adjustable clamp, c1890.
$180-360

An all steel four-pillar King's Screw, with turned bone handle, c1820.
$360-540

A turned bone handled corkscrew with dusting brush, known as the 'King's Screw', with brass barrel and steel side wind, with applied oval Royal coat-of-arms, by Heeley & Sons.
$360-540

A Victorian champagne tap, by S. Maw & Son, London, c1880, 4.5in (11.5cm) long.
$110-180

A champagne dispensing tap, in brass with ebonised turned wood handle, with Archemedian steel worm, by Edwin Wolverson, c1877.
$110-180

A double action brass barrel Thomason type corkscrew, with bone handle and applied brass plaque showing the Royal coat-of-arms, c1840.
$360-540

A George III 2-part silver wine funnel of plain design with reeded edges, by Peter & William Bateman, London 1813, slightly damaged.
$360-540

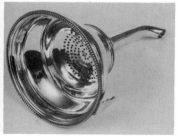

A silver wine funnel by Samuel Meriton II, London 1782, 18thC, 5in (12.5cm).
$1,000-1,500

A George III wine funnel with reeded rim, part fluted spout, London 1803, 5.5in (14cm), 4oz.
$360-540

A liqueur set in the form of a bird cage, with carrying handle, opening to release a moulded glass decanter in the form of a cockatoo, with electroplate head and glass eyes, with 8 glasses, Austrian, 18.5in (47cm) high.
$1,800-2,700

A George III wine funnel with gadrooned rim and shaped tapering spout, maker's mark S H, London 1815, 5.5in (14cm).
$720-1,000

A George III silver 2-piece wine funnel with gadrooned edge and tab to fit over the rim of a punch bowl to filter fruit juices, hall-marked, c1790.
$360-540

A silver wine funnel with fluted spout, plain strainer, marked on both pieces, London 1799.
$720-1,000

A Victorian brandy bowl with a flared rim and pouring lip, turned wood handle, maker's mark C S, London 1889, 4in (10cm).
$720-1,000

A parcel gilt wine jug, with later wood handle, the cover with bayonet fitting, formed as the head of a sphinx, with foliage finial, by Jacques Louis Clement, Kassel, German, 1793, 12in (11.5in (29.5cm) high, 915gr.
$7,000-9,000

A George IV shaped wine funnel, by Emes & Barnard, in 2 parts, the detachable simply pierced bowl with an overhanging cast fruiting vine border and vine leaf clip, the lobed body engraved with the initial S above a chased band of flowers and acanthus leaves, on a matted ground, London 1827, 6in (15cm) long, 6oz. 2dwt.
$1,000-1,500

A baluster shaped wine measure of gallon capacity, the flat circular cover inscribed Ryde Chapel and having a double-volute thumbpiece, 18thC, 12.5in (32cm).
$1,200-1,700

A mid-Victorian wine ewer, and matching goblets.
$3,600-5,500

A George III brass-bound mahogany wine cooler, with hinged lid and lead-lined interior, with slightly tapering body, the stand with associated canted tapering legs, the sides with ring and foliate carrying handles, tap missing, 17in (43cm) wide.
$3,600-5,500

A George III mahogany and brass-bound wine cooler, the hinged top above sides fitted with carrying handles, enclosing a lined interior, on square splayed legs, the stand restored, 20in (51cm) wide.
$2,700-3,600

A George III mahogany wine cooler on stand, the brass-bound octagonal body with crossbanded segmentally veneered hinged top inlaid with chevron lines and a star medallion, the stand with fluted frieze and conforming square legs with brass casters, 19in (48cm) wide.
$7,000-9,000

A George III mahogany cellaret, brass-bound and with leaded interior divisions, on stand with squared supports, brass side handles, 15.5in (39.5cm) wide.
$2,700-3,600

A George III mahogany wine cooler, inlaid with neo-classical marquetry and banded in satinwood, the lid with laurel decoration, the fluted frieze with an ornate brass ring handle above a panel with swags, paterae capped reeded pilasters, the sides with later brass swag handles, formerly on a stand, the present square tapering legs with brass casters, 25in (64cm).
$7,000-9,000

A George III mahogany and brass-bound oval wine cooler, with lined interior and lion's mask and ring carrying handles on later square tapered legs and casters, 26in (66cm) wide.
$3,600-5,500

A George III mahogany wine cooler with canted rectangular hinged top and green baize lined interior, the sides with brass carrying handles, on angled square legs with later base and restorations to legs, 24.5in (62cm) wide.
$2,700-3,600

A Georgian brass bound wine cooler.   **$1,800-2,700**

A late George III mahogany and brass bound octagonal wine cooler, the hinged lid enclosing a later fitted interior and lining, flanked by brass lion's mask handles, on turned tapering legs, 10in (51cm) wide.
$2,700-3,600

A George III mahogany wine cooler with 2 brass bands, having hinged lid with internal lead lining and brass drain tap, supported on matching stand with 4 square tapering legs and brass casters, 18in (46cm) wide.
$3,600-5,500

A Regency mahogany wine cooler with brass banding, original lead lined interior, and tap to drain melting ice.
$3,600-5,500

An Irish Regency plum-pudding mahogany wine cooler, with coffered canted rectangular hinged top enclosing a lead lined divided interior, the tapering sides with brass lion mask and ring handles, one ring missing, on later paw feet, 26.5in (67cm) wide.
$1,800-2,700

A William IV oak and ebonised wine cooler with moulded circular top and lead lined interior, above a gadrooned body and on spreading fluted shaft and square base, 26in (66cm) diam.
$3,600-5,500

A Victorian tôle peinte wine cooler, rectangular with canted corners, repainted with flower borders and stylised flowerheads, with removeable liner, twin scroll handles and on 4 spoked wheels, 24.5in (62cm) long.
$720-1,000

An early Victorian mahogany sarcophagus shaped wine cooler, with raised tambour style domed top, swivel lead lined cellarette, supported on hairy lion paw feet, 31in (78.5cm) wide.
$1,800-2,700

A William IV Old Sheffield plate wine cooler, of loosely Warwick form, the detachable rim engraved with a crest, in a bead and ovolo border, with twin entwined handles, the sides with acanthus leaf decoration, on a square base, 10in (26cm) high.
$1,800-2,700

A pair of Victorian fluted campana shaped wine coolers on rising foliate cast shaped square bases, applied with cast body bands with trailing vines incorporating crossed tendril handles, each engraved with an armorial, 12in (30.5cm).
$3,600-5,500

A pair of William IV Sheffield plate wine coolers, the campana shape bodies with melon panelling and a band of grape vines, gadroon shell leaf borders, detachable rims to the liners, moulded leaf appliqué handles on knopped circular feet, 10.5in (26.5cm).   **$2,700-3,600**

Make the most of Miller's

Unless otherwise stated, any description which refers to 'a set' or 'a pair' includes a valuation for the entire set or the pair, even though the illustration may show only a single item.

A pair of openwork wine coolers, applied with a grape vine, with short tendril stem, the sides composed of open work reeded trelliswork, liners missing, 10.5in (26.5cm) high.
$3,600-5,500

METALWARE

Gold

A 9ct gold liqueur set, by Wakeley & Wheeler, comprising: a waiter, with reeded mount, on hoof feet, 8in (20cm), a set of 4 goblets, 3.5in (8.5cm), and a single goblet, 5in (12.5cm), all initialled B and engraved Cartier, London, 1967.
$2,700-3,600

A 14ct gold toilet set, by Tiffany & Co., New York, engraved with crowns above initials N or V, c1905, 16 pieces. **$6,500-8,500**

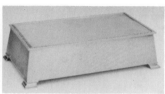

A 9ct gold cigarette box, the interior of the hinged cover engraved with a inscription 'From The Directors of Thomas W. Ward Ltd., to Arnold Carr. On completion of Fifty Years Service. 1st November, 1965', wood lined, Birmingham 1965, 8in (20cm) wide.
$2,700-3,600

Pewter

A pewter half gallon measure, by Richard Dunne, late 17thC, 11in (28cm).
$1,800-2,700

A pewter lidded flagon of Beefeater type, the muffin knopped cover with twin cusp thumbpiece stamped with a row of 4 hallmarks, the plain drum above ovolo moulded foot, c1670, 10in (25.5cm).
$1,800-2,700

A James I pewter flagon, with knopped bun cover and erect ridged thumbpiece, the plain drum on raised ovolo moulded foot, some surface pitting, c1615, 11.5in (29cm). **$1,800-2,700**

A pewter half gallon flagon, the domed lid with wrythen thumbpiece and shaped flange, the slightly tapering cylindrical body with bands of stringing, early 18thC, 11.5in (29cm).
$2,700-3,600

A pewter wrigglework pint tankard, with voluted handle terminal and splayed foot, late 17thC, 6.5in (16cm).
$3,600-5,500

A pair of pewter and brass table
candlesticks.
$360-540

A French armorial pewter
jardinière, by Louis Alegre,
Angers, with moulded rim, the
front cast with the arms of the
City of Angers, the back with
Christopher Columbus, the side
ring handles suspended through
the mouths of lion masks,
underside marked, c1820, 9in
(23cm) diam.
$1,800-2,700

A German pewter soup tureen
and cover, by A.M., with circular
foot and stem supporting the
globular body with moulded
banding and square side handles,
the fitted domed cover with urn
finial, underside marked, early
19thC, 12.5in (32cm) wide.
$3,600-5,500

A French armorial
pewter platter, cast
with the French Royal
arms enclosed within
floral garlands, the
sloping rim engraved
with scrolling vines
within a moulded
scallop edge, underside
indistinctly marked,
19thC, 20in (50cm)
long.
$1,800-2,700

A pair of French pewter sconces,
each with cartouche shaped back
plate terminating in a flame
finial, the pierced scroll arm with
spiral fluted drip pan and
campana shaped socket with
everted rim, probably 18thC, 14in
(35.5cm).
$3,600-5,500

A French pewter armorial ewer,
by Laurent Morant, Lyon, the
reeded foot supporting a knopped
stem and helmet shaped body
with moulded banding centering
an engraved coat-of-arms, the
double scroll handle with shell
finial, underside marked, 1711,
10in (26cm).
$1,800-2,700

*The arms are those of Delglat de
La Tour du Bost.*

A French pewter cistern and
basin, the cistern formed as a
dolphin, a spigot in its mouth, the
basin formed as a scallop shell
raised on tripod feet cast with
masks, the splash plate cast in
relief with Diana and Acteon, one
fin missing, probably 18thC, 23in
(59cm).
$1,800-2,700

Brass

A Turkish brass pear shaped
ewer and hinged domed cover on
4 feet with scrolling mythical
head handle and tapering lobed
spout, the lobed body with single
leaf petals on each section, 18thC,
13in (33cm).
$1,200-1,700

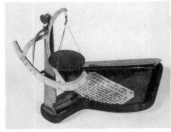

A George III brass and silvered
travelling coin balance, by V.
Anscheutz and J. Schlaff,
Denmark Street, Soho, London,
the scale from 0-36 and signed
Anscheutz & Co., No. 1620, with
original instructions, in
mahogany shaped case.
$1,000-1,500

A Flemish brass inkstand in the form of a lion, the hinged head with stylised mane, his body with stamped disc decoration, his rear leg pierced for the quill, liner missing, probably 15thC, 3.5in (8.5cm) wide.
$2,700-3,600

A Victorian coromandel brass mounted inkstand, with domed hinged superstructure, above 2 inkwells and base fitted with a single drawer, on bun feet, 11.5in (29cm) wide.
$720-1,000

A Regency style brass jardinière, with lobed and embossed body, lion's mask ring handles, paw feet, 11in (28cm).
$360-540

An Italian brass and pietra dura clock garniture, the pierced case and three-light candelabra inset with circular pietra dura plaques decorated with flowers and birds, the dial signed H. Bosi, Firenze, with French 8-day movement, late 19thC, 17in (43cm) high. **$3,600-5,500**

A pair of Adam style gilt brass coal vases and covers of oval fluted and reeded form with pineapple finials, 16.5in (42cm) high. **$2,700-3,600**

Bronze

A three-quarter life size bronze head of an elderly woman, wearing a scarf, by W. Reynolds-Stephens, on a dark marble base, 22in (56cm).
$1,000-1,500

A French bronze of Clytie, by Pierre Charles Eugène Delpech, with rich dark brown patination, on a black marble plinth, signed and inscribed London, early 20thC, 15.5in (39.5cm) high.
$900-1,500

Mujer Sentada, by Francisco Zúñiga, signed, numbered II/II, inscribed Fundación del Aguila, Mex DF, bronze with green patina, 1960, 40.5in (103cm) high.
$120,000-140,000

A French bronze bust of Minerva, with a helmet and aegis over her robe, cast from a model by Albert-Ernest Carrier-Belleuse, signed A. Carrier-Belleuse and with Valsuani Cire Perdue stamp, on mottled green marble socle, 19thC, 15.5in (39.5cm) high.
$1,800-2,700

A bronze bust of a girl with one hand to her mouth, by George van der Straeten, red/brown patination, signed and with foundry stamp, on an alabaster plinth, 7.5in (19cm) high.
$720-1,000

An Italian bronze bust of a gentleman with a moustache, from a model by Giuseppe Renda, on a moulded socle, signed and dated G. Renda settembre '94, late 19thC, 20in (51cm).
$2,700-3,600

A Belgian bronze bust of a young Bacchante woman, by Jef Lambeaux, with rich green patination, slight rubbing, 25in (63.5cm) high.
$2,700-3,600

A bronze bust of a girl holding cherries in her mouth, by George van der Straeten, red/brown patination, signed and with foundry stamp, on an alabaster base, c1910, 9in (23cm) high.
$720-1,000

Giuseppe Renda (1862-1939) studied under Toma, Lista and Solari. He executed monuments and portrait busts, but specialised primarily in bronze statuettes in an Art Nouveau style. He exhibited internationally, winning prizes and acclaim for his images of sensuous maidens, though these were later considered licentious by the Fascist regime. This bust reveals Renda's taste for the Continental Belle Epoque, with its stylish treatment of the moustache, summary and asymmetric shoulder and elegant moulded socle. Though a fashionable bronze, Renda has skilfully combined sensitive portraiture with the decorative, particularly in the delicately lined eyes, strong nose and upward tilt to the head.

A bronze figure of a fisher boy, signed on the base Lavergne, 7in (18cm) high.
$180-360

A French bronze bust of Diana, after Jean-Antoine Houdon, on waisted socle with laurel wreath moulded base, inscribed HOUDON sculpt., 19thC, 29in (73cm) high.
$3,600-5,500

A copper electrotype figure of a Nubian slave girl, by John Bell, with brown patination, signed and inscribed Elkington & Co., Founders, c1880, 21in (55cm) high.
$1,000-1,500

A bronze figure of a Grenadier Guardsman, inscribed 'J. E. Boehm Scr.', stamped Elkington, on an ebonised plinth, 1815, 23in (59cm) high.
$2,700-3,600

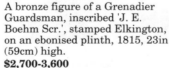

A pair of Italian bronze figures of Roman warriors in elaborate battledress, on square bases, on ebonised stands, 19thC, 17in (43.5cm) high.
$2,700-3,600

A bronze figure of the Dancing Pan with cymbals, after the Antique, on a square base, 12in (31cm) high.
$360-540

An English 'New Sculpture' bronze figure of an allegorical maiden, possibly Justice, on a stained wood socle, early 20thC, 11.5in (29.5cm) high.
$3,600-5,500

A bronze figure of a young gentleman wearing a doublet and hose, carrying a sword,19thC, 48in (122cm) high.
$7,000-9,000

A bronze figure of St Michael and Satan, by Edward William Wyon, with rich dark green/brown patination, inscribed 'Executed by E. W. Wyon after the original of Flaxman for the Art Union of London, 1842,' 20in (51cm) high.
$2,700-3,600

An English Art Union bronze figure of a boy at a stream, cast from a model by John Henry Foley, the base stamped J. H. Foley, mid-19thC, 21.5in (54.5cm) high.
$3,600-5,500

John Henry Foley R.A., 1818-1874, rose from humble origins to become one of the foremost sculptors of the Victorian era. He designed the figure of the Prince Consort and the group of 'Asia' for the Albert Memorial. He was born in Dublin, and on his death left his casts to the Schools of the Royal Dublin Society.

The Art Union of London was founded in 1837 with the high ideals of promoting the appreciation of British sculpture. The Committee decided to commission reductions of monumental sculpture, stipulating 'that the pieces should be of moderate expense and of a convenient size ... fitted for a drawing room table'. The Art Union's selection for 1846 was the present model by Foley, the monumental plaster of which had enjoyed great acclaim at the Westminster Hall Exhibition of 1844, and is now preserved by the Royal Dublin Society.

A bronze figure of a naked Bacchanalian youth, pouring wine from a skin, 9in (23cm) high.   **$360-540**

A bronze figure of a young male hunter, holding a bow and horn, wearing a loin cloth with a dead deer at his feet, after Marioton, inscribed 'Eug. Marioton, Hallalt', 27in (69cm) high.
$720-1,000

A bronze group of a young girl, restraining a setter from a game bird, with brown/black patination, by Engelbert Joseph Peiffer, signed, c1860, 14in (35cm).
$1,800-2,700

A bronze female torso, by Karin Jonzen, pale green patination, indistinctly signed, 16.5in (42cm) high.
$1,800-2,700

A bronze statuette of Bacchus and child.
$720-1,000

A bronze figure by James Butler, R.A., entitled Little Dancer Holding Her Skirt, limited edition of 12, signed, 14.5in (37cm) high.
$1,800-2,700

A bronze figure of Joan of Arc, by Henri Michel Chapu, signed F. Barbedienne Fondeur, and with the Collas reduction seal, mid-brown patination, mid-19thC, 18in (46cm).
$1,800-2,700

A bronze figure of the Farnese Hercules, standing by a tree stump, with black patination, on a rectangular base, 19thC, 15.5in (41cm) high.
$900-1,500

A pair of French School bronze cherubs, on red marble socles, with rich brown patination, mid-19thC, 33in and 34in (84cm and 87cm).
$7,000-9,000

These bronze figures are mid-19thC casts of the 1768 models by Jean Baptiste Pigalle.

A bronze figurine of a girl, in a flowing dress and plumed hat, on a shaped plinth, signed 'C. Ceribelle', 19thC, 31in (78.5cm).
$3,600-5,500

A bronze figure, by Hippolyte Moreau.
$7,000-9,000

An Austrian cold painted bronze figure of a young negro, 15.5in (40cm) high.
$2,700-3,600

A bronze figure entitled 'The Juggling Clown', signed by Francesco de Matteis, c1880.
$2,700-3,600

A bronze figurine of a young boy, standing playing a mandolin, on a plinth, stamped 'Reduction mecanique F. Barbe Dienne Fondeur', signed P. Dubois, dated 1865, 30in (76.5cm).
$3,600-5,500

A bronze figure of Mephistopheles, by Jacques Louis Gautier, signed and inscribed Duplan et Salles Ft. de Bronze, with dark brown/black patination, mid-19thC, 26in (66cm).
$1,800-2,700

Gautier was a pupil of Rude and made his debut at the Salon of 1850. Mephistopheles was first modelled in the early 1850's and was produced in several variants by the foundry Duplan et Salles, c1855.

A bronze figure of a young girl wearing a flowing dress and holding a garland of flowers, standing on a rocky circular base, inscribed 'S. Kinsburger', 25in (64cm) high.
$720-1,000

A bronze figure entitled 'La Glaneuse, by Henri Godet, with green and light brown patination, signed and stamped A1989 and with the Bronze Garanti au Titre seal, c1900, 30in (76cm).
$3,600-5,500

A French bronze figure of Henri IV, cast from a model by Baron François-Joseph Bosio, shown as a child, dressed contemporary breeches and doublet, signed B. ON BOSIO, sword blade missing, mid-19thC, 49in (125cm) high.
7,000-9,000

François-Joseph, Baron Bosio, 1768-1845, studied under Pajou in France and Canova in Rome. He was widely patronised, in particular by Bonaparte, the Bourbons and Louis Philippe. Bosio's Henri IV Enfant was originally executed in marble, commissioned by the ministre de l'Interieur for the town of Pau. It was exhibited at the Salon of 1824 and with the King's permission Bosio had a limited edition of reductions cast in bronze. A silver version was also cast, it was listed in the Cabinet du Roi in 1824, and is now in the Louvre.

A bronze figure of David with the head of Goliath, by Jean Antoinne Mercié, signed, inscribed F. Barbedienne Fondeur, stamped with the Collas reduction seal and numbered 82, with brown patination, 29in (74cm) high.
$3,600-5,500

A French bronze figure of a muse, cast from a model by Etienne-Henri Dumaige, signed H. Dumaige, 19thC, 13in (33cm) high.
$1,800-2,700

A French School bronze, entitled 'The Wishing Well', with a rich dark brown patination, on a marble plinth, signed, late 19thC, 17in (43cm).
$3,600-5,500

A French School bronze of a child offering Cupid a drink of wine, with a rich dark brown patination, on a marble base, 17in (43cm).
2,700-3,600

A bronze figure entitled 'Une Fille D'Eve', by Alfred Grévin, with pale brown patination, signed Grévin & Beer, with founder's mark E. Tassel, c1880, 23in (60cm) high.
$3,600-5,500

A French bronze figure entitled 'Soldat Spartiate', by Jean Pierre Cortot, signed and inscribed F. Barbedienne Fondeur Paris, with bronze, dark brown and green patination, 15in (38.5cm).
$1,800-2,700

Jean Pierre Cortot studied at the Ecole des Beaux Arts and won the Prix de Rome in 1809. Soldat Spartiate is a reduction cast of the marble group now in the Louvre, sometimes known as 'Soldat de Marathon', exhibited at the Salon of 1834 and cast posthumously in an edition by Ferdinand Barbedienne.

A French School bronze of Cupid stringing his bow, with a dark brown patination, on a marble plinth, late 19thC, 21in (53cm) high.
$2,700-3,600

Two French School bronze figures of Giuliano de Medici and Lorenzo de Medici, with rich dark brown patination, 16in (40.5cm) high.
$3,600-5,500

A French School bronze of two young Bacchante women, with green/brown patination, late 19thC, 19in (48cm).
$3,600-5,500

A bronze figure, entitled Fascinator, by Eugène Marioton, with mid-brown patination, signed, 33in (84cm) high.
$3,600-5,500

These bronze figures are reductions after the original marble statues in the Medici Chapel in Florence, made by the Italian master Michelangelo Buonarroti, 1475-1564. They portray the Duke of Nemours and the Duke of Urbino and are situated in the chapel above the figures of Night and Day.

A bronze figure entitled 'The Family', by Henry Etienne Dumaige, signed, with rich mid-brown patination, c1850, 21in (53cm) high.
$2,700-3,600

A bronze group of 2 putti and a young faun, signed Clodion, on green marble oval base, with dark green patination, late 19thC, 11in (28cm) high.
$720-1,000

A bronze figure of a Japanese geisha girl, by Eugène Laurent, with variegated patination, signed E. Laurent and Raingo Fes, c1880, 17in (43cm) high.
$1,800-2,700

Eugène Laurent was born in Gray on 29th April 1832, he died in Paris in 1898. He studied under Coinchon and exhibited at the Salon from 1861. He specialised in portrait busts and figures of contemporary and historical French celebrities. He sculpted the monument of Jacques Callot in Nancy and the statue of François Boucher in the Paris town hall.

A bronze figure of Pan, seated, by Jacques Antoine Theodore Coinchon, with green patination, signed, c1870, 17in (43cm).
$1,800-2,700

A bronze figure, entitled 'The Successful Hunter', by Marcel Début, with dark brown/green patination, signed, c1900, 35in (88cm) high.
$3,600-5,500

A bronze figure, entitled 'L'amour enchainant La Fortune', by Auguste Moreau, signed, stripped patination, c1900, 20in (51cm) high.
$2,700-3,600

A bronze figure of 'The Blacksmith', by Edouard Drouot, signed, with mid-brown patination, on a naturalistic base mounted on a red marble plinth, 25in (64cm) high.
$1,800-2,700

A bronze figure entitled 'Young Hunter', by Marcel Début, with rich chocolate brown patination, c1900, 26.5in (67cm) high.
$2,700-3,600

A French revolving bronze group, entitled 'Devoir, Present, Prepare, L'Avenir', of a seated man on an anvil with a woman and child holding a sword, signed Rancouler, repair to arm, 31in (79cm) high.
$7,000-9,000

A French bronze figure of a judge, cast from a model by R. Colombo, signed R. Colombo and with Bronze Garanti stamp, on a rouge marble stepped base, with bronze trim and cartouche inscribed JUGE AU CONSEIL DES DIX VENISE, late 19thC, 21.5in (54.5cm) high.
$1,800-2,700

A pair of French bronze and ivory figures of a musician and a poet, by Eustache Bernard, on onyx plinths, 19thC, 10.5in (27cm) high.
$1,800-2,700

A pair of cold painted bronze figures of Arabs, by Franz Bergman, each with Bergman stamp, on green marble plinths, tallest 15in (38cm) high.
$7,000-9,000

An Italian bronze figure of a reclining maiden, cast from a model by Vittorio Caradossi, on a green marble socle with cartouche inscribed DOLCE FAR NIENTE, PROF. V. CARADOSSI, on green marble fluted columnar pedestal, c1900, 24in (61cm).
$7,000-9,000

A German bronze figure of the nightwatchman, signed F. Bernaver, Munchen, on a mottled black circular plinth, 27in (69cm) high.
$1,200-1,700

A bronze figure of Caesar Augustus, after the Antique, standing by a putto on a dolphin, on a circular base inscribed A. MESSINA ROMA, black/green patination, 19thC, 28in (71cm) high. **$2,700-3,600**

A French bronze figure, entitled 'La Danseuse Nattova', by Serge Yourievitch, with brown patination, on a marble plinth, early 20thC, 15.5in (39.5cm) high.
$3,600-5,500

An Italian bronze figure of Spring Awakening, by Amadeo Gennarelli, signed and stamped, 20thC, 18.5in (47cm) high.
$2,700-3,600

A Norwegian bronze figure of Brunhilda on horseback, on a rocky incline, cast from a model by Stephan Sinding, signed, with founder's inscription AKT. GES. GLADENBECK-BERLIN D964, sword replaced, late 19thC, 20.5in (52cm) high.
$3,600-5,500

A bronze figure of Martha Graham, by George Aarons, rich mid-brown patination, signed and dated 1941, No. 4/12 and inscribed Modern Art Fdry. N.Y., 14in (35cm) high.
$3,600-5,500

A Hungarian bronze group of Adam and Eve, by Mark Weinberger Vedres, on a marble plinth, signed, 19thC, 16in (41cm) high.   **$3,600-5,500**

George Aarons was born in Lithuania and moved to the United States at the age of 10. His work is in the collections of the Museum of Art, Ein Harod, Israel; the Fitchburg Art Museum, Massachussetts and the Musée de St Denis, France.

A bronze figure of a cloaked medieval warrior riding a galloping horse, by Attino Prendoni, 24in (61.5cm) high.
$1,200-1,700

Gurdjan exhibited in Paris in 1945 at the Salon des Artistes Libres Arméniens. His known works include a bust of the architect, Houspian.

An Austrian School cold painted bronze of a clown and a donkey, c1900, 10in (26cm) wide.
$1,200-1,700

An Armenian bronze figure of Isadora Duncan, by Akop Gurdjan, with brown patination, signed and stamped with foundry seal Le Blanc Barbedienne, Cire Perdue, à Paris, 20thC, 18in (45cm) high.   **$1,800-2,700**

A bronze model of a First World War Cavalryman, by Pierre-Robert Christophe, signed, with rich mid-brown patination, on a mottled marble plinth, 21in (52.5cm).
$2,700-3,600

A bronze study for Europa and the Bull, by Sydney March, with dark brown patination, signed, English School, 20thC, 11.5in (29cm).
$3,600-5,500

A bronze figure of a seated bear holding a table lighter in the form of an oil lamp, after Christophe Fratin, underside of base soldered, signed with reverse 'N', 5.5in (13.5cm) high.
$360-540

A French bronze equestrian figure of Charles V, on a rouge marble base, late 19thC, 21.5in (54cm) high.
$1,800-2,700

A French bronze equestrian figure of a hussar, cast from a model by Pierre-Nicholas Tourgueneff, the hussar in First Empire uniform, signed P. Tourgueneff and inscribed Susse F. es. Ed.rs., with Susse Frères foundary stamp, plume missing, late 19thC , 22in (56cm) high.
$2,700-3,600

Pierre-Nicholas Tourgueneff, 1853 -1912, was a French sculptor of Russian extraction. He trained under the celebrated animalier and historical sculptor Fremiet.

An Austrian School cold painted bronze of an elephant tiger hunt, on a marble plinth, c1900, 12in (30.5cm).
$3,600-5,500

A bronze group of children playing with a tortoise, by Louis Ernest Barrias, signed and dated 1877, inscribed F. Barbedienne, with rich mid and dark brown patination, 5.5in (13.5cm).
$1,800-2,700

A bronze figure of an eagle, by Antoine Louis Barye, signed, with rich dark brown patination, 11in (28cm).
$2,700-3,600

A bronze figure of 2 eagles attacking a goat, by Christophe Fratin, signed, with gold and red/ brown patination, 19.5in (49.5cm).
$1,800-2,700

A French bronze animalier group of a monkey jockey astride a racehorse, on a naturalistic rectangular base signed J. GECHTER, 19thC, 5.5in (14cm) high.
$360-540

A bronzed and parcel-gilt Napoleonic eagle, with outstretched wings and clutching a ribbon-tied laurel wreath, 19thC, 38.5in (98cm) wingspan.
$2,700-3,600

A bronze group of two birds courting, by Jules Moigniez, signed, on an oval reeded base, with black patination, 8in (20cm).
$900-1,500

A bronze retriever with pheasant, by Jules Moigniez, with rich dark brown patination, 12in (30cm).
$1,800-2,700

An American bronze group of 3 terriers, cast from a model by C. Mackarness, on naturalistic ground, signed and dated C. Mackarness 1912, with Roman bronze works N-Y- stamp, 8.5in (21cm) high.
$2,700-3,600

A bronze and parcel-gilt eagle with outstretched wings and clutching a ring, 19thC, 37.5in (95.5cm) wingspan.
$2,700-3,600

A bronze group of a bird protecting its chick from a snake, by Jules Moigniez, on a reeded base, signed, with black patination, c1870, 12.5in (32cm).
$900-1,500

A bronze retriever and pheasant, by Lambert Leonard, signed, with rubbed dark brown patination, 8.5in (22cm).
$1,200-1,700

A bronze figure of a pointer dog, on a mottled black marble base, 12in (31cm) long.
$360-540

A bronze figure of a dachshund, entitled C. H. Wiseacre, signed Percy Taylor, c1920, 35.5in (90.5cm) long.
$3,600-5,500

A bronze figure of an emu, by Franz Bergman, signed Nam Greb and with seal, brown patination, c1900, 6in (16cm).
$720-1,000

A bronze group entitled Chiens Braque et Epagneau sur Faisan, by Paul Edouard Delabrierre, with green/dark brown patination, 11in (28cm).
$1,800-2,700

A cold-painted bronze model of an ibex, standing on a naturalistic rocky base, by Franz Bergman, stamped 294 Gesch and with Bergman seal, 11in (28cm).
$720-1,000

A bronze figure of a mare and foal, by Christopher Fratin, on a naturalistic base, signed, mid brown patination, c1850, 8in (20cm).
$1,800-2,700

A French bronze model of the racehorse 'Prestige', cast from a model by Henri-Louis Cordier, signed, inscribed 'Prestige', c1900, 17in (43.5cm) high.
$2,700-3,600

A bronze model of a goat, by P. J. Mêne, standing on an oval naturalistic base signed P. J. Mêne, with gold, brown and black patination, c1870, 5in (13cm).
$900-1,500

A Viennese School bronze figure of a kangaroo, with brown patination, c1900, 6in (15cm).
$720-1,000

Henri-Louis Cordier, 1853-1926, studied both under his father, the celebrated 'ethnographic' sculptor, and under Frémiet, Gérôme and Mercié. He exhibited at the Salon from 1877, and specialised in equestrian figures and studies of animals, though he did execute some ethnographic subjects. He was awarded several medals and was made a Chevalier of the Légion d'Honneur in 1903.

A bronze model of an Asian elephant, by Antoine-Louis Barye, base signed Barye and stamped 'H', with green/black patination, slightly rubbed, 19thC, 6in (15cm).
$1,000-1,500

A Italian bronze figure of a lioness on a rock, by Giacomo Merculiano, with green patination, and marble base, 15in (38cm).
$2,700-3,600

A bronze figure of a walking lion, by R*** Thomas, signed and stamped C. H. Gautier Bronzier, with rich dark green/brown patination, on a wooden plinth, 14in (37.5cm) long.
$2,700-3,600

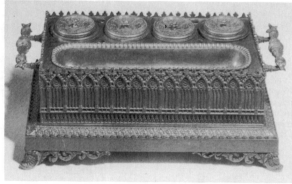

A Regency Gothic bronze standish, the plateau with 4 ink and pounce pots, nib holders and dished pen tray, the frieze with arcaded niches above bands of conforming ornament, twin handles on the sides, on foliate scroll feet, 13in (33cm) wide.
$3,600-5,500

A Paduan bronze triangular inkwell, the sides with friezes of scrolling foliate pattern, on 3 lion's paw feet, the lid with acanthus decoration, and a putto finial, 5.5in (14cm) wide.
$2,700-3,600

A pair of Viennese cold-painted bronze models of penguins, on square onyx plinths with chamfered edges, 19thC, 5in (12cm) high.
$1,200-1,700

A bronze figure of 2 stags, by Charles Valton, signed, 21in (53cm) high.
$2,700-3,600

A bronze inkstand in the Grecian manner, with central herm figure, on a breccia marble socle, 19thC.
$720-1,000

An Empire bronze inkwell, in the form of a boat, on a rouge marble platform base.
$180-360

A bronze figure of The Stag Hunt, by Pierre Jules Mêne, signed and inscribed Susse Frs Edts, with red/brown and dark brown patination, 15in (38cm) high.
$7,000-9,000

A bronze figure of a stag and doe beside a stream, by Pierre-Albert Laplanche, signed, with brown and green patination, on a green marble plinth, 18in (45cm).
$2,700-3,600

A bronze figure of a stag and doe, by Alfred Dubucand, with rich mid and green/brown patination, 11in (28.5cm).
$1,800-2,700

A Netherlands bronze snail head oil lamp, with bulbous eyes and wick emerging from trunk-shaped smiling jaws, with pale gold patina, c1600, 6.5in (16.5cm).
$3,600-5,500

An Italian bronze mortar dedicated to Pietro Bono of Perugia, inscribed around the rim in two bands PETRVS. BONVS. CANCS. GNLIS. PERVSIE. ET. VMBRIE, his coat-of-arms on one side and decorative cartouche on the other, 1618, 5in (13cm) high.
$3,600-5,500

A bronze figure of a doe, early 20thC.
$1,000-1,500

A bronzed standard lamp, in the form of an Egyptian woman, the base stamped Miroy Frères, Paris, 19thC.
$3,600-5,500

A pair of bronze game vases and covers, by Pierre Jules Mêne, signed, with brown patination, 17in (44cm) high.
$3,600-5,500

A pair of French gilt-bronze vases in the manner of Clodion, each cast with grotesque mask handles, swags and numerous playing putti, on octagonal black marble bases, 16in (41cm) high.
$1,800-2,700

A pair of French bronze models of the Medici and Borghese urns, each on square marble base, gilt patination, c1870, 14in (36cm) high.
$1,800-2,700

A pair of bronze vases, with twin handles and swan neck terminals, the bodies with raised classical friezes, on stepped bases with square plinths, 19thC, 15.5in (39.5cm) high.
$1,200-1,700

A bronze table centrepiece, by Frederic Auguste Bartholdi, of two fauns holding a basket, signed, with brown patination, 8in (20cm).
$1,800-2,700

A French bronze vase, by Léon Aimé Joachim Lecointe, the body cast in relief with Bacchante and other classical figures amongst foliage, with vine entwined handles, signed L. Lecointe, on foliate cast rising circular foot, lid missing, dated 1775, 38in (97cm) high.
$2,700-3,600

An Austrian cold-painted bronze lamp, modelled as a semi-clad lady lying on a couch smoking a cigarette, being served a drink and fanned with a palm, signed on the carpet base Chotha or Chotka, 19thC, 15in (38cm) high.
$900-1,500

A bronze mortar, with waisted body cast with heraldic devices and ring handles, possibly German, 16thC, 10in (25cm) wide. **$1,200-1,700**

Copper

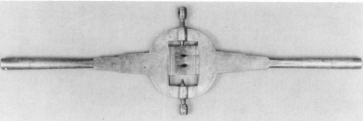

An engraved copper and brass inlaid steel screw mould, initialled D.T.S., Wurtsboro, New York, 1850, 34.5in (87.5cm) long.
$3,000-5,000

A French bronze vase, with ovoid body, stylised bird twin handles, flaring neck with everted rim, Greek key pattern border above bands of stylised Oriental ornament, the base inscribed CHRISTOFLE & CIE, late 19thC, 10in (25cm) high.
$360-540

A copper kettle, the lid with finial.
$110-180

l. A copper lidded saucepan, c1800, 4.5in (11cm).
$110-180

r. A copper coffee pot, c1790, 7.5in (19cm).
$180-360

A red patinated copper and white metal teapot, stand and burner, the teapot with ebonised turned bar handle, the body applied with white metal flowers, blossom and butterflies, the stand on 4 claw-and-ball feet, both teapot and stand stamped Gorham & Co. Y85, Cuivre, 10.5in (26.5cm) high.
$2,700-3,600

Firemarks

l. Phoenix, copper firemark, c1865-75, 9.5in (24cm) high.
$110-180

r. Salop Fire Office, lead, c1785, 7.5in (19cm).
$180-360

Iron

Sun Fire Office, lead, c1797, 6.5in (16cm).
$70-145

A sheet-iron Angel Gabriel weathervane, Hammond, New York, early 19thC, 55in (140cm) long.
$8,000-12,000

Miller's is a price
GUIDE not a price
LIST

An iron door knocker, c1800.
$70-145

A pair of cast iron classical columns, each with square top on fluted stem, with paw feet, 19thC, 51in (129.5cm).
$3,600-5,500

A set of 4 French cast iron models of owls, late 19thC, 16.5in (42cm).
$1,200-1,700

A pair of cast iron Nubian torchères, each classically draped woman holding a lamp aloft, with later light fittings, stamped Miroy Frères, Paris, on ebonised wood bases, 70.5in (178cm).
$10,000-12,000

An iron eagle door knocker, c1830. **$110-180**

Ormolu

A pair of Empire style ormolu candlesticks, each with bead-and-reel drip pan, on a reeded columnar shaft above tripartite monopodia and canted incurved triangular plinth banded with leaf tips, 13in (33cm). **$2,700-3,600**

An ormolu inkstand, in the form of a cherub playing drums, 19thC, 8in (20cm). **$1,000-1,500**

A Charles X ormolu encrier, the globular well with bands of engine turned decoration, on tripod ram's head monopodiae and concave base, 6.5in (16cm). high. **$1,000-1,500**

An Empire ormolu brûle parfum, the dish with pierced cover, on tripod ram's head monopodiae support, on concave griotte marble plinth, 8.5in (21cm) high. **$360-540**

A French ormolu encrier, in the form of a cockerel's head, with inset glass eyes, 19thC, 4.5in (11cm) high. **$360-540**

Ivory

A French ivory and gilt copper casket, with roof shaped lid, the ivory veneer bound by gilt copper straps engraved with zig-zag decoration, baluster knopped swing handle, lockplate engraved with arabesques, the lid with sliding drawer at the side, 4 sections of copper banding at one end lacking, ivory cracked, 16thC, 8in (20cm) wide. **$7,000-9,000**

A Siculo-Arabic ivory and silver mounted pyx, with central silver ringed knop, the central section with 4 double splayed mounts and hinged lockplate, the body with conforming silver mounts, some replacements to mounts, some warping to ivory, 12th/13thC, 3in (7.5cm) diam. **$7,000-9,000**

A South German ivory high relief allegorical figure group of Charity, the classically draped female figure with elaborately coiffed hair, some minor losses, late 17thC, 4in (10cm) high. **$7,000-9,000**

Turned ivory boxes and pyxes of this type were mostly produced in Sicily by Islamic artisans, during the Norman rule. The ivory was sometimes painted with decoration, and at other times as this case, was enriched with stylish metalwork. A very similar pyx is now in the Museo d'Arti Applicate del Castello Sforzesco, Milan.

An ivory baton, German or French, carved with portrait medallions and the crowned arms of France below spiral lobing, fleur-de-lys terminal, one break restored, 24in (61cm).
$1,000-1,500

The portraits shown are named as those of François II, Henry (sic) II, Charles IX and Henry III, dated 1574.

A Dieppe ivory dressing glass, applied with a bust portrait of Louis XIV, inscribed 'Ludovicus XIV Rex', with 2 small drawers to the frieze with lion mask and ring handles, and raised on lion's paw feet, 19thC, 35in (89cm) high.
$3,600-5,500

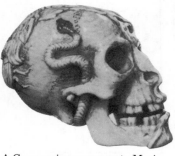

A German ivory memento Mori skull, one side of the skull covered with decomposing flesh being eaten by worms, the other revealing the skull, pierced as a rosary bead, early 17thC, 2in (5cm).
$2,700-3,600

A North Italian ivory portrait medallion of Don Juan of Austria, his head crowned with a laurel wreath, in elaborate armour and with the Order of the Golden Fleece, inscribed 'Giovanni D'Austria', in gilt bronze frame with suspension loop, late 18th/early 19thC, 4in (10cm) high.
$1,800-2,700

An Italian ivory relief of Cupid, as 'Love the Conqueror', with label on the reverse inscribed Omnia Vincit Amor, background partially broken, in Venetian parcel gilt wood frame, 17thC, 3in (7.5cm) high.
$1,800-2,700

A carved ivory open twist tapering column, with fluted spear surmount, on a stepped cylindrical hardwood socle, 11in (28cm) high.
$1,200-1,700

A Goan carved ivory group of The Virgin and Child, the babe with fingers raised in benediction, the orb base with cherub heads, traces of polychrome, 18thC, 9in (23cm) high.
$1,200-1,700

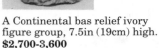

A Continental bas relief ivory figure group, 7.5in (19cm) high.
$2,700-3,600

A Spanish ivory crucifix figure, damage to fingers and crown of thorns, early 18thC, 9in (23cm), in modern velvet lined glazed case, together with ivory inscription plaque.
$1,200-1,700

A South German silver gilt mounted ivory tankard, the drum finely carved in high relief with the Triumph of Bacchus, his chariot drawn by 2 galloping stallions, late 17th/early 18thC, 7in (17.5cm) high.
$14,500-16,500

Marble

A pair of alabaster portrait busts of Brutus and Marcus Agrippa, in draped armour, on integral socles, 19thC. **$2,700-3,600**

A French marble bust of a satyr, shown with leering expression and short curled hair, horns repaired, 13in (33cm), on grey marble socle. **$3,600-5,500**

An Italian marble bust of Emperor Augustus, after the antique, with breastplate carved with confronting horsemen, 23.5in (60cm). **$10,000-12,000**

A Victorian white marble portrait bust of a woman, mid-19thC, 28in (71cm) high. **$1,200-1,700**

A Victorian marble bust of a girl, her hair tied up, raised on a low pedestal, unsigned, 23in (59cm) high. **$1,000-1,500**

A Victorian white marble portrait bust of a woman, mid-19thC, 28.5in (72cm). **$1,800-2,700**

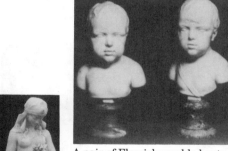

A pair of Flemish marble busts of children, 18thC, 12in (31cm) high, on socles. **$1,800-2,700**

An Italian white marble figure of a girl, standing semi-naked wearing a dress and patterned robe, holding a bunch of flowers, on circular base, 34.5in (87cm) high. **$3,600-5,500**

A pair of marble busts of Mars and Minerva, perhaps South German, 18thC, 24in (61cm) high, on socles. **$7,000-9,000**

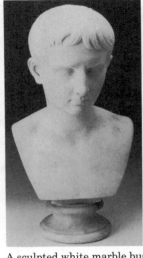

An Italian white marble bust of a maiden, signed G. Verona, late 19thC, 20in (50cm) high.
$2,700-3,600

A white marble bust of La Frileuse, after Houdon, c1880, 27.5in (70cm).
$1,800-2,700

A sculpted white marble bust of the young Caesar Augustus, on an integral socle, 19thC, 21in (53cm) high.
$1,800-2,700

A marble group of 2 putti, allegorical of Winter, in the style of Giuseppe Sanmartino, Naples, the pedestal inlaid with mottled greenish grey marble panels, 4 fingers missing, late 18thC, 26in (66cm) high.
$10,000-12,000

A white marble figure of a child, holding her dress over her head, the base signed P. Dal Negro F. Milano 1878, 37in (94cm) high.
$7,000-9,000

An Italian white marble group of a mother and child, late 19thC, 33in (83cm) high, on composition stone vermiculated pedestal, 24in (60cm) high.
$3,600-5,500

An Italian white marble group, of a young man seated on a tree trunk kissing a girl, on oval base, 19thC, 42.5in (106.5cm) high.
$2,700-3,600

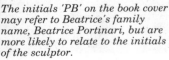

An Italian white marble and alabaster figure of Beatrice, in early Renaissance costume, her alabaster robe richly decorated with foliate arabesques, the book inscribed with the initials 'PB', on striated green marble base, with cartouche inscribed 'Beatrice', late 19thC, 41in (104cm). high.
$7,000-9,000

The initials 'PB' on the book cover may refer to Beatrice's family name, Beatrice Portinari, but are more likely to relate to the initials of the sculptor.

An English white marble figure of a nude woman, signed and dated E. Roscoe Mullins 1891, on grey onyx socle, late 19thC, 33in (84cm) high.
$3,600-5,500

An English white marble figure of Young Romilly, by Alexander Munro, the young boy shown embracing his hound, wearing medieval tunic and breeches, damages and repairs to front paws and tail of dog, with interlaced AM monogram, c1863, 37in (94cm) high.
$10,000-12,000

Alexander Munro (1825-1871) was born in Scotland, but through the patronage of Harriet, 2nd Duchess of Sutherland, studied in London and worked for Sir Charles Barry on the sculpture for the Houses of Parliament.

An Italian veined red marble column pedestal, late 19th/early 20thC, 40in (102cm) high.
$1,200-1,700

A mottled purple marble jar, of tapering cylindrical form, 10in (25cm).
$720-1,000

A pair of Italian marble reliefs of angels, one swinging a censer, the other with an incense boat, within plain borders, late 17th/early 18thC, 31 by 26in (79 by 65.5cm).
$10,000-12,000

An Italian inlaid marble table top, depicting the Doves of Pliny within concentric coloured marble frames, on slate base, 19thC, 25in (64cm) diam.
$1,800-2,700

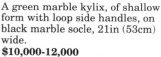

A green marble kylix, of shallow form with loop side handles, on black marble socle, 21in (53cm) wide.
$10,000-12,000

Terracotta

A pair of French cast terracotta busts of courtesans, in 18thC style, with décolleté dresses and ribbons around their necks and at their shoulders, on wood socles, 24in (61cm) high.
$7,000-9,000

A pair of serpentine marble tazzas, each on waisted socle and square base, one with broken and restored top, the other with chipped rim, late 19thC, 9.5in (24cm).   **$720-1,000**

A pair of terracotta busts of a boy and girl, by Karin Jonzen, mounted on wooden plinths,15in (38cm) high.
$720-1,000

An Anglo-Flemish terracotta statuette of an allegorical female figure, in the style of Scheemakers, holding poppies or pomegranates in her left hand, 18thC, 21in (54cm) high.
$10,000-12,000

A terracotta group of a bacchante riding a satyr, after Clodion, the nymph grasping a horn in her right hand and carrying a thyrsus over her shoulder, bearing signature of Clodion, on gilt stand, repaired, 14in (36cm).
$2,700-3,600

A French terracotta bust of a young girl, after Jacques Saly, said to be La Boudeuse, cast with a socle, 16.5in (42cm).
$3,600-5,500

A marble version of around 1750 is in the Victoria & Albert Museum. The subject is thought to be the daughter of de Troy, Director of the French Academy in Rome.

A Spanish polychrome wood male reliquary bust, perhaps St. Lawrence, with fringed collar of silver gilt thread to his gilded cope, a tassel decorating the reliquary niche with gilt metal frame, much original colour and gilding, 16thC, 23in (59cm).
$3,600-5,500

A terracotta high relief of the Baptism of Christ, attributed to Angelo Pio, Emilia, the dove of the Holy Spirit appearing above surrounded by angels, to the right dancing angels, to the left of partly draped men, in wood frame, 18thC, 19 by 26in (48 by 66cm).
$14,500-16,500

A polychrome and giltwood figure of the Virgin and Child, in the manner of Hans van Judenburg, late 15thC, 12in (31cm).
$14,500-16,500

Woodcarvings

A German limewood Corpus, with traces of red polychromy on the perizonium, arms and part legs missing, worming, 15thC, 22in (56cm) high.
$2,700-3,600

A polychrome limewood group of the Virgin and Child, probably Austrian, the Schöne Madonna with hips swung to the left in an almost S shape curve holding the Child in her left arm, some original colour beneath later overpainting, damage and restoration, c1430, 36in (92cm) high.
$14,500-16,500

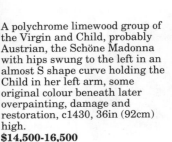

A Spanish polychrome and giltwood statue of the Virgin and Child, the Virgin standing holding the Christ Child within her left arm, some damage, 17thC, 17.5in (44cm) high.
$2,700-3,600

A set of 3 Italian giltwood statues of children, depicting Summer, Autumn and Winter, mid-19thC, 18in (46cm) high.
$2,700-3,600

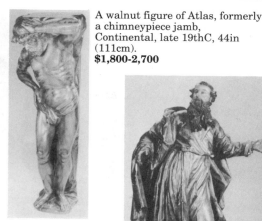

A walnut figure of Atlas, formerly a chimneypiece jamb, Continental, late 19thC, 44in (111cm).
$1,800-2,700

A South German polychrome and giltwood figure of a male saint, his arms gesturing outwards, wearing a robe, cloak and boots, on a square wood base, some chips and restorations, late 17thC, 41in (104cm) high.
$10,000-12,000

Two polychrome and giltwood angel candlesticks, with candlesticks resting on their knees, gilding worn, Tyrol, 16thC, 17 and 18.5in (43 and 47cm).
$21,000-27,000

A pair of giltwood brackets, carved as eagles, 19thC, 15in (38cm) high.
$2,700-3,600

A Flemish walnut relief of Mary Magdalene renouncing her wordly goods, damaged, late 17thC, 23.5 by 15in (60 by 38cm).
$1,200-1,700

A Netherlands oak group of the seated Virgin and Child, the Madonna holding the sandalled Child with an orb standing on her knees, restored, late 15thC, 30.5in (77cm).
$10,000-12,000

An Italian polychrome wood figure of a candle bearing angel, wearing gilt drapery with crosses painted on sash, bearing a candle holder, with base decorated with border of foliate design, on material covered base, early 16thC, 19in (49cm) high.
$7,000-9,000

A carved wood and polychrome corbel figure of a tonsured monk, a shield emblazoned on his breast, 15in (38cm) high, mounted in a frame.
$720-1,000

A Spanish wood relief of the Mocking of Christ, the slumped figure of Christ before Caiaphas and a soldier standing on a raised dais, surrounded on each side by a crowd of jeering Jews and soldiers, St. John in the background and other figures watching from the windows behind, traces of original colour, on a wood stand, early 16thC, 18in (46cm).
$7,000-9,000

An English carved and painted wood Royal coat-of-arms, mid-19thC, 70 by 73in (178 by 185cm).
$3,600-5,500

A carved wood and polychrome panel of the Royal Arms, as used by King George V, 32 by 33.5in (81 by 85cm).   **$900-1,500**

A pair of carved giltwood brackets, in the form of owls with outstretched wings, 19thC, 13in (33cm) high.   **$3,600-5,500**

A pair of South German giltwood statuettes of angels, kneeling in prayer on voluted pediments, wormed, 18thC, 10in (25cm) high.
$3,600-5,500

A Georgian carved wooden money box, as a Toby Jug figure of a seated auctioneer holding a gavel, some damage, 14in (36cm).
$3,600-5,500

ANTIQUITIES

Marble

A Roman marble relief fragment, probably from a sarcophagus, carved in high relief with a fruiting garland and a bucranium, foliate and tongue motifs above and below, 23 by 29in (59 by 74cm).
$14,500-16,500

A Roman marble head of a young woman, circa 120-20 B.C. after an original of the 4th Century B.C., 9in (23cm).
$14,500-16,500

A fragmentary Roman marble male torso, probably from a figure of Herakles, the lionskin knotted around his neck, circa 1st-2nd Century A.D.
$21,000-27,000

A Roman marble sandalled foot, circa 2nd Century A.D., 10in (25cm).
$5,000-7,000

A Roman marble head of the young Dionysus, wearing a garland of vine leaves, berries and bunches of grapes, with centrally parted hair, a fillet around his head, circa 2nd Century A.D., 12in (31cm).
$10,000-12,000

A Roman marble male portrait head, originally from a portrait bust, 2nd-3rd Century A.D., 13.5in (34cm).
$14,500-16,500

A Roman marble figure of Hermes, with drapery over his left arm, restored, circa 1st-2nd Century A.D., 52.5in (133cm).
$40,000-45,000

A Roman marble male head, the irises and pupils of the eyes incised, circa 1st Century B.C./1st Century A.D., 15.5in (39cm).
$27,000-36,000

A Luristan bronze axehead, the shaft decorated on both sides with the figure of an animal in relief, depicted holding the blade in its open mouth, 8th-7th Century B.C., 2 by 6in (5 by 15cm).
$3,600-5,500

A Roman bronze appliqué in the form of the hollow bust of Dionysus as a child, the pupils of the eyes recessed, circa 1st Century B.C/1st Century A.D., 3.5in (9cm).
$7,000-9,000

Metalware

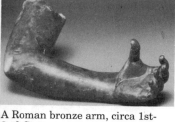

A Roman bronze arm, circa 1st-2nd Century A.D., 11in (28cm).
$3,600-5,500

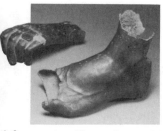

A fragmentary Roman bronze left hand and foot, the hand wearing a ring with a large oval bezel, both circa 1st-2nd Century A.D., 8in (20cm).
$3,600-5,500

An Etruscan bronze stamnos, from the Weiskirchen Group, probably made in Vulci, with tongue and bead motifs around the overhanging rim, the handles attached to 4 oval handle attachments decorated with satyr masks, each surmounted by a pair of eyes and set in a frame of stacked ivy leaves, circa 430-400 B.C., 14in (36cm).
$7,000-9,000

A Roman or early Byzantine bronze steelyard weight, probably representing Athena, the whole filled with lead, 4th-5th Century A.D., 8in (20cm).
$2,700-3,600

An Early Christian bronze right hand, holding an orb surmounted by a cross, a cross in relief on its wrist, circa 6th-7th Century A.D., 14in (36cm).
$10,000-12,000

These hands holding an orb and cross clearly derive from the hollow cast hands associated with the Phrygian God Sabazios. It is difficult to be certain about their functions. They may have been mounted on staffs as votive offerings perhaps to be paraded before the faithful when the healing powers of hands were needed.

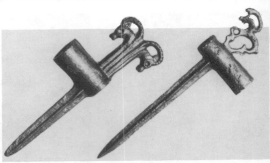

Two Scythian bronze axeheads, with animal heads projecting from one side of the shafts, 7th-6th Century B.C., 5 and 5.5in (12 and 14cm) long. **$7,000-9,000**

An Egyptian bronze figure of a cat, seated, with its tail curling round towards the right, restored, 26th Dynasty, circa 664-525 B.C., 7in (18cm).
$18,000-21,000

An Egyptian bronze figure of Harpocrates, wearing the Lock of Eternal Youth and the Crown of Upper and Lower Egypt, 30th Dynasty-Ptolemaic Period, circa 380-30 B.C., 13in (33cm).
$10,000-12,000

An Egyptian bronze figure of a cat, seated, with its tail curling round its body towards its forepaws, Saite Period, circa 664-525 B.C., 7in (18cm).
$27,000-36,000

> **Miller's is a price GUIDE not a price LIST**

A bronze vessel, in the form of a male bust, probably representing the God Dionysus, on stemmed foot, Roman Provinces, circa 3rd Century A.D., 9in (23cm).
$10,000-12,000

The flask-like mouth opening is unusual. The use of these vessels is not absolutely clear. They may have been used as an unguent vase, (balsamarium), or as a censer.

Four Scythian bronze stags, Black Sea area, 7th-6th Century B.C., 1.5 by 3.5in (4 by 9cm) each.
$10,000-12,000

Pottery

A Mycenaean pottery hydria, decorated with an octopus with long tentacles, Greece, circa 1200 B.C., 5.5in (14cm).
$10,000-12,000

A South Italian Greek pottery trefoil oinochoe, the decoration in white and yellow slip, Apulia, 4th Century B.C., 19in (48cm).
$3,600-5,500

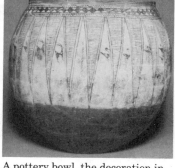

A pottery bowl, the decoration in light and dark brown slip on a cream ground, 2nd Millennium B.C., 18.6in (47cm).
$18,000-21,000

A Canosan pottery pyxis and cover, polychrome painted, chiefly in pink, blue, red and white, the cover with a pair of embracing lovers, a figure of Eros to the right, all in relief, South Italy, circa 3rd Century B.C., 5 by 11.5in (13 by 29cm).
$7,000-9,000

An Etruscan pottery panel amphora, from the La Tolfa Group, on one side a monstrous spirit, with wings on his back and feet, on the other 2 companions or followers of the spirit, the decoration with touches of applied white paint, with lid not belonging, circa 530 B.C., 13.5in (34cm).
$7,000-9,000

Miscellaneous

An Egyptian wood mask, from a sarcophagus, with traces of polychrome painting to the left and upper side of the face, Late New Kingdom, 19th Dynasty, 5.5in (14cm).   **$7,000-9,000**

A Roman iridescent green glass trefoil jug, standing on a splayed pedestal foot, with rounded body, cylindrical neck and trefoil lip, a single trail encircling the neck and another running around the base of the neck, a vertically ribbed handle attached to the shoulder and folded on to the rim, circa 4th Century A.D., 9.5in (24cm).   **$3,600-5,500**

A Roman green glass twin-handled flask, the neck with fine horizontal spiral trailing, the indented base with pontil mark, circa 4th Century A.D., 6in (15cm).   **$2,700-3,600**

The smooth chin bears no trace of a beard attachment which suggests that the mask is a female depiction. The large, widely spaced eyes with the gentle curvature of the eyebrows and exotic lips are stylistically typical of funerary art of the Ramesside era, a period when form, decoration and colour took on a more naturalistic appearance. Often the inner cover of the sarcophagus represented the owner as seen in real life and here the beautifully carved features show a young high-born woman.

Four Minoan and Mycenaean terracotta vessels, of varying types, all circa 1400 B.C., 3 to 6in (8 to 15cm).
$3,600-5,500

SEWING

A tortoiseshell étui, inlaid with mother-of-pearl, c1820, 4in (10cm) high.
$1,000-1,500

A Roman green glass wheel engraved bottle, with pear shaped body standing on a stemmed foot, funnel shaped neck and ground rim, the body with the remains of a Greek inscription, wheel cut decoration above and below, with some light weathering, repaired, 4th-5th Century A.D., 8in (20cm).
$1,800-2,700

The lid from an Egyptian anthropoid wood coffin, with yellow face and the body with polychrome painted decoration, the text, flanked by the four Sons of Horus, has a standard funerary text for a man called Irt-Hor-Rw, son of Djehutyirdis, born to Saas, Late Dynastic Period, circa 716-332 B.C., 65in (165cm).
$10,000-12,000

A horn sewing box, c1820, 14in (36cm) wide.
$720-1,000

A Bilston pink enamel étui, c1780, 3.5in (8.5cm) high.
$1,200-1,700

A gold mounted Continental porcelain needle case, painted with gilt flowers in white reserves and on a blue ground, 19thC, 4in (10.5cm) high.
$1,200-1,700

A Newton Wilson Princess of Wales lockstitch hand sewing machine, with gilt decoration and wood carrying case.
$360-540

A French opaline and ormolu sewing nest, 6.5in (16.5cm).
$1,000-1,500

A home shuttle lockstitch sewing machine. **$180-360**

A Florence Sewing Machine Co. treadle sewing machine, with black painted frame and gilt and floral decoration, in mahogany cabinet with hinged lid and double door at the front opening to treadle, American, c1870, 30in (66cm) wide. **$2,700-3,600**

A Regency boxwood model of the Royal Pavilion, with detachable sections enclosing a pin cushion and needlework implements including a thimble, 8.5in (21.5cm) high. **$2,700-3,600**

A Cookson's lockstitch sewing machine with part-plated mechanism on cast iron base and wood cover, damaged. **$1,800-2,700**

A Regency rosewood bobbin winder, with 2 drawers mounted overall with bone bobbin winders, wool winders, pin cushions and thimble stand, on bone feet, 17in (43cm) wide. **$1,800-2,700**

A Weir chain-stitch sewing machine with gilt transfers, table clamp and original instructions. **$180-360**

A Beckwith portable sewing machine, with geared crank drive, nickel-plated frame and stitchplate, stamped Beckwith S.M. Co. N.Y. Apr. 1871, by Wm. G. Beckwith and G.W. Bacon & Co. London, Eng., with table clamp. **$1,200-1,700**

A French gilt metal mounted étui case, with green ground reserved with riverscapes and foliate motifs within gilt cartouches, 4in (10cm) high, **$360-540**

A Mme. Demorest 'Fairy' sewing or running-stitch machine, the ornamentally cast iron base marked twice Patented May 13 1862, with hand-cranked gear cloth-feed and stop screw for stitch length, 5.5in (14cm) wide. **$900-1,500**

TEXTILES
Costume

A baby's bonnet with hollie point panel worked with a monogramme SB(?) and (17)83, another bonnet with asymmetric hollie point flowerspray and 2 under bonnets, all 18thC.
$360-540

A dress of blue and white striped satin, the cuffs and front trimmed with ivory satin and blue satin ribbons, with pleated train, c1870.
$720-1,000

A christening set of linen, trimmed with pleated applied linen, comprising: bonnet, bib, a pair of mittens, sleeves, 2 head bands and 2 triangular forehead panels, late 17thC, a linen square with appliqué trim.
$900-1,500

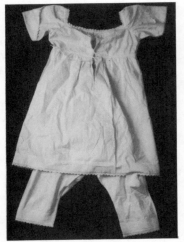

A child's linen suit, comprising: chemise and pantaloons, early 19thC.
$720-1,000

A French Au-Louvre scarlet full length dolman cape, embroidered in Turkish moresque patterns with coral, scarlet and gold thread, some discolouration to lining, one small hole, with black and scarlet woven label bearing a lion, the letter L and numbered 58030, c1895.
$1,800-2,700

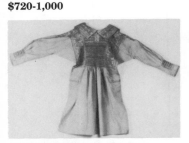

A Victorian linen smock, the bodice, sleeves, collar, cuffs and pockets embroidered with blue cotton.
$360-540

A cocktail dress of black chiffon, the front pink panel embroidered with pink, black and opalescent beads with flowers and geometric patterns, c1923.
$180-360

A Redfern brocaded evening jacket, labelled Redfern Scte. Francais, numbered 174339, the black, ivory and gold fabric covered with ferns and snakeshead lilies, brown fur shawl collar and cuffs lined in gold velvet, label slightly frayed small stain to lining, c1928.
$1,200-1,700

A Castillo for Elizabeth Arden black satin evening mantle, labelled Elizabeth Arden, New York, lined with rose pink satin, the shoulders applied with a fichu of black satin petals, American late 1950's.
$900-1,500

Two Salon Moderne silk chiffon evening gowns, one red, the other blue, boned strapless bodices, the skirts polonaises caught by 2 velvet bows to the rear, American, 1961.
$360-540

A red ground silk kossu robe, the bright red ground worked with eight dragons pursuing 'flaming pearls' amidst clouds scattered with bats and Precious Objects, above the wide lishui band, the arms and neck bordered with a dragon band, all in brightly coloured silk, 19thC, 57in (145cm).
$1,800-2,700

Sophie Gimbel was married to Adam Gimbel, owner of Sak's Fifth Avenue. She opened her own couture department in 1931 which she named Salon Moderne. In addition to her own designs she sold dresses by the major French fashion houses on a made-to-order system.

A Michel Goma embroidered oyster pink satin ballgown, unlabelled, together with a pair of Delicata shoes, and stiffened petticoat gown shortened slightly, French, c1959.
$720-1,000

Michel Goma was born in Montpellier France in 1932 and moved to Paris at the age of 19 where he tried to sell his fashion designs. He received encouragement from Christian Dior but was employed first of all by Lafaurie (1950-1958) when he bought the company and renamed it Michel Goma. He closed in 1963 and moved to Patou where he stayed until 1973.

A gown of ivory satin, printed with undulating bands of pink columbines against sea green and lilac heart shaped leaves, the sleeves and hem trimmed with lilac ruched ribbon in the Regency manner, labelled Paul Poiret à Paris, the reverse with canvas tag inscribed Mad. Saxton-Noble, 20133, the boned deep waistband inscribed Vanessa Jebb, waist sash missing, damage to underarm.
$7,000-9,000

A pair of George III shoes of blue silk and brocade, with fitted clogs.
$900-1,500

A Salon Moderne Chantilly lace evening gown, the oyster satin strapless sheath entirely covered with tiers of navy Chantilly lace, American, 1964; together with a Salon Moderne scarlet satin ball gown, with stylised scooped neckline, elbow length sleeves, full skirt falling in gathers from the hips, separate petticoat, American, 1963.
$180-360

A hand painted Ceremonial Parade Fire Hat, by Niagara Hose Company, initialled J. H., probably New York, with painted figure of an Indian Chief, mid-19thC, 7in (18cm) high.
$14,000-16,000

A hand painted Ceremonial Parade Fire Hat, by The United States Fire Company, probably Pennsylvania, with the allegorical figure of Liberty seated in a landscape, the top with initials W.R., repaired, mid-19thC, 7in (18cm) high.
$5,000-6,000

A blue sequined sheath, with blue silk underpinning overlaid with tulle, entirely covered with iridescent blue sequins, spangled tulle fichu to shoulders, probably French, c1930.
$720-1,000

A dress of fine wool, printed with stripes of slate grey alternating with striped cones, the V-shaped bodice trimmed with pleating and piping, c1840.
$720-1,000

A pair of bathing boots, the white rubber soles moulded 'Hood Seaview Bathing Made in U.S.A., size 4,' bright green satin with white trim, slight damage, c1910.
$1,200-1,700

A wide brimmed straw hat with shallow crown, lined with red silk, brocaded with flowers, with original green silk ribbons woven with garlands of flowers, c1770.
$3,600-5,500

A Bob Bugnand black satin evening coat, embroidered, beaded, jewelled Paisley botehs overall, slits to each side, Paris, 1960.
$360-540

A North American Indian seed beaded bandoleer bag, decorated with stylised geometric patterns on black and red fabric, the shoulder strap with black and patterned red fabric, probably late 19thC.
$720-1,000

Three Maison Lewis straw hats, labelled Maison Lewis, 16 Rue Royale Paris, comprising ivory straw applied with outsized daisy, ribbon streamers; a black silk and velvet with 'shaving brush' quill of feathers and white ribbon rose; another with silvered Art Deco pierced metal sunburst medallion and on ivory band, French, c1922.   **$720-1,000**

A linen coif, embroidered in black work and gilt threads, with tightly coiling stems bearing small flowerheads with various infilling patterns, English, c1600, 16in (41cm) wide.
$7,000-9,000

A cut steel and glass bead bag, English, c1850, 11.5in (29.5cm) long.   **$180-360**

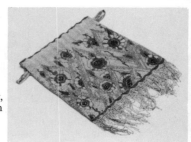

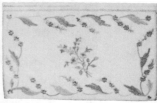

A French ivory silk wallet, embroidered in tambour stitch with coloured silks, the front, back and inside worked with sprays of roses and pansies within a leaf border, embellished with coloured spangles, lined with green silk, late 18thC.
$360-540

A cut steel miser's purse, 24in (61.5cm) long.
$180-360

An English bead bag, c1850, 8in (20cm) long.
$180-360

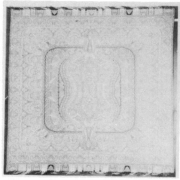

A Paisley shawl, woven with an unusual rectangular centre, the end borders woven with the initials JC, c1855, 74in (188cm) wide.
$2,700-3,600

An English glass bead and cut steel bag, c1860, 8in (20cm) long.
$110-180

A wool Paisley throw, woven in shades of blue, green and maroon centred by a cream and crimson foliate panel.
$180-360

A Paisley shawl, woven in 9 colours, with 2 central palmette tipped columns flanking a black cruciform medallion, the harlequin shawl ends woven and over-embroidered with the crest of Napoleon III above the words BIETRY in one corner and CACHEMIRE in the other, c1855, 64in (162.5cm) wide.
$1,000-1,500

At the 1855 Universal Exhibition in Paris, Anthony Berrus displayed a pivoting shawl woven by Bietry with the arms of Napoleon III woven in to the corner. The Empress Eugenie attended the Exhibition and is said to have ordered a shawl by Berrus to be woven by Bietry.

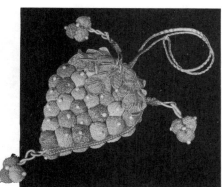

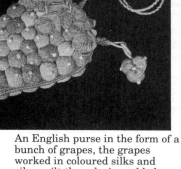

An Austrian parasol shaft, with enamelled vinaigrette finial in the shape of a sedan chair, with mirror windows, the door opening to reveal a chased and pierced vinaigrette, c1914.
$2,700-3,600

An English purse in the form of a bunch of grapes, the grapes worked in coloured silks and silver gilt threads, in padded detached buttonhole stitch embellished with seed pearls, with 3 similar pendants, the vine leaves in green silks and gilt threads, the concertina purse lined with salmon pink silk, with a pink silk and silver gilt thread plaited drawstring and handle, early 17thC, 3in (7.5cm) long.
$3,600-5,500

A silk shawl, woven with a blue field, the ends woven with snaking intertwined cones in pairs between green and blue columns, in the manner of Clabburn Son & Crisp, mid-19thC, 70in (177.5cm) wide.
$900-1,500

A parasol, the stained wood shaft tipped with an elephant's head finial of carved horn, the shade of ivory silk with black Maltese lace overlay, one tusk missing, c1916.
$180-360

A parasol, the folding ivory shaft inset with coral knots, the finial and handle of coral carved with a putto against a leafy base, the spoke guards also coral in the form of hands with a coral drop, the shade of French black lace, late 19thC.
$720-1,000

A lawyer's wig, labelled 'J. K. Methirell, Maker, 14 Bell Yard, Temple Bar, London', also with inscription 'W. J. Johnson Esq', in original tin, the name painted on the outside, and the original padlock.
$1,000-1,500

Embroidery

An English needlework picture, embroidered in coloured silks and metal threads, embellished with beads, spangles and mica strips, with a lady and gentleman in the centre standing above a pond and flanked by 2 houses, the corners each with busts within raised work frames, c1660, 17in (43.5cm) wide, framed and glazed.
$3,600-5,500

A cotton 'Log Cabin' quilt, in a Barn Raising pattern, c1935, 89 by 86in (226 by 219cm).
$3,000-4,000

A pair of appliqued cotton quilts, probably Pennsylvania, c1930, each approx. 100 by 86in (257 by 219cm).
$3,000-4,000

A French letter case, of brown silk, woven with gilt threads and coloured silks with episodes from the Fables de la Fontaine including the fox and the crow with the piece of cheese, lined with pale pink silk, late 17thC, 7in (17.5cm) wide.
$1,800-2,700

An appliqued and embroidered political wall hanging, probably New York, with central portraits of L. P. Morton, B. Harrison and George Washington, on a maroon and sapphire blue velvet ground with gold velvet borders, worn, 1889, 61 by 87in (155 by 221cm).
$6,500-8,500

An English embroidered picture, worked in coloured wools, mid-18thC, 17in (43.5cm) wide, framed and glazed.
$2,700-3,600

Lace

An English needlework picture, embroidered in coloured wools, highlighted with silks, with a spray of tulips, carnations, roses and other wild flowers, fastened by a ribbon, mid-18thC, 22in (55.5cm) high, in a carved walnut frame.
$2,700-3,600

A calico and cotton toile quilt, in a variation of the Nine Patch pattern, mid-19thC, 96 by 90in (244 by 229cm).
$600-800

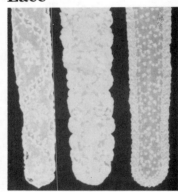

A collection of lace, including a pair of Alençon lappets, late 18thC, 4in (10cm) deep, a single Mechlin lappet, 4in (10cm) deep, and a single Brussels lappet, mid-18thC, 3in (7.5cm) deep.
$360-540

A flounce of point de gaze lace, worked with a border of flowers beneath an undulating ribbon with posies of flowers and raised petals above, c1860, 9in (22.5cm) deep, and a separate matching fragment.
$1,800-2,700

A pair of Mechlin bobbin lace cravat ends, worked with classical motifs of elegant leaves and urns, c1720.
$3,600-5,500

A deep flounce of Brussels mixed lace, worked with a border of needle lace roses among bobbin lace leaves, point de neige spotted net, late 19thC, 23in (58.5cm) deep.
$720-1,000

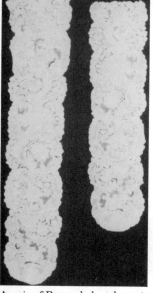

A flounce of Alençon lace, worked with a border of flowers and ivy leaves beneath oval medallions with needle lace fillings, alternating with flowersprays, in two pieces, 7in (17.5cm) deep.
$720-1,000

A flounce of Italian needle lace, worked with scrolling vines with pomegranates and flowers, 17thC, edged with 16thC vandyking, 5in (12.5cm) deep.
$360-540

A pair of Brussels lace lappets, worked with baskets of flowers, c1740, 4in (10cm) deep.
$720-1,000

A flounce of point de gaze lace, worked with a scalloped edge of roses with raised petals with patterns worked in, the flounce worked with convolvulus, lilacs and iris, many with raised petals, late 19thC, 14in (35.5cm) deep.
$3,600-5,500

Samplers

An early Victorian silk needlework sampler, 1848, 25in (64cm) wide.
$360-540

A needlework sampler, in colourful silks, by Elizabeth Taylor, 'in the eleventh year of her age', dated 1748, 13in (33cm) wide, unframed.
$900-1,500

A sampler by Hannah Mills, 'aged 12, April the 30, 1818', worked in silks with a verse 'Teach me to feel Another's Woe to hide the fault I see that Mercy I to others shew that Mercy shew to me', damaged, 13in (33.5cm) wide.
$720-1,000

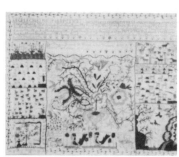

A sampler by Jane Thompson, probably American, worked in coloured silks on linen gauze, 1824, 25in (64cm) wide.
$3,600-5,500

A child's needlework sampler, inscribed 'Elizabeth Barclay her work finished 25th day of the seventh month 1725', slight damage, 12in (31cm) high, in maple frame.
$1,200-1,700

A sampler by Jane Mesman, worked in coloured silks with a verse 'See how the lillies', 1735, 16in (40.5cm) long, framed and glazed.
$1,800-2,700

A silk worked sampler, repaired, dated 1788, 12in (31cm) wide, framed and glazed.
$1,000-1,500

A sampler by Amelia Pewiner, worked in brightly coloured silks with a verse 'Misfortunes Advantageous', 18thC, 12in (31cm) wide, framed and glazed.
$720-1,000

A band sampler by Elizabeth Hoskins, aged 12 in 1799, 12in (31cm) wide.
$360-540

A silkwork sampler by Sarah Johnson, aged 10 in 1843, with 2 figures, a house, baskets of flowers and trees, within a meandering border of carnations, slight damage, 12in (31cm) wide.
$360-540

Tapestries

A George IV needlework sampler, 1820, 48in (122cm) wide.
$720-1,000

A Brussels tapestry fragment woven in wools and silks, on a brown ground, previously the border of a tapestry, reduced in size, mid-17thC, 123.5in (314cm) wide.
$7,000-9,000

COLOUR REVIEW

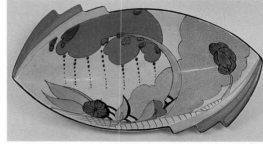

A Clarice Cliff
Solitude pattern
sugar sifter, 5.5in
(14cm) high.
$900-1,000

A pair of Clarice Cliff
Autumn design vases,
8.5in (21cm) high.
$2,700-3,200

A Clarice Cliff Tankard shaped coffee set, in Gay Day
pattern.
$1,200-1,400

A Clarice Cliff bowl, Devon pattern, Daffodil shape
475, 13in (33cm) long.
$1,200-1,400

A Clarice Cliff My Garden pattern bowl, 12in
(31cm) diam.
$450-650

A Clarice Cliff Orange House pattern,
5in (13cm) high.
$750-850

A Clarice Cliff Isis vase, in
Woodland design, 9.5in (24cm)
high.
$800-1,000

A Clarice Cliff baluster vase
Sliced Fruit pattern, 15in
(38cm) high.
$1,800-2,000

A Clarice Cliff bowl footed,
c1930, 9in (23cm) diam.
$3,600-4,000

A Clarice Cliff stepped
vase, in Latona Red
Rose pattern, 6in
(15cm) high.
$800-1,000

A Clarice Cliff large Athens shape teapot,
Diamonds pattern
$800-1,000

418

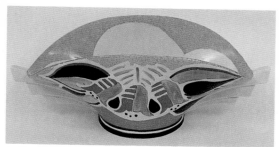

A Clarice Cliff Nuage bowl, shape No.33, 13in (33cm) wide.
$800-1,000

A Clarice Cliff Bizarre vase, c1930.
$1,000-1,200

A Clarice Cliff Bizarre model of a pig, after a model by Louis Wain, 4.5in (11cm) high.
$900-1,000

A Clarice Cliff Inspiration Bizarre Conical vase, restored, 7in (18cm).
$1,000-1,200

A Clarice Cliff floral Nuage Stamford shape biscuit barrel with lid.
$475-550

A pair of Clarice Cliff Geometric vases, 7in (17.5cm).
$2,000-2,500

A Clarice Cliff Inspiration vase, 10in (25.5cm).
$2,000-2,500

A Clarice Cliff Orange Roof Cottage, 7in (17.5cm).
$720-800

A Clarice Cliff umbrella stand.
$6,000-6,800

A Clarice Cliff mask, 7in (17.5cm).
$800-900

A Clarice Cliff Sunburst design coffee set, coffee pot 7in (17.5cm) high.
$1,700-2000

A Clarice Cliff basket vase, Bridgewater design, 13in (33cm) wide.
$1,000-1,200

A Moorcroft Leaf and Berry design flambé squat vase, c1932, 6in (15cm) high.
$1,000-1,200

A Moorcroft baraware design vase, made for Liberty, restored, c1908, 3.5in (9cm) high.
$450-650

A Moorcroft Anemone design lustre vase, made for Liberty c1909, 8in (20cm) high.
$1,500-2,000

A Walter Moorcroft yellow Hibiscus design vase, c1960, 6in (15cm) high.
$230-300

A MacIntyre Moorcroft salmon and green Carnation design vase, c1898, 12in (31cm) high.
$1,700-2,500

A Moorcroft flambé Waratah design vase, 1939, 17in (43cm) high.
$12,000-15,500

A Moorcroft saltglaze Fish design vase, dated 1931, 14in (36cm) high.
$4,000-5,000

A Moorcroft matt glaze ochre Leaf and Berry design vase, c1936, 4in (10cm) high.
$650-800

A Minton stick stand, 23in (58cm) high.
$700-900

A MacIntyre Moorcroft Florian ware Blue Tree design vase, c1902.
$2,500-4,500

A MacIntyre Moorcroft Pansy design vase, restored, c1912, 10.5in (26cm) high.
$720-1,000

A Charlotte Rhead Rhodian
pattern bowl, 10in (25.5cm).
$160-180

An Art Deco group, by Lobel Riche, c1925, 14in
(35.5cm) high.
$1,000-1,200

A Charlotte Rhead posy bowl,
6in (15cm) diam.
$70-80

An Austrian porcelain figure of
a girl, by Lenst Waliliss, c1910,
17.5in (44cm) high.
$1,600-2,000

A pair of Katshütte figures of
skiers, 11.5in (29cm) high.
$1,700-2,500

A Goldscheider ceramic figure,
c1930, 14in (35.5cm) high.
$900-1,200

A Royal Dux porcelain female
figure, Bohemian, c1910, 15.5in
(39cm) high.
$1,600-2,000

'The Hornpipe', a Royal
Doulton figure,
HN2161, 10in (25.5cm).
$550-650

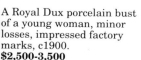

A Royal Dux porcelain bust
of a young woman, minor
losses, impressed factory
marks, c1900.
$2,500-3,500

An Austrian
porcelain figure,
c1900.
$1,600-2,000

A Rosenthal porcelain
figure of a snake charmer,
c1920. **$650-1,000**

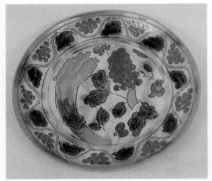

A Royal Doulton wall plaque, by Frank Brangwyn, in Harvest pattern, decorated by hand, 13in (33cm).
$450-650

A Martin Brothers salt glazed porcelain Love Birds group, dated 1902. **$8,000-9,000**

A Royal Dux two-handled vase, 16in (41cm) high.
$650-800

A Gray's Pottery Art Deco eight-piece coffee set, in yellow and black geometric pattern.
$160-280

A Susie Cooper charger, signed and dated 1934.
$2,700-3,200

A pair of Mettlach vases, 1904, 14.5in (37cm) high.
$1,200-1,400

A pair of Bermantofts vases, by V. Kremer, 11in (28cm) high.
$3,000-3,600

A figure of Bat Girl, 8.5in (21cm) high.
$650-900

A Martin Brothers bird and cover, c1913.
$2,700-3,600

A Bursley Ware tray, TL43, in shades of blue on grey, 9in (23cm) long.
$130-150

A Charlotte Rhead vase, 7in (18cm) high.
$180-210

A Royal Doulton vase, by Frank Butler, c1906, 19in (48cm) high.
$1,800-2,000

A Chiparus silvered, cold painted bronze, ivory, marble and onyx figure, 'Antinea', c1925. **$100,000-105,000**

A Ferdinand Preiss cold painted bronze, tinted ivory, marble and onyx figure, 'Ecstasy', c1930, 22in (56cm). **$7,000-10,000**

A Pierre le Faguays cold painted bronze and marble figure, 'Dancer with Thyrsus', 1920s, 22in (56cm). **$5,500-7,000**

A Ferdinand Preiss cold painted bronze, ivory and onyx figure, 1930s. **$3,000-3,600**

A Chiparus bronze and ivory 'Pierrot', with silver/grey patina, 1920s. **$6,000-9,000**

A Morante bronze figure of a dancer, 16in (41cm) high. **$1,800-2,700**

A cold painted bronze, ivory and onyx 'Dancer', c1925, 10in (25cm). **$1,200-1,800**

A Fredy Stoll silvered bronze, and marble figure, 'Daphne', c1925. **$18,000-21,000**

A Pierre Le Faguay bronze figure, 'Bacchante'. **$12,000-16,000**

r. A Ferdinand Preiss bronze and ivory 'Autumn Dancer'. **$14,500-18,000**

A Joe Descamp bronze and ivory figure, 15in (38cm) high. **$7,000-9,000**

r. A Ferdinand Preiss cold painted bronze and ivory 'Grecian with Torch'. **$5,500-7,000**

Two René Lalique drinking services: *l.* 18 pieces, after 1934. **$1,700-2,000** *r.* 29 pieces, after 1924. **$4,250-5,000**

A René Lalique opalescent glass vase, 'Orleans', marked, 8in (20cm). **$3,000-3,500**

A René Lalique opalescent glass clock, 'Inseparables', after 1926, 4.5in (12cm). **$2,500-2,800**

A Lalique moulded, frosted and enamelled glass vase, model introduced 1926, inscribed R. Lalique, 7in (18cm). **$8,500-10,000**

A René Lalique opalescent glass plate, 'Assiette Calypso', stencilled mark, after 1930. **$4,250-6,000**

l. A Lalique glass vase, 'Tournesol' after 1927. **$2,500-3,000** *r.* A Lalique perfume bottle. **$1,000-1,500**

A René Lalique glass and nickel plated metal plaque, moulded mark, slightly polished, c1925, 16in (40cm). **$10,000-12,000**

A René Lalique table decoration, 'Faisans', comprising: 2 glass candelabra and a serving dish, dish with engraved mark, chips to dish, after 1942. **$4,250-5,000**

A Lalique moulded and frosted glass vase, 1914 model, moulded and inscribed. **$2,500-3,500**

A René Lalique glass vase, 'Aras', moulded mark R. Lalique, after 1924, 9in (23cm). **$8,500-10,000**

A Lalique moulded glass perfume bottle, 1926 model, 3in (7.5cm). **$9,500-11,000**

A René Lalique black enamelled clear glass vase, wheel cut R. Lalique and engraved France No.970, 8in (20cm) high. **$11,000-12,750**

A Daum etched and wheel carved glass vase, 12in (31cm) high.
$27,000-32,000

An Emile Gallé carved vase, c1902, 11in (28cm).
$72,000-80,000

A Daum purple tinted cameo glass vase, decorated with iris, on round base, signed Daum, Nancy, 16in (41cm) high.
$4,500-5,500

A stained glass window, 'Minstrel with Cymbals' designed by William Morris, 25.5 by 19in (65 by 48cm). **$18,000-21,000**

A Morris & Co. stained glass window, designed by Edward Burne-Jones, 41in (105cm) high.
$18,000-25,000

A Sabino opalescent glass lamp, 'Suzanne Au Bain', chipped, c1930, 10in (25cm).
$2,700-3,600

A Gallé enamelled glass liquor set, inscribed E. Gallé, c1890, decanter 8.5in (21cm), stand 12.5in (32cm).
$18,000-21,000

A Gallé cameo glass vase, minor fleck at base, c1900, 13.5in (34cm) high.
$7,500-9,500

A Gallé cameo glass pilgrim vase, signed in cameo, c1900, 17in (43cm) high. **$10,000-14,500**

A Koloman Moser for E. Bakalowits & Söhne sherry jug, in dimpled glass with electroplated metal mounts c1900, 10in (25cm). **$9,000-10,000**

COLOUR REVIEW

A 'Dragonfly' leaded glass and gilt bronze table lamp, stamped Tiffany Studios New York, 23in (59cm) high. **$29,000-34,000**

A Handel reverse painted glass and cold painted metal lamp, c1920. **$16,000-19,000**

A leaded glass and bronze floor lamp, by Tiffany Studios, 1907. **$9,500-12,000**

A Handel reverse painted glass and patinated metal lamp, c1915. **$6,000-7,650**

A leaded glass and bronze table lamp 'Favrile Fabrique', by Tiffany Studios, 1923. **$9,500-12,000**

A Tiffany Favrile and bronze poinsettia border lamp shade and base, c1910. **$25,500-29,000**

A Tiffany Favrile glass and bronze peony lamp, c1910, 23in (58cm) high. **$34,000-37,000**

A Handel reverse painted glass and patinated metal lamp, c1920. **$15,500-17,000**

A Pairpoint reverse painted glass scenic sea gull lamp, c1915, 25in (64cm). **$6,000-8,500**

A Tiffany Favrile glass and gilt bronze poppy filigree lamp, c1920. **$34,000-37,000**

An Emile Gallé glass and wrought iron table lamp, with cameo signature, 20.5in (52cm) high.
$21,000-25,000

An Emile Gallé double overlaid and etched glass table lamp, 11in (28cm) high. **$12,500-18,000**

A Daum etched glass table lamp, 15in (38cm) high. **$20,000-22,000**

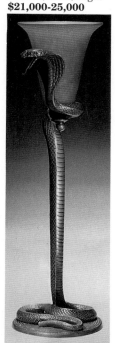

An Edgar Brandt gilt bronze table lamp, 20in (51cm) high. **$7,000-10,000**

A Daum etched and enamelled glass vase, signed Daum Nancy, 28in (71cm) high. **$22,000-27,000**

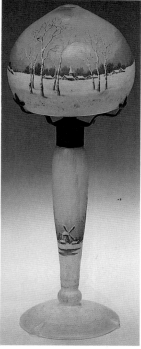

A Daum etched and enamelled table lamp, signed on base Daum Nancy, 14in (36cm) high. **$21,000-25,000**

A Daum etched and enamelled glass 'Rain' table lamp, 14in (36cm) high. **$28,000-36,000**

A Pairpoint reverse painted blown-out glass and patinated metal lamp, unsigned, c1915, 17.5in (45cm) high. **$5,500-7,000**

l. A Gallé cameo glass plafonnier, signed in cameo Gallé, c1900, 16in (41cm) diam. **$9,000-10,000**

l. A Gallé cameo glass and bronze boudoir lamp, shade and base signed, c1900, 10.5in (26cm) high. **$9,500-12,000**

A Daum etched glass and copper lamp, shade and base engraved Daum Nancy France, 1920s, 16.5in (42cm). **$9,000-12,000**

A G. Argy-Rousseau pâte-de-verre and wrought iron lamp, base and shade signed, 1926, 14.5in (37cm) high.
$40,000-45,000

A Favrile ten-light glass and bronze table lamp, by Tiffany Studios.
$24,000-28,000

A Daum etched and enamelled glass table lamp, signed on base, 12.5in (32cm) high.
$12,000-16,000

A Tiffany Studios 'Lotus' leaded glass and bronze table lamp, base stamped Tiffany Studios New York 6874, 18in (46cm) high. **$26,000-32,000**

A Le Verre Français, cameo glass and wrought iron mushroom lamp, 1920s. **$6,000-7,000**

A Daum etched glass and wrought iron chevron lamp, shade and base with engraved mark Daum Nancy France, 1920s, 12in (31cm).
$5,500-6,000

A pair of Albert Cheuret gilt bronze and alabaster tulip lamps, each inscribed Albert Cheuret, c1925.
$11,000-13,000

A Pairpoint reverse painted blown-out and patinated metal boudoir lamp, c1920.
$4,500-6,000

A Daum etched, applied and wheel carved glass vase, 10.5in (26cm) high.
$18,000-21,000

A silver plated brass tea infuser, by Christian Dell, 1924, 5in (13cm).
$3,500-4,500

A pair of Austrian silver table lamps, F. & D. Maly, marked and stamped with coat-of-arms, c1910.
$10,000-12,000

An Austrian brass lamp, c1920
$19,000-22,000

A Walker & Tolhurst silver bowl, designed by Gilbert Marks, maker's marks and London hallmarks for 1902, 2248.3gr.
$10,000-12,000

A Georg Jensen silver coffee pot, marked, c1925.
$2,000-2,500

A Charles Rennie Mackintosh fish knife and fork and dessert spoon, c1905.
$1,000-1,500

An Austrian dessert knife and fork and table fork, c1906.
$5,000-7,000

A black painted nickel plated metal and plastic table lamp, Gae Aulenti for Martinelli Luce, c1960.
$550-700

An Artificers Guild hammered silver bowl, London 1912.
$4,250-5,000

A pair of Renner and Maras wrought iron torchères, c1934.
$18,000-19,500

A pair of WMF electroplated metal candelabra and a dressing table mirror, stamped factory marks, c1900.
l. & r. **$8,500-10,000**   *c.* **$2,000-2,500**

A silver, lapis lazuli and glass cigarette box, stamped Cartier and importer's mark J.C., 1930, 7in (18cm) wide. **$3,600-4,500**

An Otto Prutscher tea and coffee service, executed by Eduard Friedmann, each piece with maker's mark, c1913. **$110,000-125,000**

A Georg Jensen silver four-piece tea and coffee set, numbered 71 and 181A, marked on bases, c1930. **$9,500-11,000**

A Frans Zwollo Snr. Art Nouveau vase, finely engraved, signed, 1899. **$10,000-12,000**

A Dagobert Peche silver coloured metal and ivory coffee pot, for the Wiener Werkstätte of 1922. **$25,000-28,000**

A Georg Jensen silver four-piece tea and coffee set, c1940. **$10,000-12,000**

A pair of Georg Jensen silver two-light candelabra, each marked 324, c1938, 9in (22cm) high, 73.5oz. **$20,000-22,000**

A Josef Hoffmann silver coloured metal and ivory teapot, with hinged cover, for the Wiener Werkstätte, c1924. **$9,000-12,000**

A Christopher Dresser, for Hukin & Heath, Aesthetic Movement electroplated sugar basin, c1880, **$1,000-1,800** and 7 cruet sets, c1880. **$5,000-6,000**

A pair of Limoges Art Nouveau enamelled copper vases, restored, c1900, 12in (31cm) high. **$5,500-7,000**

An aluminium, Bakelite and brass lamp. **$3,600-4,500**

A patinated silvered
bronze vase, stamped
Christofle B63G, c1925.
$1,000-1,200

A gilded rosewood mirror,
Wiener Werkstätte, c1925.
$20,500-24,000

A patinated and silvered bronze fish, marked
E. M. Sandoz and initialled E.R., c1920.
$10,000-13,500

A silver coloured metal box and cover,with
WW monograms and trademark, c1904.
$65,000-68,000

A brass jar and cover,
Dagobert Peche for the
Wiener Werkstätte,
c1920.
$12,000-13,500

A silver coloured metal, coral
and glass cruet set, marked,
WW monogram, c1905.
$40,000-42,500

A parcel gilt silver vase, maker's mark
of Tiffany & Co., New York, c1885,
6.5in (16.5cm), 16oz.
$22,000-25,500

Two Christofle electroplate
champagne buckets, c1935.
$2,000-2,500

A silver coloured metal dish,
Josef Hoffmann for the
Wiener Werkstätte, marked,
1927.
$6,000-7,000

A pair of WMF Art Nouveau decanters and a visiting
card tray, with factory marks, c1905.
l. & r. **$3,000-3,500**   *c.* **$2,000-2,500**

A Georg Jensen
silver vase, signed
Arno Malinowski,
7in (18cm).
$4,000-4,300

A Georg Jensen silver
coloured metal inkwell, with
glass liner, 1919.
$3,000-3,500

W.E.J. Benson copper and brass entrée and muffin dishes, on a large tray, signed.
$1,000-1,500

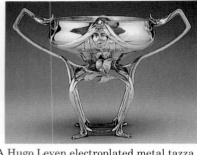

A Hugo Leven electroplated metal tazza, impressed twice with facsimile signature 'H. Leven', c1900, 12in (31cm).
$1,600-2,000

An Edgar Brandt wrought iron grille, impressed E. Brandt, c1925, 33in (84cm) high. **$4,500-6,000**

A Koch & Bergfeld, Bremen, silver and ivory covered cup, c1930, 11in (28cm) high, 23oz 10dwt.
$1,700-2,500

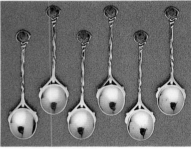

A set of 6 W.H. Haseler silver and enamel coffee spoons, for G.L. Connell, in original fitted case, 1906.
$1,700-2,500

A Tiffany Studios seventeen-piece bronze desk set, in the Zodiac pattern, all impressed Tiffany Studios/New York and numbered, lamp shade cracked and repaired, c1920. **$5,000-6,000**

A Dagobert Peche for the Wiener Werkstätte brass coupe, stamped with designer's monogram, 6in (15cm). **$3,500-5,000**

A Josef Hoffmann vase, for the Wiener Werkstätte, c1910, 6.5in (16cm).
$5,000-7,000

A Maurice Bouval Art Nouveau bronze figural tray, inscribed M. Bouval, c1900, 16in (41cm) long. **$3,050-4,250**

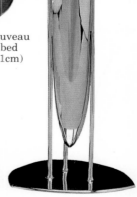

An Edgar Brandt wrought iron snake paperweight and geometric frame, stamped,1920s.
$2,500-3,500

A Jean Goulden champlevé enamelled silver box, the interior of the lid mottled turquoise, inscribed Jean Goulden, dated 1928. **$17,000-20,500**

An Archibald Knox silver and turquoise vase, for Liberty & Co. 1902.
$6,000-7,000

A George Ellwood mahogany and stained glass cabinet, for J.S. Henry, c1900, 77.5in (197cm) high. **$3,500-4,250**

A pair of Art Deco stained oak bergéres, re-upholstered, c1925, 33in (85cm). **$6,000-6,800**

A Shapland and Petter oak dresser, inlaid with pewter, mother-of-pearl and brass, possibly designed by Baillie-Scott, c1890. **$3,000-3,800**

An ebonized and painted corner cabinet, designed by Charles Rennie Mackintosh, with painted panel by Margaret Macdonald Mackintosh, c1897, 72.5in (183cm) high. **$23,000-25,500**

A double door oak and brass cabinet, attributed to Leon Jallot, c1907, 76in (193cm) high. **$3,000-3,500**

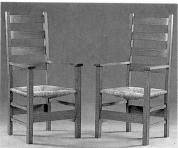

A pair of Heal's oak and rush ladderback armchairs, c1905, 48in (122cm). **$3,800-4,250**

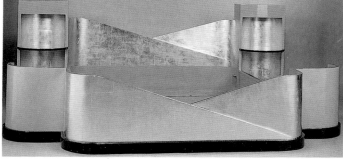

A Paul Poiret lacquered, gilt and silvered wood double bed, with nightstands and stools, c1929, 82in (208cm) long. **$7,650-10,000**

A thuya wood side cabinet, c1870, 40in (102cm) high. **$3,500-4,250**

An oak and rush high back armchair, c1907, 51in (130cm). **$4,250-5,000**

An oak and brass buffet, attributed to Leon Jallot, c1907, 52in (132cm) high. **$3,000-4,250**

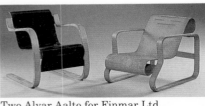

Two Alvar Aalto for Finmar Ltd., armchairs, maker's stamps, c1931. **$3,400-8,500 each**

A mahogany Art Nouveau hall stand, c1900, 104in (264cm) high. **$6,000-7,650**

A Frank Lloyd Wright oak and leather chair, c1904. **$23,800-25,500**

Four Joubert et Petit mahogany and rosewood barrel chairs, c1930. **$6,000-7,650**

A pair of leather and wood 'cloud' armchairs, some wear, c1930. **$1,200-1,500**

A Charles Rohlfs oak drop front desk, with stylised monogram, maker's logo and date 1902, 36in (92cm). **$17,850-20,500**

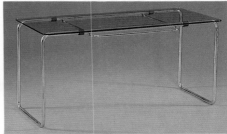

An Armand-Albert Rateau bronze and marble low table, raised on bird form supports, 40in (101.5cm). **$215,000-250,000**

A chromium plated steel and glass table, 'B 19', by Marcel Breuer for Thonet, original label, c1928, 55in (140cm). **$8,500-10,000**

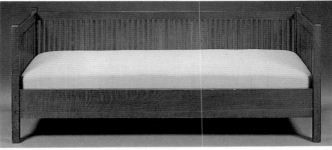

A mirrored glass and pale wood laminate coffee table, c1930. **$1,500-2,000**

An oak settle, by Gustav Stickley, model No. 291, with firm's red decal, c1908, 78in (198cm). **$12,750-14,500**

A pair of cantilever nickel plated steel, leather and glass armchairs and a coffee table, by Josef Müller, Berlin, glass replaced, table 24in (61cm) diam. **$170,000-180,000**

An Eavestaff 6-octave mini piano in Art Deco walnut case, 51in (130cm) wide, and matching stool. **$700-1,000**

A Gillow & Co. 'Stafford' satinwood and walnut wardrobe, in 3 sections, stamped Gillow & Co L5778, 87.5in (223cm) high.
$8,500-10,000

An inlaid mahogany, writing bureau, with metal attachments, c1903.
$10,000-12,000

An Edgar Brandt wrought iron and gilt bronze firescreen, c1925, 33in (84cm) high.
$15,500-17,000

A Gio Ponti rosewood, parchment and marble dining room suite, c1935, table 87.5in (223cm) long.
$22,000-25,500

A Brandt firescreen.
$18,000-20,500

A wrought iron hall stand, attributed to Paul Kiss, c1925.
$12,500-14,500

A carved mahogany dining table and 18 dining chairs, with carved foliate frames and upholstered in tooled leather, c1910.
$20,500-25,500

A wrought iron firescreen, c1925, 31in (79cm).
$5,000-7,000

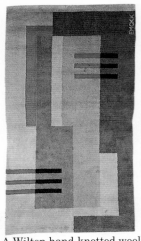

An Atelier Martine Art Deco wool carpet, signed Martine, c1923, 113 by 76in (287 by 193cm). **$5,000-7,000**

A Wilton hand-knotted woollen carpet, by Edward McKnight Kauffer, c1929, 83 by 46.5in (210 by 117cm). **$9,500-11,000**

An Art Deco wool carpet, c1923, 119 by 69in (302 by 175cm). **$2,500-3,500**

A Liberty & Co. pewter and enamel clock, designed by Archibald Knox, 8in (20cm) high. **$4,250-6,000**

A Liberty & Co. pewter clock, with copper numerals and inset with abalone shells, 18in (46cm) high. **$5,000-7,000**

An Adolf Loos brass and bevelled glass clock for J Heeg, with original movement, c1898, 19in (48cm). **$47,500-51,000**

An Art Deco diamond and black onyx desk clock, signed Cartier, Paris, No. 502, 769, 3416. **$11,000-13,000**

A Liberty & Co. mantel clock, 1903. **$5,000-8,500**

l. A Max Bill kitchen clock, with timer, for Gebrüder Junghans, Schramberg, 1951. **$1,700-2,000**

A Martin Brothers salt glazed stoneware clock case, a fantastic creature crouched beneath clock face, damage, 1874. **$4,500-6,000**

An Albin Müller patinated brass serpentine clock, designer's monogram on pendulum, c1906, 12.5in (32cm), with 2 keys. **$12,000-13,500**

An Art Deco diamond, ruby, emerald and cultured pearl clip, mounted in platinum.
$22,000-25,500

A pair of Art Deco diamond clips, set with square, baguette, bullet and old European cut diamonds, mounted in platinum.
$8,500-12,000

An Archibald Knox for Liberty pendant, c1902.
$6,800-8,500

An Art Deco diamond double clip brooch, set with pavé and round diamonds, enhanced by an old European cut diamond, mounted in platinum. **$17,500-20,500**

A silver coloured metal brooch, by Harry Bertoia, c1945.
$9,500-11,000

A silver coloured metal and coral pendant, stamped Stüber, c1908.
$1,600-2,000

An Art Deco emerald and diamond set platinum ring, 2.5ct.
$7,650-9,500

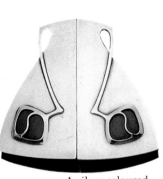

A silver coloured metal and enamel buckle, by Albrecht Holbein, c1900.
$2,500-3,000

An Art Deco diamond and gem set double clip brooch, mounted in platinum.
$9,500-11,000

A gold and rose quartz pendant, c1905.
$2,000-2,500

A silver, enamel and chalcedony stylised bird pin, Theodor Fahrner for Murrle, Bennett & Co., c1900.
$1,000-1,500

An Art Deco diamond, emerald and black onyx bracelet, mounted in platinum, 7in (18cm) long.
$17,000-20,500

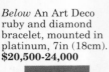

Below An Art Deco ruby and diamond bracelet, mounted in platinum, 7in (18cm). **$20,500-24,000**

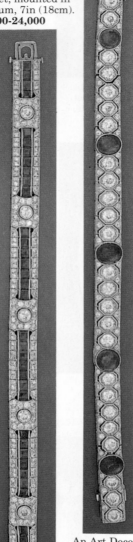

Below An Art Deco diamond and emerald bracelet, mounted in platinum, 7.5in (19cm). **$14,500-17,000**

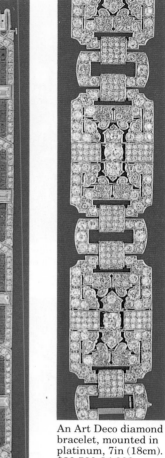

An Art Deco diamond bracelet, mounted in platinum, 7in (18cm). **$20,500-24,000**

l. An Art Deco emerald and diamond bracelet, mounted in platinum, signed Tiffany & Co, 7in (18cm). **$24,500-26,500**

An Art Deco cabochon ruby and diamond bracelet, 7in (18cm). **$25,500-30,500**

An Art Deco diamond and emerald bracelet. **$17,000-19,000**

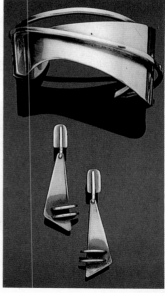

A silver coloured metal abstract brooch, stamped Ed Wiener, c1955, 3in (7.5cm). **$1,700-2,000**

An Art Deco diamond dress clip, mounted in platinum, signed by Van Cleef & Arpels, No. 37.383. **$14,500-16,000**

r. A silver coloured metal bracelet and earrings, the bracelet and one earring stamped Ed Wiener, c1947, bracelet 3in (7.5cm) max width. **$1,600-2,000**

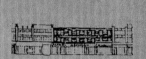
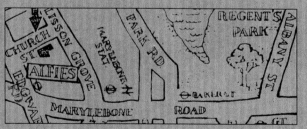

COLOUR REVIEW

A Paolo de Poli enamelled copper and wood peacock. **$2,000-3,000**

A funerary vase, by Elizabeth Fritsch, 1991. **$8,500-10,000**

A stoneware footed bowl, by Dame Lucie Rie, with a golden bronze band at the rim, impressed LR seal, c1978, 7in (18cm) diam. **$3,000-3,500**

A stoneware vase, by Dame Lucie Rie, impressed LR seal, c1978, 9in (23cm). **$6,000-7,650**

A Shino stoneware teabowl, by Toyozo Arakawa, incised signature, c1950, 5in (12.5cm) diam. **$12,000-13,500**

An earthenware vase, stamped Teco twice, model 85, 12in (30cm). **$6,800-7,800**

A stoneware inlaid sgraffito bowl, by Dame Lucie Rie, impressed LR, c1980. **$6,800-7,800**

'River and Moon Pot', by Elizabeth Fritsch, 1991. **$6,000-8,500**

A stoneware bottle form vase, by Bernard Leach, impressed BL and St. Ives seals, c1965, 14in (35cm). **$3,000-4,000**

A porcelain bowl, by Dame Lucie Rie, impressed LR seal, c1982, 6in (15cm). **$12,750-14,500**

A stoneware vase, by Hans Coper. **$5,000-8,500**

A tapestry picture, woven in coloured wools and silks depicting an urn of roses, carnations and honeysuckle resting on a plinth, mid-18thC, 12in (31cm) wide, framed.
$1,200-1,700

A Flemish tapestry covered cushion, woven in many colours with a double headed female figure, possibly Prudence, holding two goblets, late 16thC, 21in (53cm) wide; and another cushion.
$1,200-1,700

A group of 3 Aubusson tapestry portières, each depicting a ribbon-tied floral spray above flowers and foliage on a scrolling support, on an ivory ground with wide red border, 19thC, 113in (287cm) long.
$3,600-5,500

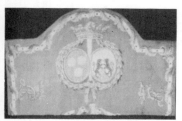

A tapestry panel for a bed head, probably Beauvais, woven in colours with 2 coats-of-arms surmounted by a coronet, each side with a monogram CB and coronet, the border of scrolling acanthus leaves and ribbons, against a dark pink ground, late 18thC, 53in (134.5cm) wide.
$1,800-2,700

An Aubusson tapestry panel for a chair seat, within a wreath frame, the border of écru, late 19thC, 29in (74cm) square.
$720-1,000

An Aubusson tapestry fragment woven in wools and silks, with a thin brown border, 116in (295cm) long.
$2,700-3,600

Miscellaneous

A pair of silk needlework pictures, 18thC, 7in (18cm) wide. **$900-1,500**

A pair of beadwork covered footstools, 12in (31cm) diam.
$720-1,000

A woolwork picture of a ship, c1840, 21.5in (54.5cm) wide.
$1,200-1,700

A collage of seaweed with baby crabs, inscribed 'Call us not weeds, we are flowers of the sea', c1850, 10in (25cm) wide.
$720-1,000

A petit point picture of a tabby
cat, 15in (38cm) wide.
$720-1,000

A patchwork coverlet, composed
of red, blue and sand coloured felt
patches, probably from uniforms,
the borders with applied felt spot
motifs, including animals, canon,
flowers, the royal coat-of-arms
and the date 1859 with the
initials FB and a heart beneath,
with vandyked edges, c1859, 56in
(142cm) square.
$360-540

A padded woolwork collage of
strawberries in a basket, 18thC,
9.5in (24cm) wide.
$1,200-1,700

A set of 4 blue velvet hangings,
with applied embroidery in silver
gilt and gilt threads, 35in (89cm)
wide; a panel worked with an urn
with a castle motif, 45in (114cm)
wide; and another with a crowned
orb, 74in (188cm) wide, late
19thC.
$7,000-9,000

A pair of English crewelwork
curtains, embroidered in shades
of green, blue, yellow and red,
with a phoenix amongst flowering
trees growing from small hillocks,
distressed, c1700, 40in (101.5cm)
wide.   **$7,000-9,000**

A Italian crimson silk border
applied with yellow silk outlined
with couched cord, with a central
crown linking curling leaves,
flanked by clumps of lilies and
other flowers, c1800, 12in (31cm)
deep.
$360-540

Did you know

*MILLER'S Antiques
Price Guide builds up
year by year to form the
most comprehensive
photo reference library
available.*

A brocatelle hanging, probably
French, woven in ivory and
crimson silk with a large scale
18thC style design of formalised
flowers and scrolling leaves, late
19thC, 51in (129.5cm) wide.
$1,800-2,700

A pair of Morris and Company
wool curtains, woven with a
repeating floral Tulip and Rose
pattern in shades of blue, cream
and rust, late 19thC, 62in
(157cm) wide.
$1,800-2,700

*Tulip and Rose was designed by
William Morris and registered as
a fabric on 20 January 1876.*

A length of crimson and white
silk damask, woven with a
repeating pattern of urns flanked
by exotic flowers and strapwork,
c1835, 21in (53.5cm) wide.
$720-1,000

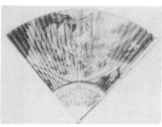

A fan, the leaf painted with a classical scene, the ivory sticks pierced and painted with a couple dining under a vine, the narrow guardsticks stained red and green and pique with silver, c1700, slight damage, 11in (28cm).
$2,700-3,600

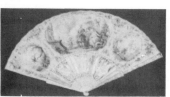

A marriage fan, the leaf painted with an allegory of love, the reverse with putti, the mother-of-pearl sticks carved, pierced, gilt and backed with mother-of-pearl, repaired, c1760, 12in (31cm).
$720-1,000

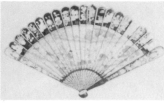

A Canton brisé fan, painted and lacquered against a gold ground, with an upper border of animals against a black ground, the reverse with a tiger hunt against a silver ground, rubbed, c1820, 7.5in (19cm), and a Canton lacquer fan box.
$1,800-2,700

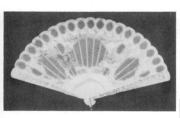

A Japanese ivory brisé fan, with pierced oval panels and lacquered in gold with figures and buildings, the guardsticks decorated with shibyama work, slight damage, c1880, 10in (25cm), in a Canton lacquer box.
$3,600-5,500

A Chinese lacquer fan of 'A Thousand Faces', the leaf painted with groups of ivory-faced figures, the guards and sticks of yellow, cream, grey, red and brown with silver and gilt painted scenes, in a lacquered case, mid-19thC.
$720-1,000

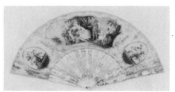

A French fan, the silk leaf painted with cherry pickers and 2 still lives of flowers, the mother-of-pearl sticks carved, pierced and gilt, repaired, c1775, 11in (28cm).
$2,700-3,600

An ivory brisé fan, painted and lacquered with a classical scene, possibly Jason, the reverse with ruins in a landscape, slight damage, c1890, 9in (23cm).
$720-1,000

A leaf painted fan with 2 asymmetrical vignette of villages, the reverse with farm buildings, the ivory sticks carved, pierced and painted with rabbits and birds amongst ferns and flowers, repaired, c1750, 11in (28cm).
$1,800-2,700

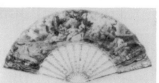

A fan, possibly South German, the leaf painted with a.king watching a harvest, the mother-of-pearl sticks carved, pierced and gilt, c1770, in contemporary shagreen box, 10.5in (26.5cm).
$2,700-3,600

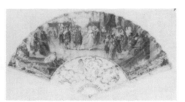

A fan, the leaf painted with a classical scene, the reverse with lovers in a landscape, the mother-of-pearl sticks carved with figures, pierced, gilt and backed with mother-of-pearl, damaged, c1750, 11.5in (29.5cm).
$1,800-2,700

A French fan, with ivory battoire sticks, carved, pierced and gilt, for the Spanish market, c1760, 10in (25cm).
$1,800-2,700

A fan, the leaf painted with chinoiserie figures in a garden, the sticks lacquered in red and gold, repaired, c1780, 12in (31cm), in a 19thC Chinese embroidered fan case.
$1,000-1,500

A handscreen, the satin leaf printed with a bird's-eye view of The Royal Victoria Infirmary, Newcastle-upon-Tyne, the metal mount set with 2 enamelled escutcheons with The Prince of Wales' crest and the arms of Newcastle, the handle set with peridots, one missing, leaf worn.
$720-1,000

A fan, the canepin leaf painted, signed Adrien-Moreau, the verso inscribed Voisin Richard, the ivory sticks finely carved and pierced, the guardsticks carved with monograms L.L., slight damage, late 19thC, 12in (31.5cm).
$4,500-5,500

A lace trimmed fan, the gauze leaf painted with a girl catching butterflies, signed F. Houghton, on curved mother-of-pearl sticks, late 19thC, 13.5in (34cm).
$500-720

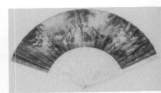

A fan, with mother-of-pearl sticks carved and pierced with figures and backed with mother-of-pearl, rubbed, c1840, 11in (28cm).
$1,500-1,700

A fan, the ivory guards carved with statues and stylised dolphins, plain shaped sticks, the leaf painted with a classical scene, 11in (28cm).
$900-1,500

A Canton brisé fan, painted and lacquered with figures in a garden against a red lacquer ground, the reverse similarly lacquered with figures in a boat, rubbed, c1820, 8in (20cm).
$4,500-6,000

A French fan, the leaf painted with a maiden by a lakeside scene attended by putti, the reverse painted with a scene of San Gregorio in a central panel, with mother-of-pearl sticks decorated with gilt putti and flowers, the gilt metal guards applied with coral busts, some missing.
$600-700

An Edwardian painted fan, 12in (30cm) long.
$110-180

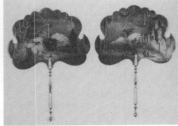

A pair of papier mâché handscreens, decorated with Turkish style street scenes, on turned giltwood handles, mid 19thC.
$500-600

An ivory brisé fan, carved in romantic style, 10in (25cm) long.
$360-600

A gold mounted and gem set tortoiseshell fan, the single guard mounted with textured gold sheath and applied with rose diamonds and cabochons in a floral design, plain, tortoiseshell sticks and ostrich feather leaf.
$700-900

RUGS & CARPETS

A Kazak rug, woven in traditional colours, with 2 rows of 10 octagons filled with hooked and geometric motifs, on a blue background (241 by 117cm)
$2,000-2,700

A Caucasian runner, the field with green, ivory, red, blue, brown and yellow diagonal rows of boteh, in a red border of stylised floral motifs, between yellow and blue floral stripes, worn and repaired, 141 by 44in (358 by 112cm).
$3,600-4,500

A Heriz carpet, with an ivory vine trellis design on a blue field, with green, ivory, blue and pink, 285 by 177in (724 by 450cm).
$54,000-63,000

A Caucasian runner, possibly kuba, the red field woven with a florette trellis pattern, the cream main border with linked star florettes, in good condition, 104 by 45in (264 by 114cm).
$2,700-3,600

A Kashan silk prayer rug, the ivory field with a vase of flowers flanked by trailing vines, deep crimson mihrab with trailing flowers, one bright blue border with leaves and flowers and several narrow borders, ends missing, 78 by 53in (198 by 135cm).
$3,600-5,500

A Beshir carpet, the dark blue field woven with a palmette trellis within multiple borders, in fair condition, 145 by 71in (369 by 180cm).
$720-1,000

A Karabagh runner, the indigo field with a rococo European design within scrolling golden frames divided by similar motifs and surrounded by floral sprays, in a narrow reciprocal Y-pattern border, minor damage, 234 by 42in (594 by 107cm).
$10,000-12,000

A Karabagh kelleh, in indigo, blackcurrant red and light blue, slight wear and repair, 218 by 79in (553 by 201cm).
$3,600-5,500

A Kazak rug, with red pointed ground, azure surround and central medallion with floral decoration within stylised border, 71 by 53in (180 by 135cm).
$360-540

A Chondzorek rug, the shaded brick-red field with 2 large indigo and sea-green panels in a shaded light blue border, corrosion and repair, 101 by 56in (256 by 142cm).
$2,700-3,600

A pair of Senneh kilims, the ivory field of each with angular floral sprays around a large serrated indigo lozenge medallion containing similar motifs radiating from a similar central ivory floral lozenge, the red spandrels similar, in a narrow rust red lozenge border between medium blue similar stripes, 87 by 48in (221 by 122cm) and 85 by 52in (216 by 132cm).
$2,700-3,600

A Qashqa'i rug, in plum red, ivory and orange, with brief inscription and the date 1319 (1901 A.D.), between orange flowerhead and serrated leaf stripes, various minor stripes, a panelled skirt and kilim strip at each end, 77 by 48in (196 by 122cm).
$2,700-3,600

A Sewan Kazak rug, the shaded brick red field in a brown border of angular rectangular panels containing stylised flowerheads and the Christian date 1916, between zig-zag stripes, slight wear, 103 by 71in (262 by 180cm).
$2,700-3,600

A Persian rug, the shaded brick field woven with floral tendrils, the dark blue main border with a palmette meander, in good condition, 78 by 48in (198 by 122cm).
$3,600-5,500

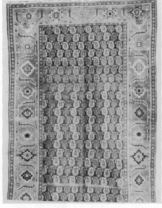

A North West Persian kelleh, the shaded indigo field with staggered rows of polychrome boteh, in a broad shaded light blue angular flowerhead and serrated leaf border, dated 1333 (1914-5 A.D.) in one corner, between brown floral and barber pole stripes, a short kilim strip at each end, 216 by 86in (549 by 218cm).
$3,600-5,500

A Ziegler carpet, the charcoal grey field with a counterposed design in a rust red flowerhead and palmette vine border between minor ivory and golden yellow floral stripes, some damage, 180 by 158 in (457 by 401cm).   **$7,000-9,000**

An East Turkestan rug, the shaded brick red field with a pictorial design of perching water fowl and a cockerel amongst flowering lotus below a large flowering tree with perching birds, repaired, 105 by 70in (271 by 178cm).
$2,700-3,600

DOLLS

Nothing in life is static and the doll market is no exception. Although prices have not risen at the very top end of the market, largely due to the lack of Japanese buyers, there have been some interesting developments, particularly in the middle of the price range. A charming Bru Jne, size 9 in original pale blue satin dress fetched $26,200 in September and in the same sale the only known example of Steiner's last patent drawing was sold for $5,450. This was of a clockwork Zouave Soldier who knelt down and fired his rifle. The curious thing about this patent is its remarkable similarity to an earlier clockwork toy produced by Theroude.

Automata also sold well in the sale, $54,200 being paid for a Vichy model of 'Pierrot Serenading the Moon', a European record price, and $47,000 for a jokey 'Peasant and Baby' also by Vichy. This was in fact of a Bohemian young man irritatedly feeding a piglet on his lap.

Wax dolls, particularly wax over composition, after being unfashionable for many years, have seen some high prices paid for those in good condition and original clothes. A beautiful large poured wax English doll of 1860 in a pretty original spotted muslin frock with blue silk sash and matching decoration on the skirt and sleeves fetched $3,400 at Christie's last year against an estimate of $850-1,200. This May $1,500 was paid for a pair of late 19thC wax over composition dolls in high quality original 18thC style fancy dress, the woman with fan and pearls, the man with tricorn hat and knee breeches. It is so unusual to find toys in an unplayed with condition, that collectors will always pay a premium for them.

Other factors that contribute to a high price are rare marks, original boxes or labels. An interesting high quality English poured wax doll we sold in May had a hitherto unknown shop stamp on its body. After extensive research we discovered that the shop stamp belonged to a fancy jeweller in Sloane Street, known to have been in business at least from 1886-1908. In spite of damaged limbs, its serenely pretty face meant it sold for $800. A pretty Pierrotti baby in good condition and attractive clothes now fetches over $850.

In the past few years we have seen a sharp rise in interest for 20thC English cloth dolls. A surprising $840 was paid for a pretty 1950s Chad Valley baby doll with sleeping eyes. In pristine condition, original knitted sewn-on clothes and tied into its labelled box, it represented a good return on its original price tag of 5/6 (50c). A couple of pairs of dolls in original boxes modelled as the Bisto Kids sold for $850 and $815. Those were cheap quality composition-headed advertising dolls again still tied in their boxes, perhaps over production accounted for them not being named on the lids, or perhaps they were such well known characters, that it was not deemed necessary.

Another curiously high price was paid for an unusually voluptuous celluloid lady doll complete with just visible painted flesh coloured stockings and high heels. Made by the Rheinische Gummi and Celluloid Fabrik and from a private collection it realised $1,150, probably a record for a celluloid doll. The same collector also sold a doll complete with original trousseau and a pretty paper covered wardrobe. These early 20thC French sets were normally not of very high quality but still a delightfully fascinating toy. Although the doll was only approximately 7 inches high, the complete wardrobe and doll with some additions sold for $1,300.

Collecting early Barbie dolls has been a new field at Christie's South Kensington. Here the appeal is equally in the boxed doll, her friends and relations as well as in their sets of lined clothes and accessories, e.g. a group of four boxed dolls with a selection of clothes fetched $1,700.

The dolls house market has remained strong throughout the year. Enormous interest was shown in the sale of the Camme Bache dolls house collection and catalogues were sold out before the sale. Although there were very few manufactured houses, all of them were fully furnished and inhabited, many with good quality pieces and unusual half-bisque doll people. Collectors were particularly interested as they came from Scandinavia, and there were many items that were typical of the Danish lifestyle but are not found in English houses. The biggest price of the sale was for an English butchers shop, once used by a 'flesher' of Dumfries. It was sold for $16,800. The dolls house and chattels sections continued to be strong throughout the year, Christie's having been building up this area, we now offer a larger selection and wider range of periods than any other auction house.

Whereas the higher priced French bébés and rare characters have tended to hold or slightly decline in price, middle and lower price range dolls in immaculate condition have been strongly sought after. The message for the recession seems to be if its pretty and perfect in its own field then its worth buying. The emotions are often uppermost in the decision to buy a doll, so the love affair between the collector and the doll has never been more important than now. A doll has to have the right look in order to appeal to a prospective owner and not remain on the shelf. Dealers are therefore becoming more cautious in their purchases and are only buying what they know they will have a ready market for.

DOLLS
Wooden

A George II wooden doll, with painted gesso covered face, nailed flax wig, legs jointed at hip and knee, block feet, cloth upper and wooden lower arms, dressed in green, pink, cream and blue, fragments of brocaded and ribbed silk and satin, lined with paper, silk stockings and boots, c1740, together with an
English waxed shoulder papier mâché doll, with black glass eyes, dark real hair, cloth body and legs, and leather arms, wearing Chinese style coat, c1830, 14 and 14.5in (36 and 37cm).
$7,000-9,000

An early German carved wooden doll, with painted hair and features, jointed body with painted yellow shoes, wearing original gold silk fringed dress and pantaloons, c1800, 6in (15cm) high.
$720-1,000

A George III wooden doll, with painted features, inserted blue eyes with dotted lashes and brows, white blonde real hair, squared hips peg jointed to straight tapering legs ending in block feet, cloth upper arms with blue kid forearms, in pink beige silk dress, restored, c1790, 13in (33cm).
$1,200-1,700

This doll is reputed to have belonged to Queen Victoria who gave it to her maid-in-waiting the Hon. Caroline Cavendish who in turn gave the doll to the aunt of the present owner.

A Grödnertal painted wooden headed doll, with yellow comb, jointed wooden body and contemporary clothes, damaged, c1820, 9in (23cm) high.
$720-1,000

A Grödnertal painted wooden headed doll, with moulded yellow comb, jointed wooden body, Welsh tweed clothes and basket, c1820, 11in (28cm) high.
$1,800-2,700

A George III wooden doll, with gessoed face, inset black enamelled eyes, brown ringlet wig, brown leather arms, articulated wooden legs, wearing a muslin skirt, voile apron, cotton underclothes, damaged, early 19thC, 18in (46cm).
$1,200-1,700

A pair of carved and painted wooden nodding figures, probably South German, with moving lower jaws, damaged, c1850, 8in (20cm) high.
$360-540

Wax

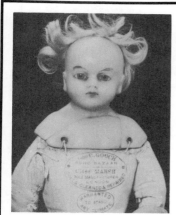

A Charles Marsh poured wax shoulder doll, with inserted blonde hair, blue lashed eyes, wax lower limbs, maker's stamp on cloth torso, damaged and restored, c1878, 18.5in (47cm).
$900-1,500

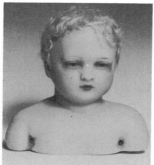

An English Pierotti wax shoulder head, with fixed blue glass eyes, closed painted mouth, inserted blonde hair, eyebrows and eyelashes, 5in (13cm).
$1,000-1,500

This shoulder head comes from a direct descendant of the Pierotti family.

A pair of wax over composition headed dolls, dressed in 18thC style, with blue eyes, blonde mohair wigs, stuffed bodies, waxed arms and composition lower legs, the man wearing black silk knee breeches, red velvet, silver braided jacket, tricorn hat, heeled shoes, the lady with open/closed mouth showing teeth, dressed in ruby pleated silk skirt with floral overdress trimmed with lace, heeled shoes and fan, damage to toe of man, 17in (43cm) high.
$1,200-1,700

A poured wax head and shoulder doll, 19thC, 17.5in (44cm) high.
$360-540

A wax over composition headed doll, with blue eyes, blonde inset mohair, stuffed body with composition limbs, moulded shoes and socks, wearing original blue silk lace and flower trimmed dress with train, posy and fan, cracks to face, c1888, 18in (46cm) high.   **$360-540**

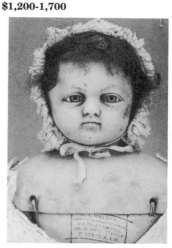

A poured wax headed child doll, with blue eyes, downturned mouth, remains of inset hair, stuffed body, wax limbs, metal eyelets and baby robe, body stamped W.J. Weedon, Importer & Manufacturer of British & Foreign Goods, 164 Sloane Street, Belgravia S.W., damaged, 23in (59cm) high.
$720-1,000

William J. Weedon is listed in Kelly's Street Directory of Chelsea, Pimlico and Belgravia as a fancy jeweller in 1886-7, 1890, 1900 and 1909.

A poured wax child doll, with fixed blue eyes, short brown inset hair, downturned mouth, stuffed body, wax limbs and contemporary blue wool dress, late 19thC, 23in (59cm) high.
$720-1,000

A Lucy Peck poured wax doll, wearing original bonnet, c1900, 27in (69cm) high.
$1,800-2,700

Bisque

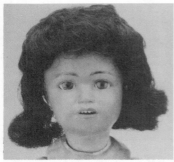

A brown bisque headed character doll, with brown eyes, dark wig and bent limbed composition body, impressed Heubach Koppelsdorf 344 3/0, replaced eyes and wig, 13in (33cm) high.
$720-1,000

A bisque headed jester doll, the wire spring and wood body with squeaker, wearing original clothes, 10.5in (26cm) high.
$360-540

A bisque headed musical poupée, with fixed blue eyes, blonde wig, original pink and white streamers with pompoms, covering a bonbon box, 12.5in (32cm) high.
$360-540

A bisque headed child doll, with blue lashed sleeping eyes, moulded and feathered brows, pierced ears, auburn wig, jointed wood and composition body, voice box and walking and kiss throwing mechanism, wearing red wool dress, coat and cape, straw bonnet and leather shoes with bee mark, impressed DEP 10, 24in (61cm) high.
$1,000-1,500

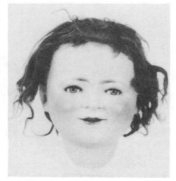

A bisque headed character doll, modelled as H.R.H. Princess Elizabeth, with blue lashed sleeping eyes, brown wig and composition toddler body, impressed Porzellanfabrik Burggrub Princess Elizabeth D.R.G.M., firing crack at neck.
$1,000-1,500

Two German shoulder parian bisque dolls, with blonde moulded hair, painted faces, cloth bodies and lower parian limbs, c1870, 16 and 17in (41 to 44cm).
$1,000-1,500

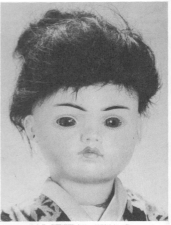

A Bähr & Pröschild bisque Oriental doll, with fixed blue glass eyes, closed mouth, black mohair wig, pierced ears, jointed wood and composition, impressed 220/3, re-dressed, eyes replaced retouching to fingers, 15in (38cm).
$1,800-2,700

A bisque headed character doll, modelled as Father Christmas, with inset eyes, original clothes and beard, impressed with an ogee curve and 6/o, 8.5in (21cm) high.   **$180-360**

A French shoulder bisque swivel head fashion doll, with fixed blue glass eyes, closed mouth, remnants of blonde real hair wig over cork pate, Gesland type body, bisque lower arm, re-dressed, one upper and lower arm missing, one foot damaged, unmarked, c1885, 10.5in (26cm).
$720-1,000

A bisque shoulder fashion doll, 19thC.
$1,000-1,500

Three all bisque Bye-Lo baby dolls and an all bisque Kewpie doll, all impressed to backs, with jointed arms and legs, early 1920s, 4 to 5in (10 to 13cm).
$1,000-1,500

A domed bisque swivel-headed doll, with feathered brows, pierced ears, blonde mohair wig, stuffed body, bisque arms, wearing original regional costume, impressed S H 905, 13.5in (34cm) high.
$1,800-2,700

A French bisque doll, with fixed spiralled blue glass eyes, closed mouth, Belton type head with long real hair wig, pierced ears, jointed wood and composition body, wearing blue lawn pleated lace trimmed dress and later bonnet, impressed 13/1 4, slight damage, 11in (28cm).
$720-1,000

A bisque headed character doll, modelled as an Oriental, with brown sleeping eyes, pierced ears, black mohair wig, jointed body and original red embroidered clothes, impressed SH 1199 DEP, 15in (38cm) high.
$2,700-3,600

An early bisque headed bébé, with brown yeux fibres, shaded lids, pierced ears, fair mohair wig, jointed wood and papier mâché body, fixed wrists, original red hat and contemporary cotton print frock, impressed and body stamped with Schmitt & Fils shield, 16in (41cm) high.
$10,000-12,000

A bisque headed character doll, with brown sleeping eyes, moulded blonde hair and bent limbed composition body and jointed wrists, dressed in whitework dress and cape, one broken finger, impressed 2048 5, by Bruno Schmidt, 18in (46cm) high.
$1,800-2,700

A bisque headed character baby doll, with blue sleeping eyes, feathered brows, brown mohair wig and bent limbed composition body, dressed in white velvet coat, marked 10 BSW, 18in (46cm) high.
$720-1,000

A group of 51 dolls house and all bisque dolls, German and French, some distressed, late 19th/early 20thC, from 1.5 to 6in (4 to 13cm). **$3,600-5,500**

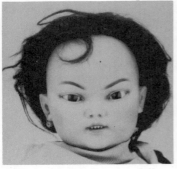

A bisque headed character doll, modelled as an Oriental, with pierced ears, black wig and jointed wood and composition body, damaged, impressed SH 1199 DEP 8, 20in (51cm) high.
$3,600-5,500

A bisque headed child doll, with feathered brows, pierced ears, blonde mohair wig, cloth covered jointed body with fixed wrists, dressed in beige silk, 11.5in (29cm) high. **$2,700-3,600**

A bisque headed child doll, with blue sleeping eyes, pierced ears, jointed body, wearing a green dress and coat, impressed S & H 1249 DEP 6, 16.5in (42cm) high.
$360-540

Bru

A Bru pressed bisque swivel-head fashion doll, the closed smiling mouth, fixed blue glass eyes, pierced ears, auburn mohair wig over cork pate, gusseted kid body with jointed wooden arms and hands, wearing original clothes and shoes, together with her trunk containing accessories, c1872.
$7,000-9,000

A bisque headed character doll, with blue sleeping eyes, moulded brows, pierced ears, blonde mohair wig, jointed body and red check wool dress, impressed 1339 S & H L.L. & S. 8., 19in (48cm) high.
$720-1,000

A Bru jeune R bisque head, with open mouth, upper teeth, weighted brown glass eyes, pierced ears, damaged, impressed BRU Jne R 9, c1892, 5in (13cm).
$720-1,000

François Gaultier

A bisque swivel-necked doll, gusseted white kid leather body, original blonde wig, underwear, modern turquoise brocade gown, probably F. Gaultier, impressed 4, c1875, 18in (46cm) high, together with a velvet pouch.
$1,800-2,700

A moulded bisque doll, with fixed blue glass eyes, red-blonde real hair wig, jointed papier mâché and wood body with straight legs, in original cream wool dress, paint scuffed, impressed 7 4. F.G. in a scroll. **$2,700-3,600**

A swivel-head pressed bisque doll, with closed mouth, fixed blue glass eyes, fair mohair wig over cork pate, kid covered wooden body with vertically jointed swivelling hips, tenon joints at knees, shoulders and elbows, bisque forearms, wearing silk and satin dress, straw bonnet and brown leather heeled boots, impressed on the shoulder F 4 G, damaged, c1865, 18in (46cm).
$7,000-9,000

A bisque character doll, with blue intaglio eyes, moulded light brown hair, curved limb composition body, in a whitework embroidered dress, some damage and repair, impressed with sunburst mark, 76 04, 6, c1910, 15in (38cm).
$1,000-1,500

Gebrüder Heubach

A bisque socket head baby boy doll, 14in (37cm) high.
$720-1,000

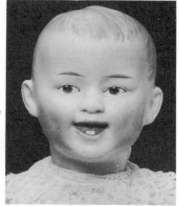

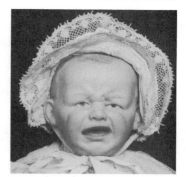

A shoulder bisque character crying doll, with open/closed mouth and simulated tongue, intaglio eyes, cloth body with composition forearms, wearing original embroidered cream silk long robe, net cape and lacy bonnet, fingers chipped, impressed 3, c1912.
$1,000-1,500

A flirty-eyed toddler character doll, Heubach 267, c1920, 28in (71cm) high.
$1,000-1,500

Jumeau

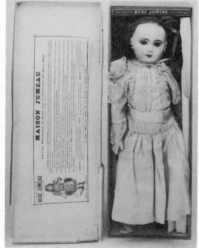

A Jumeau bisque headed bébé, with blue yeux fibres, pierced ears, brown wig, the jointed wood and papier mâché body dressed in cream silk, original cotton print shift with Bébé Jumeau ribbon, underwear, shoes and socks, stamped in red Tête Jumeau and on body in blue Jumeau Medaille d'Or, in original Jumeau box, 28in (71cm) high, with additional pair of slippers and petticoat.
$3,600-5,500

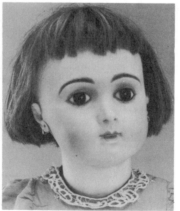

A Jumeau triste pressed bisque doll, with fixed brown glass paperweight eyes, applied and pierced ears, brown real hair over cork pate, jointed wood and composition body, wearing pink dress, stringing loose, impressed 15, c1875, 31.5in (80cm).
$14,500-16,500

An Emile Jumeau doll, wearing original clothes, c1870, 23.5in (60cm) high.
$10,000-12,000

A Jumeau bisque doll, with fixed blue glass eyes, blonde wig, jointed wood and composition body, white bonnet, chipped and cracked, stamped in red Deposé Tête Jumeau Bte S.G.D.G., c1885, 17in (43cm).
$3,600-5,500

An all bisque doll, probably Kestner, 'The Wrestler', c1890, 10.5in (26cm) high.
$2,700-3,600

A bisque doll, probably by Kestner, with open mouth and upper teeth, weighted blue glass eyes, pierced ears, fair mohair wig over original plaster pate and jointed wood and composition body, wearing cream silk dress and red wool coat and bonnet, impressed 192 4, c1910, 15in (38cm), together with her trunk, containing brush, comb and hand mirror, 2 jackets, 2 skirts, 4 items of underwear, purse bonnet and parasol, trunk 12.5in (31cm) wide.
$2,700-3,600

A Jumeau bisque doll, with brown paperweight eyes, long brown wig, jointed wood and composition body, with label to buttock, in printed floral dress and bonnet, leather pumps, paint scuffed, chipped hands, unmarked head but impressed 5, c1890, 16in (41cm). **$1,200-1,700**

A bisque character doll, with large weighted blue glass eyes, open mouth with upper teeth, original brown mohair wig, curved limb baby body, wearing later knitted pink dress and cap, arms and legs rubbed, impressed 257/64, c1916, 25in (64cm).
$1,200-1,700

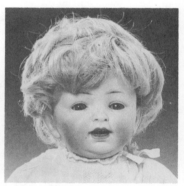

A bisque character doll, with sleeping blue eyes, open mouth with moulded upper teeth, curved limb body, wearing original dress and kid shoes, replaced wig, c1915, 13in (33cm).
$360-540

J.D. Kestner

A J.D. Kestner Bru-type bisque doll, with open/closed mouth, simulated teeth, fixed blue glass eyes, pierced ears, flattened domed head, jointed wood and composition body, wearing a cream lacy dress, impressed 121 0, c1897, 7.5in (19cm).
$1,200-1,700

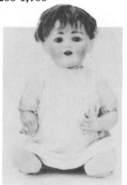

A bisque headed character baby doll with brown lashed sleeping eyes, short wig and baby's body, impressed J.D.K. 257 51, 19in (48cm) high.
$720-1,000

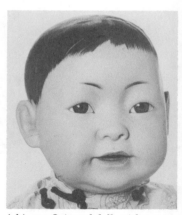

A bisque Oriental doll, with open mouth and 2 upper teeth, fixed brown glass eyes, black moulded hair and curved limb composition body, wearing yellow and white tunic, cracked, impressed 14, 16in (41cm).
$2,700-3,600

A bisque headed character doll, with blue sleeping and flirting eyes, brown mohair wig, the bent limbed composition body dressed in knitted suit, impressed J.D.K. 257, 18in (45.5cm) high.
$1,200-1,700

A bisque headed character baby doll, with open/closed mouth, blue sleeping eyes, baby's body and blue rompers, impressed F 10 211 J.D.K., 12in (31cm) high.
$1,200-1,700

A bisque headed character doll, with blue sleeping eyes, brown wig and bent limbed composition body dressed in turquoise blue cotton, impressed P.M. 914, 14in (36cm) high.
$180-360

A bisque headed character doll, with water melon mouth, sleeping side glancing googlie eyes, plaster pate, composition toddler body, starfish hands and original boots and socks, impressed J.D.K. 221, fingers damaged, 10in (25cm) high.
$3,600-5,000

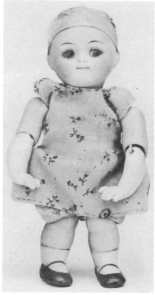

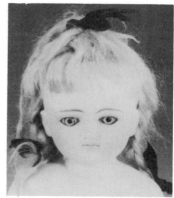

An all bisque child doll, with brown eyes, blonde mohair wig, shoulder and hip joints, moulded peach coloured socks and black two-bar shoes with bow, original blue silk lace trimmed frock and underwear, probably by Kestner, chipped and unstrung, 8in (20cm) high.   **$1,200-1,700**

An all bisque googlie-eyed character doll, with blue sleeping eyes, jointed body with moulded and painted shoes and socks, impressed 112 2, by Kestner, 5.5in (13cm) high.
$1,800-2,700

A bisque turned shoulder headed doll, with closed mouth, blue inset eyes, feathered brows, blonde mohair wig, the stuffed body with bisque limbs, dressed in underwear, impressed 8, by Kling, damaged, 18in (46cm) high.
$1,800-2,700

Use the Index

Because certain items might fit easily into any number of categories, the quickest and surest method of locating any entry is by reference to the index at the back of the book.
This has been fully cross-referenced for absolute simplicity.

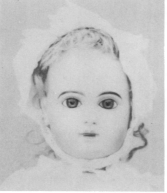

A bisque headed bébé, with closed mouth, blue yeux fibres, feathered brows, pierced ears, cork pate, blonde mohair wig, the jointed wood and composition body dressed in white shift and bonnet, impressed Déposé E 12 J, slight damage, 25in (64cm) high.
$7,000-9,000

Lenci

A Lenci painted felt doll, with brown eyes glancing to the left, blonde curly wig and original pink and white check felt clothes, Series 111, 12in (31cm) high.
$720-1,000

A pair of Lenci felt dolls, with original card and woven tags to backs, he dressed in plaid kilt, green jacket, maroon waistcoat and undershorts, white shirt, sporran, tartan socks and black shoes, tartan wool scarf, brown cap, face painted with blue eyes looking left, blonde hair, 14.5in (37cm), she with Lenci card and woven tags to back of skirt, painted face with brown eyes looking right, black hair, layered dress of net applied with cut-out felt flowers and vines in pink, red and black, black lace mantilla and red painted wood comb to hair, white socks and black shoes, 14.5in (37cm).   **$1,200-1,700**

Armand Marseille

An Armand Marseille bisque headed doll, with blue sleeping eyes, open mouth, brown hair wig, composition body, in knitted shorts and top, impressed Germany 971 A5M, 16in (41cm) high.
$720-1,000

An Armand Marseille bisque doll, with cropped black wig, jointed wood and composition body in contemporary red and white striped dress, impressed 1894 AM 8, one finger restored, c1894, 23in (59cm) high.
$1,800-2,700

A bisque headed character baby doll, with blue lashed sleeping eyes, brown mohair wig and toddler body, dressed as a boy, impressed 971 A 8 M, 18in (46cm) high.
$720-1,000

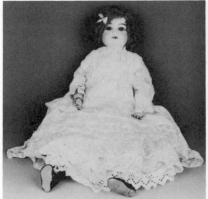

An Armand Marseille bisque socket-head girl doll, 23in (59cm) high.
$360-540

An Armand Marseille bisque socket head doll, 23in (59cm) high.
$360-540

l. An Armand Marseille bisque socket head character doll, 17in (43cm) high.
$720-1,000
r. An Armand Marseille/ Koppelsdorf bisque socket head doll, 19in (48cm).
$360-540

An Armand Marseille howling doll, cloth body with squeaker, No. AM 347, c1929, 15in (38cm) high.
$1,800-2,700

An Armand Marseille bisque socket head girl doll, 20.5in (52cm).
$360-540

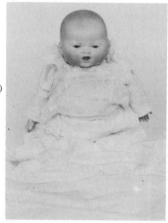

S.F.B.J.

A character doll with bisque head with raised brows, pierced ears, long hair wig, sleeping dark French eyes and jointed composition body, impressed 10, with S.F.B.J. sticker on the body, the head probably by Simon and Halbig, similar to mould No. 1159, 23in (59cm) high.
$720-1,000

An Armand Marseille jointed doll, with sleeping eyes, No. AM 390, c1900, 13in (33cm) high.
$180-360

Simon & Halbig/Kammer & Reinhardt

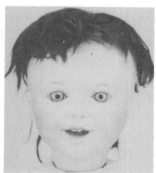

An S.F.B.J. boy doll, The Screamer, with jointed toddler body, impressed No. 233, 20in (51cm) high.
$3,600-5,000

A bisque headed character doll, with open/closed mouth, blue sleeping eyes, brown mohair wig and bent limbed composition body, impressed R SFBJ 236 Paris, body marked with SFBJ label, 19in (48cm) high.
$720-1,000

A Simon & Halbig bisque 'Santa' doll, with weighted blue glass eyes, pierced ears, blonde mohair wig, ball jointed wood and composition body, with several items of clothing, impressed 1249 DEP SANTA-8, stringing perished, unclothed, 19in (48cm) high.   **$1,000-1,500**

A Simon & Halbig bisque character doll, the long face with fixed pale blue paperweight eyes, closed mouth, long brown ringletted wig, jointed wood and composition toddler body, cream silk dress, pale aquamarine coat, cape and bonnet, impressed S 12 H, 939, restored, 19.5in (50cm) high.
$3,600-5,000

A Simon & Halbig shoulder bisque doll, with fixed spiralled brown glass eyes, closed mouth, pierced ears, moulded curly blonde hair, leather body with leather upper arms, in underskirt, cream raw silk gown, lace cap, knitted gloves, three-button brown leather boots, impressed S12H, c1890, 24.5in (62cm) high.
$1,800-2,700

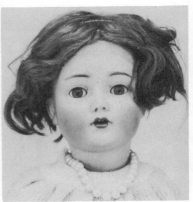

A bisque headed character doll, with blue sleeping, flirting eyes, fair mohair wig, jointed wood and composition body, rubber hands and original underclothes, impressed K*R Simon & Halbig 117N 53, 20in (51cm) high.
$1,800-2,700

An Oriental bisque doll, with almond shaped fixed brown eyes, closed mouth, black wig with pigtail, on straight limbed composition body, moulded red shoes, in contemporary gold and blue printed gown and a cardboard hat, head probably by Simon & Halbig, impressed 3/0, 12in (30cm) high.
$900-1,500

A Kammer & Reinhardt bisque doll, with brown eyes, blonde curly wig, jointed wood and composition body, in original broderie anglaise dress, ivory silk coat and wired bonnet, knitted silk socks and white leather shoes, impressed 73, 29in (73cm) high.
$1,800-2,700

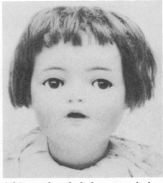

A bisque headed character baby doll, with brown lashed sleeping and flirting eyes, brown mohair wig and bent limbed composition body, marked K*R Simon & Halbig 121 56, 21in (53cm) high.
$720-1,000

Did you know

MILLER'S Antiques Price Guide builds up year by year to form the most comprehensive photo-reference system available.

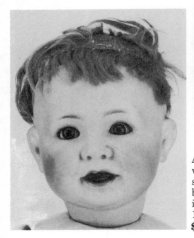

A bisque headed character doll, with open/closed mouth, blue sleeping eyes, fair mohair wig and bent limbed composition body, impressed K*R Simon & Halbig 116/A 42, 16in (41cm) high.
$1,800-2,700

A Simon & Halbig bisque swivel-necked doll, with brown eyes, short blonde wig, closed mouth, applied pierced ears, jointed German style pink kid leather body, bisque lower arms, dressed in a pink taffeta 1880's style gown, trimmed with ribbon and tulle, impressed 13 719 DEP, the breastplate impressed S 13 H 720, damaged, c1885, 29in (74cm) high. **$2,700-3,600**

A bisque headed character doll, with blue sleeping, flirting eyes, brown wig, the jointed wood and composition body with voice box, dressed in knitted outfit and brown leather shoes, impressed K*R Simon & Halbig 117N , 24.5in (62cm) high. **$1,800-2,700**

Jules Steiner

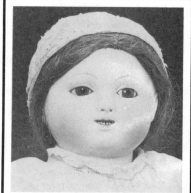

A bisque headed doll, with blue sleeping eyes, moulded brows, flapper knees with short upper leg sections and rigid arms, impressed 1159 SIMON 7 HALBIG S & H 6, 14in (36cm) high. **$1,000-1,500**

A Jules Steiner walking/crying doll, the pale bisque head with fixed blue glass eyes, brown wig over domed head, the fabric covered papier mâché body encasing the clockwork mechanism, with winding key and start/stop lever which causes the doll to agitate its arms and legs and to emit cries, damaged, c1880, 20in (51cm) high. **$1,800-2,700**

Miscellaneous

A limited edition Princess Elizabeth doll, 20.5in (52cm) high. **$1,800-2,700**

A composition Topsy doll, c1940, 12.5in (32cm) high. **$180-360**

A German three-faced doll depicting Red Riding Hood, the Wolf and the Grandmother, one bisque head showing Red Riding Hood with open/closed mouth, fixed blue glass eyes, the grandmother's lined face with smiling closed mouth and fixed blue glass eyes, the brown bisque wolf with painted slanting eyes and red moulded tongue, all under a cardboard cowl and central turning knob, the jointed wood and composition body in blue dress, white apron and top and red waistcoat, cape and lace edged red bonnet, a finely woven basket in her hand, probably by Bergner, c1895, 12.5in (32cm) high. **$7,000-9,000**

A German doll, with a five-piece body, and original clothes, 11.5in (29cm) high. **$180-360**

A painted cloth headed boy doll, with blue-grey eyes with white highlights, separate thumb section and wide hips with five-piece legs, by Kathe Kruse, Doll No. 1, no. on foot 23715, c1920, 17in (43.5cm) high. **$1,800-2,700**

A Steiff felt soldier doll, the face with glass eyes, painted mouth, cap numbered 28, oilskin boots, swivel limbs, c1915, 14in (35cm) high.
$1,200-1,700

A mask headed character doll, modelled as Snow White with black mohair wig, cloth body and original velvet and rayon dress printed 'Snow White and the Seven Dwarfs', 15in (38cm) high, and the Seven Dwarfs, in original outfits, 6.5in (16.5cm) high, all by Chad Valley.
$720-1,000

A Steiff felt soldier doll, the face with centre seam, glass eyes, painted mouth, with jointed limbs, in felt uniform and cap numbered 28, with iron cross, and sword, c1915, 14in (35cm) high.
$1,200-1,700

A pottery shoulder headed doll, with painted brown eyes, open/closed mouth with teeth, moulded hair, stuffed body, pottery arms and original Scottish solder's uniform, impressed G 7, by Goss, stamped on the body British Toy Company, and with swing ticket reading Trade Mark 'WARDOL' Registration applied for, 1915, 13.5in (34.5cm) high.
$900-1,500

Dolls House

An open pine shooting lodge, with galleried attic of 2 rooms, fully furnished, 28.5in (72.5cm) wide.
$1,000-1,500

'The Skelskoer House', with 5 bays, opening central front door with porch and balcony above, fully furnished, c1900, 39in (99cm) wide, and 2 bisque headed women with moulded hair, one in original maid's clothes.   **$2,700-3,600**

A doll's open room, probably Italian, c1770, 18in (46cm) wide.
$3,600-5,000

A German group of 'satinwood' dolls house furniture, with blue silk upholstery, including an elaborate curtained dressing table, a wardrobe with curved doors and drawers and a half-tester bed, c1870, dressing table 6.5in (16.5cm) high.
$1,200-1,700

'Patricia's House', a painted wooden open dolls house, the roof simulating red tiles, with bedroom, nursery, living room and kitchen, including furnishings, 1865, 39in (99cm) wide, and a bisque headed doll with moulded fair hair and circular hairband, 8in (20cm) high.
$2,700-3,600

A pink painted wooden dolls house, with mansard roof, the open back showing 4 rooms, and 3 bisque headed dolls and a bonnet-head baby, 29in (74cm) wide.
$1,800-2,700

'Edith's House', a painted open wooden dolls house with original wallpapers, 4 rooms, and 5 bisque dolls.
$2,700-3,600

A painted wooden two-storey dolls house, with simulated lift-off blue slate roof, and elaborate pink transfer decoration to façade, each section opening and with original striped wallpapers, embossed friezes, paper covered pelmets, net curtains, embossed gilt paper tie-backs with red cotton ribbons, and a set of printed card furniture and dolls, with Christian Hacker printed label on base and pencilled number 138/4 5, c1890, 16.5in (42cm) wide, and a bisque headed doll with high piled hair.
$2,700-3,600

'Anna's Pleasure' a painted wooden house of simulated stone with coining and sand finish, fretted window and door pediments, slate roof and wood grained door, the front removing to reveal one room, the roof lifting to show three attic rooms, furnished as a sitting room, c1860, 38in (96.5cm) wide.
$2,700-3,600

A Regency yew-wood table, 4in (10cm) diam, **$35-70**, and a Wedgwood dinner service, **$35-70 each piece**

A painted tinplate kitchen, the corner stove with hood, a painted glass window at the back, and utensils including a copper hot water bottle, possibly Märklin, late 19thC, 11.5in (29cm) wide.
$1,000-1,500

A wooden dolls house of 5 bays and 2 storeys, painted brown and grey to simulate stone with slate roof, with castellated central tower, dormer windows, hinged front, attic, windows at the sides and remains of furniture including a gilt metal fireplace, early 20thC, 47.5in (120cm) wide.
$1,000-1,500

A J. & G. Lines painted wooden dolls house, No.24, c1909, with 3 bays and 2 storeys, 32.5in (82.5cm) wide, 4 dolls house people, and 3 other dolls.
$7,000-9,000

'Lise's House', a wooden open roomed, separate storey house, painted to simulate brickwork, with elaborate semi-circular decorations above the windows, 37in (94cm) wide, and a Grödnertal doll.
$7,000-9,000

'Villa Gurre', a painted wooden dolls house with 2 bays and 2 storeys, fully furnished, c1920, 32.5in (82.5cm) wide, and 2 bisque headed dolls.
$2,700-3,600

A group of English dolls house furniture, the piano inscribed Samuel Adams, West Bromwich.
$900-1,500

Samuel Adams was a leading musical figure in West Bromwich, being both a piano tuner and dealer, and the owner of St George's Hall, where numerous concerts were held.

A selection of dolls house furniture, c1900.
$1,800-2,700

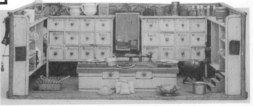

A painted wooden toy grocer's shop, with named drawers, fitted counter, bell, windows, mirror and stock, including bolts of cloth, sugar cones, food on plates, barrels, steps, baskets and items of pottery, 34in (86cm) wide. **$720-1,000**

A collection of European and English dolls house metal and beadwork furniture, damaged, c1900, fire surround 5in (12cm) wide. **$900-1,500**

A group of German dolls house furniture, c1900.
$900-1,500

A group of tinplate dolls house drawing room furniture, painted to simulate wood grain and upholstered in blue silk, by Rock and Graner, c1870, some damage, sofa 7in (18cm) long. **$900-1,500**

A painted wooden toy kitchen, with furnishings including tinplate kitchen range, water holder, cupboard, saucepans, and pottery jugs and bowls, 33in (84cm) wide. **$720-1,000**

A selection of ladies leather shoes and boots, with flower decoration. **$35-70 each**

A group of painted soft metal dolls house furniture, corner table 4in (10cm) high. **$720-1,000**

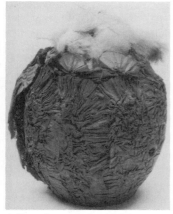

A Georgian yew-wood dresser, by Escutcheon, 11in (28cm) wide. **$180-360**

Two bronze blackamoor statues, by John Hodgson, 4.5in (11.5cm) high. **$180-360**

TOYS
Automata

A French musical rabbit in a cabbage automaton, the white fur rabbit pricking up his ears and rising from inside a fabric cabbage, key wind and stop/start mechanism and with battery compartment to illuminate the eyes, c1890. **$900-1,500**

A French musical automated scene of a carpenter, the papier mâché headed carpenter hammering at his bench in an open room, the pull-string musical and mechanical movement activated by continuously pushing the start knob, under a glass dome, dome missing, 12.5in (32cm) high. **$2,700-3,600**

A French rabbit in a lettuce automaton, the white fur covered animal with glass eyes, within lettuce leaves in a basket, clockwork movement causing him to rise pricking up his ears, movement defective, 6in (15cm) high. **$720-1,000**

A French Lambert automaton of a lady with a fan, the seated figure with a bisque Jumeau head with blue paperweight eyes, bisque lower arms and hands, dressed in exotic Oriental style outfit, when activated she fans herself and moves her left hand and head in time to the music contained in the green velvet covered base, repaired, 17.5in (45cm) high.
$3,600-5,000

A Roullet et Decamps musical drinking bear, the fur covered bear with glass eyes, lifting and pouring liquid from a metal bottle in his right hand into a beaker which he lifts to his mouth while tilting his head back and lowering his jaw, the keywind stop/start musical movement contained within the body, c1910, 16in (40cm) high.
$2,700-3,600

A Roullet et Decamps drinking bear automaton, the red fur covered glass eyed bear seated on his hind legs pouring liquid from a metal bottle into a beaker, lifting it to his face, tilting his head back and lowering his jaw, with keywind stop/start movement, 14in (36cm) high.
$2,700-3,600

A Roullet et Decamps musical automaton of a rabbit in a tree trunk, the white fur rabbit pops out of a papier mâché tree trunk decorated with leaves and grass, c1900, 9in (23cm) high.
$1,200-1,700

An automated display figure, possibly French, with a composition head and fixed blue glass eyes, open/closed mouth, on felt covered base with clockwork motors to base and figure's torso, 27in (69cm) high.
$3,600-5,000

A French walking pig automaton, covered in leather with amber and black glass eyes, wheels to feet, curled tail, clockwork mechanism driving legs and bellows within operating 'oink', 10in (25.5cm) long.
$1,000-1,500

A Decamps jumping lion automaton, early 20thC, 14in (36cm) long, and a nodding peasant on donkey figure, possibly by Roullet, with clockwork mechanism, some damage, 21in (54cm) high.
$900-1,500

A hand-operated musical automaton of 3 bisque headed dolls in original clothes playing instruments, with wooden hands and composition painted boots, impressed 52 10/0, 15in (38cm) wide.
$2,700-3,600

TEDDY BEARS

When Christie's held the world's first all Teddy Bear and Soft Toy sale in December 1985, I said during an interview that I felt the teddy bear craze would be short-lived and that I did not think that prices being achieved then would hold up over a number of years. How nice it is to be wrong.

During this recessionary period it is interesting to note that one of the most healthy areas in the toy collecting field has been in teddy bears and soft toys. Indeed, London appears to be the centre of the trade, dealers coming from Europe and particularly North America and paying bullish prices for good quality teddy bears in good condition, of all colours, makes and styles.

At the end of 1991 $2,600 was paid for a 29in 1908 white Steiff bear as the thighs were worn and it was rather dusty. Compare this price to the $3,550 paid seven months later for a normal pale gold 28in Steiff of 1906, with worn muzzle, recovered pads and no button. These two bears were both large, but we have seen similar increases in tiny ones.

A spray scent bottle inside a red 3in Schuco, fetched $935 in May. These dual purpose animals were popular in the twenties; others were made as compacts, purses, lipsticks, lighters, hot water bottles and manicure sets.

A marvellous 33in Jester bear in fine condition, with pointed cap and bell-trimmed ruff over his blue and yellow parti-coloured body fetched $5,600. There was some discussion as to his manufacture, but the probability was that he was made by Bing.

English bears, if by good makers such as Farnell, Chad Valley, Chiltern, Merrythought or Deans, sell well if in good condition. An incredibly appealing late 1930's, 20in Farnell was sold for $1,500.

German bears are still at the top of the market. A 28in Steiff of 1906 in almost perfect condition fetched $6,000, and a rare pink musical 14in Schuco of the 1920's sold for $1,800 during 1992.

As one would expect, age, quality and condition are all important, but added to these three, rarity of colour and unusual designs are also major factors in determining the price of a bear. Although loved and battered teddies are still bought for sentimental reasons, investment money is being placed in fine and rare bears.

a. An American golden plush covered teddy bear, with hump and growler, pads recovered, 32in (81cm) high. **$720-1,000**

b. 'Billy Winky', a Deans golden plush covered teddy bear, with brown glass eyes and jointed limbs, pads missing, 17in (43cm) high. **$360-540**

c. A Steiff golden plush covered teddy bear, with elongated jointed limbs, cardboard-lined feet and hump, worn, c1907, 28in (71cm) high. **$3,600-5,000**

d. A wicker pram with hood, 2 turned wooden handles and iron rimmed wheels, 29in (73.5cm) high, and a doll's wicker chair. **$180-360**

e. A light brown plush covered teddy bear, with boot button eyes, black stitched nose and claws, felt pads, jointed limbs and slight hump, 15in (38cm) high. **$180-360**

f. Two English golden plush covered teddy bears, with brown glass eyes, cloth pads and growler, one growler inoperative, pre-War, 20in (51cm) high. **$1,000-1,500**

g. A golden plush covered teddy bear, with black stitched nose, glass eyes, elongated limbs, joined claws, stitched across pads and slight hump, probably by Farnell, pads replaced, growler inoperative, c1925, 22in (56cm). **$900-1,500**

A golden plush covered teddy bear with elongated limbs, boot button eyes, wide apart ears, felt pads, pronounced snout, hump, growler and Steiff button in ear, c1907, 28in (71cm) high.
$7,000-9,000

A brown plush Steiff teddy bear, with black stitched snout, black button eyes and swivel jointed body with excelsior filling, button missing, c1908, 24.5in (62cm) high.
$7,000-9,000

A German Schuco yes/no bellboy teddy bear, with orange plush head, hands and feet, amber and black glass eyes, black stitched nose and snout, in red felt jacket and black trousers as torso and limbs, red felt cap at rakish angle, tail operating turning and nodding of head, 15in (38cm) high.   **$2,700-3,600**

A Steiff teddy bear, blonde plush with black button eyes, with button in ear, worn, 26in (66cm) high.
$2,700-3,600

'Ted' originally belonged to Miss Rosa Florella Schmidt who was the daughter of an English mother and German father. In 1914 her father left the family home in Berkshire to return to Germany whilst his wife and daughter remained in England. Unfortunately Herr Schmidt never returned (presumably killed in the war) and this bear, his parting gift to his daughter, became immensely important to the little girl as this was all she had to remember him by. The bear stayed with Rosa all her life apart from a period during World War II when she was teaching in London and decided that he would be safer if he was evacuated to the countryside.

A teddy bear, c1920, 10in (25cm) high.
$180-360

A teddy bear, 18in (46cm) high.   **$180-360**

A teddy bear, 15in (38cm) high.
$180-360

A mid brown plush Steiff teddy bear, early 20thC, 23.5in (60cm) high.
$2,700-3,600

Lead Soldiers & Figures

A boxed set of W. Britains Bedouin Arabs.
$180-360

A Britains King's Troop Royal Horse Artillery gun team, boxed, incomplete.
$360-540

A Britains mounted gun team of The Royal Artillery.
$110-180

A Britains part set of The Knights of Agincourt, comprising a herald, 2 attendants, a tournament marshal and 3 mounted knights, 5 similar mounted knights, and 19 foot knights, various conditions.
$110-180

A Britains King's Troop Royal Artillery trotting gun team, together with an outrider at full gallop, boxed.
$360-540

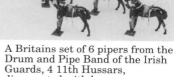

A Britains set of 6 pipers from the Drum and Pipe Band of the Irish Guards, 4 11th Hussars, dismounted with horses,
$180-360

A Britains Coronation set, with box.
$360-540

An imported wooden play box, containing 12 model legionnaires and triple-barrel cannon with lead shot, the box when opened depicts a fort under attack, marked J. Robinson & Son, 172 Regent Street, London, Importers of Scientific Novelties, Opticians and Photographers, c1900.
$360-540

A Britains Royal Navy landing party.
$110-180

A Britains collection of 15 painted lead anthropomorphic animals.
$180-360

A Britains collection of 18 mounted soldiers.
$360-540

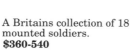

Money Banks

An American cast iron Paddy and the Pig mechanical bank, by J. & E. Stevens, the figure with a blue jacket, the pig kicks the coin placed on his snout into Paddy's mouth, the base with patent date and coin trap, c1885, 7in (18cm).
$1,800-2,700

A painted cast iron 'Paddy and the Pig' mechanical bank, by J. & E. Stevens, designed by James H. Bowen, the pig's forepaw striking a coin into the figure's mouth, dark blue coat variant, with coin trap, 7in (18cm) long.
$2,700-3,600

An American Shepherd Hardware Company Stump Speaker cast iron mechanical bank, patent date on base, some paint chipping, c1880, 10in (25cm) high.
$3,600-5,000

'Magie Bank', a German lithographed tinplate mechanical bank of a wizard, with lever operated arms, standing behind a brightly decorated table, tray missing, 7in (18cm) high.
$1,000-1,500

A German tinplate sentry bank, for Lyon's toffee, the articulated figure raises his gun to present position, moves his eyes and accepts coin when the top lever is pressed, the back with cartoon figures, minor surface wear, 9in (22cm) high. **$1,000-1,500**

A German lithographed tinplate 'Saluting Sailor' money bank, possibly by Saalheimer and Strauss, the sailor standing in front of the gun breech, with spring-loaded saluting action, coin slot 'hidden' by his left elbow and key, c1920, 7in (18cm) high.
$1,200-1,700

Tinplate

A collection of Dinky diecast toys, comprising 20 boxed and 35 unboxed cars, mixed conditions, 1945-52.
$2,700-3,600

A Tippco clockwork tinplate Mercedes 770K 'Wagen des Führers' staff car with electrically lit headlights, in black and blued steel finish, 1939, some damage, 9in (23cm) long.
$1,000-1,500

A Karl Bub clockwork lithographed tinplate four-door limousine, with chauffeur in open-front compartment, opening side doors, tinplate artillery wheels, side lamps and headlamps, finished in lined red over black, c1912, 14in (36cm) long. **$2,700-3,600**

A Corgi Batmobile, No. 267, boxed.
$180-360

A Schuco Studio 1050 tinplate
clockwork model driving school
racing car, boxed.
$180-360

A Hessmobil 1024 lithographed
tinplate limousine, c1920, 10in
(25cm) long. **$720-1,000**

A French wood and tinplate four-
seat open touring car, probably by
Jouets de Paris, with mahogany
and unpainted tin, the seats
covered in maroon silk, with cast
steering wheel and red painted
spoked wheels, and white rubber
tyres, 11.5in (29cm) long.
$1,800-2,700

A Bing lithographed tinplate
clockwork four-seat open tourer,
Cat. Ref. 10480/2, finished in
maroon with dark red and cream
lining, brake, steering front
wheels and tan 'buttoned' seats,
chauffeur missing, c1914, 10.5in
(26.5cm) long.
$1,800-2,700

A Distler lithographed tinplate
clockwork six-light saloon car
with electrically lit front indicator
and brake light, chauffeur,
opening windscreen and opening
rear doors, Cat. Ref. 667, finished
in blue over black with red lining,
one door and mascot missing,
c1920, 14in (36cm) long.
$720-1,000

A Märklin 'Der Kleine Spediteur'
clockwork cart, carrying 3 milk
churns, 3 wooden crates, paper
and string wrapped parcel, and 3
cotton sacks, 8in (21cm) long.
$2,700-3,600

A Rossignol clockwork
lithographed tinplate two-door
two-tone green roadster, with
Peugeot-style grille, registration
91-CR-921, front wheel drive and
rear wheel steering, 13in (33cm)
long.
$720-1,000

A French JEP tinplate Bugatti
racing car, finished in white,
numbered 4 and detailed in red,
with pressed tin wheels small
lithographed driver, adjustable
front axle, clockwork motor
driving rear wheels with integral
key, 16.5in 42cm) long.
$1,200-1,700

A Lehmann clockwork
lithographed tinplate EPL No.
760, racing car, finished in blue
and yellow, 6in (15cm) long.
$720-1,000

A Bing tinplate taxi, finished in
scarlet and maroon, with black
roof, hinged rear doors, adjustable
front wheels, handbrake, white
rubber tyres on spoked wheels,
clockwork motor driving rear
wheels, applied lithographed
maker's plaque to rear, worn,
c1909, 10in (26cm) long.
$3,600-5,000

A Distler clockwork lithographed
tinplate four-light limousine,
finished in blue over black, with
artillery wheels folding bevelled
glass windscreen, chauffeur,
steering, opening doors and 2
boxes on running-boards, c1920,
12in (31cm) long.
$2,700-3,600

A Distler tinplate limousine, the clockwork vehicle lithographed in dark blue with pastel blue lining, light green spoked wheels and finished in thick lacquer in parts, uniformed chauffeur, front lamps, glazed front windscreen and opening rear doors, damaged, c1920, 12in (30.5cm) long.
$1,200-1,700

A tinplate clockwork open top double decker Electric Omnibus Company bus, early 20thC.
$360-540

A Buick tinplate police car by Ichiko of Japan, with push-and-go mechanism, rotating roof lights and retractable roof radar, with original box.
$70-145

A Chad Valley lithographed tinplate single deck Greenline bus, finished in green, as a Windsor service, with hollow tin wheels, clockwork motor driving rear wheels, 12in (30cm) long.
$1,200-1,700

An André Citroen clockwork painted tinplate B2 10hp Torpedo four-seat tourer, finished in blue, with leathercloth seats and folded hood, windscreen, steering and brake, in original box inscribed 'Noel 1925', box repaired, 15in (38cm) long.
$1,800-2,700

A Minic tinplate double decker London Transport bus, in red and cream with 'Ovaltine' and 'Bovril' advertisements, and a Minic tinplate single deck Greenline bus with 'Bisto' advertisement on the back and Dorking destination board.
$180-360

A Hans Eberl tinplate clockwork limousine, lithographed in red, black and yellow, with 'pyjama' striping to rear coachwork, grey roof, running boards and mudguards, complete with driver, opening doors, glass windscreen, removable lights and key, 14in (35.5cm) long.
$1,800-2,700

A Japanese tinplate 1950 type Cadillac saloon, finished in 2-tone blue with push-and-go mechanism, in original box.
$35-70

A 'Rico' (Richards & Co) lithographed tinplate novelty turnover clown car, with 'patchwork' surface in red, blue, and yellow, pressed tin wheels with clown faces to hubs, pressed tin clown driver, clockwork motor driving rear wheels, damaged, 10.5in (26.5cm) long.
$2,700-3,600

A Bing clockwork painted tinplate two-seat motor car, Cat. Ref. 14138/4, finished in yellow with red lining and red 'buttoned' seats, with single headlamp, full-length mudguards, steering and hollow rubber tyres, c1906, 8.5in (21.5cm) long.
$1,800-2,700

A Märklin painted tin train station, with a red mansard roof, pierced windows, a hinged door, and outdoor passenger covered waiting area, a bench and a ticket office, finished in yellow on a green base, c1920, 18in (46cm) long.
$1,800-2,700

A Märklin painted tin Central Station, the central tower with hipped roof, flag, foliate eaves, and arched pierced glazed windows, with a waiting room and telegraph room, 2 hinged doors revealing candles, 14in (36cm) long.
$3,600-5,000

A Bing painted tin train station, with 6 pierced windows, a central entrance hall, a textured tiled roof and the walls painted to simulate brick, c1905, 14in (36cm) long.
$720-1,000

A Bing painted tin train station 'Central Bahnhof', with a double mansard roof, 4 hinged doors and a pierced railing surrounding the whole station, finished in cream with grey trim on a green base, 13in (33cm) long.
$1,800-2,700

A Lehmann 'Mars' No. 825 tank, in lithographed grey tinplate, with clockwork mechanism and rubber tyres, marked Jane, driver missing, c1940, 5.5in (14cm) long.
$720-1,000

A Doll & Co. tinplate rope railway, with 2 hand painted tin cars running on metal chains between ground level and mountain huts, turning handle on the side, 14in (36cm) wide.
$1,000-1,500

A Lehmann tinplate novelty 'Ski Rolf' toy, marked EPL 781, the figure dressed in blue, on mustard yellow skis, clockwork mechanism to torso, 7.5in (19cm) high, together with a Mickey Mouse clockwork handcar, with 4 wheels, lithographed red with image of Goofy running, and painted composition figures of Mickey and Minnie, 7in (18cm) long.
$2,700-3,600

A Roullet et Decamps clockwork acrobat on a tricycle, the figure with a bisque head and brown glass eyes balances on his hands on his bike, wearing a red and white silk clown costume, the clockwork mechanism activates his hands on the front wheels and the bike to move and his head moves side to side, 11in (28cm) long.   **$2,700-3,600**

A French tinplate clockwork model speedboat.
$180-360

An American Lionel painted tin
clockwork 'Speed Craft' No. 44,
with driver and passenger,
finished in white and red,
complete with a stand and
instructions, in its original box,
17in (43cm) long.
$1,200-1,700

A German
painted tin
clockwork
bicyclist toy, the
mechanism
activates the rear
tyre and the legs,
one leg missing,
8in (20cm) long.
$900-1,500

A Japanese Nomura 'Mechanised Robot', 'Robby',
battery operated tinplate toy, with silver finish,
perspex dome to head covering mechanism with 4
working pistons, antennae to sides to dome, black
rubber hands, black painted feet, legs with battery
compartments, start/stop lever to chest, in original
cardboard box, 12.5in (32cm) high, together with
a Masudaya Radicon Radio Remote Control bus,
with silver finish, black rubber tyres, in original
cardboard box, with control unit and instructions,
14in (36cm) long.   **$7,000-9,000**

A German tinplate clockwork
motorcycle and rider, by Arnold,
the side mounting rider seated on
a Mac 700 bike with coloured
lithographed details, 8in (20cm)
long.
$360-540

A Danish hand painted tinplate
fire pumper toy, finished in red,
gold, and black, with pressed tin
wheels and 2 figures, pulled by a
white horse, some paint loss, 14in
(35cm) long.
$1,800-2,700

A Wolverine painted and
lithographed tinplate clockwork
No. 48 'Zilotone', with clown
musician playing xylophone,
controlled by cam-action tune
disc, with discs for Silent Night,
The Farmer in the Dell, and
Listen to the Mocking Bird,
c1920, 7in (18cm) high.
$900-1,500

A hand painted tinplate horse
drawn carriage, possibly by
Buchner, the body finished in
cream lined blue and orange, with
opening doors, grey lined white
undercarriage and suspension,
spoked cast wheels, pulled by 2
brown painted carved wood
horses, mid-19thC.
$1,800-2,700

A Lehmann clockwork tinplate tricycle, 20thC, 5in (13cm) long.
$110-180

A German tinplate clockwork 'Mickey Mouse' organ grinder toy, probably Distler, Mickey as grinder to side, miniature Minnie to top dancing to accompany him, clockwork mechanism within bright hurdy-gurdy organ, pressed tin wheels, damaged, 8in (20cm) high.
$3,600-5,000

An American clockwork velocipede, possibly by George Hawkins and William Farr Goodwin, the tricycle decorated in red with floral stencil work and blue cast iron wheels, 9in (23cm) long.
$1,000-1,500

A painted tinplate horse drawn cabriolet, probably French, finished in yellow with black lining, with silk lined folding leathercloth hood, blue buttoned silk upholstery, rein rail, 2 whip sockets, rubber tyres and C-springs, c1890, 14in (36cm) long.
$720-1,000

Miscellaneous

A French pink suede covered clockwork walking pig, 11.5in (30cm) long.
$180-360

'Negro', a felt-covered clockwork walking figure by Schuco, dressed as a bell-hop, with on/off switch on his back, some damage, c1920, 10in (25cm) high.
$2,700-3,600

A painted wooden frog, with glass eyes, tin flippers and clockwork swimming mechanism.
$360-540

A carved carousel frog, by Herschell-Spillman Co., North Tonawanda, New York, painted green, with yellow waistcoat and orange shorts, c1914, 42in (107cm) long.
$20,000-25,000

A painted papier mâché Mickey Mouse display, probably English, the cartoon figure in characteristic pose, some paint loss to ears, c1950, 36in (92cm) high.
$1,200-1,700

A painted papier mâché Donald Duck display, probably English, c1950, slight paint loss, 26in (66cm) high.   **$720-1,000**

A painted pine rocking horse, sponge decorated in green and white, the rockers painted red with black highlights, 58in (147cm) long. **$1,200-1,400**

A matchstick construction model of an Austin Seven touring motor car, made by the late Alec Sales of Hull, reputedly using in excess of 40,000 matches to complete over a period of 18 months, 35in (89cm) long. **$180-360**

A child's carved wooden horse, painted in naturalistic colours and wearing a red fabric bridle and saddle, standing on a platform and 4 wheels, 20.5in (52cm) high. **$360-540**

A French wood and metal pull-along child's car, dark green with red and yellow striped panels, red undercarriage, wooden spoked wheels with iron rims, leather trim with brass beading, ceramic handle to draw bar, restored, c1903, 26in (66.5cm) wide. **$7,000-9,000**

An American Gendron Packard twin six pedal car, original red with black and yellow lining and black wings, wooden chassis, pressed steel body and wings, opening door, cast iron steps, bell-type headlamps, drum rear lights, opening boot, imitation dashboard, side-mounted spare wheel with cover, adjustable windscreen, imitation ignition control to wood-rimmed steering wheel, solid rubber tyres, unrestored, c1927, 65.5in (166cm) long. **$10,000-12,000**

An Italian Giordini Indianapolis pedal car, in Italian racing red with cream vinyl upholstery, pressed steel construction, chromium plated external exhausts, windscreen, imitation brake drums, electric horn, one rear view mirror, racing number 6, solid tyres, c1950, 50.5in (128cm) long. **$1,200-1,700**

A French veteran pedal car, dark blue with light blue panels and cream lining, with wooden body, steel undercarriage, radially spoked wheels with solid rubber tyres, wood rimmed steering wheel, steps, oil lamps, deep buttoned upholstery, restored, 1905, 49in (124.5cm) long. **$10,000-12,000**

A child's pedal sports car, probably by Lines Brothers, c1950. **$1,200-1,700**

An H. J. Mulliner MG two-door drophead pedal car, maroon with beige, coachbuilt with hand made aluminium panels, opening bonnet, near side door and boot, removable spats, electric lights and horn, internal handbrake, perspex windscreen, ace-type rear number plate box, chromium-plated bumber bars with overriders, solid rubber tyres, c1939, 56in (142cm) long. **$14,500-16,500**

A scratch-built Ferrari Testarossa 250 child's sports car, yellow, welded box-section steel chassis, fibreglass body, polished alloy wood-rimmed steering wheel, working lights and brakes, tonneau cover, clutchless transmission, pneumatic tyres, unused, 1958, 74in (188cm) long.
$3,600-5,000

A Phillips 4.5 litre supercharged Bentley child's electric car, British racing green, fibreglass body with wood and steel strengthening, 4-wheel cable operated drum brakes, cast aluminium dummy supercharger, electric lights, external handbrake, foot accelerator and brake pedals, gear change lever, side-mounted spare wheel, tonneau cover, pneumatic tyres, wire spoked wheels, 12-volt electric motor with belt drive to lay shaft and chain drive to back axle, c1965, 76in (193cm) long.   **$7,000-9,000**

A scratch built Bentley 3 litre pedal car, British racing green, pressed steel, part fabric covered, opening bonnet with leather strap, external handbrake lever, bucket seat, perspex windscreen, spare wheel mounted at the rear, wire spoked wheels, pneumatic tyres, c1980, 56in (142cm) long.
$3,600-5,000

An Austin J40 pedal car, red with black upholstery, heavy gauge pressed steel, dummy engine, opening boot and bonnet, handbrake, lights, pneumatic tyres, restored, c1955, 60in (152cm) long.   **$1,800-2,700**

A Lines Brothers Bullnose Morris pedal car, field grey with black mudguards, wooden chassis and wood and metal body, opening door, fold-back windscreen, adjustable seat, pressed steel wheels, rubber tyres, in original condition, c1927, 42in (107cm) long.   **$7,000-9,000**

A group of hand carved, painted wood and fabric marionettes, from the story of Alice in Wonderland, probably Pittsburgh, Pennsylvania, 6 pieces, early 20thC.
$1,000-1,200

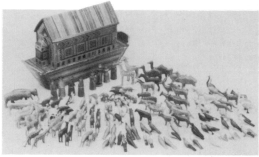

A German carved and painted wood hunting set, comprising 5 mounted figures and 10 hounds, some woodworm, c1920, figures 7in (18cm) high.
$1,800-2,700

A coloured straw-work Noah's Ark, with sliding panel and a quantity of painted wooden animals including Noah's family, damaged, 13in (33cm) long.   **$1,800-2,700**

A German painted wooden Noah's Ark, finished in cream and brown, with hollow bottom, lower storey fitted with three fenced stables, falling front, upper storey with removable front, sloping half hinged roof, with about 35 painted animals, worn, late 19thC, 22in (55cm) long.
$1,800-2,700

Models

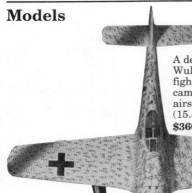

A detailed model of the Focke-Wulf Fw 190-A6 single-seater fighter, serial No. 1-5, finished in camouflage and mounted on an airstrip plinth, glazed case, 6in (15.5cm) wide.
$360-540

A flying model of the Westland Lysander, Serial No. V 9350, with fabric covered wooden airframe, glow-plug engine, carburettor and fuel tank removed, rubber tyred undercarriage and finished in RAF camouflage, 59in (150cm) wingspan.
$360-540

A large scale flying model of a Messerschmitt Me 323 'Gigant', with provision for 6 engines, 72in (183cm) long.
$720-1,000

A flying model of a Curtiss Tomahawk, engine removed, 60in (152.5cm) wingspan.
$360-540

A flying model of the Fokker D VIII parasol monoplane, Serial No. 238, with glow-plug engine, finished in green, red and yellow with Maltese crosses, 52in (132cm) wingspan.
$360-540

A detailed 1:24 scale static display model of the Supermarine Spitfire Mk. IX, Serial No. MH486, in the camouflage and markings of 132 Sqn., RAF, built by T. Scott, c1944, 19in (48cm) wingspan.
$720-1,000

A detailed flying model of the Fokker DR1, Serial No. 152/17, with glow-plug engine, finished in red, red and white stripes, and green, with Maltese crosses, 46in (117cm) wingspan.
$720-1,000

A flying model of the Supermarine Seagull prototype, finished in green and cream with RAF markings, 57in (145cm) wingspan.   **$360-540**

A detailed flying model of the Sopwith Camel, C1701, Fiji 19 glow-plug engine, 56in (142.5cm) wingspan.
$720-1,000

'Battle of Britain Flypast', a 1:144 scale aluminium model of the RAF Memorial Flight Lancaster, Spitfire and Hurricane, by Doug Vaan, 9.5in (24cm) wide.
$360-540

A Karl Bub 0-4-0 O gauge electric locomotive, No. 1-48, in green, red and pale green livery, some damage, 10.5in (26cm) long. **$110-180**

A Lionel 2-4-0 'Bild-a-Loco' electric locomotive No. 384, in black livery with brass mounts, 12in (31cm) long. **$110-180**

A German Doll et Cie tinplate model steam engine, with vertical boiler and horizontal engine, dummy boiler and mounted on a 4-wheel chassis, altered, 12.5in (32cm) wide. **$360-540**

A Bassett Lowke Gauge I electric 2-6-0 locomotive, finished in LMS maroon and black, with matching 6-wheeled tender numbered 13000 in gold, some damage, 25in (63cm) long. **$1,200-1,700**

A model of an English 1830 stagecoach, in black, blue and red livery and brass mounts, supported on a wooden plinth, 20thC, 10in (25.5cm) high. **$360-540**

A Hornby 0-Gauge 'Princess Elizabeth' 20-volt 4-6-2 locomotive and tender with original presentation box, complete with illustrated details inside lid, c1937. **$3,600-5,000**

A model of a cargo vessel, Lexden Hall, the wooden hull painted black and salmon pink, uncased, early 20thC, 102in (259cm) long. **$3,600-5,000**

A pine five-masted schooner, The Gaspe Trader, mounted on a shaped wood stand, c1930, 53in (135cm) long. **$3,000-4,000**

GAMES
Chess Sets

A Cantonese red and natural ivory chess set, each carved piece on pierced concentric ball pedestal bases, kings 7in (17cm) high, together with a highly decorated lacquered chess/backgammon board with mother-of-pearl white squares, and a vellum-covered carrying case, late 19thC. **$720-1,000**

A four-handed chess set, comprising 4 tournament sized sets of Staunton pattern, one of natural ivory, one red stained ivory, one boxwood, and one ebony, with a booklet containing 'Rules and a List of Members of the London Four-Handed Chess Club', and another blue covered booklet with gold lettering 'Rules of the Game of Four-Handed Chess', and with large folding chess board of mahogany with satinwood and ebony squares, in an oak case with brass handles, some damage, c1880, kings 4.5in (11.5cm) high. **$5,000-8,000**

Miscellaneous Games

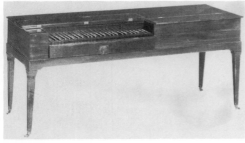

A 'Novelty Merchantman' Crane by the Exhibit Supply Co. Chicago, the crane takes the form of the bow end of a merchant ship with the grab as a derrick mounted on the foredeck, contained in glazed wood and cast iron case, 71in (180cm) high.
$900-1,500

A JEP platform car racing game, with circular track around which 5 small cast racers spin by lever mechanism, with lid, box base covered in black textured paper, 10.5in (27cm) wide.
$720-1,000

A Bryans Quadmatic Allwin, with 2 Elevenses Allwins, a 7-cup Allwin with 5 winning and 2 losing cups, and a U-Win Allwin with one large U-shaped winning cup and 2 smaller losing cups, 66in (167.5cm) high.
$1,200-1,700

MUSIC
Musical Instruments

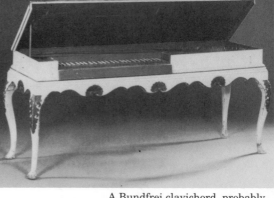

A Bundfrei clavichord, by Pehr Lindholm, Stockholm, the facia board of mahogany with boxwood stringing, the case of mahogany, the four and a half octave keyboard with ebony naturals and bone overlaid accidentals, on frame stand with square tapered legs, labelled on the soundboard Förfardigadt af Pehr Lindholm, Instrumentmakare Stockholm ar 1792, 64in (163.5cm) long.
$10,000-12,000

> Clavichords were the first stringed instruments with keyboards, the predecessor of the piano.

A Bundfrei clavichord, probably Danish, the interior and the keyboard surround painted red, the 5 octave keyboard with ebony naturals and ivory overlaid accidentals, bistrung throughout and with additional 4ft. stringing in the bass up to f, on 4 cabriole legs carved with gilded acanthus leaves on the knees, inscribed Factum Anno 1768, Rep. 1918 Hockauf, 69in (175cm) long, c1770.
$14,500-16,500

A mahogany cased baby grand piano, by Bechstein with plain repolished case, no. 240228, 59in (149.5cm) wide, together with a mahogany duet stool.
$2,700-3,600

A walnut cased baby grand piano by Hagspiel, Dresden, with ripple mouldings and 2 brass pedals on a lyre-shaped support, raised on 3 tapered octagonal legs with brass casters, 70in (177cm) long.
$2,700-3,600

A grand piano, by Bechstein, model B, no. 105019, the ebonised case with tapering octagonal legs and brass casters, 80in (203cm) long.
$1,800-2,700

A boudoir grand piano, by Bechstein, the walnut case on 3 pairs of tapering square legs with brass casters, 81in (205.5cm) long.
$3,600-5,000

An English chamber barrel organ, on a stand containing spare barrel, c1800, 51in (130cm) high.
$1,800-2,700

A grand piano, by John Broadwood & Son, in a crossbanded mahogany case with satinwood interior and inscribed nameboard, on a mahogany trestle stand with brass casters, c1806, 89.5in (227cm) long.
$7,000-9,000

An Art Deco style walnut cased baby grand piano, by Monington & Veston of London, on inlaid block supports, with iron frame overstrung movement, no. 60013, 50in (127cm) long.
$2,700-3,600

A rare German 32in Polyphon Concerto orchestrion, the coin-operated 101 key movement playing on side and bass drums, cymbals, 10 tubular bells and symmetrical piano, driven by massive spring, contained in stained wood case with double doors at the front with etched glass panels, pediment above with trade name, on matching base with drop front for disc storage together with 10 metal discs, restored, c1905, 103.5in (262cm) high.
$40,000-45,000

The Polyphon Concerto was the largest of the Polyphon disc machines and was only produced in very limited numbers. Regina imported the Polyphon Concerto and sold it in the U.S.A. as the Regina Sublims.

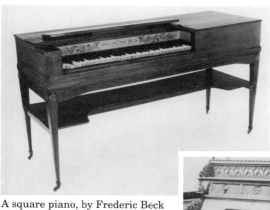

A square piano, by Frederic Beck of Broad Street, Soho, with mahogany and inlaid case-on-stand, with square tapering supports and brass paterae headers, dated 1790.
$1,800-2,700

A Gothic revival straight strung piano, by Gebruder Knake, Munster, the oak case pierced and carved, with brass candle arms and side handles, 64in (162.5cm) wide.
$1,800-2,700

A Seybold & Hohner 'Magic Organa' automatic accordian, the paper roll mechanism operated by foot pedal, contained in original case with separate case for foot pedal and with 7 paper rolls.
$3,600-5,000

A Tanzbar automatic concertina, by A. Zuleger of Leipzig, the paper roll mechanism operated by crank lever mounted on the side in conjunction with bellows, complete with rewind handle, and 12 paper rolls, 10in (26cm) wide.
$1,200-1,700

The foot operated vacuum pump was designed to be operated unobtrusively. The vacuum supply tube could be connected from the separate foot pump to the accordian by running the tube up the operator's trouser leg, through his shirt, and out through his shirt sleeve, at which point it was connected to the accordian.

A violin, by Sebastian Vuillaume, Paris, labelled Jean Baptiste Vuillaume à Paris, 3 rue Demours-Ternes JBV 1965, with the certificate of Hulmuth A. Keller, Philadelphia, 7th April 1969, the one-piece back of medium curl descending from left to right, the ribs of similar curl, the head of faint narrow curl, the table of fine grain in the centre opening out towards the flanks, the varnish of a red brown colour, the back 14in (36cm) long, in a case with outer canvas cover.
$10,000-12,000

A violin, by Emile Laurent, labelled Fait par Emile Laurent/à Paris l'an 1928, inscribed by the maker, the 2-piece back of medium curl, the ribs and scroll similar, the table of open grain, red colour varnish over a golden ground, the back 14in (36cm) long.
$3,600-5,000

An Italian violin, school of Gabrielli, attributed to Pier Lorenzo Vangelisti, the 2-piece back of broad figure, similar ribs, the scroll of plain wood, the table of medium to open grain, dark golden varnish over a lighter ground, the back 14in (36cm) long, with a letter from W. E. Hill & Sons dated 18 May 1953.
$14,500-16,500

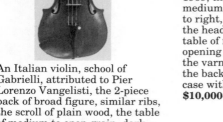

A gold mounted violin bow, by François Nicolas Voirin, branded F. N. Voirin à Paris, the round stick mounted with a gold and ebony frog with Paris eye and gold-sheathed adjuster, 60.5gr.
$14,500-16,500

A self-rehairing viola bow, Pajeot/Maire style, unbranded, the round stick mounted with a nickel and ebony frog and adjuster, 64gr.
$2,700-3,600

A Cremona school violin, with exceptionally wide lower bouts, the 2-piece back of wood cut on the slab of narrow horizontal curl, the ribs of similar wood, the head probably later of medium curl, the table of medium to fine grain, golden brown varnish, c1700, the back 14.5in (36cm).
$7,000-9,000

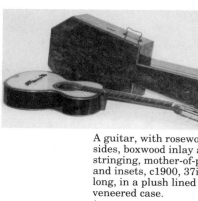

An English seven-keyed Serpent, the body of leather bound wood, brass mounts, brass keys with circular covers, ivory bushed fingerholes, one missing, brass crook, ivory and brass mouthpiece from another instrument, c1835, 102in (259cm) long.
$3,600-5,000

A guitar, with rosewood back and sides, boxwood inlay and stringing, mother-of-pearl bands and insets, c1900, 37in (94cm) long, in a plush lined burr walnut veneered case.
$360-540

A six-course guitar, ascribed to Francesco Sanguino, the table with extensive inlays in mother-of-pearl and various woods both around the sound hole, c1780, 18.5in (47cm) long.
$10,000-12,000

A walnut and giltwood harp, by Jackson, 7 Molesworth Street, Dublin, with 8 foot pedals, the maker's name inscribed on the brass harmonica curve, 66in (167.5cm) high.
$1,200-1,700

A Regency bird's-eye maple harp, by I. & I. Erat, with gilt-gesso neo-Grecque mouldings, the brass plate engraved I. & I. Erat, patent Harp Manufacturers, 23 Berners Street, London, No. 2217, 68in (172.5cm) high.
$27,000-36,000

A cross strung harp, inscribed Harpe S** G Lyon B**, Pleyel Wolff Lyon & Cie, Paris, 73in (185cm) high.
$7,000-9,000

An 11-keyed boxwood oboe, probably German, with detachable top finial, ivory mounts, brass keys with circular covers, c1860, 21.5in (55cm) long.
$1,800-2,700

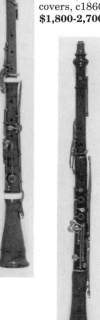

A 10-keyed boxwood oboe, by Jacques Nonon, Paris, with onion and cotton reel finial, brass mounts, brass keys including the Brille key, the Eflat key with duplicate touchpiece, stamped Nonon, Paris, with the device of a treble clef, 22in (56cm) long.
$2,700-3,600

Musical Boxes

A Swiss orchestral cylinder musical box, with 16in (41cm) cylinder playing 8 airs, with snare drum, 8 bells and castanets in sight by Nicole Frères, No. 43590, retailed by John A. Mills, London, in floral marquetry rosewood case with gilt brass side handles, 19thC, 26in (66cm) wide. **$3,600-5,000**

A Swiss Sublime Harmony interchangeable cylinder musical box-on-stand, each of the six 39cm cylinders playing a selection of 8 popular airs, raised on 4 ebonised wood cabriole legs, 50in (127cm) long.
$18,000-21,000

A Grand Format musical box, by Nicole Frères, No. 32027, playing 4 overtures (Freischutz, Robert le Diable, William Tell and La Fille du Regiment), Gamme No. 1500, with lever wind, 3-wing governor, engraved tune sheet, Imhof & Mukle instructions for key-wind boxes, and label on base, the rosewood veneered case inlaid on front and lid in brass, enamel and mother-of-pearl, 28.5in (72cm) wide, on a later fitted walnut stand with turned legs.
$27,000-36,000

A Polyphon disc musical box, the coin-operated movement with periphery drive and twin combs, contained in upright wood case with glazed door at the front, and sides with coin chute and winding handle, surmounted by shaped pediment, c1900, 48in (122cm) high, and 12 metal discs.
$7,000-9,000

A German Symphonion 'rococo' disc musical box, the sublime harmonie comb arrangement contained in ornately mounded wood case with velvet lined lid interior inset with coloured silk print of an amorous couple, c1905, 19in (48cm) wide, with approximately 38 metal discs.
$3,600-5,000

A Swiss figured walnut, amboyna and eboniséd cased Sublime Harmony musical box, the 13in (33cm) interchangeable brass cylinder and 2 comb movement playing 6 airs, with butterfly shaped fly wheel, no. 15976, the case inlaid with mother-of-pearl and brass, with kingwood banding and strung with ebony and box, and with gilt brass foliate cast fixed handles to the sides, 19thC, 40in (102cm) long.
$3,600-5,000

A Swiss and English Bremond mandoline, interchangeable cylinder musical box-on-stand, each of the six 33cm cylinders playing 6 airs as indicated by pointer and listed on tune sheet, contained in walnut veneered case and mounted on non-original aesthetic movement mahogany table with 2 cylinder storage drawers in the front, c1880, 41in (104cm) wide.
$7,000-9,000

Phonographs

A 'Puck' type phonograph, with green and gold painted base cast as a mermaid, floating reproducer, flower horn, maker's carton, instruction sheet and dealer's letter dated 1908.
$1,800-2,700

The letter, sent out by the United Phonograph Co., of 5 Helmet Row, E.C., indicates that the phonograph was being offered as a promotional scheme with an option to 12 cylinders.
A circular on the instruction sheet offers a free gramophone to the purchaser of 50 cylinders, or to a customer selling 8 phonographs among friends. By July 1908, a company with large stocks of Puck phonographs would have been very anxious to dispose of them by any means.

A cabinet phonograph, incorporating a Model A Edison Triumph mechanism 45035 with 2-speed pulley and Diamond C reproducer connected via telescopic tapered brass arm to a flower horn within the cabinet, with approximately 24 two minute and four minute cylinders, 49in (124.5cm) high.
$2,700-3,600

An Edison Fireside phonograph, Model A, no. 93470, with Model R large diaphragm reproducer, no. 10 Cygnet horn, now with Music Master style transfer, substitute crane, repolished pale oak case and replica Model K reproducer, gear cover missing.
$2,700-3,600

An Edison 'Red Gem' phonograph, model D, no. 359142, with Model K reproducer, on an oak plinth beneath a bentwood cover with carrying handle, together with a red painted 'Fireside' horn and horn crane.
$720-1,000

An Edison 'Gem' phonograph, cased with aluminium horn and 12 rolls, winding handle missing.
$360-540

An Edison Concert phonograph, Model A No. C6840, now with combination pulley, standard and slip-on Concert mandrel, C reproducer with adapter, Triton motor, Edison Bell plaque, oak case with banner transfer and brass carrying handles, and large brass horn with folding tripod stand, 40in (102cm) long.
$1,800-2,700

Gramophones

A Dulcephone horn gramophone, with Dulcephone single-spring motor in walnut case with carved mouldings, Dulcephone (Lindstroem 'Reform') soundbox on ball-jointed arm and green flower horn.
$720-1,000

Dulcephone was the main brand name of Barnett Samuel up to 1914. Although both motor and back bracket are cast with the name this machine is clearly of Lindstroem manufacture.

A Monarch Senior gramophone by Gramophone & Typewriter Co., with original brass horn, c1904.
$1,800-2,700

An 'Academy' mahogany gramophone, the cabinet decorated with white string inlay and transferred urn and swags, hinged lid opening to reveal turn table, with 2 doors which open to reveal speakers, supported on 4 square tapered splay legs and circular platform, 20thC.
$360-540

A Peter Pan alarm clock gramophone, c1925.
$2,700-3,600

483

An HMV Model 510 cabinet gramophone, with Lumière pleated diaphragm, quadruple spring motor and quarter veneered oak case with ebony stringing to doors, horizontally divided record compartment, and cabriole legs, c1924, 43.5in (110cm) high.
$2,700-3,600

A 'Trade Mark' gramophone, by the Gramophone Company, no. 5219, with March '98 Patent date, Clark-Johnson soundbox no. J19297, lacquered brass horn, leather elbow, record clamp, winding crank and cam-and-spring brake, the oak case with Gramophone Co. and Wallace Ash, Southsea transfers, c1898, a teak carrying case, a 7in Berliner record of God Save the Queen, and 4 other Berliner records, 2 cracked.
$3,600-5,000

A Cliftophone bijou grand gramophone, in oak cabinet on twist turned legs, with Cliftophone horizontal soundbox, internal wood horn with transfer enclosing panelled doors and gilt fittings, c1924, 32.5in (82cm) high.
$720-1,000

An EMG handmade gramophone, the papier-mâché horn with 28in (71cm) diameter mouth, and an oak case with 12in (31cm) turntable, c1930.
$3,600-5,000

A German double spring gramophone, with Art Nouveau light oak case and painted tin horn, 23in (59cm) diam.
$720-1,000

A Columbia disc gramophone, with original brass horn, c1912.
$1,800-2,700

A Klingsor gramophone, in oak case with pierced door to upper compartment containing horn aperture and strings and Klingsor soundbox in lower compartment with sloping flap, 27in (69cm) high.
$1,200-1,700

A horn gramophone, by H.M.V., with 12in turntable, Exhibition soundbox, mahogany horn and base with trade transfers, together with needle tin and accredited dealer enamelled badge, c1912.   **$720-1,000**

A Mark XB 'Tropical' handmade gramophone, by EMG Handmade Gramophones Ltd., 6 Newman St., with four-spring soundbox, Paillard GGR double-spring motor, crossbanded oak case and two-piece papier-mâché horn, 29.5in (75cm) diam.
$3,600-5,000

A 'His Master's Voice' horn gramophone, with patent dates for 1905 and examination date for 1913, 28in (71cm) high.
$1,200-1,700

A Victorian penny-in-the-slot type Polyphon, by Nicole Frères, the twin combs playing 15.5in (39cm) discs, in an upright walnut cabinet with architectural features, 34in (86cm) high, and 30 discs of popular songs, etc., in an oak case.
$10,000-12,000

A walnut cased wall mounted penny-in-slot Polyphon disc player, playing discs of 20in (50cm) diam., with a plaque on the side inscribed 'Drop A Penny In The Slot - Nicole Frères - Leipzig', the base set with a drawer, and on baluster turned and tapering front supports, 51in (130cm) high, together with 24 discs.   **$7,000-9,000**

Miscellaneous

A William and Mary silver mounted shagreen instrument case, with shallow drawer and narrow silver borders, the elaborate hinges and lockplate engraved with stylised flowers and pierced with kidney shaped motifs, the slightly raised cover with applied oval plaque engraved with the arms of the Barber Surgeons' Company and with the initials ME and dated 1695, the mounts unmarked, the interior inscribed indistinctly in ink 'This Box with Instruments Bought June 9th, 1695'.
$7,000-9,000

Without doubt the most important instrument case to have survived is that applied with the enamelled coat-of-arms of King Henry VIII, now in the collection of The Worshipful Company of Barbers, and given to them by the King, probably in 1512. The case also bears the arms of the Barbers' Company and below it the badge of the Fellowship of Surgeons. During the reign of Henry VIII the two were incorporated becoming the Barber-Surgeons' Company in 1540.

A similar instrument case to the present shagreen example, also engraved with the Barber-Surgeon's Arms and with the initials IK, possibly for John Knight, sergeant-surgeon to King Charles II in 1661, is also in the collection of the The Worshipful Company of Barbers.

An Ami Continental II two hundred selection jukebox, with traditional domed glass cover, c1962.
$2,700-3,600

A German 19.5in (49cm) Polyphon disc musical box, 19thC, 48in (122cm) high, together with 10in discs.
$7,000-9,000

BOXES

A mahogany and marquetry tea caddy, with a hinged brass handle, c1790, 8in (20cm) wide.
$720-1,000

A George III mahogany tea caddy, with folding brass handle, interior with 3 compartments and pen tray, on bun feet, 9.5in (24cm).
$360-540

A Queen Anne walnut tea caddy, inlaid with geometric fruitwood banding, the interior with 2 divisions, with waved apron, on shaped bracket feet, the right side rising to reveal secret drawer, the base inscribed in pencil JBG twice, 11in (28cm) wide.
$1,800-2,700

A George III tea caddy, the interior with hinged lid, plush velvet and 2 lidded compartments, 5in (13cm) high.
$720-1,000

A late George III tortoiseshell tea caddy, with canted angles, on silver plated ball feet, one replaced, 6in (16cm).
$720-1,000

A Georgian fruitwood tea caddy, in the form of an apple, the stalk forming the handle 5in (13cm) high.
$1,800-2,700

A George III mirror panelled diamond shaped tea caddy, with interior lid, small crack, 7.5in (19cm).
$720-1,000

A George III burr yew and boxwood banded tea caddy, with ivory escutcheon, 5in (13cm) high.
$110-180

A Tiffany Favrile glass and bronze glove box, the hinged framework with beaded edges enclosing bronze filigree in the Grape Vine pattern and green and white striated opalescent glass, impressed Tiffany Studios/New York/827, c1915, 14in (35cm) long.
$2,000-3,000

A Regency rosewood tea caddy, with sarcophagus formed lid, box string inlaid, 2 sectioned interior, metal handles and feet, inscribed to the inner 'In the memory of the late William Foster Esquire'.
$180-360

A George III harewood tea caddy, the cover with floral patera, the front with ivory escutcheon and sprays of lily of the valley and mysotis, 6.5in (16cm) wide.
$720-1,000

A Regency penwork tea caddy.
$1,200-1,700

A Regency tortoiseshell tea caddy, with moulded 'starburst' front, the interior with 2 lidded compartments, 6.5in (16cm) wide.
$1,200-1,700

A tortoiseshell veneered hexagonal tea caddy, the domed top surmounted by a button finial, with a plinth base, veneer chipped, c1810, 5in (13cm) wide.
$720-1,000

A rosewood tea caddy, with sarcophagus formed lid, squat circular feet, with 2 interior sections plus cut glass mixing bowl, early 19thC.
$180-360

A pair of George III mahogany knife boxes, crossbanded and with chequer stringing, with serpentine fronts and fitted interiors, on ogee bracket feet, 15.5in (39cm) high.
$2,700-3,600

A pair of George III mahogany knife boxes, painted in polychrome with river landscapes, urns, flowerheads, foliage and lambrequin swags, with later converted interiors, 14.5in (37cm) high.
$3,600-5,000

A pair of Georgian mahogany serpentine front knife boxes, the hinged sloping covers having brass lion's mask ring handles, enclosing fitted interiors with boxwood stringing, 15in (39cm) high. **$2,700-3,600**

A Georgian mahogany knife box, with serpentine front, the top with shell inlay, converted for stationery. **$720-1,000**

A pair of George III inlaid mahogany cutlery boxes, each with serpentine fronts and fitted interiors, late 18thC, 14.5in (37cm) high.
$3,600-5,000

A 4 compartment smoker's box, on 4 elaborate scroll feet, the centre with matchbox holder on pedestal base, the interior of the compartments with grille between, 11.5in (29cm) long.
$1,800-2,700

A Sheraton inlaid and crossbanded knife box, with fitted interior. the sloping lift-up lid with shell inlay patera, 9in (23cm) wide. **$900-1,500**

A mahogany studded shoe snuff box, c1840, 5.5in (14cm) wide.
$180-360

Two similar shagreen mounted knife boxes, with plush lined fitted interiors, containing 12 Hanoverian pattern table spoons, John Gorham, London, 1750, 24 steel bladed knives, with indistinct maker's mark and lion passant, all crested and with shell capped handles and wave mouldings, mid-18thC.
$10,000-12,000

A late Victorian biscuit box, with straight fluted panels alternating with stamped foliage, fruit and scroll panels, the hinged domed cover with rounded rectangular finial, on an integral stand with 4 bun feet, maker's mark B.G. & Co. Ltd., Sheffield 1897, 7.5 by 5.5in (19 by 14cm), 1120gr.
$1,800-2,700

An early 19thC
mahogany
decanter box,
11in (28cm) wide.
$720-1,000

A smoker's box, carved in the form of a cabin trunk,
with twin handles, the interior fitted with 2 trays, one
with a canister and cigar holders, the top tray fitted
with a meerschaum pipe bowl, a vesta case and 2
further cigar cases, 19thC, 14in (36cm) wide.
$2,700-3,600

A mother-of-pearl and silver
inlaid tortoiseshell snuff box,
probably French, damaged, c1780,
3in (8cm) long, together with
another mother-of-pearl inlaid
and silver piquet point
tortoiseshell snuff box, probably
French, silver gilt mounts,
damaged, mid-18thC, 3in (8cm)
wide. **$720-1,000**

A German silver mounted snuff
box, painted with a goldfinch, a
great tit, 2 bullfinches and a
shrike attacking a fledgling,
chipped and cracked, perhaps
Höchst, c1770, 3.5in (9cm) wide.
$2,700-3,600

A French enamel double snuff
box, waisted, one cover painted
with the bust of a lady, the other
with a farming scene, 19thC,
3.5in (9cm).
$720-1,000

A rococo gold mounted hardstone
snuff box, of cartouche form, with
figured agate panels, the sides
chased with scrolls and flowers on
a stippled ground, maker's initials
P.V., 3in (8cm). **$1,200-1,700**

A Mauchline ware cheroot box,
signed, c1840, 3in (8cm) wide.
$180-360

A monkey snuff box, 18thC, 3.5in
(9cm) wide.
$360-540

A Mauchline ware snuff box, pen
worked and painted, 3in (8cm)
wide.
$180-360

A 19thC Continental micro-
mosaic and gilt metal snuff box,
the lid with finely detailed plaque
of the Pliny doves, within engine
turned panels with foliate angles,
3in (8cm), pseudo hallmarks,
$1,800-2,700

A French snuff box, overlaid with
gilt on a maroon ground, the
cover centred by a medallion of a
classical scene, 19thC, 3in (8cm).
$360-540

A coquilla nut snuff man, 18thC, 3in (8cm) high.
$360-540

A Victorian trinket box, the front applied with a well cut and enamelled reverse crystal intaglio of a bulldog, the back sliding to reveal a gilt lined drawer, Thomas Johnson, London 1881, 3.5in (9cm).
$3,600-5,000

A yew wood stationery casket, in the form of a house, with hinged lid and architectural windows fitted with painted glass panes, worn, 19thC, 7.5in (19cm) high.
$1,800-2,700

A Charles II blue grey and red painted boarded box, with hinged top, the panelled front carved with tulips amidst scrolling foliage, repair to top, partially redecorated, the right side later incised CF 1691, 24in (61cm) wide.
$3,600-5,000

The carving is similar to that on a chest of c1660 from Ottery St. Mary, Devon, and closely related to a group of chests, chairs and other items made in Ipswich, Massachusetts by William Searle, who was born and trained in Ottery St. Mary and moved to Ipswich by 1663; and Thomas Dennis (working in Ipswich 1668-1706). These English examples seem to represent a prototype for the Massachusetts style.

An enamel box, possibly Limoges, with allegorical scenes and The Rape of Europa on the lid, early 19thC.
$1,800-2,700

An articulated fish shaped box, with red stone eyes, unmarked, early 19thC, 5in (13cm), in a fish shaped sharkskin covered box.
$360-540

A fruitwood casket, inlaid with brass piqué work, inscribed Mary Bales, James Bales, January 17th 1826, Massingham, Norfolk, John Bales, and Jane Bales, 5.5in (14cm) wide.
$720-1,000

A gilt mounted tortoiseshell portrait box, with carved basketwork design and mounted on the inside cover with a portrait miniature of a gentleman wearing a scarlet waistcoat, c1760, 2.5in (6cm).   **$720-1,000**

A walnut and brass bound stationery cabinet, enclosing a leather covered writing surface and an arrangement of pigeon-holes, with 3 small drawers and a pair of glass ink bottles, c1880, 16.5in (42cm) wide.
$1,800-2,700

A Nuremburg steel miniature strong box, engraved with figures amidst formal scrolling foliage, lid mounted lock and with ball feet, 4.5in (11cm) long.
$1,800-2,700

TRANSPORT
Vehicles

A Starley and Jeffries 'Ariel' Ordinary bicycle, all metal with large main wheel, 45in (114cm) diam, fitted inside with eye-holes threaded with spokes attached to central hub, central tension bar, metal spine attached to small wheel, 22in (56cm) diam, simple wooden handles linked to central steering head and simple metal pedals, detached, c1872.
$2,700-3,600

A vintage Dursley Pederson lady's bicycle, with original overpainted frame, wheels 26in (66cm) diam.
$2,700-3,600

A gentleman's cross frame safety bicycle, with solid tyres, adjustable pedals with replaced rubbers, foot rests on front forks, leather sprung saddle and mudguard to rear wheel, c1870, wheel 28in (71cm) diam.
$2,700-3,600

A Victorian tricycle, pedal and chain drive, foot rests on front forks, lever band brake to rear axle, also activated by left foot pedal on frame, adjustable pedals, sprung saddle and turned wooden handlebar grips, with 24in (61cm) front wheel, 40in (102cm) rear wheels.
$7,000-9,000

An English child's tricycle, the cast iron frame stamped Hughes Birm., with shaped handlebars, solid rubber tyres and shaped metal seat, the pedals acting on the front axle, early 20thC.
$720-1,000

An 'Open Lot' gipsy caravan, with canvas external cover, fixed back with single window and an open frame front, with additional decorated side panels and crown board, mounted on 2 pairs of 36in (92cm) wheels with contemporary shafts, the interior with individual panels, rear mounted bed with under cupboards and drawers, painted in typical fashion, 138in (336cm) long.
$3,600-5,000

A Canadian clinker built canoe, of copper pinned mahogany planks over oak frames, 168in (427cm) long.
$1,800-2,700

Built at Peterborough, Victoria, c1906, with 7 planks a side and frames at 6in (15cm) spacing, this canoe has been rescued and restored, (some frames require replacing) and has original metal work, the gunwale information plate is missing.

An 1885 Wagonette, by Woodall & Son of London, with detachable saloon top, finished in black livery with red coachlining and navy blue upholstery.
$7,000-9,000

Originally the property of Squire Carter, High Sheriff of Hampshire and acquired from the coach house of the family home.

An 1886 dog cart, by Morgan & Co. Ltd., of Longacre, with leaf springs, iron tyres and wooden wheels, 54in (137cm) diam.
$2,700-3,600

A popular vehicle in the late 19thC, with back-to-back seating designed to allow sportsmen to carry their dogs beneath the seats and much used on country estates.

A horsedrawn landau, by Woodall & Son, of Orchard Street, London, mounted on rubber tyres and equipped with skimpy flared mudguards with spoon brakes to the rear tyres, c1860.
$10,000-12,000

This well preserved Landau from London coachbuilders Woodall & Son was originally the property of Squire Carter, High Sheriff of Hampshire and came from the coach house of the family home. It still carries the family crest of the Red Lion on the doors.

Leather and Luggage

A Scandinavian 2-man racing sledge, with painted pine body, metal mounts and runners, 84in (213cm).
$360-540

A Louis Vuitton double opening office trunk, covered in LV monogram material, brass and leather bound, leather carrying handle, with key, interior with fitted sliding tray for typewriter, brown felt covered compartments with straps for files, paper and envelopes, labelled LV Paris, London No. 811908, 26in (66cm) high.
$2,700-3,600

A Louis Vuitton cabin trunk, the monogrammed cloth covered case with brass and leather mounts, fitted with 6 drawers, hanging compartment and shoe box, 1930s.
$2,700-3,600

A Japanese double foliot travelling alarm clock and case, posted lacquered iron movement with fusees for the gong and strike and spring barrel for the alarm, verge escapement with 2 foliots, engraved brass case with a fixed silvered chapter ring, on a wood stand with key drawer and a glazed wood travelling case with sliding front panel, 18thC, 8in (20cm) high.   **$7,000-9,000**

Leather & Luggage

The condition of luggage is very important, as with most things, and items must be very fine in order to achieve top prices. Dressing cases and other items with fittings must be complete.

The highest demand continues to be for fine quality luggage by the top makers and unusual items for a particular function such as the office trunk, fishing rod box and drinks cases.

A Louis Vuitton gentleman's fitted dressing case, covered in brown leather with matching carrying handle, brass lock and catches, interior lined with black morocco, fully fitted interior with lift-out manicure set complete, each item stamped LV, the case stamped in gold LV, Paris London No. 736272, lock No. 047814, 17.5in (44cm) long.
$3,600-5,000

A Continental tortoiseshell and silver travelling inkstand, the exterior with sloping hinged lid, side carrying handles, on circular feet, the front with 2 hinged doors concealing 2 trays, the interior with mirrored lid, 2 glass bottles, folding pencil, tweezers, funnel, etc., 19thC, 4in (10cm).
$900-1,500

A Louis Vuitton lady's fitted dressing case, covered in red grained leather with matching carrying handle, brass lock and catches, interior lined in fine red leather fitted with 8 silver topped crystal containers each stamped LV and engraved monogram GM, 11 tortoiseshell fittings, 2 small circular containers each with gold inlaid monogram GM, 7 fitted matching red leather boxes, standing mirror and incomplete manicure set, the case stamped Louis Vuitton, Made in France 820176, lock No 053221, 21in (53cm) long.
$7,000-9,000

A Louis Vuitton cabin trunk, the interior with a removable tray, 44in (111cm) wide.
$1,800-2,700

> Miller's is a price
> GUIDE not a price
> LIST

SPORT
Cricket

A group of 9 posters produced by various newspapers in the 1930s, printed in red and black with banner headlines such as 'G.O. Allen Sensational Bowling', 'Allen's Mistake' and 'Allen made no Mistake', some tears and wear at folds, one with printed date, 18th August 1936, all from the M.C.C. Australasian Tour 1936-37.
$2,700-3,600

A cast iron slot machine, pre-WWI, 68in (173cm) high.
$1,800-2,700

A pair of M.C.C. white metal and enamelled cufflinks, engraved 'West Indies 1948' and 'G.O.A.'
$360-540

These cufflinks belonged to Gubby Allen.

Football

A maroon Scotland -v- England International cap, 1893.
$720-1,000

A collection of Gubby Allen's detailed engagement diaries from 1925-88, including 2 with presentation inscriptions from Pelham Warner, 1945 and 1946, together with an autograph notebook detailing Allen's play from 1914-21, whilst at Eton, and 5 fixture notebooks from Eton, 71 in all, including a diary of the Australian tour, 1936-37.
$3,600-5,000

A blue Scotland -v- Wales International cap, 1889, a blue Scottish Football League cap 1893, a purple Glasgow -v- Sheffield cap, 1891, a brown Glasgow -v- Edinburgh cap, 1892, a Scotland -v- Ireland 1886 embroidered cloth jersey badge, 5 various Renfrewshire F.A. embroidered jersey badges, 1885-1888, and a silver medal, the obverse engraved with a scene of a footballer, the reverse inscribed Thompson, 1887.
$1,800-2,700

A blue Scotland -v- England International cap, 1923.
$360-540
The above cap was awarded to Denis Lawson, St. Mirren. It was his only appearance in the International arena. An outside right by nature, his professional career started with St. Mirren in 1920, thereafter Cardiff City in 1923, Springfield F.C., U.S.A., 1926 Wigan Borough, 1927, and Clyde 1928-29.

A 15ct gold and enamel medal, the obverse inscribed 'From Aston Villa F.C. Presented to James Cowan', the reverse inscribed 'Presented to James Cowan by the Directors of The Aston Villa Football Club, in Recognition of His Long and Valued Services, 1890-1903', with ring suspension.
$700-1,000

A set of 108 Bowman Football cards, 1948.
$5,000-5,500

A portrait of Red Grange, produced by Goudey Chewing Gum Company of Boston, 1933.
$2,000-2,500

A bronze figure of a footballer, in aggressive pose, inscribed E. Drouot, early 20thC, 13in (33cm) high.
$1,800-2,700

F.A. Cup Final, 18.4.23, first Wembley Final, Royal Box edition programme, bound in gilt tooled blue morocco.
$1,800-2,700

A set of 14 Mayo Football cards, c1895.
$2,000-2,500

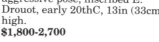

A set of 144 Bowman Football cards, 1952.
$8,500-10,000

A 10ct gold and enamel medal, the obverse inscribed 'U.S.F.A.' the reverse inscribed 'Dr. I. Schriecker, Vice-Pres. Federation Internationale De Football Assn.', with ring suspension and brooch ribbon, in original case. A.A.S., won by A.
$720-1,000

Fishing

The thumb magnifier, by Fosters of Ashbourne, to fix on the thumb and to help tying flies, as shown in 1921 catalogue.
$35-70

A 5in unnamed sea reel, probably designed and made by Slater, 1930s. **$70-145**

A Shaw's fly-fishing knife, Fred Shaw was the fly-fishing winner in 1905.
$110-180

An Allcocks Silver Superb reel, c1953. **$35-70**

A 3in Hardy Perfect, with ivorine handle, c1917.
$110-180

A 4.5in wide drum salmon reel, marked and sold by Harrods, 1920s.
$70-145

A 4.25in Hardy Silex No. 2, c1911.
$110-180

A 3in Hardy Perfect, narrow drum reel, with ivorine handle, 1912.
$180-360

A 4.25in Hardy Perfect reel, brass faced, brass rimmed unperforated back, 1900.
$360-540

A 2.5in Hardy Uniqua, Spitfire model from WWII, manufactured by Jimmy Smith.
$110-180

A 3in Hardy Perfect narrow drum reel, with no ball bearings, Eunoch model, agate lineguard, c1918.
$180-360

A 4in Hardy Silex No. 2, with
brass brake on rim, c1915.
$110-180

A 3.25in Hardy Silex No. 2 reel, with red
handle on the edge, c1919. **$110-180**

A 3.5in brass faced Hardy Perfect, c1900.
$360-540

A 4in Wallace & Watson of Hexham reel,
with elaborate mechanism. **$110-180**

A 3in Hardy Uniqua reel, with
ivorine handle and horseshoe
latch, c1905. **$110-180**

l. A Julius Vom Hofe ebonite and
nickel muliplier reel, with
counterbalanced crank, sliding
click and insciption 'Julius Vom
Hofe, pat. Nov. 17 '85, Oct. 8
1889', the foot stamped 3.5,
2.25in.
$180-360
r. A Julius Vom Hofe ebonite and
plated multiplier reel, with
counterbalanced crank, sliding
click, raised pillars and
inscription 'Julius Vom Hofe pat.
June 15 '86, October 5th 1889',
the foot stamped 4, 2.25in.
$360-540

A 3in Hardy Perfect, reel in
superb condition, with box, c1960.
$110-180

A 4.25in Hardy Perfect salmon fly
reel, with circular revolving line
guide, ivorine handle and alloy
foot, 1917 check. **$180-360**

A 2.75in Hardy Silex Multiplier
casting reel, with ebonite handle
ivorine thumb bar, knurled rim
check with brass brake indicator
and brass foot.
$720-1,000

A 2.5in Hardy brass crankwind
fly reel, with tapered horn handle
on curved crank arm stamped
'Hardy's Alnwick', fixed check,
brass foot, 1890s.
$360-540

A 2.5in Hardy platewind
gunmetal reel, with enclosed oval
logo, horn handle and fixed check.
$180-360

LIGHTING

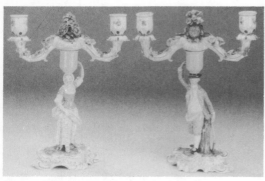

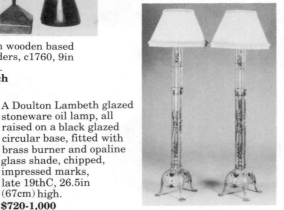

A pair of Meissen figure candlesticks, raised on a scroll moulded base picked out in turquoise, puce and gilt, crossed swords mark in underglaze blue, incised and impressed numbers, late 19thC, 11in (28cm) high.
$2,700-3,600

A pair of Bilston enamelled candlesticks, c1780.
$1,000-1,500

A pair of Derby candlestick figures of cherubs, restored, c1770, 7in (17.5cm).
$1,000-1,500

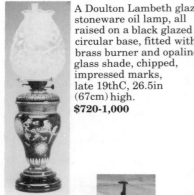

Three English wooden based rushlight holders, c1760, 9in (22.5cm) high.
$180-360 each

Two English porcelain lamp bases, decorated with gilding, with later matched baluster columns painted with either bands or sprays of flowers, fitted for electricity, some damage, c1830, 23in (58cm) high.
$1,800-2,700

A Doulton Lambeth glazed stoneware oil lamp, all raised on a black glazed circular base, fitted with brass burner and opaline glass shade, chipped, impressed marks, late 19thC, 26.5in (67cm) high.
$720-1,000

A matched pair of Victorian steel lamps, with modern pale yellow cloth shades with tasselled fringes, fitted for electricity, 59.5in (151cm) high, excluding fittings and shades.
$1,800-2,700

A wrought iron rushlight holder, 18thC.
$720-1,000

A metalware tin lantern, c1800, 10in (26cm) high.
$180-360

A porcelain Pierrot night light, c1920, 7.5in (18.5cm) high.
$360-540

A Victorian giltmetal 18-light chandelier, with foliate corona sexpartite rigid spirally twisted shaft supports, the circlet with scrolling foliate branches above a cast boss, the central section possibly replaced, 38in (97cm) high.
$1,800-2,700

A cut crystal electric table lamp, with cut crystal shade, c1920.
$180-360

A chrome and glass table lamp, on a black base, c1930, 24in (61.5cm) high.
$360-540

A heavy cut glass mushroom shaped electric table lamp, on a plated base with 2 bulb sockets and chain pulls, c1920, 18in (46cm) high.
$360-540

A Pairpoint reverse painted glass and patinated metal lamp, with Exeter shade signed L. H. Gorham, base signed Pairpoint and numbered D3094, 21in (54cm) high.
$2,500-3,500

A brass table lamp with original beaded shade, c1920, 19.5in (49.5cm) high.
$180-360

An Edwardian spelter lamp, with flambeau glass shade, probably gas originally, 22in (56cm) high.
$180-360

A Handel reverse painted glass and patinated metal Boudoir lamp, shade signed Handel 6989 RC, base with Handel label, c1915, 15.5in (38.5cm) high.
$1,000-1,500

A pair of Georgian style candlestick lamps, with original painted glass shades, c1920, 14.5in (37cm) high.
$180-360

A dentist's lamp, 38in (96.5cm) high.
$360-540

A French carved wood classical revival lamp, c1910, 27.5in (70cm) high, with French shade.
$180-360

An Art Deco plaster cat lamp, with lined black and white silk shade, 30in (76cm) high.
$180-360

A Victorian Arts and Crafts iron candle lamp and shade, 9.5in (24cm) high.
$110-180

A Handel reverse painted glass and patinated metal Boudoir lamp, shade enamelled 6712 Handel, base with impressed mark H, 1915, 14in (35cm) high.
$1,200-1,500

A modern leaded glass and bronze lamp, after a design attributed to Louis C. Tiffany, 17.5in (44.5cm) high.
$3,000-4,000

A brass Art Nouveau angel lamp, with lace shade, originally gas, 21in (53.5cm) high.
$180-360

A French original Art Nouveau iron dragon table lamp, 12in (31cm) high.   **$180-360**

A pair of Art Nouveau iron lily candlesticks, 9in (23cm) high.
$180-360

A modern leaded glass and bronze lamp, after the Wisteria design by Louis C. Tiffany, 25.5in (65cm) high.
$7,500-9,500

Miller's is a price GUIDE not a price LIST

A Victorian spelter cherub lamp, with flambeau shade, 12in (31cm) high.
$180-360

A Tiffany Studios bronze adjustable lamp base with a Steuben amber iridescent glass shade, base impressed Tiffany Studios/New York/473, shade with printed mark, c1915, 29in (74cm) high.
$2,000-3,000

An Art Nouveau bronzed iron lamp, with beaded shade made of original celluloid plastic, 25in (64cm) high.
$180-360

A pair of French bronze and parcel gilt candlestick bases, the columns with winged caryatid figures and foliage, the tripod concave bases modelled with wolves' heads, on paw feet, with acanthus leaf chased stand, 19thC, 15in (38cm) high.
$1,000-1,500

A Tiffany Favrile glass and bronze Bridge lamp, the shade inscribed I.C.T., base impressed Tiffany Studios/New York/678, 55.5in (141cm) high.
$2,000-2,500

A pair of bronze candelabra of mermen, probably English, each kneeling bearded figure set on a rocky outcrop supporting scrolled foliate branches, brown patination, finely chased surface and detail, late 19thC, 15in (37cm) high.
$3,600-5,000

A gilt bronze hall lantern, the engraved panes with anthemion crestings, with foliate scroll corona, late 19thC, 33in (83.5cm) high.
$1,200-1,700

A pair of Edwardian brass candlesticks, 8in (20cm) high.
$70-145

A set of 3 Harrods copper lily wall lights, with a hanging centre light, c1901, centre light 14in (36cm) diam.
$360-540

A pair of French chandeliers, probably Paris, in Louis XV manner, each for 24 lights, with moulded glass balusters and a gilt bronze cage, hung with drops, c1885, 66in (167.5cm) high.
$21,000-27,000

A pair of Art Nouveau brass wall lights, with milk glass shades, 15in (38cm) wide.
$720-1,000

A pair of Second Empire ormolu three-light wall appliqué, each with a pierced foliate backplate, the scrolling branches supported by a wreath emanating from a lion's mask with foliate drilled nozzles, 10in (25cm) high.
$1,800-2,700

A Continental five-light chandelier, with a gilt metal frame adorned with numerous graduated chains of cut glass beads and prism drops, bordered with curving leaf shape mounts, 34in (86cm) high.
$1,000-1,500

A pair of brass piano candle holders, to screw on to the piano, 9in (23cm) high.
$70-145

A pair of Arts and Crafts polished steel wall lights, 11.5in (29.5cm) high. **$360-540**

A pair of brass piano candle holders, weighted at the base, 7in (17.5cm) high.
$110-180

A French Art Nouveau ironwork lantern, with replacement glass, 15.5in (40cm) high.
$180-360

A brass gas pole, with original transfer printed pink shade.
$110-180

A pair of Art Deco chrome and glass wall lights, 9.5in (24cm) high. **$110-180**

An Art Deco original leaded glass, iron and brass hall lantern, 19in (48cm) high.
$180-360

A French cream painted brass hall lantern, the bulbous tapering body with 6 glass panels in a beaded bell husk cast frame, c1900, 37in (94cm) high.
$3,600-5,000

A pair of giltwood twin branch wall lights, each carved with a dove and scallop shell on a ribbon tied backplate, 53in (134cm) high.
$3,600-5,000

A pair of brass candle sconces, signed, c1900.
$360-540

A pair of leaded glass ceiling lights, c1920, 22in (56cm) wide.
$360-540

A brass hanging lantern, the sides with arched bevelled glass panels centred by a star burst below an acanthus scroll cresting, suspended by 6 scrolled supports, 28in (71cm) high.
$2,700-3,600

A Georgian design gilt bronze cylindrical hall lantern, the glazed body with beaded rims and ribs, hung with flower swags, 31in (78cm) high.
$1,800-2,700

A bronzed plaster cherub with beaded shades, cherub 11in (28cm).
$180-360

A gilt metal and glass light, 15.5in (39cm) high.
$720-1,000

A pair of oak barley twist candlesticks, c1930, 14.5in (37cm) high.
$110-180

A pair of the Empire style gilt brass candelabra, 19thC, slight damage, 22.5in (57.5cm) high.
$1,000-1,500

A pair of Empire style gilt metal five-branch candelabra, 30in (76cm) high.
$1,800-2,700

An oviform grey veined onyx column lamp, on a square base, c1920.
$360-540

A pair of Jacobean style pewter candlesticks, marked, c1930, 10in (25cm) high.
$110-180

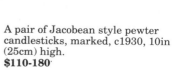

CRAFTS

A stoneware coiled and pinched vase, by Betty Blandino, oxide painted with ochre, brown and grey sponged glazes, impressed BB seal, c1991, 10.5in (26cm) high.
$360-540

An Abuja Pottery stoneware plate, by Michael Cardew, with everted rim, incised linear decoration, brown glazed body beneath cream details, impressed MC with Abuja Pottery seal, 10in (25cm) high.
$180-360

A Kingwood earthenware baluster vase, by Michael Cardew, the upper section covered in a grey-brown glaze with cream brushwork and incised decoration, beneath a fine translucent cream glaze, impressed with MC and Kingwood Pottery seals.
$1,200-1,700

A Michael Cardew bowl, painted with fish in brown reserved against an olive green ground, impressed Wenford Bridge seal and MC mark, c1970, 10in (25cm) diam.
$1,000-1,500

A stoneware slab built vase, by Ian Ault, with combed textured sides and applied wide collar, covered in an olive green and mushroom coloured pink tinted glaze, impressed IA seal, 12in (30cm) high.
$720-1,000

An earthenware bowl, by Michael Cardew, on a short foot, the interior covered in a mottled yellow ochre and olive green glaze, the exterior dark brown over yellow, with yellow brushwork, minor chips to rim, impressed MC with Winchcombe Pottery seal, 11.5in (29cm) diam.
$1,200-1,700

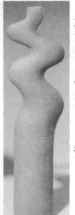

A porcelain 'Pot with Wave' vase, by Joanna Constantinidis, the foot with horizontal combed decoration, covered in a matt saggar fired pale brown glaze, impressed C seal, 1981, 17in (43.5cm) high.
$1,000-1,500

A stoneware coffee pot, by Michael Cardew, covered in a dark green glaze, incised through to body with cross-hatching and linear decoration, impressed MC and Wenford Bridge seals, 10in (25cm) high.　　**$360-540**

A stoneware bowl, by Hans Coper, the interior covered in a matt manganese slip pooling to reveal translucent white glaze beneath, the buff coloured exterior burnished and textured, impressed with HC seal, 6in (15cm) diam.
$1,200-1,700

A stoneware bowl, by Hans Coper, the interior with matt manganese running and pooling glaze revealing translucent white glaze beneath, the matt buff-coloured exterior burnished and textured, minor chips, impressed with HC seal, 7in (18cm) diam.
$1,800-2,700

A stoneware vase, by Joanna Constantinidis, covered in a yellow ochre and mottled brown glaze with iron-brown speckles, impressed C seal, 20in (51cm) high.
$720-1,000

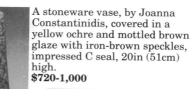

A stoneware jug, by Ray Finch, with yellow and black speckled body beneath metallic brown, impressed seal, 11in (27.5cm) high.
$180-360

'The Rose and Crown', a stoneware slab built pub, by Ian Gregory, applied with elaborate architectural and figurative motifs, salt glazed in beige and brown with green, blue and yellow highlights, 27in (89cm) high.
$720-1,000

A stoneware 'Body Pot', by Joanna Constantinidis, covered in a saggar fired pitted metallic glaze, impressed C seal, 1974, 21.5in (55cm) high.
$1,800-2,700

A stoneware vase, by Joanna Constantinidis, with irregular rim, with incised spiralling decoration, covered in a mottled iron-brown glaze, impressed C seal, 19in (49cm) high.
$720-1,000

A tea bowl, by Ewen Henderson, of various laminated clays textured with pink, brown, green and ochre slips, glazes and oxides, 1991, 4in (10.5cm) high.
$360-540

A raku water container, by Keiko Hasegawa, with iron grey body covered in a mottled mushroom-coloured crackled and pitted glaze with lustrous metallic splashes, impressed potter's seal, 6in (15.5cm) high. **$360-540**

A stoneware bowl, speckled grey with a rust brown rim, impressed HH seal, 6in (15.5cm) diam.
$180-360

A porcelain bowl, by Marian Gaunce, laminated in green, purple and blue clays, the rim with purple laminated chequered pattern, 5in (12cm) high.
$360-540

A stoneware bowl, olive green, the interior with bird design, glaze flakes to rim, impressed HH seal, 11in (28cm) diam.
$720-1,000

A stoneware bowl, speckled green-grey with a brown circular motif, impressed HH seal, 6in (15cm) diam.
$360-540

An earthenware bowl, decorated with 3 engraved fishes, brown and green, impressed HH seal, 7in (18.5cm) diam.
$720-1,000

A porcellaneous beaker, with pale grey glaze, decorated with a band of brown and blue lines, impressed HH seal, 4in (10.5cm) high. **$180-360**

A stoneware vase, by Janet Leach, covered in a speckled oatmeal run and pooled glaze, impressed JL with St. Ives Pottery seal, 5in (12cm) high.
$180-360

An inlaid stoneware plate, by Tatsuo Shimaok, the interior inlaid in pale green slip with herringbone pattern and stylised with iron brown rim, the underside covered in a mottled brown and olive green glaze, impressed seal, 12in (31cm) diam.
$720-1,000

A stoneware vase, by William Staite Murray, covered in a pitted mottled olive green glaze stopping short of the foot, with iron brown details, impressed M seal, 7.5in (19cm) high.
$360-540

A stoneware cut-sided vase, by Malcolm Pepper, covered in a thick crackled pale grey glaze, impressed seal obscured by glaze, 10.5in (26cm) high.
$110-180

A large stoneware oviform vase, by Malcolm Pepper, covered in a finely crackled grey glaze beneath a brushed white glaze with cobalt blue brushwork, with impressed seal, 11.5in (29cm) high.
$180-360

A stoneware bowl, by Takeshi Yasuda, green with raised white decoration and some running brown glaze, c1980, 6in (15cm) diam.
$180-360

A thickly potted cylindrical stoneware vase, by Alan Wallwork, covered in an oatmeal and lavender grey glaze, 19.5in (50cm) high.
$180-360

A stoneware vase, by Alan Wallwork, with uneven V-shaped rim, covered in a mottled pale olive green glaze with large iron brown flecks, inscribed AW, 15.5in (39cm) high.
$360-540

An earthenware water pot, with textured vertical bands, 12in (31cm).
$360-540

A stoneware vase, by William Staite Murray, with prominent potting rings, the interior covered in a crackled brown glaze, the exterior in a crackled mushroom coloured glaze with olive green and blue decoration, impressed M seal, 6in (15cm) high.
$360-540

An exhibition standard 7.25in gauge model of the Texas and Pacific Railroad 4-4-0 locomotive and tender, No.34, by M. Pavie, 84in (213cm) long. **$15,300-17,000**

A Bing hand painted tinplate limousine, minor paint loss and over-varnishing, original cardboard box, c1908. **$18,700-20,500**

A dolls perambulator, late 19thC. **$85-150**

A German dolls open kitchen filled with accessories, mainly 19thC, 22.5in (57cm)wide. **$6,00-6,800**

A Steiff white plush teddy bear,with blank metal button in left ear, 23in (59cm). **$3,500-4,250** flying a Steiff display aeroplane, canvas on wooden frame, 48in (122cm). **$850-1,700**

A 5in gauge model of the Great Western Railway River Class 2-4-0 locomotive and tender, No.76, 'Wye' modelled as modified c1896 by R.F. Richards, Southsea, 54in (137cm) long. **$7,650-9,500**

A scratch built model of an omnibus. **$100-150**

An important Admiralty Dockyard model of a 96-Gun Second Rate Ship-of-the-Line, the fruitwood frame with exposed planking to hull and exposed plank deck, c1700, 33.5in (85cm) long. **$306,000-340,000**

A child's pedal car, by Lines Bros (Tri-ang), 2-speed drive and solid rubber tyres, partially restored, 1950s. **$300-400**

A 7.25in gauge model of the Great Western Railway 14XX Class 0-4-2 side tank locomotive, by I.R. Holder, 45in (114cm) long. **$15,500-20,500**

A model First Rate Ship-of-the-Line, H.M.S. Majestic, late 18thC, 33in (84cm) long. **$51,000-60,000**

A Gustave Vichy musical automaton of a negro fruit seller, c1870, in display case.
$34,000-37,500

A Jumeau bisque headed two-faced doll, wearing late 19thC clothes, 18in (46cm) high.
$8,500-10,000

A Roullet et Decamps musical automaton, c1880, 23in (59cm) high.
$13,500-17,000

A leather headed clockwork musical automaton, by Vichy.
$15,500-17,000

A German papier mâché doll, c1860, 15.5in (39cm).
$1,500-1,700

A European bisque headed lady doll, with poured head, wood and composition jointed body, unmarked, 22in (56cm) high.
$24,000-27,000

A composition headed clockwork musical automaton, by Vichy, 18in (46cm) high.
$5,000-8,500

An Armand Marseille 1920s flapper doll, No. 390, 18in (45cm) high.
$425-600

A Lenci boudoir doll, in original organza dress, garters with roses, stockings, shoes trimmed with roses, c1920, 28in (71cm) high, with original box. **$3,000-3,500**

A Leopold Lambert musical automaton , with papier mâché head, c1890, 23in (59cm) high.
$19,000-24,000

An Emile Jumeau all original doll, c1870, 14.5in (37cm) high.
$3,250-4,250

A Jules Steiner Bourgoin pressed bisque doll, unstrung, replacement wig, incised Steiner, c1882. **$4,500-7,000**

A folding pine room box, representing a drawing, with original wooden set of furniture, German, c1880, 11in (28cm) wide. **$1,600-2,000**

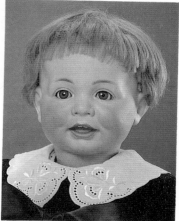

A Kammer & Reinhardt bisque character doll, c1910. **$4,500-6,000**

A Simon & Halbig bisque headed character doll. **$1,500-2,000** with accessories. **$750-1,000** *CSK*

A Jumeau bisque doll, in muslin frock, some damage, impressed Depose, 10, 23in (59cm). **$10,000-12,000**

A Scandinavian painted wooden grocer's shop, dated 1883. **$1,000-1,500**

A Simon & Halbig Mulatto bisque character doll, c1910. **$2,700-3,600**

'Anna's Pleasure', a painted wooden dolls house, c1860, 38in (96.5cm) wide. **$3,000-4,500**

A J.D. Kestner Oriental doll, impressed F.10, 243 JDK, c1914, 13in (33cm). **$3,600-4,500**

'Villa Lily', a painted wooden dolls house, with Walterhausen furniture. **$5,500-7,000**

A Kammer & Reinhardt character doll, damage to wig, impressed 101 K*R 46, c1910. **$4,500-5,500**

'The Dennis House' a painted wooden dolls house, possibly American, c1880. **$6,000-7,000**

A South Italian Greek pottery krater, Apulia, circa 4th Century B.C.
$10,000-13,500

An Hellenistic terracotta figure, 4th-3rd Century B.C., 7.5in (19cm).
$8,500-10,000

A Roman marble cinerarium, Italy, Tiberian or early Claudian period, circa 20-40 A.D., 16in (41cm) long.
$18,000-21,250

An Egyptian limestone relief fragment, depicting a retinue of musicians, Amarna Period, circa 1372-1355 B.C., 21in (53cm) long.
$17,000-20,500

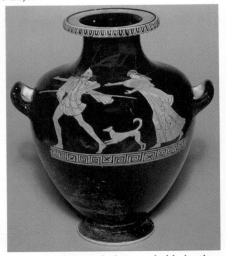

A Greek red figure kalpis, probably by the Tithonos painter, Attic, early 5th Century B.C.   **$46,750-51,000**

A Visigothic bronze buckle, circa 6th Century A.D., 4in (10cm) high.
$3,500-5,000

A Roman marble vase, with bell shaped lid, circa 1st Century A.D., 19.5in (50cm) high.
$26,350-30,000

A Greek bronze peplophoros, circa 460 B.C., 4in (10cm).
$20,500-24,000

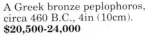

A Roman ivory miniature Corinthian capital, circa 1st-2nd Century A.D., 2in (4.5cm).
$2,250-2,500

An Etruscan bronze figure of a kouros, circa 520-500 B.C., 4.5in (11.5cm).
$7,500-11,000

A Roman marble head of Eros.
$17,000-20,500

A young girl, by Richard Schwager, signed and dated 1868, 4in (10cm) high.
$7,000-8,000

Colonel Black, by George Engleheart, c1753-1829, with plaited hair reverse, 2in (5cm).
$2,700-3,600

Charles and Samuel Black, by Abraham Daniel, died 1806, 4in (10cm) high. **$6,000-9,000**

A lady, by John Smart, 1742-1811, initialled and dated 1800, 3in (8cm). **$21,000-27,000**

A lady, by John Smart, dated 1788, 3in (8cm) high.
£32,000-36,000

An Officer, by John Smart.
$20,000-27,000

A lady, by Jeremiah Meyer, R.A., 1735-1789, in a silver gilt frame with enamel border, 2.5in (6cm) high. **$4,500-5,500**

An Officer, by Frederick Buck, 1771-c1840, 2.5in (6cm) high.
$1,200-1,500

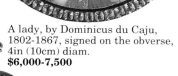

A lady, by Dominicus du Caju, 1802-1867, signed on the obverse, 4in (10cm) diam.
$6,000-7,500

Two girls, in a double sided gold locket, by George Engleheart, 1750-1829, 1.5in (4cm) high.
$9,500-11,000

r. Frederica, Duchess of York, in a gold frame, by William Grimaldi, 1751-1830, 3in (7cm) high.
$5,500-7,000

Above An Officer, wearing the uniform of the 65th Foot, in gilt metal frame, by Abraham Daniel, died 1805, 3in (8cm) high.
$5,500-7,000

COLOUR REVIEW

An early ivory study of a baku, unsigned, 18thC, 3in (7cm). **$24,000-27,000**

A pair of inlaid and lacquered wood vases, on giltwood stands, Meiji period, 25.5in (65cm). **$9,500-12,000**

l. A wood kiseruzutsu, with Tomobako, by Hokkyo Sessai, late 19thC. **$12,000-13,500**

A pair of Japanese wood vases, inlaid in ivory, horn, mother-of-pearl, ebony and with metal studs, minor cracks, 21in (53cm). **$3,500-5,000**

An ivory study of a Dutchman, unsigned, 18thC, 4in (9.5cm). **$3,500-4,250**

A cloisonné vase, by Namigawa Sosuke, the rims mounted in shakudo, signed in a silver wire seal, Meiji period, 8in (20cm). **$34,000-42,500**

A recumbent jade horse, Ming Dynasty or later, 8in (20cm) long. **$5,000-8,500**

A pair of Peking glass vases, Jiaqing. **$12,000-15,500**

An ivory figure, 18thC. **$5,000-7,000**

A jadeite bowl and cover, on 3 cabriole legs and crisply carved with mask handles suspending loose rings, the cover surmounted by a seated qilin finial, 5.5in (13.5cm) wide, on wood stand. **$12,000-13,500**

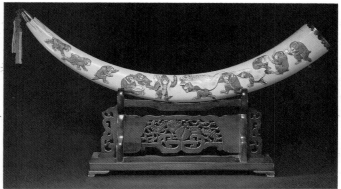

An ivory tusk, carved in relief with monkeys dressed as shishimai and sambaso dancers, the reverse with lions and tiger fighting, carved wood stand, signed Kizawa, Meiji period, 36.5in (92cm). **$8,000-9,000**

An ivory monkey, holding a fruit, signed in relief seal Ishikawa, Meiji period, 4.5in (11cm). **$10,000-12,000**

A lacquer tobako-bon, decorated in gold, small chips, 19thC, 10in (25cm). **$6,000-7,500**

A silver mounted ivory and shibayama tankard, Meiji period. **$4,500-5,500**

An embellished gilt bronze vase, cast as 2 phoenix, Qianlong, 19.5in (49cm) high. **$21,000-25,000**

Above A gold lacquer, two-case inro, by Shiomi Masanari, 19thC. **$21,000-23,000**

A suzuribako, decorated in gold and silver, chipped, 18th/19thC. **$6,000-7,500**

A pair of enamelled silver and shibayama vases, Meiji period, 13in (33cm). **$9,000-10,000**

Below A lacquer kogo, 19thC, 3in (8cm). **$1,700-2,000**

l. A gold lacquer box and cover, 19thC, 4in (10cm). **$20,000-21,000**

An Imperial gilt bronze mirror, Qianlong. **$3,600-4,500**

A komai style gilt bronze shrine, decorated in gold, base marked Kusa, Meiji period. **$9,000-10,000**

An Export cabinet-on-stand, elaborately decorated, 17thC, 32in (82cm). **$51,000-68,000**

A roironuri ground inro-dansu, old damage, unsigned, 19thC. **$127,500-136,000**

A composite lacquer sage-jubako, some damage, 18thC, 12in (30.5cm) high. **$8,500-10,000**

A lacquered palanquin, with gold hiramakie on a roironuri ground, gilt fittings, 19thC, the case 41.5in (105cm) long. **$51,000-60,000**

A shibayama style kodansu, the silver ground carved in relief, minor restorations, signed on the nashiji ground base Masayoshi, late 19thC, 12in (30.5cm) high. **$42,500-51,000**

l. A satsuma vase, signed Keishu ga, blue satsuma mon, late 19thC, 24in (61.5cm) high. **$37,500-42,500**

A composite lacquer sage-jubako, c1800, 9.5in (24.5cm) high. **$6,000-7,500**

A lacquer vase and cover, minor old damage, signed Sadatoshi, late 19thC, 10.5in (26cm) high. **$34,000-51,000**

A Continental neo-classical ormolu, blue glass and cut glass, twelve-light chandelier, early 19thC, 48in (122cm) high. **$20,000-22,000**

A pair of gilt bronze wall lights, each with three-candle nozzles, supported by winged female terms from anthemion backplates, 9in (23cm). **$3,600-4,500**

A Restauration gilt bronze mounted etched glass hanging light, c1820, 13.5in (34cm) high. **$9,000-10,000**

A painted glass and gilt bronze hanging light, with screw-in candle nozzle, mid-19thC, 13in (33cm) wide. **$12,000-12,500**

A pair of Empire ormolu and marble seven-light candelabra, fitted for electricity, early 19thC, 44.5in (112cm) high. **$80,000-90,000**

A pair of Regency gilt metal and tôle peinte chinoiserie decorated five-light candelabra, c1820, 22in (56cm) high. **$20,000-27,000**

A pair of Restauration gilt bronze candlesticks, with anthemion cast nozzles, c1815, 8in (20cm) high. **$4,500-5,500**

A French gilt brass twenty four-light chandelier, 19thC, 53in (135cm) high. **$16,500-18,000**

A pair of Empire bronze, gilt bronze and marble candlesticks, c1810, 17in (43cm) high. **$22,000-25,000**

A pair of Empire gilt bronze wall lights, c1815, 7in (18cm). **$2,700-3,600**

A set of 6 brass and glass wall lights, each with three nozzles, 19thC, 8in (20cm).
$4,500-5,500

A pair of gilt bronze table candelabra, each with a pair of detachable scrolling arms, mid-19thC, 16in (41cm) high.
$7,000-9,000

A pair of early Louis XVI gilt bronze wall lights, c1775, 18in (46cm) high.
$7,000-9,000

A Baltic glass and gilt bronze chandelier, part 1800, 50in (127cm) high.
$7,000-10,000

A pair of ormolu and bronze ten-light candelabra, with foliate nozzles and drip pans, wired for electricity, late 19thC, 43in (109cm) high.
$28,000-30,000

A George III cut glass mounted oval mirror, with two-light girandole.
$40,000-45,000

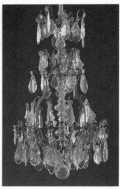

A Louis XV gilt bronze and glass chandelier, mid-18thC, some restoration, 45in (115cm) high. **$6,000-9,000**

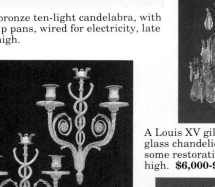

r. A set of 4 ormolu twin-light wall applique, 20thC, 16.5in (42cm) high.
$5,500-7,000

A pair of Napoleon III parcel gilt and silvered Egyptian revival bronze torchéres.
$7,000-9,000

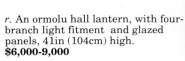

l. A pair of Louis XV ormolu two-light candelabra, mid-18thC, 18in (46cm) high. **$15,000-18,000**

r. An ormolu hall lantern, with four-branch light fitment and glazed panels, 41in (104cm) high.
$6,000-9,000

A New Hebrides wood slit drum, 96in (244cm).
$8,500-10,000

A Kuba ceremonial drinking cup, 7in (18cm) high.
$4,250-5,000

A Mossi ivory pendant, 8in (20cm) high.
$3,500-5,000

A face mask, remains of red and white pigment, 12.5in (32cm) high.
$5,000-6,000

A Songe face mask, pierced along the perimeter for attachment, 20in (51cm) high.
$7,500-9,500

An Easter Island club,
$6,000-7,500

An anthropomorphic Kuba cup, areas of encrustation.
$76,500-85,000

A fang spoon, aged dark brown patina, 6in (15cm) long.
$34,000-37,500

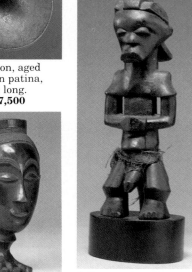

A Kuba cup.
$2,000-3,000

A Fang male reliquary guardian figure.
$48,500-51,000

A Lower Sepik river male figure.
$44,000-51,000

A Senufo figure of a hornbill.
$34,000-42,500

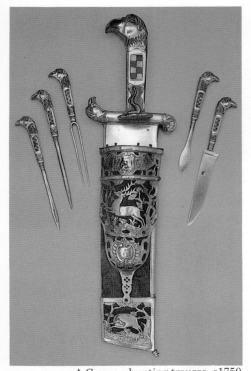

A German hunting trousse, c1750.
$18,700-22,000

l. An etched state glaive.
$18,700-22,000

Two German
officers' daggers,
WWII.
$150-250 each

A German etched state
halberd, on original wooden
staff, c1625, head 23.5in
(60cm).
$22,000-25,500

A German etched comb morion,
Nuremberg, c1700, 10.5in (26cm).
$9,500-11,000

An early fluted blued steel close
helmet, some replacements, probably
Innsbruck, c1520, 11.5in (29cm) high.
$29,000-34,000

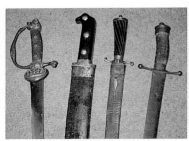

German hunting swords, c1740-
1800.
$170-1,200 each

A Chinese brass cannon, 25in (64cm) barrel.
$1,700-2,250

An English sabretache, 20th
Hussars. **$680-780**

A French
hunting sword,
for exhibition,
c1860.
**$25,500-
30,500**

BOW-WELL ANTIQUES
EDINBURGH

WE BUY & SELL, EXPORT & IMPORT

**Scottish pebble jewellery, Scottish regalia,
early Scottish pottery, Scottish pictures and paintings,
silver and plate, clocks and scientific instruments,
furniture, light fittings and glass.**

103-105 WEST BOW, EDINBURGH EH1 2JP
(Between the Grassmarket and The Royal Mile)

Shop hours 10am-5pm Monday-Saturday

**Tel: 031-225 3335
Fax: 031-665 2839
Mobile: 0831 106768**

ALL CREDIT CARDS ACCEPTED

A brass barrelled flintlock blunderbuss
pistol, c1780.
$2,000-2,700

A .400 self-opening sidelock ejector rifle, No. 25057, 25.5in
(65cm) chopper-lump barrels, by J. Purdey & Sons, in its oak
and leather case with canvas outer cover.
$50,000-60,000

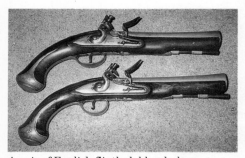

A pair of English flintlock blunderbuss
coaching pistols, with crest of Baronet Hume-
Purves Campbell, signed Joyner, London,
c1765. **$3,600-4,500**

A cased percussion pepperbox
revolver, by Blissett, c1840.
$1,600-1,800

Three Japanese swords, with
wakisashi blades, 19thC, 20 to
22in (51 to 56cm) long.
$550-800 each

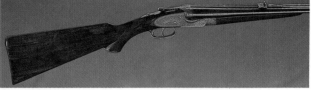

A .240 flanged 'Royal' model detachable sidelock ejector gun,
No. 31445, 25in (64cm) chopper-lump barrels, by Holland &
Holland. **$20,000-27,000**

A .318 'Royal' model detachable sidelock ejector rifle, No.
35011, 25in (64cm) chopper-lump barrels, with pistol grip
and cheek piece, in its oak and leather case with canvas
outer cover, by Holland & Holland. **$30,000-36,000**

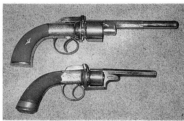

Two English Transitional percussion
revolvers, c1830.
$450-550 each

An English double barrelled percussion pistol, in
original case with accessories, in near mint
condition, c1840. **$1,800-2,500**

A Japanese lacquer saddle, a pair of iron abumi,
stirrup leathers, a crupper, saddle flaps, felt and
silk traces, bridle and bit, variously decorated.
$17,000-20,000

A pair of North American Indian beaded moccasins, in very good condition, 19thC, 10in (25cm). **$360-450**

A silk work basket, late 18thC. **$2,700-3,000**

An embroidered purse, re-lined, late 16thC. **$1,500-2,000**

An Italian embroidered cushion cover, c1700. **$6,000-7,000**

A French polychromatic beaded watch case, c1790. **$1,200-1,500**

A painted fan, with mother-of-pearl sticks carved and pierced with dancing figures, c1760, 11in (28cm). **$4,500-5,500**

A hand painted fan, early 20thC. **$320-360**

A French polychromatic beaded patch box, c1790. **$800-1,000**

Three Flemish tapestry covered cushions, late 16thC. **$6,000-7,500**

A French portrait miniature case, c1790, 3.5in (9cm). **$1,000-1,200**

A French painted paper leaf fan, with ivory sticks carved and pierced with figures, c1784, 20.5in (52cm). **$9,000-10,000**

A Beauvais tapestry covered cushion, early 18thC, 33in (84cm) square. **$10,000-12,000**

l. A French painted silk leaf fan, with ivory sticks, 18thC, 20in (51cm). **$5,500-6,000**

519

A Balenciaga chiné taffeta cocktail dress, with tie belt and matching stole, c1954. **$350-450**

A Christian Dior faille dress, jacket and stole, c1956. **$3,000-3,500**

A Christian Dior embroidered taffeta ball gown, c1954. **$450-600**

A Christian Dior figured silk dress, c1957. **$700-775**

A Christian Dior sequined cocktail dress, c1956. **$4,250-5,000**

A French beaded court robe, c1926. **$8,500-10,000**

A Christian Dior wool ensemble, with mink collar, c1953. **$3,500-4,250**

A Christian Dior beaded silk faille dress, c1955. **$1,350-1,500**

A Christian Dior organza strapless dress, with bolero jacket, c1956. **$1,100-1,200**

A Doucet silk faille mantle, c1911. **$850-1,000**

A Christian Dior embroidered organdie dress, c1953. **$1,500-1,600**

A Christian Dior tulle ball gown, c1954. **$9,500-11,000**

l. A Michel Goma embroidered taffeta ball gown, c1960. **$700-770**

l. A Christian Dior chiné ball gown, c1953. **$2,250-2,500**

A pair of Italian polychrome silk needlework and metal thread embroidered wall panels, both distressed, c1800. **$8,000-9,000**

An English needlework picture, mid-17thC, 12 by 17in (31 by 43cm). **$5,500-7,000**

An Antwerp historical tapestry, depicting the story of Augustus sacrificing at an altar, inscribed IGNOTO DEO, late 17thC, 119 by 165in (302 by 419cm). **$21,000-25,000**

A Brussels baroque biblical tapestry, depicting Gideon selecting his army to fight the Midianites, late 16th/early 17thC, 135 by 241in (343 by 612cm). **$45,000-54,000**

A Brussels silk and wool mythological tapestry, early 18thC, 178 by 129in (452 by 328cm). **$30,000-35,000**

An embroidered portrait miniature and mount, late 16th/early 17thC, wooden base and velvet possibly later, 9 by 8in (23 by 20cm). **$1,500-2,500**

l. A woolwork picture of a ship, with cushion sails, c1840, in original frame, 20.5 by 16in (51 by 41cm). **$1,800-2,500**

An English needlework picture, framed and glazed, mid-17thC. **$13,000-16,000**

A French 'overture' chamber barrel organ, mid-19thC.
$5,000-8,500

A pin barrel organ, with fusee mechanism, early 19thC. **$1,350-2,000**

A 'Standard' 7in (17.5cm) gramophone, c1900.
$450-600

A pair of drawing room barrel pianos, with 10 tunes. **$2,500-5,000 each**

A German Komet penny-in-the-slot disc musical box, c1900.
$10,000-13,500

A musical game, by Ann Young of Edinburgh, patented 1801.
$1,350-1,500

A German polyphon disc musical box, c1910.
$7,000-8,500

An Italian violin, by Andrea Guarneri, Cremona, c1674.
$68,000-76,500

An Italian violin, by Enrico Rocca, Genoa, 1911.
$56,000-64,500

A Jacob Bertsche grand piano, with 6 pedals, 4 gilt Turkish headed monopodia, tapering to gilt feet, with music stand, c1815, 89 by 48in (226 by 122cm). **$36,000-45,000**

A two-keyed oboe, Dresden, 1798. **$2,700-4,500**

A Robert Woffington single manual harpsichord, Dublin, c1770, 88.5 by 39in (225 by 99cm). **$55,000-60,000**

A Jacob and Abraham Kirckman single manual harpsichord, London 1772, 99 by 39in (252 by 99cm). **$45,000-55,000**

A Conrad Graf grand piano, with labelled gilt metal frame, 4 pedals, and 3 baluster legs, c1835, 97 by 49.5in (246 by 125cm). **$25,000-35,000**

A Jacob & Abraham Kirckman, two manual harpsichord, London 1789, 94.5 by 39in (240 by 99cm). **$100,000-110,000**

A Noblet Frères two-keyed boxwood oboe, c1840. **$2,700-3,600**

A polygonal virginals, with four octave keyboard, possibly Venetian, 17thC, outer case with late 19thC painted decoration, 61.5 by 20in (156 by 51cm). **$21,000-27,000**

A Tabriz carpet, kilim strip at one end, 125 by 87in (317 by 221cm). **$4,250-5,000**

A Kirman carpet, 163 by 124in (414 by 315cm). **$2,500-3,500**

A Sarouk carpet, with scrolling vine around a concentric medallion, 124 by 85in (315 by 216cm).
$12,000-13,500

A Ziegler carpet, some wear, damage and repair. **$3,500-5,000**

A Ziegler carpet, repairable splits, 100 by 93in (254 by 236cm). **$23,000-24,500**

A Heriz carpet, restored, late 19thC, 201 by 142 in (510 by 360cm).
$37,500-42,500

A Dabir Kashan carpet, early 20thC, 212in (538cm).
$18,500-20,500

A Ziegler carpet, slightly stained, minute repairs, 199in (505cm). **$13,500-20,500**

A silk and metallic thread brocade prayer rug, Isphahan or Kashan, 17thC.
$18,000-21,000

A Seychour runner, North East Caucasus, minor repairs, late 19thC, 120in (305cm) long.
$9,000-10,000

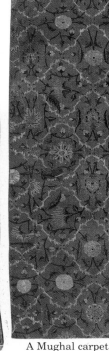

A silk and metallic thread velvet panel, Kashan or Isphahan, early 17thC, 78in (198cm).
$230,000-250,000

An Armenian Kazak rug, some repairs, dated 1841. 113in (287cm) long.
$6,000-9,000

A Khotan rug, East Turkestan, early 19thC, 92in (234cm).
$9,000-10,000

A Kazak prayer rug, South West Caucasus, late 19thC, 55in (140cm) long. **$7,000-9,000**

A Shirvan prayer rug, dated 1306 (1888), repaired, 49in (125cm).
$15,000-18,000

A Mughal carpet fragment, early 17thC.
$62,000-72,000

A Directoire Aubusson carpet, restored and rewoven throughout, late 18thC, 116 by 113in (295 by 287cm). **$40,000-45,000**

A Kazak rug, South West Caucasus, late 19thC, 59 by 49in (150 by 125cm). **$9,000-10,000**

A Gabbeh rug, South Persia, late 19thC, 80 by 51in (203 by 130cm). **$6,000-7,000**

A Perpedil prayer rug, North East Caucasus, worn with some holes, early 19thC, 92 by 43in (234 by 109cm). **$4,000-4,500**

A Yomud Okbash, West Turkestan wool rug, c1800, 23 by 18in (59 by 46cm). **$40,000-45,000**

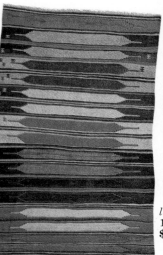

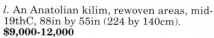

A Qashqa'i wool rug, South West Persia, worn, mid-19thC, 80 by 62in (203 by 157cm). **$9,000-10,000**

A Karagashli rug, North East Caucasus, late 19thC. **$28,000-32,000**

l. An Anatolian kilim, rewoven areas, mid-19thC, 88in by 55in (224 by 140cm). **$9,000-12,000**

An Aubusson rug, Napoléon III, 109 by 76in (276 by 194cm). **$10,000-14,500**

A Kurdish woven carpet, from Khorassan area, Saumak and plain weave banding, c1940. **$2,000-2,700**

A Charles X Aubusson carpet, restorations, c1825, 112 by 95in (285 by 241cm). **$45,000-54,000**

A Shirvan runner, East Caucasus, 121in (307cm) long. **$5,500-7,000**

A Khorassan carpet fragment, 17thC, 126in (320cm) long. **$54,000-63,000**

An Aubusson carpet, early 20thC, 170in (432cm). **$27,000-30,000**

l. A Kazak rug, West Caucasus, 41 by 33in (104 by 83cm). **$4,000-4,500**

A title lobby card for the film The Mummy, Universal, 1932, in good condition, 11 by 14in (28 by 36cm). **$11,000-13,000**

Orson Welles working scripts for Citizen Kane and The American, dated 4/30/40-5/9/40, together with another for The Magnificent Ambersons, 1942. **$12,000-14,500**

A 'He Who Kills, Zuni Fetish Doll', 1975. **$4,500-6,000**

The Poor Little Rich Girl, 20th Century Fox, 1936, linen backed, in good condition, 81in (206cm) square. **$4,500-6,000**

l. A poster for The Oregon Trail, Republic, 1936, linen backed, in good condition, 41 by 27in (104 by 69cm). **$11,000-12,000**

A 'Thing's Box' from TV's The Addams Family, 1964-66, together with 4 photographs and a letter from Mrs Jackie Coogan. **$22,000-25,000**

A Bill Melendez celluloid from It was a Short Summer Charlie Brown, 1969. **$2,700-3,600**

Below. A Walt Disney celluloid from Winnie the Pooh and the Blustery Day, 1968. **$5,500-7,000**

r. A Bill Melendez celluloid from It's The Great Pumpkin Charlie Brown, 1966, 11 by 13.5in (28 by 34cm). **$5,500-7,000**

ORIENTAL
Bamboo & Wood

A sagemono, in the form of wood rolled makimono, inlaid with takaramono, in wood and stag antler, damaged, Asakusa School, unsigned, 19thC, 5in (12cm).
$720-1,000

A wood carving of a horse, with a blanket tied to its girth, nicks to top of tail and himotoshi, unsigned, 19thC, 2in (5cm).
$1,800-2,700

A boxwood group of 5 turtles, in the style of Chuichi (Tadakazu), one forming a base for the others to clamber upon, their eyes inlaid, unsigned, late 19thC, 2in (5cm).
$1,200-1,700

A Japanese giltwood and lacquer figure of a Buddha, seated in dhyanasana, the hair dressed in tight knots, the overlapping robes falling over his legs and forming the base, cracked, chipped and worn, 15in (38cm) high.
$1,200-1,700

A boxwood okimono of a snake and turtle, the turtle emerging from its shell as the snake winds around it, the wood lightly stained and the eyes inlaid, signed in an oval reserve Shomin, late 19thC, 2.5in (6cm).
$2,700-3,600

A Chinese lacquered and painted wood figure of a seated multi-armed Buddha, wearing a hat with hanging masks at the back, 3 arms broken and repaired, 17th/18thC, 7.5in (19cm) high.
$360-540

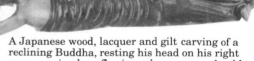

A Japanese wood, lacquer and gilt carving of a reclining Buddha, resting his head on his right arm, wearing long flowing robe over one shoulder, the hair worn in tight curls, chipped and worn, 18th/19thC, 20.5in (52cm) long.   **$720-1,000**

Two bamboo carvings, one comprising a group of 2 happy figures holding auspicious attributes including a double gourd, a turtle and a lotus stem, small chip, 18/19thC, 7.5in (19cm) high, the other carved as a mythical treetrunk raft, with an openwork fruiting and flowering branch growing from the gunwales of the hull, and small figures standing on the deck, small loss, 18thC, 8.5in (21cm) long.
$1,800-2,700

A wood okimono of shibunkin, by Chikuju, the group of long tailed goldfish naturalistically carved, the eyes inlaid in horn, signed on a horn tablet, Meiji period, 10in (25cm).   **$3,600-5,000**

A Chinese bamboo brush pot, carved to the exterior with a panel of sages being entertained by musicians in a garden landscape, the reverse with birds perched among flowering prunus and bamboo, cracked, Daoguang mark and of the period, 3in (8cm) diam.   **$720-1,000**

Cloisonné & Enamel

A Japanese cloisonné enamel plaque, showing irises in colours, on black ground, Meiji period, 9 by 7in (23 by 18cm), the hardwood frame relief carved with dragons amongst waves.
$720-1,000

A pair of cloisonné enamel vases, decorated with panels of irises and baskets of flowers on each of the 4 raised panels, against the dark blue ground, small blisters, impressed Daikoku's head rebus, Meiji period, 6in (15cm).
$1,000-1,500

A pair of cloisonné vases, decorated in musen-jippo with irises on a pale cream ground, the rims mounted in shakudo, inlaid mark of Ando Jubei, Meiji period, 9.5in (24cm).
$1,800-2,700

A pair of blue and white cloisonné enamel and gilt bronze jardinières, decorated on either side, a ruyi collar at the shoulder, applied at either side with loose-ring double animal head handles, pitted, late Qing Dynasty, 22in (56cm) diam.
$5,000-7,000

A cloisonné enamel meiping, decorated with red, pink, yellow, blue, white and green stylised lotus flowers among scrolling foliage, on a blue ground with ruyi heads around the short neck, 18th/19thC, 12in (30.5cm) high.
$1,800-2,700

A cloisonné enamel dish, decorated in gold and silver wire with a central landscape panel, inlaid lozenge mark of Hayashi Kodenji, Meiji period, with original fitted wood box, 7in (18cm).
$5,000-7,000

A Canton enamel supper set, the central dish painted in famille rose enamels, with Shou-hsing and other figures in a landscape, the 8 fan shaped subsidiary dishes with similar decoration, 18thC, 17in (43cm).
$360-540

A Chinese cloisonné vase, mid-19thC, 14in (36cm) high.
$720-1,000

Furniture

A Chinese export padouk wood bureau, enclosing a fitted interior, on later shaped bracket feet, the base incised SDR 42, mid-18thC, 37in (94cm) wide.
$2,700-3,600

A Japanese carved hardwood and lacquer side cabinet, with a pagoda pediment, numerous galleried shelves, cupboards and drawers each with a lacquer panel and mounted carved ivory, allover decorated with open carved phoenix and flowering branches, 84in (213cm) high.
$1,000-1,500

A Chinese export black lacquer and lac burgaute brass cabinet, enclosing shelves and a pair of drawers, c1800, 40in (102cm) wide.
$1,800-2,700

A Chinese Export black lacquer small secrétaire cabinet, gilt decorated with shell and scroll cornice above a pair of panel doors enclosing shelves and 2 short drawers, the base with hinged writing surface and pen rest, on stand with 4 turned supports, 61in (155cm).
$1,800-2,700

A Chinese export black and gilt lacquered chest-on-stand, the stand with acanthus scroll carved X-shaped supports joined by stretchers, early 19thC.
$1,000-1,500

A Chinese black lacquer cabinet, set with hardstones and mother-of-pearl, 38.5in (97cm) square, with later ebonised stand.
$1,000-1,500

A Chinese ebonised padouk wood side cabinet, inlaid in copper wire, mother-of-pearl, ivory and bone, with brass flat hinges and door plates, on key pattern carved bracket feet, door set with white metal plaque inscribed 'Lock Hing Curios & Arts, Hong Kong. Established 1870', 46in (117cm) wide.   **$1,000-1,500**

A nest of 4 Chinese hardwood occasional tables.
$720-1,000

A Japanese parquetry and lacquer table cabinet, late 19thC, 18in (46cm) wide.
$720-1,000

A Chinese huang huali altar table, the cleated top above a stylised pierced and carved frieze, on square legs with scroll feet, late 19thC, 53.5in (136cm) wide.
$1,000-1,500

A Chinese huang huali davenport, profusely carved, the top revealing 3 small drawers, the sides with a pen drawer above 8 opposing drawers and pierced dragon brackets, on a platform base with claw-and-ball feet, some damage, late 19thC, 33in (84cm) wide. **$720-1,000**

A Chinese four-fold painted hide screen, with pagodas, figures, boats and floral vase motifs, within a nailed gilt hide border, distressed, 19thC, each fold 75 by 23in (191 by 59cm). **$2,700-3,600**

A Chinese brown lacquer six-fold screen, late 19thC, 78in by 15in (198 by 38cm). **$1,800-2,700**

A nest of 4 Chinese hardwood tea tables, the borders and legs carved as bamboo, the aprons pierced and carved with scrolling fruiting foliage, 15 to 8.5in (38 to 21cm). **$720-1,000**

An inlaid hardwood screen, carved with lotus and inlaid in bone and mother-of-pearl, with numerous fighting frogs, Meiji period, 70.5 by 67in (178 by 170cm). **$7,000-9,000**

A Chinese two-fold screen, each panel decorated with onlaid cloisonné vases and censers containing flowers and fruiting sprays, on a coral coloured lacquer ground, within a hardwood frame decorated with a band of key-pattern, 69.5in (178cm) high. **$1,800-2,700**

A Chinese huang huali centre table, the top with a burr wood panel within concentric bandings, the carved and pierced frieze above 6 supports, joined by pierced stretchers, on stylised carved feet, 19thC, 53.5in (135cm) diam. **$1,800-2,700**

An Oriental carved hardwood jardinière stand, with inset rouge marble top, pierced side aprons, shaped legs and cross stretcher, 19thC, 10in (25cm) diam. **$180-360**

An Anglo-Chinese rosewood hall table, with pink veined marble inset top, on cabriole front supports, with carved shell and leafage ornament and scroll toes, on serpentine fronted plinth base, 19thC, 50in (127cm) long. **$2,700-3,600**

A black and gold lacquer painting table, braced at each end by twin stretchers, decorated by an allover design of gold lacquer scrolling stylised lotus, Wanli, 36in (91cm). **$7,000-9,000**

An Oriental carved hardwood jardinière stand, with inset rouge marble top, pierced side aprons, under gallery, supported on circular legs with claw and ball feet, 16in (41cm) square.
$360-540

A pair of Chinese 2-tier hardwood urn stands, the aprons, legs and edges all carved to simulate bamboo, 18in (46cm) square.
$1,200-1,700

A Chinese Export black lacquer work table, decorated in gilt throughout in traditional manner, 25in (64cm) wide.
$1,000-1,500

An Oriental carved hardwood plant stand, with inset marble panel, on 4 cabriole legs, 19in (48cm) high.
$360-540

An Oriental carved hardwood jardinière stand, with inset rouge marble top, floral carved side apron, shaped legs and pierced floral under gallery, 19thC, 36in (92cm) high.   **$360-540**

Two lacquered armchairs, and a lacquered square table, each decorated in gilding with figures and flowers on a black lacquer ground.
$1,800-2,700

Inros

A three-case wood inro, decorated in relief and lacquered with an eagle perched on rocks, damaged, 19thC, 3.5in (8cm).
$720-1,000

A two-case wood inro, decorated in gold, silver and black hiramakie with tigers among bamboo, late 19thC, 2.5in (7cm) and an attached ivory netsuke of karashishi, cracked, 18thC.
$1,800-2,700

A five-case lacquer inro, bearing a kinji ground, decorated in gold and silver takamakie, hiramakie, gold foil and kirigane with a flowercart filled with cherry blossoms and camelia, scratches, with coral bead ojime, and guri lacquer manju netsuke, chipped, 19thC, 3.5in (9cm).
$1,200-1,700

A four-case inro, decorated in gold togidashi, takamakie, kirigane and gold leaf, with a flight of cranes above a ship, signed Kajikawa saku, 19thC, 3.5in (9cm), with a lacquer hako-netsuke showing a ferry boat.
$3,600-5,000

A three-case inro, decorated in gold hiramakie and nashiji, on a roi ronuri ground with characters, and a wood netsuke of a seated figure, 19thC, 2.5in (7cm).
$1,000-1,500

A Japanese ivory okimono of Tenku emerging from an egg, 4in (10cm) wide.
$360-540

Ivory

A pair of ivory tusk vases, carved in relief with a monkey trainer, musicians and dancers beneath cherry blossom, mounted on wood bases, Meiji period, 10.5in (26cm).
$2,700-3,600

A Japanese ivory group, of a standing sage holding a staff in one hand and stroking his beard with the other while looking at a butterfly perched on the frond of a palm tree issuing from rockwork, the details stained black, on oval base, minor damage, signed on red lacquer reserve Kogyoku, 5.5in (14cm) high.
$1,000-1,500

An ivory tusk vase and cover, carved overall in high relief with quail and millet, the quail with stained plumage, some cracks, signed on a mother-of-pearl tablet Yoshikazu, Meiji period, 7in (18cm).   **$3,600-5,000**

A Japanese carved ivory group of 3 figures on a log raft, one with an oar and a bundle of sticks, one seated, and a child with gourd, late 19thC, 10in (25cm) high, with plinth.
$720-1,000

A Japanese ivory carving of a warrior, mounted on the back of a rearing stallion, both horse and rider with heads turned to the right, the warrior with his right arm raised above his head, the details stained black, sword missing, old damage, 5in (13cm) long, with stand.   **$1,000-1,500**

A Japanese wood and ivory group, of a street entertainer with his assistant, red lacquered signature to base, Meiji, 9in (23cm) high.
$1,800-2,700

An ivory group of bananas, by Banshu, the fruit attached to a stem, naturalistically carved and stained, signed, Meiji period, 7in (18cm).
$1,800-2,700

An ivory study of a rabbit, seated facing ahead and with its ears drawn back for compactness, the ivory bearing a good colour and the eyes inlaid, chipped, Kyoto, late 18thC, 2in (5cm).   **$2,700-3,600**

An ivory tusk carving of a kneeling man struggling with an octopus, a woman and child escaping behind his back, Meiji period, 10in (25cm) long, on wood stand.
$1,200-1,700

A Japanese ivory carving of a kangaroo, carrying her young in her pouch, inlaid eyes, set on a wood stand, 6in (15cm) high.
$180-360

A large ivory okimono of a man and two boys, the man standing with one child holding a rabbit at his feet, the other boy on his back, with an elaborate revolving wood stand, the figure signed Atsumochi, Meiji period, 31in (79cm) overall height.
$7,000-9,000

An ivory and lacquerwork carving of a leaping carp, the fish flexed upon its tail, the ivory head, gills and fins finely rendered, its body painted to simulate scales, repaired, Meiji period, 6in (15cm), on wood stand.
$1,800-2,700

An ivory model of a Kakemono, by Hidemasa of Osaka, opening to reveal Okame seated, throwing beans to exorcise an oni who climbs over the top of the scroll, a hanging pole at the base, the ivory is slightly worn and of a good colour, signed, early 19thC, 2.5in (6cm).
$1,000-1,500

A pair of Japanese ivory bezique counters, both carved in sunken low relief with monkeys playing with crab and toad, the tabs with further apes, Meiji period, signed, 4in (10cm).
$360-540

Three Chinese ivory seals, 2 surmounted by Buddhistic lions, one by a mythical animal with a bifurcated tail, on rectangular or oval bases, and an oval soapstone seal surmounted by a rabbit beside a cabbage, 18thC and later, 2in (5cm) high.
$720-1,000

Jade & Agate

A white jade deer cup, the scallop shaped cup resting on a short foliate foot, a deer's head with delicate pointed ears and short beard carved at the pointed end, chipped, 18thC, 3.5in (9cm) wide, with padded box.
$3,600-5,000

A pale celadon jade pierced censer and cover, the body and domed cover crisply carved and incised in openwork with scrolling peony flowers and 3 peony stem handles, on a flaring openwork base, 18thC, 5in (13cm), with wood stand.
$7,000-9,000

A Chinese moss agate peach shaped libation cup, with chilong handle, carved to the exterior with leafy tendrils, 4.5in (11cm) wide.
$360-540

A carved jade dragon plaque, of domed oval form, carved in relief with a dragon amidst lotus, mounted as a table screen, in a well carved pierced wood stand, Kangxi, 12in (31cm).
$1,800-2,700

A speckled burnt jade figure of an elephant, draped with a decorative tasselled howdah, surmounted by a young boy grasping a lotus stem, and another standing at its rear holding a vase, the pale cream jade richly speckled with black flecks, repaired, probably Ming Dynasty, 7.5in (19cm) long.
$2,700-3,600

Lacquer

A lacquer coffer, decorated in gold and black and mother-of-pearl with foliate panels, flaked, c1600, 9in (23cm).   **$2,700-3,600**

A lacquer comb and hairpin, signed Ryushin Sei, Meiji period, the pin 6.5in (16cm).
$1,200-1,700

A Japanese lacquer picnic set, comprising 3 flat square boxes and covers and 4 triangular trays, each decorated to simulate different wood samples, in a fitted lacquer casket of hinged vertical square section, covered in herringbone pattern and coloured raffia, with open side panels, early 20thC, 10in (25cm) high.
$360-540

A japanese gold lacquer figure of Hotei, seated on his sack holding a peach in one hand, his robes decorated in hiramakie and black, on a gilt metal base, damaged, 8in (20cm) high.   **$180-360**

An Export lacquer coffer, decorated in gold takamakie, hiramakie, kirigane and inlaid mother-of-pearl, with shaped panels showing palaces and gardens, birds and flowers reserved on a nashiji ground, chipped, mid-17thC, 52in (132cm) long, on a later English stand. **$18,000-21,000**

A Chinese red lacquer sewing box and cover, incised with figures in a landscape of trees, 13in (33cm) diam. **$360-540**

A pair of red lacquer drums and stands, the drums painted and gilt with lotus scrolls, the stands with dragon head terminals, drums 26.5in (67cm) wide. **$2,700-3,600**

A gold lacquer saddle, decorated on the nashiji ground in gold takamakie, hiramakie and foil with ho-o, chipped, 18th/19thC, 15in (38cm) long. **$7,000-9,000**

Metal

A bronze study of a lion, its teeth bared in a roar, impressed seal Seiya saku, Meiji period, 20in (51cm), with wood base. **$1,800-2,700**

Two bronze figures of a warrior and a falconer, each in flowing robes with floral medallions, the warrior brandishing a drawn sword, the other holding a hawk balanced on a perch, gilt details, bearing a rich dark patina, on wood stands, one missing a weapon, both signed Gyoko, Meiji period. **$7,000-9,000**

A Japanese bronze model of a walking camel, signed, 12in (31cm) high. **$2,700-3,600**

An Oriental bronze cauldron, decorated with figures and clouds, having elephant mask and trunk handles, 18in (46cm) diam. **$180-360**

A Japanese bronze group of a seated monkey gazing at a lotus bud held in one hand, the fur markings well defined, 7in (18cm) high. **$360-540**

A Japanese inlaid bronze bowl, of flower form, the exterior decorated in low relief with crested water birds wading among lotus, heightened in gilt, signed, Meiji period, 8in (20cm) diam. **$900-1,500**

A bronze elephant, cast with wrinkled skin, the trunk raised with a pair of ivory tusks, impressed seal Seiya saku, Meiji period, 17.5in (44cm) long. **$720-1,000**

A Japanese bronze lobed jardinière, on 8 elephant head feet, inscribed Dai Nippon, Bunsei Nensei, Sei Minju, 24.5in (62cm) diam.
$3,600-5,000

A Japanese silver coloured metal and shibyama two-handled vase, cover and liner, the body inlaid in mother-of-pearl and polished hardstones, on a gold lacquered ground applied with two dragon shaped metal handles, the white metal shoulders, domed quatrefoil foot and domed cover decorated with champlevé enamelled sprays of flowers, the cover with hawk shaped knop, indistinct seal mark to base, damaged, 10.5in (26cm) high.
$3,600-5,000

A bronze two-handled vase, cast with archaic designs below central roundels of kylins, with gilt details, 19thC, 16in (41cm).
$1,200-1,700

Two Japanese bronze models of crayfish, realistically modelled with their tails tucked under their bodies, their antennae slightly raised, old wear, 8.5in (21cm) long.   **$720-1,000**

A Japanese inlaid bronze vase, the exterior decorated with a continuous panel of a pagoda among pine trees below a key-fret style border and above 3 lotus flowerheads and scrolling foliage, on tripod feet, signed, Meiji period, 3in (8cm).   **$720-1,000**

A Japanese patinated bronze group of quail, coloured in copper, shakudo and gilt, mounted on a carved wood base, signed Yoshitani sei, late 19thC, 14in (35cm) long.
$2,700-3,600

A Japanese bronze articulated model of a crab, the details of claws and body naturalistically rendered, 4in (10cm) wide.   **$1,000-1,500**

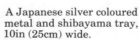

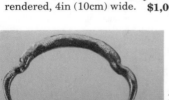

An inlaid iron tetsubin, 19thC, 7in (18cm).
$720-1,000

A Japanese silver coloured metal and shibayama tray, 10in (25cm) wide.
$3,600-5,000

A Japanese bronze model of a warrior, dressed in robes decorated in relief with dragons among clouds, with a long and short sword to his side, pole missing, 24in (61cm) high.
$720-1,000

A Japanese bronze model of a swimming carp, supported on its fins, the head turned slightly to the left, gilt inlaid eyes, signed, 8in (20cm) long. **$2,700-3,600**

Netsuke

A wood and ivory nesuke of a skull, thigh bone and lotus bud resting on a large lotus leaf, 1.5in (4cm) wide.
$360-540

An ivory netsuke of Onna Daruma, seated on a removable circular mat, signed Mitsutsugu, 19thC, 1.5in (4cm).
$720-1,000

Two ivory netsuke, the first being a Manju, carved in relief with Konoha Tengu balancing a spinning top on his nose, signed Gyokugi, the second is a fishergirl with a large octopus on her back, signed Gyokkosai, both 19thC, 1.5 and 2in (4 and 5cm).
$1,800-2,700

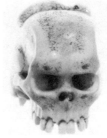

An ivory netsuke of a spider on a melon, with a vine leaf and bud, 19thC, 1.5in (4cm).
$360-540

A marine ivory netsuke of coiled snake resting on a skull, 1.5in (4cm) long. **$360-540**

A set of 3 boxwood mask netsuke, representing Okame, Usofuki and Kannon, each crisply carved in lightly stained and patinated wood, a bar on the back forming the himotoshi, signed Sogaku to, c1900, 1.5in (4cm).
$1,800-2,700

Snuff Bottles

An agate thumbprint snuff bottle, of pebble shape, the stone with grey and white bands, c1800.
$720-1,000

A macaroni agate snuff bottle, of flattened ovoid form, on an oval foot rim. **$360-540**

An agate snuff bottle, the smoky grey stone carved with vertical reeding, gilt metal mounted stopper. **$720-1,000**

An agate snuff bottle, carved with a sage beneath a willow tree, the reverse with figures and peaches, mask and ring handles carved in low relief.
$1,000-1,500

A coloured ivory snuff bottle, carved in relief with a figure on a rearing horse, colleagues standing back in alarm under plantain and willow branches, incised Qianlong mark, 20thC.
$900-1,500

A puddingstone snuff bottle, the mottled stone with circular inclusions, c1800.
$360-540

A cinnabar lacquer snuff bottle, carved with Shou Lao standing beneath a pine tree, the reverse with a maiden, restored, c1800.
$360-540

A lacquer burgauté snuff bottle, of flattened pear form, decorated using minute chips of gilt metal and mother-of-pearl, in shades of blue and green, with circular flower panels reserved against a diaper pattern ground.
$360-540

A moulded porcelain snuff bottle, finely modelled with 9 dogs-of-Fo gambolling with brocade balls, against a cloud pierced ground, all coloured cinnabar red with gilt detail, mark and period of Jiaqing.
$720-1,000

A red overlay glass snuff bottle, carved with animals of the Zodiac over a bubble suffused ground, c1780.
$720-1,000

A porcelain snuff bottle, formed as a folded lotus leaf with reeds and birds, c1850.
$360-540

A puddingstone snuff bottle, of stout squared form, the stone with mottled light and dark inclusions.
$360-540

A blue overlay glass snuff bottle, decorated with figures beneath bamboo and prunus over a bubble suffused ground, c1800.
$720-1,000

A porcelain snuff bottle, enamelled with 2 dragons chasing a flaming pearl amidst clouds and waves, silver coloured metal mount and stopper, the six-character mark painted in iron red on base, mark and period of Guangxu. **$720-1,000**

An agate snuff bottle, of flattened stout ovoid form, carved using speckled brown and ochre inclusions in the pale grey stone with various animal subjects, c1800. **$720-1,000**

A Peking glass snuff bottle, imitation nephrite, finely polished discoidal form, 18thC.
$360-540

Did you know

MILLER'S Antiques Price Guide builds up year by year to form the most comprehensive photo reference library available.

Tsuba

An iron tsuba, carved in relief with the large head of a nio expelling a wasp from his nose, his scarf of inlaid brass and other details gilt, the reverse with 3 birds in shishiaibori, inscribed on 2 inlaid silver tablets Hamano Noriyuki, 19thC, 3.5in (9cm).
$2,700-3,600

A copper tsuba, carved in relief with Daruma floating on waves, his hossu floating on the reverse, beneath gouged clouds, details in shibuichi, signed with a kakihan, early 19thC, 3in (8cm).
$1,800-2,700

An associated pair of sukashi tsuba for a daisho, each in the form of 2 encircling oxen, their tails curling to form a rim, one with a rope halter, 18thC, 3in (8cm).
$1,200-1,700

A ko-kinko yamagane sukashi tsuba, of mokko form, carved and pierced as a stylised flower, with tomobako and certificate, Muromachi period, 16thC, 2.5in (6cm).
$1,000-1,500

The certificate describes the tsuba as tachi-shi and dates it 1470-1570.

Miscellaneous

A Japanese embroidered silk picture, very finely worked with a study of a peasant woman carrying a bundle of reeds, Meiji/Taisho period, 19 by 12in (48 by 31cm) framed and glazed.
$720-1,000

A Chinese red, green and cream 3-tiered box with canted corners, containing shaped smaller boxes and covers, decorated within red lacquer pierced container modelled as a table, the cover carved in relief with figures in pavillion gardens in a mountainous river landscape, within a band of key and cell-pattern, old damage and restoration, Qianlong, 7in (18cm) high. **$1,800-2,700**

TRIBAL ART

Although during the past year the percentage of unsold lots in tribal art sales has on average increased, this has for the most part been due to the reluctance of sellers to part with good quality material rather than a real decline in auction values or interest from buyers. When top quality lots have appeared in the salerooms they have still commanded very high prices, particularly if they have not been seen on the market before. For example, a Songye stool which surfaced from the collection of a Belgian colonial family sold at Christie's in the last few months for $187,000, against an estimate of $100,000-140,000, more than had been realised for a similar stool sold during the 'peak' of the market in 1987. The McCarty-Cooper tribal sale at Christie's New York was a great test of the market as almost every item had been purchased during the past seven years, many having been bought for sums which, even at the peak of the market, had caused quite a stir. In the event, the sale result came as a great relief to dealers and collectors, several lots exceeding expectations and exceeding the prices McCarty-Cooper had paid for them at the peak of the market. A Fang figure purchased in New York for $71,500 in November 1984 sold for $440,000.

There has been no reduction in the number of fakes appearing in the auction rooms during the past year and rumours have been rife at the auction views. This has meant those lots with a good provenance have been at a premium, sometimes commanding several times the price of a lot without history; for example, the Ashanti pottery lamp known to have been in the Pitt Rivers Museum at the beginning of the century realised $7,100 against an estimate of $3,000-5,000.

Stories of important tribal artefacts turning up in the country and being bought for a song have been circulating for many years but the current scarcity of good quality material has also led to the phenomenon of extraordinary excitement being generated when a piece, even of mediocre quality, turns up at a provincial saleroom, often realising several times its likely auction price at a specialised sale in London. A Maori bowl for which a dealer is reputed to have paid $15,300 in a country sale was sold in London for $3,400 recently, a cautionary tale for would-be bargain hunters.

African art has been the most difficult area during the past year. It has always accounted for 50% or more of the lots in tribal sales and despite the scarcity of top quality material in the sales there has been no shortage of mediocre or bad African art. Zaire and Gabon have continued to command the highest prices but again only for the very best material. The market for Yoruba art has suffered more than most with no shortage of material, even the very best examples having met with little interest from buyers. By contrast, the art of South Africa has increased dramatically in value with a number of long standing collectors recently turning their attention to this area; consequently today headrests, snuff bottles and unusual knobkerries are frequently fetching four figure sums which, a few years ago, could have been bought for a few hundred dollars or less.

The demand for American Indian and Eskimo art has not diminished and competition between serious American collectors is often fierce. A pair of Seminole moccasins estimated at $1,500-2,500 were sold in London recently for $34,000 after a battle between telephone bidders. Artefacts from the turn of the century have become more acceptable to the modest collector, with items made for 'Wild West' shows early this century being in demand.

The market for Pre-Columbian material is still poor in London with the majority of material available being heavily restored or simply fake. Many of the fakes are themselves now antique and whilst buyers exist prepared to pay modest sums for decorative pots, prices rarely exceed a few hundred dollars.

Polynesian art has remained popular with record breaking prices for top lots. A Fiji headrest from the Methodist Missionary Society which had sold for $11,000 in June 1987 was sold recently for $77,000. Such high prices have led to an increase in the number of high quality Polynesian fakes appearing on the market though this is by no means a new phenomenon. A Hawaiian style figure thought to be the work of the famous carver James Little who worked at the beginning of this century and which was published as genuine as recently as 1967 sold this year for $1,900.

New Guinea art has not been in short supply, the vast majority dating from the 1960's or later, and whilst there are still buyers interested for its decorative quality, prices rarely exceed $850, though carvings with a provenance going back to the early years of this century, or even later for more remote areas of the island, can still bring several thousand dollars.

With very few named carvers and many objects which defy classification, tribal art has never been a field for the investor. Its relatively small group of enthusiastic collectors frequently pay far in excess of what might be considered a reasonable sum for a fine and rare carving in the not unreasonable belief that they may not get another chance to buy such a piece again. As a result tribal art has remained relatively unaffected by the recent decline in prices seen in the Impressionist and Contemporary Art markets.

Tribal Art

A Sierre Leone soapstone figure, nomoli, forearms missing, 16thC, 6in (15cm) high.
$1,000-1,500

A Maori feather box, carved at each end in high relief with a tiki figure, the remaining surface covered with notched scrolls, concentric circles and linked chain ornament, dark patina, cracked and repaired, 18.5in (47cm) wide.
$2,700-3,600

A Krinjabo terracotta funerary head, blackish patina, minor damage, 9in (23cm) high.
$1,800-2,700

An Ashanti pottery lamp, modelled as a maternity figure, the mother seated on a large stool which forms the lamp, her large flat head with features modelled in relief, holding the child who stands between her legs, neck repaired, 9in (23cm) high.
$7,000-9,000

A group of 7 ibeji from Abeokuta, 2 pairs of females, another pair, male and female, wearing various coloured bead and coconut shell ornaments, and a male with incised apron, all on square bases, 8.5 to 9in (21 to 22cm) high.
$720-1,000

A Yoruba bowl, for ifa divination, agere ifa, crusty patina, from Iseyin, 8in (20cm) high.
$720-1,000

Birds appear to be a popular motif for the supports of agere ifa in the Iseyin area, carved in various modes from realistic to the stylised. Our example is conceived as a series of triangular forms, the wings to tail tip as the central triangle with 2 smaller triangles to complete the tail.

A Californian basket, woven with 7 cactus-like motifs in dark fibre on a pale ground, plaited rim, perhaps Washo, 9.5in (23cm) diam.
$1,000-1,500

A Lulua figure, crouched with the hands placed behind the ears, the arms and legs forming a continuous curve, 3 horns carved about the coiffure, the narrow face with open mouth and spectacle type eyes, glossy dark brown patina, c1890, 9in (22cm) high.
$7,000-9,000

A rare Nilotic fibre doll, the elaborate coiffure formed as 2 large wings of plaited fibre, 4 strands of pink and blue beads above the carved wooden breasts set in gum, knotted fibre buttocks, multiple strands of red and white striped beads retaining a skin loin cloth, reddish patina, 8.5in (21cm) high.
$1,000-1,500

A Mangaia turret adze, the basalt blade secured with finely plaited coir, the broad shaft and base of oval section, the latter pierced with 28 square apertures, carved allover with chevrons and crosses, damaged, 21in (53cm) high.
$1,800-2,700

An Anyi pottery vessel, the 2 spouts each modelled in relief with a head, one with lobed coiffure the other ridged, raised scarification to the necks and faces, the spherical body modelled in relief with 2 splayed recumbent figures, old label, 13in (33cm) high.
$360-540

A rare documented carving, by James Little, the standing figure carved in the Kona style, with hands on the hips, the forked head, lateral panels and teeth each with serrated edges and showing extensive traces of blue paint, 20in (51cm) high.
$2,700-3,600

A Maori post figure, standing with the arms carved in relief and hands placed on the abdomen, the face with engraved and blackened tattoo ornament, the body with notched scrolls, 3 sides of the tall base with carved scrolls, notched edges along 2 corners, mid-19thC, 36in (91cm) high.
$2,700-3,600

Two Maori figures, one standing with the arms free of the body and the hands on the abdomen, the other with elongated head, the arms in relief, each with the surface carved extensively with notched bands, each with old label with monogram AEC damaged, 21.5 and 27in (54 and 67.5cm) long.
$2,700-3,600

A Canadian Indian beaded birchbark vase, of hexagonal section and baluster form, the silk covered bark sewn with various foliate and geometric motifs in coloured beads incorporating the date 1888, in fine condition, with glass dome, 7in (17.5cm) high.
$720-1,000

Three Letti figures, each crouching with the arms folded across the knees, the 2 largest each with forked headdress carved with scrolls, the rectangular bases similarly carved, the smallest with tuft to the top of the head, 4 to 7.5in (10 to 18.5cm) high.
$1,800-2,700

A Bobo animal mask, with concentric circular eyes, long ears and pierced triangular mouth, painted in black, red and white, minor damage, 16in (40cm) long.
$360-540

A Tonga basket, of compressed spherical form, ornamented with cross hatched triangles in plaited coir, damaged, 18in (45cm) diam.
$3,600-5,000

A Colima pottery dog, standing with pierced open mouth showing many teeth, pierced nostrils, the ears pinched and pierced, the tail curved over the plump body, restored, 14.5in (37cm) long.
$1,800-2,700

A brass presentation 'King Plate' of crescent form, a pierced circle at each end with an emu and a kangaroo respectively, inscribed 'Presented to Queen Grace Of The Nyungar 11th May. 1881. Tamulgani Outstation', the border with stamped crescents and circlets, pierced twice for suspension, 9in (22cm) wide.
$900-1,500

A New Caledonia ceremonial axe, the rectangular nephrite blade secured to the wood head with finely bound plaited coir, 2 bands of woven flying fox fur about the top of the shaft, dark glossy patina, 25.5in (65cm) long.
$1,800-2,700

A roll of Santa Cruz feather money, tavau, the long band of fibre sewn with the brilliant red feathers of the small honey bird, Myzomela cardinalis, suspending clusters of Job's tears and fibre tassels. **$1,800-2,700**

A Haida mountain goat horn spoon, the handle carved as a bear, a mask on its abdomen, its ears flanking the bird head finial, 19thC, 8in (20cm) long.
$1,200-1,700

A Solomon Islands ceremonial paddle, the blade carved as a bonito, the open mouth with carved teeth grasping the shaft, the eyes and body with inset fretted pearl shell inlay, similar shell inlay to the tapered finial and crescent crossbar, black painted embellishments, 6 inlays missing, 59in (150cm) long.
$3,600-5,000

A Mangaia adze, the small stone blade lashed with plaited coconut fibre to the cylindrical shaft which is carved with 39 bands of stylised figures, damaged finial, 28in (71cm) long.
$900-1,500

A brass presentation 'King Plate' of crescent form, 8.5in (21cm) wide.
$1,800-2,700

A Haida mountain goat horn spoon, the handle carved as a chief wearing ceremonial hat in the jaws of a killer whale whose body is incised on the back of the bowl, 8in (20cm) high.
$1,800-2,700

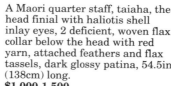

A Maori quarter staff, taiaha, the head finial with haliotis shell inlay eyes, 2 deficient, woven flax collar below the head with red yarn, attached feathers and flax tassels, dark glossy patina, 54.5in (138cm) long.
$1,000-1,500

A Marquesas pipe, the bowl carved as a stylised figure, his hands before him flanking a panel carved with angular geometric motifs, the stem carved with a stylised supine figure, dark glossy patina, crack to stem, 6.5in (15.5cm) long.
$2,700-3,600

A rare Easter Island club, ua, the Janus head finial with eyes recessed for inlay, grooved coiffure, slightly flared shaft, 44in (111cm) long.
$7,000-9,000

A Fiji kava bowl, on 11 tapered
cylindrical legs, pierced
triangular lug to underside,
glossy patina, 27in (69cm) diam.
$1,800-2,700

Two nautilus shell vessels, each
covered with hatched triangles
and other geometric designs in
brown resin, each pierced twice
for twisted fibre cord, inscribed on
the inside 52/11935, with old
museum label Nicobar or
Andaman Islands, 8 and 7.5in (20
and 18cm) long.
$1,200-1,700

An Anang (Ibibio) mask, of oval
form, with twisted features, a
crooked nose, the mouth to one
side, pierced oval eyes below the
domed forehead, the crescent
coiffure with outer notched edge,
some fibre about the pierced
border, black patina, minor
restorations and eroded border,
12in (30cm) high.
$720-1,000

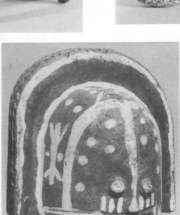

A rare Tetela-Sungu Janus
helmet mask, each face with
small features carved in relief,
rectangular eye holes flanking the
mouth, the median crest with 3
rows of holes for insertion of
feathers, missing, the whole
painted reddish brown with bold
geometric design in white, native
hide repair to the rim, pierced
about the border, 12.5in (32cm)
high.   **$1,800-2,700**

A Yoruba headdress, for the
Egungun masquerade, with a
hare carved behind the large ears
and a waisted ornament in front,
medicine bottles carved on the
forehead of the bearded face, the
whole painted in colours, by the
Eshubiyi household of Abeokuto,
damaged, 18.5in (47cm) high.
$720-1,000

A North West Coast
mountain sheep horn
spoon, the flat handle
with applied white metal
panel with engraved
creature, beaver's tail and
a plaque below, some
unfinished carving to the
underside, c1900, 10.5in
(26cm) high.
$720-1,000

A Luba shankadi axe,
the metal blade inset in
the mouth of the carved
head which has an
elaborate coiffure
embellished with inset
brass upholstery nails,
16in (40cm) high.
$1,800-2,700

An Ekoi Janus headdress, each
skin covered face pierced for the
eyes and mouth and coloured a
reddish orange, applied above
with 4 carved figures, and 2 inset
mirrors, each figure with
articulated arms and painted in
colours, the flared circular base
pierced 4 times, 19.5in (49cm)
high.   **$1,000-1,500**

Two New Ireland bird finials, for
dance staffs, each carved as the
head of a hornbill with some red
and black painted motifs and
panel at the rear, inset shell-
opercula eyes, one with cassowary
feathers bound at the next with
twisted fibre, also suspending
shells and feathers on strands of
beads, the other with fibre bound
with barkcloth, 7 and 10.5in (18
and 26cm) long.   **$2,700-3,600**

A Bijugo buffalo mask headdress, the face pierced horizontally at the jaws to show the inset tongue, the nose and eyes encrusted with mud, the flared base with wing like ears and attached plaited and twisted fibre binding, painted red triangles within black borders about the jaws and back of head, the remainder painted black and white, minor old damage, 23in (58cm) high. **$360-540**

A Fang staff, with standing figure finial, the face with applied circular metal eyes and tall brass collar, the shaft of square section below 4 flared knops, dark glossy patina, 27.5in (70cm) high. **$1,800-2,700**

A Vanuatu head, nambuci, the wood shaft with applied head of mud, fibre and cobwebs, coloured black, white and orange, the fibre top knot blackened, 2 inset curved boar's tusks flanking the mouth, from the Small Nambas of South Central Malekula, 27in (68cm) long. **$1,800-2,700**

Part of a New Ireland mask, carved as a squatting figure with shell opercula inlay eyes, the jowls encrusted with fibre and mud, the limbs spread eagled flanked by 2 wing like panels, pierced at the centre, the base with old label, various deficiencies, 20.5in (52cm) wide. **$1,800-2,700**

A Tonga 'Paddle' club, culacula, the broad blade and upper shaft carved allover with asymmetric design with panels of triangles, lozenges, rectangles, a zigzag spiral and other motifs, raised transverse ridge to each side, the grip carved with bands of zigzags above the flared butt, fine dark glossy patina, minor repair, 47in (118cm) long. **$7,000-9,000**

A pair of Eastern Great Lakes moccasins, of smoked buckskin, the uppers embroidered with curved motif in red and blue dyed porcupine quill. **$7,000-9,000**

An Athapaskan beaded cloth octopus bag, red wool tassels on triple green glass bead fringe, plaited fibre carrying strap, c1880, 21in (53cm) long. **$2,700-3,600**

A Huron birchbark dish, with oblong centre and flared sides with shaped borders, the whole embroidered in coloured moosehair with exotic flowersprays, minor damage, 10.5in (26cm) long. **$180-360**

A Senufo helmet mask, the carved horns each with 4 applied white metal bands, a female figure seated upon a crescent each side obscuring part of the serrated median crest, cloth panel with sewn cowrie shells pendant at the back, from the Boundiali region, 13.5in (35cm) high without attachments. **$3,600-5,000**

ISLAMIC WORKS OF ART

Three Turkish brass candlesticks, the centre of which rises to a faceted stem with plain and tulip-shaped bosses below the similarly shaped mouth with flared serrated rim, slight damage, 17thC, largest 15in (37.5cm) high. **$3,600-5,000**

A Mamluk Pottery baluster vase, the white exterior painted with a broad band of Mamluk 'thuluth' inscription, the gaps between the letters painted black, a band of roundels around the shoulder and stripes around the neck, restored, 14thC, 6in (16cm) high. **$2,700-3,600**

The inscription reads 'al-'izz al-da'im wa'l-iqbal' (perpetual glory and good fortune).

An Herati silver inlaid bronze stem, heavily cast with medial ridge, the upper section with a repeating lozenge lattice of palmettes, rubbed, 13thC, 14in (35.5cm) high. **$2,700-3,600**

The personal seal of Major General Sir Willoughby Keane of Ghuznee (sic) and Cappoquin, the pale yellow agate finely carved with scrolling vine around the elegant 'nasta'liq' inscription, in original gold mount with repoussé dense foliage and walrus ivory round handle with waisted shaft, dated AD 1839, 4in (10.5cm) high. **$2,700-3,600**

A Mamluk brass gulla tray, with pierced floral decoration, the interstices filled with palmettes and flowering vine around engraved roundels with birds flying around rosettes, the central sunken roundel surrounded by a 'thuluth' honorific inscription inscription interrupted by rosette roundels, outer lobed motif stripe, rubbed, 15thC, 17.5in (45cm) diam. **$10,000-12,000**

An early Safavid tinned copper Dervish's bowl (kashkul), with inscription, each side carved with a panel of elaborate palmettes, the rim with similar minor band, associated tinned brass complex link chain with swivelling attachments, rubbed, late 15thC, 8in (20.5cm) long. **$7,000-9,000**

An East Persian pierced bronze jardinière, the sides with a broad band of pierced interlaced arabesques enclosing stylised knotted roundels, an arcaded band below, a band of 'kufic' inscription around the mouth with inner linked roundel band, slight damage, 13thC, 5in (12.5cm) diam. **$1,800-2,700**

An Ottoman mother-of-pearl and tortoiseshell veneered pen box, the upper edge with zigzag motifs made from rhino horn and walrus ivory, the lower edge similar with ebony and bone, the top of the lower section with silver and hardwood banding, later silver hinges and hooks, velvet lining, damaged, 17thC, 12.5in (31.5cm) long. **$3,600-5,000**

An Ottoman enamelled copper jar and cover, imitating the Continental porcelain original, the jar of broad baluster form on spreading foot, the cover of shallow double domed form, 'tombak' floral knop, the green sides painted with gold scrolling leafy vine around white cusped cartouches with floral sprays, the interior plain white, slight damage, c1850, 7in (18cm) high. **$2,700-3,600**

RUSSIAN WORKS OF ART

A Russian porcelain egg, painted within a gilt frame joined by a turquoise ground and gilt diaper band, 3.5in (9cm) high, with a cover and stand; and a Russian porcelain egg, painted with Christ's ascension from the grave, reserved on a gold ground, 3in (7.5cm) high, on a stand.
$720-1,000

A Russian pottery egg, painted with Christ holding the cross, enamelled in colours on a gold ground, the reverse with a monogram X.L., ring mount, 4.5in (11.5cm) high.
$720-1,000

Mother of God Vladimirskaia, realistically painted, with parcel gilt oklad, repoussé and engraved with stylised foliage scrolls and arabesques, maker's mark illegible, in a glazed kiot, Moscow, 1892, 12in (31cm) high.
$3,600-5,000

A Russian Imperial Glass Factory engraved and cut glass goblet, the bowl engraved with a profile portrait of Tzarina Elizabeth Petrovna, 9in (22.5cm) high.
$1,800-2,700

A pair of Russian engraved wine glasses, each decorated with a crowned shield medallion with an eagle divided by a chevron, the reverse with ribbon tied foliage on a spiral stem on a domed foot, 9in (22.5cm) high.
$1,000-1,500

A Russian cut glass wine glass, gilt with a profile portrait of Marshal Kukuzov, beneath a gilt key pattern band above a fluted lower part and on a faceted knop and fluted stem, 7.5in (19cm) high.
$2,700-3,600

A Russian cut glass mug, with gilt rim and handle, 4in (10cm) high.
$2,700-3,600

A composite 12-piece silver toilette set, comprising: a dish and beaker with gilt interiors, a covered powder box with original puff, 2 patch boxes, 2 candlesticks, a silver covered pentray, and 4 silver mounted perfume bottles, all with the engraved initials JC, the beaker by Efim Siderov, St Petersburg, one patch box Moscow 1852, unknown maker's Cyrillic initals FV, the remainder St Petersburg, various makers, various later years, in a lined fitted wooden case, the hinged lid stamped in Russian 'Vladimirov, SPB, Nevskii prospekt no. 31', with brass handles and catches, on a stand, dish 8in (20.5cm) long.
$7,000-9,000

A silver trompe l'oeil cigar box, engraved and chased overall to simulate tobacco tax bands and brand name with seals, by Petr Miliukov, Moscow 1896, 5.5in (14cm) long.
$3,600-5,000

A Russian icon of the Mother of God of the Burning Bush, 12in (31cm) high.
$720-1,000

DECORATIVE ARTS

It is generally accepted that Art Nouveau was born out of the Arts and Crafts Movement and peaked during the late 1890s and 1900s. By the onset of WWI, its demise was certain, but during this very short span of time a revolution in design had taken place. Artists and designers were inspired by the free forms and sinuous lines which were to become synonymous with the Art Nouveau style. Having discovered a new found freedom from the ordered but over fussy Victorian ideas of decoration they set out to explore and exploit this freedom.

In France Emile Gallé and Daum were the leading exponents of the art of cameo glass. Many of their designs were inspired by the delicate plant form motifs found in Japanese art. Whilst the asymmetrical inlaid and marquetry furniture designs of Louis Marjorelle display a totally new and uninhibited approach.

Credit must be given to Arthur Lasenby Liberty, the creator of the famous London store whose far-sighted approach to retailing led him to commission the work of individual artists, the most notable of whom is Archibald Knox, whose fluid, though more restrained work in silver, pewter and jewellery has come to epitomise the English style of Art Nouveau.

The semi-clad, slightly innocent but teasingly erotic portrayal of the female form was surely the most oft-repeated image of the era, whether captured on the canvas by Toulouse Lautrec, incorporated in poster designs by Alphonse Mucha or cast with free flowing hair amidst floral motifs in the pewter designs of the German company W.M.F. Though today we may find Art Nouveau charming and almost coquettish, there is no doubt that at the time the Art Nouveau style appealed largely to the Bohemian and avant garde. One cannot help but imagine that amongst polite post-Victorian society the portrayal of sensuously half-clad females may have 'sat' rather uncomfortably.

It was impossible for the gently poetic forms of Art Nouveau to survive alongside the horror of war. The Art Deco artists emerging after WWI eschewed the romantic forms of Art Nouveau, preferring the sharper angles, straighter lines and more austere materials which reflected the machine age fast growing up around them. They looked to, and were influenced by, Hollywood and its stars. In Egypt, the discovery of Tutankhamen's tomb explains the strong Egyptian forms seen in the sculpture and ceramics of the period. Sometimes called 'The Jazz Age' , it was certainly 'Art imitating life' - with an immediacy as never before. The tantalus was replaced by the cocktail shaker. Ladies danced The Charleston in revealing beaded dresses. Fashionable society travelled in limousines adorned with the stylised mascots designed by René Lalique. The mass production techniques he employed in his glass making allow today's collectors the opportunity to build collections of his work. His jewellery designs though were unique. He combined the use of non-precious materials with the rarest of gems to produce what can only be described as sculpture to adorn the body. His work, and the work of many contemporary artists, was displayed at the Paris Exhibition of 1926 from whence the term 'Style Moderne' evolved.

Whether one's passion is for Jungenstil from Germany, Art Nouveau from France, style Liberty from England or Art Deco, described through a myriad of terms which evoke the style, there is no doubting the immense appeal of the artifacts of these times to today's collectors.

Arts and Crafts furniture has for some time been emerging as a major interest to collectors. Individually designed and made, it is

A Clarice Cliff Fern pot, decorated with swirls, 3.5in (9cm) high.
$360-540

almost always of fine quality and if unsigned can often be attributed to the artist responsible.

Bronze and bronze and ivory figures by Preiss, Chiparus, Colinet, Lorenzl, Zack and others have a sustaining appeal. The hand finishing techniques involved make them prohibitively expensive to reproduce today and although copies do exist, it is rarely without some sacrifice to quality.

Whilst the work of the larger pottery companies such as Moorcroft and Doulton have always found a ready market, the smaller ones have sometimes struggled to achieve the same level of interest. I am pleased and not a bit surprised to see a resurgence of interest in the Royal Lancastrian lustre wares produced by the Pilkington Co., the Isnic inspired designs of the Burmantofts factory and the scraffito decorated wares of Della Robia, amongst others.

It is not surprising that the output of the Art Nouveau and Deco Movements was so finite when one considers the very short time span involved. Whilst the finest examples of work by the major artists are out of reach of the average buyer, it is still possible for a discerning novice with modest resources to acquire good examples of the work of the less famous designers. Examples across the spectrum are available to the new collector, who would be well advised to seek the assistance of a reputable dealer whose stock is sympathetic to their taste and who can guide them at their pace.

ART NOUVEAU

Arts and Crafts Furniture

A Scottish Arts & Crafts oak bureau bookcase, by G. Laird, Glasgow.
$1,000-1,500

An Arts & Crafts buffet, 55in (139.5cm) wide.
$720-1,000

An Arts & Crafts oak bureau, standing on 4 reeded legs, 27in (68.5cm) wide.
$360-540

An oak bureau by Sidney Barnsley, with a fitted interior, with frieze drawer and 2 panelled cupboard doors, on moulded trestle ends with arched apron, 34in (86cm) wide.
$3,600-5,000

A Neo-Gothic carved and inlaid oak hanging cabinet, 41in (104cm) wide.
$3,600-5,000

A pair of oak side cabinets, with parquetry decoration, stamped Gillow & Co. 2344, 65in (164.5cm) wide, with single pedestal en suite stamped Gillow & Co. 2343.
$10,000-12,000

An Arts & Crafts oak bureau, with a fitted interior of pigeon-holes and 2 drawers, above 3 long similarly panelled drawers, on bracket feet, 36in (91.5cm) wide.
$1,800-2,700

An oak inlaid dwarf cabinet, by J. P. White, designed by M. H. Baillie-Scott, the cupboard door with pewter and fruitwood inlay, c1904, 20in (51cm) wide.
$2,700-3,600

A mahogany and satinwood breakfront cabinet, the design attributed to Thomas E. Collcutt, the marquetry to Stephen Webb, with original red velvet interior, stamped Collinson & Lock, 900, c1885, 65in (165cm) wide.
$3,600-5,000

A corner cabinet, by Heal & Son, on a plinth base, 21.5in (54cm) wide.
$720-1,000

Four dining chairs and one carver, by George Walton, 40in (101.5cm) high.
$360-540

An Arts & Crafts high backed elbow chair in dark oak, with solid seat.
$180-360

A pair of oak side chairs, designed by J. P. Seddon, the moulded arched backs with carved leaf motifs, upholstered backs and seats, stamped Seddon, New Bond Street, 9969.
$3,600-5,000

An oak low chair, by Arthur Simpson of Kendal, the curving arched back with pierced motif, with similarly curved seat on square section arched legs, damaged.
$720-1,000

A set of 7 oak Arts & Crafts dining chairs, including an open armchair.   **$1,800-2,700**

A set of 6 oak side chairs, designed by A. W. N. Pugin, on turned and chamfered legs joined by chamfered stretchers, upholstered in brown hide, with casters on front legs.
$2,700-3,600

An oak adjustable open armchair, upholstered in embroidered fabric, supported by Y-shaped arm and legs sections carved and pierced, on brass casters, late 19thC.
$1,800-2,700

A set of 8 chairs, including 2 carvers, by Ernest Gimson, with barber's pole inlay, tapering grille backs and upholstered drop-in seats, 38in (96cm) high.
$3,600-5,000

An oak 'Manxman' piano, by John Broadway & Sons, designed by M. H. Baillie-Scott, with wrought iron hinge plates and drop handles, brass and wrought iron candle brackets, panelled base, the case inscribed J. B. & Sons, movement no. 95972, c1899, 56.5in (142.5cm) wide.
$10,000-12,000

A walnut occasional table with ebony feet, by Gordon Russell, 23in (58cm) wide.
$720-1,000

GEORGE HENRY WALTON (1867-1933)

Closely associated with the Arts & Crafts movement, George Walton spent the first ten years of his career in Glasgow. In 1888, after little formal training, he established retail premises and workshop for his own business, 'George Walton & Co., Ecclesiastical and House Decorators'.

Design commissions from this period included Clutha glass for James Couper & Son, stained glass panels for William Burrell, furniture and interiors for Liberty & Co. and the refurbishment of Miss Cranston's Argyll and Buchanan Street Tearooms.

In 1898 Walton moved to London and concurrently set up business in York. He received a major commission to redesign a series of interiors for Kodak in Glasgow, Brussels, Vienna, Milan, Moscow, Leningrad and London, and later widened his range of activities by turning his hand to architecture, designing and building houses in Wales, London, France and Oxfordshire.

A pine wardrobe, designed by E. W. Godwin, the panelled front with 2 studded brass bands and central cupboard door enclosing a single fitted shelf, above a long drawer with central circular escutcheon and drop ring handles on channelled square section legs and casters, 60in (152.5cm) wide.
$21,000-27,000

This wardrobe was probably designed for Castle Dromore, County Limerick, Ireland. The door fittings are identical to those illustrated in the drawings of Godwin's door furniture for Dromore in the Drawings Collection at the Royal Institute of British Architects.

An Arts & Crafts mahogany framed four-fold draught screen, with embossed board panels decorated and gilt with pomegranates and meandering foliage, 75in (190.5cm) wide.
$720-1,000

An Arts & Crafts oak sideboard, the finialled ledge back with copper panel, quadrant tiers and slatted sides above a rectangular top and 2 frieze drawers and arched recess below, flanked by 2 panelled doors with carved tree motifs, on block feet, stamped Maple & Co. Ltd. in drawer and Nos. 4053, 2547, 1, design, to the reverse.
$1,200-1,700

An Arts & Crafts oak smoking cupboard with coppered hinges, marked Rd 39192, c1885, 12in (30.5cm) wide.
$70-145

An oak writing desk, designed by George Walton, the rectangular top above 3 drawers, on square tapering supports, c1900, 37in (94cm) high.
$1,000-1,500

A Thebes mahogany stool, 17in (43cm) square.
$360-540

A pair of highback ash armchairs, by Clisset, designed by Ernest Gimson, with ladderbacks above rush seats, on turned tapering legs joined with turned stretchers.
$1,000-1,500

A mahogany gateleg table, by Kenton & Co., designed by Ernest Gimson, the sides with Rose and Briar palmwood inlay, c1891, 32in (81.5cm) wide extended.
$3,600-5,000

An Arts & Crafts ebonised card table, 36in (91.5cm) wide.
$720-1,000

An oak side table, designed by Gordon Russell, 33.5in (85cm) wide.
$360-540

An Arts & Crafts hall table/ bureau, in the manner of Gustav Stickley, the 2 drawers with copper handles, 49in (124.5cm) wide.   **$1,000-1,500**

An oak chequered inlaid wardrobe, possibly designed by M. H. Baillie-Scott, 85in (216cm) wide, and a matching chest with 2 hinged lids above a pair of doors and 3 drawers, on octagonal supports, 55in (139.5cm) high, both with copper
$2,700-3,600

A mahogany and cane newspaper basket, designed by Sir Edwin Lutyens, with carved 'rope' decoration and cane panels, the rectangular basket on 4 square section legs, each pair joined with single plain stetcher, on casters, 32in (81cm) wide.
$7,000-9,000

This newspaper basket was designed by Sir Edwin Lutyens for his own use, certainly at 13 Mansfield Street, where he lived from September 1919, however it may have been designed earlier while he was living in Bedford Square. His daughter, Mary Lutyens, remembers the piece being in constant use.

English Furniture

A marquetry cabinet, profusely decorated.
$7,000-9,000

An inlaid armchair, 22in (55.5cm) wide. **$720-1,000**

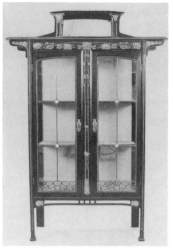

A Glasgow-style mahogany display cabinet, with a pair of stained and leaded glass doors, 69in (175cm) high.
$1,800-2,700

A breakfront cabinet, on arched trestle ends, with metal plaque Liberty & Co., London, 48in (122.5cm) wide.
$1,000-1,500

Continental Furniture

A polished mahogany bedroom suite, designed by Carlo Zen, comprising:
A pair of bedside cabinets, each set with marble plaque, and shaped panelled cupboard door carved with stylised floral motifs, on arched bracket feet, with original labels, Carlo Zen, Milano, 17in (43.5cm) wide. **$3,600-5,000**
A matching double bed, the front panel elaborately carved with a flowerspray, the back panel with original label, Carlo Zen, Milano, 46in (117cm) wide. **$3,600-5,000**
A large matching wardrobe, with floral brass lock-plates, 77in (196cm) wide.   **$3,600-5,000**

A carved mahogany mirror, by V. Epeaux, the glass enclosed in a curvilinear framework of apple blossom, 63.5in (161cm) high.
$7,000-9,000

A black and white painted cabinet, by Wiener Werkstätte, designed by Josef Hoffmann, c1910, 34in (86cm) wide.
$1,800-2,700

This piece is part of a suite of furniture designed for the home of Heinrich Bohler, Vienna.

Textiles

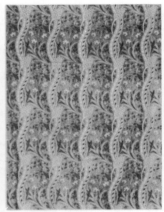

Three curtains, by Morris & Co., 'Violet & Columbine' design, woven wool and mohair in a repeating design of pink and red flowerheads amid entwined green foliage on dark blue ground, 67in (170cm) wide.
$3,600-5,000

A curtain, by Morris & Co., 'Daffodil', designed by J. H. Dearle, in printed cotton with braid border, with repeating pattern of daffodils and wild flowers between waved stylised vines in various greens, yellows and pinks, on smoke blue ground, 18in (45cm) wide.
$720-1,000

A wall hanging designed by Walter Crane, 'The Four Seasons', in woven silk on cotton, with repeating design of roundels enclosing classical figures, surrounded by figures representing the four seasons, c1893, 44in (111cm) wide.
$7,000-9,000

Glass

A Gallé vase, overlaid in green and brown and etched with seed pods and leaves, cameo signature, c1900, 5in (13cm) high.
$720-1,000

A woven wool curtain, the design attributed to B. J. Talbert, with repeating floral design, dark olive green ground with sage green, rust and beige, 49in (125cm) wide.
$1,000-1,500

A French cameo glass vase, with a lustrous pink and green ground, overlaid and etched in green with pendant fuchsias and foliage, indecipherable incised mark, c1900, 16in (40cm) high.
$1,000-1,500

A Tiffany Favrile glass floriform vase, inscribed L.C. Tiffany Favrile, 947 J, c1915, 13.5in (34cm) high.
$1,500-2,000

A Gallé bottle and stopper, enamelled with small polychrome flowers on gilt stems, repeated on the button stopper, crack to neck, painted mark Emile Gallé, c1900, 4in (10cm) high.
$720-1,000

A Daum, Nancy, cameo pedestal bowl, decorated with flowers and foliage in shades of red on an amber ground, 4.5in (11cm) high.
$1,200-1,700

Iridescent Glass

An iridescent glass vase, probably Austrian, of Persian inspiration, decorated with a band of gilt calligraphy on a vermiculé ground, divided by 3 lugs, the short trumpet neck gilt with scrolls, painted mark 515/2, late 19thC, 6in (15cm) high.
$720-1,000

A Loetz-style iridescent glass compôte with a metal stand.
$360-540

Two Austrian iridescent glass inkwells, with brass stylised decoration on the lids, c1900, 2in (5cm) high.
$360-540 each

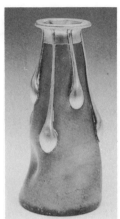

A Loetz-style iridescent glass vase, applied with a dot and thin line pattern in a deep blue on a mottled green ground, slight rubbing to neck, unmarked, 5in (13.3cm) high. **$720-1,000**

A miniature Tiffany Favrile iridescent glass vase, in a pale amber glass decorated with millefiori cane flowers amongst green lily pads and trails, on a gilt ground, engraved L.C.T., 8429A, c1906, 1.5in (4cm) high.
$360-540

A Tiffany-style iridescent glass vase, with green shading to blue iridescence, with Sterling silver mounts to the rim pendant with stylised droplets, mount stamped L. Sterling, glass unmarked, 6in (15cm) high.
$720-1,000

Lighting

A copper, brass and coloured glass lamp, 37in (94cm) high.
$360-540

A bronze table lamp, by Thomas Elsely, designed by C.F.A. Voysey, the base incorporating a heart-shaped lever switch with inverted collar, the tulip-shaped stem with central disc knop, the hemispherical shaped shade supported on scrolling brackets, fitted for electricity, c1904, 19.5in (49cm) high.
$2,700-3,600

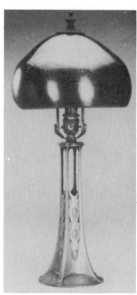

A W.M.F. pewter lamp, fitted with an onion-shaped purple, blue and green iridescent glass shade, base stamped W.M.F., c1905, 20.5in (52cm) high.
$1,200-1,700

A cantilevered brass desk lamp, 15.5in (39cm) high.
$180-360

A French glass lamp, signed, c1900.
$720-1,000

A copper and brass oil lamp, by W. A. S. Benson, supported on 3 high looped handles extending to the base, raised on a tripod stand, with overlapping copper shaped sheets forming the shade, slight damage, unmarked, c1890, 12in (31cm) high.
$720-1,000

Silver

A silver handled brush.
$110-180

A Hukin & Heath sugar scoop, 5in (13cm) long.   **$110-180**

A Liberty & Co. lightly hammered silver four-handled bowl, attributed to Rex Silver, stamped L&Co., with Birmingham hallmarks for 1900, 5.5in (14cm) high, 910gr.
$1,800-2,700

A silver and enamel jewellery box, 11in (28cm) long.   **$1,800-2,700**

A pair of candlesticks, hallmark 1910, 5.5in (14cm) high.
$720-1,000

A William Hutton & Sons Ltd., silver and enamel frame, embossed with typical Art Nouveau motifs, the recesses above filled with green and blue enamel, wood back, stamped factory marks, damaged, Rd: 404508, London 1902.
$1,800-2,700

A Hukin & Heath silver sugar bowl, designed by Dr. Christopher Dresser, with engraved crest, stamped with maker's marks JWH, JTH and London hallmarks for 1881, 5.5in (14cm) 195gr.
$900-1,500

An Art Nouveau silver ewer, maker's mark of Shreve, Crump & Low Co. Inc., 11in (28.5cm) high, 26.5oz.
$3,000-4,000

A pair of Art Nouveau silver photograph frames, Birmingham 1903, 12 by 10in (31 by 25cm).
$1,800-2,700

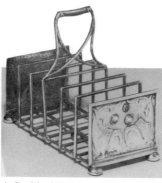

A Guild of Handicraft silver toast rack, on bun feet, the end panels with repoussé decoration of stylised fish and cabochon turquoises, stamped maker's marks G of H Ltd., with London hallmarks for 1904, 5in (13cm) high, 230gr.
$2,700-3,600

A pair of silver novelty pepperettes, by Goldsmiths & Silversmiths Company, in the form of champagne bottles, the corks engraved as smiling faces, on vestigial feet and circular bases, London 1908, 3.5in (9cm).
$360-540

A Georg Jensen fruit dish, on short cylindrical foot, with 2 cast and applied stylised floral handles, with stamped marks GJ No. 618 and Denmark Sterling, 12.5in (32cm) wide, 1,240gr.
$3,600-5,000

A Tiffany and Co. Japanesque jug, the copper body applied with 3 Sterling silver fish, one swimming amongst silver fronds, the others amongst engraved fronds, above a lobster and below 2 dragonflies, stamped Tiffany and Co., 8844 Makers 2678 Sterling Silver, Other Metals 925-1000 over T, 5.5 pints, 8.5in (21cm high.
$18,000-21,000

A set of 6 Liberty & Co. silver coffee spoons, the terminal of each decorated with stylised honesty, stamped maker's mark L&Co., with Birmingham hallmarks for 1907, in fitted case, 80gr.
$360-540

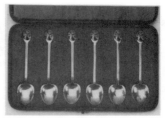

A set of 6 Liberty Cymric spoons, with heart shaped bowls, reeded stems and pierced oval terminals enamelled with foliage, in original fitted case, stamped maker's marks, Birmingham 1902, 4in (10cm) long.
$180-360

A Tiffany & Co. silver repoussé and chased rococo style coffee pot, of Turkish form, marked beneath Tiffany & Co. 5401 M 4145 Sterling silver, 9in (23cm) high, 15oz.
$1,000-1,500

An Art Nouveau ten-piece silver backed dressing table set, in original leatherbound velvet and satin lined fitted case, stamped maker's marks, London 1901/2.
$1,800-2,700

An H.G. Murphy silver tazza, the base applied with 2 shields bearing coats-of-arms and the inscription 'From Colfes Grammar School to Sir Lulham and Lady Pound on the opening of the New Science Building, Founders Day 1929', stamped with maker's marks HGM, with London hallmarks for 1929, 6.5in (17cm) high, 875gr.
$1,800-2,700

A four-piece tea and coffee set, Arts and crafts style, with bulbous cylindrical hammered finish, with applied rosettes, pad supports, the pots with composition handles and buttons, Birmingham 1925/26, 46oz.
$900-1,500

A Guild of Handicraft hammered silver inkwell, 3.5in (9cm) high.
$360-540

Silver Plate

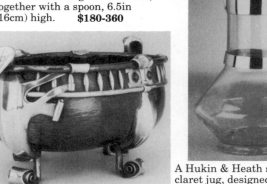

A preserve jar and cover, the frosted glass body decorated to simulate a drum, the elecroplate lid surmounted by a drummer boy, all supported on a bright cut stand terminating in 3 bun feet, together with a spoon, 6.5in (16cm) high. **$180-360**

A white metal and copper jardinière, designed by Oliver Baker, 13.5in (35cm) long.
$2,700-3,600

A Walker & Hall four-piece electroplated tea service, designed by David Mellor, the base stamped Walker & Hall, 53722 with flag monogram, 6.5in (16cm) high. **$900-1,500**

A Hukin & Heath electroplated tankard designed by Dr. Christopher Dresser, with ebonised bar handle, stamped maker's marks H&H 2089.
$720-1,000

A Hukin & Heath silver mounted claret jug, designed by Dr. Christopher Dresser, with ebonised bar handle, stamped maker's marks JWH, JTH with London hallmarks for 1881, and date registration lozenge for 9th May 1881, 8.5in (21cm) high.
$2,700-3,600

A James Dixon & Sons electroplated toast rack, designed by Dr. Christopher Dresser, stamped with James Dixon & Sons marks and facsimile signature Chr. Dresser, 68, 6.5in (17cm) long. **$7,000-9,000**

A Hukin & Heath electroplated double bonbon dish, designed by Dr. Christopher Dresser, stamped H&H 2223, c1881, 5.5in (14cm) high. **$900-1,500**

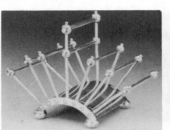

A Hukin & Heath electroplated toast rack, designed by Christopher Dresser, stamped maker's mark, signs of wear, H&H 2555, 1880s, 5in (13cm).
$720-1,000

A Hukin & Heath electroplated twin sweetmeat bowl, designed by Dr. Christopher Dresser, on 4 spike feet, stamped with maker's mark H&H 2523, 10.5in (27cm) long. **$1,000-1,500**

Pewter

A W.M.F. silver plated pewter champagne bucket, signed and dated 1906.
$1,800-2,700

A W.M.F. silvered pewter bowl, with swing handle, and green glass liner, stamped marks, 10in (25cm) wide.
$900-1,500

A W.M.F. round silver box, 5in (13cm) diam.
$360-540

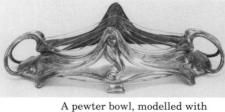

A pewter bowl, modelled with female heads and swirling draperies and cut glass liner.
$360-540

A Liberty & Co., pewter and enamel clock, c1900, 7.5in (19cm) high.
$2,700-3,600

A Liberty & Co., Tudric pewter clock, the arched top cast with heart shaped leaves, their stems flanking the tapering rectangular body, the copper dial above 2 blue enamelled cabochons, stamped marks, 8in (20cm).
$1,800-2,700

A pair of Tudric candlesticks, attributed to Archibald Knox, 5.5in (14cm) high.
$180-360

A Liberty & Co. pewter and enamel clock, 4.5in (11cm) high.
$1,200-1,700

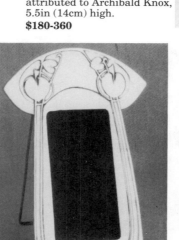

A Tudric pewter picture frame, with stylised honesty decoration, 10in (25cm) high.
$1,200-1,700

A Liberty & Co., pewter and enamel clock, 8in (20cm) high.
$2,700-3,600

A Liberty & Co. hammered pewter rose bowl, the design attributed to Oliver Baker, set with 5 green glass studs, on 5 curved legs and trefoil feet, stamped English Pewter made by Liberty & Co, 01130, 6.6in (16cm) high.
$720-1,000

A German pewter top claret jug, 11.5in (29cm) high.
$720-1,000

A W.M.F. pewter jug, 12in (31cm) high.
$110-180

A W.M.F. pewter dressing table mirror, 12.5in (32cm) high.
$360-540

A W.M.F. pewter inkstand, 8in (20cm) wide.
$720-1,000

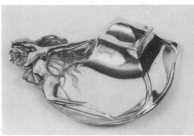

A German green glass and pewter claret jug, 14in (36cm) high.
$360-540

A Tudric pewter tea set, tray 18.5 by 11.5in (47 by 29cm).
$720-1,000

A Continental pewter plaque, with central dished panel chased with the head of pre-Raphaelite maiden, flanked by curved uprights pendant with husks with stepped cresting, the reverse initialled EP and stamped 279, 8.5in (21cm) wide.
$180-360

A W.M.F. electroplated pewter tazza, 12.5in (32cm) high.
$720-1,000

A Tudric pewter vase, cast in relief with sprays of honesty and bearing the inscription 'For Old Times Sake', stamped marks, 8in (20cm) high.   **$180-360**

Miscellaneous Metalware

Two Art Nouveau gilt metal plaques, on wooden surrounds.
$720-1,000

A copper box, with ship on lid, attributed to John Pearson, 8in (20cm) long.
$180-360

A Benham & Froud copper coffee pot, designed by Dr. Christopher Dresser, with ebonised handle, stamped with maker's mark, c1884, 8.5in (22cm) high.
$900-1,500

A copper charger, by John Pearson, 20in (51cm) diam.
$360-540

An Artificer's Guild hammered gilded copper bowl, designed by Edward Spencer, with inscription 'To Edward & Ellen Packard, Wedded 50 years, May 23rd 1917, with the love from their sons and daughters, Charles, Katherine, Winifred, Celia, Reginald, Nina, Walter, Sylvia, Phyllis, Harold', on 5 bun feet, numbered 891, 11in (28cm) diam.
$1,800-2,700

An Art Nouveau two-handled French copper jug, 19.5in (50cm) high.
$360-540

An Art Nouveau brass note pad holder, 7.5in (19cm) high.
$35-70

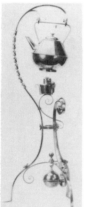

A Benham and Froud copper and brass kettle-on-stand, on domed tripartite foot, the scrolling openwork column arching over to form hooks from which the kettle is suspended, stamped maker's mark, 32in (81cm) high.
$360-540

A pair of polished steel twin branched candelabra, by Alfred Bucknell, c1920, 14in (35cm) high.
$3,600-5,000

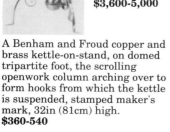

A Tiffany bronze tripod base candlestick with green glass interior, numbered 22322, 10in (25cm) high.   **$400-500**

A pair of polished steel firedogs, attributed to Alfred Bucknell, each bud finial above hammered and fluted perpendicular, on trestle feet, 22.5in (57cm) high.
$900-1,500

A pair of Arts and Crafts copper framed mirrors, the central plate flanked by twin Celtic style motifs, 19in (48cm) high.
$360-540

A set of polished steel fire irons, attributed to Thornton & Downer comprising: a poker, pair of tongs, a shovel, a brush, supported on square section stand with 3 arched legs, bands of engraved decoration, 25in (64cm) high.
$1,800-2,700

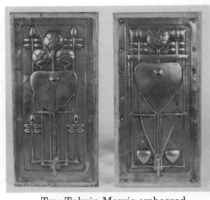

Two Talwin Morris embossed brass finger plates, each with a central motif of a heart imposed on a stylised foliate grid of blooming and budding roses, cracked, c1893, 11 by 15in (28 by 38cm).
$360-540

Jewellery

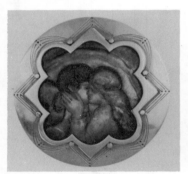

A silver and enamel brooch, by Phoebe Anna Ramsay Traquair, the central plique à jour enamel panel with 2 lovers in medieval costume embracing, coloured in blue, green, pink, brown and yellow with touches of gold, enclosed within a silver mount with single bar pin, the enamel inscribed to the reverse 'The Kiss' and with P.R.T. monogram, the silver mount for Edinburgh 1935, 2in (5cm) diam.
$2,700-3,600

Born in Dublin in 1852 and married in 1873 to Ramsay Traquair, the keeper of the National Gallery of Scotland, Phoebe Traquair was one of the most renowned enamelists of her time and possibly the best known after Alexander Fisher. Her work, often of a religious nature, was regularly featured in exhibitions and in 'The Studio' magazine. She carried out many important commissions including work for St. Mary's Cathedral in Edinburgh, the National Gallery of Scotland and for Sir Robert Lorimer. She may also have worked for Omar Ramsden. In 1883 she remarried, her full name becoming Phoebe Anna Traquair Reid. She died in 1936.

A citrine single stone and diamond pendant/brooch, with frosted crystal and diamond surround to a diamond and gem-set suspension, with detachable fittings for conversion to a clasp.
$900-1,500

An Arts & Crafts chalcedony, amethyst and mother-of-pearl openwork pendant with matching drop and neck chain; and a chalcedony, chrysoprase and marcasite articulated drop brooch/pendant.
$720-1,000

Continental Ceramics

An Amphora ware mirror, 12in (31cm) high.   **$180-360**

A ceramic figure with sea shells, by Ernst Whallis, 16.5in (42cm) high.   **$900-1,500**

A Royal Dux ceramic figure on a sea shell, 14in (36cm) high.
$360-540

A terracotta lamp by Goldscheider, 28in (71.5cm) high.
$2,700-3,600

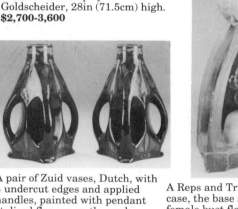

A pair of German tiles, both depicting maidens with flowing hair in coloured glazes, the Muse of Music playing a harp, and the Muse of Dancing, having raised outlines, 5in (14cm) wide, framed.
$1,200-1,700

A pair of Zuid vases, Dutch, with 4 undercut edges and applied handles, painted with pendant stylised flowers on the neck, painted mark made in Zuid, Holland, J. H. and incised 213, 8.5in (22cm) high.
$720-1,000

A Reps and Trinte pottery clock case, the base supporting a female bust flanked by 2 floral buttresses beneath triangular face, impressed marks and incised Shellmacher, damaged, early 20thC, 21in (53cm) high.
$1,200-1,700

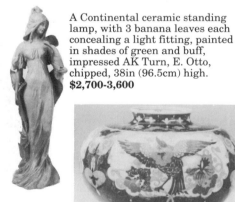

A Continental ceramic standing lamp, with 3 banana leaves each concealing a light fitting, painted in shades of green and buff, impressed AK Turn, E. Otto, chipped, 38in (96.5cm) high.
$2,700-3,600

A Clement Massier turquoise glazed earthenware jardinière and stand, of organic design moulded in relief with leaves, flowers and branches, the oviform bowl on cylindrical stand, impressed factory marks, 37in (94cm) high.
$2,700-3,600

A Rozenberg vase, painted in rich polychrome colours, black printed factory mark and year symbol of a flower, Rozenberg, den Haag, a cross in a square, 372, c1913, 6in (15.5cm) high.
$360-540

A pair of Rozenberg vases, decorated in rich polychrome colours, black painted factory mark and year symbol of a flower, Rozenberg, den Haag, cross in a square, 472, c1913, 8.5in (21.5cm) high.
$720-1,000

British Art Pottery

A vase by C. H. Brannam, c1885, 10in (25cm) high.
$180-360

A blue frog, by C. H. Brannam, 3in (7.5cm) high.
$110-180

A green vase by C. H. Brannam, with 6 handles, 1903, 6.5in (16cm) high.
$180-360

A Bretby 'copperette' jug, 12in (31cm) high.
$180-360

A pair of spill vases, by C. H. Brannam, converting to candlesticks, 10in (25cm) high.
$360-540

A Watcombe cheese dish, attributed to Christopher Dresser, 6.5in (16.5cm) high.
$180-360

A Burmantofts vase, decorated with dragons, by V. Kremer, 9.5in (24cm) high.
$720-1,000

A Bretby spill vase, decorated with a stork and bamboo, yellow coloured, 12in (31cm) high.
$110-180

An early Burmantofts turquoise blue planter, No. 1082, 7in (18cm) high.
$180-360

A figure of The Brighton Wet Nurse, with nodding head and suspended body, dressed in a cloak and gown baring a bosom to a babe in arms, standing on a circular base marked Rye B4, 6in (15cm) high. **$360-540**

An Ault vase, by Christopher Dresser, 12in (31cm) high.
$180-360

A pair of Bretby pottery vases, with applied horn and insect decoration, No. 1470, 14in (35.5cm) high.
$720-1,000

A Burmantofts pottery ewer, 10in (25cm) high.
$180-360

A Burmantofts green pottery vase, with Gothic decoration, 9.5in (24cm) high.
$180-360

A vase by Thomas Forester, 8in (20cm) high.
$180-360

A Linthorpe pouring vessel, designed by Christopher Dresser, covered in a mottled and streaked green glaze, impressed Linthorpe, .312, facsimile signature Chr. Dresser with Linthorpe Pottery seal, 6.5in (16.5cm) high.
$900-1,500

A Linthorpe pottery vase, after a design by Christopher Dresser, in a streaked brown glaze, with a pierced flower and foliage in the centre in green, stamped Chr. Dresser, HT, c1880, 8.5in (21.5cm) high.
$720-1,000

A Minton porcelain vase, designed by Christopher Dresser, painted in gold, green, yellow, blue, black and orange enamels, restored, 11.5in (29cm) high.
$3,600-5,000

A Linthorpe vase, by Clara Pringle, 9.5in (24cm) high.
$360-540

A Linthorpe vase, designed by Christopher Dresser, impressed with a spiralling feather design, covered in an olive green glaze, impressed Linthorpe with facsimile signature Chr. Dresser, 298 and HT monogram, 7.5in (19cm) high.
$720-1,000

A pair of Martin Brothers stoneware panels, the arched forms impressed and incised with profile images of Cower and Chaucer, each against a patterned background, covered in a salt glaze in shades of blue and brown, indistinct marks and date, 17in (43cm) long. **$900-1,500**

A pair of Minton Art Pottery moon flasks, painted in blue with frogs and fish or birds and rabbits within chevron bands, the short cylindrical neck flanked by a pair of loop handles, impressed, printed and painted marks, c1870, 8.5in (21.5cm) high. **$900-1,500**

A Martin Brothers jug, in a mottled blue/green on a brown ground, the neck with a band of vertical incised lines, incised Martin Bros., London & Southall, 2-1894, chip to spout, c1894, 8.5in (21.5cm) high. **$720-1,000**

A Martin Brothers vase, painted with spiny fish and eels swimming amongst water weeds and other aquatic life, in shades of grey and brown on a buff ground, incised Martin Bros, London & Southall, 10-1891, repaired, 7.5in (19cm) high; and a miniature Martin Ware vase. **$720-1,000**

A Linthorpe vase, by Christopher Dresser, shape No. 24, 12.5in (32cm) high. **$360-540**

A Martin Brothers stoneware tobacco jar and cover, modelled as a comic bird with curly plumage, standing erect with eyes closed, glazed in shades of blue and buff, base incised Martin Bros London & Southall, cover incised Martin 30.8.81 London & Southall, repaired, 12in (31cm) high. **$2,700-3,600**

A Minton Art Pottery studio moon flask, one side with painted head and shoulders portrait of a girl in the style of W. S. Coleman, framed by a band of holly, the reverse in dark blue, impressed Minton 1498 and printed mark Minton's Art Pottery Studio Kensington Gore, damaged, 14in (35cm) high. **$900-1,500**

A set of 20 Minton stoneware tiles, designed by A. W. N. Pugin, the ochre ground with brown and black glazed decoration of quatrefoil reserve with central flowerhead within foliate motifs, reverse with moulded marks Minton & Co., Stoke-upon-Trent, Patent, each tile 6in (15cm) square. **$1,000-1,500**

A Minton Seccessionist jardinière, decorated in purple, turquoise and green, repeated around the body, impressed and printed factory marks, Mintons, No. 72, c1910, 13in (32.5cm) high.
$1,200-1,700

A Minton stoneware bread plate, designed by A. W. N. Pugin, with inscription 'Waste Not, Want Not', covered in rust and blue encaustic glazes, stamped 430, 13in (33cm) diam. **$1,800-2,700**

A William de Morgan two-tile panel of a manned galley within a classical harbour, with turquoise, green, amethyst and yellow glazes, c1880, 12in (31cm) long.
$1,800-2,700

A William de Morgan deep red lustre bowl, decorated by Fred Passenger, with decoration of an eagle attacking a grotesque lizard within a scrolling foliate border, painted FP initials, c1890, (25cm) diam.
$1,200-1,700

A Minton Seccessionist jardinière, after a design by Léon V. Solon and John W. Wadsworth, decorated in turquoise above printed scrolling green foliage, moulded Minton's, England, impressed factory marks and date cypher, damaged, 12.5in (32cm) high. **$360-540**

A William de Morgan oviform vase, painted in turquoise, tones of blue, grey, black, and dark red on a cream ground, damaged, unmarked, 16in (40cm) high.
$3,600-5,000

A William de Morgan four-tile panel of 2 snakes amongst flowering foliage against turquoise ground, with green, puce and amethyst glazes, chipped, each impressed WM, Merton Abbey seal, c1882, 16in (41cm) square.
$2,700-3,600

A Pilkington's red vase, 5.5in (13.5cm) high.
$360-540

A Bernard Moore enamelled flambé plate, the centre painted and enamelled with the bust of a female figure, the face in profile, hands clasped in prayer, with an inscription in a halo, on a flambé ground, overpainted hands and face, painted monogram B.M., circular frame, 10in (25.5cm) diam. **$360-540**

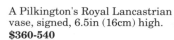

A Pilkington's Royal Lancastrian lustre charger, by Mycock, inscribed on reverse, c1900, 11.5in (29cm) diam.
$1,800-2,700

A Pilkington's Royal Lancastrian vase, signed, 6.5in (16cm) high.
$360-540

A collection of William de Morgan tiles, decorated with a parrot, flowers, guinea fowl, great curassow, pelican with fish, and ships, some lustre and some polychrome, various marks, two 8in (20cm) square the others 6in (15cm) square. **$3,600-5,000**

A Pilkington's vase, 6in (15cm) high. **$110-180**

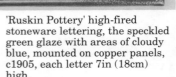

A Pilkington's Royal Lancastrian 'Vermillion' glaze vase, moulded with fish amongst waves on a green ground under a speckled orange glaze, impressed factory marks, c1920, 8in (20cm) high; and a similar vase, after a design by William S. Mycock and modelled by E. T. Radford, with a mottled green and speckled orange glaze, impressed factory marks E.T.R., painted monogram and year cypher, c1929, 7in (18cm) high. **$360-540**

'Ruskin Pottery' high-fired stoneware lettering, the speckled green glaze with areas of cloudy blue, mounted on copper panels, c1905, each letter 7in (18cm) high. **$7,000-9,000**

These are the original letters used at the Ruskin Pottery factory.

A Royal Lancastrian uranium glazed vase, by Richard Joyce, 5in (13cm) high. **$720-1,000**

A Ruskin plate, with incised mark, 6in (15cm) diam. **$35-70**

A Ruskin lustre vase, dated 1922, 8in (20cm) high. **$110-180**

A Ruskin blue vase, c1930, 5.5in (14cm) high. **$110-180**

A Rye Pottery 'Sussex Pig', lead glazed mainly in blue, having a hook-on head inscribed with the motto 'Wun't be druv', 4.5in (11.5cm) long. **$360-540**

A Wedgwood Fairyland lustre 'Elves and Bell Branch' bowl, after a design by Daisy Makeig-Jones, decorated with elves and fairies dancing and amongst tall grass against a black ground with a gilt spider's web, printed Portland vase mark England, painted number Z4968, minor rubbing, c1920, 3in (7.5cm) high.
$900-1,500

A pair of Shelley 'Intarsio' ware vases, after a design by Walter Slater, decorated with stylised pink flowerheads amongst interlinked foliage in green, brown, and blue, printed mark Late Foley, Shelley, England, Intarsio and painted number 544 3617, c1915, 6.5in (16cm) high.
$360-540

A Rye Pottery vase, with flared neck, applied with daffodils and leaves, marked on base Sussex Ware Rye, 6in (15cm) high.
$180-360

A pair of Wedgwood Fairyland lustre vases, afer a design by Daisy Makeig-Jones, each decorated with the 'Imps on a Bridge and Tree House' pattern, against a flame red ground, Portland vase mark Wedgwood, Made In England and painted number Z5481, c1920, 10in (26cm) high.
$7,000-9,000

A Pilkington's Royal Lancastrian lustre wall plaque, after a design by Walter Crane and painted by Charles E. Cundall, with a peacock standing with its tail displayed, in copper lustre with red details on a mauve ground, the reverse with 4 copper lustre floral motifs, damaged impressed factory 'P' and Bee mark, VII, and lustre monograms, c1907.
$900-1,500

A Wileman & Co. 'Intarsio' jug, after a design by Frederick Rhead, modelled as the body of a bird with an Egyptian style head, in typical palette, raised on 3 feet, printed factory mark Intarsio, Registration No. 330274, painted No. 3076, c1900, 5in (13.5cm) high.   **$360-540**

A Wedgwood Fairyland lustre 'Woodland Bridge' bowl, after a design by Daisy Makeig-Jones, decorated outside with orange, yellow, green and purple shrubs on a black ground, the interior with the 'Fairy with Large Hat' pattern, cobwebs in the trees, fairies and elves amongst the toadstools on the banks of a river, gilt printed factory mark and painted number Z4968, c1920, 6in (16cm) diam.
$3,600-5,000

A tapering vase, the body applied with branches, acorns and oak leaves, marked on base S.R.W. Rye, 4in (10cm) high.
$110-180

A Wileman & Co. 'Intarsio' jardinière, after a design by Frederick Rhead, decorated with a frieze of geese between foliate bands, in typical colours printed factory mark Intarsio, Registration No. 330400, printed No. 3143, c1900, 7in (18cm) high.
$900-1,500

A Rye Pottery bowl, the brown body profusely covered with applied green hops, the rim banded with petite leaves, marked on base Rye Sussex, dated 1919, 8in (20cm) diam.
$360-540

Moorcroft

Moorcroft pottery is very much in vogue at the moment. This British pottery was first made by William Moorcroft at the factory of James MacIntyre in 1898.

From the start it was important to Moorcroft that ornament was used to accentuate form. Each piece was thrown on the potters wheel to produce the forms and variety he wanted. William then drew each design himself. His drawings were outlined in slip and practically every piece was signed.

While at MacIntyre's William became known for his Florian ware. His recognition grew rapidly on both sides of the Atlantic and his work was sold at Tiffany of New York and Liberty of London. In 1904 he won his first gold medal at St. Louis.

In 1913 William left James MacIntyre to build his own workship at Cobridge and to found the private company of W. Moorcroft Ltd., which still flourishes today.

As you delve deeper into the history of this pottery you wonder just how many different shapes and designs there are, when you think, at last you've seen them all, low and behold you find another!

The quality of the workmanship is so precise, sharp, clear and distinct that, to the observer, other types of pottery look primitive by comparison. Each piece portrays a variety of pure colour. Design preference is of an individual taste, but the landscape, trees and toadstool outweigh most for popularity. For absolute brilliance the flambé pieces are unrivalled. The rare and exotic waratah and protea have much appeal, but probably the early wisteria on a white ground, because of its simplicity and incredible beauty, is a favourite with most people. Another popular choice is the pomegranate - this particular design is probably the one which is most associated with Moorcroft pottery, because it was in production continually between 1910 & 1940.

William Moorcroft's pottery has proved to be an extremely good investment from both a financial and collector's point of view. While the value of other potteries tend to rise and fall with current trends, Moorcroft has always risen steadily. With the prevalent strong market both here and abroad, past and present prices and performance point to a continued growth for the future.

In each category of art, great masters stand out in their field. In art pottery William Moorcroft stands alone with his genius as the consummate master potter.

His artistry will leave an everlasting legacy of beauty for the World to enjoy.

A Moorcroft two-handled Blue Pansy design biscuit barrel, c1929, 7in (17.5cm) high.
$900-1,500

A MacIntyre Moorcroft Blue Poppy design salad bowl and servers, c1902, 10in (25cm) diam.
$1,200-1,700

A W. R. Jacobs & Co. biscuit tin, moulded in a Moorcroft shape and transfer decorated with the pomegranate design, 6in (16cm) high.
$110-180

A Moorcroft Pomegranate design octagonal bowl, c1925, 10in (25cm) diam.   **$720-1,000**

A MacIntyre Moorcroft Yellow Cornflower design tobacco jar, c1910, 6in (15cm) diam.
$1,000-1,500

A Moorcroft exhibition pomegranate ginger jar, 1927, 12in (31cm) diam.
$7,000-9,000

A MacIntyre Moorcroft blue 18thC design teapot, c1906.
$720-1,000

A MacIntyre footed bowl, the exterior decorated with sprays of blue pansies on a green ground, impressed factory marks, signed in green, rim restored, 9in (22.5cm) diam.
$360-540

A Moorcroft yacht design meat dish, c1934, 16.5in (42cm) long.
$110-180

The yacht design was introduced by William Moorcroft in 1934, taken from an original sketch by his daughter, Beatrice Moorcroft.

A MacIntyre Moorcroft Florian ware blue on Blue Tulip design jug, c1901, 12in (31cm) high.
$1,200-1,700

A Lise B. Moorcroft Toadstool design plaque, dated 1990, 16in (41cm) diam.
$360-540

Lise B. Moorcroft is the daughter of Walter Moorcroft, who ran the factory from 1945-1986 and the granddaughter of the founder, William Moorcroft.

A Moorcroft pottery jardinière, with Florian style daisy and poppy decoration in green, blue and yellow glazes, with two loop handles, impressed Cambridge factory mark, and green painted signature, c1916, 10in (25cm) wide. **$1,800-2,700**

A Moorcroft Claremont Toadstool design vase, decorated in shades of yellow, mauve and blue on a mottled green ground, impressed Moorcroft, Burslem, 1914, signed in green, 4.5in (11cm) high.
$720-1,000

A Moorcroft small Blue Pansy design jardinière, c1928, 4in (10cm) high.
$360-540

A Moorcroft pink Flamminian design teapot with cup, saucer and plate, c1914.
$360-540

A Walter Moorcroft Caribbean design mug, c1962, 4.5in (11cm) high.   **$180-360**

A MacIntyre Moorcroft Aurelian design coffee pot, c1897, 7in (17.5cm) high.
$720-1,000

A Moorcroft blue teapot, c1918, 6in (15cm) high.
$110-180

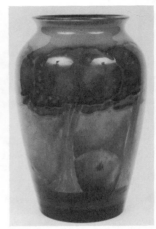

A Moorcroft saltglaze pink waving corn landscape vase, c1934, 11in (28cm) high.
$3,600-5,000

A MacIntyre Moorcroft two-handled Tulip and Forget-me-not design vase, c1902, 9in (23cm) high.
$1,800-2,700

A Moorcroft Eventide tree design vase, c1928, 6in (15cm) high.
$1,800-2,700

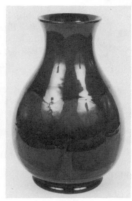

A MacIntyre Moorcroft Alhambra design crocus vase, c1903, 6in (15cm) high.
$900-1,500

A Moorcroft ochre Spring Flower design vase, c1936, 9.5in (24cm) high.
$900-1,500

A Moorcroft Moonlight blue tree design vase, c1925, 9in (23cm) high.
$1,800-2,700

A MacIntyre Moorcroft Aurelian design vase, c1897, 12in (31cm) high.
$720-1,000

A Moorcroft two-handled inverted baluster shaped vase, painted with the Brown Chrysanthemum pattern on a green ground, with green W. Moorcroft signature, c1915, 9in (23cm) high.
$1,800-2,700

A Moorcroft pomegranate design vase, c1928, 9.5in (24cm) high.
$720-1,000

A pair of Moorcroft MacIntyre double-gourd shaped vases painted with the Brown Chrysanthemum pattern on a green ground, printed marks and W. Moorcroft signature in green, impressed 166, 12in (31cm) high.
$2,700-3,600

A Moorcroft Pomegranate design vase, c1930, 9in (23cm) high.
$720-1,000

A MacIntyre Moorcroft blue on blue Cornflower design vase, c1901, 5in (13cm) high.
$360-540

A Moorcroft saltglaze Spring Flower design vase, c1936, 6in (15cm) high.
$720-1,000

A Moorcroft MacIntyre Liberty smoker's set, damaged, c1903, 17in (43cm) wide.
$1,800-2,700

A Moorcroft blue panel saltglaze vase, dated 1941, 9in (23cm) high.
$1,200-1,700

A Walter Moorcroft Dahlia design vase, c1959, 8in (20cm) high.
$360-540

Doulton

Anthea, a Royal Doulton figure, HN 1526, green printed and painted marks, 1932-38, 7in (18cm) high.
$720-1,000

A Marlene Dietrich wall mask, with brown eyes and hair, and pale pink lips, marked HN 1591, 8in (20cm) long.
$360-540

Autumn, HN 314, model number 222, introduced in 1918, withdrawn in 1938, 7.5in (19cm) high.
$360-540

A Royal Doulton figure, Lady Fayre, HN 1265, green printed and red painted marks, c1928-38, 5.5in (14cm) high.
$360-540

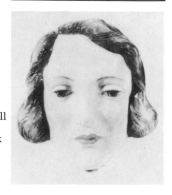

A Doulton Burns punch bowl, 9in (23cm) diam.
$110-180

Scotties, HN 1281, designed by L. Harradine, introduced in 1928, withdrawn in 1938, ear damaged, 5in (13cm) high.
$720-1,000

Easter Day, HN 2039, a Royal Doulton figure, designed by M. Davies, introduced in 1949, withdrawn in 1969.
$180-360

Griselda, a Royal Doulton figure, 1947-53, 6in (15cm) high.
$360-540

Memories, a Royal Doulton figure, 1949-59, 6in (15cm) high.
$180-360

Modena, HN 1846, a Royal Doulton figure, withdrawn 1949, cracked.
$180-360

Capt. Hook, D 6597, a Royal Doulton figure, designed by M. Henks and D. Biggs, introduced in 1965, withdrawn in 1971, 7in (18cm) high.
$360-540

The Laird, HN 2361, a Royal Doulton figure, designed by M. Nicoll, introduced in 1969.
$70-145

Coppelia, a Royal Doulton porcelain figurine, HN 2115, 7in (18cm) high.
$180-360

Francine, a Royal Doulton figure, designed by J. Bromley, introduced in 1922, discontinued in 1981, 5.5in (14cm) high.
$70-145

A Doulton Lambeth jug to commemorate Emin Pasha, Relief Expedition 1887-1889, with a portrait of H. M. Stanley, 8in (20cm) high.
$360-540

A Royal Doulton figure of a seated bulldog with a Union Jack draped over its back, printed factory marks, 4in (10cm) high.
$360-540

A pair of Doulton stoneware vases, decorated by Hannah Barlow, with bands of deer within stylised foliage borders, impressed mark and date 1885, 9.5in (24cm) high.
$1,000-1,500

A Royal Doulton Chang vase, covered in a thick crackled mottled white, black, red, ochre glaze running over mottled shades of ochre, red, blue and black, printed marks Chang, Royal Doulton, Noke, 4.5in (11cm) high.
$720-1,000

A pair of Royal Doulton baluster vases, with mottled green glaze and raised design of stylised flowers and foliage.
$360-540

A Royal Doulton teapot and cover commemorating Lord Nelson, blue ground with brown glazed rope twist handle and spout, with raised decoration of the head of the Admiral, the other side depicting the Victory, and inscribed around the neck, 'England Expects Every Man Will Do His Duty', monogrammed Ap., 5in (13cm) high.
$180-360

A Royal Doulton urn with Grecian figures, 13in (33cm) high.
$360-540

A Doulton Studio ware vase, c1930, 7in (18cm) high.
$110-180

A pair of Royal Doulton toy vases, hand painted with a country scene, c1910, 1.5in (4cm) high.
$360-540

A Royal Doulton vase, decorated with a continuous floriate pattern in blue, white and gilt, against a shaded ground, 18.5in (47cm) high.
$360-540

A pair of Lambeth Doulton stoneware vases, decorated by Florence Barlow in green slip with black grouse, incised marks, F.E.B., 14in (36cm) high.
$1,000-1,500

A pair of Doulton stoneware vases, 11in (28cm) high.
$360-540

ART DECO
Furniture

A Heal's oak cabinet, designed by Ambrose Heal, the drawers with heart shaped pulls, with inlaid plaque Heal & Son Makers, London W, 44.5in (113cm) wide.
$1,800-2,700

An upholstered 'shell' armchair, the padded back and seat in the form of a scallop shell, with scrolling 'nautilus shell' arms and with a fringe apron, c1930.
$900-1,500

A Makers of Simple Furniture birchwood chest of drawers, designed by Gerald Summers, with retailer's label Bowmans Bros., Ltd., Complete House Furnishers, Camden Town, London N.W.1, 27in (69cm) wide.
$720-1,000

Four Isokon stacking plywood chairs and a table, designed by Marcel Breuer, c1936, table 54in (137cm) wide.
$3,600-5,000

A burr maple sideboard, the design attributed to Ray Hille, 44.5in (113cm) wide.
$900-1,500

A Hille sideboard, the design attributed to Ray Hille, the burr-veneer fronted sideboard with 4 short drawers flanked by single cupboard doors, each with stylised carved leaf handles and enclosing a single fitted shelf, on 4 bowed carved legs, stamped Hille, 66in (167.5cm) wide.
$1,000-1,500

A Makers of Simple Furniture birchwood millinery chest, designed by Gerald Summers, on platform base, with retailer's label Bowman Bros. Ltd., Complete House Furnishers, Camden Town, London N.W.1., 27in (69cm) wide.
$720-1,000

An ebonised and sycamore cheval glass-cum-dressing table, supported at the side by a bow-front cupboard inlaid with polka dots, 41in (102cm) wide; and a matching upholstered stool, the cupboard bearing the label of Marcus Adams, 6 Granville Place, Portman Square.
$900-1,500

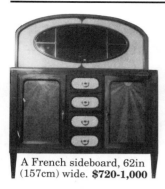

A French sideboard, 62in (157cm) wide. **$720-1,000**

A burr maple sideboard, the design attributed to Ray Hille, 54in (137cm) wide. **$1,200-1,700**

A Heal's oak dining table, designed by Ambrose Heal, 57in (145cm) wide. **$2,700-3,600**

Lalique Glass

A French daybed, with mattress covered in black and white zebra skin with matching cylindrical cushion, on 4 tapering fluted legs, 1930s, 74in (188cm) long. **$2,700-3,600**

A Lalique 'Figurines et Voiles' box and cover, moulded with a band of classically draped figures holding roses and swirling lengths of material, heightened in red, the lid with 2 similar figures, damaged, moulded mark R. Lalique, made in France, c1930, 3in (7.5cm) high.
$360-540

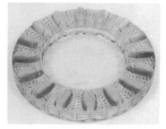

A Lalique 'Filix' glass bowl, the deep well moulded outside with a band of large fern leaves picked out with frosting, wheel engraved R. Lalique, France, c1927, 13in (33cm) diam.
$720-1,000

An opalescent Lalique glass ashtray, with beetle design, 5.5in (14cm) diam. **$360-540**

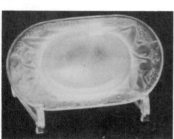

A Lalique 'Medicis' glass ashtray, with 2 pairs of naked female figures amongst flowers, moulded mark R. Lalique, engraved R. Lalique, France, No. 280, c1925, 6in (15cm) long.
$360-540

A Lalique 'Enfants' box and cover, moulded outside with a band of nude children holding a weight above their heads on a blue stained ground, the lid moulded with 5 tiers of rose bands similarly coloured, stencilled mark R. Lalique, France, c1930, 3in (7.5cm) high.
$360-540

A Lalique 'Ondines' opalescent glass plate, moulded underneath with 6 mermaids in swirling water on the border, wheel engraved R. Lalique, France, engraved No. 3003, c1922, 11in (28cm) diam. **$1,000-1,500**

A Lalique 'Roger' box and cover, moulded with long-tailed exotic birds perched in branches amongst clear glass discs, engraved Lalique, France, c1927, 5in (13cm) diam.
$360-540

A Lalique clock, the circular dial with black enamelled chapters, engraved 'R. Lalique, France', with chrome base enclosing light fitting, 7in (18cm) high.
$1,800-2,700

A Lalique 'Prunes' glass vase, moulded in high relief with an opalescent band of rounded fruits on leafy branches, damaged, wheel engraved R. Lalique, France, c1930, 7in (18cm) high.
$3,600-5,000

'Suzanne', a Rene Lalique opalescent figurine, of a naked maiden, her arms outstretched and holding her robes, chipped, moulded R. Lalique signature, 9in (23cm) high.
$10,000-12,000

A Lalique amber moulded vase shaped table lamp, modelled as a stylised artichoke, engraved in script R. Lalique, France, 9in (23cm) high.
$2,700-3,600

A Lalique 'Ceylan' vase, moulded with opalescent pairs of budgerigars below foliage wheel, engraved mark R. Lalique, 9.5in (24cm) high.   **$1,800-2,700**

A Lalique 'Saint Francois' opalescent glass vase, moulded outside with birds perched in leafy branches, damaged, stencil mark R. Lalique, France, c1930, 7in (18cm) high.
$1,000-1,500

A Lalique 'Epis No. 1' stained glass plate, the border moulded and stained in blue with a repeated band of wheatears, with a fluted radiating centre, moulded R. Lalique, engraved France, c1922, 12.5in (31.5cm) diam.
$180-360

Glass

An amber glass trinket set in the form of a butterfly, comprising: a tray, 3 boxes and lids, and 2 candlesticks.   **$35-70**

A pink frosted glass flower holder with a figure, 8.5in (21cm) diam.
$70-145

A Sabino blue glass vase, moulded with overlapping peacock feather motifs in low relief with slight frosting, incised Sabino, France, c1930, 8in (20cm) high.   **$360-540**

A glass mascot, minor chips, unmarked, 1930s, 5.5in (14cm) high.
$360-540

A Verlys frosted and opalescent glass plafonier, moulded with 3 large sunflowers and foliage, moulded mark Verly, France, 1930s, 14in (36cm) high.
$360-540

A red glass Ashay car mascot, 5in (13cm) high.
$360-540

A Dubarry scent bottle and stopper, moulded in relief with sunburst motif, in original fitted box with lithographed interior, 4in (10cm) high.
$35-70

A Sabino iridescent moulded glass vase, modelled with classical Bacchic scene, chipped, engraved Sabino, Paris, 9in (23cm) diam.
$720-1,000

Three John Walsh engraved glass wares, after a design by Clyne Farquharson, each engraved with polished stylised leaf forms on sinuous stems, in a clear glass, comprising:
a gently tapering vase, a wide flared bowl, and a high sided bowl, the vase incised Clyne Farquharson, NRD, 8in (20cm) high; the flared bowl incised Clyne Farquharson and with a limited edition number 23/250, 36, 12in (31cm) diam., the other unmarked 8in (20cm) diam.
$720-1,000

An Etling opalescent model of a Penguin, damaged, moulded Etling, 203, France, 5in (13cm) high.
$360-540

A Continental glass vase, internally decorated with birds in flight in blue on a speckled white ground graduating to red at the neck, unmarked, 20thC, 7in (18cm) high.
$360-540

An Orrefors 'Graal' vase, by E. Hald, internally decorated with scaly green and brown fish swimming amid reeds, etched to base Orrefors Sweden Graal 26416 Edward Hald, 5.5in (14cm) high.
$1,200-1,700

Metalware

A spelter figure lamp, c1930, 13.5in (34cm) high.
$360-540

A spelter figure holding a clock, c1930, 22in (56cm) high.
$360-540

A stylised figure of a deer, by Hagenauer, 14in (36cm) long.   **$720-1,000**

An aluminium and brass sailing ornament, with 3 graduated stylised sailing boats in aluminium, on a brass and wood base, 12in (30.5cm) high.
$360-540

A spelter figure of a bird on a base, signed Rochard, 16in (41cm) wide.
$360-540

A chrome metal figure with a cigarette lighter, 9.5in (24cm) wide.
$180-360

A plated metal smoker's companion, in the form of an aeroplane, consisting of 2 cigarette cases, 4 ashtrays and a cigar cutter, 10in (25cm) wide.
$1,200-1,700

Jewellery

An Art Deco style diamond and ruby set cocktail bracelet, each link alternately set with brilliant cut diamonds and square cut rubies.
$3,600-5,000

A lady's Art Deco style platinum and diamond wristwatch, the jewelled lever movement inscribed 'Garrard', the case with diamond surround and diamond openwork panel shoulders, to cordette straps, in maker's stamped case.
$1,200-1,700

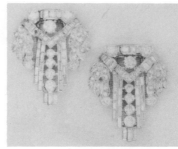

A pair of diamond set dress clips, each in a leafage and geometric pierced design, set with small cut and baguette diamonds with the principal diamonds mounted at the centre in the Art Deco taste.
$2,700-3,600

An opal and diamond brooch, the cut opal stone set in a surround of cut diamonds, the mount in a fan pierced geometric design in the Art Deco taste, c1920.
$2,700-3,600

A diamond set platinum cocktail watch, the silvered dial with black Arabic numerals inscribed 'Crusader Swiss Made', within a border pave set with numerous small diamonds, with pierced angular shaped shoulders set with further diamonds, on an articulated bracelet strap.
$1,200-1,700

A lady's pavé diamond wristwatch, with diamond graduated panel shoulders, to a 9ct. white gold Brazilian link bracelet, the rectangular dial with Arabic numerals.
$360-540

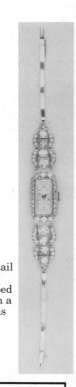

Did you know

MILLER'S Antiques Price Guide builds up year by year to form the most comprehensive photo reference library available.

Bronze and Ivory

'One man and his lion', a green patinated spelter figure, cast from a model by M. Le Verrier, on a marble base, restored, with engraved signature M. Le Verrier, 20.5in (52cm) high.
$3,600-5,000

A Preiss bronze and ivory figure, on a stepped green and black onyx base, lacking hands, signed in the maquette, c1930, 5in (13cm) high.
$1,200-1,700

A P. Tereszczuk bronze inkwell, with a young girl crossing a stream, a basket in each hand, signed, c1920, 12.5in (32cm) wide.
$180-360

A silvered bronze figure, by Helène Grünne, indistinct foundry mark, 1920s, 11.5in (29cm) high.
$1,200-1,700

'Dancer', a bronze and ivory figure, cast and carved from a model by Gerdago, her costume with gold patination, and cold painted geometric decoration in red and shades of blue, on an oval green onyx base, decoration rubbed, signed in the bronze A. R. Gerdago, 13in (33cm) high.
$7,000-9,000

An enamelled bronze and ivory dancer, in red and black shoes, her dress decorated in orange, red, blue, green, black and gilt flowerheads, a wide-brimmed hat similarly painted, raised on a stepped oval green onyx base, incised Austria on the base, 1920s, 12.5in (32cm) high.
$3,600-5,000

A chrome plated sculpture of a reclining figure, worn, stamped A. Reimann, Ges Gesch, made in Germany, 5.5in (14cm) long.
$720-1,000

A Dutch brass model of a woman dancing, on an oval base, signed Th. A. Vos., and 'Kunst-Bronsgieterij 'De Kroon', Haarlem', 19in (48cm) high.
$360-540

Thomas Vos was born in Groningen in the Netherlands in 1887. Having learnt to sculpt in Brussels, he worked principally on figures of women, animals and children until his death in Haarlem in 1948.

An ashtray with a figure of a boy, 6in (15cm) high. **$1,000-1,500**

A Lorenzl silvered bronze and ivory figure of a dancing girl, painted with bell-formed blue flowers and green foliage, raised on a green onyx base, damaged, moulded mark Lorenzl, painted Crejo, 1920s, 14.5in (37cm) high.
$3,600-5,000

British Ceramics

A Burleigh jug with parrot design, c1930, 8in (20cm) high.
$110-180

A Hancock vase, with pomegranate pattern, 10in (25cm) high. **$180-360**

A Carlton Ware blue toilet jug and bowl set, with chinoiserie pattern, printed mark in blue.
$360-540

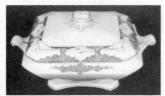

A Crown Ducal vegetable dish, decorated in red trees pattern, c1925.
$35-70

Two Carlton Ware dishes, with Pink Daisy design, 4.5in (11cm) wide. **$35-70 each**

A Hancock vase, decorated with Autumn design, 7in (18cm) high.
$180-360

A Carlton Ware vase, with stylised flower heads in polychrome enamels, c1930, 9in (23cm) high.
$360-540

A Burleigh jug with fox and stork design, 8in (20cm) high.
$180-360

A Burleigh jug with kingfisher pattern, c1930.
$110-180

A Carlton Ware bowl, and a drainer, with Water Lily design, 9.5in (24cm) and 8.5in (22cm) wide.
$70-145 each

A pair of Carlton Ware porcelain vases, painted with pairs of swallows and stylised foliage, polychrome on pastel blue ground with gilt details, the interior covered in mauve glaze, printed marks Carlton Ware, Made in England, 'Trade Mark', 10in (25cm) high.   **$720-1,000**

A Royal Cauldron fruit bowl, c1935, 9in (23cm) diam.
$110-180

A Carlton Ware teapot, milk jug and sugar bowl, in Water Lily pattern, c1930.
$180-360

A Carlton Ware blue coffee service, decorated in jewelled enamels and gilt with exotic birds and with wisteria, with gilt interiors, comprising: coffee pot and cover, two-handled sucrier and cover, cream jug and 6 coffee cups and saucers, printed mark in black.
$360-540

Three Gray's Paris jugs, with geometric design by Susie Cooper.
$360-540 each

A Hancock part coffee service.   **$180-360**

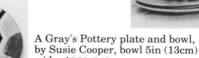

A Gray's Pottery plate and bowl, by Susie Cooper, bowl 5in (13cm) wide. **$360-540**
plate **$180-360**

A Carlton Ware tête-à-tête, each piece with a speckled pale blue ground heightened with gilding, applied with solid gilt ribbed handles, comprising: teapot and cover, 2 cups and saucers, jug, sugar bowl, jam pot and cover, plate, and biscuit barrel and cover, printed marks, 1930s.
$720-1,000

A pair of Compton Pottery stoneware bookends, each trefoil form with relief decoration of a butterfly, on semi-circular base, covered in a matt green glaze with black, ochre and yellow painted decoration, impressed seal Compton Pottery, Guildford, c1945, 5in (12cm) high.
$360-540

A Susie Cooper cased part coffee set, each piece painted with wash and solid bands in mixed grey, brown and blue, comprising: 6 coffee cans, 6 saucers and 6 electroplated shell moulded spoons with blue bead ends, in a fitted case, printed factory marks A. Susie Cooper Production, Crown Works, Burslem, England, cans 2in (5.5in) high.
$360-540

A Maling ware fruit bowl, 8.5in (21cm) diam.
$180-360

A Maling ware oval dish in the Stork design, decorated by Janet Taylor, c1932, 10in (25cm) wide.
$180-360

A Hancock bowl, with Pomegranate pattern, 9in (23cm) diam.
$180-360

A pair of Hancock vases, in Cremorne pattern, 11in (28cm) high. **$180-360**

A Gray's Pottery lamp base, painted with golfers, c1930, 6in (16cm) high.
$1,000-1,500

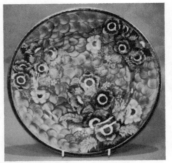

A Maling ware wall plaque, decorated in the Anemone pattern, c1936, 11in (28cm) diam.
$180-360

A Gray's Pottery teapot, with Cubist face design, decorated with orange and yellow enamel, 4.5in (12cm) high.
$360-540

A Maling ware ginger jar, c1950, 8in (20cm) high.
$110-180

A Hancock bowl, with Water Lily pattern, 9in (23cm) diam.
$180-360

A Poole pottery jug, with geometric design, 6in (15cm) high.
$110-180

A Maling ware oval bread basket decorated in the Gladioli pattern, c1936, 11in (28cm) wide.
$180-360

A Maling ware wall pocket in the Michaelmas Daisy pattern, c1938, 9in (23cm) high.
$180-360

A Poole pottery bowl, 1960s.
$35-70

A Radford ware vase, with tree design, c1930, 10in (25cm) high.
$110-180

A Shelley tea set for two, Oxford shape, with green leaf motif, No. 12387, c1935.
$180-360

'Travel', a Wedgwood 44 piece dinner service, designed by Eric Ravilious, grey ground transfer printed in black and heightened in blue enamel, printed marks Travel, designed by Ravilious, Wedgwood of Etruria & Barlaston, Made in England, c1953, dinner plate 10in (25cm) diam.
$3,600-5,000

A Radford ware jug and vase, c1930.
$35-70 each

A Shelley banded jam pot, 4.5in (11cm) high.
$35-70

A Poole pottery teapot stand, c1930.
$35-70

A Shelley nursery plate, with Mabel Lucie Attwell design, printed in colours with a little girl standing with her doll beneath an umbrella, watching a parade of pixies, with inscription 'Fairy folk with tiny wings flying all over my plates and things', printed factory marks, 8in (20cm) diam.
$180-360

A Staffordshire model of a cat, after a design by Louis Wain, in green, yellow, red, blue and black, slight rubbing, impressed and overpainted facsimile signature on the back, stamped Made in England and impressed registration mark, 1920s, 5in (13cm) high.
$720-1,000

A Czechoslovakian vase, 8in (20cm) high.
$70-145

A W. H. Grindley coffee service of 15 pieces.
$180-360

Clarice Cliff

A Clarice Cliff plate by Graham Sutherland, impressed mark, 1934, 9in (23cm) diam.
$180-360

A Clarice Cliff Athens shaped jug, with Sliced Fruit pattern, 8in (20cm) high.
$360-540

A Clarice Cliff plate, with Laura Knight design, from the Artists in Industry range, 9in (23cm) diam.
$900-1,500

A Clarice Cliff jug, in Gibraltar pattern, 4in (10cm) high.
$900-1,500

A Clarice Cliff Newport Pottery Bizarre 'Inspiration-Persian' pottery charger, decorated with quatrefoil flowerhead within a border of scrolls in mottled blue, green, apricot and lilac glazes, inscribed in brown, 13in (34cm) diam.
$900-1,500

A set of 3 graduated Clarice Cliff meat plates, each designed by Ernest Proctor and painted in pink, green, black and blue with abstract waves and coils, printed and impressed marks, 1934, largest 18.5in (47cm) wide.
$1,000-1,500

A Clarice Cliff Newport Pottery Fantasque Melon pattern Lotus jug, printed mark and facsimile signature in black, 11.5in (29cm) high.
$900-1,500

A Clarice Cliff Athens shape teapot, decorated with umbrellas and rain, 7in (18cm) high.
$720-1,000

A Clarice Cliff Oceanic jug, with Windbells pattern, 6in (15cm) high.   **$180-360**

A Clarice Cliff Athens shape teapot, decorated with Berries, 4.5in (11cm) high.
$360-540

A Clarice Cliff Lotus pattern jug, Goldstone painted, 6.5in (16cm) high.
$180-360

A Clarice Cliff, Newport Pottery teapot in the form of a Teepee, by Betty Silvester, moulded with moose and leaves, the spout in the form of a Red Indian, the handle as a totem pole, inscribed under the base, Greetings from Canada, 7in (18cm) high.
$1,200-1,700

A Clarice Cliff Newport Pottery Bizarre pattern globular shaped vase, decorated with a landscape, castle, flowers and leaves, banded, impressed number 370, 6in (15cm) diam.
$720-1,000

A Clarice Cliff 'Café au Lait' Bizarre vase, the brown speckled ground decorated with the Red Roofs pattern, Shape 358, printed marks, c1931, 8in (20cm) high.
$720-1,000

A Clarice Cliff vase, decorated with umbrellas and rain, shape 342, 8in (20cm) high.
$1,000-1,500

A Clarice Cliff Newport Pottery Latona vase, the globular body with a graduated ringed neck, painted with blue, pink, green, yellow and black flowers above a yellow band, black printed factory mark, c1930, 8in (20cm) high.
$720-1,000

A Clarice Cliff Flora pattern vase, shape No. 342, 7.5in (19cm) high.
$1,000-1,500

A Clarice Cliff Geometric Lotus vase, painted with a wide band of repeated angular shapes within rectangular panels, in purple, orange, brown and yellow betwen orange bands, black printed factory mark, c1930, 11in (28cm) high.
$720-1,000

A Clarice Cliff geometric pattern vase, shape No. 355, 8in (20cm) high.
$720-1,000

A Clarice Cliff Newport Pottery, Latona candlestick, painted with stylised blue, pink, green, yellow and black flowers with a yellow band below, black printed factory mark, remains of paper label, c1930, 8in (20cm) high.
$360-540

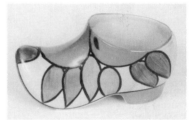

A Clarice Cliff sabot, c1932.
$180-360

A Clarice Cliff swan, 10.5in (26cm) wide.
$720-1,000

A Clarice Cliff conical pepper pot, decorated with pink pearls, 3in (8cm) high.
$35-70

Continental Ceramics

A Clarice Cliff Newport Pottery Bizarre Sunray pattern confiture and cover of plain cylindrical form, printed mark in black, 3in (8cm) over knop.
$720-1,000

A Wilkinson & Sons Clarice Cliff Bizarre Gayday bowl, 5.5in (14cm) diam., and 3 Bizarre mugs, 2 decorated in Fantasque and Nasturtium pattern, 3.5in (9cm) high.
$720-1,000

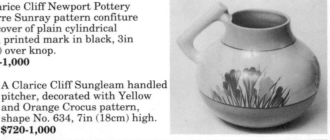

A Clarice Cliff Sungleam handled pitcher, decorated with Yellow and Orange Crocus pattern, shape No. 634, 7in (18cm) high.
$720-1,000

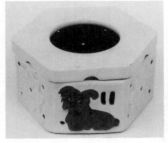

An Art Deco ceramic night light holder.
$35-70

A Goldscheider terracotta wall mask, with black printed marks, impressed 1107, 1930s, 8in (20cm) high.
$720-1,000

A cat by Georges Jacques Adnet, c1930, 14in (36cm) high.
$720-1,000

A Goldscheider figure of a boy, c1920, 10in (25cm) high.
$360-540

A Goldscheider ashtray, formed of interlinked circles with a recess in the rim applied with a female head with orange curly hair on the edge, stamped Goldscheider Wien, c1925, 10in (25cm) wide.
$720-1,000

A French porcelain box and cover, signed, with 'France Editions Etling Paris' on base, 5in (13cm) diam.   **$110-180**

A Royal Dux Ballet Russe figure, c1928, 12in (31cm) high.
$720-1,000

A Rosenthal porcelain figure, naturalistically modelled and coloured as a female nude reclining on a rock, green printed and painted marks, c1934, 16in (41cm) wide.
$1,800-2,700

A Saint Clément Ged Condé polar bear, c1920, 11in (28cm) wide.
$360-540

A Saint Clément Ged Condé fish, with white crackle glaze, c1920, 10.5in (26cm) wide.
$180-360

> **Miller's is a price GUIDE not a price LIST**

A Boch Frères Keramis Ch. Catteau figure of 'The Skaters', 13in (33cm) high.
$360-540

A Royal Dux porcelain group, in dark blue with gilt detailing, raised on a scallop edged circular base, applied pink triangular mark, stamped Made in Czechoslovakia, 2993 4, c1930, 12in (31cm) high.
$720-1,000

A Rosenthal porcelain figure of Pierrot, 12in (31cm) wide.
$1,800-2,700

A French white porcelain figure, signed, 13in (33cm) high.
$720-1,000

A Lenci earthenware group, modelled as a naked adolescent girl seated at the foot of a kneeling woman wearing a flowing blue robe and cream scarf spangled with gilt stars, minor glaze chips, painted factory mark, 1938, 16in (41cm) high.
$720-1,000

A Goebels Pottery set of ashtrays and a jockey cigarette box, decorated in orange and black, box 6in (15cm) high. **$35-70 each**

A Goldscheider Butterfly model of a figure, after a design by Lorenzl, incised marks Goldscheider, Wien, Lorenzl, 5917 515 4, facsimile signature on the base, 1930s, 10in (25cm) high.
$900-1,500

PAPIER MACHE

A papier mâché pencil box, 8in (20cm) long.
$35-70

A papier mâché box, inlaid with mother-of-pearl, 9.5in (24cm) long.
$35-70

A mid-Victorian shell inlaid and parcel gilt papier mâché and iron bedstead, the uprights and foot uprights similarly decorated, restored, 60in (153cm) wide.
$3,600-5,000

A papier mâché shaped snuff box, 'The Ring Master', c1850, 3in (7cm) wide.
$360-540

A papier mâché snuff box, c1840, 3in (7.5cm) wide.
$900-1,500

A papier mâché box, 7in (17.5cm) wide.
$35-70

A papier mâché shaped snuff box, c1850, 3in (7.5cm) wide.
$900-1,500

A Victorian papier mâché table top, painted after Landseer's 'Dignity and Impudence'.
$180-360

A papier mâché snuff box, c1840, 3in (7.5cm) wide.
$900-1,500

A papier mâché crumb scoop, 10.5in (26.5cm) wide.
$70-145

A Victorian black lacquered papier mâché tilt-top table, probably Birmingham, 47.5in (120cm) diam.
$3,600-5,000

A pair of Victorian black lacquered papier mâché tilt-top tables, with mother-of-pearl, painted, and gilt floral decoration.
$1,800-2,700

A papier mâché blotter, 9in (22.5cm) high.
$110-180

A Victorian green and gilt papier mâché cradle style planter, with a metal liner to the boat-shaped panel sides, on an open scroll base with gilt flowers.
$3,600-5,000

A Victorian papier mâché tray, the centre painted with an extensive Italian landscape, in a gilt foliate and floral reserve border, the back signed indistinctly 'Mechi', 4 Leadenhall St., London, 32in (81cm) wide.
$180-360

KITCHENALIA

A Georgian salt box, 17.5in (44.5cm) high.
$360-540

A pair of fruitwood nutcrackers, with printed label EVAN-THOMAS COLLECTION, numbered in ink 51, 18thC, 5in (12cm) long.
$360-540

A Welsh spoon rack with spoons, in staircase form, with a shaped apron, 18thC.
$360-540

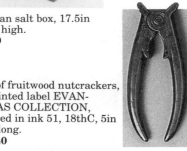

A pair of late Victorian Avery Pole Scales, in brass and cast blackened wrought metal, the centre stand supporting a brass balance rail with pans and holders.
$360-540

A pair of Queen Anne yew nutcrackers, carved with a hare and incised with a shepherd, a fox, a cat and a seated bird, dated 1708, 8in (21cm) long.
$1,200-1,700

A pair of boxwood nutcrackers, modelled as a bishop's head and a stylised bird and animal, carved with the legend 'He that is willing/peace for to make/must be indifferent/and no partie take', the body bearing a fleur-de-lys below a coronet, c1600, 8in (21cm) long.
$2,700-3,600

A brass and glass wall mounted towel rail.
$110-180

TOOLS

A glazed wall display cabinet of I. Sorby's 'Punch' brand tools, including hand and tenon saw, turnscrews, chisels, gouges, pincers, secateurs, draw-knife, spirit level, adjustable spanner and ratchet brace, 43.5in (110cm) high.
$3,600-5,000

A carved wood moulding plane, 19thC, 18.5in (47cm) long.
$720-1,000

A universal cutting frame.
$360-540

This is of overhung pattern similar to Evans of Birch, but ungeared. The jockey pulleys are mounted on tubular supports through which the driving band runs. The object seems to be to prevent the band coming off, in which it succeeds. It is clearly by one of the professional makers. No other of this pattern has been recorded.

An epicycloidal cutting frame, with 17 change wheels and 11 cutters, in a fitted mahogany chest with drawer and brass drop handles at ends.
$1,800-2,700

A slope-top mahogany cabinet, with till top and 2 drawers, containing 151 O/T slide rest tools (mostly fancy forms), 8 various adaptors, 71 small and 78 large O/T drills.
$2,700-3,600

A Swedish brass plated plough, of composite beech, fruitwood and mahogany with brass screw stems and nuts, the full-length depth stop adjusted by key-operated rack and pinion, with compartment in fence for adjusting and locking keys, fence engraved C. G. Hermanson and C.G.H., 1883.
$720-1,000

A violin plane with plain and toothing cutters, another with plain cutter, both with Preston cutters, another with plain and toothing cutters, the lever and cutters with TZ monogram, longest 2in (5cm) long, and 5 various other cutters.
$720-1,000

A Norris A32 thumb plane, of steel-soled gunmetal with rosewood infill and wedge, twin-thread Patent Adjustment, Norris cutter, traces of lacquer on gunmetal and Buck & Ryan stamp on heel, 7in (17.5cm) long.
$2,700-3,600

A slope top mahogany chest, fitted for tools.
$3,600-5,000

ARTISTS' MATERIALS

A pair of artist's treen hands, with articulated joints, 10in (25cm) high.
$720-1,000

A Winsor & Newton mahogany artist's box, the cover leather lined and gilt decorated, with remains of watercolour blocks, 3 ceramic slabs and drawer to base, 12in (31cm) wide.
$180-360

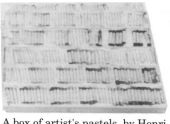

A box of artist's pastels, by Henri Roche, comprising 5 trays of numerous individually numbered colour sticks.
$360-540

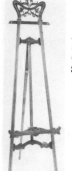

A late Victorian Arts & Crafts stained beech wood easel, 75.5in (192cm) high.
$1,200-1,700

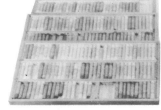

A box of Grumbacher artist's pastels, comprising 4 trays of numerous individually numbered colour sticks.
$360-540

An artist's oak studio easel, by Reeves & Sons, with winding mechanism, 19thC, 76in (193cm) high.
$900-1,500

An artist's oak studio easel, with winding mechanism, late 19thC, 77in (195cm) high.
$720-1,000

An artist's oak studio easel, with an adjustable shelf and winding mechanism, 19thC, 84in (213.5cm) high.
$720-1,000

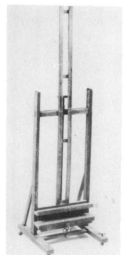

An artist's oak studio easel, by J. Bryce Smith, with adjustable shelf above a materials shelf and winding mechanism, 19thC, 92in (234cm) high.
$720-1,000

An artist's oak studio easel, by Young & Co., with winding mechanism, 102in (259cm) high.
$720-1,000

Make the most of Miller's

Unless otherwise stated, any description which refers to 'a set' or 'a pair' includes a valuation for the entire set or the pair, even though the illustration may show only a single item.

PENS

A Swan 445/90 silver grey lizard skin effect leverless pen, c1938, and a Waterman's No. 92 brown lizard skin effect lever filled pen, with decorated cap and barrel bands, clip missing, c1933.
$180-360

A Conklin Endura Symetric green marble pen, with Toledo nib, c1930.
$110-180

A Mabie Todd gold plated eye dropper pen, with 'puffball' decoration and ladder-fed No. 2 nib, c1915.
$180-360

A lacquered Dunhill Namiki lever fill pen, with Maki-E design of 2 birds beside a wood fence and foliage, a similar scene without birds on the cap, lacquered ball clip, lever, nib section, cap band and original Dunhill Namiki No. 3 nib, cap cracked.
$720-1,000

A Mabie Todd 14ct self filler pen, with No. 2 nib, c1918. **$360-540**

A Conway-Stewart 22 Floral pen, with Conway-Stewart nib, c1955.
$180-360

A De la Rue lapis blue 5501-96 pen, with 3/81 nib, c1935, and a black/pearl 1743-22 lever filler pen, with No. 4 nib, clip missing, c1934.
$180-360

A lacquered Dunhill pyramid shaped pencil, with design of an ocean-going ship in full sail and metal lead surround, base with legend Dunhill-Paris-Fabrication-Japonaise.
$1,800-2,700

A Mabie Todd brown marble and white chased button fill L205/47 pen.
$70-145

A Parker 9ct. 61 Flammé pen, c1974.
$360-540

A Parker black and pearl Duofold pencil and a yellow-metal and black banded Fyne Point propelling pencil.
$110-180

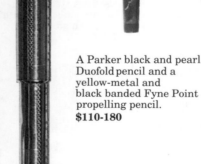

A Parker gold plated lady's pen, with Parker fountain pen nib, c1921.
$110-180

A Mont Blanc black 6M safety pen, with No. 6 nib, c1922.
$720-1,000

A Parker black/pearl Lucky Curve Junior pen, with 18ct nib, c1924.
$70-145

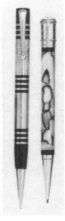

A Mont Blanc black 1 EF safety pen, with No. 1 nib, c1922.
$360-540

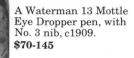

A Waterman 9ct gold cased Line and Dot 52 pen and pencil set, with No. 2 nib, 1929 and 1930.
$360-540

A Waterman silver overlaid 52.5 Line and Dot pen, with No. 2 nib, 1922.
$360-540

A Waterman 13 Mottle Eye Dropper pen, with No. 3 nib, c1909.
$70-145

A red Parker Lucky Curve Senior pen, with Duofold pen nib, c1927.
$110-180

A Waterman 9ct gold overlaid 42 safety pen, with fluted decoration and No. 2 nib, damaged, 1924.
$360-540

A silver overlaid eye dropper fill pen, with ornate floral decoration on barrel, plain cap with one chased band, c1900.
$70-145

A Parker red button fill Duofold pen and a red button fill Duofold Junior pen.
$70-145

EPHEMERA
Pop Ephemera

A brooch of white and baguette white rhinestones, worn on stage by Marvin Gaye, 2in (5cm) wide; a black leather wallet made by Givenchy, with printed gilt inscription inside 'To Marvin With All My Love, Faith, 4-2-'83'; a printed handbill for Marvin Gaye and Tammi Terrell at the Cocoanut Grove, c1967-70; 2 tour jackets for the Marvin Gaye Concert Tour '83; a printed proclamation from the Mayor of Buffalo declaring Friday, May 13th, 1983 to be Marvin Gaye Day; a pair of brass goblets used on stage by Marvin Gaye during his last tour (one damaged); and a portrait of Marvin Gaye, signed A. Cross 5-21-83, mixed media, 20in (51cm) wide; and related material.
$720-1,000

A publicity photograph of The Beatles, in a recording studio, c1963, signed by each member of the group in blue biro, 11in (28cm) wide.
$1,000-1,500

A black felt hat trimmed with an American Indian style band of leather and metal decorated with circular panels stamped with a star motif; and a matching belt, the buckle stamped with a steer-head motif, worn by Hendrix on stage, c1963.
$7,000-9,000

An original sketch by Marvin Gaye for the album cover 'In Our Lifetime', 1980, in black and blue ink, 7in (18cm) wide, mounted together with a copy of the final album cover, an explanatory statement from the artist commissioned to design the sleeve and a colour picture of the singer, framed and glazed, 24in (61cm) wide.
$1,000-1,500

Mick Jagger's Victorian coat, in black cut velvet and red, brown and gold paisley design; and an affidavit confirming provenance.
$2,700-3,600

A Dezo Hoffmann publicity photograph, 1963, signed by each member of The Beatles in blue biro, 8 by 10in (20.5 by 25cm) wide.
$1,000-1,500

A Jimi Hendrix concert poster for Hastings Pier, Sunday 22nd October, 7.30-11, 1967, featuring Jimi Hendrix Experience plus full supporting program (sic), 20in (50.5cm) wide.
$3,600-5,000

An autographed slip of paper inscribed 'Thanks for the Roses, The Beatles, Paul, John, Ringo, George', 3 by 5in (7.5 by 12.5cm).
$360-540

A brown velvet stage jacket decorated at the shoulders with embroidered orange, yellow and green flowerheads and mirrored sequins; accompanied by a copy of Black Stars Magazine, January 1975, featuring several photographs of Gaye wearing a similar jacket on stage at Chicago's Amphitheatre; and a copy of Step News International, May 1976, featuring a photograph of Gaye on the front cover wearing this jacket at a Charity Concert in Radio City Music Hall, New York, where he was presented with a US State Department Ambassador of Good Will award by Shirley Temple Black.
$900-1,500

A bank cheque signed by Jimi Hendrix, 1968, together with 4 original colour slides of Jimi on stage, c1970.
$1,000-1,500

A piece of writing paper illustrated with a pencil portrait of Jimi Hendrix, signed and inscribed 'Love to you forever thank you - I wish you the Best of Love constantly Jimi Hendrix EXP', and 'Backwards Noel Redding xxx', and 'love Mitch xxx', 5.5in (14cm) wide.
$1,800-2,700

The Beatles E.P., Twist and Shout, 1963, signed on the back cover by all 4 members of the group.
$1,000-1,500

A black felt trilby, signed and inscribed on the underside of the brim 'All My Love Michael Jackson' and stamped with artist's name in gilt lettering on inside band; accompanied by a letter of authenticity from MJJ Productions and a colour photograph of Jackson wearing a similar hat.
$1,800-2,700

The Isley Brothers' matching 2-piece Western-style stage suits in suede and leather, in 3 different colours of suede, burgundy, black and turquoise, each trimmed at the cuffs, shoulders and seams with gold or silver coloured leather; and one pair of corresponding gold and turquoise suede platform shoes; and 2 zebra-striped sleeveless stage tops, one with a matching scarf, worn on stage by Marvin, Kelly and Ronald Isley; and 2 photographs of Ronald Isley wearing the burgundy suit from the Isley Brothers Souvenir Book, 1976.
$1,000-1,500

Michael Jackson's leather jacket, in black with matching quilted lining, fringes on arms and back, elaborately decorated overall with silver studs, with Maxfield Los Angeles label, size 42.
$18,000-21,000

Worn by the singer for the 'Moonwalker' video.

A Coral Records promotional postcard, 1958, signed by Buddy Holly, Joe Mauldin and Jerry Allison, 3.5in (8.5cm) wide; and a collection of promotional postcards and miniature publicity photographs of various recording artists and film stars, c1955, mounted in an album.
$900-1,500

A half length publicity photograph of Elvis Presley, signed and inscribed 'To Linda Best Wishes Elvis Presley', c1960, 4.5in (11cm) wide.
$360-540

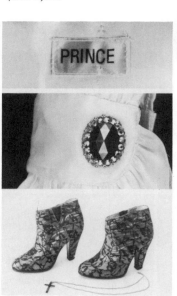

A Michael Jackson phonograph, made by Vanity Fair, 1984, with instruction leaflet, in original box, 12.5in (32cm) wide.
$110-180

A complete stage outfit from the Purple Rain Tour, 1984, comprising: an ornate purple lurex coat, a pair of high-waisted trousers, a matching pair of high-heeled ankle boots, a white shirt with Prince label in purple stitched inside, and a gilt metal crucifix and chain, worn by Prince, and an illustrated souvenir concert programme from the same tour.
$21,000-27,000

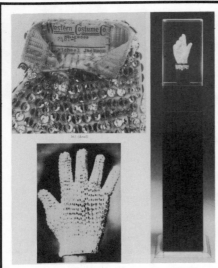

A rhinestone stage glove, with Western Costume Co. Hollywood woven label, printed with the artist's name Michael Jackson and order number 2481-1, stitched inside, fastening at the cuff with a single hook, thought to have been worn by Michael Jackson at the 1984 Grammy Award ceremonies, February 28th 1984, where he won 8 Grammy Awards and to the USA For Africa We Are The World recording session, January 28th 1985; and a custom-made rotating display case of black and clear perspex, 59in (149.5cm) high.
$27,000-36,000

Michael Jackson's rhinestone glove is probably the most recognisable piece of Rock and Roll costume of the 1980s.

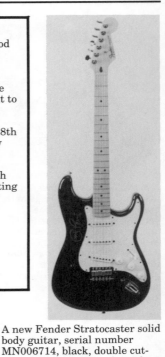

A new Fender Stratocaster solid body guitar, serial number MN006714, black, double cutaway body, 4 bolt maple neck, headstock face with Fender logo, 21 fret fingerboard with black dot marker inlays, 3 single coil pickups, selector switch, 3 controls, tremolo bridge/tailboard and white pickguard, signed and inscribed on the body Eric Clapton '91.
$1,800-2,700

A single-sided acetate for Black Star, 20th Century Fox Film Corp. white label with typescript details giving title of song by Elvis Presley and Orchestra, 78 rpm; accompanied by a letter from Sid King of Sid King & The Five Strings stating that Presley had given him this acetate in the 1960s.
$7,000-9,000

Sid King and his band were friends with Elvis and shared the billing at a number of venues in the 1950s.

Elvis Presley's custom made pendant with monogram T.C.B. (Taking Care of Business), set above a lightning bolt motif on a rope work chain; and a cloth concert banner from 'Elvis Summer Tour', Las Vegas, c1970.
$1,000-1,500

The bolt of lightning was taken from the comic strip Captain Marvel Jnr. Elvis gave T.C.B. necklaces to the male members of his entourage and T.L.C. necklaces (Tender Loving Care) to the female associates.

A black shirt worn by Prince on stage, 1986, with a postcard showing him wearing a similar garment.
$1,800-2,700

According to information supplied, this was obtained at a concert in the Sportpaleis Ahoy, Rotterdam on 19th August 1986, having been thrown into the audience by Prince.

A Rolling Stones illustrated souvenir concert programme, 1965, signed by Mick Jagger, Brian Jones, Charlie Watts, Keith Richards and Bill Wyman, and 6 of the other performers; and a page from an autograph book signed by Brian Jones, 2 tickets for the Odeon Theatre, Southend-on-Sea; and related material.
$1,800-2,700

A drumskin, with Remo head signed and annotated by Phil Collins in black felt tip pen, 'As used on the 'Serious' album sessions. Thanks for your help!', and with cartoon self portrait, 8.5in (21.5cm) diam., with an accompanying signed letter from Phil Collins, framed and glazed, 12in (30cm) wide. **$1,000-1,500**

Two printed rayon bandannas allegedly worn by Jimi Hendrix at the Isle of Wight Festival; accompanied by a letter of authenticity stating that Hendrix gave them away back stage; and a photograph of Hendrix wearing similar scarves on stage. **$1,800-2,700**

A B.C. Rich Bich 10 string solid body electric guitar, serial No. 82011, red finish, c1980; and a letter stating that it was purchased from Jamie Crompton, a guitarist in Suzi Quatro's band, who was given the guitar by Suzi Quatro. **$2,700-3,600**

A single-breasted multi-coloured striped jacket worn by Keith Richards, c1967, and a copy of a letter stating that Richards gave this jacket to his personal assistant Tony Sanchez in the early 1970s. **$1,800-2,700**

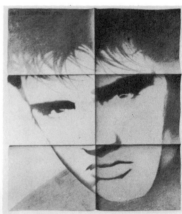

A silk screen proof print of Elvis Presley by David Oxtoby, 'Golden Years - Elvis', titled and signed by the artist in pencil, 18in (46cm) wide, framed. **$360-540**

Michael Jackson's sequined jacket, in black with matching lining, gold-coloured buttons decorated with the American eagle, the right shoulder embellished with chain and studded, black leather strap. **$21,000-27,000**

Worn by the singer in the well-known cola commercial.

A 'gold' disc, 'Stuck On You', presented to Elvis Presley, the single mounted above a plaque bearing the R.I.A.A. Certified Sales Award and inscribed Presented to Elvis Presley to commemorate the sale of more than one million copies of the RCA Records single record 'Stuck On You', 13in (33cm) wide, framed. **$1,000-1,500**

A signed and inscribed colour picture of Bruce Springsteen, used on the cover of the album 'Darkness on the Edge of Town'. **$110-180**

Posters and Postcards

Advertisements, chromo for Toni-Kola, showing people drinking with a negro tourist being surprised at finding the product, 1908.
$35-70

Cheshire, RP, unloading the electric car at Runcorn, by Hall, 1906.
$35-70

H-T-L Santa with 32 lights, pale purple robe.
$35-70

Sarawak RP of Sir Charles Vyner Brooke, with block of 4 1-c purple, and special cachet Kuching 1938.
$35-70

> **Miller's is a price GUIDE not a price LIST**

Tom Browne, Davidson 2599 complete, Pa Learns To Ride A Horse.
$35-70

Novelty, Opening Comedy Cards, all with double flap opening to show full picture, topics including Drinking, Romance, etc. published by W.S.S.B., Nos. 312, 314, 315, 317, 325-327.
$35-70

Nazi, Unser Deutches Heer (Our German Forces), a card game for troops in the field exactly like Happy Families, consisting of 12 sets of 4 cards, comprising good action photos of infantry, cavalry, panzers, mountain troops, Hitler with soldiers etc., in original carton.
$70-145

Exhibitions, a set of 6 Chromos for the 1897 Stockholm Exhibition, by Anna Palm, showing Industry Hall, Tourist Pavilion, Infantry, Old Ships etc.
$70-145

Longley Chilton, Art Deco Girls, published by A. G. & Co., Series 442.
$35-70

Black and white advertisements, News of the World Bioscope Wagon with traction engine, published by Taunt's.
$35-70

Disney

Pluto and a cat surprised, unknown production, c1940, 10in (25cm) wide.
$3,600-5,000

Bashful Playing An Accordian, from Snow White and the Seven Dwarfs, 1937, framed, 6in (15cm) wide. **$1,200-1,700**

Peter Pan, Captain Hook feels the tip of his hook and Tinkerbell points downwards as she flies along, 1953, largest 16in (41cm) wide. **$2,700-3,600**

A sketch of Roger Rabbit, signed and inscribed 'From Roger Rabbit Via Richard Williams, May 18th 1990', coloured pencil on paper, unframed, 11.5in (29cm) wide. **$1,800-2,700**

Peter Pan dressed in an Indian headdress, Wendy half-length, and Wendy three-quarter length, 1953, 12.5in (32cm) wide. **$2,700-3,600**

Doc talks to Snow White through the window, from Snow White and the Seven Dwarfs, 1937, 8in (20cm) wide. **$7,000-9,000**

Dopey looks bashful, from Snow White and the Seven Dwarfs, 1937, 5in (12.5cm) wide. **$2,700-3,600**

An illustrated première programme for Walt Disney's Snow White and the Seven Dwarfs, Cathay Circle Theatre, Los Angeles, California, December 21st, 1937, with pull-out poster, illustrations, original wrappers. **$360-540**

Grumpy plays the piano, from Snow White and the Seven Dwarfs, 1937, 7in (17.5cm) wide. **$2,700-3,600**

A piece of card signed and inscribed To Marie Rose, Our Best Walt Disney, 5in (12.5cm) wide. **$360-540**

Mickey Plays Papa, 1934, 11.5in (29cm) wide. **$3,600-5,000**

Two celluloids for American TV each depicting Mickey Mouse as The Sorcerer's Apprentice, one of Mickey surrounded by brooms carrying pails of water, the other of Mickey being reprimanded by the sorcerer, both gouache on celluloid, 10.5in (26cm) square. **$720-1,000**

Lady runs to the Tramp, from The Lady and the Tramp, 1955, 13in (33cm) wide. **$2,700-3,600**

A German lithographic tinplate mechanical bank with lever action eyes and extending tongue operated by pressing Mickey's right ear, probably made by Saalheimer & Strauss, c1930, 7in (17.5cm) high.
$14,500-16,500

Mickey, Pluto and Donald, Studio Wartime Art, c1942, 7.5in (18.5cm) wide.
$3,600-5,000

Lady in a muzzle, Jock glaring, the Tramp digging and the Tramp standing with his head cocked to one side, from The Lady and the Tramp, 1955, 16in (41cm) wide.
$3,600-5,000

Cross Reference

For a further selection of money banks, see page 468

Mickey Mouse and Minnie, from The Klondike Kid, 1932, 9in (22.5cm) wide.
$3,600-5,000

Film and Theatre

A painted plaster portrait model of Christopher Reeve as Superman in a flying pose, 26in (66cm) long.
$360-540

A printed souvenir menu for the Grand Order of Water Rats House Dinner, at the Savoy Hotel, London, September 21st 1947, with illustrated cover featuring guests of honour, Laurel and Hardy, autographed in blue ink; and 2 group photographs of the occasion, and similar souvenir menus.
$1,800-2,700

A postcard of Charlie Chaplin, signed in white ink.
$180-360

A red and white striped cotton jacket, stamped MGM Wardrobe and inscribed Gene Kelly inside the collar, possibly worn by Kelly in the 1952 MGM film Singing in the Rain; and a still photograph of Kelly wearing a similar striped jacket in the film.
$360-540

A signed and inscribed postcard of Robert Ryan.
$35-70

A signed sepia photograph of Laurel and Hardy, 1930, 10in (25cm) wide.
$900-1,500

An American one sheet poster for The Empire Strikes Back, 20th Century Fox, 1981, signed by Harrison Ford, Dave Prowse, Billy Dee Williams, Carrie Fisher, Mark Hamill, Peter Mayhew, Anthony Daniels, Kenny Baker and George Lucas, framed, 27in (68cm) wide.
$1,800-2,700

According to the vendor who worked on the film, only three posters were signed by the cast, and each of these posters had a different image. This poster was won at a raffle held during the 'End of Picture' party.

A pair of painted rubber pointed ear tops, worn by Leonard Nimoy to look like Mr Spock's Vulcan ears in the TV series Star Trek, mounted on board, ears 2.5in (6cm) high.
$1,800-2,700

Astaire and Kelly, signed by Fred Astaire and Gene Kelly, full length in dancing pose, 8in (20cm) wide.
$110-180

Noel Coward's full length dressing gown of black and gold silk, monogram N.C. on breast pocket; together with a letter stating that it was given to the actor Ronnie Ward after a charity matinée performance at Drury Lane, when Ward shared a dressing room with his friend Noel Coward.　**$2,700-3,600**

A prototype robotic head of painted gold rubber for the character C-3PO from Star Wars, 1977, 20th Century Fox, 9in (22.5cm) wide.
$720-1,000

A grotesque creature head, of polyurethane foam with isocylate coating finished in acrylic airbrush, with resin teeth and detailed 2-layered jaw, used in the 1986 20th Century Fox film Aliens.　**$1,800-2,700**

A guardsman's bearskin cap, with metal plume-ring on left side, c1939, 15in (38cm) high, and a photograph of the Cowardly Lion, the Tin Man and the Scarecrow dressed in Winkie guard uniform in the Witch's castle, 10in (25cm) wide.
$3,600-5,000

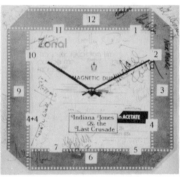

A novelty souvenir clock for the film Indiana Jones & The Last Crusade, made out of a film box, the lid forming the face, signed by Steven Spielberg, George Lucas, Alison Doody, Denholm Elliott, Tom Stoppard, Harrison Ford and 11 other members of the cast and crew, 11.5in (29cm) square.
$1,800-2,700

A set of 10 limited edition Bert Stern colour portrait photographs of Marilyn Monroe, taken in 1962, 6 weeks before her death, printed in 1978, each signed by the photographer on the margin and numbered 231/250, 19in (48cm) square; a corresponding printed index, and a printed title page, produced by Shorewood Atelier For Woodbine Books Inc. New York, N.Y., inscribed with the number of the set 231/250.
$3,600-5,000

ARMS AND ARMOUR
Armour

An Italian composite etched full foot armour, including later close helmet, on a stand, c1600.
$10,000-12,000

A German composite full armour, partly early 16thC, the helmet mid-16thC, on a stand with mail shirt,.
$10,000-12,000

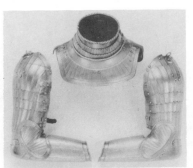

An Italian fluted gorget 'Alla Tedesca', with a composed pair of South German fluted 'Maximillian' full arm defences, damaged, c1520.
$3,600-5,000

A pair of Italian cuisses, c1520.
$3,600-5,000

A cabasset, formed in one piece, with 'pear stalk' finial to crown, brass rosettes around base, cleaned and restored, c1600.
$360-540

A visored bascinet in late 14thC style, 10.5in (26.5cm) high.
$3,600-5,000

A cuirass, probably German, with steel breastplate and backplate, both with brass studs around the perimeter, and a leather waist strap with brass buckle, c1870.
$720-1,000

An Italian fluted close helmet, adapted for the Giuoco del Ponte, the one piece skull embossed with a spray of 11 flutes and punched with the letters GP, early 16thC with later additions, 11in (28cm) high.   **$7,000-9,000**

A Cromwellian lobster tail steel helmet, the skull with 6 flutes, 4 piece articulated neck lames with large steel rivets, pierced ear flaps, and an adjustable nasal bar, initialled M.
$900-1,500

Two identical heavy steel breastplates, each with 10 brass studs around the perimeter, and 2 prominent brass fastening studs on the front, one plate stamped 585 at one armhole.
$360-540

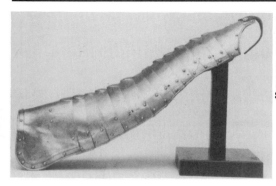

A composite crinet for a horse armour, made of 14 plates moving on sliding rivets, restored, 16thC, 31in (78.5cm).
$1,000-1,500

A Civil War steel helmet, with peeked hinged visor applied with large brass rivets, a single ridge to the skull extending down to a single socket plume holder.
$900-1,500

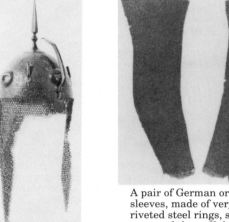

An Indo Persian steel helmet Khula Khud, the one piece skull embossed with masks, foliage and gilding, together with a matching shield, 18in (46cm) diam., and a fore-arm guard.
$900-1,500

A pair of German or Italian mail sleeves, made of very small riveted steel rings, shaped for the arm, and the cuffs bordered with riveted brass rings of the same size, damaged, 24in (61cm).
$900-1,500

A cabasset, formed in one piece, with 'pear stalk' finial to crown, brass rosettes around base, cleaned and restored, c1600.
$360-540

A cabasset, formed in one piece, with 'pear stalk' finial to crown, brass rosettes around base, the brim with a trace of crowned armourer's mark, cleaned and restored, c1600.
$360-540

Crossbows

A Flemish sporting crossbow, with robust steel bow and original string, the string hook inscribed 'I. Gernay', early 18thC, 41.5in (105.5cm) without windlass.
$1,200-1,700

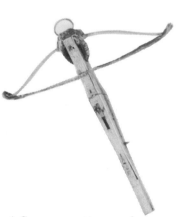

A German sporting crossbow, with detached steel bow, with original string and stirrup, late 17thC, together with 6 crossbow bolts, damaged, 26.5in (67.5cm).
$3,600-5,000

Daggers

A Lowland Scottish Quillon dagger, with tapering double edged blade, late 16thC, 16.5in (42cm).
$1,800-2,700

The reverse side of the blade bears a label inscribed 'Dagger from Battle of Pinkie fought September 1547 recovered from bank of River Esk August 2 1924'.

A kidney or ballock dagger, possibly English, damaged, c1500, 9in (23cm).
$3 600-5,000

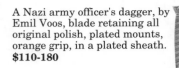

A Nazi army officer's dagger, by Emil Voos, blade retaining all original polish, plated mounts, orange grip, in a plated sheath.
$110-180

A Nazi Luftwaffe officer's dagger, 2nd pattern, the blade retaining all original polish, grey metal mounts, wire bound yellow grip, bullion dress knot, in its grey metal sheath.
$360-540

A Nazi SS dagger, by Robert Klaas, with inscription on blade, some wear.
$110-180

An unmarked Bowie and sheath, blade worn, 5.5in (14cm).
$110-180

A Victorian Gothic dagger, with double edged straight blade etched with foliate scrolls, solid copper gilt hilt, decorated with entwined serpents at base, diced pattern to grip, oval pommel with scrolled decoration, in brown leather covered metal sheath with 3 copper gilt foliate scrolled gothic mounts, blade 7in (18cm).
$360-540

A Nazi Red Cross man's dagger, original polish on the blade, plated mounts, in its black painted metal sheath with plated mounts and original leather frog, some wear.
$360-540

A Sheffield Bowie, for the American market, stag horn grip, nickel silver guard and clipped pointed blade, leather sheath, marked 'George Butler, Trinity Works', 19thC, blade 6in (15cm).
$110-180

Swords

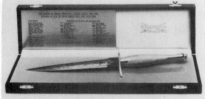

A presentation commemorative SAS dagger, a copy of the First Model Fairbairn Sykes fighting knife, the blade blued with gilt inscription and quotation, the hilt and guard gilt, in a presentaiton case with brass plate listing the regimental battle honours, actions and relevant dates, London 1991.
$1,200-1,700

This presentation dagger is part of a Limited Edition of 50, specially produced by the Wilkinson Sword Company to commemorate the 50th Anniversary of the SAS, the remainder only being made available to serving or ex-members of the Regiment. This dagger, numbered 1 of 50, is being offered for auction by the organisers of the Golden Jubilee, and all proceeds will be donated to the SAS Regimental Charities.

A selection of Scottish basket hilted swords.
$360-540 each

A Spanish military sword rapier with Bilboa hilt, c1780, 33in (84cm).
$360-540

A British Royal Naval flag officer's sword, the mameluke hilt with ivory grips and gilt brass guard, in its nickel plated scabbard, c1850, blade 31in (79cm).
$900-1,500

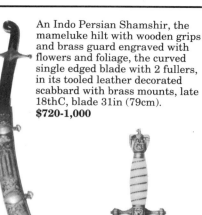

An Indo Persian Shamshir, the mameluke hilt with wooden grips and brass guard engraved with flowers and foliage, the curved single edged blade with 2 fullers, in its tooled leather decorated scabbard with brass mounts, late 18thC, blade 31in (79cm).
$720-1,000

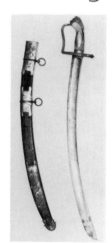

A silver mounted Peninsular War, presentation sword by Rundell, Bridge and Rundell, London, with inscription, 1811, the double edged blade 32in (81cm).
$3,600-5,000

A Nazi naval officer's dirk, with plain double fluted blade, brass mounts, wire bound white grip, in its brass sheath.
$360-540

A Scottish military backsword, etched in large script 'Sans Peur Et Sans Reproche', iron three-quarter basket guard pierced with traditional patterns, wire bound fishskin covered grip, domed pommel, age wear, part of guard removed, late 18thC.
$360-540

A Shamshir mounted in 2 colours of gold and encrusted with diamonds, presented by Abd-ul-Medshid, Sultan of Turkey, to Prince Alexander Couza, Hospodar of Moldavia and Wallachia, with slender blade of watered steel, the hilt encased in gold, enriched with encrusted patterns of rose diamonds and chased with foliage, in leather-covered wooden scabbard with gold mounts decorated en suite, and complete with its original gold bullion knot, blade repaired, some diamonds lacking, blade 33in (84cm), in its original fitted case.
$21,000-27,000

A Peninsula War period officer's sword, the single channelled curved blade engraved with flowers, leaves, martial trophies and other motifs, with crowned G.R. monogram and coat-of-arms, inscribed Major Walter Ross, and Mackintosh & Birnie, London, the gilt brass hilt with inscription, damage to hilt, 37in (94cm).
$3,600-5,000

A silver gilt Mameluke sword hilt, the quillons cast and chiselled as lions' heads, the eyes of semi-precious stones, gilding worn, 19thC, 8in (20cm) long.
$1,200-1,700

A Spanish sword believed to have belonged to Fernando Fernandez de Velasco y Sonanes, a claimant to the throne of Charles VII.
$3,600-5,000

An experimental military combination percussion underhammer pistol and cavalry sword, c1860, blade 35.5in (90.5cm).
$2,700-3,600

A Japanese wakizashi, the bronzed metal handle inlaid with prunus blossom and bamboo in gilt metal, blade signed, 30in (76cm).
$1,200-1,700

Blunderbuss

A flintlock blunderbuss, with brass barrel and mounts, spring loaded bayonet, the action and barrel signed 'Dakyn, Nottingham', the figured walnut stock with engraved butt plate, 18thC, 31in (79cm).
$1,800-2,700

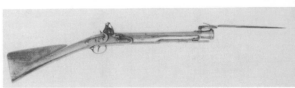

A George III flintlock blunderbuss, by Archer, the action incorporating a half cock, with early safety mechanism, the slightly flared brass barrel stamped with Victorian and Georgian proof marks, top mounted triangular spring bayonet, full walnut stock with brass furniture, and ramrod, 29in (74cm) overall length.
$1,800-2,700

Sporting Guns

A 19 bore German or Austrian half stocked flintlock sporting gun, part round, part octagonal barrel with 'spider' foresight, plain lock with 'banana' style lockplate, swan necked cock and pan without frizzen bridle, plain brass furniture and figured walnut stock with horn forend tip, grip tail guard and flat bottomed butt with characteristic cheekpiece, c1780, barrel 36.5in (94cm).
$1,200-1,700

A double barrelled percussion sporting gun, by Parker Field, inscribed 'Makers to Her Majesty 233 Holborn', and gold rectangular poinçon of W. Parker Field & Sons, signed, c1850, 32in (81cm).
$1,000-1,500

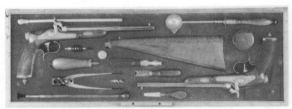

A cased double barrelled tubelock sporting gun, by Joseph Manton of Hanover Square, London, London Proof, No. 8884, barrelsmith's mark of William Fullerd, maker's stamps, patent case hardened locks engraved and signed Joseph Manton Patent, c1821, some damage, 34in (87cm).
$3,600-5,000

A cased pair of German percussion sporting pistols with detachable stock, by Jacob Kuchenreuter, Regensburg, Liège Proof, with blued and sighted octagonal barrels rifled with 7 grooves, the top flats inlaid with silver scrolls and signed in full in silver, in their brass bound oak case, lined with green baize and containing all but one of the original accessories, mid-19thC, case 30in (76in) long.
$10,000-12,000

Pistols

A French flintlock holster pistol, by Piraube Aux Galleries à Paris, stock worn, gilt faded in parts, c1725, 20in (50.5cm).
$7,000-9,000

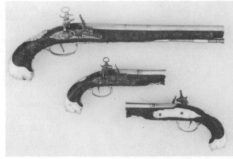

A German flintlock Kalthoff-system rifled repeating pistol, by Jan Sander, Hanover, c1680, 24in (60.5cm).
$18,000-21,000

A set of Spanish or Neapolitan pistols, comprising a holster pistol and 2 pocket pistols, with silver gilt mounts, inscribed, mid-18thC, largest 15in (38.5cm).
$10,000-12,000

Revolvers

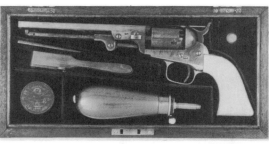

A Birmingham proved 60 bore 6 shot self cocking bar hammer percussion transitional revolver, the octagonal barrel rifled with 9 deep grooves and marked 'Improved Revolver', c1860, barrel 6in (15cm). **$360-540**

A cased Colt London Model 1849 pocket revolver, No. 647, .31 calibre, London proof, inscribed 'Address Col. Colt London', 1854, 6in (15cm). **$2,700-3,600**

A cased Colt London Model 1849 pocket percussion revolver, No. 3958, inscribed 'Address Col. Colt London', London proof, 1854, barrel 5in (12.5cm). **$2,700-3,600**

A 150 bore English 6 shot self cocking bar hammer percussion transitional revolver, the barrel marked 'Improved Revolver', c1855, together with a Dixon patent top revolver flask, an ebony handled turnscrew, pewter oil bottle, cap tin and iron pincer type mould, barrel 3.75in (9cm). **$1,200-1,700**

A pinfire, 4 barrelled pepperbox revolver, by Le Faucheux à Paris, the frame ornately engraved with foliage, underhammer action with ring trigger, 8in (20cm) overall. **$360-540**

Medals and Orders

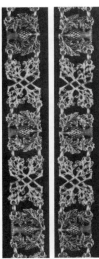

A 5 shot .31 SA percussion pocket revolver, No. 795, the barrel stamped Bacon Mfg Co. Norwich Conn, some wear and cleaned bright, 8.5in (21.5cm). **$360-540**

A Knight of Hanover's Waterloo pair, Lieutenant Colonel G. Desbrowe, Grenadier Guards, 1815. **$7,000-9,000**

The Most Ancient and Most Noble Order of the Thistle (K.T.), Knight's Collar, unmarked but probably by John Campbell of Lundie, 18thC. **$110,000-115,000**

A Bombardment of Acre pair, Lieutenant General T. G. Higgins, Royal Artillery, 1793. **$7,000-9,000**

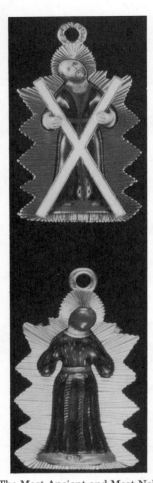

Queen Margherita, wife of King Umberto I, presentation brooch, by Musy Padre e Figli of Turin, silver gilt and enamel, in the form of an oval badge set with cushion diamonds around the edge, the centre with superimposed royal initial set with rose diamonds, crown above, the base set with stones, in a leather case, Italian, early 20thC. **$2,700-3,600**

A Peninsular War and Waterloo pair, Lieutenant Colonel Lord Charles Fitzroy, P.C., M.P., Grenadier Guards and D.A.A.G., later Vice Chamberlain of the Household, Military General Service, 1793, Waterloo, 1815. **$7,000-9,000**

The Most Ancient and Most Noble Order of the Thistle (K.T.), St Andrew Jewel, by John James Edington of Portland Street, Soho Square, London, the integral suspension loop fully hallmarked and bearing the unusual sun-in-splendour goldmark as well as the date letter k for 1825-26, with 2 further marks on the reverse of the green ground, c1825, 2.5in (6cm) high. **$37,400-42,500**

A Waterloo medal, awarded to Corporal Thomas Greasly, Royal Artillery Driver, with original steel clip-ring and ribbon, 1815. **$360-540**

A Crimean War and Indian Mutiny group to a Highlander officer, including dirk, skean dhu and plaid brooch, Lieutenant Colonel Neil Campbell, Cameron Highlanders, all contained within a large glazed display case. **$7,000-9,000**

Order of the Iron Crown, Grand Cross collar chain, by Rothe of Vienna, in gold and enamel, with 37 alternating oak leaf wreaths, Iron Crowns of Lombardy and arabesques, in a fitted case, Austrian. **$14,500-16,500**

Army small gold medal for Nive, 1813, Lieut. Col. James D. West, 1st Regt. Ft. Gds., in circular glazed case, with swivel suspension and a contemporary riband buckle. **$7,000-9,000**

Badges & Plates

A pair of white metal collar badges of the 2nd Cheshire Engineer Volunteers.
$180-360

A Georgian other ranks oval brass shoulder belt plate of The 60th (R. American) Regt., '60' within crowned oval garter.
$360-540

A Victorian other ranks white metal headdress badge of the Sheffield Engineer Volunteers.
$180-360

137 World War II cloth shoulder titles and divisional signs etc., sewn into the lining of a W.R.N.S. other ranks blue jacket, with composition buttons, jacket with minor wear and moth.
$720-1,000

An officer's badge of the 4th Gurkhas, 'IV' and bugle in the centre of a Maltese Cross resting on crossed kukris, adapted as a desk ornament, 2.5in (6.5cm) wide.   **$360-540**

An officer's gilt badge of the 1st City of London Engineers.
$180-360

A helmet plate of the 1st Durham Volunteers, Royal Engineers.
$180-360

An other ranks' white metal badge.
$110-180

A Victorian R.E. officer's silver cloak clasp, Birmingham 1892.
$180-360

A cast silver plated glengarry badge of the Scottish Engineers CTC.
$180-360

A badge of the 1st Middlesex Engineer Vols.
$180-360

Headddress

An Austrian Dragoons officer's helmet.
$1,800-2,700

An Austrian Dragoons officer's helmet, the sides of the gilt comb unpainted and lacking chin scales and lining.
$1,000-1,500

A Prussian Infantry officer's quality pickelhaube, of heavy leather with gilt/brass mounts including spike with crosspiece base, fastened with star-shaped studs, flat chin scales, and a German officer's green leather pouch with pouchbelt, both with gilt metal fittings, c1850.
$1,000-1,500

A Victorian officer's gilt helmet of The 6th Dragoon Guards (Carabiniers), with gilt mounts, leather backed chin chain and ear rosettes, silver plated helmet plate, padded silk lining, white hair plume with rosette, some damage and worn.
$1,200-1,700

A helmet of the 1st Oxfordshire Light Horse Volunteers, of black cloth with red horsehair mane and tuft to the white metal comb, white metal lower edge to patent leather peak, and crown above the badge.
$1,800-2,700

The helmet is fitted with rose pattern side bosses of white metal with matching chin chain lined with velvet and a small rose hook at back for hooking it up.

An officer's helmet of the 2nd Life Guards, complete with chin chain and plume, the elaborate plate having the white metal field to the enamel cross within the Garter, top finial missing.
$3,600-5,000

This helmet belonged to Lieutenant Colonel the Hon. Malcolm Bowes-Lyon (Uncle of Queen Elizabeth the Queen Mother), who served in the Boer War and in the Great War, and was wounded.

A trooper's/NCO's chapka of the Austrian 1st Ulans, with crimson top trimmed with yellow braid, brass chin scales lacking strap ends, eagle front plate and falling hair plume with brass cockade, c1900.
$360-540

An officer's shako of the Royal Dock Yard Battalion, black felt sides and top, black patent leather peak and head band, silver lace top band, gilt laurel and oak wreath plate, leather and silk lining, worn, c1850.
$1,000-1,500

An officer's green shako of The Scottish Rifles, black lace and plaited cord trim, patent leather peak, blackened bugle badge, corded boss bearing blackened mullet, black over green feather plume in socket, patent leather chinstrap.   **$360-540**

An officer's busby of the Royal Gloucestershire Hussars, by Hawkes, 14 Piccadilly, with scarlet bag and crimson and gold cord lines around busby, gilt covered chin chain lined with red velvet and fastening to fine gilt lion's mask bosses and white over red plume with gilt socket and ring and black metal plume case, c1880.
$720-1,000

An officer's pattern Second Empire chapka of the French 7th Lancers, with blue cloth top, large numbered front plate, chin chain and a crimson hair plume.
$720-1,000

A George VI officer's side cap of the Royal Horse Guards, gilt piping, scarlet top, embroidered badge, gilt buttons.
$180-360

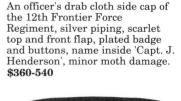

An officer's drab cloth side cap of the 12th Frontier Force Regiment, silver piping, scarlet top and front flap, plated badge and buttons, name inside 'Capt. J. Henderson', minor moth damage.
$360-540

An officer's blue smoking cap of the 1st Bombay Lancers, scarlet top with gilt braid trim, embroidered '1' on crossed lances badge, plain silk buttons, some wear and moth.
$360-540

An officer's peaked cap of the Scots Guards, embroidered peak, red, white and blue silk headband, gilt and silver plated badge with green enamelled centre.
$180-360

A German steel helmet of the Great War, a trench knife, knucklebow and shaped grip of cast alloy with leather sheath, and a water bottle, probably of a British officer, c1900.
$360-540

An officer's black shako of the South Regiment of West York Yeomanry, with silver lace band and black silk cockade, with white metal ball button, front and back peaks of plain black leather, and a drooping black horsehair plume, with a brass ring, minor refurbishments, some damage, c1825, plume 19in (48cm) long.
$1,800-2,700

This regiment later became the Yorkshire Dragoons.

A cocked hat of an officer of the Royal Dragoons, with large elaborate star loop and regimental mounted gilt button, large tassels and white silk lining, trade label of Catter & Co., 56 Pall Mall, London, in its black metal case, with brass plate engraved Walter B. Barttelot, Esqr., Royal Dragoons, c1841, case 17in (43cm) high.
$720-1,000

A post-1902 officer's silver plated helmet of The Life Guards, silver plated spike, gilt and silver plated helmet plate, with good red and blue enamelled centre, leather backed chin chain and ear rosettes, leather and silk lining, white hair plume with plain white metal rosette, some minor damage and repairs.
$2,700-3,600

An officer's chapka of Austrian Ulans, with crimson cloth top, ornate chin scales, eagle front plate, and falling hair plume with cockade, c1880.
$720-1,000

An officer's pattern blue pillbox cap of the East Lothian Yeomanry Cavalry, with gold lace band, an ornate figure in gold to the top and a lining of quilted crimson silk, and a scarlet jacket of the same with very dark blue collar and pointed cuffs, trimmed with gold lace, and matching piping to the back seams, 11 small gilt buttons down the front and winged shoulder cords of twisted gold chain gimp, c1880.
$180-360

Uniforms

An Irish Volunteer colour and tassel, of red silk with a bullion fringe and embroidered with roses, thistles, foliage and a crown incorporating beads and fur, above a harp and with red and gold tassel, some wear, c1798, 22in (56cm) wide.
$7,000-9,000

Three Victorian practice Standards of the Household Cavalry, of crimson silk damask painted with the same designs as the actual Standards and edged on 3 sides with yellow worsted fringe, 2 being of the Union Flowers pattern and the other of the Royal Arms pattern, some damage, each 33in (84cm) wide, excluding fringe.
$1,200-1,700

A pre-1922 officer's full dress drab tunic of the 124th Baluchistan Infantry, scarlet facings, gilt lace and braid trim, shoulder cords. **$110-180**

A post-1902 Lieutenant's full dress blue jacket of The Royal Horse Artillery, scarlet collar, gilt cord and lace trim, including 17 loops with ball buttons to chest, shoulder cords, embroidered collar grenades, name inside 'N. M. McLeod, 27.7.12'; and 2 pairs of matching breeches with broad scarlet stripe.
$720-1,000

A heavy dark green velour table cover, edged all round with wide regimental gold lace and bearing the richly embroidered ornaments from one side of an officer's shabraque of the 14th Light Dragoons, consisting of regimental number XIV and two VR cyphers, each with Royal crest superimposed, 68in (172.5cm) long.
$720-1,000

The uniform of an officer of the Royal Horse Guards, including a dress helmet with skull of German silver, a polished steel cuirass, a pair of Wellington boots and wooden stretchers, blue tunic, blue trousers with gold lace at the seams, 2 pairs white leather pantaloons, shabracque, Sam Browne belt and straps, 2 mess waistcoats, various accessories, all contained in a patent zinc lined damp-proof trunk, 1882; and a uniform of a member of the Royal Company of Archers, including bonnet, cap, tunic, frock coat, trousers and 2 belts and blue serge uniform worn in the Egypt 1882 campaign.
$10,000-12,000

An officer's blue full dress jacket of the Royal Maylor Cavalry, with scarlet facings, silver Russia braid trimming, white metal curb chain wings, and plated buttons with 'RMC' and Prince of Wales' plumes, coronet and motto, 'R. Bateman' on the lining, c1830.
$1,800-2,700

An officer's bearskin of the Irish Guards, St. Patrick's blue feather plume, velvet backed graduated link gilt chin chain, leather lining.
$720-1,000

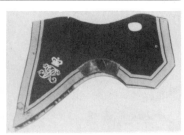

The shabraque of an officer of the Long Melford Troop of the Suffolk Yeomanry Cavalry, in dark blue cloth with scarlet cloth borders, with large VR cypher in white and crimson silk embroidery beneath crown in coloured silk embroidery, the points lined with black coach-hide.
$1,200-1,700

An officer's dark blue full dress coatee of the King's Cheshire Yeomanry, with scarlet facings and white metal buttons, with 'KCY' within a crowned Garter Star with motto, the collar and cuffs trimmed with silver lace and the back seams with Russia decoration, c1825.
$1,000-1,500

A Lieutenant's full dress scarlet tunic of The Queen's Royal Regiment (West Surrey), with blue facings, gilt lace and braid trim, shoulder cords, gilt collar badges, Paschal lamb on torso, gilt buttons, and a pair of overalls with narrow scarlet stripe, some damage, c1925.
$180-360

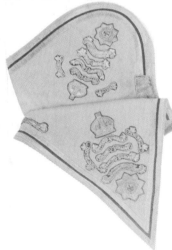

A North American Indian beaded waistcoat, the front of black velvet with elaborate floral decoration worked in polychrome beads, plain calico lining and red tie fastenings to front, 19thC.
$1,000-1,500

A post World War I officer's scarlet cloth shabraque of the Royal Horse Guards, embroidered crown, 10 battle honour scrolls 'Dettingen' to 'Paardeburg', and Garter star in each quarter, additional scroll 'France and Flanders 1914-18' along the back edge, gilt lace border with blue central stripe.
$720-1,000

A complete other rank's full dress Elcho grey uniform of the London Scottish, comprising: glengarry cap, doublet, plaid, leather sporran, leather waistbelt with white metal waist belt clasp.
$360-540

A sabretache of the Royal North Devon Yeomanry Cavalry, with its foul weather cover and in its tin case.
$1,000-1,500

A Victorian embroidered crimson damask drum banner of the Household Cavalry, bearing the Royal Arms, with silk backing, 48in (122cm) long.   **$360-540**

A Lancashire Hussars officer's full dress blue jacket and pélisse embellished with gold cord, and crimson netherwear with gold lace stripes, both jackets with crimson silk lining, together with their crimson and gold barrel-sash and a set of gold caplines with large acorn terminals.
$1,800-2,700

JEWELLERY

A sapphire and cultured pearl flowerhead brooch.
$70-145

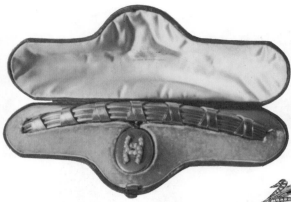

A Victorian yellow gold hollow articulated link bracelet with X-mounts, with gold locket, in fitted
$2,700-3,600

A ruby and diamond brooch, set with rubies with a principal diamond at the foremost flowerhead, the back spray set with small circular cut diamonds, one diamond lacking.
$1,800-2,700

A star brooch, set with rose diamonds, cut diamonds and chip diamonds.
$3,600-5,000

A 15ct gold and seed pearl swallow brooch.
$720-1,000

A 9 ct gold brooch, with cabochon polished amethyst bodies.
$360-540

A gold, opal and rose diamond set locket, glazed within.   **$180-360**

A Victorian yellow gold necklace, with alternate malachite and triple gold vine leaf panels, 20in (50.5cm) long, in fitted red leather case.   **$3,600-5,000**

A solitaire diamond set platinum ring, 2.75ct. with an inclusion and fissures.
$3,600-5,000

A gentleman's claw set diamond ring, 3ct.
$3,600-5,000

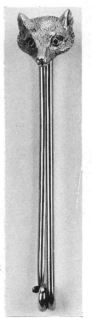

A late Victorian fox's mask stock pin, the mask set with 2 ruby chips for the eyes, on a 9ct gold bar.
$180-360

TUNBRIDGE WARE

A Tunbridge Ware pencil box, by
Thomas Barton, c1870, 8.5in
(21.5cm) long.
$180-360

Two Tunbridge Ware stamp
boxes:
l. by Thomas Barton, with stamp
stuck on, 1.5in (4cm) high.
$110-180
r. the Queen's head in tesserae,
1.5in (4cm) high.
$180-360

A Tunbridge Ware writing box,
with inkwell, the mosaic possibly
of Edward, Prince of Wales,
wearing a kilt, holding a parrot in
one hand and a dog in the other,
the design possibly taken from a
Berlin woolwork pattern, c1850,
10in (25cm) long.
$1,200-1,700

A Tunbrige Ware glove box, by
Thomas Barton, labelled, c1875,
9.5in (24cm) long.
$360-540

A Tunbridge Ware box, depicting
a lion, 3.5in (9cm) long.
$180-360

A Tunbridge Ware stationery box,
by T. Barton, with a label on the
base, c1870, 4in (10cm) high.
$720-1,000

A Tunbridge Ware snuff box,
c1860, 3in (8cm) diam.
$180-360

A Tunbridge Ware basket, c1860,
4.5in (11.5cm) wide.
$180-360

A Tunbridge Ware stationery box,
by Edmund Nye, labelled, 6.5in
(16.5cm) wide.
$720-1,000

A Tunbridge Ware caddy, with
single compartment, 4.5in (12cm)
square.
$360-540

A Tunbridge Ware tea caddy with
an unusual border, c1850, 8.5in
(21.5cm) long.
$720-1,000

Two Tunbridge Ware boxes, 4in
(10cm) long.
$110-180 each

Two Tunbridge Ware boxes, c1850, larger 4.5in
(11.5cm) long.   **$180-360 each**

A Tunbridge Ware watch stand, c1865, 3.5in (9cm) square.
$180-360

A pair of Tunbridge Ware book ends, c1840.
$360-540

Two Tunbridge Ware waxes, smallest 0.5in (1cm) high.
$35-70

A Tunbridge Ware counter box, 2.5in (6cm) high, **£100-145,** and a Tunbridge Ware nutmeg grater, 1.5in (4cm) high.
$110-180

Two Tunbridge Ware teapot pin cushions, c1870, 1.5in (4cm) high.   **$180-360 each**

A Tunbridge Ware oak book rack, with cube mosaic ends, 12.5in (32cm) long.
$180-360

A Tunbridge Ware book mark, 1in (2.5cm) diam.   **$35-70**

A late Georgian marquetry cribbage board, with Masonic emblem, 12in (31cm) long.
$180-360

Tunbridge Ware match strikers, the centre inscribed 'Go To Bed', c1835, 2in (6.5cm) high.
$110-180 each

A Tunbridge Ware ruler, c1840, 15in (38cm) long.
$110-180

A group of Tunbridge Ware sewing items, comprising: pin cushions, tape measure, and pin wheel.   **$110-180 each**

A Tunbridge Ware letter opener, c1860, 9.5in (24cm) long.
$35-70

DIRECTORY OF INTERNATIONAL AUCTIONEERS

This directory is by no means complete. Any auctioneer who holds frequent sales should contact us for inclusion in the 1992 Edition. Entries must be received by April 1991. There is, of course, no charge for this listing. Entries will be repeated in subsequent editions unless we are requested otherwise.

America

Acorn Farm Antiques,
15466 Oak Road, Carmel,
IN 46032
Tel: (317) 846-2383

ALA Moanastampt Cain (David H Martin),
1236 Ala Moana Boulevard,
Honolulu, HI 96814

Alabama Auction Room Inc,
2112 Fifth Avenue North,
Birmingham, AL 35203
Tel: (205) 252-4073

B Altman & Co,
34th & Fifth Avenue, New York,
NY 10016
Tel: (212) OR 9 7800 ext 550 & 322

Ames Art Galleries,
8729 Wilshire Boulevard, Beverly
Hills, CA 9021
Tel: (213) 655-5611/652-3820

Arnette's Auction Galleries Inc,
310 West Castle Street,
Murfreesboro, TN 37130
Tel: (615) 893-3725

Associated Appraisers Inc,
915 Industrial Bank Building,
Providence, RI 02906
Tel: (401) 331-9391

Atlanta's ABCD Auction Gallery
(Clark, Bate and Depew),
1 North Clarendon Avenue,
Antioch, IL 30002
Tel: (312) 294-8264

Bakers Auction,
14100 Paramount Boulevard,
Paramount, CA 90723
Tel: (213) 531-1524

Barridoff Galleries,
242 Middle Street, Portland,
ME 04 101
Tel: (207) 772-5011

C T Bevensee Auction Service,
PO Box 492, Botsford, CT 06404
Tel: (203) 426-6698

Frank H. Boos Gallery, Inc.,
420 Enterprise Ct., Bloomfield
Hills, MI 48013

Richard A Bourne Co Inc,
Corporation Street, PO Box 141/A,
Hyannis Port, MA 02647
Tel: (617) 775-0797

Bridges Antiques and Auctions,
Highway 46, PO Box 52A,
Sanford, FL 32771
Tel: (305) 323-2801/322-0095

George C Brilant & Co,
191 King Street, Charleston,
SC 29401

R W Bronstein Corp,
3666 Main Street, Buffalo,
NY 14226
Tel: (716) 835-7666/7408

Brookline Auction Gallery,
Proctor Hill Road, Route 130,
Brookline, NH 03033
Tel: (603) 673-4474/4153

Brzostek's Auction Service,
2052 Lamson Road, Phoenix,
NY 13135
Tel: (315) 678-2542

Buckingham Galleries Ltd,
4350 Dawson Street, San Diego,
CA 92115
Tel: (714) 283-7286

Bushell's Auction,
2006 2nd Avenue, Seattle,
WA 98121
Tel: (206) 622-5833

L Butterfield,
605 W Midland, Bay City,
MI 48706
Tel: (517) 684-3229

Butterfield,
808 N La, Cienega Boulevard, Los
Angeles, CA 90069

Butterfield & Butterfield,
1244 Sutter Street, San Francisco,
CA 94109
Tel: (415) 673-1362

California Book Auction Galleries,
358 Golden Gate Avenue, San
Francisco, CA 94102
Tel: (415) 775-0424

C B Charles Galleries Inc,
825 Woodward Avenue, Pontiac,
MI 48053
Tel: (313) 338-9023

Chatsworth Auction Rooms,
151 Mamaroneck Avenue,
Mamaroneck, NY 10543

Christie, Manson & Wood
International Inc,
502 Park Avenue, New York
Tel: (212) 826-2388 Telex: 620721

Christie's East,
219 East 67th Street, New York,
NY 10021
Tel: (212) 570-4141

Representative Offices:
California:
9350 Wilshire Boulevard, Beverly
Hills, CA 902 12
Tel: (213) 275-5534

Florida:
225 Fern Street, West Palm Beach,
FL 33401
Tel: (305) 833-6592

Mid-Atlantic:
638 Morris Avenue, Bryn Mawr,
PA 19010
Tel: (215) 525-5493

Washington:
1422 27th Street NW, Washington,
DC 20007
Tel: (202) 965-2066

Midwest:
46 East Elm Street, Chicago,
IL 60611
Tel: (312) 787-2765

Fred Clark Auctioneer Inc,
PO Box 124, Route 14, Scotland,
CT 06264
Tel: (203) 423-3939/0594

Cockrum Auctions,
2701 North Highway 94,
St Charles, MO 63301
Tel: (314) 723-9511

George Cole, Auctioneers and
Appraisers,
14 Green Street, Kingston,
NY 12401
Tel: (914) 338-2367

Coleman Auction Galleries,
525 East 72nd Street, New York,
NY 10021
Tel: (212) 879-1415

Conestoga Auction Company Inc,
PO Box 1, Manheim, PA 17545
Tel: (717) 898-7284

Cook's Auction Gallery,
Route 58, Halifax, MA 02338
Tel: (617) 293-3445/866-3243

Coquina Auction Barn
40 S Atlantic Avenue, Ormond
Beach, FL 32074

Danny's Antique Auction Service
(Pat Lusardi),
Route 46, Belvidere, NH 07823
Tel: (201) 757-7278

Douglas Galleries,
Route 5, South Deerfield,
MA 01373
Tel: (413) 665-2877

William Doyle,
175 East 87th Street, New York,
NY 10128
Tel: (212) 427-2730

DuMochelle Art Galleries,
409 East Jefferson, Detroit,
MI 48226
Tel: (313) 963-6255

John C Edelmann Galleries Inc,
123 East 77th Street, New York,
NY 10021
Tel: (212) 628-1700/1735

Robert C Eldred Co Inc,
Box 796, East Dennis, MA 02641
Tel: (617) 385-3116/3377

The Fine Arts Company of
Philadelphia Inc,
2317 Chestnut Street,
Philadelphia, PA 19103
Tel: (215) 564-3644

Fordem Galleries Inc,
3829 Lorain Avenue, Cleveland,
OH 44113
Tel: (216) 281-3563

George S Foster III,
Route 28, Epsom, NH 03234
Tel: (603) 736-9240

Jack Francis Auctions,
200 Market Street, Suite 107,
Lowell, MA 01852
Tel: (508) 441-9708

S T Freeman & Co,
1808 Chestnut Street,
Philadelphia, PA 19103
Tel: (215) 563-9275

Col K R French and Co Inc,
166 Bedford Road, Armonk,
NY 10504
Tel: (914) 273-3674

Garth's Auctions Inc,
2690 Stratford Road, Delaware,
OH 43015
Tel: (614) 362-4771/369-5085

Gilbert Auctions,
River Road, Garrison, NY 10524
Tel: (914) 424-3657

Morten M Goldberg,
215 N Rampart Street, New
Orleans, LA 70112
Tel: (504) 522-8364

Gramercy Auction Galleries,
52 East 13th Street, New York,
NY 10003
Tel: (212) 477-5656

Grandma's House,
4712 Dudley, Wheatridge,
CO 80033
Tel: (303) 423-3640/534-2847

The William Haber Art Collection
Inc,
139-11 Queens Boulevard,
Jamaica, NY 11435
Tel: (212) 739-1000

Charlton Hall Galleries Inc,
930 Gervais Street, Columbia,
SC 29201
Tel: (803) 252-7927/779-5678

Hampton Auction Gallery,
201 Harwick Street, Belvidere,
NH 07823
Tel: (201) 475-2928

Hanzel,
1120 S Michigan Avenue, Chicago,
IL 60605
Tel: (312) 922-6234

Harbor Auction Gallery,
238 Bank Street, New London,
CT 06355
Tel: (203) 443-0868

Harmer's of San Francisco Inc,
49 Geary Street, San Francisco,
CA 94102
Tel: (415) 391-8244

Harris Auction Galleries,
873-875 North Howard Street,
Baltimore, MD 21201
Tel: (301) 728-7040

Hart,
2311 Westheimer, Houston,
TX 77098
Tel: (713) 524-2979/523-7389

Hauswedeil & Nolte,
225 West Central Park, New York,
NY 10024
Tel: (212) 787-7245

G Ray Hawkins,
7224 Melrose Avenue, Los
Angeles, CA 90046
Tel: (213) 550-1504

Elwood Heller & Son Auctioneer,
151 Main Street, Lebanon,
NJ 08833
Tel: (201) 23 62 195

William F Hill Auction Sales,
Route 16, East Hardwick,
VT 05834
Tel: (802) 472-6308

Leslie Hindman,
215 West Ohio Street, Chicago,
iL 60610
Tel: (312) 670-0010

The House Clinic,
PO Box 13013A, Orlando, Fl 32859
Tel: (305) 859-1770/851-2979

Co Raymond W Huber,
211 North Monroe, Montpelier,
OH 43543

F B Hubley Et Co,
364 Broadway, Cambridge,
MA 02100
Tel: (617) 876-2030

Iroquois Auctions,
Box 66, Broad Street, Port Henry,
NY 12974
Tel: (518) 942-3355

It's About Time,
375 Park Avenue, Glencoe,
IL 60022
Tel: (312) 835-2012

Louis Joseph Auction Gallery
(Richard L Ryan),
575 Washington Street, Brookline,
MA 02146
Tel: (617) 277-0740

Joy Luke,
The Gallery, 300 East Grove
Street, Bloomington, IL 61701

Julia's Auction Service,
Route 201, Skowhegan Road,
Fairfield, ME 04937
Tel: (207) 453-9725

Sibylle Kaldewey,
225 West Central Park, New York,
NY 10024
Tel: (212) 787-7245

Kelley's Auction Service,
PO Box 125, Woburn, MA 01801
Tel: (617) 272-9167

Kennedy Antique Auction
Galleries Inc,
1088 Huff Road, Atlanta,
GA 30318
Tel: (404) 351-4464

Kinzie Galleries Auction Service,
1002 3rd Avenue, Duncansville,
PA 16835
Tel: (814) 695-3479

La Salle,
2083 Union Street, San Francisco,
CA 94123
Tel: (415) 931-9200

L A Landry (Robert Landry),
94 Main Street, Essex, MA 01929
Tel: (603) 744-5811

Jo Anna Larson,
POB 0, Antioch, IL 60002
Tel: (312) 395-0963

Levins Auction Exchange,
414 Camp Street, New Orleans,
LA 70130

Lipton,
1108 Fort Street, Honolulu,
HI 96813
Tel: (808) 533-4320

F S Long & Sons,
3126 East 3rd Street, Dayton,
OH 45403

R L Loveless Associates Inc,
4223 Clover Street, Honeoye Falls,
NY 14472
Tel: (716) 624-1648/1556

Lubin Galleries,
30 West 26th Street, New York,
NY 10010
Tel: (212) 924-3777

Main Auction Galleries,
137 West 4th Street, Cincinnati,
OH 45202
Tel: (513) 621-1280

Maison Auction Co Inc,
128 East Street, Wallingford,
CT 06492
Tel: (203) 269-8007

Joel L Malter & Co Inc,
Suite 518, 16661 Ventura
Boulevard, Encino, CA 91316
Tel: (213) 784-7772/2181

Manhattan Galleries,
1415 Third Avenue, New York,
NY 10028
Tel: (212) 744-2844

Mapes,
1600 West Vestal Parkway,
Vestal, NY 13850
Tel: (607) 754-9193

David W Mapes Inc,
82 Front Street, Binghamton,
NY 13905
Tel: (607) 724-6741/862-9365

Marvin H Newman,
426 South Robertson Boulevard,
Los Angeles, CA 90048
Tel: (213) 273-4840/378-2095

Mechanical Music Center Inc,
25 Kings Highway North, Darien,
CT 06820
Tel: (203) 655-9510

Milwaukee Auction Galleries,
4747 West Bradley Road,
Milwaukee, WI 53223
Tel: (414) 355-5054

Wayne Mock Inc,
Box 37, Tamworth, NH 03886
Tel: (603) 323-8057

William F Moon & Co,
12 Lewis Road, RFD 1, North
Attleboro, MA 02760
Tel: (617) 761-8003

New England Rare Coin Auctions,
89 Devonshire Street, Boston,
MA 02109
Tel: (617) 227-8800

Kurt Niven,
1444 Oak Lawn, Suite 525, Dallas,
TX 75207
Tel: (214) 741-4252

Northgate Gallery,
5520 Highway 153, Chattanooga,
TN 37443
Tel: (615) 842-4177

O'Gallerie Inc,
537 SE Ash Street, Portland,
OR 97214
Tel: (503) 238-0202

Th J Owen & Sons,
1111 East Street NW, Washington,
DC 20004

Palmer Auction Service,
Lucas, KS 67648

Park City Auction Service,
925 Wood Street, Bridgeport,
CT 06604
Tel: (203) 333-5251

Pennypacker Auction Centre,
1540 New Holland Road,
Kenhorst, Reading, PA 19607
Tel: (215) 777-5890/6121

Peyton Place Antiques,
819 Lovett Boulevard, Houston,
TX 77006
Tel: (713) 523-4841

Phillips,
867 Madison Avenue, New York,
NY 10021
Tel: (212) 570-4830

525 East 72nd Street, New York,
NY10021
Tel: (212) 570-4852

Representative Office:
6 Faneuil Hall, Marketplace,
Boston, MA 02109
Tel: (617) 227-6145

Pollack,
2780 NE 183 Street, Miami,
FL 33160
Tel: (305) 931-4476

Quickie Auction House,
Route 3, Osseo, MN 55369
Tel: (612) 428-4378

R & S Estate Liquidations,
Box 205, Newton Center,
MA 02159
Tel: (617) 244-6616

C Gilbert Richards,
Garrison, NY 10524
Tel: (914) 424-3657

Bill Rinaldi Auctions,
Bedell Road, Poughkeepsie,
NY 12601
Tel: (914) 454-9613

Roan Inc,
Box 118, RD 3, Logan Station,
PA 17728
Tel: (717) 494-0170

Rockland Auction Services Inc,
72 Pomona Road, Suffern,
NY 10901
Tel: (914) 354-3914/2723

Rome Auction Gallery (Sandra A
Louis Caropreso),
Route 2, Highway 53, Rome,
GA 30161

Rose Galleries Inc,
1123 West County Road B,
Roseville, MN 55113
Tel: (612) 484-1415

Rosvall Auction Company,
1238 & 1248 South Broadway,
Denver, CO 80210
Tel: (303) 777-2032/722-4028

Sigmund Rothschild,
27 West 67th Street, New York,
NY 10023
Tel: (212) 873-5522

Vince Runowich Auctions,
2312 4th Street North, St
Petersburg, FL 33704
Tel: (813) 895-3548

Safran's Antique Galleries Ltd,
930 Gervais Street, Columbia,
SC 29201
Tel: (803) 252-7927

Sage Auction Gallery,
Route 9A, Chester, CT 06412
Tel: (203) 526-3036

San Antonio Auction Gallery,
5096 Bianco, San Antonio,
TX 78216
Tel: (512) 342-3800

Emory Sanders,
New London, NH 03257
Tel: (603) 526-6326

Sandwich Auction House,
15 Tupper Road, Sandwich,
MA 02563
Tel: (617) 888-1926/5675

San Francisco Auction Gallery,
1217 Sutter Street, San Francisco,
CA 94109
Tel: (415) 441-3800

Schafer Auction Gallery,
82 Bradley Road, Madison,
CT 06443
Tel: (203) 245-4173

Schmidt's Antiques,
5138 West Michigan Avenue,
Ypsilanti, MI 48 197
Tel: (313) 434-2660

K C Self,
53 Victory Lane, Los Angeles,
CA 95030
Tel: (213) 354-4238

B J Selkirk & Sons,
4166 Olive Street, St Louis,
MO 63108
Tel: (314) 533-1700

Shore Galleries Inc,
3318 West Devon, Lincolnwood,
IL 60659
Tel: (312) 676-2900

Shute's Auction Gallery,
70 Accord Park Drive, Norwell,
MA 02061
Tel: (617) 871-3414/238-0586

Ronald Siefert,
RFD, Buskirk, NY 12028
Tel: (518) 686-9375

Robert A Siegel Auction Galleries
Inc,
120 East 56th Street, New York,
NY 10022
Tel: (212) 753-6421/2/3

Robert W Skinner Inc,
Main Street, Bolton, MA 01740
Tel: (617) 779-5528

585 Boylston Street,
Boston, MA 02116
Tel: (617) 236-1700

C G Sloan & Co,
715 13th Street NW, Washington,
DC 20005
Tel: (202) 628-1468

Branch Office:
403 North Charles Street,
Baltimore, MD 21201
Tel: (301) 547-1177

Sotheby,
101 Newbury Street, Boston,
MA 02116
Tel: (617) 247-2851

Sotheby Park Bernet Inc,
980 Madison Avenue, New York,
NY 10021
Tel: (212) 472-3400

1334 York Avenue, New York,
NY 10021

171 East 84th Street, New York,
NY 10028

Mid-Atlantic:
1630 Locust Street, Philadelphia,
PA 19103
Tel: (215) 735-7886

Washington:
2903 M Street NW, Washington,
DC 20007
Tel: (202) 298-8400

Southeast:
155 Worth Avenue, Palm Beach,
FL 33480
Tel: (305) 658-3555

Classic Auction Gallery
(formerly Sterling Auctions),
62 No. 2nd Avenue, Raritan,
NJ 08869
Tel: (201) 526-6024

Midwest:
700 North Michigan Avenue,
Chicago, IL 60611
Tel: (312) 280-0185

Southwest:
Galleria Post Oak,
5015 Westheimer Road, Houston,
TX 77056
Tel: (713) 623-0010

Northwest:
210 Post Street, San Francisco,
CA 94108
Tel: (415) 986-4982

Pacific Area:
Suite 117, 850 West Hind Drive,
Honolulu, Hawaii 96821
Tel: (808) 373-9166

Stack's Rare Coin Auctions,
123 West 57th Street, New York,
NY 10019
Tel: (212) 583-2580

Stremmel Auctions Inc,
2152 Prater Way, Sparks,
NV 89431
Tel: (702) 331-1035

Summit Auction Rooms,
47-49 Summit Avenue, Summit,
NJ 07901

Superior Stamp & Coin Co Inc,
9301 Wiltshire Boulevard,
Beverly Hills, CA 90210
Tel: (213) 272-0851/278-9740

Swann Galleries Inc,
104 East 26th Street, New York,
NY 10021
Tel: (212) 254-4710

Philip Swedler & Son,
850 Grand Avenue, New Haven,
CT 06511
Tel: (203) 624-2202/562-5065

Tait Auction Studio,
1209 Howard Avenue,
Burlingame, CA 94010
Tel: (415) 343-4793

Tepper Galleries,
110 East 25th Street, New York,
NY 10010
Tel: (212) 677-5300/1/2

Louis Trailman Auction Co,
1519 Spruce Street, Philadelphia,
PA 19102
Tel: (215) K1 5 4500

Trend Galleries Inc,
2784 Merrick Road, Bellmore,
NY 11710
Tel: (516) 221-5588

Trosby Auction Galleries,
81 Peachtree Park Drive, Atlanta,
GA 30326
Tel: (404) 351-4400

Valle-McLeod Gallery,
3303 Kirby Drive, Houston,
TX 77098
Tel: (713) 523-8309/8310

The Watnot Auction,
Box 78, Mellenville, NY 12544
Tel: (518) 672-7576

Adam A Wechsler & Son,
905-9 East Street NW,
Washington, DC 20004
Tel: (202) 628-1281

White Plains Auction Rooms,
572 North Broadway, White
Plains, NY 10603
Tel: (914) 428-2255

Henry Willis,
22 Main Street, Marshfield,
MA 02050
Tel: (617) 834 7774

The Wilson Galleries,
PO Box 102, Ford Defiance,
VA 24437
Tel: (703) 885-4292

Helen Winter Associates,
355 Farmington Avenue,
Plainville, CT 06062
Tel: (203) 747-0714/677-0848

Richard Withington Inc,
Hillsboro, NH 03244
Tel: (603) 464-3232

Wolf,
13015 Larchmere Boulevard,
Shaker Heights, OH 44120
Tel: (216) 231-3888

Richard Wolffers Inc,
127 Kearney Street, San
Francisco, CA 94 108
Tel: (415) 781-5127

Young,
56 Market Street, Portsmouth,
NH 03801
Tel: (603) 436-8773

Samuel Yudkin & Associates,
1125 King Street, Alexandria,
VA 22314
Tel: (703) 549-9330

Australia

ASA Stamps Co Pty Ltd,
138-140 Rundle Mall, National
Bank Building, Adelaide, South
Australia 5001
Tel: 223-2951

Associated Auctioneers Pty Ltd,
800-810 Parramatta Road,
Lewisham, New South Wales 2049
Tel: 560-5899

G J Brain Auctioneers Pty Ltd,
122 Harrington Street, Sydney,
New South Wales 2000
Tel: 271701

Bright Slater Pty Ltd,
Box 205 GPO, Lower Ground
Floor, Brisbane Club Building,
Isles Lane, Brisbane, Queensland
4000
Tel: 312415

Christie, Manson & Woods
(Australia) Ltd,
298 New South Head Road, Double
Bay, Sydney, New South Wales
2028
Tel: 326-1422

William S Ellenden Pty Ltd,
67-73 Wentworth Avenue,
Sydney, New South Wales 2000
Tel: 211-4035/211-4477

Bruce Granger Auctions,
10 Hopetoun Street, Huristone
Park, New South Wales 2193
Tel: 559-4767

Johnson Bros Auctioneers & Real
Estate Agents,
328 Main Road, Glenorchy,
Tasmania 7011
Tel: 725166 492909

James A Johnson & Co,
92 Boronia Road, Vermont,
Victoria 3133
Tel: 877-2754/874-3632

Jolly Barry Pty Ltd,
212 Glenmore Road, Paddington,
New South Wales 2021
Tel: 357-4494

James R Lawson Pty Ltd,
236 Castlereagh Street, Sydney,
New South Wales
Tel: 266408

Mason Greene & Associates,
91-101 Leveson Street, North
Melbourne, Victoria 3051
Tel: 329-9911

Mercantile Art Auctions,
317 Pacific Highway, North Sydey,
New South Wales 2060
Tel: 922-3610/922-3608

James R Newall Auctions Pty Ltd,
164 Military Road, Neutral Bay,
New South Wales 2089
Tel: 903023/902587 (Sydney ex)

P L Pickles & Co Pty Ltd
655 Pacific Highway, Killara, New
South Wales 2071
Tel: 498-8069/498-2775

Sotheby Parke Bernet Group Ltd,
115 Collins Street, Melbourne,
Victoria 3000
Tel: (03) 63 39 00

H E Wells & Sons,
326 Rokeby Road, Subiaco, West
Australia
Tel: 3819448/3819040

Young Family Estates Pty Ltd,
229 Camberwell Road, East
Hawthorn, Melbourne 2123
Tel: 821433

New Zealand

Devereaux & Culley Ltd,
200 Dominion Road, Mt Eden,
Auckland
Tel: 687429/687112

Alex Harris Ltd,
PO Box 510, 377 Princes Street,
Dunedin
Tel: 773955/740703

Roger Moat Ltd,
College Hill and Beaumont Street,
Auckland
Tel: 37 1588/37 1686/37 1595

New Zealand Stamp Auctions,
PO Box 3496, Queen and
Wyndham Streets, Auckland
Tel: 375490/375498

Alistair Robb Coin Auctions,
La Aitken Street, Box 3705,
Wellington
Tel: 727-141

Dunbar Sloane Ltd,
32 Waring Taylor Street,
Wellington
Tel: 721-367

Thornton Auctions Ltd,
89 Albert Street, Auckland 1
Tel: 30888 (3 lines)

Daniel J Visser,
109 and 90 Worchester Street,
Christchurch
Tel: 68853/67297

Austria

Christie's,
Ziehrerplatz 4/22, A-1030 Vienna
Tel: (0222) 73 26 44

Belgium

Christie, Manson & Woods
(Belgium) Ltd,
33 Boulevard de Waterloo, B-1000
Brussels
Tel: (02) 512-8765/512-8830

Sotheby Parke Bernet Belgium,
Rue de l'Abbaye 32, 1050 Brussels
Tel: 343 50 07

Canada

A-1 Auctioneer Evaluation
Services Ltd,
PO Box 926, Saint John,
NB E2L 4C3
Tel: (508) 762-0559

Appleton Auctioneers Ltd,
1238 Seymour Street, Vancouver,
BC V6B 3N9
Tel: (604) 685-1715

Ashton Auction Service,
PO Box 500, Ashton, Ontario,
K0A 180
Tel: (613) 257-1575

Canada Book Auctions,
35 Front Street East, Toronto,
Ontario M5E 1B3
Tel: (416) 368-4326

Christie's International Ltd,
Suite 2002, 1055 West Georgia
Street, Vancouver, BC V6E 3P3
Tel: (604) 685-2126

Miller & Johnson Auctioneers Ltd,
2882 Gottingen Street, Halifax,
Nova Scotia B3K 3E2
Tel: (902) 425-3366/425-3606

Phillips Ward-Price Ltd,
76 Davenport Road, Toronto,
Ontario M5R 1H3
Tel: (416) 923-9876

Sotheby Parke Bernet (Canada)
Inc,
156 Front Street, Toronto, Ontario
M5J 2L6
Tel: (416) 596-0300
Representative:
David Brown,
2321 Granville Street, Vancouver,
BC V6H 3G4
Tel: (604) 736-6363

Denmark

Kunsthallens,
Kunstauktioner A/S,
Købmagergade 11 DK 1150
Copenhagen
Tel: (01) 13 85 69

Nellemann & Thomsen,
Neilgade 45, DK-8000 Aarhus
Tel: (06) 12 06 66/12 00 02

France

Ader, Picard, Tajan,
12 rue Favart, 75002 Paris
Tel: 261.80.07

Artus,
15 rue de la Grange-Batelière,
75009 Paris
Tel: 523.12.03

Audap,
32 rue Drouot, 75009 Paris
Tel: 742.78.01

Bondu,
17 rue Drouot, 75009 Paris
Tel: 770.36.16

Boscher, Gossart,
3 rue d'Amboise, 75009 Paris
Tel: 260.87.87

Briest,
15 rue Drouot, 75009 Paris
Tel: 770.66.29

de Cagny,
4 rue Drouot, 75009 Paris
Tel: 246.00.07

Charbonneaux,
134 rue du Faubourg Saint-
Honoré, 75008 Paris
Tel: 359.66.57

Chayette,
10 rue Rossini, 75009 Paris
Tel: 770.38.89

Delaporte, Rieunier,
159 rue Montmartre, 75002 Paris
Tel: 508.41.83

Delorme,
3 rue Penthièvre, 75008 Paris
Tel: 265.57.63

Godeau,
32 rue Drouot, 75009 Paris
Tel: 770.67.68

Gros,
22 rue Drouot, 75009 Paris
Tel: 770.83.04

Langlade,
12 rue Descombes, 75017 Paris
Tel: 227.00.91

Loudmer, Poulain,
73 rue de Faubourg Saint-Honoré,
75008 Paris
Tel: 266.90.01

Maignan,
6 rue de la Michodière, 75002 Paris
Tel: 742.71.52

Maringe,
16 rue de Provence, 75009 Paris
Tel: 770.61.15

Marlio,
7 rue Ernest-Renan, 75015 Paris
Tel: 734.81.13

Paul Martin & Jacques Martin,
3 impasse des Chevau-Legers,
78000 Versailles
Tel: 950.58.08

Bonhams, Baron Foran,
Duc de Saint-Bar, 2 rue Bellanger,
92200 Neuilly sur Seine
Tel: (1) 637-1329

Christie's, Princess Jeanne-Marie
de Broglie,
17 rue de Lille, 75007 Paris
Tel: (331) 261-1247

Sotheby's, Rear Admiral J A
Templeton-Cotill, CB,
3 rue de Miromesnil, 75008 Paris
Tel: (1) 266-4060

Monaco

Sotheby Parke Bernet Group,
PO Box 45, Sporting d'Hiver, Place
du Casino, Monte Carlo
Tel: (93) 30 88 80

Hong Kong

Sotheby Parke Bernet (Hong
Kong) Ltd,
PO Box 83, 705 Lane Crawford
House, 64-70 Queen's Road
Central, Hong Kong
Tel: 22-5454

Italy

Christie's (International) SA,
Palazzo Massimo Lancellotti,
Piazza Navona 114, 00186 Rome
Tel: 6541217

Christie's (Italy) SR1,
9 Via Borgogna, 20144 Milan
Tel: 794712

Finarte SPA,
Piazzetta Bossi 4, 20121 Milan
Tel: 877041

Finarte SPA,
Via delle Quattro, Fontane 20,
Rome
Tel: 463564

Palazzo International delle Aste ed
Esposizioni SPA,
Palazzo Corsini, Il Prato 56,
Florence
Tel: 293000

Sotheby Parke Bernet Italia,
26 Via Gino Capponi, 50121
Florence
Tel: 571410

Sotheby Parke Bernet Italia,
Via Montenapoleone 3, 20121
Milan
Tel: 783907

Sotheby Parke Bernet Italia,
Palazzo Taverna, Via di Monte
Giordano 36, 00186 Rome
Tel: 656 1670/6547400

The Netherlands

Christie, Manson & Woods Ltd,
Rokin 91, 1012 KL Amsterdam
Tel: (020) 23 15 05

Sotheby Mak Van Waay BV,
102 Rokin 1012, KZ Amsterdam
Tel: 24 62 15

Van Dieten Stamp Auctions BV,
2 Tournooiveld, 2511 CX The
Hague
Tel: 70-464312/70-648658

Singapore & Malaysia
Victor & Morris Pte Ltd,
39 Talok Ayer Street, Republic of
Singapore
Tel: 94844

South Africa
Ashbey's Galleries,
43-47 Church Street, Cape Town
8001
Tel: 22-7527

Claremart Auction Centre,
47 Main Road, Claremont, Cape
Town 7700
Tel: 66-8826/66-8804

Ford & Van Niekerk Pty Ltd
156 Main Road, PO Box 8,
Plumstead, Cape Town
Tel: 71-3384

Sotheby Parke Bernet South
Africa Pty Ltd,
Total House, Smit and Rissik
Streets, PO Box 310010,
Braamfontein 2017
Tel: 39-3726

Spain
Juan R Cayon,
41 Fuencarral, Madrid 14
Tel: 221 08 32/221 43 72/222 95 98

Christie's International Ltd,
Casado del Alisal 5, Madrid
Tel: (01) 228-9300

Sotheby Parke Bernet & Co,
Scursal de Espana, Calle del
Prado 18, Madrid 14
Tel: 232-6488/232-6572

Switzerland
Daniel Beney,
Avenue des Mousquines 2,
CH-1005 Lausanne
Tel: (021) 22 28 64

Blanc,
Arcade Hotel Beau-Rivage, Box
84, CH-1001 Lausanne
Tel: (021) 27 32 55/26 86 20

Christie's (International) SA,
8 Place de la Taconnerie, CH-1204
Geneva
Tel: (022) 28 25 44

Steinwiesplatz,
CH-8032 Zurich
Tel: (01) 69 05 05

Auktionshaus Doblaschofsky AG,
Monbijoustrasse 28/30, CH-3001
Berne
Tel: (031) 25 23 72/73/74

Galerie Fischer,
Haldenstrasse 19, CH-6006
Lucerne
Tel: (041) 22 57 72/73

Germann Auktionshaus,
Zeitweg 67, CH-8032 Zurich
Tel: (01) 32 83 58/32 01 12

Haus der Bücher AG,
Baumleingasse 18, CH-4051 Basel
Tel: (061) 23 30 88

Adolph Hess AG,
Haldenstrasse 5, CH-6006 Lucerne
Tel: (041) 22 43 92/22 45 35

Auktionshaus Peter Ineichen,
CF Meyerstrasse 14, CH-8002
Zurich
Tel: (01) 201-3017

Galerie Koller AG,
Ramistrasse 8, CH-8001 Zurich
Tel: (01) 47 50 40

Koller St Gallen,
St Gallen
Tel: (071) 23 42 40

Kornfeld & Co,
Laupenstrasse 49, CH-3008 Berne
Tel: (031) 25 46 73

Phillips Son & Neale SA,
6 Rue de la Cité, CH-1204 Geneva
Tel: (022) 28 68 28

Christian Rosset,
Salle des Ventes, 29 Rue du Rhone,
CH-1204 Geneva
Tel: (022) 28 96 33/34

Schweizerische Gesellschaft der
Freunde von Kunstauktionen,
11 Werdmühlestrasse, CH-8001
Zurich
Tel: (01) 211-4789

Sotheby Parke Bernet AG,
20 Bleicherweg, CH-8022 Zurich
Tel: (01) 202-0011

24 Rue de la Cité, CH-1024 Geneva
Tel: (022) 21 33 77

Dr Erich Steinfels, Auktionen,
Rämistrasse 6, CH-8001 Zurich
Tel: (01) 252-1233 (wine) &
(01) 34 1233 (fine art)

Frank Sternberg,
Bahnhofstrasse 84, CH-8001
Zurich
Tel: (01) 211-7980

Jürg Stucker Gallery Ltd,
Alter Aargauerstalden 30,
CH-3006 Berne
Tel: (031) 44 00 44

Uto Auktions AG,
Lavaterstrasse 11, CH-8027
Zurich
Tel: (01) 202-9444

West Germany
Galerie Gerda Bassenge,
Erdener Strasses 5a, D-1000 West
Berlin 33
Tel: (030) 892 19 32/891 29 09

Kunstauktionen Waltraud Boltz,
Bahnhof Strasse 25-27, D-8580
Bayreuth
Tel: (0921) 206 16

Brandes,
Wolfenbütteler Strasse 12, D-3300
Braunschweig 1
Tel: (0531) 737 32

Gernot Dorau,
Johann-Georg Strasse 2, D-1000
Berlin 31
Tel: (030) 892 61 98

F Dörling,
Neuer Wall 40-41, D-2000
Hamburg 36
Tel: (040) 36 46 70/36 52 82

Roland A Exner,
Kunsthandel-Auktionen,
Am Ihmeufer, D-3000
Hannover 91
Tel: (0511) 44 44 84

Hartung & Karl,
Karolinenplatz 5a, D-8000
Munich 2
Tel: (089) 28 40 34

Hauswedell & Nolte,
Pöseldorfer Weg 1, D-2000
Hamburg 13
Tel: (040) 44 83 66

Karl & Faber,
Amiraplatz 3 (Luitpoldblock),
D-8000 Munich 2
Tel: (089) 22 18 65/66

Graf Klenau Ohg Nachf,
Maximilian Strasse 32, D-8000
Munich 1
Tel: (089) 22 22 81/82

Numismatik Lanz München,
Promenadeplatz 9, D-8000
Munich 2
Tel: (089) 29 90 70

Kunsthaus Lempertz,
Neumarkt 3, D-5000 Cologne 1
Tel: (0221) 21 02 51/52

Stuttgarter Kunstauktionshaus,
Dr Fritz Nagel,
Mörikestrasse 17-19, D-7000
Stuttgart 1
Tel: (0711) 61 33 87/77

Neumeister Münchener
Kunstauktionshaus KG,
Barer Strasse 37, D-8000
Munich 40
Tel: (089) 28 30 11

Petzold KG- Photographica,
Maximilian Strasse 36, D-8900
Augsburg 11
Tel: (0821) 3 37 25

Reiss & Auvermann,
Zum Talblick 2, D-6246
Glashütten im Taunus 1
Tel: (06174) 69 47/48

Gus Schiele Auktions-Galerie,
Ottostrasse 7 (Neuer Kunstblock),
D-8000 Munich 2
Tel: (089) 59 41 92

Galerie,
Paulinen Strasse 47, D-7000
Stuttgart 1
Tel: (0711) 61 63 77

J A Stargardt,
Universitäts Strasse 27, D-3550
Marburg
Tel: (06421) 234 52

Auktionshaus Tietjen & Co,
Spitaler Strasse 30, D-2000
Hamburg 1
Tel: (040) 33 03 68/69

Aachener Auktionshaus, Crott &
Schmelzer,
Pont Strasse 21, Aachen
Tel: (0241) 369 00

Kunstauktionen Rainer
Baumann,
Obere Woerthstrasse 7-11,
Nuremburg
Tel: (0911) 20 48 47

August Bödiger oHG,
Oxford Strasse 4, Bonn
Tel: (0228) 63 69 40

Bolland & Marotz,
Feldören 19, Bremen
Tel: (0421) 32 18 11

Bongartz Gelgen Auktionen,
Münsterplatz 27, Aachen
Tel: (0241) 206 19

Christie's International Ltd,
Düsseldorf:
Alt Pempelfort 11a, D-4000
Düsseldorf
Tel: (0211) 35 05 77

Hamburg:
Wenzelstrasse 21, D-2000
Hamburg 60
Tel: (4940) 279-0866

Munich:
Maximilianstrasse 20, D-8000
Munich 22
Tel: (089) 22 95 39

Württemberg:
Schloss Langenburg, D-7183
Langenburg

Sotheby Parke Bernet GmbH,
Munich:
Odeonsplatz 16, D-8000 Munich 22
Tel: (089) 22 23 75/6

Kunstauktion Jürgen Fischer,
Alexander Strasse 11, Heilbronn
Tel: (07 131) 785 23

Galerie Göbig,
Ritterhaus Strasse 5 (am
Thermalbad ad Nauheim)
Tel: (Frankfurt) (611) 77 40 80

Knut Günther,
Auf der Körnerwiese 19-21,
Frankfurt
Tel: (611) 55 32 92/55 70 22

Antiquitaeten Lothar Heubel,
Odenthaler Strasse 371, Cologne
Tel: (0221) 60 18 25

Hildener Auktionshaus und
Kunstgalerie,
Klusenhof 12, Hilden
Tel: (02103) 602 00